GAAP GUIDE, VOLUME II

Restatement and Analysis of
Current FASB Standards and Other Current FASB, EITF,
and AICPA Announcements

JAN R. WILLIAMS, Ph.D., CPA

JOSEPH V. CARCELLO, Ph.D., CPA, CMA, CIA

TERRY L. NEAL, Ph.D., CPA

JUDITH WEISS, CPA

CCH
a Wolters Kluwer business

This publication is designed to provide accurate and authoritative information in regard to the subject matter covered. It is sold with the understanding that the publisher is not engaged in rendering legal, accounting, or other professional services. If legal advice or other professional assistance is required, the services of a competent professional person should be sought.

>—From a *Declaration of Principles* jointly adopted by a Committee of the American Bar Association and a Committee of Publishers and Associations

ISBN: 978-0-8080-2644-0 (set)

ISBN: 978-0-8080-2646-4

© 2011 CCH. All Rights Reserved.
4025 W. Peterson Avenue
Chicago, IL 60646-6085
1 800 248 3248
http://CCHGroup.com

No claim is made to original government works; however, within this Product or Publication, the following are subject to CCH's copyright: (1) the gathering, compilation, and arrangement of such government materials; (2) the magnetic translation and digital conversion of data, if applicable; (3) the historical, statutory and other notes and references; and (4) the commentary and other materials.

Portions of this work were published in a previous edition.

Printed in the United States of America

Contents

Our Peer Review Policy — xi
Peer Review Statement — xiii
Preface — xv
About the Authors — xvii
About the Accounting Standards Codification and the Former GAAP Hierarchy — xix

VOLUME I

Generally Accepted Accounting Principles

Chapter 1	ASC 105—Generally Accepted Accounting Principles	**1003**
Chapter 2	ASC 205—Presentation of Financial Statements	**2001**
Chapter 3	ASC 210—Balance Sheet	**3001**
Chapter 4	ASC 215—Statement of Shareholder Equity	**4001**
Chapter 5	ASC 220—Comprehensive Income	**5001**
Chapter 6	ASC 225—Income Statement	**6001**
Chapter 7	ASC 230—Statement of Cash Flows	**7001**
Chapter 8	ASC 235—Accounting Policies and Standards	**8001**
Chapter 9	ASC 250—Accounting Changes and Error Corrections	**9001**
Chapter 10	ASC 255—Changing Prices	**10,001**
Chapter 11	ASC 260—Earnings Per Share	**11,001**
Chapter 12	ASC 270—Interim Reporting	**12,001**
Chapter 13	ASC 272—Limited Liability Entities	**13,001**
Chapter 14	ASC 274—Personal Financial Statements	**14,001**
Chapter 15	ASC 275—Risks and Uncertainties	**15,001**
Chapter 16	ASC 280—Segment Reporting	**16,001**
Chapter 17	ASC 305—Cash and Cash Equivalents	**17,001**
Chapter 18	ASC 310—Receivables	**18,001**
Chapter 19	ASC 320—Investments—Debt and Equity Securities	**19,001**
Chapter 20	ASC 323—Investments—Equity Method and Joint Ventures	**20,001**
Chapter 21	ASC 325—Investments—Other	**21,001**
Chapter 22	ASC 330—Inventory	**22,001**
Chapter 23	ASC 340—Deferred Costs and Other Assets	**23,001**
Chapter 24	ASC 350—Intangibles—Goodwill and Other	**24,001**

Chapter 25	ASC 360—Property, Plant, and Equipment	25,001
Chapter 26	ASC 405—Liabilities	26,001
Chapter 27	ASC 410—Asset Retirement and Environmental Obligations	27,001
Chapter 28	ASC 420—Exit or Disposal Cost Obligations	28,001
Chapter 29	ASC 430—Deferred Revenue	29,001
Chapter 30	ASC 440—Commitments	30,001
Chapter 31	ASC 450—Contingencies	31,001
Chapter 32	ASC 460—Guarantees	32,001
Chapter 33	ASC 470—Debt	33,001
Chapter 34	ASC 480—Distinguishing Liabilities From Equity	34,001
Chapter 35	ASC 505—Equity	35,001
Chapter 36	ASC 605—Revenue Recognition	36,001
Chapter 37	ASC 705—Cost of Sales and Services	37,001
Chapter 38	ASC 710—Compensation—General	38,001
Chapter 39	ASC 712—Compensation—Noretirement Postemployment Benefits	39,001
Chapter 40	ASC 715—Compensation—Retirement Benefits	40,001

VOLUME II

Chapter 41	ASC 718—Compensation—Stock Compensation	41,001
Chapter 42	ASC 720—Other Expenses	42,001
Chapter 43	ASC 730—Research and Development	43,001
Chapter 44	ASC 740—Income Taxes	44,001
Chapter 45	ASC 805—Business Combinations	45,001
Chapter 46	ASC 808—Collaborative Arrangements	46,001
Chapter 47	ASC 810—Consolidation	47,001
Chapter 48	ASC 815—Derivatives and Hedging	48,001
Chapter 49	ASC 820—Fair Value Measurement	49,001
Chapter 50	ASC 825—Financial Instruments	50,001
Chapter 51	ASC 830—Foreign Currency Matters	51,001
Chapter 52	ASC 835—Interest	52,001
Chapter 53	ASC 840—Leases	53,001
Chapter 54	ASC 845—Nonmonetary Transactions	54,001
Chapter 55	ASC 850—Related Party Disclosures	55,001
Chapter 56	ASC 852—Reorganizations	56,001
Chapter 57	ASC 855—Subsequent Events	57,001
Chapter 58	ASC 860—Transfers and Servicing	58,001

Appendices

Appendix A	ASC 912—Contractors—Federal Government	**59,003**
Appendix B	ASC 915—Development Stage Entities	**60,001**
Appendix C	ASC 92X—Entertainment	**61,001**
Appendix D	ASC 93X—Extractive Activities	**62,001**
Appendix E	ASC 94X—Financial Services	**63,001**
Appendix F	ASC 952—Franchisors	**64,001**
Appendix G	ASC 954—Health Care Entities	**65,001**
Appendix H	ASC 958—Not-For-Profit Entities	**66,001**
Appendix I	ASC 962—Plan Accounting	**67,001**
Appendix J	ASC 970—Real Estate—General	**68,001**
Appendix K	ASC 976—Real Estate—Retail Land	**69,001**
Appendix L	ASC 980—Regulated Operations	**70,001**
Appendix M	ASC 985—Software	**71,001**

Accounting Resources on the Web **72,001**

For the most recent activities of the FASB and the AICPA, refer to the GAAP *Update Service* and the GAAP *Library* (www.CCHGroup.com).

CHAPTER 41
ASC 718—COMPENSATION—STOCK COMPENSATION

CONTENTS

Part I: General Guidance	41,003
Overview	41,003
ASC 718-10: Overall	41,003
Background	41,003
Employee Stock Option Plan	41,004
Restricted Stock Plan	41,004
Performance-Based Stock Plan	41,004
Stock Appreciation Rights	41,004
Employee Stock Purchase Plan	41,004
Compensatory Plans	41,004
Recognition and Measurement Principles	41,005
Measurement of Awards Classified as Equity—Public Company	41,005
Valuation Techniques for Share Options and Other Similar Instruments	41,007
Illustration of Application of Lattice Model to Valuing an Employee Stock Option	41,007
Illustration of Application of Lattice Model—Early Exercise with Fully Vested Options	41,008
Illustration of Application of Lattice Model—Early Exercise and Cliff Vesting	41,008
Illustration of Application of Black-Scholes-Merton Model to Valuing an Employee Stock Option	41,009
Selecting Assumptions for Use in an Option-Pricing Model	41,010
Consideration of Market, Performance, and Service Conditions	41,013
Illustration of Accounting for a Stock Option with a Market Condition	41,013
Illustration of Accounting for a Stock Option with Performance Conditions	41,016
Reload Options	41,017
Measurement of Awards Classified as Equity—Nonpublic Company	41,017
Illustration of Accounting for a Stock Option Award by a Private Company—Company Unable to Estimate Its Expected Stock Price Volatility	41,018
Recognition of Compensation Cost for an Award Accounted for as an Equity Instrument	41,020
ASC 718-20: Awards Classified as Equity	41,021
Modifications of Awards of Equity Instruments	41,021
ASC 718-30: Awards Classified as Liabilities	41,022
Measurement of Awards Classified as Liabilities	41,022
Illustration of the Accounting for Stock Appreciation Rights to be Settled in Cash—Recognition of a Liability	41,023

41,001

41,002 ASC 718—Compensation—Stock Compensation

Disclosure Requirements	41,024
ASC 718-50: Employee Share Purchase Plans	41,027
Noncompensatory Plans	41,027
Illustration of an Employee Share Purchase Plan	41,028
ASC 718-740: Income Taxes	41,029
Accounting for Tax Effects of Share-Based Compensation Awards	41,029
Illustration of Accounting for a Stock Option with a Service Condition—Including Treatment of Income Tax Effects and Presentation in Statement of Cash Flows	41,029
Part II: Interpretive Guidance	41,032
ASC 718-10: Overall	41,032
ASC 718-10-25-3	
Accounting for Payroll Taxes Associated with Stock Option Exercises	41,032
ASC 718-10-25-5	
Practical Accommodation to the Application of Grant Date as Defined in ASC 718	41,032
ASC 718-10-25-14A, 65-02	
Effect of Denominating the Exercise Price of a Share-Based Payment Award in the Currency of the Market in Which the Underlying Equity Security Trades	41,033
ASC 718-10-25-22	
Recognition and Measurement of Employer Payroll Taxes on Employee Stock-Based Compensation	41,034
ASC 718-10-S25-1, S99-2; ASC 505-50-S25-3	
Escrowed Share Arrangements and the Presumption of Compensation	41,034
ASC 718-10-35-9, 35-10, 35-11, 65-1	
Classification and Measurement of Freestanding Financial Instruments Originally Issued in Exchange for Employee Services under ASC 718	41,035
ASC 718-10-35-15	
Classification of Options and Similar Instruments Issued as Employee Compensation That Allow for Cash Settlement upon the Occurrence of a Contingent Event	41,037
ASC 718-40: Employee Stock Ownership Plans	41,038
ASC 718-40-05-2 through 05-4, 15-2 through 15-4, 25-2 through 25-6, 25-9 through 25-17, 25-19, through 25-20 through 25-21, 30-1 through 30-5, 35-1, 40-2 through 40-7, 45-2 through 45-9, 50-1, 55-1 through 55-33	
Employers' Accounting for Employee Stock Ownership Plans	41,038
ASC 718-50: Employee Share Purchase Plans	41,056
ASC 718-50-30-1 through 30-3, 35-1 through 35-2, 55-2 through 55-9, 55-22 through 55-33	
Accounting under ASC 718 for Certain Employee Stock Purchase Plans with a Look-Back Option	41,056
ASC 718-740: Income Taxes	41,060
ASC 718-740-45-8 through 45-12	
Accounting for Income Tax Benefits of Dividends on Share-Based Payment Awards	41,060
ISSUES GRANDFATHERED UNDER THE CODIFICATION	

Employee Stock Ownership Plans	**41,062**
SOP 76-3	
Accounting Practices for Certain Employee Stock Ownership Plans	**41,062**
EITF Issue 89-8	
Expense Recognition for Employee Stock Ownership Plans	**41,064**
EITF Issue 89-12	
Earnings-per-Share Issues Related to Convertible Preferred Stock Held by an Employee Stock Ownership Plan	**41,066**
EITF Issue 92-3	
Earnings-per-Share Treatment of Tax Benefits for Dividends on Unallocated Stock Held by an Employee Stock Ownership Plan	**41,070**

PART I: GENERAL GUIDANCE

OVERVIEW

An entity may pay for goods or services by issuing its stock. Although stock can be issued as compensation for many types of goods or services, the accounting treatment of stock issued in exchange for employee services, especially stock options, has been particularly controversial. In some instances, the stock issued to employees does not include compensation (noncompensatory plan); in other instances, the stock issued to employees includes compensation (compensatory plan). A *compensatory plan* is one in which services rendered by employees are partially compensated for by the issuance of stock. The measurement of compensation expense included in compensatory plans is the primary problem encountered in accounting for stock issued to employees.

ASC 718-10: OVERALL

BACKGROUND

GAAP for issuances of stock as compensation to employees is found in ASC 718. ASC 718 applies to all share-based payment transactions in which an entity compensates employees by issuing its shares, share options, or other equity instruments or by issuing liabilities to an employee in amounts based, at least in part, on the price of the entity's shares or other equity instruments or that require or may require settlement by issuing the entity's equity shares or other equity instruments. In addition, ASC 805 (Business Combinations) provides guidance on whether a share-based payment award issued as part of an acquisition is part of the acquisition price or is for continued service. If the share-based payment award is part of the consideration transferred then the applicable accounting guidance is ASC 805; otherwise, the guidance in ASC 718 is applicable (ASC 718-10-15-6).

ASC 718 provides guidance in accounting for the issuance of employee stock options, restricted stock, performance-based stock issuances, stock appreciation rights, and employee stock purchase plans. Descriptions of the more common types of plans follow.

Employee Stock Option Plan

In a stock option plan, an employee is granted the right to purchase a fixed number of shares at a certain price during a specified period (ASC Glossary).

Restricted Stock Plan

Shares that have been issued under a restricted stock plan cannot be sold for a period of time due to a contractual or governmental restriction. In the case of shares issued to employees, a limitation on the ability to sell the shares typically results from the shares not yet being vested. The employee may be prohibited (restricted) from selling the shares until the employee meets a service or performance condition (ASC Glossary).

Performance-Based Stock Plan

A stock award where a pertinent provision of the award (e.g., vesting, exercisability, exercise price) is affected by whether one or more performance targets are achieved (ASC Glossary).

Stock Appreciation Rights

Under a stock appreciation rights plan, employees receive an amount equal to the increase in the value of a specified number of shares over a specified period of time. This amount usually is paid in cash, although it can be issued in the form of stock.

Employee Stock Purchase Plan

Employee stock purchase plans are a type of employee benefit permitted by the Internal Revenue Code. These types of plans are typically established as either a stock bonus plan or a stock bonus plan combined with a money purchase pension plan and are designed to invest in the employer's stock (ASC Glossary).

COMPENSATORY PLANS

Compensatory plans give rise to compensation, usually out of an offer or agreement by a corporation to issue shares to one or more officers or employees (grantees) at a stated price that is less than the prevailing market price. Under ASC 718, the issuance of equity instruments (stock and options) in exchange for employee services is recognized at the instruments' fair value in an entity's primary financial statements. ASC 718 relates to the accounting for the issuance of equity instruments in exchange for employee services and the resulting recognition of compensation expense.

PRACTICE POINTER: The SEC issued Staff Accounting Bulletin No. 107 (SAB 107), *Share-Based Payment*, in March 2005. SAB 107 is designed to provide guidance to public companies in applying GAAP related to share-based payments to employees and non-employees. Although SEC pronouncements typically are not covered in the *GAAP Guide*, this edition is covering selected excerpts of SAB 107 because of the complexity of GAAP related to the accounting for share-based payments and because SAB 107 provides detailed and specific guidance in accounting for these types of payments.

Public companies are required to recognize compensation cost for equity instruments based on the grant-date fair value of those instruments. The resulting compensation cost is recognized as an expense over the period that the employee must work in order to be entitled to the award. The grant-date fair value of the equity instrument is estimated using an option-pricing model (e.g., the Black-Scholes model, a binomial model), adjusted to reflect the unique characteristics of the equity instrument. Nonpublic companies also must recognize compensation expense based on the grant-date fair value of the equity instrument issued, though some variation in how this principle is applied may be required due to the inability to determine the fair value of the equity instrument at its date of issuance.

PRACTICE POINTER: SAB 107 indicates that compensation expense for share-based payment arrangements with employees should appear in the same income statement line item as cash-based compensation paid to employees. Some companies might want to highlight the non-cash portion of employee compensation expense (i.e., the expense as a result of a share-based payment arrangement). SAB 107 indicates that companies could make this disclosure as a parenthetical notation to the appropriate income statement line item, in the cash flow statement, in the financial statement notes, or in the MD&A.

Recognition and Measurement Principles

The cost of services received from employees in exchange for awards of share-based compensation generally shall be measured at the fair value of the equity instruments issued or at the fair value of the liabilities incurred. The fair value of the liabilities incurred in share-based transactions with employees shall be remeasured at the end of each reporting period until settlement (ASC 718-10-30-3).

Share-based payments awarded to an employee of the reporting entity by a related party or other holder of an economic interest in the entity as compensation for services provided to the entity are share-based transactions to be accounted for under ASC 718 unless the transfer is clearly for a purpose other than compensation for services to the reporting entity. The substance of such a transaction is that the economic interest holder makes a capital contribution to the reporting entity and that entity makes a share-based payment to its employee in exchange for services rendered (ASC 718-10-15-4).

Measurement of Awards Classified as Equity—Public Company

For equity instruments awarded to employees, the measurement objective is to estimate the fair value at the grant date of the equity instruments that the entity is obligated to issue when employees have rendered the required service and have satisfied any other conditions required to earn the right to benefit from the instruments. To satisfy this measurement objective, the restrictions and conditions inherent in equity instruments awarded to employees are treated differently depending on whether they continue in effect after the requisite service period. A restriction that continues in effect (e.g., the inability to transfer vested equity share options to third parties or inability to sell vested shares for a period of time) is considered in estimating the fair value of the instruments at the grant date. For equity share options and similar instruments, the effect of nontransferability is taken into account by reflecting the effects of expected exercise by employees and post-vesting employment termination behavior in estimating the option's expected term, and the option's expected term affects the estimate of the option's fair value (ASC 718-10-30-6, 10).

In contrast, a restriction that results from the forfeitability of instruments to which employees have not yet earned the right (e.g., the inability to exercise a nonvested equity share option or to sell nonvested shares) is *not* reflected in estimating the fair value of the related instruments at the grant date. Rather, those restrictions are taken into account by recognizing compensation cost only for awards for which employees render the requisite service (ASC 718-10-30-11).

Ordinarily, awards and share-based employee compensation specify a performance and/or service condition that must be satisfied for an employee to earn the right to benefit from the award. No compensation cost is recognized for instruments that employees forfeit because a service condition or performance condition is not satisfied. Some awards contain a market condition. The effect of a market condition is reflected in the grant-date fair value of the award. Compensation cost is recognized for an award with a market condition provided that the requisite service is rendered, regardless of whether the market condition is satisfied (ASC 718-10-30-12, 14).

The effects on grant-date fair value of service and performance conditions that apply only during the requisite service period are reflected based on the outcomes of those conditions (ASC 718-10-30-13).

A nonvested equity share or nonvested equity share unit awarded to an employee shall be measured at its fair value as if it were vested and issued on the grant date. A restricted share awarded to an employee (i.e., a share that will be restricted after the employee has a vested right to it) shall be measured at its fair value, which is the same amount for which a similarly restricted share would be issued to a third party (ASC 718-10-30-17, 18, 19).

The fair value of an equity share option or similar instrument shall be measured based on the observable market value of an option with the same or similar terms and conditions if one is available. Otherwise, the fair value of an equity share option or similar instrument is estimated using a valuation technique such as an option-pricing model (ASC 718-10-30-7, 8, 9). The valuation technique used should possess all of the following characteristics:

- It is applied in a manner consistent with the fair value measurement objective and other requirements of ASC 718;
- It is based on established principles of financial economic theory and generally applied in that field; and

- It reflects all substantive characteristics of the instrument (ASC 718-10-15-11).

The estimated fair value of the instrument at grant date does not take into account the effect on fair value of vesting conditions and other restrictions that apply only during the requisite service period. Under the fair-value-based method required by ASC 718, the effect of vesting restrictions that apply only during the requisite service period is reflected by recognizing compensation cost only for instruments for which the requisite service is rendered (ASC 718-10-55-12).

PRACTICE POINTER: SAB 107 indicates that only rarely will there be only one acceptable method of determining the fair value of a share-based payment arrangement. SAB 107 also indicates that estimates of fair value are not intended to predict future events. As long as a reasonable and appropriate process was used to estimate fair value, a difference (no matter how significant) between the estimate of fair value and actual future events does not necessarily reflect on the reasonableness of the original estimates.

Valuation Techniques for Share Options and Other Similar Instruments

A lattice model (e.g., a binomial model) and a closed-form model (e.g., the Black-Scholes-Merton formula) are among the valuation techniques that meet the criteria required by ASC 718 for estimating the fair values of employee share options and similar instruments. ASC 718 does not specify a preference for a particular valuation technique or model for estimating the fair value of employee share options and similar instruments (ASC 718-10-55-16, 17).

Illustration of Application of Lattice Model to Valuing an Employee Stock Option

This example illustrates the valuation of stock options using the binomial model, a lattice-based option-pricing model. Aqua Resources Inc. grants fully vested stock options with an exercise price of $25 and a term of five years. The owner of the option can therefore purchase shares of stock for $25 for the next five years until the option expires. There is a 75% probability that the price of the security will increase by 16% each year and a 25% probability that the price will decline by 14% each year. Aqua Resources uses a discount rate of 6%. The bold numbers indicate the expected share prices, and the corresponding numbers below are the option value calculations.

If the share price exceeds $25 by Year 5, the option holder will realize a gain of the net amount upon exercise of the option. For example, if the share price increases all five years, the holder will net $27.51 ($52.51 - $25) upon exercise. If the share price falls below $25 by Year 5, the option holder will not exercise since the share price is less than the exercise price.

To calculate the option value at the time of grant, Entity X first determines the option value at the expiration period and then works backward to the date of the grant. For example, assume that in Year 4, the share price has increased to

$45.27 based on the aforementioned estimates. In this case, the option holder has an asset that will either rise to a share price of $52.51 (total five-year net increase of $27.51) or fall to a share price of $38.93 (total five-year net increase of $13.93). The respective probability of these outcomes is 75% and 25%. Using a discount rate of 6%, the value of the option in Year 4 will be $22.75, as calculated below:

Year 4: [(75% × $27.51)/1.06] + [(25% × $13.93)/1.06] = $22.75

Continuing to work backward, the option value at the grant date is determined as follows:

Year 3: [(75% × $22.75)/1.06] + [(25% × $10.77)/1.06] = $18.63
Year 2: [(75% × $18.63)/1.06] + [(25% × $8.26)/1.06] = $15.13
Year 1: [(75% × $15.13)/1.06] + [(25% × $6.30)/1.06] = $12.19
Grant Date: [(75% × $12.19)/1.06] + [(25% × $4.78)/1.06] = **$ 9.76**

Thus, the value of the option is based on the expected share price at each node of the lattice. Note that when the share price does not exceed the exercise price at Year 5, the option has no value since the option would simply expire unexercised. Accordingly, there is no real risk of loss to the owner; the higher the probability of an increase in stock price, the higher the value of the option. Also note that one of the advantages of the binomial model is that it can use different volatility estimates for different time periods; however, different volatilities are not used in this illustration.

Illustration of Application of Lattice Model—Early Exercise of Fully Vested Options

Using the same information as in the previous example, we allow for the early exercise of the options. Assume that there is an expectation of early exercise when the underlying share price reaches 1.3 times the exercise price. As shown, when the price exceeds $32.50 ($25 × 1.3), employees will exercise their options, stopping the binomial tree from expanding. The underlined share prices indicate where early exercise takes place. The shaded areas represent the portion of the binomial tree that is no longer relevant due to early exercise.

For example, if the share price increases in Years 1 and 2, the value of the option would be $33.64 in Year 2. Because the price now exceeds $32.50, the option holder is assumed to exercise the option early, and no further increases in share value are possible. Therefore, the total net increase is calculated as $8.64 ($33.64 - $25), and the option value at grant date falls from $9.76 to $6.14 as a result of early exercise:

Year 1: [(75% × $8.64)/1.06] + [(25% × $5.2)/1.06] = $7.34
Grant Date: [(75% × $7.34)/1.06] + [(25% × $4.00)/1.06] = **$6.14**

Illustration of Application of Lattice Model—Early Exercise and Cliff Vesting

Using the same information as in the previous examples, we now assume three-year cliff vesting. This extends the life of the option and increases its value from $6.14 to $7.57. Early exercise cannot occur in Year 2 even though the share price may exceed $32.50 by that time, as indicated by the double-underlined share price. The single-underlined share prices indicate where early exercise is allowed and does take place, and the shaded areas represent the portion of the binomial tree that is no longer relevant due to early exercise. The option value at grant date is calculated in the same manner as illustrated previously.

The Black-Scholes-Merton formula assumes that option exercises occur at the end of an option's contractual term and that expected volatility, expected dividends, and risk-free interest rates are constant over the option's term. This formula must be adjusted to take into account certain characteristics of employee share options and similar instruments that are not consistent with the formula's assumptions (e.g., the ability to exercise before the end of the option's contractual term) (ASC 718-10-55-18).

OBSERVATION: A closed-form model (e.g., Black-Scholes-Merton) is not always appropriate for valuing an employee share option. For example, if an option's exercise is conditional on the entity's stock price rising a certain amount, SAB 107 indicates that a closed-form model would not be appropriate.

Illustration of Application of Black-Scholes-Merton Model to Valuing an Employee Stock Option

Optical Vision Inc. issues 100,000 stock options to its employees on January 1, 20X7. Optical Vision expects its stock price volatility to be relatively constant over time, and it does not expect the risk-free interest rate to fluctuate greatly from its present level. Optical Vision's current dividend yield (d) is 1%, and management plans to maintain a relatively constant dividend yield. Optical Vision will value its issuance of stock options using the Black-Scholes-Merton option pricing method.

Optical Vision's current stock price (S) is $30 per share, and the exercise price (E) of the option is $30 (i.e., as is often the case, the exercise price of the options is set equal to the stock's market price on the date the options are granted). The expected term (T) of the options is 8 years, and the riskfree interest rate (r) is 4%. Optical Vision expects its stock price volatility (σ) (the standard deviation of Optical Vision's daily stock price) to be 50% over the expected term of the option.

The Black-Scholes-Merton formula to value this option is:

$N(d1$ or $d2)$ = the cumulative normal density function - the probability that a particular number falls at or below $d1$ or $d2$, respectively

where:

ln = the natural logarithm

Therefore, Optical Vision will calculate the value of 1 stock option to be:

Therefore, the fair value of the options issued by Optical Vision Inc. on January 1, 20X7 is $1,599,000 ($15.99 × 100,000).

In contrast to the Black-Scholes-Merton formula, a lattice model can be designed to accommodate dynamic assumptions of expected volatility and dividends over the option's contractual term and estimates of expected option exercise patterns during the option's contractual term. This includes the effect of black-out periods. As a result, a lattice model more fully reflects the substantive characteristics of a particular employee share option or similar instrument (ASC 718-10-55-18).

An entity should change the valuation technique it uses to estimate fair value if it concludes that a different technique is likely to result in a better estimate of fair value (ASC 718-10-55-20).

PRACTICE POINTER: Some entities may not initially use a lattice model because they have not previously captured the data necessary to apply such a model. However, after changing their systems to capture the needed data, such an entity should change to a lattice model from the Black-Scholes-Merton model if the entity concludes that a lattice model provides a better estimate of fair value.

Selecting Assumptions for Use in an Option-Pricing Model

If an observable market price is not available for a share option or similar instrument with the same or similar terms and conditions, the fair value of the instrument shall be estimated using a valuation technique or model that meets the criteria of ASC 718 (discussed previously) and takes into account at least the following:

- The exercise price of the option;
- The expected term of the option, considering the option's term and employees' expected exercise behavior and postvesting termination behavior;
- The current price of the underlying share;
- The expected volatility of the price of the underlying share for the expected term of the option;
- The expected dividends on the underlying share for the expected term of the option; and
- The risk-free interest rate(s) for the expected term of the option (ASC 718-10-55-21).

There may be a range of reasonable estimates of expected volatility, dividends, and term of the option. If no amount within the range is more or less likely than any other amount, the average of the amounts within the range, referred to as the expected value, should be used (ASC 718-10-55-21).

OBSERVATION: SAB 107 indicates that a company may appropriately conclude that its past experience with the exercise of options by employees is the best estimate of future exercise behavior. In this instance, it is appropriate to use the company's historical exercise experience in estimating the option's expected term.

In certain circumstances, historical information may not be available. If this is the case, the entity might base expectations about future volatility on the average volatilities of similar entities for an appropriate period following their going public (ASC 718-10-55-25).

The valuation technique an entity selects to estimate fair value for a particular type of instrument should be used consistently and should not be changed unless a different valuation technique is expected to produce a better estimate of fair value. Assumptions used to estimate the fair value of instruments granted to employees also should be determined in a consistent manner from period to period (ASC 718-10-55-27).

> **OBSERVATION:** SAB 107 indicates that a change in the model or technique used to determine fair value would *not* be considered a change in accounting principle. However, the SEC indicates that companies should not change valuation models or techniques frequently.

A U.S. entity issuing an option on its own shares must use as the risk-free interest rate the implied yields currently available from the U.S. Treasury zero-coupon yield curve over the contractual term of the option if the entity is using a lattice model incorporating the option's contractual term. If the entity is using a closed-form model, the risk-free interest rate is the implied yield currently available on U.S. Treasury zero-coupon issues with a remaining term equal to the expected term used in the model to value the options (ASC 718-10-55-28).

The expected term of an employee share option or similar instrument is the period of time for which the instrument is expected to be outstanding. In most cases, the expected term is shorter than the option's contractual term because employees typically exercise options before the end of the contractual period (ASC 718-10-55-29). The expected term is an assumption in the closed-form model. If an entity uses a lattice model that has been modified to take into account an option's contractual term and employees' expected exercise and post-vesting employment termination behavior, the expected term is estimated based on the resulting output of the lattice (ASC 718-10-55-30).

> **PRACTICE POINTER:** SAB 107 indicates that the expected term can be estimated based on (1) the company's historical option exercise experience, (2) exercise patterns of employees in similar industries, or (3) as an output of a lattice model where the expected term can then be used as an input into the Black-Scholes-Merton model. (Note that a lattice model could also be used to value the option itself).

Other factors that may affect expectations about employees' exercise and post-vesting employment termination behavior include:

- The vesting period of the award (the expected term of the award cannot be less than this);
- Employees' historical exercise and post-vesting employment termination behavior for similar grants;
- Expected volatility of the price of the underlying share;
- Blackout periods and other coexisting arrangements, such as agreements that allow for exercise to automatically occur during blackout periods if certain conditions are satisfied; and
- Employees' ages, lengths of service, and home jurisdictions (ASC 718-10-55-31).

Aggregating individual awards into relatively homogeneous groups with respect to exercise and post-vesting employment termination behaviors and estimating the fair value of the options granted to each group separately reduces potential misstatement. An entity shall aggregate individual awards into relatively homogeneous groups with respect to exercise and post-vesting employment termination behaviors regardless of the valuation technique or model used to estimate fair value (ASC 718-10-55-34).

OBSERVATION: SAB 107 indicates that a reasonable estimate of fair value can be developed using as few as two groups. Groups should be identified based on differences in expected exercise behavior. Two possible groups where exercise behavior will likely differ are executives and non-executives.

Volatility is a measure of the amount by which a financial variable, such as share price, has fluctuated (i.e., historical volatility) or can be expected to fluctuate (i.e., expected volatility) during a period. Option-pricing models require expected volatility as an assumption because an option's value is dependent on potential share returns over the option's term. The higher the volatility, the more the returns on the shares can be expected to vary. An entity's estimate of expected volatility should be reasonable and supportable (ASC 718-10-55-36).

Factors that should be considered in estimating expected volatility include:

- Volatility in the share price, including potential changes in the entity's share price in the future (e.g., as a result of reversion to the average level of volatility of other similar companies);
- Implied volatility of the share price determined by the market prices of traded options or other traded financial instruments, such as outstanding convertible debt;
- For public companies, the length of time an entity's shares have been publicly traded;
- Appropriate and regular intervals for price observations; and
- Corporate and capital structure, recognizing that entities with greater levels of debt tend to have higher volatility (ASC 718-10-55-37).

> **PRACTICE POINTER:** Some entities have exchange-traded financial instruments (e.g., exchange-traded options) that can be used to derive implied (stock price) volatility. SAB 107 encourages public companies to consider such implied volatility in estimating expected volatility. For example, the SEC indicates that a company with exchange-traded options could rely heavily, possibly even exclusively, on the implied volatility in these options, as evidenced by the option's price, in estimating expected volatility for the purpose of applying ASC 718.

> **OBSERVATION:** SAB 107 indicates that daily, weekly, or monthly price observations may provide a sufficient basis to estimate expected volatility. The SEC also indicates that weekly or monthly price observations are more appropriate than daily price observations if the stock is thinly traded. A public company listed on an organized stock exchange would generally use daily price observations to estimate volatility.

Consideration of Market, Performance, and Service Conditions

Analysis of the market, performance, or service conditions that are explicit or implicit in the terms of an award is required to determine the requisite service period over which compensation cost is recognized and whether recognized compensation cost may be reversed if an award fails to vest or become exercisable (ASC 718-10-55-61).

Vesting or exercisability may be conditional on satisfying two or more types of conditions: a market condition and a performance or service condition. Alternatively, vesting may be conditional on satisfying one of the two or more types of conditions. Regardless of the nature and number of conditions that must be satisfied, the existence of a market condition requires recognition of compensation cost if the requisite service is rendered, even if the market condition is never satisfied (ASC 718-10-55-62).

Market, performance, and service conditions may affect an award's exercise price, contractual term, quantity, conversion ratio, or other pertinent factors that are relevant in measuring an award's fair value. For instance, an award's quantity may double, or an award's contractual term may be extended, if a company-wide revenue target is achieved. Market conditions that affect an award's fair value are included in the estimate of grant-date fair value. Performance or service conditions that only affect vesting are excluded from the estimate of grant-date fair value, but all other performance or service conditions that affect an award's fair value are included in the estimate of grant-date fair value (ASC 718-10-55-64).

> **Illustration of Accounting for a Stock Option with a Market Condition**
>
> Beta Company grants share options whose exercise price varies with an index of the share prices of a group of entities in the same industry. This qualifies as a market condition per ASC 718. Assume that on January 1, 20X7, Beta grants 50

share options on its common stock with an initial exercise price of $20 to each of 500 employees. The share options have a maximum term of ten years. The exercise price of the share options increases or decreases on December 31 of each year by the same percentage that the index has increased or decreased during the year. For example, if the peer group index increased by 10% in 20X7, the exercise price of the share options during 20X8 would increase to $22 ($20 × 1.10). Assume that, on January 1, 20X7, the peer group index is 500 and the dividend yield on the index is 1%.

Each indexed share option may be analyzed as a share option to exchange 0.04 (20/500) "shares" of the peer group index for a share of Beta stock—that is, to exchange one noncash asset for another. The intrinsic value of a share option to exchange .04 "shares" of the peer group index for a share of Beta stock also equals the difference between the prices of the two assets exchanged.

To illustrate the equivalence of an indexed share option and the share option above, assume that an employee exercises the indexed share option when Beta's share price has increased 100% to $40 and the peer group Index has increased 70% from 500 to 850. Thus, the exercise price of the indexed share option is $34 ($20 × 1.70).

Price of Beta share	$40.00
Less: Exercise price of share option	34.00
Intrinsic value of indexed share option	$ 6.00

That is the same as the intrinsic value of a share option to exchange .04 shares of the index for 1 share of Beta stock:

Price of Beta share	$40.00
Less: Price of a share of the peer group index (.04 × $850)	34.00
Intrinsic value at exchange	$ 6.00

Option-pricing models can be extended to value a share option to exchange one asset for another. The volatility of a share option to exchange two noncash assets is based on their cross-volatility, the relationship between the volatilities of the prices of the assets to be exchanged. In a share option with an exercise price payable in cash, the amount of cash to be paid has zero volatility, so only the volatility of the stock needs to be considered in estimating that option's fair value. In contrast, when two noncash assets are involved, the fair value of a share option depends on possible movements in the prices of both assets. In this example, fair value depends on the cross-volatility of a share of the peer group index and a share of Beta stock. Historical cross-volatility can be computed directly based on measures of Beta's share price in shares of the peer group index. For example, Beta's share price was 0.04 shares at the grant date and 0.0471 (40/850) shares at the exercise date. Those share amounts then are used to compute crossvolatility. Cross-volatility can also be computed indirectly based on the respective volatilities of Beta stock and the peer group index and the correlation between them.

In a share option with an exercise price payable in cash, the assumed risk-free interest rate (discount rate) represents the return on cash that will not be paid until exercise. In this example, an equivalent share of the index, rather than cash, is what will not be "paid" until exercise. Therefore, the dividend yield on the peer group index of 1% is used in place of the risk-free interest rate as an input to the option-pricing model.

The initial exercise price for the indexed share option is the value of an equivalent share of the peer group index, which is $20 (0.04 × $500). The fair value of each share option would be based on relevant inputs.

The indexed share options have a three-year explicit service period. The market condition affects the grant-date fair value of the award and its exercisability; however, vesting is based solely on the explicit service period of three years. The at-the-money nature of the award makes the derived service period irrelevant in determining the requisite service period in this example; therefore, the requisite service period of the award is three years based on the explicit service period. The accrual of compensation cost would be based on the number of options for which the requisite service is expected to be rendered, and that cost would be recognized over the requisite service period.

An award may be indexed to a factor in addition to the entity's share price. If that factor is not a market, performance, or service condition, that award is classified as a liability for purposes of ASC 718. An example of this is an award of options whose exercise prices are indexed to the market price of a commodity (ASC 718-10-55-65).

The requisite service period for an award that has only a service condition is presumed to be the vesting period unless there is clear evidence to the contrary. An employee's share-based payment award becomes vested at the date that the employee's right to receive or retain equity shares, other equity instruments, or cash under the award is no longer contingent on satisfaction of either a performance condition or a service condition. Any unrecognized compensation cost shall be recognized when an award becomes vested. If the award includes no market, performance, or service conditions, the entire amount of compensation cost is recognized when the award is granted (ASC 718-10-55-67, 68).

A requisite service period may be explicit, implicit, or derived. An explicit service period is one that is stated in the terms of the share-based payment award. An implicit service period is one that may be inferred from an analysis of an award's terms. A derived service period is based on a market condition in a share-based payment award that affects exercisability, exercise price, or the employee's ability to retain the award. A derived service period is inferred from the application of certain techniques used to estimate fair value (ASC 718-10-55-69, 70, 71).

An award with a combination of market, performance, or service conditions may contain multiple explicit, implicit, or derived service periods. For such an award, the estimate of the requisite service period is based on an analysis of (1) all vesting and exercisability conditions; (2) all explicit, implicit, and derived service periods; and (3) the probability that performance or service conditions will be satisfied. For example, if vesting or exercisability is based on satisfying *both* a market condition and a performance or service condition and it is probable that the performance or service condition will be satisfied, an initial estimate of the requisite service period generally is the *longest* of the explicit, implicit, or derived service periods. If vesting or exercisability is based on satisfying *either* a market condition or a performance or service condition and it is probable that the performance or service condition will be satisfied, the initial estimate of the requisite service period generally is the *shortest* of the explicit, implicit, or derived service periods (ASC 718-10-55-72, 73).

Compensation cost ultimately recognized is equal to the grant-date fair value of the award based on the actual outcome of the performance or service condition. The proper accounting for a change in the initial estimate of the requisite service period depends on whether that change would affect the grant-date fair value of the award that is to be recognized as compensation. For example, if the quantity of instruments for which the requisite service is expected to be rendered changes because a vesting condition becomes probable of satisfaction or if the grant-date fair value of an instrument changes because another performance or service condition becomes probable of satisfaction, the cumulative effect on current and prior periods of those changes in estimates is recognized in the period of change. In contrast, if compensation cost is already being attributed over an initially estimated requisite service period and that period changes because another market, performance, or service condition becomes the basis for the requisite service period, any unrecognized compensation cost at the time of the change is recognized prospectively over the revised requisite service period, if any (ASC 718-10-55-77, 78).

Illustration of Accounting for a Stock Option with Performance Conditions

This example illustrates the computation of compensation cost if Alpha Company grants an award of share options with multiple performance conditions. Under the award, employees vest in differing numbers of options depending on the amount by which the market share of one of Alpha's products increases over a three-year period (the options cannot vest before the end of the three-year period).

On January 1, 20X7, Alpha grants to each of its 500 employees an award of up to 150 ten-year-term share options on its common stock. If market share increases by at least 4% by December 31, 20X9, each employee vests in at least 50 share options at that date. If market share increases by at least 8%, another 50 share options vest, for a total of 100. If market share increases by more than 16%, all 150 share options vest. Assume that Alpha's share price on January 1, 20X7, is $20, and the grant-date fair value per share option is $15.

The compensation cost of the award depends on the estimated number of options that will vest. Alpha must determine whether it is probable (probable as defined in ASC 450) that any performance condition will be achieved, that is, whether market share growth will be at least 4% over the three-year period. Accruals of compensation cost are initially based on the probable outcome of the performance conditions—in this case, different levels of market share growth over the three-year vesting period—and adjusted for subsequent changes in the estimated or actual outcome. If Alpha determines that no performance condition is probable of achievement (that is, market share growth is expected to be less than 4%), then no compensation cost is recognized; however, Alpha is required to reassess at each reporting date whether achievement of any performance condition is probable and would begin recognizing compensation cost if and when achievement becomes probable.

Accruals of cost must be based on the probable outcome of performance conditions. Accordingly, Alpha cannot base accruals of compensation cost on an amount that is not a possible outcome (and thus cannot be the probable outcome). For example, if Alpha estimates a 90%, 45%, and 15% likelihood that market share growth will be at least 4%, 8%, and 16%, respectively, it would not try to determine a weighted average of the possible outcomes because that number of shares is not a possible outcome.

The table below shows the compensation cost that would be recognized in 20X7, 20X8, and 20X9, if Alpha estimates at the grant date that it is probable that market share will increase at least 4 but less than 8% (that is, each employee would receive 50 share options). That estimate remains unchanged until the end of 20X9, when Alpha's market share has actually increased over the three-year period by more than 8%. Thus, each employee vests in 100 share options.

Through 20X7, Alpha's estimated and actual forfeiture rate is 5%. Alpha therefore estimates that 429 employees (500 × .95^3) will remain in service until the vesting date. (If actual forfeiture rates differ from estimated forfeiture rates, Alpha would adjust its estimate of expected forfeiture rates which would affect the recognition of compensation cost.) The compensation cost of the award is initially estimated based on the number of options expected to vest, which in turn is based on the expected level of performance and the fair value of each option. The amount of compensation cost recognized (or attributed) when achievement of a performance condition is probable depends on the relative satisfaction of the performance condition based on performance to date. Alpha determines that recognizing compensation cost ratably over the three-year vesting period is appropriate with one-third of the value of the award recognized each year.

Share Option with Performance Condition—Number of Share Options Varies

Year	Total Value of Award	Pretax Cost for Year	Cumulative Pretax Cost
20X7	$321,750 ($15 × 50 × 429)	$107,250 ($321,750 × 1/3)	$107,250
20X8	$321,750 ($15 × 50 × 429)	$107,250 [($321,750 × 2/3)- $107,250]	$214,500
20X9	$643,500 ($15 × 100 × 429)	$429,000 ($643,500 - $214,500)	$643,500

Reload Options

Some companies issue new options to employees when an employee uses existing shares of the company's stock to exercise a stock option rather than paying in cash. Additional options are issued equal to the number of shares used to pay for the shares purchased under a previous stock option grant (ASC Glossary). The effect of a reload feature in terms of an award shall not be included in estimating the grant-date fair value of the award. A subsequent grant of reload options shall be accounted for as a separate award when the reload options are granted (ASC 718-10-30-23).

Measurement of Awards Classified as Equity—Nonpublic Company

As was the case for a public company, stock or options issued by a nonpublic company in exchange for employee services should be recorded at fair value. In determining the fair value of a stock option, the volatility of the underlying stock needs to be estimated. This can often be difficult for a nonpublic company, given the lack of trading of these shares and their illiquid market. Therefore, a nonpublic entity must exercise judgment in selecting a method to estimate expected volatility and might do so by basing its expected volatility on the average volatilities of similar public entities (ASC 718-10-55-25).

In other instances, a nonpublic entity may not be able to reasonably estimate the fair value of its equity share options and other instruments because it is not practicable to estimate the expected volatility of its share price. In this circumstance, the entity shall account for the equity share options and similar instruments based on a value calculated using the historical volatility of an appropriate industry sector index. If the complexity of the terms of an equity share option or other equity instrument precludes making a reasonable estimate of fair value, the option or instrument shall be accounted for based on its intrinsic value, remeasured at each reporting date through the date of exercise or other settlement. The intrinsic value method shall continue to be used, even if the entity subsequently concludes that a reasonable estimate of fair value can be made (ASC 718-10-55-25, 27).

As discussed previously, if it is not practicable for a nonpublic entity to estimate its stock price volatility, the entity may estimate its stock price volatility using an industry-sector index (the calculated value method) (ASC 718-10-55-52). For purposes of applying ASC 718, it is not practicable for a nonpublic entity to estimate the expected volatility of its share price if it is unable to obtain sufficient historical information about past volatility, or other information on which to base a reasonable and supportable estimate of expected volatility at the grant date of the award without undue cost and effort. In that situation, ASC 718 requires the nonpublic entity to estimate a value of its equity share options and similar instruments by substituting the historical volatility of the appropriate industry sector index for the expected share price volatility as an assumption in its valuation model. There are many different indices available to consider in selecting an appropriate industry sector index. An appropriate index is one that is representative of the industry sector in which the nonpublic entity operates and that also reflects, if possible, the size of the entity. In *no* circumstance shall a nonpublic entity use a broad-based market index, such as the S&P 500, Russell 3000®, or Dow Jones Wilshire 5000, because these indices are sufficiently diversified as to be *not* representative of the industry sector(s) in which the nonpublic entity operates (ASC 718-10-55-55, 56).

Illustration of Accounting for a Stock Option Award by a Private Company—Company Unable to Estimate Its Expected Stock Price Volatility

Talisman Inc. is a small, private company that develops, markets, and distributes computer software. On January 1, 20X6, Talisman issues 200 stock options to each of its 75 employees. Talisman's share price on January 1, 20X6, is valued at $5, and the exercise price is $5 on that date. The options cliff vest in three years, and the contractual term of the options is seven years. Although the contractual term of the options is seven years, Talisman expects the term of the options to be four years (i.e., Talisman expects the options to be exercised early). Talisman assumes no forfeitures over the next three years (a simplifying assumption for this example), and expects to pay no dividends. We assume away income taxes.

> **PRACTICE POINTER:** The AICPA has issued a practice aid, Valuation of Privately-Held-Company Equity Securities Issued as Compensation, that is likely to be helpful in valuing equity securities of privately-held companies where these securities are issued as compensation.

Talisman does not maintain an internal market for its shares, and its shares are rarely traded privately. The last time Talisman issued equity shares was in 20W7, and it has never issued convertible debt securities. In addition, Talisman is unable to identify any similar public companies. As such, Talisman is unable to estimate the expected volatility of its share price—a key input to valuing its employee stock options on January 1, 20X6. Therefore, Talisman will value the options it has issued using the *calculated value method*.

Under the calculated value method, the historical volatility of an appropriate industry sector index is used instead of the company's own stock price volatility. Talisman operates exclusively in the software industry. Using the Dow Jones Indexes Web site and the Industry Classification Benchmark tab on this Web site, Talisman determines that its operations fit within the software subsector of the software and computer services sector. Talisman, based on its share price and contributed capital, would be classified as a small-cap company within the index. Talisman therefore selects the small-cap version of the software index as an appropriate industry sector index. Again, using the Dow Jones Indexes Web site, Talisman obtains the daily closing total return values from the index from January 1, 20X1, through December 31, 20X5 (five years of daily total return values). Using the five years of daily total return values, Talisman computes the annualized historical volatility of the software index to be 30%. This 30% volatility is an input to the option pricing model used by Talisman, and the computed value of the options granted by Talisman is $3.25 per share.

Talisman would make the following journal entries at December 31, 20X6, 20X7, and 20X8:

Compensation cost [(200 × 75 × $3.25) / 3]	16,250	
Additional paid-in capital		16,250

—To recognize compensation cost.

All of the stock options are exercised on December 31, 20X9. Talisman would record the following entry (Talisman issues no-par common stock).

Cash (200 × 75 × $5)	75,000	
Additional paid-in capital	48,750	
Common stock		123,750

—To record the issuance of common stock upon exercise of stock options and to reclassify previously recorded additional paid-in capital.

Recognition of Compensation Cost for an Award Accounted for as an Equity Instrument

Compensation cost associated with an award of share-based employee compensation classified as equity is recognized over the requisite service period with a corresponding credit to equity (usually paid-in capital). The requisite service period is that period during which the employee is required to provide service in exchange for the award (i.e., the vesting period). The service period is estimated based on an analysis of the terms of the share-based payment award. The requisite service period may be explicitly stated or it may be implicit, being inferred from analysis of other terms of the award (ASC 718-10-35-2, 5).

The total amount of compensation cost recognized at the end of the requisite service period for an award of share-based compensation is based on the number of instruments for which the requisite service has been rendered. An entity shall base initial accruals of compensation cost on the estimated number of instruments for which the requisite service is expected to be rendered. That estimate should be revised if subsequent information indicates that the actual number of instruments is likely to differ from the previous estimate. The cumulative effect on current and prior periods of a change in the estimated number of instruments for which the requisite service is expected to be or has been rendered shall be recognized as compensation cost in the period of the change (ASC 718-10-35-3).

Accruals of compensation cost for an award with a performance condition shall be based on the probable outcome of that performance condition. Compensation cost is accrued if it is probable that the performance condition will be achieved and is not accrued if it is not probable that the performance condition will be achieved. Previously recognized compensation is not reversed if an employee share option for which the requisite service has been rendered expires unexercised (ASC 718-10-25-20; 718-10-35-3).

The entity shall make its best estimate of the requisite service period at the grant date and shall base accruals of compensation cost on that period. That initial estimate is adjusted in light of changes in facts and circumstances. If an award requires satisfaction of one or more market, performance, or service conditions (or a combination of these), compensation cost is recognized if the requisite service is rendered. No compensation cost is recognized if the requisite service is not rendered (ASC 718-10-30-25, 26).

Performance or service conditions that affect vesting are not reflected in estimating the fair value of an award at the grant-date because those conditions are restrictions that result from the forfeitability of instruments to which employees have not yet earned the right. The effect of a market condition is reflected, however, in estimating the fair value of an award at the grant date. Market, performance, and service conditions (or a combination of these) may affect the award's exercise price, contractual term, quantity, conversion ratio, or other factors that are considered in measuring an award's grant-date fair value. That fair value shall be estimated for each possible outcome of such a performance or service condition, and the final measure of compensation shall be based on the amount estimated at the grant date for the condition or outcome that is actually satisfied (ASC 718-10-30-27).

ASC 718-20: AWARDS CLASSIFIED AS EQUITY

MODIFICATIONS OF AWARDS OF EQUITY INSTRUMENTS

A modification of the terms or conditions of an equity award shall be treated as an exchange of the original award for a new award. The effects of a modification are measured as follows:

- Incremental compensation cost is measured as the excess, if any, of the fair value of the modified award over the fair value of the original award immediately before its terms are modified, based on the share price and other pertinent factors as of that date. The effect of the modification on the number of instruments expected to vest also shall be reflected in determining incremental compensation cost.

- Total recognized compensation cost for an equity award shall at least equal the fair value of the award at the grant-date unless at the date of the modification the performance or service conditions of the original award are not expected to be satisfied. Total compensation cost measured at the date of the modification shall be (1) the portion of the grant-date fair value of the original award for which the requisite service is expected to be rendered at that date plus (2) the incremental cost resulting from the modification.

- A change in compensation cost for an equity award measured at intrinsic value shall be measured by comparing the intrinsic value of the modified award, if any, with the intrinsic value of the original award, if any, immediately before the modification (ASC 718-20-35-3).

Cancellation of an award accompanied by the concurrent grant of a replacement award or other valuable consideration is accounted for as a modification of the terms of the cancelled award. Incremental compensation cost is measured as the excess of the fair value of the replacement award or other valuable consideration over the fair value of the cancelled award at the cancellation date (ASC 718-20-35-8).

A cancellation of an award that is not accompanied by the concurrent grant of a replacement award or issuance of other valuable consideration is accounted for as a repurchase for no consideration. Any previously unrecognized compensation cost is recognized at the cancellation date (ASC 718-20-35-9). In other circumstances, the entity may pay cash to repurchase an equity award. The cash payment is charged against equity as long as the amount paid does not exceed the fair value of the equity instruments on the date of payment. Additional compensation cost is recognized if the cash payment exceeds the fair value of the equity instruments. Also, any previously unrecognized compensation cost is recognized at the repurchase date (ASC 718-20-35-7).

ASC 718-30: AWARDS CLASSIFIED AS LIABILITIES

MEASUREMENT OF AWARDS CLASSIFIED AS LIABILITIES

In determining whether an instrument shall be classified as a liability or equity, the entity shall apply generally accepted accounting principles applicable to financial instruments issued in transactions that do not involve share-based payments. ASC 480 (Distinguishing Liabilities from Equity) provides guidance for making this determination (ASC 718-10-25-6, 7).

An award may be indexed to a factor in addition to the entity's share price. If the additional factor is not a market, performance, or service condition, the award is classified as a liability for purposes of applying ASC 718, and the additional factor shall be reflected in estimating the fair value of the award (ASC 718-10-25-13).

The determination of whether a share-based payment award should be accounted for as an equity instrument or as a liability shall reflect the substance of the award and any related arrangement. Generally, the written terms provide the best evidence of the substantive terms of an award, but an entity's past practice may indicate that the substantive terms differ from its written terms (ASC 718-10-25-15).

The measurement objective for liabilities incurred under share-based compensation arrangements is the same as the measurement objective for equity instruments awarded to employees as described previously. The measurement date for liability instruments, however, is the date of settlement. Liabilities incurred under share-based payment arrangements are remeasured at the end of each reporting period until they are settled (ASC 718-30-30-1).

A public entity shall measure a liability award under a share-based payment arrangement based on the award's fair value remeasured at each reporting date until settlement. Compensation cost for each period is based on the change in the fair value of the instrument for each reporting period. A nonpublic entity shall make a policy decision regarding whether to measure all of its liabilities incurred under share-based payment arrangements at fair value or measure all such liabilities at intrinsic value. Regardless of the method selected, a nonpublic entity shall remeasure its liabilities under share-based payment arrangements at each reporting date until settlement (ASC 718-30-35-3, 4).

Changes in the fair value (or intrinsic value for a nonpublic entity that elects that method) of a liability incurred under a share-based payment arrangement that occur during the requisite service period shall be recognized as compensation cost over that period. The percentage of the fair value (or intrinsic value) that is accrued as compensation cost at the end of each period shall equal the percentage of the requisite service that has been rendered to that date. Changes in the fair value (intrinsic value) of a liability that occur after the end of the requisite service period are compensation cost of the period in which the changes occur (ASC 718-30-35-2).

Illustration of the Accounting for Stock Appreciation Rights to be Settled in Cash—Recognition of a Liability

Ultimate Metrics International is a public company that grants 750,000 share appreciation rights (SARs) to its employees on January 1, 20X8. Each holder of an SAR is to receive in cash the increase in Ultimate Metrics stock price above $15 per share (Ultimate Metrics' stock price on January 1, 20X8). Ultimate Metrics determines the fair value of the SAR grant on January 1, 20X8, in the same manner as if it had issued 750,000 stock options (i.e., an option-pricing model is used). Using an acceptable option-pricing model, Ultimate Metrics computes the fair value of each SAR as $7.50. The SARs cliff vest at the end of three years. Ultimate Metrics expects forfeitures of 7% of the SARs each year, and actual forfeitures equal expected forfeitures. As a result, Ultimate Metrics expects 603,268 (750,000 × .93^3) of the SARs to vest, and the fair value of the SAR award on January 1, 20X8, is $4,524,510 [(603,268 × $7.50]. Ultimate Metrics' tax rate is 35%.

Because the SARs are to be settled in cash, Ultimate Metrics must record a liability. In addition, ASC 718 requires the liability to be remeasured at each reporting date through the date of settlement of the SARs (this period includes the vesting period and any period after the vesting date until the SARs are settled).

The fair value of the SARs is $11.25 at December 31, 20X8, and the resulting fair value of the award is $6,786,765 (603,268 × $11.25). Ultimate Metrics will recognize $2,262,255 ($6,786,765 ÷ 3), one-third of the total fair value, as compensation cost during 20x8. The journal entries recorded at December 31, 20X8, are:

Compensation cost ($6,786,765 ÷ 3)	2,262,255	
Share-based compensation liability		2,262,255
—To recognize compensation cost.		
Deferred tax asset ($2,262,255 × .35)	791,789	
Deferred tax benefit		791,789
—To recognize a deferred tax asset for the temporary difference.		

The fair value of the SARs is $6.75 at December 31, 20X9, and the resulting fair value of the award is $4,072,059 (603,268 × $6.75). Ultimate Metrics will recognize two-thirds of this amount, $2,714,706, as a liability at December 31, 20X9. Compensation cost recognized during 20X9 is $2,714,706 less the amount of compensation cost recognized during 20X8. The journal entries recorded at December 31, 20x9, are:

Compensation cost ($2,714,706 - $2,262,255)	452,451	
Share-based compensation liability		452,451
—To recognize compensation cost.		
Deferred tax asset ($452,451 × .35)	158,358	
Deferred tax benefit		158,358
—To recognize a deferred tax asset for the temporary difference.		

The fair value of the SARs is $12.50 at December 31, 20Y0, and the resulting fair value of the award is $7,540,850 (603,268 × $12.50). The liability at

December 31, 20Y0, is this entire amount because the award is now fully vested. Compensation cost recognized during 20Y0 is $7,540,850 less the amounts recognized in 20X8 and 20X9. The journal entries recorded at December 31, 20Y0, are:

Compensation cost ($7,540,850 - $2,262,255 - 452,451)	4,826,144	
Share-based compensation liability		4,826,144

—To recognize compensation cost.

Deferred tax asset ($4,826,144 × .35)	1,689,150	
Deferred tax benefit		1,689,150

—To recognize a deferred tax asset for the temporary difference.

All of the SARs are exercised on December 31, 20Y0, and Ultimate Metrics International settles its $7,540,850 liability by making a cash payment. The journal entries are:

Share-based compensation liability (2,262,255 + 452,451 + 4,826,144)	7,540,850	
Cash		7,540,850

—To record the cash payment to employees upon the exercise of the SARs.

Deferred tax benefit (791,789 + 158,358 + 1,689,150)	2,639,297	
Deferred tax asset		2,639,297

—To write off the deferred tax asset related to the SARs.

Income taxes payable	2,639,297	
Income taxes expense		2,639,297

—To record the current tax benefit provided by the exercise of the SARs.

Disclosure Requirements

An entity with one or more share-based payment arrangements must disclose information that enables users of the financial statements to understand:

- The nature and terms of such arrangements that existed during the period and the potential effects of those arrangements on shareholders;
- The effect of compensation cost arising from share-based payment arrangements on the income statement;
- The method of estimating the fair value of the goods or services received, or the fair value of the equity instruments granted, during the period; and
- The cash flow effects of share-based payment arrangements (ASC 718-10-50-1).

Some entities maintain multiple share-based payment arrangements, and these different arrangements may include different types of awards. The above disclosures should be made separately for different share-based payment arrangements if differences in the types of awards make such disclosure necessary (ASC 505-50-50-1).

The minimum information needed to achieve ASC 718's disclosure objectives is (ASC 718-10-50-2):

ASC 718—Compensation—Stock Compensation

- A description of the share-based payment arrangements, including the general terms of the awards under the arrangements. This includes the method used for measuring compensation cost from share-based payments with employees.
- For the most recent year for which an income statement is presented:
  - The number and weighted-average exercise prices for each of the following groups of share options or share units:
    (1) Those outstanding at the beginning of the year.
    (2) Those outstanding at the end of the year.
    (3) Those exercisable or convertible at the end of the year.
    (4) Those granted during the year.
    (5) Those exercised or converted, forfeited, or expired during the year.
  - The number and weighted-average grant-date fair value (or calculated value or intrinsic value for a nonpublic entity that uses either of those approaches) for instruments not covered by the disclosures in the previous paragraph (e.g., nonvested stock). The following disclosures should be made:
    (1) Nonvested shares at the beginning of the year.
    (2) Nonvested shares at the end of the year.
    (3) Shares granted, vested, and forfeited during the year.
- For each year for which an income statement is presented:
  - The weighted-average grant-date fair value (or calculated value or intrinsic value for a nonpublic entity that uses either of those approaches) of equity options or other equity instruments granted during the year.
  - The total intrinsic value of options exercised, share units converted, share-based liabilities paid, and the total fair value of shares vested during the year.
- For fully vested share options (units) and share options (units) expected to vest at the date of the latest balance sheet:
  - The number, weighted-average exercise price (conversion ratio), aggregate intrinsic value, and weighted-average remaining contractual term of options (units) outstanding.
  - The number, weighted-average exercise price (conversion ratio), aggregate intrinsic value (only for public companies), and weighted-average remaining contractual term of options (units) currently exercisable (or convertible).
- For each year for which an income statement is presented (these disclosures are not required for a nonpublic company using the intrinsic value method):

- A description of the method used during the year to estimate the fair value (calculated value) of awards under share-based payment arrangements.
- A description of the significant assumptions used during the year to estimate the fair value (calculated value) of share-based compensation awards, including:
    (1) Expected term of share options and similar instruments and the method used to incorporate the contractual term for the instruments and employees' expected exercise and post-vesting employment termination behavior into the fair value of the instrument.
    (2) Expected volatility of the entity's shares and the method used to estimate it. A nonpublic company using the calculated value method must disclose why it could not estimate the volatility of its stock, the industry sector index used, why that index was chosen, and how the index was used to calculate volatility.
    (3) Expected dividends.
    (4) Risk-free rate(s).
    (5) Any discount, and how it was estimated, for post-vesting restrictions on the sale of stock received.
- An entity that grants equity or liability instruments under multiple share-based payment arrangements with employees shall provide the information specified above separately for different types of awards to the extent that differences in the characteristics of awards make separate disclosure important for an understanding of the entity's use of share-based compensation.
- For each year for which an income statement is presented:
    - Total compensation cost for share-based payment arrangements recognized in income as well as the total recognized tax benefit related thereto, and the total compensation cost capitalized as part of the cost of an asset.
    - A description of significant modifications, including the terms of the modifications, the number of employees affected, and the total incremental compensation cost resulting from the modifications.
- As of the latest balance sheet date, the total compensation cost related to nonvested awards not yet recognized and the weighted-average period over which this compensation cost is expected to be recognized.
- If not separately disclosed elsewhere, the amount of cash received from the exercise of share options and similar instruments granted under share-based payment arrangements and the tax benefit realized from stock options exercised during the year.
- If not separately disclosed elsewhere, the amount of cash used to settle equity instruments granted under share-based payment arrangements.

- A description of the entity's policy for issuing shares upon share option exercise, including the source of those shares (e.g., newly issued shares or treasury stock). If the entity expects to repurchase shares in the following annual period, the entity shall disclose an estimate of the amount of shares (or range) to be repurchased during that period.

OBSERVATION: Given that many companies buy back stock in order to offset the potential earnings per share dilution that would otherwise result from the issuance of stock when options are exercised, the required disclosure of the amount of shares to be repurchased during the next year is likely to be closely followed by financial analysts.

ASC 718-50: EMPLOYEE SHARE PURCHASE PLANS

NONCOMPENSATORY PLANS

Certain stock purchase plans are not intended to compensate employees. For example, a corporation may intend to raise additional capital or to diversify its ownership to include employees and officers. A plan is *noncompensatory* if the cash received per share is very close to the amount of cash that would be received if the same deal were offered to all shareholders. In these types of transactions, a company generally does not recognize any compensation cost.

An employee share purchase plan that satisfies all of the following criteria does not give rise to recognizable compensation cost:

- The plan satisfies at least one of the following conditions:

  — The terms of the plan are no more favorable than those available to all holders of the same class of shares.

  — Any purchase discount from the market price does not exceed the per-share amount of share issuance costs that would have been incurred to raise a significant amount of capital by a public offering. (A purchase discount of 5% or less from the market price is considered to comply with this condition without justification. A purchase discount greater than 5% that cannot be justified under this condition results in compensation cost for the entire amount of the discount.)

- Substantially all employees that meet limited qualifications may participate on an equitable basis.

- The plan incorporates no option features, other than the following:

  — Employees are permitted a short time (not over 31 days) after the purchase price has been fixed to enroll in the plan.

  — The purchase price is based solely on the market price of the shares at the date of purchase, and employees are permitted to cancel participation before the purchase date and obtain a refund of amounts previously paid (ASC 718-50-25-1).

A provision that establishes the purchase price as an amount based on the lesser of the equity share's market price at date of grant or its market price at date of purchase is an example of an option feature that causes the plan to be compensatory. Similarly, a plan in which the purchase price is based on the share's market price at the grant date and that permits a participating employee to cancel participation before the purchase date and obtain a refund of amounts previously paid contains an option feature that causes the plan to be compensatory (ASC 718-50-25-2).

The requisite service period for any compensation cost resulting from an employee share purchase plan is the period over which the employee participates in the plan and pays for the shares (ASC 718-50-25-3).

The portion of the fair value of an instrument attributed to employee service is net of any amount that an employer pays for that instrument when it is granted. For example, if an employee pays $25 at the grant date for an option with a fair value at that date of $100, the amount attributed to employee service is $75 (ASC 718-10-30-3).

Illustration of an Employee Share Purchase Plan

Stein Inc. plans to adopt an employee share purchase plan on January 1, 20X6. Stein wants its employee share purchase plan to be noncompensatory. Under the terms of the plan, all employees who have completed six months of service will be eligible to participate in the plan. Employees will be able to purchase up to $8,000 of Stein Inc.'s common stock each year at an eight percent discount from its market price at the date of purchase. The per share amount of share issuance costs to raise a significant amount of capital by selling stock through a public offering is five percent of Stein's share price. Stein is considering three different alternatives for offering a share discount to existing holders of its common stock.

Alternative 1 Stein Inc. would allow its current common stockholders to purchase up to $8,000 of its stock on a yearly basis at a three percent discount from its market price on the date of purchase. The employee stock purchase plan would be compensatory because the discount offered to employees (eight percent) is larger than the discount offered to existing stockholders (three percent). Therefore, the entire eight percent discount offered to employees would be viewed as compensatory (i.e., compensation expense would be recognized for the full amount of the eight percent discount when employees purchase shares under the plan).

Alternative 2 Stein Inc. would allow its current common stockholders to purchase up to $8,000 of its stock on a yearly basis at an eight percent discount from its market price on the date of purchase. The employee stock purchase plan would be non-compensatory because the discount offered to employees is the same as the discount offered to existing stockholders.

Alternative 3 Stein Inc. would allow its current common stockholders to reinvest dividends received in new shares of common stock. Existing stockholders could buy up to $8,000 of new shares of common stock using dividends received at a discount of eight percent. Since Stein Inc.'s common stock is widely-held, very few existing shareholders would receive dividends equal to $8,000. Therefore, most shareholders would not be able to get the benefit of purchasing $8,000 of stock at an eight percent discount, whereas all employees meeting minimal eligibility requirements would receive this benefit. As a result, this plan would be viewed as compensatory and compensation expense would be recognized for the full amount of the eight percent discount when employees purchase shares under the plan.

ASC 718-740: INCOME TAXES

ACCOUNTING FOR TAX EFFECTS OF SHARE-BASED COMPENSATION AWARDS

Tax deductions generally arise in different amounts and in different periods from compensation costs recognized in financial statements. The cumulative effect of compensation cost recognized for instruments classified as equity that ordinarily would result in a future tax deduction are considered to be deductible temporary differences in applying ASC 740 (Income Taxes). ASC 740 requires a deferred tax asset to be evaluated for future realization and to be reduced by a valuation allowance if it is more likely than not that some portion or all of the deferred tax asset will not be realized. Differences between the deductible temporary difference computed pursuant to ASC 718 (described previously) and the tax deduction that would result based on the current fair value of the entity's shares shall not be considered in measuring the gross deferred tax asset or determining the need for a valuation allowance for a deferred tax asset recognized under ASC 718 (ASC 718-740-05-04; 718-740-25-2; 718-740-30-2).

If a deduction reported on a tax return for an award of equity instrument exceeds the cumulative compensation cost for those instruments recognized for financial reporting (referred to in ASC 718 as the excess tax benefit), any resulting realized tax benefits that exceed the previously recognized deferred tax asset for those instruments are recognized as paid-in capital (ASC 718-740-35-3).

The amount deductible on the employer's tax return may be less than the cumulative compensation cost recognized for financial reporting purposes. The write-off of a deferred tax asset related to that deficiency, net of any related valuation allowance, is first offset to the extent of any remaining additional paid-in capital from excess tax benefits from previous awards accounted for in accordance with the requirements under previous GAAP. Any remaining balance of the write-off of a deferred tax asset related to a tax deficiency shall be recognized in the income statement (ASC 718-740-35-5; 718-740-45-04).

Illustration of Accounting for a Stock Option with a Service Condition—Including Treatment of Income Tax Effects and Presentation in Statement of Cash Flows

Diaz Inc. is a public company that awards 2,000,000 stock options to 4,000 different employees (each employee received 500 options) on January 1, 20X6. The term of the options is seven years, and they vest in full in three years (cliff vesting). These options are not classified as incentive tax options for tax purposes. Diaz Inc.'s tax rate is 35%. Diaz Inc.'s stock price on January 1, 20X6, is $50 per share, and the option's exercise price is also $50. Diaz expects that 5%

41,030 ASC 718—Compensation—Stock Compensation

of the options will be forfeited (due to turnover) in each of the next three years. Using a lattice-based valuation model, the fair value of the options on January 1, 20X6, is $24.75.

Diaz Inc. expects 1,714,750 of the options to vest over the three year period (2,000,000 × .95³). Under ASC 718 compensation cost is only recognized for those share options where a performance or service condition is met. In this case, the service condition is that each of the 4,000 employees that receive options must work through December 31, 20X8. Estimated total compensation cost is $42,440,062 ($1,714,750×$24.75).

During 20X6 Diaz experienced only a four percent employee turnover rate. However, at 12/31/X6 Diaz still expects the employee turnover rate to average five percent over the X6-X8 period (i.e., the estimate of total compensation cost developed at 1/1/X6 is not changed). Diaz Inc. would prepare the following journal entries at December 31, 20X6:

Compensation cost ($42,440,062 / 3)	14,146,687	
Additional paid-in capital		14,146,687

—To recognize compensation cost in 20X6.

Deferred tax asset ($14,146,687 × .35)	4,951,340	
Deferred tax benefit		4,951,340

—To recognize deferred tax benefit for the temporary difference related to compensation cost.

Note that the net effect of the above entries is that Diaz Inc.'s net income in 20X6 is reduced by $9,195,347 ($14,146,687 - $4,951,340).

During 20X7 employee turnover again runs at a 4% annual rate. Diaz Inc. now expects an average employee turnover of four percent over the X6-X8 period. As such, Diaz computes a new estimate of total compensation cost which is $43,794,432 [(2,000,000 × .96³) × $24.75]. Diaz Inc. will recognize compensation cost in 20X7 so that the sum of compensation cost recognized in 20X6 and 20X7 will equal two-thirds of $43,794,432. Diaz Inc. would prepare the following journal entries at December 31, 20X7:

Compensation cost		
[($43,794,432 × 2/3) - $14,146,687]	15,049,601	
Additional paid-in capital		15,049,601

—To recognize compensation cost in 20X7.

Deferred tax asset ($15,049,601 × .35)	5,267,360	
Deferred tax benefit		5,267,360

—To recognize deferred tax benefit for the temporary difference related to compensation cost.

The turnover during 20X8 is 4%. Diaz Inc. would prepare the following journal entries at December 31, 20X8:

Compensation cost ($43,794,432 / 3)	14,598,144	
Additional paid-in capital		14,598,144

—To recognize compensation cost in 20X8.

Deferred tax asset ($14,598,144 × .35)	5,109,351	
Deferred tax benefit		5,109,351

—To recognize deferred tax benefit for the temporary difference related to compensation cost.

All 1,769,472 (2,000,000 × .96³) vested options are exercised on December 31, 20Y1. Diaz Inc.'s stock price is $120 on December 31, 20Y1. Diaz Inc. would prepare the following journal entry (Diaz issues no par common stock):

Cash (1,769,472 × $50)	88,473,600	
Additional paid-in capital ($14,146,687 + $15,049,601 + $14,598,144)	43,794,432	
Common stock		132,268,032

—To record the issuance of common stock upon the exercise of the stock options and to reclassify previously recorded additional paid-in capital.

Income Tax Effects

Diaz Inc. is able to deduct the difference between the market price of the stock on the date the options are exercised, $120, and the exercise price of the option, $50, on its federal income tax return. The tax benefits from deductions in excess of compensation cost recognized are recorded as credits to additional paid-in capital. The tax deductible amount is $123,863,040 [($120 - $50) × 1,769,472]. The tax benefit realized by Diaz Inc. is $43,352,064 ($123,863,040 × .35) (assuming sufficient taxable income to fully realize the tax deduction). Diaz Inc. would make the following journal entry at December 31, 20Y1, to record the tax consequences related to the exercise of the stock options:

Deferred tax expense ($4,951,340 + $5,267,360 + $5,109,351)	15,328,051	
Deferred tax asset		15,328,051

—To write off the deferred tax asset related to stock options exercised.

Income taxes payable ($123,863,040 × .35)	43,352,064	
Income tax expense ($43,794,432 × .35)		15,328,051
Additional paid-in capital [($123,863,040 - $43,794,432) × .35]		28,024,013

—To adjust taxes currently payable and current tax expense to recognize the current tax benefit from deductible compensation cost when the options are exercised.

Presentation of Income Tax Effects in Statement of Cash Flows

The tax benefits received as a result of the tax deductible amount exceeding recognized compensation cost is shown as a cash inflow from financing activities. In its 20Y1 Statement of Cash Flows, Diaz Inc. would present a cash inflow of $28,024,013 from excess tax benefits as a result of the exercise of stock options.

PART II: INTERPRETIVE GUIDANCE

ASC 718-10: OVERALL

ASC 718-10-25-3 Accounting for Payroll Taxes Associated with Stock Option Exercises

The FASB staff was asked to clarify the accounting for payroll taxes paid by an employer under the Federal Insurance Contributions Act (FICA) and Medicare taxes that the employer pays when an employee exercises stock options.

The FASB staff believes that because the difference between the exercise price paid by an employee and the fair value of the acquired stock on the exercise date is treated as if it were compensation paid to the employee, payroll taxes on those amounts should be recognized as operating expenses and included in the income statement.

ASC 718-10-25-5 Practical Accommodation to the Application of Grant Date as Defined in ASC 718

BACKGROUND

The *grant date* of a share-based payment award is defined in Appendix E of ASC 718 based on certain criteria, one of which is the concept that an employer and employee have a "mutual understanding" of a share-based payment award's most important terms. That concept was initially included in the definition of the grant date in FAS-123 (Accounting for Stock-Based Compensation).

In practice, an award's grant date is the date on which an award is approved in accordance with an entity's corporate governance provisions if the approved grant is communicated to the entity's employees within a short period of time after the award's approval. Communicating the key terms and conditions of an award to employees receiving share-based payments immediately after the board of directors' approval or the approval of management with the relevant authority may be difficult for many companies with large numbers of employees that are located in different geographic locations, because the companies prefer to communicate with their employees personally.

To address those concerns, the FASB believes that there should be a *practical* solution to the manner in which the concept of "mutual understanding" is applied. Because this solution is unique to the circumstances described, the concepts in this FSP should *not* be applied by analogy to other concepts in ASC 718 or other generally accepted accounting principles.

ACCOUNTING GUIDANCE

It is presumed that there is a mutual understanding of the key terms and conditions of an award made to an individual employee at the date an award is approved by the board of directors or management with the relevant authority if all the other criteria in the definition of the grant date *and* the following two conditions have been met:

1. The award was made unilaterally so that a recipient is *unable* to negotiate its key terms and conditions with the employer.

2. It is expected that the employer will communicate the award's key terms and conditions to the individual recipients within a short period of time from the date on which the award was approved (i.e., within a reasonable period of time in which an entity could communicate information about the awards to the recipients in accordance with the entity's customary human resource practices).

ASC 718-10-25-14A, 65-02 Effect of Denominating the Exercise Price of a Share-Based Payment Award in the Currency of the Market in Which the Underlying Equity Security Trades

OVERVIEW

Guidance on the classification of share-based payment awards as equity or a liability is provided in ASC 718, *Compensation—Stock Compensation*. The exercise price of employee stock options granted by a public company to its employees is usually denominated in the currency in which the underlying equity securities trade. Such awards are usually classified in equity. However, ASC 718-10-25-13 provides that if an award is indexed to a factor that is "not a market, performance, or service condition, the award should be classified as a liability . . . ."

Share-based awards of public companies that regularly raise capital in a country other than their home country and whose securities trade on an exchange in that foreign country frequently are denominated in the foreign country's functional currency, which may differ from the issuer's functional currency, the functional currency of the subsidiary that has issued the share-based payment awards, or the currency in which the employees receiving the awards are paid. Under the guidance in ASC 718-10-25-13, if an award is indexed "to a factor in addition to the entity's share price" and that "additional factor is not a market, performance, or service condition, the award shall be classified as a liability." Because there is no guidance in ASC 718 regarding which currency is considered the "ordinary" currency of a share-based payment award that qualifies for classification in equity, some believe that it is the issuer's functional currency, while others believe that it is the functional currency of the country in which the shares are traded. Therefore, the question has been raised whether awards denominated in the currency of the market in which the underlying equity security trades should be classified as equity or as liability awards.

SCOPE

The following guidance applies to share-based payment awards accounted for under the scope of ASC 718.

ACCOUNTING GUIDANCE

Equity treatment of an employee share-based payment award is appropriate if an award is denominated in the currency of a market in which a substantial portion of the entity's equity securities are traded and all of the other criteria for classification in equity have been met

An employee share-based payment award denominated in a currency other than the functional currency of the foreign operation or in the currency in which the employee is paid should *not* be classified in equity because it contains a condition that is *not* a market, performance, or service condition. Such an award should be accounted for as a liability.

EFFECTIVE DATE AND TRANSITION

This guidance is effective for fiscal years, and interim periods within those years, beginning on or after December 15, 2010. It should be applied through a cumulative effect adjustment to the opening balance of retained earnings for all awards that are outstanding as of the beginning of the fiscal year in which the guidance is initially applied.

Early adoption of the guidance is permitted. An entity that elects early adoption in a fiscal period other than the first reporting period of the entity's fiscal year is required to apply the guidance *retrospectively* from the beginning of its fiscal year. Presentation of the transition disclosures in ASC 250, *Accounting Changes and Error Corrections* (250-10-50-1 through 50-3) is required.

ASC 718-10-25-22 Recognition and Measurement of Employer Payroll Taxes on Employee Stock-Based Compensation

BACKGROUND

As a result of the increased use of employee stock options as a means of compensating employees and the rapid growth of the market value of stock in certain sectors of the economy, the significance of payroll taxes incurred by employers on employee stock-based compensation is increasing. Under the guidance in ASC 718-10-25-23, employers are required to recognize an expense for payroll taxes incurred in connection with stock-based compensation. There is no guidance, however, on when the employer should recognize that expense. Currently, employers recognize a cost when an event, such an employee's exercise of a stock option, results in a payment to the taxing authority. Some question whether the timing of cost recognition for an employer's payroll taxes on stock-based compensation under the guidance in ASC 718 is appropriate.

ACCOUNTING ISSUE

When should an employer recognize a liability and the corresponding cost for employer payroll taxes on employee stock-based compensation?

ACCOUNTING GUIDANCE

Employers should recognize a liability for payroll taxes on an employee's stock-based compensation on the date that the measurement and payment of the tax to the taxing authority is triggered. For example, in the case of a nonqualified option in the United States, a liability would generally be recognized on the exercise date.

ASC 718-10-S25-1, S99-2; ASC 505-50-S25-3 Escrowed Share Arrangements and the Presumption of Compensation

As a result of requests for clarification of the SEC staff's position regarding the presumption that escrowed share arrangements represent compensation for certain shareholders, the SEC Staff Observer made the following announcement regarding such arrangements.

Sometimes when an entity has an initial public offering or enters into another transaction to raise capital, some of the entity's shareholders may agree to put a portion of their shares in escrow. An escrowed share arrangement can occur between a company and its shareholders or between the shareholders and new investors. Under the terms of some escrowed share arrangements, the shares are released back to the shareholders only if specified criteria related to performance are met.

In the past, the SEC staff has held the view that there is a presumption that an escrowed share arrangement that involves the release of shares to certain shareholders when those shareholders have met certain criteria related to performance is compensatory and that it is like a reverse stock split under which shareholders subsequently receive a restricted stock award under a plan based on performance.

To determine whether the presumption of compensation has been overcome, a registrant should consider the substance of an arrangement and whether a shareholder has entered into the arrangement for a purpose that is not related to, or contingent on, continued employment. For example, as a condition of a financing transaction, an investor may request that specific shareholders who own a significant portion of an entity's shares and who also may be the entity's officers or directors participate in an escrowed share arrangement. Under those circumstances, if the shares are released or cancelled, regardless of whether a shareholder's employment will continue, the facts and circumstances may indicate that the arrangement was entered into by the shareholders to make the financing transaction possible and *not* for the purpose of compensation. The SEC staff believes that if the presumption that an escrow arrangement is compensatory has been overcome based on the facts and circumstances, the arrangement should be recognized and measured based on its nature and accounted for as a reduction of proceeds allocated to newly issued securities.

The SEC staff also believes that consistent with the principle stated in ASC 805-10-55-25, if shares in an escrowed share arrangement are automatically forfeited on the termination of employment of a participant in the arrangement, such an arrangement is considered to be compensatory.

ASC 718-10-35-9, 35-10, 35-11, 65-1 Classification and Measurement of Freestanding Financial Instruments Originally Issued in Exchange for Employee Services under ASC 718)

OVERVIEW

This guidance has been issued for the following reasons:
- To defer the requirement in ASC 718 that freestanding financial instruments accounted for under the guidance in ASC 718 that were conveyed to a holder by an employer and linked to the holder's employment should be accounted for in accordance with the recognition and measurement guidance in other applicable generally accepted accounting principles (GAAP) if the instrument's rights no longer are linked to the holder's employment.

- To supersede the guidance in FSP EITF 00-19-1 (Application of EITF Issue No. 00-19 to Freestanding Financial Instruments Originally Issued as Employee Compensation).

- To amend the guidance in ASC 815-10-15-74 and Statement 133 Implementation Issue No. C3 (Scope Exceptions: Exception Related to Share-Based Payment Arrangements) by adding a footnote to both documents stating that this guidance defers the guidance in ASC 718-10-35-13 under certain circumstances for employee awards and provides additional guidance for awards that no longer are within the scope of ASC 718. Such awards should be analyzed to determine whether they should be accounted for under the guidance in ASC 815.

Entities that offer stock-based compensation to employees are required to account for such arrangements under the guidance in ASC 718; however, ASC 718 provides that the rights conveyed by freestanding instruments issued under those arrangements are *excluded* from the scope of ASC 718 if the holder's rights under the instruments no longer are linked to the holder's employment by the issuer. According to the guidance in ASC 718-10-35-13, those instruments should be accounted for under the measurement and recognition guidance in other applicable GAAP. The guidance in ASC 718-10-35-13 through 35-14 and the related footnotes 123 and 124 provide guidance as to when an award no longer is linked to employment.

To determine whether a financial instrument should be classified as a liability or equity, examples of differences between the accounting in ASC 718 and that in other GAAP are discussed in paragraphs B119-B135 of FAS-123(R) (not included in the ASC). As a result of those differences, freestanding financial instruments initially accounted for as equity under the guidance in ASC 718 or as liabilities may be classified differently under other GAAP. Those differences may be related to practical exceptions in ASC 718, some of which have been carried over from the existing literature on stock compensation as interim guidance while the FASB continues its work on a project related to the distinction between liabilities and equity and the unique nature of the employee-employer relationship.

The requirement in ASC 718 that instruments no longer linked to employment be evaluated under other GAAP was based on the view that the recognition and measurement principles used to account for freestanding financial instruments should be the same regardless of how they were acquired by a holder. Because the FASB's project considering the distinction between liabilities and equity could change other applicable GAAP significantly, the FASB decided to defer the requirement in ASC 718 that freestanding financial instruments no longer linked to a holder's employment be accounted for under the measurement and recognition principles of other applicable GAAP.

ACCOUNTING GUIDANCE

The recognition and measurement guidance in ASC 718 for freestanding financial instruments issued to employees in exchange for their past or future services that currently is being applied or that was applied to such instruments when ASC 718 was initially adopted should continue to apply for the life of those instruments, unless the instrument's terms are modified or a holder is no longer employed by the entity. Modifications should be accounted for in accordance with the guidance in ASC 718-10-35-14. After an instrument has been modified, it should be accounted for in accordance with the recognition and measurement guidance of other applicable GAAP.

When the guidance herein is applied, financial instruments issued, in whole or in part, as consideration for the delivery of goods or services, *not* employee services, should *not* be considered to have been issued in exchange for employee services regardless of whether the award's recipient was an employee on the grant date.

ASC 718-10-35-15 Classification of Options and Similar Instruments Issued as Employee Compensation That Allow for Cash Settlement upon the Occurrence of a Event

BACKGROUND

The subject of this guidance is the classification of options and similar instruments issued to employees as compensation that can be settled in cash when a contingent event occurs. ASC 718-10-25-11 are amended by this guidance.

This issue was addressed because under some share-based payment plans, cash settlement of an option or similar instrument is required if a contingent event occurs. Settlement of an option in cash is required or permitted, at a holder's option, if the issuer has a change in control or another event affecting its liquidity occurs or if the holder dies or becomes disabled. Under APB-25 (Accounting for Stock Issued to Employees), as interpreted, an option or similar instrument would have been classified as a liability or as equity based on an assessment of the *probability* that an event requiring cash settlement, such as a change of control, would occur. Therefore, an option or similar instrument would have been classified as equity if it had been determined that occurrence of a contingent event was *not* probable *and not* under the employee's control. In contrast, under the guidance in ASC 718-10-25-11, options or similar instruments must be classified as liabilities if settlement in cash or other assets is required "under any circumstances." Because cash settlement of an entity's options or similar instruments issued as employee compensation *may* be required on the occurrence of a change in control, those instruments would have to be classified as liabilities under the guidance in ASC 718-10-25-11.

ACCOUNTING GUIDANCE

This guidance amends the guidance in ASC 718-10-25-11 to incorporate the notion that the conditions in those paragraphs would *not* be met until the occurrence of a contingent event requiring cash settlement that is *not* under an employee's control, such as an initial public offering, becomes *probable*.

An option or similar instrument should be accounted for as a modification from equity to a liability award if that instrument is reclassified from equity to a liability, because it becomes *probable* that an event requiring cash settlement will occur. On the date it becomes probable that a contingent event will occur, the issuer should:

- Recognize a share-based liability equal to the portion of the award attributed to past service (considering a provision, if any, for accelerated vesting) multiplied by the award's fair value on that date.
- Charge an offsetting debit to equity if the liability is equal to or less than the amount previously recognized in equity.
- Recognize compensation cost for an amount, if any, by which the liability exceeds the amount previously recognized in equity.

Total compensation cost recognized for an award that has a contingent cash settlement feature must be at least equal to the award's fair value at the grant date.

This guidance, which applies only to options or similar instruments issued in connection with employee compensation arrangements, should *not* be applied by analogy to instruments that are *not* related to employee share-based arrangements.

AMENDMENT OF ASC 718-10-25-11

The following footnotes are being added to ASC 718-10-25-11:

- "A cash settlement feature that can be exercised only upon the occurrence of a contingent event that is outside the employee's control (such as an initial public offering) would not meet condition (b) until it becomes probable that event will occur."
- "SEC registrants are required to consider the guidance in ASR 268. Under that guidance, options and similar instruments subject to mandatory redemption requirements or whose redemption is outside the control of the issuer are classified outside permanent equity."

ASC 718-40: EMPLOYEE STOCK OWNERSHIP PLANS

ASC 718-40-05-2 through 05-4, 15-2 through 15-4, 25-2 through 25-6, 25-9 through 25-17, 25-19, through 25-20 through 25-21, 30-1 through 30-5, 35-1, 40-2 through 40-7, 45-2 through 45-9, 50-1, 55-1 through 55-33) Employers' Accounting for Employee Stock Ownership Plans

BACKGROUND

An employee stock ownership plan (ESOP) is an employee benefit plan described by the Employee Retirement Income Security Act (ERISA) of 1974 and the Internal Revenue Code of 1986. An ESOP can be either a qualified stock bonus plan or a combination of a qualified stock bonus plan and a money purchase pension plan. In both cases, the ESOP is expected to invest primarily in stock of the sponsoring employer.

SOP 76-3, which was issued in December 1976, primarily provided accounting and reporting guidance for leveraged ESOPs. ASC 718-40, which supersedes it, must be applied for ESOP shares acquired after December 30, 1992; at the company's discretion, it can be applied to ESOP shares acquired before December 31, 1992. Alternatively, SOP 76-3 can continue to be applied to ESOP shares acquired before December 31, 1992. A number of changes affecting ESOPs occurred between the release of SOP 76-3 and the issuance of ASC 718-40. For instance, Congress passed a number of laws affecting ESOPs, and numerous regulatory changes in this area have emanated from the Internal Revenue Service and from the U.S. Department of Labor. A number of these changes sparked a substantial growth in the number of ESOPs. Not only has the number of ESOPs grown, but also their complexity has increased. ESOPs are now formed for a number of different purposes:

- To fund a matching program for one or more employee benefit plans of the sponsor (e.g., 401(k) savings plan, formula-based profit-sharing plan)
- To raise new capital or to create a market for the existing stock
- To replace benefits lost from the termination of other employee benefit plans (e.g., retirement plans, other postretirement benefit plans)
- To help finance a leveraged buy-out
- To be used by owners to terminate their ownership interests in the entity on a tax-advantaged basis
- To be used as a deterrent against hostile takeovers

The financing of ESOPs also has changed significantly since SOP 76-3 was issued. When SOP 76-3 was issued, ESOP borrowing was typically from an outside lender. In today's environment, it is not unusual for an ESOP to be internally leveraged (the ESOP borrows from the employer sponsoring the ESOP, with or without an outside loan to the employer). In addition, some ESOPs use dividends on shares held by the ESOP largely to fund required debt payments. When SOP 76-3 was issued, most debt repayments were funded through employer contributions.

Finally, the guidance in ASC 718-40 was issued to resolve some continuing controversies regarding the measurement of compensation cost and how dividends on shares held by the ESOP should be treated. Those two issues had been problematic since the issuance of SOP 76-3.

ACCOUNTING GUIDANCE

The conclusions in ASC 718-40 apply to all ESOPs, both leveraged and nonleveraged and provides guidance to employers that sponsor ESOPs. The accounting for leveraged and nonleveraged ESOPs is discussed separately on the following pages. In addition, pension reversion ESOPs and the disclosures required by the guidance in ASC 718-40 are discussed.

Accounting for Leveraged ESOPs

A leveraged ESOP borrows money to acquire shares of the employer sponsoring the ESOP. An ESOP may borrow either from the employer sponsor or directly from an outside lender. The shares acquired from the debt proceeds initially are held in a suspense account (i.e., they are not immediately allocated to the accounts of employees participating in the ESOP). The ESOP's debt is liquidated through (*a*) contributions of the employer to the ESOP and (*b*) dividends on the employer's stock held by the ESOP. As the ESOP's debt is repaid, shares are released from the suspense account. Released shares must be allocated to participants' accounts by the end of the ESOP's fiscal year.

Purchase of Shares

The ESOP may purchase either newly issued shares or treasury shares from the employer. The employer should record the issuance or sale of shares to the ESOP at the time it occurs, based on the fair value of its shares at that time. The offsetting debit is to unearned ESOP shares, a contra-equity account, which is to be shown as a separate line item on the employer's balance sheet.

In some cases, the ESOP may acquire shares of the employer through secondary market purchases. Even in this case, the employer should debit unearned ESOP shares for the cost of the shares purchased by the ESOP. If the ESOP is internally leveraged (i.e., the ESOP has borrowed from the employer), the offsetting credit recorded by the employer is to cash. If the ESOP is externally leveraged (i.e., the ESOP has borrowed directly from an outside lender), the offsetting credit recorded by the employer is to an appropriately titled debt account.

Illustration of Issuance of ESOP Shares as a Form of Employee Compensation

Pfeiffer, Bryant & Co. sponsors an ESOP for its employees. During the first quarter of 20X4, the employees of Pfeiffer, Bryant & Co. earn the right to receive 10,000 shares. The ESOP holds 25,000 shares of Pfeiffer Bryant's stock, acquired at an average cost of $20 per share. Pfeiffer Bryant's stock price was $22 at 1/1/X4, $29 at 3/31/X4, and was $25 on average during the first quarter of 20X4. Pfeiffer Bryant would record this transaction as follows:

Compensation cost (10,000 × $25)	$250,000	
Unearned ESOP shares (10,000 × $20)		$200,000
Additional paid-in capital		50,000

Release of ESOP Shares—General

ESOP shares are released for one or more of three purposes: (1) to compensate employees directly, (2) to settle a liability for other employee benefits, and (3) to replace dividends on allocated shares when these dividends are used to pay debt service.

The allocation of shares to employees typically is based on employee service. The number of shares to be released for each period (quarter or year) of employee service is usually specified in ESOP documents. As employees provide services, the release of ESOP shares is earned (hence they are committed to be released whether or not they have yet to be legally released). ESOP shares are legally released for distribution to participant accounts when debt payments are made.

When shares are committed to be released (which may occur before the shares are legally released), unearned ESOP shares should be credited for the cost of the shares to be released. The offsetting debit, which is based on the fair value of the shares, depends on the purpose for which the ESOP shares are being released. If the committed-to-be-released shares relate to employee compensation, the debit is to compensation cost. If the committed-to-be-released shares relate to the settlement of a liability for other employee benefits, the debit is to employee benefits payable. If the committed-to-be-released shares are to replace dividends on allocated shares, the debit is to dividends payable. Therefore, in most cases, the debit for committed-to-be-released shares, which is based on fair value, will differ from the credit for these same shares, which is based on cost. This difference is accounted for as a debit or credit to shareholders' equity, typically through the use of the additional paid-in capital account.

Release of ESOP Shares—Direct Compensation of Employees

As employees provide services over the accounting period (quarter or year), they ratably earn the right to receive ESOP shares. In essence, the commitment to release shares occurs ratably throughout the period. Therefore, compensation cost should be measured based on the average fair value of the stock over the relevant time period. Compensation cost recognized in previous interim periods should not be changed to reflect changes in the stock's fair value in later interim periods in the same fiscal year.

Release of ESOP Shares—Satisfaction of Other Employee Benefits

In some cases, an employer will settle its liability to provide other employee benefits by allocating shares of stock held by the ESOP to participant accounts. For example, some employers may allocate ESOP shares to satisfy a commitment to fund a 401(k) plan or a profit-sharing plan. The employer should recognize the expense and the liability for employee benefits (e.g., 401(k) contributions, profit-sharing contributions) in the same manner as if the ESOP was not used to fund the benefit. The employer should debit the liability account (for employee benefits) when ESOP shares are committed to be released to settle the liability. The number of shares to be released depends on the amount of the liability and the fair value of the ESOP shares at the time the liability is settled.

Release of ESOP Shares—Replacement of Dividends on Allocated Shares When Such Dividends Are Used to Service Debt

Dividends on shares of stock already allocated to participants' accounts can be used to service debt. However, if dividends on allocated shares are used in this manner, unallocated shares with a fair value equal to the dividends diverted must be allocated to participants' accounts.

When shares are committed to be released to replace the dividends on allocated shares used for debt service, the employer should debit dividends payable. In addition, only those dividends that pertain to shares already allocated are charged to retained earnings.

Determination of Fair Value

A number of the provisions of ASC 718-40 require the use of the fair value of the employer's stock. The fair value of such stock is the amount that would be received in a sale, in the normal course of business, between a willing buyer and a willing seller. If the stock is publicly traded, the market price of the stock is the best estimate of fair value. If the employer's stock is not publicly traded, the employer's best estimate of fair value should be used.

Dividends on Unallocated ESOP Shares

Dividends declared on unallocated ESOP shares are not charged against retained earnings by the employer. If dividends on unallocated shares are used for debt service, the employer debits debt and/or interest payable (the credit is to cash). In some cases, dividends on unallocated shares may be paid to participants or added to participants' accounts. In these cases, the offsetting debit is to compensation cost.

Dividends on Allocated ESOP Shares

Dividends declared on allocated ESOP shares are charged against retained earnings by the employer. The employer can satisfy its liability for the distribution of dividends in one of three ways: (1) by contributing cash to participant accounts; (2) by contributing additional shares, with a fair value equal to the amount of the dividends, to participant accounts; or (3) by releasing ESOP shares held in suspense, with a fair value equal to the amount of the dividends, to participant accounts.

Redemption of ESOP Shares

Employers are required to offer a put option to holders of ESOP shares that are not readily tradable (required for both leveraged and nonleveraged ESOPs). The employer is required to purchase the employee's stock at its fair value at the time the put option is exercised. The employer would record its purchase of the employee's stock in a manner identical to the purchase of treasury shares.

Reporting of Debt and Interest—General

The employer's accounting for ESOP-related debt and interest depends on the type of ESOP debt. The three types of ESOP-related debt can be described as follows:

1. *Direct loan* The loan is from an outside lender to the ESOP.
2. *Indirect loan* The loan is from the employer to the ESOP, and the employer borrows a comparable sum from an outside lender.
3. *Employer loan* The loan is from the employer to the ESOP. There is no related outside borrowing by the employer.

Reporting of Debt and Interest—Direct Loan

The ESOP's liability to the lender should be recorded by the employer (in essence, the ESOP's debt is treated as the debt of the employer). In addition, accrued interest payable on the loan is recorded by the employer. Cash payments that the employer makes to the ESOP, which are to be used to service debt payments, are recorded as a reduction in the related debt and the accrued interest payable amounts. The employer should record the reduction in these two liability accounts when the ESOP remits a loan or interest payment to the lending institution. The source of the cash contribution from the employer to the ESOP does not affect this accounting treatment (i.e., the accounting treatment is as specified above, regardless of whether the source of cash is an employer contribution or dividends on ESOP stock).

Recording of Debt and Interest—Indirect Loan

Because the employer borrows from an outside lender, the employer obviously records this borrowing as a liability. In addition, in the case of an indirect loan, the ESOP has borrowed from the employer (typically an amount equal to what the employer has borrowed from an outside lender). Although the employer has a loan receivable from the ESOP, the employer does not recognize this asset in its financial statements. Because the employer does not record the loan receivable, the employer also does not recognize interest income. The employer may make a cash contribution to the ESOP for the purpose of funding the ESOP's debt repayments—concurrent payments from the ESOP back to the employer. Neither the cash contribution from the employer to the ESOP nor the concurrent debt repayment from the ESOP to the employer is recognized in the employer's financial statements.

Recording of Debt and Interest—Employer Loan

The employer has made a loan to the ESOP, and the employer has not borrowed a comparable amount from an unrelated lender. Although the employer has a note receivable, it is not recognized in the employer's financial statements. Therefore, interest income also is not recognized. (The ESOP's note payable and related interest cost also are not recognized in the employer's financial statements.)

Earnings per Share

Shares that are committed to be released are treated as outstanding in computing both basic and diluted EPS. Shares not committed to be released are not treated as outstanding in either computation.

ESOPs holding convertible preferred stock may encounter the following unique EPS issues (however, some complexity in this area has been reduced by the issuance of ASC 260-10:

- How to compute the number of shares outstanding for the application of the if-converted method
- How earnings applicable to common stock in if-converted computations should be adjusted for the effects of dividends on allocated shares used for debt service
- Whether prior periods' EPS should be restated for a change in the conversion ratio

Convertible preferred stock—Number of common shares outstanding The number of common shares that would be issued on conversion of preferred stock, where the convertible preferred stock is committed to be released, should be considered outstanding for the purpose of applying the if-converted method. This treatment applies to the computation of both basic and diluted EPS (assuming the effects are dilutive).

A participant's account balance may contain convertible preferred stock when it is withdrawn. The participant may be entitled to receive either (*a*) common stock or (b) cash with a value equal to (1) the fair value of convertible preferred stock or (2) a stated minimum value per share. The common stock that would have been issuable (upon conversion) may have a fair value that is less than the fair value of the convertible preferred stock or less than the stated minimum value per share. If this is the case, the participant will receive common stock or cash with a value greater than the fair value of the common stock that would have been issuable given the stated conversion rate. The presumption is that any shortfall will be made up by the issue of additional shares of common stock. However, this assumption can be overcome if past experience or a stated policy indicates that any shortfall will be paid in cash.

When the employee applies the if-converted method, the number of common shares issuable on assumed conversion is the greater of:

- The shares issuable at the stated conversion rate *or*
- The shares issuable if participants were to withdraw the convertible preferred shares from their accounts.

The shares issuable, if participants were to withdraw the convertible preferred shares from their accounts, are to be computed as the ratio of:

- The average fair value of the convertible stock or, if greater, its stated minimum value *to*
- The average fair value of the common stock.

Convertible preferred stock—Adjustment to earnings If employers use dividends on allocated shares to pay debt service, earnings applicable to common shares should be adjusted for the purpose of applying the if-converted method. Earnings applicable to common stock would be adjusted for the difference (net of tax) between:

- The amount of compensation cost reported *and*
- The amount of compensation cost that would have been reported if the allocated shares had been converted to common stock at the beginning of the period.

Convertible preferred stock—Changes in conversion rates Earnings per share for prior periods should not be restated for changes in conversion rates.

Accounting for income taxes Differences between book ESOP-related expense and the ESOP-related expense allowed for tax purposes may result from the following:

- The fair value of committed-to-be-released shares is different from the cost of these shares *and/or*
- The timing of expense recognition is different for book purposes than for tax purposes.

In either case, the guidance in ASC 740 should be followed. The tax effects of differences between book and tax reporting are to be recognized as a component of stockholders' equity (i.e., these differences do not give rise to deferred tax assets and liabilities).

If the cost of shares committed to be released exceeds their fair value, the expense deductible for tax purposes will exceed the book expense. The tax effect of this difference should be credited to stockholders' equity. If the cost of shares committed to be released is less than their fair value, the expense deductible for book purposes will exceed the expense deductible for tax purposes. The tax effect of this difference should be charged to stockholders' equity to the extent that prior credits to stockholder's equity that are related to cost exceeding the fair value of shares that were committed to be released in previous years.

Dividends paid on ESOP shares frequently result in a tax deduction. The tax-advantaged nature of ESOPs is a contributing factor behind their growth. The tax benefit of tax-deductible dividends on allocated ESOP shares is to be recorded as a reduction in income tax expense from continuing operations.

Accounting for terminations If an ESOP is terminated, either in whole or in part, all outstanding debt related to the shares terminated must be repaid or refinanced. The ESOP may repay the debt through one or more of the following sources:

- Employer contributions
- Dividends on ESOP shares
- Proceeds from selling suspense shares, either to the employer or to another party

The number of suspense shares the employer may purchase is limited. The employer can purchase only those shares that have a fair value equal to the applicable unpaid debt. Any shares that remain must be allocated to participants' accounts.

For example, if the ESOP sells suspense shares and uses the proceeds to repay the debt, the employer would account for this transaction as follows:

- Debit the book value of the debt and the accrued interest payable that relate to the shares being terminated.
- Credit unearned ESOP shares for the cost of the shares being terminated.
- Debit or credit any resulting difference to paid-in capital.

If the employer reacquires the suspense shares, the employer should account for the purchase in a manner similar to the purchase of treasury stock. The employer debits treasury stock based on the fair value of the suspense shares acquired (on the date the employer reacquires them). The employer credits unearned ESOP shares based on their cost. Any difference between the cost and the fair value of the suspense shares reacquired is assigned to paid-in capital.

If the fair value of the suspense shares on the termination date of the ESOP is greater than the ESOP's unpaid debt, the remaining suspense shares are released to participants. The release of these remaining suspense shares to participants is charged to compensation cost. The charge is equal to the fair value of the shares released to participants, determined as of the date the ESOP-related debt is extinguished.

Accounting for Nonleveraged ESOPs

A nonleveraged ESOP is less complex than a leveraged ESOP, and the accounting guidance on it is less complex and less voluminous. An employer contributes shares of its stock or cash to the ESOP for the benefit of employees. If the employer's contribution is cash, the ESOP uses the cash contribution to purchase employer securities. The employer shares that are donated or acquired by the ESOP may be outstanding shares, treasury shares, or newly issued shares. The shares held by the ESOP are allocated to participants' accounts; they are held by the ESOP and are distributed to employees at a future date (e.g., termination, and retirement). Shares obtained by the ESOP must be allocated to individual accounts by the ESOP's fiscal year-end.

Purchase of Shares

The employer records compensation cost based on the contribution that the terms of the plan require the employer make to the ESOP in the reporting period. Compensation cost includes the fair value of shares contributed, the fair value of shares committed to be contributed, cash contributed, and cash committed to be contributed.

Dividends

The employer should record a charge to retained earnings for dividends declared on shares held by a nonleveraged ESOP, with one exception to this requirement: Dividends on suspense account shares held by a pension reversion ESOP are to be accounted for in a manner similar to dividends on suspense account shares held by a leveraged ESOP.

Redemptions

As was the case with leveraged ESOPs, the employer is required to provide ESOP participants with put options if the employer shares held by the ESOP are not readily tradable. If a participant exercises his or her put option, the employer is to record the reacquisition of its stock from the participant in a manner similar to the purchase of treasury stock.

Earnings per Share

In general, all shares held by a nonleveraged ESOP are to be treated as outstanding by the employer in computing its EPS, with one exception: Suspense account shares of a pension reversion ESOP should not be treated as outstanding until they are committed to be released to participants' accounts.

Income Taxes

Compensation cost for financial reporting purposes may be accrued earlier than it is deductible for tax purposes, which creates a FAS-109 temporary difference.

Accounting for Pension Reversion ESOPs

An employer may terminate a defined benefit pension plan and recapture excess pension plan assets, although such a reversion of pension plan assets exposes the employer to an excise tax on the reversion of the pension assets. The employer may avoid some of the excise tax by transferring the pension assets to an ESOP (either new or existing, either leveraged or nonleveraged). The ESOP uses the (reverted) pension plan assets to acquire shares of the employer or to retire ESOP-related debt.

The ESOP may use the pension assets it receives to acquire shares of the employer. If the shares are acquired from the employer (either new shares or treasury shares), the employer would debit unearned ESOP shares (the offsetting credit is to common stock or treasury stock). If the shares are acquired on the secondary market, the employer would still debit unearned ESOP shares (the offsetting credit is to cash).

The ESOP may use the pension plan assets received on the reversion to repay debt. If this is the case, ESOP shares will be committed to be released from the suspense account. The guidance for leveraged ESOPs should be followed in determining the appropriate accounting. For instance, the employer will record the reduction in debt as it is repaid. The employer also will reduce the account "unearned ESOP shares" as these shares are committed to be released. How these committed-to-be-released shares are used determines the offsetting debit (see the earlier discussion on this issue for leveraged ESOPs).

Disclosures

An employer that sponsors an ESOP (both for leveraged and nonleveraged plans) is required to make the following disclosures:

1. A description of the ESOP, employee groups covered, the method of determining contributions, and the nature and effects of any significant changes that would affect comparability across periods
2. The accounting policies followed by the ESOP, which include the method of determining compensation, the classification of dividends on ESOP shares, and the treatment of ESOP shares for EPS computations
3. The amount of compensation cost for the period
4. As of the balance sheet date, the number of (*a*) allocated shares, (*b*) committed-to-be-released shares, and (*c*) suspense shares
5. As of the balance sheet date, the fair value of unearned ESOP shares
6. The existence and nature of any repurchase obligation (if such an obligation exists, the fair value of shares already allocated that are subject to the repurchase obligation)

Shares of an ESOP acquired before December 31, 1992, can continue to be accounted for under the provisions of SOP 76-3. For employers that elect to continue to account for these "old shares" under SOP 76-3, the disclosures required by items 2 and 4 above need to be made separately for shares accounted for under SOP 93-6 and SOP 76-3. Also, the fair value of unearned ESOP shares as of the balance sheet date (item 5) does not have to be disclosed for "old shares."

For leveraged and pension reversion ESOPs only, the following additional disclosures are required:

- The basis for releasing shares
- How dividends on allocated and unallocated shares are used

41,048 ASC 718—Compensation—Stock Compensation

Examples

Appendix A of SOP 93-6 provides a number of detailed examples on the application of this Statement. Accounting is illustrated for the following types of ESOPs: (1) a common-stock leveraged ESOP with a direct loan, (2) a common-stock leveraged ESOP used to fund the employer's match of a 401(k) savings plan with an indirect loan, (3) a common-stock nonleveraged ESOP, (4) a convertible-preferred-stock leveraged ESOP with a direct loan, and (5) a convertible, preferred stock, leveraged ESOP used to fund a 401(k) savings plan with an employer loan. The guidance in ASC 718-40 includes an example of an ESOP termination and of the required ESOP note disclosures. The first illustration that follows is a simplified example of the accounting for a common-stock leveraged ESOP with a direct loan; the second illustration is for a common-stock nonleveraged ESOP.

Illustration of a Common-Stock Leveraged ESOP with a Direct Loan

Neal and Neel (N&N) established a common-stock leveraged ESOP with a direct loan on January 1, 20X4. Relevant information regarding the ESOP is as follows:

1. The ESOP borrows $2,500,000 from an outside lender at 8% for four years. The proceeds are used to purchase 50,000 shares of newly issued N&N stock that has a market value of $50 per share.

2. The ESOP will fund the debt service with cash contributions from N&N and with dividends on the employer stock it holds.

3. Dividends on all shares of stock held by the ESOP, allocated and unallocated, are used for debt service.

4. N&N makes cash contributions to the ESOP at the end of each year.

5. The average market price of N&N's common stock during each year is as follows: 20X4, $54; 20X5, $47; 20X6, $56; 20X7, $60.

6. At the end of each quarter, N&N pays dividends of $.50 per share on its common stock. Therefore, dividends on ESOP shares are $100,000 per year (50,000 shares × $.50 dividend per share per quarter × 4 quarters per year). Because dividends on allocated shares are used for debt service, N&N must provide the ESOP with additional shares of common stock. The number of additional shares of common stock required is determined by dividing the dividends on allocated shares by the average market price of N&N's stock.

7. Both principal and interest payments on the ESOP's debt are due in equal annual installments at the end of each year. Yearly debt service is as follows:

Table 1—Debt Service

Year	Principal	Interest	Total Debt Service
20X4	$554,802	$200,000	$754,802
20X5	599,186	155,616	754,802
20X6	647,121	107,681	754,802
20X7	698,891	55,911	754,802
Total	$2,500,000	$519,208	$3,019,208

8. The number of shares of N&N stock released to participants' accounts each year is as follows:

Table 2—Shares Released for Compensation and Dividends

Year	Dividends	Compensation	Total
20X4	0	12,500	12,500
20X5	532	11,968	12,500
20X6	893	11,607	12,500
20X7	1250	11,250	12,500

The number of shares released for dividends is determined by dividing the amount of dividends on allocated shares (which are being used for debt service) by the average market price of the common stock during the year in question. For example, in the year 20X5, 12,500 shares of common stock were allocated (see Table 3 below). Dividends on these 12,500 shares are $25,000 (12,500 shares × $2 per year). Dividing $25,000 by $47 (the average market price of N&N's common stock during 20X5) results in the issuance of 532 shares during 20X5 to replace the dividends on allocated shares used for debt service. In this example, the remaining shares are released as compensation to ESOP participants.

9. Shares released and allocated are based on total debt service payments made during the year (both principal and interest). Because 25% of debt service payments are made in each year, 25% of the shares (12,500) are released each year. Shares released in a particular year are allocated to participants' accounts during the next year. See Table 3.

Table 3—Shares Released and Allocated

Year	Cumulative Number of Shares Released	Allocated	Average Shares Released	Year-End Suspense Shares
20X4	12,500	0	6,250	37,500
20X5	25,000	12,500	18,750	25,000
20X6	37,500	25,000	31,250	12,500
20X7	50,000	37,500	43,750	0

10. N&N's income before giving effect to the ESOP is as follows: 20X4, $2,600,000; 20X5, $2,800,000; 20X6, $3,100,000; 20X7, $3,200,000.

11. All interest cost and compensation cost are charged to expense each year.

12. Excluding ESOP shares, the weighted average equivalent number of shares outstanding is 2,000,000 each year.

13. N&N's combined statutory tax rate is 36% each year.

14. The only book/tax difference is that associated with the ESOP.

15. No valuation allowance is necessary for any deferred tax asset.

The following tables and journal entries illustrate the results of applying SOP 93-6.

Table 4—Summary of the Effects of Applying SOP 93-6

Year	Principal	Unearned ESOP Shares	Paid-In Capital	Dividends	Interest Expense	Compensation Expense	Cash
Notes:	(1)	(2)	(3)	(4)	(1)	(5)	(6)
20X4	$ 554,802	$ (625,000)	$ (50,000)	$ 0	$200,000	$ 675,000	$(754,802)
20X5	599,186	(625,000)	37,500	25,000	155,616	562,496	(754,802)
20X6	647,121	(625,000)	(75,000)	50,000	107,681	649,992	(754,802)
20X7	698,891	(625,000)	(125,000)	75,000	55,911	675,000	(754,802)
Total	$2,500,000	$(2,500,000)	$(212,500)	$150,000	$519,208	$2,562,488	$(3,019,208)

Notes:

(1) Principal paid and interest expense from Table 1.
(2) The credit to unearned ESOP shares is calculated by multiplying the number of ESOP shares released each year (12,500) by the cost of these shares to the ESOP ($50 per share).
(3) The debit or credit to paid-in capital is computed by multiplying the number of ESOP shares released each year (12,500) by the difference between the average market price per share (for the particular year) and the cost per share ($50). For example, in 20X4 this calculation resulted in a $50,000 credit [($54 - $50) × 12,500].
(4) The dividend amount is calculated by multiplying the cumulative number of shares allocated (see Table 3) by the dividend per share, $2 per year.
(5) Compensation expense is computed by multiplying the number of shares released for compensation (see Table 2) by the average market price per share (for the particular year).
(6) The cash disbursed each year comprises a yearly contribution of $654,802 and $100,000 of dividends. Also note that this amount equals the yearly debt service.

Table 5—Tax Computations

	20X4	20X5	20X6	20X7
Current provision:				
Income before ESOP	$2,600,000	$2,800,000	$3,100,000	$3,200,000
ESOP contribution	(654,802)	(654,802)	(654,802)	(654,802)
ESOP dividends	(100,000)	(100,000)	(100,000)	(100,000)
Taxable income	$1,845,198	$2,045,198	$2,345,198	$2,445,198
Multiplied by 36%	664,271	736,271	844,271	880,271
Deferred provision:				
Reduction in unearned ESOP shares for financial reporting	$625,000	$625,000	$625,000	$625,000
Related tax deduction(1)	554,802	599,186	647,121	698,891
Difference	$(70,198)	$(25,814)	$22,121	$73,891
Tax rate	36%	36%	36%	36%
Deferred tax expense (benefit)	$(25,271)	$(9,293)	$7,964	$26,601

Notes:

(1) The tax deduction in computing the deferred income tax provision is equal to the amount of the principal repayment.

Table 6—Reconciliation of Effective Tax Rate to Provision for Income Taxes

	20X4	20X5	20X6	20X7
Pretax income[1]	$1,725,000	$2,081,888	$2,342,327	$2,469,089
Tax at 36% (statutory rate)	621,000	749,480	843,238	888,872
Benefit of ESOP dividends[2]	0	(9,000)	(18,000)	(27,000)
Effect of difference between average fair value and cost of released shares[3]	18,000	—	13,500[4]	45,000
Provision as reported	$639,000	$740,480	$838,738	$906,872

Notes:

(1) See Table 7 for the computation of the pretax income.
(2) Computed by multiplying the yearly ESOP dividend amount (see Table 4) by the statutory tax rate, 36%.
(3) Computed by multiplying the number of shares released during the year (12,500 each year) by the difference between the average market value during the year and the cost of the ESOP shares and then multiplying this amount by the statutory tax rate. This computation is as follows for 20X4: [12,500 × ($54 - $50) × 36%]. This amount cannot be negative; therefore, this amount is zero during any year in which the cost of the ESOP shares exceeds the average market value during the year (e.g., year 20X5).
(4) Computed as explained in item 3 minus the excess cost of the ESOP shares released in year 20X5 over their fair value multiplied by the tax rate. The entire computation is [(($56 - $50) × 12,500) × 36%] - [(($50 - $47) × 12,500) × 36%].

Table 7—Tax and EPS Computations

	20X4	20X5	20X6	20X7
Income before ESOP	$2,600,000	$2,800,000	$3,100,000	$3,200,000
Interest expense	(200,000)	(155,616)	(107,681)	(55,911)
Compensation expense	(675,000)	(562,496)	(649,992)	(675,000)
Pretax income	$1,725,000	$2,081,888	$2,342,327	$2,469,089
Provision for income tax:				
Currently payable	$664,271	$736,273	$844,271	$880,271
Deferred	(25,271)	(9,293)	7,964	26,601
Shareholders' equity[1]	0	13,500	(13,500)	0
Total	$639,000	$740,480	$838,735	$906,872
Net income	$1,086,000	$1,341,408	$1,503,592	$1,562,217
Average shares outstanding[2]	2,006,250	2,018,750	2,031,250	2,043,750

41,052 ASC 718—Compensation—Stock Compensation

	20X4	20X5	20X6	20X7
Earnings per share	$0.54	$0.66	$0.74	$0.76

Notes:

(1) Calculated by multiplying the shares released during the year (12,500) by the excess of ESOP cost over the average market value of the stock ($50 - $47) and then multiplying this amount by the statutory tax rate (36%). This amount reverses in full in 20X6 since the fair value of the N&N stock in that year, $56, is more than $3 above the cost of N&N's stock to the ESOP, $50.

(2) Calculated by adding the cumulative average number of shares released in each year (see Table 3) to the weighted average number of common shares otherwise outstanding.

Journal Entries

January 1, 20X4 (Date N&N Establishes the ESOP)

Cash	$2,500,000	
Debt		$2,500,000

[To record the ESOP loan]

Unearned ESOP shares (contra-equity)	$2,500,000	
Common stock and paid-in capital		$2,500,000

[To record the issuance of 50,000 shares to the ESOP at $50 per share—the fair value of the stock at the time it is issued]

December 31, 20X4

Interest expense	$200,000	
Accrued interest payable		$200,000

[To record interest expense]

Accrued interest payable	$200,000	
Debt	554,802	
Cash		$754,802

[To record the debt payment. The cash disbursement consists of $100,000 of dividends (none of which is charged to retained earnings in 20X4, because none of the shares has yet to be allocated) and $654,802 of additional employer contributions to the ESOP.]

Compensation expense	$675,000	
Paid-in capital		$ 50,000
Unearned ESOP shares		625,000

[To record release of 12,500 shares at average fair value of $54. The ESOP's cost is $50.]

Deferred tax asset	$ 25,271	
Provision for income taxes	639,000	
Income taxes payable		$664,271

[To record income taxes for 20X4; see Tables 5-7 for the computations of these amounts]

December 31, 20X5

Interest expense	$155,616	
Accrued interest payable		$155,616

[To record interest expense]

Accrued interest payable	$155,616	

Debt	599,186	
Cash		$754,802

[To record the debt payment. The cash disbursement consists of $100,000 of dividends ($25,000 of which is charged to retained earnings in 20X5 (see Table 4)) and $654,802 of additional employer contributions to the ESOP.]

Retained earnings	$25,000	
Dividends payable		$25,000

[To record declaration of a $2.00-per-share dividend on 12,500 allocated shares]

Compensation expense	$562,500*	
Dividends payable	25,000	
Paid-in capital	37,500	
Unearned ESOP shares		$625,000

[To record the release of 12,500 shares (11,968 for compensation and 532 for dividends) at an average fair value of $47 per share. The per-share cost is $50.]

* $4 rounding difference

Deferred tax asset	$9,293	
Provision for income taxes	740,480	
Paid-in capital		$13,500
Income taxes payable		736,273

[To record income taxes for the year 20X5; see Tables 5-7 for the computations of these amounts.]

December 31, 20X6

Interest expense	$107,681	
Accrued interest payable		$107,681

[To record interest expense]

Accrued interest payable	$107,681	
Debt	647,121	
Cash		$754,802

[To record the debt payment. The cash disbursement consists of $100,000 of dividends ($50,000 of which is charged to retained earnings in 20X6 (see Table 4)) and $654,802 of additional employer contributions to the ESOP.]

Retained earnings	$50,000	
Dividends payable		$50,000

[To record declaration of a $2.00-per-share dividend on 25,000 allocated shares]

Compensation expense	$650,000*	
Dividends payable	50,000	
Paid-in capital		$75,000
Unearned ESOP shares		625,000

[To record the release of 12,500 shares (11,607 for compensation and 893 for dividends) at an average fair value of $56 per share. The per-share cost is $50.]

* $8 rounding difference

Provision for income taxes	$838,735	
Paid-in capital	13,500	
Deferred income taxes		$ 7,964

| | Income taxes payable | | 844,271 |

[To record income taxes for 20X6; see Tables 5-7 for the computations of these amounts.]

December 31, 20X7

Interest expense		$55,911	
Accrued interest payable			$55,911

[To record interest expense]

Accrued interest payable		$ 55,911	
Debt		698,891	
Cash			$754,802

[To record the debt payment. The cash disbursement consists of $100,000 of dividends ($75,000 of which is charged to retained earnings in 20X7 (see Table 4)) and $654,802 of additional employer contributions to the ESOP.]

Retained earnings		$75,000	
Dividends payable			$75,000

[To record declaration of a $2.00-per-share dividend on 37,500 allocated shares]

Compensation expense		$675,000	
Dividends payable		75,000	
Paid-in capital			$125,000
Unearned ESOP shares			625,000

[To record the release of 12,500 shares (11,250 for compensation and 1,250 for dividends) at an average fair value of $60 per share. The per-share cost is $50.]

Provision for income taxes		$906,872	
Deferred income taxes			$ 26,601
Income taxes payable			880,271

[To record income taxes for 2002; see Tables 5-7 for the computations of these amounts]

Illustration of a Common-Stock Nonleveraged ESOP

Melton, Inc. established a common-stock nonleveraged ESOP on January 1, 20X4. Melton is to contribute 15% of its pretax profit before ESOP-related charges as of the end of each of the next four years. The ESOP will use this contribution to purchase newly issued shares at the current market price (the year-end price, since contributions to the ESOP are made at year-end). Melton's stock price at December 31 of each year is as follows: 20X4, $52; 20X5, $49; 20X6, $54; 20X7, $63. With the exception of these new facts, all of the relevant facts are identical to the assumptions used in the previous illustration. The following table and journal entries illustrate the results of applying SOP 93-6.

Table 1—Summary of the Effects of Applying SOP 93-6

Year	Compensation Expense	Dividends	Number of ESOP Shares Purchased	Cumulative ESOP Shares
Notes:	(1)	(2)	(3)	(4)
20X4	$390,000	$ —	7,500	7,500
20X5	420,000	15,000	8,571	16,071
20X6	465,000	32,142	8,611	24,682

ASC 718—Compensation—Stock Compensation 41,055

Year	Compensation Expense	Dividends	Number of ESOP Shares Purchased	Cumulative ESOP Shares
20X7	480,000	49,364	7,619	32,301

Notes:

(1) Compensation expense is equal to pretax profit before ESOP-related charges multiplied by 15%.
(2) Dividends are equal to cumulative ESOP shares, as of the beginning of the year, multiplied by the annual dividend per share, $2.
(3) The number of ESOP shares purchased is computed by dividing the yearly employer contribution (i.e., compensation expense) by the year-end market price of Melton's common stock. For example, in 20X4, 7,500 shares are purchased ($390,000/$52 per share).
(4) Cumulative ESOP shares are shares held at the beginning of the year plus shares purchased during the year.

Journal Entries

December 31, 20X4

Compensation expense	$390,000	
Common stock and paid-in capital		$390,000

[To record Melton's contribution, the sale of shares to the ESOP, and compensation expense]

Provision for income taxes	$795,600	
Income taxes payable		$795,600

[To record income taxes at 36% on taxable income of $2,210,000 ($2,600,000 of pre-ESOP income less $390,000 of compensation expense)]

December 31, 20X5

Compensation expense	$420,000	
Retained earnings	15,000	
Common stock and paid-in capital		$420,000
Dividends payable		15,000

[To record Melton's contribution, the sale of shares to the ESOP, declaration of dividends, and compensation expense]

Dividends payable	$15,000	
Cash		$15,000

[To record the payment of dividends]

Provision for income taxes	$856,800	
Income taxes payable		$856,800

[To record income taxes at 36% on taxable income of $2,380,000 ($2,800,000 of pre-ESOP income less $420,000 of compensation expense)]

December 31, 20X6

Compensation expense	$465,000	
Retained earnings	32,142	
Common stock and paid-in capital		$465,000
Dividends payable		32,142

[To record Melton's contribution, the sale of shares to the ESOP, declaration of dividends, and compensation expense]

Dividends payable	$32,142	

Cash		$32,142
[To record the payment of dividends]		
Provision for income taxes	$948,600	
Income taxes payable		$948,600
[To record income taxes at 36% on taxable income of $2,635,000 ($3,100,000 of pre-ESOP income less $465,000 of compensation expense)]		

December 31, 20X7

Compensation expense	$480,000	
Retained earnings	49,364	
Common stock and paid-in capital		$480,000
Dividends payable		49,364
[To record Melton's contribution, the sale of shares to the ESOP, declaration of dividends, and compensation expense]		
Dividends payable	$49,364	
Cash		$49,364
[To record the payment of dividends]		
Provision for income taxes	$979,200	
Income taxes payable		$979,200
[To record income taxes at 36% on taxable income of $2,720,000 ($3,200,000 of pre-ESOP income less $480,000 of compensation expense)]		

ASC 718-50 Employee Share Purchase Plans

ASC 718-50-30-1 through 30-3, 35-1 through 35-2, 55-2 through 55-9, 55-22 through 55-33 Accounting under ASC 718 for Certain Employee Stock Purchase Plans with a Look-Back Option

BACKGROUND

ASC 718 states that the objective of the fair value method of accounting for stock-based compensation is to estimate the fair value of the equity instrument—based on the stock price and other measurement assumptions at the grant date—that is issued in exchange for employee services. This objective also applies to the fair value measurement of grants under a compensatory employee stock purchase plan (ESPP).

A *look-back option* is a feature that provides the employee a choice of purchasing stock at two or more times (e.g., an option to purchase stock at 85% of the stock price at the grant date or at a later exercise date). Section 423 of the Internal Revenue Code provides that the employee will not be immediately taxed on the difference between the fair value of the stock and a discounted purchase price if the following requirements are met:

- The option price is not less than 85% of the market price when the option is granted or when the option is exercised.
- The choice does not have a term in excess of 27 months.

The criteria for evaluating whether an ESPP qualifies for noncompensatory treatment are established in ASC 718-50-25-1; if it does, the employer is not required to recognize compensation expense. If an ESPP satisfies *all* of the following criteria, the discount from market price to the employee is not stock-based compensation and simply reduces the proceeds from issuing the shares of stock:

- The plan incorporates no option features.
- The discount from the market prices does not exceed the greater of (*a*) a per-share discount that would be reasonable in an offer of stock to stockholders or others or (*b*) the per-share amount of stock issuance costs avoided by not having to raise a significant amount of capital by a public offering of the stock.
- Substantially all full-time employees meeting limited employment qualifications may participate on an equitable basis.

A look-back option is one feature that causes an ESPP to be considered compensatory. In reaching this conclusion, the FASB observed that a look-back option can have substantial value, because it enables the employee to purchase the stock for an amount that *could be* significantly less than the fair value at the date of purchase. A look-back option is not an essential element of a plan aimed at promoting broad employee stock ownership; a purchase discount also provides incentive for participation. Based on these observations, the FASB concluded that broad-based plans that contain look-back options cannot be treated as noncompensatory.

ACCOUNTING GUIDANCE

The following guidance responds to three questions concerning the different types of ESPP plans with look-back options described above. Following is a recap of Illustration 19 of FAS-123(R)) and an analysis of the three questions and the FASB's response.

Illustration of Look-Back Option without Dividends

On January 1, 2004, Company S offered employees the opportunity to purchase its stock at either 85% of the current price ($50) or 85% of the price at the end of the year when the options expire. For purposes of valuing the option, expected volatility is assumed to be .30, and the risk-free interest rate for the next 12 months is 6.8%.

The value of this look-back option can be estimated at the grant date by combining its two components, as follows:

1. 15% of a share of nonvested stock
2. 85% of a 1-year call option held with an exercise price of $50

The option holder will receive value of at least 15% of a share of stock upon exercise, regardless of the stock price after the grant date. In this example, the stock price is $50 when the grant is made. If the price falls to $40 and the option is exercised at that price, the holder pays $34 ($40 × .85) and receives value of $6, which is 15% of the market price at the date of exercise. On the other hand, if the market price increases to $60, the holder can purchase stock at only $42.50 ($50 × .85) and receive value of $17.50 ($60 - $42.50).

ASC 718—Compensation—Stock Compensation

Using an option-pricing model to value the look-back option under the stated assumptions (e.g., .30 expected volatility and 6.8% risk-free interest rate) results in the following:

15% of a share of nonvested stock ($50 × .15)	$7.50
Call on 85% of a share of stock with an exercise price of $50 ($7.56 × .85)	6.43
Total grant date value	$13.93

This calculation is based on the idea that the value of the look-back option consists of two components: (1) the 15% reduction from a $50 market value ($7.50) and (2) 85% of a call option with an exercise price of $50. The $7.56 figure in the second component is the value of the call option as computed by an option-pricing model.

Illustration of Look-Back Option with Dividends

This example assumes the same facts as in the previous case, except that Company S pays a 2.5% annual dividend quarterly (i.e., .625% per quarter). Calculation of the value of the look-back option is similar to the calculation in the previous illustration, except that the components are *reduced to reflect the dividends that the holder of the option does not receive* during the term of the option. The value of the two components of the option is calculated as follows:

15% of a share of nonvested stock ($50 × .15 × .9754)	$7.32
Call on 85% of a share of stock, $50 exercise price, 2.5% dividend yield ($6.78 × .85)	5.76
Total grant date value	$13.08

The first component is the minimum benefit to the holder, regardless of the price of the stock at the exercise date. The second component is the additional benefit to the holder if the stock price exceeds $50 at the exercise date. The $6.78 in the second component is the value of the call option as computed by an option-pricing model.

Questions and Answers

Question 1: Illustration 19 of FAS-123(R)) provides the only specific guidance on measuring the compensation cost associated with an award under a compensatory ESPP with a look-back option. Is the fair value measurement technique described in that illustration applicable to all types of ESPPs with a look-back option?

Answer: No. The measurement approach in FAS-123(R), Illustration 19, was intended to illustrate how the fair value of an award under a basic type of ESPP with a look-back option could be determined at the grant date by focusing on the substance of the arrangement and valuing each feature of the award separately. The fundamental components of a look-back option may differ from plan to plan, affecting the individual calculations. For example, the illustration in FAS-123(R) assumes that the number of shares that may be purchased is fixed at the grant date based on the grant date stock price and the amount the employee elects to have withheld (Type A plan). Some plans (e.g., Type B plans) do not fix the number of shares that the employee is permitted to purchase, requiring modification to the determination of fair value.

Question 2: How should the Illustration 19 measurement approach be modified to determine the fair value of an ESPP award plan with a Type B look-back option (i.e., the plan does *not* fix the number of shares that an employee is permitted to purchase)?

Answer: In a Type A plan, the number of shares an employee is permitted to purchase is limited to the number based on the price of the stock at the origin of the agreement. For example, if an employee had $4,250 withheld from salary, and the plan permitted him or her to purchase shares at 85% of the $50 current stock price, he or she could purchase 100 shares, as follows:

$$\$4,250 / (85\% \times \$50) = 100 \text{ shares}$$

In a Type B plan, the employee is permitted to purchase as many shares as the $4,250 withheld will permit. If, for example, the market price falls to $30, the employee is not limited to purchasing 100 shares and may actually purchase 167 shares, determined as follows:

$$\$4,250 / (85\% \times \$30) = 167 \text{ shares}$$

Following the FAS-123(R), Illustration 19, approach of combining the components of the plan, and using the same underlying assumptions as in that illustration, the value of the Type B option is calculated at the grant date as follows:

15% of a share of nonvested stock ($50 × 15%)	$7.50
One-year call on 85% of a share of stock, exercise price of $50 ($7.56 × 85%)	6.43
One-year put on 15% of a share of stock, exercise price of $50 ($4.27 × 15%)	.64
	$14.57

This Illustration is the same as that presented earlier (the "no dividend" case) with the addition of a third component: a one-year put option on the employer's stock, valued with a standard option-pricing model. The same assumptions are applied. This has the effect of adding $.64 to the value of the option, raising the total to $14.57 ($7.50 + $6.43 + $.64).

Total compensation is measured at the grant date based on the number of shares that can be purchased using the total withholdings and the grant date market price, rather than on the potentially greater number of shares that may be purchased if the market price falls. For example, in the above Illustration, an employee who had $1,275 withheld could purchase 30 shares based on the grant date price [$1,275/($50 × .85)], and total compensation expense recognized for that employee would be $437 (30 × $14.57).

Question 3: The characteristics of Type A and Type B plans are incorporated into other types of ESPP plans with a look-back option. The measurement approach in Illustration 19 of FAS-123(R) for a Type A plan, as modified by Question 2 for a Type B plan, forms the basis for determining the fair value of the award under the other types of ESPP with a look-back option. What additional modifications are necessary to determine the fair value of awards under other types of ESPPs?

Answer: The fair value of an award under an ESPP plan with a look-back option with multiple purchase periods (Type C plan) should be determined in the same manner as an award under a graded vesting stock option plan. Such awards under a two-year plan with purchase periods at the end of each year would be valued as having two separate options, both starting with the initial grant date and having different lives (12 and 24 months, respectively).

This same approach should be used to value ESPP awards with multiple purchase periods that incorporate reset or rollover mechanisms (Type D and Type E plans). At the date the reset or rollover mechanism becomes effective, the terms of the award have been modified. This is, in substance, an exchange of the original award for a new award with different terms. Similarly, an election by an employee to increase withholdings (Types F, G, and H plans) is a modification of the terms of the award, which is similar to an exchange of the original award for a new award with different terms.

The guidance in ASC 718-50) indicates that a modification of the terms of an award that makes it more valuable should be treated as an exchange of the original award for a new award. In substance, the employer repurchases the original instrument by issuing a new instrument of greater value and incurs additional compensation cost for that incremental value.

A Type I plan permits an employee to increase withholdings retroactively. An employee may elect not to participate, or to participate at a minimal level, until just before the exercise date. This makes it difficult to determine when there is a mutual understanding of the terms of the award and, thus, when the grant date actually occurs. In this situation, the later date when the employee remits an amount to the company should be considered the grant date for purposes of valuing the option.

Changes in compensation resulting from salary increases, commissions, or bonus payments are not plan modifications and do not represent changes in the terms of the plan. The only incremental compensation cost is that which results from the additional shares that may be purchased with the additional amounts withheld.

ASC 718-740: Income Taxes

ASC 718-740-45-8 through 45-12 Accounting for Income Tax Benefits of Dividends on Share-Based Payment Awards

BACKGROUND

A share-based payment arrangement may include a "dividend protection" provision under which employees may be entitled to receive, for example, (a) dividends or dividend equivalents on *nonvested* equity shares and *nonvested* equity share units during the vesting period, (b) payments equal to dividends on equity shares underlying an outstanding option, or (c) exercise price reductions of share options based on dividends paid on the underlying equity shares while an option is outstanding.

Under the guidance in ASC 718, employers charge the payment of dividends or dividend equivalents to employees on nonvested shares to retained earnings, but in some cases, those amounts are treated as deductible compensation cost for income tax purposes. The FASB staff has received questions regarding the accounting for income tax benefits related to the dividend payments discussed above.

SCOPE

The guidance in this Issue applies to share-based payment arrangements with dividend protection features under which employees have a right receive: (1) dividends or dividend equivalents during the vesting period on awards of nonvested shares and nonvested share units, all of which are classified as equity; or (2) equity share options until the awards are exercised. Some entities have been treating those dividends, nonvested equity units, and outstanding equity share options as deductible compensation for income tax purposes while charging those dividends to retained earnings under the provisions in ASC 718, Share-Based Payment (Revised December 2004)), thus providing employers with an income tax deduction.

ACCOUNTING ISSUE

How should an entity recognize an income tax benefit it receives on dividends or dividend equivalents that are: (1) paid to employees that hold nonvested shares, nonvested share units, or outstanding share options, all of which are classified as equity; and (2) charged to retained earnings under the provisions of ASC 718?

ACCOUNTING GUIDANCE

- Additional paid-in capital should be *increased* by an amount equal to a *realized* income tax benefit from dividends or dividend equivalents that have been charged to retained earnings and paid to employees for nonvested equity shares, nonvested equity share units, and outstanding equity share options that are classified as equity.

- The amount recognized in additional paid-in capital should be included in a pool of *excess tax benefits* available to absorb potential future tax deficiencies on share-based payment awards discussed in ASC 718-740-35-5.

To reach that conclusion, the fact that such dividends or dividend equivalents paid to employees for nonvested equity shares, nonvested equity share units, and outstanding equity share options that are charged to retained earning may result in a tax deduction *before* the related tax benefit has actually been realized was taken into account because, for example, an employer may have a net operating loss carryforward. According to the guidance in ASC 718-740-25-10, an entity would *not* recognize an income tax benefit until income taxes payable have been reduced by the deduction. Consequently, *unrealized* income tax benefits from dividends on employee share-based payment awards should *not* be included in the pool of excess tax benefits available to absorb tax deficiencies on share-based payment awards.

Under the guidance in ASC 718, dividend equivalents paid to employees for nonvested equity shares, nonvested equity share units, and outstanding equity share options related to awards that are expected to vest are charged to retained earnings. Dividends and dividend equivalents related to awards that are *not* expected to vest are recognized as compensation cost. If an entity changes its estimates of forfeitures or actual forfeitures vary from previous estimates, dividends and dividend equivalents are reclassified between retained earnings and compensation cost in a subsequent period. An entity's pool of excess tax benefits available to absorb tax deficiencies would increase or decrease as a result of adjustments to additional paid-in capital by an amount that matches the amount of reclassifications between retained earnings and compensation cost. Further, if an entity's estimated forfeitures increase or actual forfeitures are greater than estimated, the amount of tax benefits from dividends that have been reclassified from additional paid-in capital to the income statement to reduce income tax expense or to increase an entity's income tax benefit should be restricted to the amount of the entity's pool of excess tax benefits available to absorb deficiencies on the date on which a reclassification occurs.

ISSUES GRANDFATHERED UNDER THE CODIFICATION

NOTE: SOP 93-6 supersedes SOP 76-3 and nullifies the consensus positions in this Issue. However, under the SOP's transition provisions, employers that elect not to apply SOP 93-6 to shares purchased before December 31, 1992, can continue to apply the provisions of SOP 76-3 and applicable EITF consensus positions to those shares.

EMPLOYEE STOCK OWNERSHIP PLANS

SOP 76-3 Accounting Practices for Certain Employee Stock Ownership Plans

BACKGROUND

An employee stock ownership plan (ESOP) is an employee benefit plan sponsored under the provisions of the Employee Retirement Income Security Act (ERISA) of 1974. An ESOP can be either a qualified stock bonus plan or a combination of a qualified stock bonus plan and a money purchase pension plan. In both cases, the ESOP is expected to invest primarily in "qualifying employer securities."

At the time SOP 76-3 was issued, there were two essential differences between an ESOP and other qualified stock bonus plans. First, the ESOP generally is permitted to borrow money for the purpose of purchasing the employer's stock. Second, the allowable investment tax credit percentage that the employer can claim may increase by as much as 1.5% if that amount is contributed to the ESOP.

In borrowing money for the purpose of purchasing the employer's stock, the ESOP typically borrows from a bank or another commercial lender. The employer shares purchased can be outstanding shares, treasury shares, or newly issued shares. The ESOP holds these shares until they are distributed to employees. The shares may be allocated to individual employees even though the actual shares may not be distributed until a later date. In some cases, the ESOP issues notes to existing shareholders in exchange for their stock.

The employer typically collateralizes the ESOP debt by pledging the stock (purchased from the debt proceeds), and by either guaranteeing or committing to make ESOP contributions sufficient to service the related debt. The employer's annual contribution to the ESOP is tax-deductible (subject to certain limitations). The employer's annual contribution is used to fund (1) amortization of the debt principal, (2) interest payments on the debt, (3) working capital needs, and (4) other expenses. If the employer's annual ESOP contribution exceeds items 1 through 4, the excess can be used to purchase additional employer securities.

SOP 76-3 was issued because several accounting questions arose relating to ESOPs that borrowed money from a bank or other lender to acquire shares, or that issued notes directly to existing shareholders in exchange for their shares.

ACCOUNTING GUIDANCE

The provisions of SOP 76-3 were largely superseded by SOP 93-6 (Employers' Accounting for Employee Stock Ownership Plans). However, shares acquired by an ESOP before December 31, 1992, or shares acquired after that date that were committed to be released before the beginning of the year in which SOP 93-6 was adopted, can continue to be accounted for under the guidance in SOP 76-3.

If the employer has either guaranteed or committed to funding the ESOP in a manner sufficient to cover debt service payments, the related debt (i.e., obligation of the ESOP) is to be recorded as a liability on the employer's balance sheet. AcSEC concluded that the employer's guarantee or commitment was in substance the assumption of the ESOP's debt; as such, the related debt amount should be shown as a liability in the employer's financial statements.

The offsetting debit that the employer records upon recognizing a liability for the ESOP's debt is to shareholders' equity. The employer does not recognize the assets of the ESOP; employees of the ESOP—not the employer—own these assets.

As the ESOP makes payments on its debt, the employer is to reduce its liability. As the employer reduces its liability, the offsetting credit is to shareholders' equity. Symmetry should exist between the liability for ESOP-related debt and the corresponding entry to shareholders' equity.

The annual ESOP contribution (or contribution commitment) that the employer makes is recognized as an expense. This requirement applies to all ESOPs—whether the ESOP has borrowed money from a bank or another lender or has issued a note directly to existing shareholders for their shares. The employer's contribution or contribution commitment is recognized in the year it was made, regardless of whether such contribution is concurrently used to reduce the ESOP's debt.

The expense is to be divided between interest expense and compensation expense, and the employer should disclose the interest rate and terms of the ESOP's debt in its financial statements (since SOP 76-3 essentially views such debt as that of the employer).

The employer should treat all shares held by the ESOP as outstanding for the purpose of calculating the employer's EPS (whether or not the shares have been allocated to individual employees). The employer should charge all dividends pertaining to shares held by the ESOP to retained earnings.

If the employer receives any additional investment tax credit (ITC) as a result of an ESOP contribution, such incremental ITC is to be recorded as a reduction in income tax expense in the year that the applicable ESOP contribution is made. This accounting treatment applies, regardless of the method generally utilized by the employer in accounting for the ITC (flow-through or deferral) for property acquisitions.

EITF Issue 89-8 Expense Recognition for Employee Stock Ownership Plans

BACKGROUND

An employer may establish a leveraged employee stock ownership plan (ESOP) to benefit its employees by granting them shares of its stock. The employer also realizes tax benefits on its contributions to the ESOP.

A leveraged ESOP is established by forming a trust that borrows money to acquire shares of the employer's stock, which are restricted to common stock and convertible preferred stock. Usually, the ESOP borrows from a financial institution and pledges the stock as security. Alternatively, the employer may borrow from a financial institution, and, in turn, lend the money to the trust to purchase the employer's stock. When the employer recognizes the ESOP debt as a liability, an equivalent amount is recognized as a debit in shareholders' equity, similar to unearned compensation, as discussed in paragraph 14 of APB-25. In both cases, the debt is serviced with proceeds from employer contributions to the ESOP and dividends on unallocated shares of the employer's stock. As payments are made on the debt, shares are released and allocated to employees' individual accounts, and the debit in shareholders' equity is reduced. The amount of shares to be released and allocated to employees is based on a percentage of the total number of shares the ESOP purchased. The percentage may be determined in one of two ways:

1. The ratio of principal and interest paid in the current period to the total principal and interest to be paid.

2. The ratio of principal paid in the current period to the total debt principal.

SOP 76-3 was the primary source of guidance when this Issue was discussed. It viewed a leveraged ESOP as a deferred compensation plan and provided that annual expense be based on the amount contributed or committed to be contributed for the year. Because the structure of ESOPs had changed since the issuance of the SOP in 1976, the guidance on expense recognition needed to be updated. Specifically, because loan repayment terms had changed, loan repayments on ESOPs were not always level over the term of the loan, with some repayment schedules tied to an employer's expected cash flow or compensation costs. Other repayment schedules required only interest payments in early years, with principal payments delayed for a number of years, or otherwise had nonlevel repayment terms. Some debt agreements permitted voluntary prepayments or required prepayments if the employer's cash flow exceeded certain amounts. Some questioned whether such changes in repayment terms should affect an employer's expense recognition for contributions to a plan.

ACCOUNTING ISSUE

How should an employer recognize expense for contributions to an ESOP?

EITF CONSENSUS

1. Expense recognition for contributions to an ESOP should be as follows for shares acquired after December 14, 1989:

    a. Recognize contributions to an ESOP as expense in accordance with the shares-allocated method, discussed below, for shares with level and nonlevel repayment terms. Under the shares allocated

    b. method, interest expense is recognized each period as incurred. Expense related to the principal portion (the compensation element) is recognized based on the cost of shares allocated for the period.

    c. It is computed as follows:

    $$\frac{\text{Shares allocated for the period}}{\text{Total shares purchased}} \times \text{Original principal}$$

    + Interest incurred for the period = Expense related to the principal

    b. Reduce compensation expense recognized each period by dividends used to service the ESOP debt.

2. Expense recognition for contributions to an existing ESOP for shares acquired before December 15, 1989, should be as follows:

    a. The current method may continue to be used if cumulative expense, before dividends are deducted, is at least equal to 80% of cumulative expense under the shares-allocated method before dividends are deducted.

    b. Recognize an additional amount in the current period if cumulative expense under the current method is less than 80% of cumulative expense under the shares-allocated method (total cumulative expense should equal 80% of expense under the shares-allocated method).

    c. Expense recognition should not be reduced if the cumulative amount under the current method exceeds 80% of the amount under the shares-allocated method.

3. Report the effect of initial application of this consensus as a cumulative effect of a change in accounting principle, in accordance with APB-20.

4. Adjust the debit in shareholders' equity related to the ESOP loan for the difference between the periodic expense and cash contributions, if any, in each period.

SEC OBSERVER COMMENT

The SEC Observer stated that SEC registrants should fully disclose their method of accounting for ESOPs in accordance with the pension plan disclosure requirements in paragraph 65 of FAS-87. Accordingly, the following information should be disclosed:

- A description of the plan, including employee groups covered
- The basis for determining contributions
- The nature and effect of significant matters affecting comparability of information for all periods presented
- The cost of contributions to the ESOP recognized during the period

In addition, the SEC staff expects the following information to be disclosed for each period presented:

- Actual interest incurred on ESOP debt
- Amount contributed to the ESOP
- Amount of dividends paid by the ESOP on shares held by the ESOP for ESOP debt service

The SEC Observer suggested that registrants consider the need to discuss the potential effect of leveraged ESOPs in the results of operations and liquidity sections of "Management's Discussion and Analysis of Financial Condition and Results of Operations," as required by Item 303 of Regulation S-K. An example is a large scheduled increase in contributions to an ESOP.

At a meeting subsequent to the issuance of SOP 93-6, the SEC Observer stated that the above disclosure requirements should continue to be made by registrants for shares grandfathered from the accounting provisions of that SOP.

DISCUSSION

The Task Force believed that the shares-allocated method is consistent with the guidance in paragraph 9 of SOP 76-3, which required the employer's expense to be the amount contributed or committed to be contributed to the ESOP for the year. (The employer is committed to the extent that interest is accrued and shares are allocated.) Task Force members noted that if shares are allocated based on principal, expense recognition is the same whether the cash payments or shares-allocated methods are used.

The Task Force noted that sometimes the debt payments, the allocation of related shares to participants, and the period over which participants earned those shares may not occur in the same reporting period. If this is the case, the employer may have to accrue or defer compensation expense recognition. The cost of shares should be recognized in the period in which they were earned, regardless of whether debt payments were made in that period. However, expense recognition for prepaid debt should not be deferred for more than one period. Accruals and deferrals should be consistent. Interest should be charged as incurred.

EITF Issue 89-12 Earnings-per-Share Issues Related to Convertible Preferred Stock Held by an Employee Stock Ownership Plan

BACKGROUND

An employer sponsoring an ESOP issues high-yield convertible preferred stock to the ESOP, which finances that purchase with debt. The ESOP repays the debt by using the dividends from the convertible preferred stock and the employer's contributions. In accordance with the guidance in SOP 76-3, the employer charges such dividends to retained earnings.

The employer may redeem the convertible preferred stock in common stock, cash, or a combination of both at a redemption price that equal's the stock's initial value. Each share may be converted into a fixed number of shares of common stock. The employer also may guarantee ESOP participants that on retirement or termination they will receive at least the redemption price in common stock, cash, or a combination of both.

ACCOUNTING ISSUES

The EITF discussed the following issues related to the calculation of EPS under the if-converted method:

1. Should convertible preferred shares issued to an ESOP be considered common stock equivalents?

2. Should net income be reduced by the additional ESOP contribution that would be necessary to meet the debt service requirement if the preferred stock is assumed to be converted, thus eliminating the availability of dividends on the convertible preferred stock?

3. If the employer guarantees that participants will receive at least the redemption price of the preferred stock on retirement or termination, should the number of shares assumed to be outstanding be increased, and if so, to what extent, if the market price of the underlying common stock is less than the redemption price of the preferred stock?

4. What would be the effect on the answer in Issue 3 if the redemption price guarantee can be paid in cash?

EITF CONSENSUS

The EITF reached the following consensus positions, which apply regardless of how the convertible stock is classified in the employer's balance sheet. (Publicly held companies must classify convertible shares as temporary equity. In addition, the if-converted method should not be applied if it is antidilutive.)

1. FAS-128 nullified the consensus in Issue 1.

2. If the preferred stock is assumed to be converted, dividends on those shares would no longer be paid and the ESOP would receive only dividends on the common stock into which the shares were converted. As a result, the employer would have to make an additional contribution to the ESOP for debt service. The employer should therefore adjust net income for the difference between the current dividends on the convertible preferred stock and the dividends on the common stock considered outstanding under the if-converted method. EITF members noted that under the provisions of some employee benefit plans, an employer may be required to make other nondiscretionary adjustments related to the conversion of preferred stock and the additional ESOP contribution.

3. The calculation of EPS in paragraph 63 of APB-15 and FAS-128, which requires using the market price at the end of the reporting period to determine the number of shares to be issued, applies if the market price of the underlying common stock is less than the guaranteed value of the convertible stock. The number of common shares to be used in calculating EPS under the if-converted method is the sum of the following: for unallocated shares—the number of common shares based on the stated conversion, *plus* for allocated shares—the number of common shares equivalent to the redemption value, but not less than the number of shares at the stated conversion rate for convertible preferred stock allocated as of the reporting date. As required in paragraph 63 APB 15, EPS for prior periods should be restated if the number of shares issued or contingently issuable changes as a result of changes in the market price.

4. An employer that is required or has the ability and intent to satisfy a guarantee in cash should use the stated conversion rate for all shares in calculating EPS; the employer need not assume the issuance of additional shares for the guarantee feature.

OBSERVATION: The disclosure requirements in FIN-45 (Guarantor's Accounting and Disclosure Requirements for Guarantees, Including Indirect Guarantees of Indebtedness to Others) apply to guarantees of the value of the preferred stock by employers that continue to apply the guidance in SOP 76-3 to shares acquired before January 1, 1993. The other provisions of FIN-45 do *not* affect the consensuses in this Issue.

SEC OBSERVER COMMENT

The SEC Observer noted that registrants should not analogize these consensus positions to other situations involving the calculation of EPS. In addition, registrants should apply the consensus positions retroactively to EPS calculations for all periods presented in SEC filings subsequent to the consensus. Although the SEC staff would accept the calculations required in the consensus, the SEC staff will deal with unusual situations based on the specific case.

FASB STAFF COMMENT

The FASB staff stated that consensus positions 2, 3, and 4 apply to basic (referred to as "primary" when this Issue was discussed) and diluted EPS calculations if the convertible preferred stock is a common stock equivalent.

DISCUSSION

Issue 2 In computing diluted EPS under the provisions of APB-15 (and FAS-128) a convertible security is assumed to have been converted at the beginning of the period, thus requiring appropriate adjustments to net income. In the case of convertible preferred stock held by an ESOP, if it is assumed that the stock has been converted to common stock, the ESOP will receive dividends on the common stock, but dividends from preferred shares would no longer be available to the ESOP for debt service. Consequently, the employer's contribution for debt service would increase to compensate for a potential deficiency resulting from the difference between dividends on the preferred stock and on the common stock. To illustrate, assume that an ESOP has an annual debt service requirement of $2,000,000, and dividends on the employer's preferred stock held by the ESOP are $1,000,000. The employer would thus contribute $1,000,000 for debt service. However, if it is assumed that (a) the ESOP converts the preferred stock, (b) dividends from the common stock are only $600,000, and (c) there is no change in the debt service requirement, the employer would have to increase the debt service contribution by $400,000 to make up the deficiency.

The EITF's consensus was based on the view that regardless of the source of the proceeds (i.e., whether from dividends on the preferred stock or from an additional employer contribution), the ESOP made debt service payments during the year. Because dividends on the preferred stock would not have been available during the year—as a result of the assumed conversion of the preferred stock at the beginning of the year—it is assumed that the deficiency between the higher dividends on the preferred stock and the dividends on the common stock into which it is converted is made up by an additional employer contribution, which is considered a nondiscretionary adjustment to net income in accordance with paragraph 51 of APB-15.

Issue 3 Sometimes an ESOP that invests in the employer's convertible securities guarantees that the value the employee would receive at the time of conversion would not be less than a specified amount per share of preferred stock. To illustrate, assume the following: A preferred stock that is convertible into common stock on a one-for-one basis has a guarantee that the employee would receive at least $12 for each share of preferred stock at the date of conversion. If an employee converts 100 shares of preferred stock when the fair value of the common stock is more than $12 per share, the employee would receive 100 shares of common stock. If, however, the common stock's fair value is less than the $12 per share guaranteed minimum value, the employee would receive additional shares or cash so that the total value received is equal to the guaranteed amount. For example, at $10 per share, the employee would receive 120 shares of common stock, 100 shares of common stock plus $200, or a combination of common stock and cash worth $1,200.

The following illustrates the EITF's consensus on Issue 3. An ESOP holds 100,000 shares of convertible preferred stock, of which 60,000 shares are allocated to participants and 40,000 shares are unallocated. One share of preferred stock is convertible into two shares of common stock, and participants are guaranteed a market value of common stock equivalent to $10 per preferred share. On December 31, 1989, the market price per share of common stock is $4. The number of shares to be included in diluted EPS is calculated as follows:

Unallocated shares:
    40,000 shares × 2   80,000

Allocated shares:
    Guaranteed value (60,000 shares × $10) $600,000
    Market price per share $ 4

Shares required to satisfy guarantee ($600,000/$4)	150,000	
Shares based on conversion rate (60,000 shares × 2)	120,000	
Shares used:		150,000
		230,000

Issue 4 The consensus reached by the Task Force analogized to the guidance in paragraph 6 of FIN-31, which dealt with whether stock appreciation rights that are payable in stock or in cash should be considered common stock equivalents. Under the Interpretation, the decision was made based on "the terms most likely to be elected based on the facts available each period." FAS-128 carried forward that guidance but provides that it should be presumed that settlement will be in common stock. The potential common shares would, therefore, be included in diluted EPS. The presumption that the rights will be paid in stock may be overcome based on past experience and on the company's stated policy that the rights will be paid partially or wholly in cash. Similarly, this consensus depends on the requirement or the employer's ability and expressed intent to satisfy the guarantee in cash.

EITF Issue 92-3 Earnings-per-Share Treatment of Tax Benefits for Dividends on Unallocated Stock Held by an Employee Stock Ownership Plan

BACKGROUND

Under current federal income tax laws, an employer that sponsors an employee stock ownership plan (ESOP) is entitled to deduct dividends on stock held by the ESOP in computing the employer's corporate taxable income. When this Issue was discussed in March 1992, FAS-109 had just been issued but its application was not required until 1993. Consequently, companies were accounting for income taxes based on the guidance in APB-11, FAS-96, or had early adopted FAS-109. Under paragraph 37 of FAS-109 (ASC 740-20-45-3), tax benefits related to dividends on unallocated ESOP shares must be credited directly to retained earnings. That requirement is similar to the requirement in APB-11, except that APB-11 does not distinguish between allocated and unallocated shares. FAS-96 required recognizing the benefit as a reduction of income tax expense.

ACCOUNTING ISSUES

- In computing EPS, should entities applying the provisions of FAS-109 adjust net income for tax benefits related to dividends on unallocated common stock held by an ESOP?
- Should the same treatment apply to convertible preferred stock ESOPs when computing EPS under the if-converted method?

EITF CONSENSUS

- In computing EPS, companies applying FAS-109 should not adjust net income for tax benefits related to dividends on unallocated common stock held by an ESOP, because under FAS-109, tax benefits on such shares must be charged to retained earnings.

- The same treatment applies to convertible preferred stock ESOPs in computing EPS under the if-converted method.

DISCUSSION

The Task Force's consensus positions on this Issue were based on the view that the amount used in EPS computations should be consistent with the calculation of net income based on the provisions of FAS-109.

This consensus was nullified by SOP 93-6 for shares acquired by an ESOP *after* December 31, 1992.

CHAPTER 42
ASC 720—OTHER EXPENSES

CONTENTS

Part I: General Guidance	42,001
ASC 720-25: Contributions Made	42,001
Overview	42,001
ASC 720-30: Real and Personal Property Taxes	42,002
Overview	42,002
Background	42,002
Accounting and Reporting Standards	42,003
Illustration of Accounting and Reporting Standards for Property Taxes	42,004
Part II: Interpretive Guidance	42,004
ASC 720-15: Startup Costs	42,004
ASC 720-15-15-1 through 15-5, 25-1, 55-1, 55-3, 55-5, 55-7, 55-9, 55-10	
Reporting on the Costs of Start-Up Activities	42,004
ASC 720-20: Insurance Costs	42,006
ASC 720-20-05-2 through 05-8, 15-4 through 15-6, 15-8, 25-2 through 25-12, 25-14, 30-2; 35-2 through 35-5, 35-8 through 35-10, 45-1, 50-1, 55-3 through 55-12, 55-14 through 55-20; ASC 450-30-60-4; ASC 954-720-25-4A	
Accounting for Claims-Made Insurance and Retroactive Insurance Contracts by the Insured Entity	42,006
ASC 720-40: Electronic Equipment Waste Obligations	42,013
ASC 720-40-05-1 through 05-4, 15-1, 25-1 through 25-3, 35-1, 55-2 through 55-3; ASC 410-20-15-2 through 15-3, 55-23 through 55-30, 55-64 through 55-67	
Accounting for Electronic Equipment Waste Obligations	42,013
ASC 720-50: Fees Paid to the Federal Government by Pharmaceutical Manufacturers and Health Insurers	42,015
ASC 720-50-05-1 through 05-4, 15-1, 25-1, 45-1, 65-1through 65-2	
Fees Paid to the Federal Government by Pharmaceutical Manufacturers and Health Insurers	42,015

PART I: GENERAL GUIDANCE

ASC 720-25: CONTRIBUTIONS MADE

OVERVIEW

The guidance in ASC 720-25 applies to contributions of gifts and other assets, including unconditional promises to give (ASC 720-25-15-2). The guidance in ASC 720-25 does not apply to: (1) exchange transactions where each party transfers assets and other consideration of equal value, (2) transfers where the entity is an agent, trustee, or intermediary rather than a donor, (3) tax exemptions, incentives, or abatements, and (4) asset transfers from a government to a business (ASC 720-25-15-3).

A contribution made to an entity shall be recorded at fair value, whether the contribution is of assets or is the settlement or cancellation of a liability (ASC 720-25-30-1). A gain or loss is recognized if the fair value of the asset contributed differs from its recorded value (ASC 720-25-25-2). If the unconditional promise to give is expected to be paid within one year, it can be recorded at net settlement value (ASC 720-25-30-2).

A contribution is recognized as an expense in the period it is made. If the contribution is an asset, assets are decreased; if the contribution is an unconditional promise to give, a liability is increased (ASC 720-25-25-1).

ASC 720-30: REAL AND PERSONAL PROPERTY TAXES

OVERVIEW

Generally, the basis for recognizing expense for property taxes is monthly accrual on the taxpayers' books over the fiscal period of the taxing authority for which the taxes are levied. At the end of the accounting period, the financial statements will show the appropriate accrual or prepayment.

BACKGROUND

FASB Concepts Statements (CONs) constitute the FASB's conceptual framework. In CON-6 (Elements of Financial Statements), *liabilities* are defined as probable future sacrifices of economic benefits arising from present obligations of a particular entity to transfer assets or provide services to other entities in the future as a result of past transactions or events. A liability has three essential characteristics:

> It embodies a present duty or responsibility to one or more other entities that entails settlement by probable future transfer of assets at a specified or determinable date, on occurrence of a specific event, or on demand.
>
> The duty or responsibility obligates a particular entity, leaving it little or no discretion to avoid the future sacrifice.
>
> The transaction or other event obligating the entity has already happened.

Unlike excise tax, income tax, and Social Security tax, which are directly related to particular business events, real and personal property taxes are based on an assessed valuation of property as of a given date, as determined by law. For this reason, the legal liability for such taxes generally is considered to accrue when a specific event occurs, rather than over a period of time. Following are several dates that have been suggested as the point in time in which property taxes legally accrue (ASC 720-30-25-1):

- Assessment date
- Beginning of the taxing authority's fiscal year
- End of the taxing authority's fiscal year
- Date on which the tax becomes a lien on the property
- Date the tax is levied

- Date(s) the tax is payable
- Date the tax becomes delinquent
- Tax period appearing on a tax bill

The date most widely accepted as obligating the entity is the date of assessment of the taxes by the appropriate taxing authority.

ACCOUNTING AND REPORTING STANDARDS

Although many states have different laws or precedents as to when the legal liability accrues for real and personal property taxes, the general rule is that it accrues on the date the taxes are assessed (ASC 720-30-25-1). The exact amount of tax may not be known on the assessment date, however, and a reasonable estimate must be made. The inability to determine the exact amount of real and personal property taxes is not an acceptable reason for not recognizing an existing tax liability (ASC 720-30-25-6).

In those cases in which the accrued amount is subject to a great deal of uncertainty, the liability should be described as estimated. Whether the amount of the accrued tax liability for real and personal property taxes is known or estimated, it should be reported as a current liability in the balance sheet (ASC 720-30-45-1).

A monthly accrual over the fiscal period of the taxing authority is considered the most acceptable basis for recording real and personal property taxes. This results in the appropriate accrual or prepayment at any closing date (ASC 720-30-25-7). An adjustment to the estimated tax liability of a prior year is made when the exact amount is determined. This adjustment is made in the income statement of the period in which the exact amount is determined, either as an adjustment to the current year's provision or as a separate item on the income statement.

In most circumstances, however, real and personal property taxes are considered an expense of doing business and are reported in the appropriate income statement (a) as an operating expense, (b) as a deduction from income, or (c) allocated to several expense accounts, such as manufacturing overhead and general and administrative expenses. As a general rule, real and personal property taxes should not be combined with income taxes (ASC 720-30-45-2, 3).

PRACTICE POINTER: In interim financial reports, estimate the end-of-period liability in order to estimate the expense for the year. Reflect adjustments to the amount of the estimate in the interim period during which the adjustment becomes known.

Property taxes on property held for resale to customers or under construction are typically capitalized.

OBSERVATION: The promulgated GAAP do not describe the criteria for capitalizing or not capitalizing real estate taxes.

Illustration of Accounting and Reporting Standards for Property Taxes

On October 1, 20X5, the City assesses $12,000 of property taxes on Wilson, Inc., for the fiscal year, October 1, 20X5-September 30, 20X6. Wilson records the assessment as follows:

Oct. 1, 20X5

Deferred property taxes	12,000	
Property taxes payable		12,000

At December 31, 20X5, the end of Wilson's financial reporting year, Wilson adjusts the deferred property taxes account by recognizing three months of expense, as follows:

Dec. 31, 20X5

Property tax expense	3,000	
Deferred property taxes		3,000

At February 1, 20X6, Wilson pays the property taxes and makes the following entry:

Feb. 1, 20X6

Property taxes payable	12,000	
Cash		12,000

Throughout, or at the end of 20X6, the remaining nine months of property taxes are recognized as expense:

Various dates, 20X6

Property tax expense	9,000	
Deferred property taxes		9,000

PART II: INTERPRETIVE GUIDANCE

ASC 720-15: Startup Costs

ASC 720-15-15-1 through 15-5, 25-1, 55-1, 55-3, 55-5, 55-7, 55-9, 55-10 Reporting on the Costs of Start-Up Activities

BACKGROUND

"Reporting on the Costs of Start-Up Activities," was the second in a series of projects under which the AICPA's Accounting Standards Exective Committee (AcSEC) considered how to report on costs of activities that are undertaken to create future economic benefits. The first project resulted in the issuance of the Statement of Position, "Reporting on Advertising Costs," (see Chapter 23, *ASC 340—Deferred Costs and Other Assets*).

Start-up activities are defined broadly as onetime activities related to all of the following:

- Opening a new facility
- Introducing a new product or service
- Conducting business in a new territory
- Conducting business with a new class of customer or beneficiary
- Initiating a new process in an existing facility
- Commencing some new operation
- Organizing a new entity (i.e., organization costs)

In practice, start-up costs are referred to in different ways, including pre-operating costs and organization costs.

Certain costs are not considered start-up costs and should be accounted for in accordance with existing authoritative accounting pronouncements. They include the following:

- Costs of acquiring or constructing long-lived assets and getting them ready for their intended use
- Costs of acquiring or producing inventory
- Costs of acquiring intangible assets
- Costs related to internally developed assets
- Costs that are covered by ASC 730
- Costs of fund-raising incurred by not-for-profit organizations
- Costs of raising capital
- Costs of advertising
- Costs incurred in connection with existing contracts in accordance with ASC 605-35

ACCOUNTING STANDARDS

Costs of start-up activities, including organization costs should be expensed as incurred.

PRACTICE POINTER: This guidance continues a general trend (begun with ASC 730-10) of expensing costs with uncertain amounts, timing, or future cash flows. The costs associated with start-up activities, although clearly incurred with the expectation of generating future benefits, may not meet the definition of an asset or may not be measurable with sufficient accuracy because of the following:

- The expenditure fails to generate future benefits (i.e., no asset).
- The timing of any future benefits that might be generated is uncertain (i.e., measurement difficulties in valuing the resulting asset).
- The amount of such future benefits may not exceed the costs of generating those benefits (i.e., no asset).

The conclusion that costs of start-up activities should be expensed as incurred has been incorporated in the following guidance:

- ASC 605-35, Accounting for Performance of Construction-Type and Certain Production-Type Contracts;
- ASC 908, Accounting for Developmental and Preoperating Costs, Purchases and Exchanges of Take-off and Landing Slots, and Airframe Modifications;
- ASC 908, Audits of Airlines;
- ASC 910, Construction Contractors;
- ASC 912, Audits of Federal Government Contractors;
- ASC 924, Audits of Casinos;
- ASC 946, Foreign Currency Accounting and Financial Statement Presentation for Investment Companies;
- ASC 946, Audits of Investment Companies.

ASC 720-20: Insurance Costs

ASC 720-20-05-2 through 05-8, 15-4 through 15-6, 15-8, 25-2 through 25-12, 25-14, 30-2; 35-2 through 35-5, 35-8 through 35-10, 45-1, 50-1, 55-3 through 55-12, 55-14 through 55-20; ASC 450-30-60-4; ASC 954-720-25-4A Accounting for Claims-Made Insurance and Retroactive Insurance Contracts by the Insured Entity

BACKGROUND

Companies generally purchase claims-made policies to cover product, directors and officers (D&O), and malpractice liabilities. Such coverage insures an entity for claims reported during the policy's term, depending on the policy's retroactive date. Two categories of claims are covered: (*a*) retroactive claims for incidents that occurred *before* the policy's term and reported during its term or (*b*) *prospective* claims for incidents that occur and are reported during the policy's term.

Claims-made policies are generally renewed annually. If a company ceases its operations, it can purchase tail insurance, which insures the entity against claims made *after* the policy has terminated. By renewing its policy annually and purchasing tail insurance, if needed, a company can convert a claims-made policy to one based on occurrence so that the company is covered for any claims made against it. Because the date of occurrence is usually irrelevant in determining whether a claim is covered, a claims-made policy is usually the only form of insurance that covers exposures for which it is difficult to determine the date of occurrence and occurrences that may extend over long periods of time. Some companies that purchase such insurance are frequently unaware of outstanding unasserted claims of liabilities that do not meet the recognition criteria in ASC 450 or other generally accepted accounting principles (GAAP). Consequently, no liability has been recognized for such claims, including incurred but not reported (IBNR) claims. Other companies that purchase claims-made coverage may know about potential claims related to specific incidents, and may choose to specifically include those unasserted claims under the coverage or to exclude them.

ASC 720—Other Expenses **42,007**

The following guidance does *not* apply to reinsurance transactions.

ACCOUNTING ISSUES

1. How should an insured entity, such as a manufacturer, retailer, service company, or financial institution, including an insurance company that purchases insurance *not* related to its core insurance operations, account for a purchased retroactive insurance policy to cover a liability for a *past* event recognized in accordance with ASC 450, and does that transaction result in a gain being recognized?

2. Does a claims-made insurance policy correspond to a purchased retroactive insurance policy covered by the consensus in Issue 1?

3a. Should an insured entity recognize a liability at the balance sheet date for IBNR claims?

3b. If it is impossible to reasonably estimate the probable losses from IBNR claims and the number of incidents cannot be reasonably estimated, may a liability be accrued based on the estimated cost of purchasing tail coverage to insure the entity for events that occur during the period of the claims-made policy but that are *not* reported to the insurance carrier in that period?

4a. If an entity's fiscal year and the term of a prospective policy are the same, how should both of the following be accounted for: (*a*) the IBNR liability in subsequent periods in which the entity purchases another claims-made insurance policy that covers a portion of losses included in the IBNR liability, and (*b*) the premiums for the subsequent claims-made insurance policy?

4b. What is the accounting effect on a conclusion reached on Issue 4(a) if a prospective claims-made policy's term is *not* the same as the entity's fiscal year?

5. What disclosures should be made by companies insured under claims-made policies?

ACCOUNTING GUIDANCE

1. The guidance below applies only to retroactive insurance contracts that (*a*) do not legally extinguish an entity's liability, (*b*) meet the conditions in ASC 450 for indemnification against loss or liability, (*c*) indemnify the insured against loss or liability for liabilities that were incurred as a result of a past event, for example, environmental remediation liabilities, and (*d*) are not reinsurance transactions.

Under the guidance in ASC 450-20-05-3, entities are required to determine whether an insurance contract results in a transfer of insurance risk. The guidance for insurance enterprises in ASC 944-20 may be useful in making that determination. Under that guidance, reinsurance contracts that do *not* transfer insurance risk should be accounted for as deposits.

Although ASC 944-20 applies only to insurance companies, purchased retroactive insurance contracts that indemnify an insured should be accounted for in a manner similar to that provided in ASC 944-20 for retroactive reinsurance contracts. The guidance in ASC 944-605-25-35 should be applied, if appropriate, based on the facts and circumstances of the specific transaction.

Amounts paid for retroactive insurance should be expensed immediately, and a receivable should be recognized at the same time for expected recoveries related to the underlying event. If a receivable exceeds the amount paid for the insurance, there is a deferred gain, which should be amortized using the interest method over the estimated period that the entity expects to recover substantially all amounts due under the terms of the insurance contract, provided the amount and timing of the insurance recoveries can be reasonably estimated. If not, a deferred gain should be amortized based on the proportion of actual recoveries to total estimated recoveries.

A gain should *not* be recognized and a related liability should *not* be derecognized immediately, because the liability has not been completely extinguished. Amounts receivable on an insurance policy should *not* be offset against a liability for a past insurable event, because those amounts do *not* meet the criteria in ASC 210-20-45-1 for offsetting. Legal and other costs covered under purchased insurance contracts should be accounted for in a consistent manner in the related asset and liability accounts. For example, if the costs are covered under the term of the insurance contracts and the entity's policy is to accrue such costs, they should also be included in the insurance receivable.

2. A claims-made insurance policy contains a retroactive provision if it provides coverage for specific, known claims that were reportable by an insured entity to the insurance carrier before the period of the policy, such as asserted claims, unasserted claims, or known previous events and circumstances, if any, that might result in a specific asserted or unasserted claim.

Retroactive and prospective provisions of such policies should be accounted for separately, if practicable. Otherwise, an entire policy should be accounted for as a retroactive contract in accordance with the guidance in ASC 944-605-25-35. Claims-made insurance policies that do *not* include retroactive provisions should be accounted for on a *prospective* basis based on the guidance in 4(a) and 4(b) below.

ASC 944-20-15-34B states that under a claims-made policy, an *insured event* is the act of *reporting* to an insurer a loss covered by a policy during the period stated in the policy. Therefore, *prospective* claims-made insurance policies cover only losses reported to an insurer during the term of a policy. A policy with a retroactive provision covers insured events that occurred or were reportable *before* the term of the policy and, therefore, covers claims for specific, known claims that were reportable before the policy's effective date. The fact that a liability for IBNR claims has been recognized is *not* a conclusive factor in determining whether a claims-made insurance policy does or does not contain a retroactive provision.

All the relevant facts and circumstances should be considered in determining whether a claims-made policy includes a retroactive provision. The following are indicators that a policy does *not* contain a retroactive provision (i.e., it does not cover previously reportable claims) and should be accounted for on a prospective basis, but no one indicator is conclusive:

a. The insured always purchases claims-made insurance policies for the type of risk that is insured, and tail coverage for prior periods and prior policies can be easily obtained at a reasonable cost compared to tail coverage that does not contain retroactive provisions offered to similar companies.

b. The claims-made policy covers unknown risks for a finite or limited time period, because (*a*) the claims are incurred during the policy's period and paid shortly after the end of the policy's period, (*b*) the policy covers a limited time period, (*c*) claims-made insurance is the most easily available coverage for this type of insurance risk, and (*d*) it is difficult to determine the date on which the type of risk covered under the policy will occur.

c. The claims-made insurance policy has clear indicators *not* subject to interpretation, negotiation, or manipulation, that a claim is covered under the policy, such as, a provision requiring an insured (*a*) to notify the insurance carrier of an asserted claim or that an incident occurred during the policy term, or (*b*) to represent that it was not aware of such an incident when the claims-made policy was purchased.

d. The claims-made policy's premium is *not* significantly higher than that for a policy that could be purchased by a similar entity with similar insurance risks that does not know of any circumstances or events that would result in claims, except for a typical number of claims incurred but not reported (IBNR).

e. The policy's premium may be based on estimates and predictions based on the insured's past experience, but not on estimates of settlements of specific, known events expected to be recovered under the policy.

f. The current year's premium does *not* significantly exceed the amount charged in previous years, except for increases in the amount or type of coverage.

g. The policy is purchased primarily to cover insurance risk, *not* as a financing arrangement. Such claims-made policies usually include (*a*) no adjustments based on experience, and (*b*) coverage of the final loss from a claim once it has been made, regardless of when the claim is settled.

h. If a claims-made insurance policy has a specified retroactive date before the relationship with the insurer begins, the period from the specified retroactive date to the date the claims-made relationship with the insurer begins is short or is covered by other insurance.

The guidance in 1 above is *not* intended to preclude prospective accounting for claims-made policies or portions of those policies that contain only prospective provisions even though the guidance applies in situations in which an insured entity uses the policy to finance known losses that occurred or were reportable *before* entering into the insurance contract. In addition, an insured entity that enters into multiple claims-made insurance contracts at the same time should consider whether to combine the insurance contracts so it can determine how to account for them. ASC 944-20-15-40 provides guidance on those matters.

ASC 720—Other Expenses

3a. Under the guidance in ASC 450-20-25-2, entities that insure certain risks using a claims-made approach are required to recognize a liability for probable losses from IBNR claims and incidents if a loss is *probable* and *reasonably estimable*. ASC 450-20-55-10 through 55-17 provides implementation guidance for litigation, claims, and assessments.

3b. If an entity has not purchased tail insurance coverage, the estimated cost of such coverage is irrelevant in determining a loss accrual, because netting an insurance receivable against a claim liability is prohibited under the guidance in ASC 210-20-45-1. However, if an insured entity had a unilateral option to purchase tail coverage at a premium that does not exceed a specified fixed maximum amount, the entity could record a receivable for expected insurance recoveries (after considering deductibles and the policy's limits) for the insurable portion of the IBNR liability under the tail coverage. The cost of the expected premium for tail coverage should be recorded. Nevertheless, the need to determine whether an additional liability should be accrued as a result of policy limits and other factors is *not* eliminated by purchasing tail coverage.

4a. If an entity's fiscal year and the policy's year are the same, it should recognize the expense of of the annual premium based on a combination of any of the following:

    a. Accruing the IBNR liability;

    b. Accruing expected increases in insurance recoveries;

    c. Amortizing the insurance premium on a pro rata basis over the year.

A liability for unusual claims or incidents and related insurance recoveries should be recognized in the interim period in which they become known.

Under this approach, usual recurring losses are accounted for in the interim period as part of annual reporting, so that expected changes, if any, in the IBNR liability and related insurance recoveries not related to specific events can be spread over the whole year. But unusual material losses should be accounted for as separate items and recognized as they occur. It is assumed under this approach that the purchase of a one-year term claims-made insurance policy is a recurring event and that the premium will be paid on the first day of each policy year.

If an entity's fiscal year and the policy's term are the same, an entity's liability at year-end for IBNR is related to the entity's obligation for claims and incidents that were incurred *before* the year-end but that will be reportable after year-end. Policyholders that purchase claims-made policies consisting of *prospective* provisions should account for those policies as follows:

    a. At the *beginning* of the fiscal year, a prepaid expense should be recognized for the total premium paid for the new policy.

    b. At the *beginning* of the fiscal year, the IBNR liability as of the end of the fiscal year should be estimated by considering claims and incidents that occurred before the year-end but that will *not* be reportable until after the year-end. That amount should be roughly the IBNR liability at the beginning of the year plus adjustments to the IBNR liability for relevant

ASC 720—Other Expenses **42,011**

historical patterns and possible adjustments, if any, due to new factors that have been identified, such as major changes in products, manufacturing processes, or risk management systems.

c. The estimated annual expense should be computed as the sum of (*a*) the premium paid for the claims-made policy, (*b*) the difference between the IBNR liability at the beginning of the year and the estimated amount at the end of the year, and (*c*) the difference between the beginning insurance recoverable related to the IBNR liability and estimated amount at the end of the year.

That estimated amount should be recognized in interim periods using a method that best represents the manner in which the benefits of the insurance coverage are used up and the IBNR liability is incurred. Liabilities for specific claims incurred during the year not included in the estimated IBNR liability should be recognized as an expense in interim periods in which they are incurred. The method should be selected by considering the relevant facts and circumstances and should be applied consistently.

d. The estimated year-end IBNR liability should be reviewed at interim reporting dates. Routine adjustments of the estimated liability should be recognized ratably in each of the remaining interim periods. But significant adjustments of the year-end IBNR liability should be recognized in an interim period in which events and circumstances indicate that unusual claims and incidents occurred *before* the end of that interim period but that will probably not be reported until after year-end and, therefore, will *not* be covered under the existing claims-made policy.

e. Unusual claims and incidents that have occurred *before* the end of an interim period but that will probably be reported *before* the year-end do *not* affect net income if they are covered under an existing policy. The asset under the insurance claim and the liability for the incident should be presented on the balance sheet.

f. An entity should evaluate recognized insurance recoverables, if any, that are related to IBNR liabilities or to specific incurred claims and adjust them, if necessary, based on changes in circumstances. See ASC 410-30-35-8 for guidance on the recognition of receivables for expected insurance recoveries

Prepaid insurance should *not* be offset against a recognized IBNR liability or a liability incurred as a result of a past insurable event unless the conditions in ASC 210-20.

4b. If an entity's fiscal year and policy year are *not* the same, the accrual in interim periods should be based on the entity's estimated premium for the claims-made policy expected to be purchased later in that fiscal year. At year-end, the entity should recognize the following: (*a*) an IBNR *liability* for the obligation for claims and incidents that occurred *before* year-end but that will be reported *after* year-end, (*c*) an insurance recoverable for outstanding claims, if any, that are reimbursable und an existing claims-made policy, and (*c*) an *asset*

42,012 ASC 720—Other Expenses

for prepaid insurance premiums for coverage of claims and incidents that will occur *after* year-end, but will be reported *before* the current policy expires. Policyholders that purchase claims-made policies with terms that are *not* the same as the entity's fiscal year should account for those policies as follows:

a. The estimated premium for a new claims-made policy expected to be purchased during the fiscal year should be estimated at the *beginning* of the fiscal year. The portion of the future premium relating to coverage for claims or incidents that will occur *after* the end of the fiscal year but that will be reported *before* the new claims-made policy expires should also be estimated. That amount is the estimated prepaid asset at end of the fiscal year. An estimate of the future premium considers the effect of past claims and incidents that are expected to affect the amount of the premium and the effect of historical patterns and relevant new factors, such as a major change in products, manufacturing processes, or risk management systems.

b. At the *beginning* of the fiscal year, the IBNR liability as of the end of the fiscal year should be estimated by considering claims and incidents that will be incurred before the year-end but that will not be reportable until after the year-end. That amount should be roughly the IBNR liability at the beginning of the year plus adjustments for relevant historical patterns and possibly additional adjustments if the entity has identified new factors that would affect the IBNR liability, such as major changes in products, manufacturing processes, or risk management systems.

c. The estimated annual expense should be computed as the sum of (*a*) the balance of the premium cost of the claims-made policy that expires during the year, (*b*) the difference the estimated premium cost for a new claims-made policy, (*c*) the difference between the beginning IBNR liability and the estimated IBNR liability at year-end, and (*d*) the difference between the beginning and estimated ending insurance receivable related to the IBNR liability. That estimated annual expense should be recognized ratably in interim periods using a method that best represents the manner in which the benefits of the insurance coverage are used up and the IBNR liability is incurred. That method should be appropriate based on the relevant facts and circumstances and should be applied consistently. Liabilities for specific claims incurred during the year that are not included in the estimated IBNR liability should be recognized as expense in the period in which they are incurred.

d. The estimated year-end IBNR liability should be reviewed at interim reporting dates. Routine adjustments of the estimated liability, such as adjustments of the estimated future premium to reflect the actual cost should be recognized ratably in the remaining interim periods. But significant adjustments of the year-end IBNR liability should be recognized in an interim period in which events and circumstances indicate that unusual claims and incidents occurred before the end of that interim period but that will probably not be reportable until after the subsequent interim period.

ASC 720—Other Expenses   42,013

e. An entity should evaluate assets related to insurance recoverables, if any, that are related to an IBNR liability or to specific incurred claims and should adjust them, if necessary, based on changes in circumstances. See ASC 410-30-35-8 through 35-11 for guidance related to the recognition of receivables for expected insurance recoveries.

f. Unusual claims and incidents incurred before the end of an interim period but that will probably be reported before the new claims-made policy expires do *not* affect net income if they will be covered by insurance. Both the asset under an insurance claim and a liability for the incident should be presented in the balance sheet.

5. If an entity changes from occurrence-based insurance to claims-made insurance or elects to significantly reduce or eliminate its insurance coverage, disclosure is required under the guidance ASC 450-20-50-3 if it is at least reasonably possible that a loss has been incurred. That paragraph also includes a discussion of disclosures for unasserted claims.

ASC 720-40: Electronic Equipment Waste Obligations

ASC 720-40-05-1 through 05-4, 15-1, 25-1 through 25-3, 35-1, 55-2 through 55-3;
ASC 410-20-15-2 through 15-3, 55-23 through 55-30, 55-64 through 55-67
Accounting for Electronic Equipment Waste Obligations

BACKGROUND

The following guidance addresses the accounting for obligations related to the European Union's Directive 2002/96/EC on Waste Electrical and Electronic Equipment (the Directive). The Directive refers to two types of waste: (1) "new waste," the term used for products put on the market *after* August 13, 2005, and (2) "historical waste" equipment, the term used for all products that have been on the market on or *before* August 13, 2005. For the purpose of financing the cost of historical waste, the Directive differentiates between such waste from households and from commercial users.

The guidance discussed here applies only to *historical* waste. The guidance in ASC 720-40 applies to historical waste from private households, while the guidance in ASC 410-20 applies to historical waste from commercial users. Under the Directive the costs related to new waste will be assumed by the producers of such equipment. The following two questions are addressed under the guidance that follows: (1) should commercial users of electronic equipment or producers of such equipment that sell to private households and to commercial users recognize the Directive's effects on historical waste management under U.S. GAAP and (2) if so, when and how should those effects be accounted for?

ACCOUNTING GUIDANCE

Historical Waste Equipment Held by Commercial Users

The Directive provides that a commercial user retains a waste management obligation for historical waste until it replaces the equipment. At the time of replacement, that obligation may be transferred to the entity that has produced the newly acquired equipment, subject to the laws adopted by applicable EU-member countries. A commercial user that does not replace the equipment retains the obligation until the equipment's disposition. Under the Directive, however, EU-member countries have the option of requiring commercial users to retain an obligation for a portion of or all costs associated with historical waste even if the equipment is replaced. In that case, a commercial user may retain a portion or all of the obligation until disposing of the equipment. Therefore, for all intents and purposes, commercial users may be obligated to incur the costs of retiring assets that meet the definition of historical waste equipment.

Commercial users should apply the provisions ASC 410-20 and the related guidance in ASC 410-20-25 and 20-55 to obligations related to historical waste because they are, in effect, asset retirement obligations. The guidance in ASC 410-20-25-1-5, 30-1, 35-1 through 35-2; ASC 360-10-35-18 through 35-19 applies to the initial recognition and measurement of a liability and the cost of asset retirement. Recognition of that obligation is required regardless of a commercial user's intent and ability to replace the equipment and transfer the obligation. The obligation may be transferred to the producer of replacement equipment, depending on the laws of the applicable EU-member country, and if so, would be reflected in the asset's purchase price.

The cost related to an asset's retirement should be capitalized when a liability related to historical waste is initially recognized by increasing the related asset's carrying amount by the same amount as the liability. The guidance in ASC 410-20-35-3 through 35-8, which requires recognition of changes in the amount of an obligation as a result of the passage of time and changes in the timing or amount of the original estimate of undiscounted cash flows, should be applied in periods following the initial accounting for the liability.

A commercial user that subsequently replaces equipment and transfers its obligation for historical waste to the producer of the newly acquired equipment should determine, based on the fair value of the asset retirement obligation, how much of the purchase price is related to the newly acquired equipment and how much is related to the transferred asset retirement obligation. The cost basis of the newly acquired equipment should equal the difference between the amount paid and the fair value of the obligation transferred. The transferred liability should be removed from the commercial user's balance sheet and a gain or loss should be recognized for the difference between the carrying amount of the liability at the date that replacement equipment was purchased and the portion of the purchase price related to the transferred obligation. Producers of replacement equipment that accept the transfer of and obligation related to historical waste and for whom recycling of electronic waste equipment is *not* a revenue-producing activity should recognize revenue on a net basis based on the amount received less the fair value of the transferred liability for historical waste. The producer should derecognize the transferred obligation when it is settled. Producers that do conduct such recycling as a revenue-producing activity should measure revenue earned on the sale of replacement equipment and the assumption of the obligation based on the guidance in ASC 605-25-05; 05-15, 05-25, 05-30, 05-50, 05-55. In EU countries where commercial users retain their historical waste obligations when purchasing replacement equipment, *no* portion of the purchase price of newly acquired equipment should be allocated to the liability, which remains on the commercial user's balance sheet until it is settled.

Historical Waste Held by Private Households

The guidance in this section is not related to the guidance for asset retirement in ASC 410-20. Under the Directive, historical waste held by private households should be financed collectively by producers that are sellers in the market during each measurement period, which should be defined by each EU member. The amount to be financed is not affected by the volume of equipment qualifying as historical waste sold by electronic equipment producers in the market before the measuring period. Producers will be required to contribute proportionate amounts based on their shares of the market by type of equipment. Each EU-member country will determine the exact method of computation. For example, if the amount of the liability of each producer in the market is computed based on its respective share of the market by type of equipment sold during a measurement period, a producer would recognize a liability for its obligation and an offsetting amount as an expense over the measurement period based on its portion of the estimated total costs of the waste management program to be allocated and its estimated market share. Each producer is required to adjust its liability as information about the actual cost of the program and the producer's actual respective market share becomes available. Because an obligation is triggered by participation in the market during the measurement period, a producer should *not* recognize an obligation *before* that period begins.

ASC 720-50: Fees Paid to the Federal Government by Pharmaceutical Manufacturers and Health Insurers

ASC 720-50-05-1 through 05-4, 15-1, 25-1, 45-1, 65-1through 65-2 Fees Paid to the Federal Government by Pharmaceutical Manufacturers and Health Insurers

BACKGROUND

Under the requirements of the Patient Protection and Affordable Care Act and the Health Care and Education Reconciliation Act (the Acts), which were signed into law in March 2010, companies in the pharmaceutical manufacturing industry will be required to pay an annual fee for each calendar year beginning on or after January 1, 2011. Health insurers will be required to pay an annual fee beginning on or after January 1, 2014.

The pharmaceutical industry's total fee, which ranges between $2.5 and $4.1 billion, will be allocated to individual entities in the industry based on the amount of their branded prescription drug sales for the preceding year as a percentage of the industry's total branded prescription drug sales during that period. A portion of an entity's payments to the U.S. Treasury department become payable when an entity has a gross receipt from branded prescription drug sales to any specified government program or based on coverage under any government program within each calendar year that begins on or after January 1, 2011. Subject to when the pharmaceutical manufacturing industry becomes obligated to pay the fee, it is expected that entities in that industry will recognize their pro rated portion of the fee in the annual period in which the fee is due.

Entities in the industry generally consider the fee to be an annual cost of participating in the government programs for the year in which the payment is due and that the amount of sales in the prior year is used only as a means of allocating the fee among the entities in the industry based on their market share in the government programs. The SEC staff has indicated that it would not object if entities in the industry recognize the annual fee over the calendar year when it is paid by allocating the fee on a straight-line basis or based on another method that provides a better allocation of the cost or revenue reduction over the benefit period.

The annual fee that will be paid by entities in the health insurance industry will be allocated to individual health insurers based on the ratio of the amount of net premiums that an entity has written during the preceding year to the amount of health insurance for any U.S. health risk written during the preceding calendar year. A portion of a health insurance entity's annual fee becomes payable to the U.S. Treasury department when that entity provides health insurance for any U.S. health risk for each calendar year beginning on or after January 1, 2014.

Although there is agreement on the annual periods in which those fees will be recognized, there are different opinions about: (1) how to classify those annual fees in reporting entities' income statements; and (2) whether to expense the entire annual fees when a liability is recognized for those fees or whether to recognize an asset for the fee that would be amortized over the calendar year.

SCOPE

The guidance herein applies to all entities in the pharmaceutical manufacturing industry and to health insurers subject to the annual fee, as defined under the Acts. Before analogizing to the following accounting guidance, the facts and circumstances of other fee arrangements should be considered

ACCOUNTING GUIDANCE

Pharmaceutical manufacturers should estimate and recognize a liability for the full amount of the annual fee discussed in ASC 720-50-05-1 through 05-2 when the first qualifying sale has been made. Likewise, health insurers should estimate and recognize a liability for the full amount of the annual fee discussed in ASC 720-50-05-3 through 05-4 once the entity has provided qualifying health insurance in the applicable calendar year in which the fee is payable. Pharmaceutical manufacturers and health insurers should recognize a corresponding amount as a deferred cost that should be amortized to expense on a straight line basis unless another method provides a better allocation of the fee over the year in which it is payable. The annual fee paid to the U.S. Treasury does not correspond to a cost related to the acquisition of policies that conforms with the definition of an *acquisition cost* in ASC 944-30. Pharmaceutical manufacturers and health insurer should account for the annual fee as an operating expense.

Transition Method and Disclosures

1. Pharmaceutical entities—The above guidance should be effective for calendar years that begin after December 31, 2010. Entities are not required to evaluate their existing policies related to similar fees assessed by governmental authorities.

2. Health insurers—The above guidance should be effective for calendar years that begin after December 31, 2013. Entities are not required to evaluate their existing policies related to similar fees assessed by governmental authorities.

CHAPTER 43
ASC 730—RESEARCH AND DEVELOPMENT

CONTENTS

Part I: General Guidance	43,001
ASC 730-10: Overall	43,001
Overview	43,001
Background	43,001
Accounting and Reporting Research and Development—General Standards	43,002
Illustration of Determining R&D Expense	43,003
Disclosure	43,003
ASC 730-20: Research and Development Arrangements	43,004
Research and Development Arrangements	43,004
Contract	43,004
Nature of Obligation	43,004
Obligation for Contractual Services	43,006
Financial Statement Disclosure	43,007
Part II: Interpretive Guidance	43,007
ASC 730-20: Research and Development Arrangements	43,007
ASC 730-20-25-13 through 25-14, 35-1, 65-1; ASC 730-10-55-3	
Accounting for Nonrefundable Advance Payments for Goods or Services to Be Used in Future Research and Development Activities	43,007

PART I: GENERAL GUIDANCE

ASC 730-10: OVERALL

OVERVIEW

Research and development (R&D) cost is carefully defined in the authoritative accounting literature. Once R&D costs are appropriately identified, GAAP require that they be expensed in the period incurred. Some costs related to R&D activities, however, are appropriately capitalized and carried forward as assets if they have alternative future uses. R&D-related assets typically include items of property, plant, and equipment and intangible assets used in the ongoing R&D effort of the enterprise.

BACKGROUND

Research is the planned efforts of a company to discover new information that will help create a new product, service, process, or technique or vastly improve one in current use. *Development* takes the findings generated by research and formulates a plan to create the desired item or to improve an existing one. Development in the context of this area of GAAP does not include normal improvements in existing operations (ASC Glossary). The following specific activities are *not* covered by the provisions of ASC 730:

- Activities that are unique to the extractive industries, such as prospecting, exploration, drilling, mining, and similar functions. Research and development activities of companies in extractive industries that are comparable in nature to other companies, such as the development or improvement of techniques and processes, *are* covered (ASC 730-10-15-4).
- Research and development performed under contract for others, including indirect costs that are specifically reimbursable under a contract (ASC 730-10-15-4).

PRACTICE POINTER: R&D does not include market research and testing, because these items specifically relate to the selling and marketing operations of a company. In addition, general and administrative expenses not *directly* related to the R&D activities are not included in R&D.

Because of the high degree of uncertainty of any resulting future benefit, the underlying basic principle in accounting for R&D is conservatism. Since at the time of performing R&D there is uncertainty concerning future success, the most conservative approach is to expense the item in the period incurred.

ASC 730 does not apply if research and development assets are acquired in a business combination, or if they are acquired in an acquisition of a business or nonprofit activity by a not-for-profit entity (ASC 730-10-25-1). ASC 805 applies to the accounting for these assets and requires that tangible and intangible assets used in research and development are measured at fair value, regardless of whether these assets have an alternative future use. In future periods, tangible assets acquired in a business combination that are used in research and development activities are accounted for as are other similar tangible assets. In future periods, intangible assets acquired in a business combination that are used in research and development activities are accounted for in a similar manner to other intangible assets (ASC 730-10-15-4).

ACCOUNTING AND REPORTING RESEARCH AND DEVELOPMENT—GENERAL STANDARDS

All R&D costs covered by GAAP are expensed in the period when they are incurred (ASC 730-10-25-1). Assets used in R&D activity, such as machinery, equipment, facilities, and patents that have alternative future uses either in R&D activities or otherwise are capitalized. Depreciation and amortization on such capitalized R&D-related assets is charged to R&D expense. All expenditures in conjunction with an R&D project, including personnel costs, materials, equipment, facilities, and intangibles, for which the company has no alternative future use beyond the specific project for which the items were purchased, are expensed. Indirect costs, including general and administrative expenses, which are *directly* related to the R&D project also are expensed when incurred (ASC 730-10-25-2).

Illustration of Determining R&D Expense

Lambert, Inc. develops new products and, therefore, engages in extensive research and development activities. Following is a description of current period expenditures related to a current Lambert project:

1.	Material and labor directly related to the project	$150,000
2.	Purchase of machinery and equipment required to carry out the project:	
	a. Useful only for this project	75,000
	b. Useful for this and other R&D projects over an estimated five-year period	90,000
3.	Contract services acquired	15,000
4.	Overhead and administration allocation	50,000

Assuming the overhead and administration allocation is for activities closely related to the project, and assuming depreciation of machinery and equipment by the straight-line method with no expected salvage value, the R&D expense for the year is:

Material and labor	$150,000
Machinery and equipment	75,000
Depreciation of machinery and equipment ($90,000/5 years)	18,000
Contract services	15,000
Overhead and administration	50,000
R&D expense	$308,000

The machinery and equipment with alternative future uses ($90,000 – $18,000 = $72,000 book value) is considered an asset available for use in future periods.

PRACTICE POINTER: ASC 730 does not require assets related to R&D that have alternative future uses in R&D, production, or other activities to be expensed in the period incurred. Typical assets with alternative future uses include machinery, equipment, facilities, patents, and copyrights. Include amortization and depreciation of these assets in R&D expense as long as the assets are used in R&D activities. No asset described as "research and development" should appear in the balance sheet. Present R&D-related assets that are included in the balance sheet in the normal asset categories they represent—plant assets, intangible assets, etc.

Research and development costs acquired by the acquisition method in a business combination are assigned their fair values, if any, in accordance with ASC 805 (Business Combinations).

Disclosure

The amount of R&D charged to expense for the period must be disclosed in the financial statements for each period presented (ASC 730-10-50-1).

43,004 ASC 730—Research and Development

ASC 730-20: RESEARCH AND DEVELOPMENT ARRANGEMENTS

RESEARCH AND DEVELOPMENT ARRANGEMENTS

ASC 730 also covers an enterprise's research and development arrangements that are partially or completely funded by other parties. In this respect, a typical arrangement is for the parties to set up a limited partnership through which the R&D activities related to a specific project are funded. Although the limited partnership arrangement is used in ASC 730 for illustrative purposes, the legal structure of an R&D arrangement may take a variety of forms and is sometimes influenced by income tax implications and securities regulations (ASC 730-20-05-10).

In a typical R&D arrangement, an enterprise that has the basic technology for a particular project is the general partner and manages the R&D activities. The limited partners, who may or may not be related parties, provide all or part of the funds to complete the project. If the funds are not sufficient, the arrangement may allow or require the general partner to either (*a*) sell additional limited partnership interest or (*b*) use its own funds to complete the project. In addition, some funds may be provided in the form of loans or advances to the limited partnership. The repayment of the loans or advances may be guaranteed by the partnership (ASC 730-20-05-2, 3).

Contract

The actual R&D activities usually are performed by the enterprise or a related party, under a contract with the limited partnership. The contract price is either fixed or cost plus a fixed or percentage fee and is performed on a *best efforts* basis, with no guarantee of ultimate success. The legal ownership of the results of the project vests with partnership (ASC 730-20-05-4). Frequently, the enterprise has an option to acquire the partnership's interest in the project or to obtain exclusive use of the results of the project (ASC 730-20-05-5). If the project is a success, the enterprise will usually exercise its option to acquire the project. Under some circumstances, however, even if the project is unsuccessful, the enterprise may still have reason to acquire the project, in spite of the fact that it is not legally required to do so. For example, the enterprise may want to prevent the final results of the project becoming available to a competitor (ASC 730-20-05-7).

Many of the liabilities and obligations that an enterprise undertakes in an R&D project that is funded by others are specified in the agreements. Some liabilities and obligations, however, may exist in substance but may not be reduced to writing. For example, future payments by the enterprise to other parties for royalties or the acquisition of the partnership's interest in the project may, in substance, represent (*a*) the repayment of a loan or (*b*) the purchase price of a specific asset (ASC 730-20-05-9).

Nature of Obligation

In R&D arrangements that are partially or completely funded by other parties, accounting and reporting for R&D costs depend upon the nature of the obligation that an enterprise incurs in the arrangement. The nature of the obligation in such R&D arrangements can be classified in one of the following categories:

- The obligation is solely to perform contractual services.
- The obligation represents a liability to repay all of the funds provided by the other parties.
- The obligation is partly to perform contractual services and partly a liability to repay some, but not all, of the funds provided by the other parties.

If the nature of the obligation incurred by an enterprise is solely to perform contractual services, all R&D costs are charged to *cost of sales*. If the nature of the obligation represents a liability to repay all of the funds provided by the other parties, all R&D costs are charged to *expense* when incurred.

If the nature of the obligation incurred by an enterprise is partly a liability and partly the performance of contractual services, R&D costs are charged partly to expense and partly to cost of sales. The portion charged to cost of sales is related to the funds provided by the other parties that do not have to be repaid by the enterprise. The portion charged to expense is related to the funds provided by the other parties that *are* likely to be repaid by the enterprise. Under ASC 730, the portion charged to expense is referred to as the enterprise's portion of the R&D costs. Under the provisions of ASC 730, an enterprise shall charge its portion of the R&D costs to expense in the same manner as the liability is incurred. Thus, if the liability arises on a pro rata basis, the enterprise's portion of the R&D costs shall be charged to expense in the same manner. If the liability arises as the initial funds are expended, the enterprise's portion of the R&D costs shall be charged to expense in the same manner (ASC 730-20-25-7).

ASC 730 provides guidance in determining the nature of the obligation that an enterprise incurs in R&D arrangements that are partially or completely funded by other parties. An enterprise is required to report in its financial statements the estimated liability, if any, incurred in an R&D arrangement that is partially or completely funded by other parties. The estimated liability shall include any contractually defined obligations and any obligations not contractually defined but otherwise reasonably evident (ASC 730-20-25-3, 5).

An important criterion in determining an enterprise's obligation is whether the financial risk involved in an R&D arrangement has been substantively transferred to other parties. To the extent that the enterprise is committed to repay any of the funds provided by the other parties regardless of the outcome of the research and development, all or part of the risk has not been transferred (ASC 730-20-25-4).

Under the provisions of ASC 730, if significant indications exist that the enterprise is *likely* to repay any funds, it is presumed that a liability has been incurred. This presumption can be overcome only by substantial evidence to the contrary. Circumstances in which significant indications exist that the enterprise is likely to repay funds and a liability is presumed are as follows (ASC 730-20-25-6):

- Regardless of the success of the R&D project, the enterprise has indicated the intent to repay all or part of the funds provided by other parties.
- If it failed to repay any of the funds, the enterprise would suffer a *severe economic penalty.* Under ASC 730, an economic penalty is *severe* if an enterprise would probably elect, under normal business circumstances, to repay the funds rather than to incur the penalty.
- At the inception of the R&D arrangement, a material related party relationship, as defined in ASC 850 (Related Party Disclosures), exists between the enterprise and any of the parties funding the R&D project.
- At the inception of the R&D arrangement, the project is substantially complete. Under this circumstance, the financial risks involved in the R&D project are already known to all parties.

An obligation may represent a liability whether it is payable in cash, securities, or by some other means (ASC 730-20-25-3).

Obligation for Contractual Services

If substantially all of the financial risks of the R&D project are transferred to the other parties and the enterprise is not committed to repay any of the funds provided by the other parties, the enterprise shall account for its obligation as contractual R&D services. If repayment by the enterprise of any of the funds provided by the other parties depends on the availability of a future economic benefit to the enterprise, the enterprise shall also account for its obligation as contractual R&D services. In these circumstances, the financial risks of the R&D arrangement have clearly been transferred to others and the enterprise is only obligated to perform contractual R&D services (ASC 730-20-25-8).

Frequently, an enterprise makes a loan or advance to the other parties that is designated to be repaid as a reduction of the purchase price for the results of the project, or as a reduction of future royalty payments from the enterprise. In this event, the portion of the loan or advance that is designated to be repaid as a reduction of the purchase price for the results of the project, or as a reduction of future royalties, shall be accounted for by the enterprise as R&D expense, unless it can be attributed to activities other than R&D, such as marketing or advertising (ASC 730-20-25-11).

At or before the completion of the R&D project, the enterprise may elect to exercise its option to purchase the partnership's interest, or to obtain exclusive rights to the results of the project. The enterprise shall account for the purchase of the partnership's interest, or the exclusive rights, in accordance with existing GAAP. Thus, any asset that results from the R&D project shall be assigned its fair value, and intangible assets shall be accounted for in accordance with ASC 350 (Intangibles - Goodwill and Other) (ASC 730-20-25-9, 10).

If an enterprise is required to issue warrants or similar instruments in connection with the R&D arrangement, a portion of the funds provided by the other parties shall be recorded as paid-in capital. The amount capitalized as paid-in capital shall be equal to the fair market value of the warrants or other instruments at the date the R&D arrangement is consummated (ASC 730-20-25-12).

Financial Statement Disclosure

Notes to the financial statements shall include the following disclosures for R&D arrangements that are accounted for as contracts to perform R&D services for others (ASC 730-20-50-1):

- The terms of the significant agreements relating to the R&D arrangement, including purchase provisions, license agreements, royalty arrangements, and commitments to provide additional funds as of the date of each balance sheet presented
- The amount of R&D costs incurred and compensation earned during the period for such R&D arrangements for each income statement presented

PART II: INTERPRETIVE GUIDANCE

ASC 730-20: RESEARCH AND DEVELOPMENT ARRANGEMENTS

ASC 730-20-25-13 through 25-14, 35-1, 65-1; ASC 730-10-55-3 Accounting for Nonrefundable Advance Payments for Goods or Services to Be Used in Future Research and Development Activities

BACKGROUND

The following guidance addresses the accounting for *nonrefundable* portions of prepayments made by entities involved in research and development activities (R&D entities) related to purchases of goods and services that will be used in an entity's future activities, such as prepayments to contract research organizations (CROs), which perform clinical trial management services. Prepayments to CROs are generally for activities, such as for per-patient clinical trial treatment costs and travel costs of a CRO's personnel. In addition, CROs often enter into contracts with third parties to deliver goods or services to an R&D entity and must pay those third parties even if the R&D activities are terminated. Advance payments are usually made three to six months *before* an R&D entity's activities begin.

R&D entities usually purchase goods and services for a specific project and can not use them for another future project. A portion of the prepayment may sometimes be refundable, but usually some portion of an advance payment is nonrefundable.

There is diversity in the way that R&D entities account for the nonrefundable portion of advance payments. Some defer those prepayments until the R&D activities have been performed while others expense them as the payments are made.

SCOPE

The guidance herein applies only to *nonrefundable* advance payments for goods and services to be used or rendered in future R&D activities under executory contractual arrangements. The accounting guidance in ASC 730, Research and

Development, applies to nonrefundable advance payments for materials, equipment, facilities, and purchased intangible assets having an alternative future use in an entity's future R&D activities.

ACCOUNTING ISSUE

Should *nonrefundable* advance payments for goods or services that will be used or rendered for research and development activities be expensed when the advance payment is made or when the research and development equity has been performed?

ACCOUNTING GUIDANCE

R&D entities should defer and capitalize as assets *nonrefundable* advance payments for goods and services that will be used or rendered in an entity's future R&D activities under an executory contractual arrangement.

Nonrefundable advance payment for materials, equipment, facilities, and purchased intangible assets that have an alternative future use in future research and development projects or for other purposes should be accounted for according to the guidance in ASC 730-10. Nonrefundable advance payments that have been capitalized should be recognized as an expense when the related goods have been delivered or the services have been performed.

Entities should continue to evaluate whether they expect that purchased goods will be delivered and purchased services will be rendered. If the goods and services will *not* be used in an entity's future R&D activities, capitalized advanced payments for those goods or services should be expensed.

The above guidance does not apply to *refundable* advance payments for future R&D activities and should *not* be applied by analogy to other types of advance payments.

CHAPTER 44
ASC 740—INCOME TAXES

CONTENTS

Part I: General Guidance	44,003
Overview	44,003
Background	44,004
ASC 740-10: Overall	44,004
The Asset/Liability Method	44,004
General Provisions of ASC 740	44,005
Scope	44,005
Basic Principles of the Asset/Liability Method	44,005
Temporary Differences	44,006
Taxable and Deductible Temporary Differences	44,007
Table 44-1: Examples of Taxable and Deductible Temporary Differences	44,008
Recognizing and Measuring Deferred Tax Assets and Liabilities	44,008
Valuation Allowance and Tax-Planning Strategies	44,009
Applicable Tax Rate	44,010
Tax Planning Strategies	44,011
Negative Evidence	44,011
Positive Evidence	44,012
Specialized Applications of ASC 740	44,012
Change in Tax Status	44,013
Regulated Enterprises	44,013
Business Combinations	44,013
Quasi-Reorganizations	44,013
Separate Financial Statements of a Subsidiary	44,014
Miscellaneous Topics	44,014
Accounting for Tax Effects of Share-Based Compensation Awards	44,014
Financial Statement Presentation and Disclosure Issues	44,015
Disclosures	44,016
Illustration of Major Provisions of ASC 740	44,017
Exhibit A: Analysis of Cumulative Temporary Differences and Deferred Taxes, 20X8	44,018
Exhibit B: Analysis of Cumulative Temporary Differences and Deferred Taxes, 20X9	44,020
Exhibit C: Analysis of Cumulative Temporary Differences and Deferred Taxes, 20Y0	44,021
Exhibit D: Financial Statement Presentation of Income Taxes, 20X8-20Y0	44,023
Uncertain Tax Positions	44,025
Scope	44,025
Recognition	44,026
Measurement	44,026

Effect of ASC 740 on Evaluation of Deferred Tax Assets	**44,027**
Subsequent Recognition	**44,027**
Derecognition	**44,027**
Treatment of Interest and Penalties	**44,027**
Financial Statement Classification	**44,028**
Disclosure Requirements	**44,029**
Implementation Guidance	**44,029**
Illustration—Measuring Benefit of a Tax Position	**44,030**
Illustration—Measurement when Uncertainty Exists Surrounding the Timing of Tax Deductibility	**44,030**
ASC 740-20: Intraperiod Tax Allocation	**44,031**
Intraperiod Tax Allocation	**44,031**
ASC 740-30: Other Considerations or Special Areas	**44,032**
Income Taxes in Special Areas	**44,032**
ASC 740-270: Interim Reporting	**44,034**
Accounting for Income Taxes in Interim Periods	**44,034**
Illustration of Quarterly Income Tax Calculation	**44,034**
Part II: Interpretive Guidance	**44,034**
ASC 740-10: Overall	**44,034**
ASC 740-10-25-9	
Definition of *Settlement* in FASB Interpretation No. 48	**44,034**
ASC 740-10-25-34, 50-4, 55-2 through 55-6, 55-15 through 55-22, 55-25, 55-40 through 55-41, 55-48, 55-59 through 55-65, 55-79 through 55-80, 55-163 through 55-164, 55-168 through 55-169, 55-213 through 55-216; ASC 740-20-55-1 through 55-7; ASC 942-740-35-1 through 35-3; ASC 942-852-55-2 through 55-6; ASC 855-10-60-2	
A Guide to Implementation of ASC 740 on Accounting for Income Taxes	**44,035**
ASC 740-10-25-39 through 25-40, 30-14	
Accounting for Tax Credits Related to Dividend Payments in Accordance with ASC 740	**44,041**
ASC 740-10-25-41	
Measurement in the Consolidated Financial Statements of a Parent of the Tax Effects Related to the Operations of a Foreign Subsidiary That Receives Tax Credits Related to Dividend Payments	**44,043**
ASC 840-30-35-48 through 35-52; ASC 740-10-25-43	
Tax Reform Act of 1986: Issues Related to the Alternative Minimum Tax	**44,044**
ASC 740-10-25-48	
Effect of a Retroactive Change in Enacted Tax Rates That Is Included in Income from Continuing Operations	**44,045**
ASC 740-10-25-50, 25-51, 25-22 through 25-24, 52-55, S25-1, S99-3, 55-171 through 55-201, 55-203 through 55-204, 55-76	
Accounting for Acquired Temporary Differences in Certain Purchase Transactions That Are Not Accounted for as Business Combinations	**44,047**
ASC 740-10-45-21; ASC 740-20-45-11	
Accounting by a Company for the Income Tax Effects of Transactions among or with Its Shareholders under ASC 740	**44,051**
ASC 740-10-45-18, 25-47	
Adjustment Due to Effect of a Change in Tax Laws or Rates	**44,054**

ASC 740—Income Taxes **44,003**

ASC 740-10-55-26, 55-140 through 55-144, 15-4, 05-5
    Application of ASC 740 to a State Tax Based on the Greater of a Franchise Tax or an Income Tax 44,054

ASC 740-10-55-27 through 55-30, 55-146 through 55-148
    Application of ASC 740, Accounting for Income Taxes, to the Tax Deduction on Qualified Production Activities Provided by the American Jobs Creation Act of 2004 44,056

ASC 740-10-55-50, 25-31
    Temporary Differences Related to LIFO Inventory and Tax-to-Tax Differences 44,057

ASC 740-10-55-51
    Income Tax Consequences of Issuing Convertible Debt with a Beneficial Conversion Feature 44,057

ASC 740-10-55-53, 25-31
    Intraperiod Tax Allocation of the Tax Effect of Pretax Income from Continuing Operations 44,059

ASC 740-10-55-69, 55-70, 55-71
    Classification of Payment Made to IRS to Retain Fiscal Year 44,059

ASC 740-10-55-73 through 55-74, 15-4
    Accounting for Tax Effects of Dividends in France in Accordance with ASC 740 44,060

ASC 740-30: Other Considerations or Special Areas 44,062

ASC 740-30-25-10
    Recognition of Deferred Tax Assets for a Parent Company's Excess Tax Basis in the Stock of a Subsidiary That Is Accounted for as a Discontinued Operation 44,062

ASC 740-270: Interim Reporting 44,062

ASC 740-270-55-51
    Accounting in Interim Periods for Changes in Income Tax Rates 44,062

PART I: GENERAL GUIDANCE

OVERVIEW

The tax consequences of many transactions recognized in the financial statements are included in determining income taxes currently payable in the same accounting period. Sometimes, however, tax laws differ from the recognition and measurement requirements of financial reporting standards. Differences arise between the tax bases of assets or liabilities and their reported amounts in the financial statements. These differences are called *temporary differences* and they give rise to deferred tax assets and liabilities.

Temporary differences ordinarily reverse when the related asset is recovered or the related liability is settled. A *deferred tax liability* or *deferred tax asset* represents the increase or decrease in taxes payable or refundable in future years as a result of temporary differences and carryforwards at the end of the current year.

The objectives of accounting for income taxes are to recognize:

- The amount of taxes payable or refundable for the current year.
- The deferred tax liabilities and assets that result from future tax consequences of events that have been recognized in the enterprise's financial statements or tax returns.

BACKGROUND

Accounting for income taxes is strongly influenced by the fact that some transactions are treated differently for financial reporting purposes and for income tax purposes. Other transactions are treated the same way in financial reporting and for income tax purposes, but not in the same accounting periods. Differences in timing are referred to as temporary differences and are reconciled in the financial statements by the recognition of deferred tax assets and liabilities.

For several decades, deferred tax assets and liabilities were recognized in the financial statements by the deferred method which placed primarily emphasis on the matching of revenues and expenses. Income tax expense was determined by applying the current tax rate to pretax accounting income. Any differences between the resulting expense and the amount of income taxes payable in the current period were adjustments to deferred income taxes. The deferred method focused first on the income statement, and adjustment to balance sheet elements were determined by the measurement of income tax expense.

The Financial Accounting Standards Board significantly changed this approach when it changed accounting for income taxes from the deferred method to the asset/liability method, frequently referred to as simply the liability method. The liability method places primary emphasis on the valuation of the elements of the balance sheet—deferred tax assets and liabilities. The amount of income tax expense currently payable or refundable, plus or minus the changes in deferred tax assets and liabilities, is the amount of income tax expense recognized in the income statement for a financial reporting period. The liability method focuses first on the balance sheet, and the amount of income tax expense is determined by changes in the elements of the balance sheet.

ASC 740-10: OVERALL

THE ASSET/LIABILITY METHOD

ASC 740 requires income taxes to be accounted for by the asset/liability method. Its main effects on financial statements include the following:

- Emphasis is on the recognition and measurement of deferred tax assets and liabilities. Deferred income tax expense is determined residually (i.e., as the difference between the beginning and required ending balances in deferred tax assets and liabilities for the period).
- Deferred tax asset and liability amounts are remeasured when tax rates change to approximate more closely the amounts at which those assets and liabilities will be realized or settled.
- Deferred tax assets are recognized for operating loss and other carryforwards. Deferred tax assets are subject to reduction by a valuation allow-

ance if evidence indicates that it is *more likely than not* that some or all of the deferred tax assets will not be realized. Determining this valuation allowance is similar to accounting for reductions in receivables to net realizable value.

- Disclosure requirements result in the presentation of a significant amount of information in the notes to the financial statements.

GENERAL PROVISIONS OF ASC 740

Scope

ASC 740 requires what traditionally has been referred to as "comprehensive income tax allocation," as opposed to partial allocation or nonallocation. This means that the income tax effects of all revenues, expenses, gains, losses, and other events that create differences between the tax bases of assets and liabilities and their amounts for financial reporting are required to be recognized (ASC 740-10-05-1).

ASC 740 is applicable to:

- Domestic federal income taxes and foreign, state, and local taxes based on income.
- An enterprise's domestic and foreign operations that are consolidated, combined, or accounted for by the equity method. ASC 740 provides guidance for determining the tax bases of assets and liabilities for financial reporting purposes.
- Foreign enterprises in preparing financial statements in accordance with U.S. GAAP. (ASC 740-10-15-2; 740-10-15-3).

Three important financial statement issues are specifically set aside and not covered by ASC 740:

1. Accounting for the investment tax credit (ITC)
2. Accounting for income taxes in interim periods
3. Discounting deferred income taxes

Accounting for the ITC and accounting for income taxes in interim periods are covered by other authoritative pronouncements. Discounting of deferred income taxes is not permitted.

Basic Principles of the Asset/Liability Method

The objectives of accounting for income taxes are identified in terms of elements of the balance sheet (ASC 740-10-10-1):

- To recognize the amount of taxes currently payable or refundable
- To recognize the deferred tax assets and liabilities for the future tax consequences of events that have been recognized in the financial statements or in tax returns

This emphasis on the balance sheet is consistent with the liability method of accounting for income taxes incorporated ASC 740.

Four basic principles are particularly important in understanding the liability method for accounting for income taxes. Each of the following basic principles focuses on the elements of the balance sheet relating to income taxes (ASC 740-10-25-2; 740-10-30-2):

1. Recognize a *tax liability or asset* for the amount of taxes currently payable or refundable, based on the provisions of ASC 740.

2. Recognize a *deferred tax liability or asset* for the estimated future tax effects of temporary differences or carryforwards. ASC 740 provides guidance for determining the tax bases of assets and liabilities for financial reporting purposes.

3. Measure *current* and *deferred tax assets* and *liabilities* based on provisions of enacted tax laws.

4. Reduce the amount of any deferred *tax assets* by a valuation allowance, if necessary, based on available evidence.

The following are exceptions to the four basic principles (ASC 740-10-25-3):

- Certain exceptions to the requirements for recognition of deferred tax assets and liabilities for particular areas, notably the investments in foreign subsidiaries and joint ventures
- Special transitional procedures for temporary differences related to deposits in statutory reserve funds by U.S. steamship enterprises
- Accounting for leveraged leases as required by ASC 840 (Leases)
- Prohibition of the recognition of a deferred tax liability related to goodwill for which amortization is not deductible for tax purposes
- Accounting for income taxes under ASC 810 (Consolidation)
- Prohibition of the recognition of a deferred tax liability for differences related to assets and liabilities accounted for under ASC 830 (Foreign Currency Matters)

Temporary Differences

Deferred tax assets and liabilities that result from temporary differences are based on the assumption that assets and liabilities in an entity's balance sheet eventually will be realized or settled at their recorded amounts (ASC 740-10-25-20).

The following major categories of temporary differences refer to events that result in differences between the tax bases of assets and liabilities and their reported amounts in the financial statements (ASC 740-10-25-20):

- Revenues or gains that are taxable <u>after</u> they are recognized in accounting income (e.g., receivables from installment sales)
- Expenses or losses that are deductible for tax purposes <u>after</u> they are recognized in accounting income (e.g., a product warranty liability)

- Revenues or gains that are taxable before they are recognized in accounting income (e.g., subscriptions received in advance)
- Expenses or losses that are deductible for tax purposes before they are recognized in accounting income (e.g., depreciation expense)

Other less common examples of temporary differences are:

- Investment tax credits accounted for by the deferred method.
- Business combinations accounted for by the acquisition method.

Taxable and Deductible Temporary Differences

An important distinction in applying the procedures required to account for income taxes by the asset/liability method under ASC 740 is the difference between *taxable* and *deductible* temporary differences. A *taxable temporary difference* is one that will result in the payment of income taxes in the future when the temporary difference reverses. A *deductible temporary difference* is one that will result in reduced income taxes in future years when the temporary difference reverses (ASC 740-10-05-8). Taxable temporary differences give rise to deferred tax liabilities; deductible temporary differences give rise to deferred tax assets. Table 740-1 further illustrates this important difference between taxable and deductible temporary differences.

The expanded definition of *temporary differences* includes some items that do not appear in the company's balance sheet. For example, a company may expense organization costs when they are incurred but recognize them as a tax deduction in a later year. Between the two events, no balance-sheet item exists for this type of temporary difference (ASC 740-10-25-25, 26).

The identification of temporary differences may require significant professional judgment. Similar items may be temporary differences in one instance and not in another. For example, the excess of the cash surrender value of life insurance over premiums paid is a temporary difference and results in deferred taxes if the cash surrender value is expected to be recovered by surrendering the policy, but it is not a temporary difference and does not result in deferred taxes if the asset is expected to be recovered upon the death of the insured (ASC 740-10-25-30). Management intent and professional judgment are important factors in making the appropriate determination of the nature of assets and liabilities of this type.

PRACTICE POINTER: Developing a system for identifying and tracking the amounts of all temporary differences and carryforwards is an important implementation issue for ASC 740. Theoretically, differences should be identified by comparing items and amounts in the entity's balance sheets for accounting purposes and for tax purposes. Many companies do not maintain tax-basis balance sheets, though this may be the most logical way to identify and track temporary differences in relatively complex situations.

Table 44-1: Examples of Taxable and Deductible Temporary Differences

Nature of Temporary Difference	Explanation	Deferred Tax
Taxable Temporary Differences		
Depreciable assets	Use of modified accelerated cost recovery system (MACRS) for tax purposes and straight-line for accounting purposes makes the tax basis of the asset less than the accounting basis	Liability, to be paid as MACRS deduction becomes less than straight-line depreciation
Installment sale receivable	Sales recognized for accounting purposes at transaction date and deferred for tax purposes until collection, resulting in a difference between the tax and accounting basis of the installment receivable	Liability, to be paid when the sale is recognized for tax purposes
Deductible Temporary Differences		
Warranty liability	Expense recognized on accrual basis for accounting purposes and on cash basis for tax purposes, resulting in a liability that is recognized for financial reporting purposes but has a zero basis for tax purposes	Asset, to be recovered when deduction is recognized for tax purposes
Accounts receivable/ allowance for doubtful accounts	Expense recognized on an accrual basis for accounting purposes and deferred for tax purposes	Asset, to be recovered when uncollectible account is written off for tax purposes

Certain differences between the tax basis and the accounting basis of assets and liabilities will not result in taxable or deductible amounts in future years, and no deferred tax asset or liability should be recognized (ASC 740-10-05-9). These differences are often referred to as permanent differences, although that term is not used in ASC 740.

Recognizing and Measuring Deferred Tax Assets and Liabilities

The emphasis placed on the balance sheet by the asset/liability method of accounting for income taxes is evident from the focus on the recognition of deferred tax liabilities and assets. The change in these liabilities and assets is combined with the income taxes currently payable or refundable to determine income tax expense (ASC 740-10-30-3).

Five steps are required to complete the annual computation of deferred tax liabilities and assets (ASC 740-10-30-5):

1. Identify the types and amounts of existing temporary differences and the nature and amount of each type of operating loss and tax credit carryforward and the remaining length of the carryforward period.

2. Measure the total deferred tax liability for taxable temporary differences using the applicable tax rate.

3. Measure the total deferred tax asset for deductible temporary differences and operating loss carryforwards using the applicable tax rate.

4. Measure deferred tax assets for each type of tax credit carryforward.

5. Reduce deferred tax assets by a valuation allowance if it is more likely than not that some or all of the deferred tax assets will not be realized.

Valuation Allowance and Tax-Planning Strategies

Determining the need for and calculating the amount of the valuation allowance requires the following steps at the end of each accounting period (ASC 740-10-30-18):

1. Determine the amount of the deferred tax asset recognized on each deductible temporary difference, operating loss, and tax credit carryforward. (These are not offset by the deferred tax liability on taxable temporary differences.)

2. Assess the sources of future taxable income which may be available to recognize the deductible differences and carryforwards by considering the following:

    PRACTICE POINTER: The four sources of income are organized differently here than in ASC 740 in order to emphasize the implementation of the standard. In identifying income to support the recognition of deferred tax assets (and thereby supporting a case that an allowance is not required), a logical approach is to consider sources of income in order from the most objective to the least objective. Income in prior carryback years is most objective, followed by the income from the reversal of taxable temporary differences, income resulting from tax planning strategies, and finally, future income from other sources.

    a. Taxable income in prior carryback year(s) if carryback is permitted under tax law

    b. Future reversals of existing taxable temporary differences

    c. Tax planning strategies that would make income available at appropriate times in the future that would otherwise not be available

    d. Future taxable income exclusive of reversing differences and carryforwards

3. Based on all available evidence, make a judgment concerning the realizability of the deferred tax asset.

4. Record the amount of the valuation allowance, or change in the valuation allowance (the example below assumes that the allowance is being recorded for the first time or is being increased for $100,000).

Income tax expense	$100,000	
Allowance to reduce deferred tax asset to lower recoverable value		$100,000

> **OBSERVATION:** ASC 740 relaxes the criteria for recognizing deferred tax assets by requiring the recognition of deferred tax assets for all deductible temporary differences and all operating loss and tax credit carryforwards. An important adjunct to this provision, however, is the requirement to determine the need for, and amount of, a valuation allowance to reduce the deferred tax asset to its realizable value. The valuation allowance aspects of current GAAP require significant judgment on the part of accountants and auditors of financial statements. A valuation allowance is required if it is more likely than not that some or all of the deferred tax assets will not be realized. *More likely than not* is defined as a likelihood of more than 50%.

Applicable Tax Rate

Reference to the applicable tax rate is made in the four steps identified above. The *applicable tax rate* is that rate expected to apply to taxable income in the periods in which the deferred tax liability or asset is expected to be settled or realized based on enacted tax law. If the entity's taxable income is low enough to make the graduated tax rates a significant factor, the entity uses the average graduated tax rate applicable to the amount of estimated annual taxable income in the periods in which the deferred tax liability or asset is expected to be settled or realized (ASC 740-10-10-3). For example, if a company has taxable temporary differences of $20,000 that are expected to reverse in a year when no other income is expected, the applicable tax rate under current tax law is 15% and the deferred tax liability is:

$$\$20,000 \times 15\% = \$3,000$$

If the taxable temporary differences total $60,000, graduated tax rates become a factor (the tax rate changes at $50,000); deferred taxes are $10,000:

$50,000 × 15%	=	$ 7,500
$10,000 × 25%	=	2,500
		$10,000

The average applicable tax rate is 16.67%.

$$\$10,000 / \$60,000 = 16.67\%$$

> **PRACTICE POINTER:** Determining the applicable tax rate may be a very simple task, or it may require careful analysis and professional judgment. When an entity has been consistently profitable at sufficiently high levels that graduated tax rates are not a significant factor, use the single flat tax rate at which all income is used to compute the amount of deferred taxes on cumulative tempo-

rary differences. If a company experiences intermittent tax loss and tax income years, or if the company is consistently profitable at a level low enough that the graduated tax rates are a significant factor, greater judgment is required to determine the applicable tax rate.

Deferred tax assets and liabilities are remeasured at the end of each accounting period and adjusted for changes in the amounts of cumulative temporary differences and for changes in the applicable income tax rate, as well as for other changes in the tax law (ASC 740-10-35-4). As a result of this procedure, the deferred tax provision is a combination of two elements:

1. The change in deferred taxes because of the change in the amounts of temporary differences
2. The change in deferred taxes because of a change in the tax rate caused by new enacted rates or a change in the applicability of graduated tax rates (or other changes in the tax law)

Treating the change in income tax rates in this manner is consistent with accounting for a change in estimate under ASC 250 (Accounting Changes and Error Corrections).

Tax Planning Strategies

Consideration of tax planning strategies is also required by ASC 740. Tax planning strategies are an important part of determining the need for, and the amount of, the valuation allowance for deferred tax assets. Tax-planning strategies as actions that (ASC 740-10-30-19):

- Are prudent and feasible
- The entity might not ordinarily take, but *would* take to prevent an operating loss or tax credit carryforward from expiring before it is used
- Would result in the realization of deferred tax assets

Examples include actions the entity could take to accelerate taxable income to utilize expiring carryforwards, to change the character of taxable or deductible amounts from ordinary income or loss to capital gain or loss, and to switch from tax-exempt to taxable investments.

Negative Evidence

If negative evidence is present, such as cumulative losses in recent years, it is difficult to conclude that a valuation allowance is not necessary. Other examples of negative evidence are (ASC 740-10-30-21):

- A history of operating loss or tax credit carryforwards expiring before they are used
- Losses expected in early future years
- Unsettled circumstances that, if unfavorably resolved, would adversely affect future operations and profit levels on a continuing basis in future years

- A carryback or carryforward period that is so short that it significantly limits the probability of realizing deferred tax assets

Positive Evidence

Positive evidence supports a conclusion that a valuation allowance is *not required*. Examples of positive evidence are (ASC 740-10-30-22):

- Existing contracts or firm sales backlog that will produce more than enough taxable income to realize the deferred tax asset based on existing sales prices and cost structures

- An excess of appreciated asset value over the tax basis of the entity's net assets in an amount sufficient to realize the deferred tax asset

- A strong earnings history exclusive of the loss that created the future deductible amount, coupled with evidence indicating that the loss is an aberration rather than a continuing condition

---

PRACTICE POINTER: Projecting the reversal of temporary differences for each future year individually is commonly referred to as "scheduling." Does ASC 740 require scheduling? On the one hand, the requirement to recognize deferred tax assets and liabilities for all taxable and deductible temporary differences, as well as for all carryforwards, seems to diminish or eliminate the need to schedule. Also, using a flat tax rate in determining the amount of deferred tax assets and liabilities, as described earlier, diminishes the need to schedule individual future years. On the other hand, scheduling may help determine the need for, and amount of, a valuation allowance, including the consideration of tax-planning strategies. To determine the availability of taxable income in the appropriate years—to take advantage of deferred tax assets and to make the judgments concerning the valuation allowance—projecting taxable income from known or estimated sources by year may still be important.

Professional judgment is required in considering the relative impact of negative and positive evidence to determine the need for, and amount of, the valuation allowance for deferred tax assets. The weight given the effect of negative and positive evidence should be commensurate with the extent to which it can be objectively verified. The more negative evidence exists, the more positive evidence is needed to conclude that a valuation allowance is not required (ASC 740-10-30-23).

The effect of a change in the valuation allowance that results from a change in circumstances, which in turn causes a change in judgment about the realizability of the related deferred tax asset, is included in income from continuing operations with limited exceptions (ASC 740-10-42-20).

SPECIALIZED APPLICATIONS OF ASC 740

Several specialized applications of ASC 740 are summarized briefly below.

Change in Tax Status

An enterprise's tax status may change from nontaxable to taxable or taxable to nontaxable. A deferred tax liability or asset shall be recognized for temporary differences at the date that a nontaxable enterprise becomes a taxable enterprise. A deferred tax liability or asset shall be eliminated at the date an enterprise becomes a nontaxable enterprise (ASC 740-10-25-32).

Regulated Enterprises

Regulated enterprises are *not* exempt from the requirements of ASC 740. Specifically, ASC 740 (ASC 740-10-25-1):

- Prohibits net-of-tax accounting and reporting
- Requires recognition of a deferred tax liability for tax benefits that flow through to customers when temporary differences originate and for the equity component of the allowance for funds used during construction
- Requires adjustment of a deferred tax liability or asset for an enacted change in tax laws or rates

If as a result of an action by a regulator, it is probable that the future increase or decrease in taxes payable for items (2) and (3) above will be restored from or returned to customers through future rates, an asset or a liability is recognized for that probable future revenue or reduction in future revenue in accordance with ASC 980 (Regulated Operations). That asset or liability is a temporary difference for which a deferred tax liability or asset is required.

Business Combinations

A deferred tax asset or liability is recognized as of the acquisition date for an acquired entity's taxable or deductible temporary differences or operating loss or tax credit carryforwards. Taxable or deductible temporary differences occur when there are differences between the tax bases and the recognized values of assets acquired and liabilities assumed in a business combination. The acquirer must assess the need for a valuation allowance related to any acquired deferred tax asset (ASC 805-740-25-3).

A change in a valuation allowance for an acquired entity's deferred tax asset that occurs during the measurement period and results from new information about fact and circumstances that existed at the acquisition date shall be recognized with a corresponding reduction to goodwill. Once goodwill is reduced to zero, any additional change in the valuation allowance shall be recognized as a bargain purchase. All other changes to the valuation allowance shall be reported as a reduction or increase to income tax expense (ASC 805-740-45-2).

Quasi-Reorganizations

The tax benefits of deductible temporary differences and carryforwards as of the date of a quasi-reorganization ordinarily are reported as a direct addition to contributed capital if the tax benefits are recognized in subsequent years. The only exception is for enterprises that previously adopted ASC 740 and affected a quasi-reorganization involving only the elimination of a deficit in retained earnings by a noncurrent reduction in contributed capital prior to adopting ASC 740. For those enterprises, subsequent recognition of the tax benefit of prior deductible temporary differences and carryforwards is included in income, reported as required by ASC 740, and then reclassified from retained earnings to contributed capital (ASC 852-740-45-3).

Separate Financial Statements of a Subsidiary

The allocation of income taxes among the members of a group of entities that file a consolidated tax return must be based on a method that is systematic, rational, and consistent with the broad principles established in ASC 740, although ASC 740 does not require a single allocation method. A method that allocates current and deferred taxes to members of the group by applying ASC 740 to each member as if it were a separate taxpayer meets those criteria. Examples of methods that are *not* consistent with the broad principles of ASC 740 include (ASC 740-10-30-28):

- A method that allocates only current taxes payable to a member of the group that has taxable temporary differences
- A method that allocates deferred taxes to a member of the group using a method fundamentally different from the asset and liability method
- A method that allocates no current or deferred tax expense to a member of the group that has taxable income because the consolidated group has no current or deferred tax expense

Miscellaneous Topics

ASC 740 indicates that deferred taxes should not be discounted (ASC 740-10-30-8), and that offsetting of assets and liabilities (including tax assets and liabilities) is prohibited unless a legal right of setoff exists (ASC 210-20-05-1).

ASC 740-30 indicates several situations in which deferred taxes are not recognized for certain temporary differences unless it becomes apparent that those differences will reverse in the foreseeable future.

ASC 740 guides the accounting for the tax effects of share-based compensation awards which are accounted for under ASC 718 (Compensation - Stock Compensation).

Accounting for Tax Effects of Share-Based Compensation Awards

Tax deductions generally arise in different amounts and in different periods from compensation costs recognized in financial statements. The cumulative effect of compensation cost recognized for instruments classified as equity that ordinarily would result in a future tax deduction are considered to be deductible temporary differences in applying ASC 740. ASC 740 requires a deferred tax asset to be evaluated for future realization and to be reduced by a valuation allowance if it is more likely than not that some portion or all of the deferred tax asset will not be realized. Differences between the deductible temporary difference computed pursuant to ASC 718 and the tax deduction that would result based on the current fair value of the entity's shares shall not be considered in measuring the gross deferred tax asset or determining the need for a valuation allowance for a deferred tax asset recognized under ASC 718 (ASC 718-740-05-04; 718-740-25-2; 718-740-30-2).

If a deduction reported on a tax return for an award of equity instrument exceeds the cumulative compensation cost for those instruments recognized for financial reporting (referred to in ASC 718 as the excess tax benefit), any resulting realized tax benefits that exceed the previously recognized deferred tax asset for those instruments are recognized as paid-in capital (ASC 718-740-35-3).

The amount deductible on the employer's tax return may be less than the cumulative compensation cost recognized for financial reporting purposes. The write-off of a deferred tax asset related to that deficiency, net of any related valuation allowance, is first offset to the extent of any remaining additional paid-in capital from excess tax benefits from previous awards accounted for in accordance with the requirements under previous GAAP. Any remaining balance of the write-off of a deferred tax asset related to a tax deficiency shall be recognized in the income statement. (ASC 718-740-35-5; 718-740-45-04).

> **OBSERVATION:** The special applications discussed in this section illustrate the pervasive nature of accounting for income taxes. Income tax considerations affect many parts of the financial statements and many kinds of business transactions. This dimension of accounting for income taxes makes ASC 740 a very important pronouncement and accounts, at least partially, for the long and difficult process of making the transition from the deferred method to the asset/liability method.

FINANCIAL STATEMENT PRESENTATION AND DISCLOSURE ISSUES

ASC 740 requires deferred tax assets and liabilities to be presented in a classified balance sheet in current and noncurrent categories. The following policies are included for applying this requirement (ASC 740-10-45-4):

- If the temporary difference giving rise to the deferred tax asset or liability is reflected in a balance sheet asset or liability, the classification of the deferred tax is governed by the related asset or liability. For example, deferred taxes on the temporary difference for depreciable assets is classified as noncurrent because the related asset (i.e., property, plant and equipment) is noncurrent.

- If the deferred tax does not relate to an underlying asset or liability on the balance sheet, classification is based on the expected timing of reversal. For example, if organization costs are expensed when incurred for accounting purposes but deferred and deducted later for tax purposes, there is no related balance sheet asset or liability. (ASC 740-10-55-77).

- For a particular taxpaying component of an enterprise and within a particular tax jurisdiction (e.g., federal and state), all current deferred tax liabilities and assets are offset and presented as a single amount; the same procedure is followed for all noncurrent deferred tax liabilities and assets.

Deferred tax liabilities and assets that are attributable to different taxpaying components of the enterprise or to different tax jurisdictions are *not* offset.

OBSERVATION: The classification of deferred tax assets and liabilities as current or noncurrent based on the underlying asset is conceptually inferior to classifying them based on the expected timing of the receipt or payment of taxes. The latter approach is conceptually stronger in terms of the intent of the current/noncurrent classification—namely, to isolate as current those assets and liabilities expected to have cash flow consequences in the near future. Classifying a deferred tax asset or liability based on the underlying asset or liability appears to have been part of an effort by the FASB to reduce complexity and eliminate, to the extent possible, procedures that would require scheduling of taxable income for individual future years in determining the amounts of deferred tax assets and liabilities and their classifications.

Disclosures

The following components of the net deferred tax liability or asset recognized in an enterprise's balance sheet must be disclosed (ASC 740-10-50-2):

- The total of all deferred tax liabilities for taxable temporary differences
- The total of all deferred tax assets for deductible temporary differences and loss and tax credit carryforwards
- The total valuation allowance recognized for deferred tax assets
- The net change during the year in the total valuation allowance

Disclosure of significant components of income tax expense attributable to continuing operations for each year presented is required in the financial statements or related notes (ASC 740-10-50-9):

- Current tax expense or benefit
- Deferred tax expense or benefit
- Investment tax credit
- Government grants (to the extent recognized as reductions in income tax expense)
- Tax benefits of operating loss carryforwards
- Tax expense that results from allocating tax benefits
- Adjustments to a deferred tax liability or asset for enacted changes in tax laws or rates or for a change in the tax status of the enterprise
- Adjustments of the beginning balance of the valuation allowance because of a change in circumstances that causes a change in judgment about the realizability of the related deferred tax asset in the future

---

OBSERVATION: The effect of two unique features of the asset/liability method can be seen in the disclosure requirements listed above. The seventh item requires disclosure of the amount of the adjustment to deferred tax assets and liabilities for enacted changes in tax laws or rates. The eighth item requires disclosure of the amount of the adjustment of the beginning balance of the valuation allowance on deferred tax assets made as a result of a change in judgment about the realizability of that item.

The amount of income tax expense or benefit allocated to continuing operations and amounts separately allocated to other items shall be disclosed for each year for which those items are presented.

Several distinctions are made in the disclosures required by public enterprises and those required by nonpublic enterprises. The two most significant ones are summarized as follows (ASC 740-10-50-6, 8, 12, 13):

	Public/Nonpublic Company Disclosures	
	Public	Nonpublic
Temporary Differences and Carryforwards	Approximation of tax effect of each type	Description of types
Statutory Reconciliation	Reconciliation in percentages or dollars	Description of major reconciling items

Companies with operating loss and tax credit carryforwards must disclose the amount and expiration dates. Disclosure is also required for any portion of the valuation allowance for deferred tax assets for which subsequently recognized tax benefits will be credited directly to contributed equity (ASC 740-10-50-3).

An entity that is a member of a group that files a consolidated tax return shall disclose the following in its separately issued financial statements (ASC 740-10-50-17):

- The aggregate amount of current and deferred tax expense for each statement of earnings presented and the amount of any tax-related balances due to or from affiliates as of the date of each statement of financial position presented

- The principal provisions of the method by which the consolidated amount of current and deferred tax expense is allocated to members of the group and the nature and effect of any changes in that method during the year

---

Illustration of Major Provisions of ASC 740

This illustration considers Power Company for three consecutive years, with the objective of preparing the year-end income tax accrual and income tax information for the company's financial statements. Power Company's first year of operations is 20X8. During that year, the company reported $160,000 of pretax accounting income. Permanent and temporary differences are combined with pretax financial income to derive taxable income, as follows:

Pretax financial income	$160,000
Permanent difference:	
Interest on municipal securities	(5,000)
Pretax financial income subject to tax	$155,000

Temporary differences:

Depreciation	(28,000)
Warranties	10,000
Revenue received in advance	7,000
Taxable income	$144,000

The $5,000 interest on municipal securities represents nontaxable income, and the $28,000 depreciation temporary difference represents the excess of accelerated write-off for tax purposes over straight-line depreciation for financial reporting purposes. Warranties are expensed at the time of sale on an estimated basis, but are deductible for income tax purposes only when paid. In 20X8, $10,000 more was accrued than paid. Revenue received in advance is taxable at the time received, but is deferred for financial reporting purposes until earned. In 20X8, $7,000 was received that was not earned by year-end. Depreciation is a *taxable temporary difference* that reduces current tax payable and gives rise to a deferred tax liability. The warranties and revenue received in advance are *deductible temporary differences* that increase current tax payable and give rise to deferred tax assets.

Exhibit A presents analyses that facilitate the preparation of the year-end tax accrual, as well as information for the financial statements. Similar analyses are used for each of the three years in this Illustration. The analysis in the upper portion of Exhibit A "rolls forward" the amount of the temporary differences from the beginning to the end of the year. Because 20X8 is the first year for Power Company, the beginning balances are all zero. The change column includes the amounts used in the earlier calculation to determine taxable income from pretax accounting income. The numbers without parentheses are deductible temporary differences; those in parentheses are taxable temporary differences. The company is in a net taxable temporary difference position at the end of the year because the net amount of temporary differences is $(11,000), due to the large amount of the depreciation difference.

EXHIBIT A: Analysis of Cumulative Temporary Differences and Deferred Taxes, 20X8

The lower portion of Exhibit A converts these temporary differences to amounts of deferred income taxes based on those differences. Again, the beginning balances are all zero and the ending balances are computed at 34%, the assumed income tax rate for 20X8 in this Illustration. The amounts in parentheses are deferred tax liabilities, based on taxable temporary differences. The numbers without parentheses are deferred tax assets, based on deductible temporary differences.

The classification columns on the lower right side of Exhibit A separate the ending balances into current and noncurrent for balance sheet classification purposes. This distinction is based on the asset or liability (if one exists) underlying the temporary difference. If no such asset or liability exists, classification is based on the timing of the expected cash flow. In this case, the warranty period is assumed to be five years, so the related temporary difference is noncurrent, as is depreciation, because of the noncurrent classification of the underlying plant assets. The revenue received in advance is expected to be earned in the coming period, and thus is a current asset.

The December 31, 20X8, entry to record the income tax accrual for Power Company is as follows:

Dec. 31, 20X8

Income tax expense ($48,960 + $3,740)	$52,700	
Deferred income tax—Current	2,380	
Income tax payable ($144,000 × 34%)		$48,960
Deferred income tax—Noncurrent		6,120

Notice that the amounts of deferred income taxes—current and noncurrent—are taken from the lower analysis in Exhibit A. The income tax payable is determined by multiplying the $144,000 taxable income by the 34% tax rate. An important point to understand is that income tax expense is determined last: It is the net of the other three numbers and can be computed only after the remaining elements of the entry have been determined.

An important step to complete before moving to 20X9 is a proof of the numbers obtained, commonly referred to as a *statutory rate reconciliation*. For 20X8, this calculation is as follows:

Pretax financial income @ statutory rate ($160,000 × 34%)	$54,400
Less: Permanent differences ($5,000 × 34%)	(1,700)
Income tax expense	$52,700

Effects of these calculations on the balance sheet and income statement will be considered after all three years of analysis are completed.

Power Company's second year of operations is 20X9, in which pretax financial income is $150,000. Municipal interest is $12,000 and temporary differences for depreciation and warranties are $(35,000) and $12,000, respectively. Of the revenue received in advance in 20X8, $5,000 is earned and an additional $9,000 is received in 20X9 that is expected to be earned in 20Y0. A new temporary difference is the litigation loss that results from the $10,000 accrual on an estimated basis for accounting purposes. This loss will be deductible for tax purposes when the suit is settled, which is expected to occur in 20Y0.

Taxable income for 20X9 is determined as follows:

Pretax financial income	$150,000
Permanent difference:	
Interest on municipal securities	(12,000)
Pretax financial income subject to tax	$13,800
Temporary differences:	
Depreciation	(35,000)
Warranties	12,000
Revenue received in advance ($9,000 − $5,000)	4,000
Litigation loss	10,000
Taxable income	$12,900

Exhibit B includes a 20X9 analysis similar to the 20X8 analysis in Exhibit A. During 20X9, new tax legislation increases the income tax rate for 20X9 and all future years to 40%. The amounts in 20X9 simply are moved forward from the end of 20X8. In the lower portion of Exhibit B, the change column is calculated by determining the change required to move the beginning balance to the desired ending balance. The litigation loss is classified as current because of its expected settlement in 20Y0, when it will be deductible for income tax purposes.

The entry to record income taxes at the end of 20X9 is as follows:

Dec. 31, 20X9

Income tax expense ($51,600 + $4,260)	55,860	
Deferred income tax—Current ($8,400 − $2,380)	6,020	
Income tax payable ($129,000 × 40%)		51,600
Deferred income tax—Noncurrent ($16,400 − $6,120)		10,280

Notice that the debits and credits to deferred income tax—current and noncurrent, respectively—are calculated as the changes in those accounts. It is not necessary to deal with that consideration in 20X8 because it was the company's first year. The desired ending balances of current and noncurrent deferred income taxes from Exhibit B are compared with the balances from Exhibit A and the differences are debited or credited into the deferred tax accounts, as appropriate, to produce the desired ending balances. For example, deferred income tax—noncurrent must have a credit (liability) balance of $16,400 at the end of 20X9. The account began with a credit balance of $6,120, requiring a credit of $10,280 in the year-end tax accrual. Similarly, the required debit (asset) balance for deferred income taxes—current is $8,400; with a debit balance of $2,380 at the end of 20X8, the adjustment is $6,020 ($8,400 − $2,380). This illustrates the basic approach of the liability method of accounting for income taxes: The desired balance sheet figures are determined first and the expense is recognized in the amount required to meet the balance sheet objective.

EXHIBIT B: Analysis of Cumulative Temporary Differences and Deferred Taxes, 20X9

The statutory rate reconciliation has an additional component in 20X9, because of the tax rate change from 34% to 40%. This change has the effect of increasing deferred taxes and, therefore, tax expense, as indicated in the following reconciliation:

Pretax financial income at statutory rate ($150,000 × 40%)	$ 60,000
Less: Permanent differences ($12,000 × 40%)	(4,800)
Plus: Tax increase on beginning cumulative temporary differences [$11,000 × (40% − 34%)]	660
Income tax expense	$ 55,860

Notice that the adjustment for the tax increase is calculated only for the beginning balance of cumulative temporary differences. The temporary differences originating in 20X9 have already been taxed at 40%. As indicated earlier, the balance sheet and income statement presentation of deferred tax information will be considered after the analysis for 20Y0.

During the third year of this Illustration, Power Company's activities took a significant downturn. Because of negative economic trends and a loss of several important contracts, the company reported a pretax financial *loss* of $275,000.

An analysis of the pretax financial loss, permanent and temporary differences, and the amount of loss for tax purposes are analyzed as follows:

Pretax financial (loss)	$(275,000)
Permanent difference:	
Interest on municipal securities	(15,000)
Pretax financial (loss) subject to tax	$(290,000)
Temporary differences:	
Depreciation	(40,000)
Warranties	18,000
Revenue received in advance ($15,000 – $10,000)	5,000
Litigation loss	(10,000)
Taxable (loss)	$(317,000)

This analysis is similar to those for 20X8 and 20X9, except for the negative amount of pretax financial loss. Revenue of $10,000 received in advance that was previously taxed was recognized in accounting income and an additional $15,000 was received that was deferred for accounting purposes, but taxed currently. The litigation of 20X9 was completed and the $10,000 loss was deducted for tax purposes.

Notice that the loss for tax purposes is $317,000. Assume that Power Company decides to carry back the loss to the extent possible and receive a refund for income taxes paid in the carryback period. Under current tax law, the loss can be carried back only two years, the entire life of Power Company. The amount of the refund to be received is $100,560:

20X8: $144,000 × 34%	=		$ 48,960
20X9: $129,000 × 40%	=		5,600
			$100,560

The determination of deferred tax balances in Exhibit C is similar to those in the two previous exhibits with modifications necessary to include the loss carryforward of $44,000, which is determined by subtracting the amount of loss that is carried back from the total loss for tax purposes for 20Y0:

$$\$317{,}000 - (\$144{,}000 + \$129{,}000) = \$44{,}000$$

EXHIBIT C: Analysis of Cumulative Temporary Differences and Deferred Taxes, 20Y0

A category for the loss carryforward has been added to the analysis at the top of Exhibit C and the $44,000 loss carryforward in 20Y0 has been included. The loss carryforward gives rise to a deferred tax asset, as indicated in the analysis at the bottom of Exhibit C. This item is classified as noncurrent on the assumption that, given the large loss encountered by Power Company in 20Y0, it will be several years before the company returns to profitable operations and is able to recognize the benefit of the loss carryforward. That item is treated in the same manner as a deductible temporary difference for purposes of determining deferred tax assets and liabilities.

PRACTICE POINTER: Accumulating the information required to implement ASC 740 is facilitated by preparing a workpaper like those in Exhibits A, B, and C. Such a workpaper includes the following major components:

- A record of the cumulative temporary differences and carryforwards, including:
  - Separation of temporary differences into taxable and deductible categories
  - Beginning balances, the increase or decrease in the cumulative temporary differences, and the ending balances
- A record of cumulative amounts of carryforwards identified by year
- A record of deferred income taxes, including:
  - Separate classifications of deferred tax liabilities and assets
  - Beginning balances, ending balances, and the resulting changes in deferred taxes for the year
  - The classification of the ending balances of deferred tax assets and liabilities into current and noncurrent balance sheet categories

The journal entry to record income taxes at the end of 20Y0 is as follows:

Dec. 31, 20Y0

Receivable for past income taxes [($144,000 × 34%) + ($129,000 × 40%)]	$100,560	
Deferred income tax—Noncurrent ($16,400 – $7,600)	8,800	
Deferred income tax—Current ($8,400 – $6,400)		$ 2,000
Income tax benefit ($100,560 + $6,800)		107,360

As shown in the two right-hand columns of Exhibits B and C, the balances of both deferred income taxes—current (debit) and deferred income taxes—noncurrent (credit) declined from 20X9 to 20Y0. The two most significant differences are the reversal of the temporary difference from the litigation loss and the inclusion of the loss carryforward, both of which are relatively large amounts.

In the journal entry above, income tax expense has been replaced by the account income tax benefit, which indicates the positive impact (loss reduction) of using the 20Y0 loss to receive the refund of 20X8 and 20X9 income taxes and to offset income taxes that would otherwise have to be paid after 20Y0.

The 20Y0 statutory rate reconciliation can now be prepared as follows:

Pretax financial (loss) at statutory rate [($275,000) × 40%]	$(110,000)
Less: Permanent differences ($15,000 × 40%)	(6,000)
Plus: Loss carryback at 34% [$144,000 × (40% – 34%)]	8,640
Income tax (benefit)	$(107,360)

The last item in the reconciliation, identified as "loss carryback at 34%," is required because the 20X8 part of the carryback was determined at 34%, the 20X8 income tax rate, rather than the current (20Y0) rate of 40%.

Now that the three-year analysis of the cumulative temporary differences and the loss carryforward, the related deferred tax assets and liabilities, and the year-end journal entries to record income taxes is completed, attention should be focused on the amounts that will be presented in the balance sheet and income statement. That information is presented in Exhibit D. For each year, a portion of deferred taxes appears in the current asset section of the balance sheet. This amount represents the net amount of deferred taxes on temporary differences on assets and liabilities that are classified as current in the balance sheet. In addition, in 20Y0, a current asset is presented for the $100,560 receivable of 20X8 and 20X9 taxes resulting from the 20Y0 carryback. For 20X8 and 20X9, a current liability is presented for income taxes payable—$48,960 and $51,600 in 20X8 and 20X9, respectively.

Among noncurrent liabilities, each year includes a deferred tax amount that represents deferred taxes resulting from temporary differences classified as noncurrent, and from the loss carryforward. The amount of noncurrent deferred taxes declines between 20X9 and 20Y0 because of the loss carryforward, which partially offsets the large deferred tax liability related to the depreciation temporary difference for the first time in 20Y0.

The income statement presentation for each year displays pretax financial income (loss), followed by income tax expense (benefit), separated into current and deferred components. In 20X8 and 20X9, income tax expense reduces the amount of net income reported, as would be expected given the profitability reported by the company in those years. In 20Y0, however, the benefit of the carryback and carryforward results in a reduction in the amount of loss that would otherwise have been reported because of the refund of past taxes and the anticipation of reduced taxes in the future, when the carryforward is realized.

To examine the accounting procedures required when a valuation allowance is established for deferred tax assets, return to Exhibit C. Assume that, after careful consideration, management determines it is more likely than not that 25% of the deferred tax assets will not be realized. This requires a valuation allowance of $10,000, determined as follows, based on the information from Exhibit C:

EXHIBIT D: Financial Statement Presentation of Income Taxes, 20X8-20Y0

Balance Sheet

	20X8	20X9	20Y0
Current assets:			
Receivable for past income taxes			$ 100,560
Deferred income taxes	$2,380	$8,400	6,400
Current liabilities:			
Income taxes payable	48,960	51,600	
Noncurrent liabilities:			
Deferred income taxes	6,120	16,400	7,600

Income Statement

	20X8	20X9	20Y0
Income (loss):			
Before income tax	$160,000	$150,000	$(275,000)
Income tax expense (benefit):			
Current	48,960	51,600	(100,560)
Deferred	3,740	4,260	(6,800)
	52,700	55,860	(107,360)

44,024   ASC 740—Income Taxes

Balance Sheet

	20X8	20X9	20Y0
Net income (loss)	$107,300	$94,140	$(167,640)

Current deferred tax assets:			
Revenue received in advance			$ 6,400
Noncurrent deferred tax assets:			
Warranties		$16,000	
Loss carryforward		17,600	33,600
			$40,000
Valuation allowance: 25% × $40,000			$10,000
Allocation to current/noncurrent:			
Current: ($6,400/$40,000) × $10,000			$ 1,600
Noncurrent: ($33,600/$40,000) × $10,000			8,400
			$10,000

This allocation results in a $1,600 reduction in the current deferred tax asset and a $8,400 addition to the net noncurrent deferred tax liability. In the following comparative analysis, the impact of the valuation allowance is determined as indicated in the right-hand column, and is compared with the figures presented earlier without a valuation allowance in the left-hand column.

	Without Valuation Allowance	With Valuation Allowance
Current deferred tax asset	$ 6,400	$ 6,400
Less: Allowance	0	(1,600)
	$ 6,400	$ 4,800
Noncurrent deferred tax liability:		
Asset component	$33,600	$ 33,600
Less: Allowance	0	(8,400)
	$33,600	$ 25,200
Liability component	(41,200)	(41,200)
	$ (7,600)	$(16,000)
Total deferred tax	$ (1,200)	$(11,200)

The difference between the totals in the two columns is $10,000, exactly the amount of the valuation allowance.

The journal entry to record income taxes at the end of 20Y0 under these revised assumptions, and including the valuation allowance, is as follows:

Dec. 31, 20Y0

Receivable for past income taxes [($144,000 × 34%) + ($129,000 × 40%)]	$100,560	
Deferred income tax—Noncurrent ($16,400 – $7,600)	8,800	
Allowance to reduce deferred tax assets to lower recoverable value		$10,000
Deferred income tax—Current ($8,400 – $6,400)		2,000
Income tax benefit ($100,560 + $6,800 – $10,000)		97,360

The statutory rate reconciliation for 20Y0, including the recognition of the valuation allowance, is as follows:

Pretax financial income (loss) at statutory rate [($275,000) × 40%]	$(110,000)
Less: Permanent differences ($15,000 × 40%)	(6,000)
Plus: Loss carryback at 34% [$144,000 × (40% – 34%)]	8,640
Increase in valuation allowance	10,000
Income tax (benefit)	$ (97,360)

The valuation allowance is evaluated at the end of each year, considering positive and negative evidence about whether the asset will be realized. At that time, the allowance will either be increased or reduced; reduction could result in the complete elimination of the allowance if positive evidence indicates that the value of the deferred tax assets is no longer impaired and the allowance is no longer required.

UNCERTAIN TAX POSITIONS

ASC 740 recognizes that the ultimate deductibility of positions taken on tax returns is often uncertain. Guidance is provided on when tax positions claimed by an entity can be recognized (recognition) and guidance on the dollar amount at which those positions are recorded (measurement). Differences between tax positions taken in a tax return and recognized in accordance with ASC 740 will generally result in an increase in income taxes currently payable or a reduction in an income tax refund receivable or an increase in a deferred tax liability or a decrease in a deferred tax asset.

Scope

Because income taxes primarily affect business enterprises, ASC 740 is most applicable to for-profit businesses. However, ASC 740 also applies, assuming income taxes are an issue, to not-for-profit entities and pass-through entities (e.g., real estate investment trusts and investment companies).

A tax position is a position taken in a tax return already filed or to be filed in the future and that affects the determination of current or deferred income tax assets or liabilities (in either annual or quarterly financial statements). The effects of a tax position can result in either a permanent reduction in taxes payable or a reduction in the deferral of taxes payable to a future period, or can increase the realizability of deferred tax assets. Examples of tax positions include shifting income from one tax jurisdiction to another, the inclusion and characterization of income, and the recognition of deductions (ASC Glossary).

Recognition

The definition of the appropriate unit of account for analyzing uncertain tax positions is judgmental. In exercising this judgment, the entity should consider both how it prepares and supports its tax return, as well as the likely approach taken by the relevant taxing authority in defining the unit of account for the entity (ASC 740-10-25-13).

The entity should initially recognize the effects on the financial statements of a tax position when it is more likely than not (i.e., greater than a 50% likelihood) that the claimed tax position will be upheld by the relevant taxing authority, including any appeals or litigation. The evaluation of whether the tax position is more likely than not to be upheld should be based on the technical merits of the position (ASC 740-10-25-6). In making this evaluation, the entity should:

- Consider the facts, circumstances, and information that exist at the reporting date (ASC 740-10-25-10).
- Presume that the tax position will be evaluated by the relevant taxing authority, and that this authority will have full knowledge of the facts and circumstances surrounding the position (ASC 740-10-25-7).
- Evaluate the technical merits of a tax position based on tax legislation, statutes, and related legislative intent (implementing regulations and rulings and case law) (ASC 740-10-25-7).
- Consider each tax position on its own—that is, do not consider the possibility of offset or aggregation (ASC 740-10-25-7).

The benefits associated with tax positions that are not more-likely-than-not to be upheld are not recognized in the financial statements. Rather, a liability for the additional tax that taxing authorities are likely to assess is recognized in the financial statements.

Measurement

Before the financial statement effects of a tax position are recognized, the entity must conclude that it is more-likely-than-not that the tax position will be upheld by the relevant taxing authority. For each tax position, the entity is to consider the possible dollar amounts that might be realized upon settlement with the appropriate taxing authority (i.e., there is an implicit assumption that the tax return will be audited and that all tax positions will be evaluated). The entity is to estimate the probabilities associated with each possible settlement of the tax position. The amount recognized in the financial statements is the largest amount where the probability of ultimate receipt exceeds 50% (ASC 740-10-30-7).

> **PRACTICE POINTER:** Very few tax disputes are litigated and even fewer are litigated to the court of "last resort." Therefore, assuming the tax position is more-likely-than-not to be upheld, the amount recognized related to the tax position is often the amount that the entity would settle for in a negotiation with taxing authorities ASC 740-10-55-4.

Effect of ASC 740 on Evaluation of Deferred Tax Assets

To realize a deferred tax asset, an entity must have taxable income in the future. Some entities plan to use one or more tax-planning strategies to provide taxable income in the future. ASC 740 is to be applied in evaluating the amount of any future taxable income as a result of using a tax-planning strategy (ASC 740-10-30-20).

> **PRACTICE POINTER:** To the extent that future taxable income as a result of applying a tax-planning strategy is not more-likely-than-not to be realized, the entity may have to increase the valuation allowance associated with any recognized deferred tax asset.

Subsequent Recognition

A tax position may not be more-likely-than-not to be upheld at the time the position is initially taken, but circumstances may change in the future such that the tax position becomes more-likely-than-not to be upheld. The financial statement effects of the tax position are to be recognized in the first interim period that any of the following conditions occur: (1) it is now more-likely-than-not that the tax position will be upheld by the relevant taxing authority, (2) the entity has negotiated a settlement of the tax position with the taxing authority, or (3) the statute of limitations for the taxing authority to challenge the claimed tax position has expired (ASC 740-10-25-8).

Any such change in the evaluation of the realizability of a tax position should result from the receipt of new information, not from a new evaluation of information that existed at the time the tax position was originally taken (ASC 740-10-25-14).

Derecognition

If circumstances change and an unrecognized tax position is no longer more-likely-than-not to be recognized, the financial statement effects of the tax position are to be derecognized in the first period when this change occurs. An entity cannot use a valuation allowance account as a substitute for derecognizing the financial statement effects of the tax position (ASC 740-10-40-2).

Treatment of Interest and Penalties

Most taxing authorities require interest to be paid on an underpayment of income taxes. If a tax position is deemed not more-likely-than-not to be realized, the entity should begin accruing interest from the first period where the relevant taxing authority would begin to impose interest. Interest is computed by applying the relevant statutory tax rate to the difference between the tax position taken in the income tax return and the tax position recognized per the provisions of ASC 740-10 (i.e., essentially the difference between the tax position taken in the tax return and the tax position that is likely to be eventually upheld by the relevant taxing authority) (ASC 740-10-30-29).

An entity may take a tax position in its return that does not even meet the minimum statutory threshold for the avoidance of penalties. In this case, the entity should recognize an expense for the amount of the statutory penalty in the period in which the tax position is taken. If circumstances change and the more-likely-than-not threshold is met, a settlement with the taxing authorities is reached, or the statute of limitations for examining prior tax returns lapses, than previously recognized interest and penalties should be derecognized (ASC 740-10-25-57).

The recognition of interest that result from the application of ASC 740 can be treated as either income tax expense or interest expense, and penalties can be treated as either income tax expense or in another expense classification. The entity is given discretion in categorizing interest and penalties. However, the categorization of interest and penalties must be consistently applied (ASC 740-10-45-25). In addition, the entity must disclose its policy on how it treats interest and penalties in its financial statements (ASC 740-10-50-19).

Financial Statement Classification

An unrecognized tax benefit exists for the difference between a position taken on a tax return and the amount recognized under the provisions of ASC 740. Essentially, tax positions that are unlikely to be upheld are not recognized in the financial statements and are labeled as unrecognized tax benefits. An unrecognized tax position creates a liability for financial reporting purposes (or reduces an income tax refund receivable or a net operating loss carryforward). The liability reflects the fact that an entity is paying a taxing authority less (based on the filed tax return) than is likely to eventually be owed because certain tax positions are unlikely to be upheld. A liability associated with an unrecognized tax position is to be shown as a current liability if the entity expects to pay cash within one year or within the operating cycle, if longer (ASC 740-10-25-16; 740-10-45-11).

The application of ASC 740 also may affect the recognition of deferred tax assets and liabilities. Taxable and deductible temporary differences result from the difference between the book basis of assets and liabilities and the tax basis of those same assets and liabilities. Taxable and deductible temporary differences, formerly based on the tax treatment used in the tax return, are based on the tax treatment that is likely to ultimately be upheld by the relevant taxing authorities (ASC 740-10-25-17).

Disclosure Requirements

A table reconciling the total amounts of unrecognized tax benefits from the beginning to the end of the year must be included for each annual reporting period. At a minimum, this table must include (ASC 740-10-50-15):

- The gross amounts of increases and decreases in unrecognized tax benefits as a result of tax positions taken in the current and prior periods. An unrecognized tax benefit results from a tax position claimed on a tax return that is not given financial statement effect because it is not more-likely-than-not that the tax position will be upheld by taxing authorities.
- The gross amounts of decreases in unrecognized tax benefits resulting from settlements with taxing authorities.
- The gross amounts of decreases in unrecognized tax benefits resulting from a lapse in the statute of limitations.

In addition to the above, the entity must disclose the total amount of unrecognized tax benefits that would affect the entity's tax rate if they were recognized and the total amount of interest and penalties included in the income statement and the balance sheet (ASC 740-10-50-15). Moreover, if the entity has any unrecognized tax benefits where the amount of these unrecognized benefits may significantly increase or decrease over the next year, the entity must disclose (ASC 740-10-50-15):

- A description of the uncertainty.
- A description of the event that could change the amount of unrecognized tax benefits.
- An estimate of the amount by which the unrecognized tax benefit may change (range) or a statement that an estimate of this range cannot be developed.

The entity also must disclose the tax years that are still subject to examination by the taxing authorities (ASC 740-10-50-15).

Implementation Guidance

Subsequent to the issuance of ASC 740-10, the FASB implementation guidance on accounting for uncertainty in income taxes and amend disclosures for nonpublic entities (ASC 740-10).

Following are the key provisions of this guidance:

- If income taxes paid by the entity are attributable to the entity, the transaction should be accounted for consistent with the guidance for uncertainty in income taxes in ASC 740-10. If income taxes paid by the entity are attributable to the owners, the transaction should be recorded as a transaction with the owners. The determination of attribution should be made for each jurisdiction where the entity is subject to income taxes and is determined on the basis of laws and regulations of each jurisdiction.
- Management determination of the taxable status of the entity, including its status as a pass-through entity or tax-exempt not-for-profit entity, is a

tax position subject to the standards required for accounting for uncertainty in income taxes.

- A reporting entity must consider the tax positions of all entities within a related group of entities regardless of the tax status of the reporting entity.
- The disclosures required by ASC 740-10-15(a)-(b) are eliminated for non-public entities. These disclosures require a tabular reconciliation of the total amount of unrecognized tax benefits at the beginning and end of the period and disclosure of the total amount of unrecognized tax benefits that, if recognized would affect the effective tax rate.

OBSERVATION: The elimination of the disclosure requirements above resulted from users of private company financial statement indicating that these disclosures do not provide decision-useful information. Their elimination reduces the cost of preparing private company financial statements without eliminating information useful to decision makers. The elimination of these disclosures does not apply to public companies.

Illustration—Measuring Benefit of a Tax Position

Hust and Jacony Inc. have taken a tax position that results in a $80 million tax benefit. Hust and Jacony conclude that it is more-likely-than-not (more than a 50% likelihood) that its claimed tax position will be upheld by the relevant taxing authority and, as such, the benefit associated with the tax position should be recognized. However, Hust and Jacoby believe that it may not receive the full $80 million tax benefit. In determining the amount of tax benefit to record in its financial statements, Hust and Jacoby estimate potential outcomes and the probabilities associated with those outcomes. Hust and Jacoby develop the following schedule:

Estimated Outcome	Individual Probability	Cumulative Probability
$80 million	10%	10%
60 million	15%	25%
50 million	40%	65%
40 million	20%	85%
20 million	15%	100%

Hust and Jacoby would record a benefit associated with this tax position of $50 million because this is the largest benefit that has more than a 50% cumulative probability of being received.

Illustration—Measurement when Uncertainty Exists Surrounding the Timing of Tax Deductibility

Neel and Neal Inc. (N&N) purchase a separately identifiable intangible asset for $4.5 million on 1-1-X7. The intangible asset has an indefinite life for financial reporting purposes and is therefore not being amortized. The tax treatment related to the timing of the deductibility of the intangible asset is ambiguous—

there is some support for an immediate expensing of the intangible asset, but other sources suggest that the intangible is to be amortized over 15 years. N&N deduct the entire cost of the intangible asset in 20X7 for tax purposes.

N&N conclude that realization of the tax benefit associated with deducting the cost of the intangible asset is more-likely-than-not and, therefore, a tax benefit is to be recognized in the financial statements. The only uncertainty is whether the entire tax benefit is recognizable in 20X7 or ratably over the next 15 years.

N&N estimates that it has a 35% likelihood of being able to deduct the entire cost of the intangible asset in 20X7. If immediate expensing is not allowed, deductibility through periodic amortization over the next 15 years would be allowed. The tax benefit that is more than 50% likely of being realized is associated with amortization over 15 years (the probability of immediate expensing being supported is only 35%). Therefore, the tax benefit is the tax savings associated with a $300,000 ($4.5 million ÷ 15 years) in 20X7.

N&N would recognize the following on its 12-31-X7 financial statements:

- A deferred tax liability related for the tax effects of the difference between the book basis of the intangible asset ($4.5 million) and the tax basis of the intangible asset ($4.2 million) (The tax basis of the intangible asset is computed based on the provisions of ASC 740, not on the amount deducted in the tax return.)
- An income tax liability for the tax effects of the difference between the deduction claimed on the tax return ($4.5 million) and the appropriate deduction determined based on the provisions of ASC 740 ($300 thousand)

In addition, N&N must evaluate whether to accrue interest and penalties because the amount claimed on the tax return exceeds the amount that is supportable under the provisions of ASC 740 (i.e., the amount that has a greater than 50% likelihood of being ultimately realized).

ASC 740-20: INTRAPERIOD TAX ALLOCATION

INTRAPERIOD TAX ALLOCATION

Income tax expense or benefit for the year shall be allocated among continuing operations, discontinued operations, extraordinary items, and items charged or credited directly to shareholders' equity. The amount allocated to continuing operations is the tax effect of the pretax income or loss from continuing operations that occurred during the year, plus or minus income tax effects of:

- Changes in circumstances that cause a change in judgment about the realization of deferred tax assets
- Changes in tax laws or rates
- Changes in tax status
- Tax deductible dividends paid to shareholders, except for dividends paid on unallocated shares held by an employee stock ownership plan (ESOP)

The remainder is allocated to items other than continuing operations (ASC 740-20-45-2).

The tax effects of the following items are charged or credited directly to the related components of stockholders' equity (ASC 740-20-45-11):

- Adjustments of the opening balance of retained earnings for certain changes in accounting principles or to correct an error
- Gains and losses included in comprehensive income but excluded from net income
- An increase or decrease in contributed capital
- Expenses for employee stock options recognized differently for accounting and tax purposes
- Dividends that are paid on unallocated shares held by an ESOP and that are charged to retained earnings
- Deductible temporary differences and carryforwards that existed at the date of a quasi-reorganization

Generally, the tax benefit of an operating loss carryforward or carryback is reported in the same manner as the source of the income or loss in the current year, and not in the same manner as (*a*) the source of the operating loss carryforward or taxes paid in a prior year or (*b*) the source of expected future income that will result in realization of deferred tax assets for an operating loss carryforward from the current year. Exceptions to this general rule are:

- Tax effects of deductible temporary differences and carryforwards that existed at the date of a purchase business combination and for which a tax benefit is recognized initially in subsequent years in accordance with ASC 805-740-25-3.
- Tax effects of deductible temporary differences and carryforwards that are allocated to shareholders' equity in accordance with ASC 740-20-45-11. (See previous list.)

If there is only one item other than continuing operations, the portion of income tax expense or benefit that remains after the allocation to continuing operations is allocated to that item. If there are two or more items, the amount that remains after the allocation to continuing operations is allocated among those other items in proportion to their individual effects on income tax expense or benefit for the year (ASC 740-20-45-14).

ASC 740-30: OTHER CONSIDERATIONS OR SPECIAL AREAS

INCOME TAXES IN SPECIAL AREAS

A deferred tax liability is not recognized for the following temporary differences, unless it becomes apparent that they will reverse in the foreseeable future (ASC 740-30-25-3):

- An excess of the amount for financial reporting over the tax basis of an investment in a foreign subsidiary or a foreign corporate joint venture as defined in the ASC Glossary that is essentially permanent in nature

- For a domestic subsidiary or a domestic corporate joint venture that is essentially permanent in duration, undistributed earnings that arose in fiscal years beginning on or before December 15, 1992
- "Bad debt reserves" for tax purposes of U.S. savings and loan associations and other qualified thrifts that arose in tax years beginning before December 31, 1987
- Policyholders' surplus of stock life insurance companies that arose in fiscal years beginning on or before December 15, 1992

Whenever a deferred tax liability is not recognized because of one of these exceptions, the following information is required to be disclosed (ASC 942-740-50-1):

- A description of the types of temporary differences for which a deferred tax liability has not been recognized and the types of events that would cause those temporary differences to become taxable
- The cumulative amount of each type of temporary difference
- The amount of the unrecognized deferred tax liability for temporary differences related to investments in foreign subsidiaries and foreign corporate joint ventures that are essentially permanent in duration if determination of that liability is practicable, or a statement that determination is not practicable
- The amount of the deferred tax liability for temporary differences other than those in item (3) above that is not recognized

A deferred tax liability is recognized for the following types of taxable temporary differences (ASC 740-30-25-2; 942-740-25-2):

- An excess of the amount of accounting basis over the tax basis of an investment in a domestic subsidiary that arises in fiscal years beginning after December 15, 1992
- An excess of the amount for accounting purposes over the tax basis of an investment in a 50%-or-less-owned investee except as provided in ASC 740 for a foreign corporate joint venture that is essentially permanent in nature
- "Bad debt reserves" for tax purposes of U.S. savings and loan associations and other qualified thrifts that arise in tax years beginning after December 31, 1987

Whether an excess of the amount for accounting purposes over the tax basis of an investment in a more-than-50%-owned domestic subsidiary is a taxable temporary diffcrence must be assessed. It is not a taxable temporary difference if the tax law provides a means by which the reported amount of that investment can be recovered tax free and the enterprise expects that it will ultimately use that means (ASC 740-30-25-7).

A deferred tax asset is recognized for an excess of the tax basis over the amount for accounting purposes of an investment in a subsidiary or corporate joint venture that is essentially permanent in duration only if it is apparent that the temporary difference will reverse in the foreseeable future (ASC 740-30-25-9).

… ASC 740—Income Taxes

ASC 740-270: INTERIM REPORTING

ACCOUNTING FOR INCOME TAXES IN INTERIM PERIODS

ASC 740 provides guidance in accounting for income taxes in interim periods in accordance with the provisions of ASC 270. Generally an entity is required to estimate the annual effective tax rate to use to determine the interim period income tax provision, applied on a cumulative year-to-date basis (ASC 740-270-30-4-5).

Illustration of Quarterly Income Tax Calculation

Valentine, Inc. reports pretax income for the first two quarters of 20X9 as follows: January-March, $500,000; April-June, $450,000. At the end of the first quarter, management estimates that its effective annual income tax rate will be 40%. At the end of the second quarter, this estimate had been revised to 38%.

Income tax expense for the first quarter is calculated as follows:

$$\$500{,}000 \times 40\% = \$200{,}000$$

Income tax expense for the second quarter is determined by applying the revised estimate of the effective annual income tax rate to the cumulative pretax income to date and subtracting the amount recognized as income tax expense in the first quarter:

$$[(\$500{,}000 + \$450{,}000) \times 38\%] - \$200{,}000 = \$161{,}000$$

This same process is followed for the remaining quarters of the year: cumulative income to date × the estimated annual income tax rate − previous quarters' tax expense = current quarter expense.

PART II: INTERPRETIVE GUIDANCE

ASC 740-10: Overall

ASC 740-10-25-9 Definition of *Settlement* in FASB Interpretation No. 48
BACKGROUND

The FASB directed the FASB staff to draft this guidance, which amends the guidance in ASC 740-10, because constituents have asked the staff whether an entity may recognize a tax benefit that it previously had decided should not be recognized if the only change that has occurred is the completion of a tax authority's examination or audit. Constituents have also asked for clarification of the following information in ASC 740-10:

- The meaning of the term *ultimate settlement* in ASC 740-10-30-7;
- The meaning of the terms *ultimately settled* and *negotiation* in ASC 740-10-40-3;
- The concept stated in ASC 740-10-35-2 that "a tax position need not be legally extinguished and its resolution need not be certain to subsequently recognize or measure the position."

This guidance amends the guidance in ASC 740 by clarifying that a taxing authority's examination effectively could result in the settlement of a tax position. Judgment is required in determining whether a tax position is effectively settled, because examinations occur in different ways. That determination should be made separately for each individual tax position, but an entity may conclude that all its tax positions in a specific tax year have effectively been settled.

ACCOUNTING GUIDANCE

In applying the guidance in ASC 740-10-40-3, the benefit of a tax position should be recognized when it is considered to be effectively settled. All of the following conditions should be evaluated to determine whether an effective settlement has occurred:

1. The taxing authority's examination procedures have been completed, including all appeals and administrative reviews related to the tax position that the taxing authority is required or expected to perform;
2. The entity does *not* intend to appeal or litigate any aspect of the tax position included in the completed examination;
3. Assuming that the taxing authority has full knowledge of all the relevant information, the entity believes that the possibility that the taxing authority would reexamine any aspect of the tax position is remote based on the taxing authority's commonly understood policy on reopening closed examinations and the tax position's specific circumstances.

Further, to be considered effectively settled through examination, the taxing authority need not have specifically reviewed or examined the tax position in the tax years under examination. Nevertheless, a tax position's effective settlement as a result of an examination does not mean that it is an effective settlement of a similar or identical tax position that has *not* been examined.

If at a later date, an entity becomes aware that a tax position that it had considered effectively settled may be examined or reexamined, the entity should reevaluate the tax position in accordance with the guidance in ASC 740-10, because the tax position should no longer be considered to be effectively settled.

Based on information obtained during the examination process, an entity may change its judgment about the technical merits of a tax position and wish to apply that view to similar tax positions taken in other periods. However, an entity should not change its judgment about the technical merits of a tax position in other periods based exclusively on the conditions for effective settlement stated above.

A number of changes are made to the terms *ultimate settlement* or *ultimately settled*, in ASC 740-10 to conform to this guidance. The term *effectively settled* replaces the term *ultimately settled* when it is used in the Interpretation to describe recognition. Likewise, the terms *settlement* or *settled* replace the terms *ultimate settlement* or *ultimately settled* when they are used in the Interpretation to describe measurement.

ASC 740-10-25-34, 50-4, 55-2 through 55-6, 55-15 through 55-22, 55-25, 55-40 through 55-41, 55-48, 55-59 through 55-65, 55-79 through 55-80, 55-163 through

55-164, 55-168 through 55-169, 55-213 through 55-216; ASC 740-20-55-1 through 55-7; ASC 942-740-35-1 through 35-3; ASC 942-852-55-2 through 55-6; ASC 855-10-60-2 A Guide to Implementation of ASC 740 on Accounting for Income Taxes

ACCOUNTING GUIDANCE

Scheduling

Question 1: When is it necessary to schedule reversal patterns of existing temporary differences?

Answer: Scheduling individual years in terms of reversals of temporary differences is required under ASC 740 in the following circumstances:

- Deferred taxes that do not relate to a specific asset or liability are classified as current or noncurrent based on the timing of their reversal.

- When deferred tax assets are recognized without consideration of offsetting, after which an assessment is required concerning the need for a valuation allowance. The timing of reversal of temporary differences may be an important consideration in determining the need for and amount of a valuation allowance on deferred tax assets.

- When tax rate changes are phased in, which will often require scheduling.

In scheduling the reversal of temporary differences, consistency and minimizing complexity are particularly important considerations. The same methods should be used for all temporary differences in a particular category for a particular tax jurisdiction.

Question 2: The guidance in ASC 740 states that future originating temporary differences for existing depreciable assets and their subsequent reversals are a factor in assessing the likelihood of future realization of a tax benefit of deductible temporary differences and carry forwards. Should future originating and reversing temporary differences always be scheduled for purposes of determining the need for a valuation allowance for deferred tax assets related to existing deductible temporary differences and carryforwards?

Answer: Not necessarily. There are four possible sources of taxable income to support the realizability of deferred tax assets. When it can easily be demonstrated that future taxable income will be sufficient, scheduling is generally not necessary. However, if reversal of taxable temporary differences is the basis for a realization assumption for deferred tax assets, the timing of reversal is important and may require scheduling.

Question 3: Does ASC 740 require separate deferred tax computations for each state or local tax jurisdiction?

Answer: As a general rule, the answer is "yes," if there are significant differences between the tax laws of the different jurisdictions involved. In the United States, however, many state and local income taxes are based on U.S. federal income tax, and aggregate computations of deferred tax assets and liabilities may be appropriate.

Question 4: An enterprise may have a basis under the tax law for claiming certain deductions (e.g., repair expense) on its income tax return. It may have recognized a liability (including interest) for the probable disallowance of that deduction that, if disallowed, would be capitalized for tax purposes and deductible in future years. How should an item like this be considered in the scheduling of future taxable or deductible differences?

Answer: If expenses are disallowed, taxable income of that year is higher, which provides a source of taxable income for purposes of assessing the need for a valuation allowance for deductible temporary differences. Taxable income after the year of disallowance will be lower because of annual deductions attributable to those capitalized amounts. A deductible amount for the accrued interest is scheduled for the future year in which that interest is expected to be deductible (i.e., when the underlying issues are expected to be settled with the tax authority).

Question 5: A change in tax law may require a change in accounting method for tax purposes (e.g., the uniform cost capitalization rules required by the Tax Reform Act of 1986). For calendar-year taxpayers, inventories on hand at the beginning of 1987 are revalued under the new rules, and the initial catch-up adjustment is deferred and taken into taxable income over not more than four years. Does the deferral of the initial catch-up adjustment for a change in accounting method for tax purposes give rise to a temporary difference?

Answer: Yes. The uniform cost capitalization rules initially resulted in two temporary differences—one related to the additional amounts initially capitalized into inventory for tax expense and one related to the deferred income for tax purposes that results from the initial catch-up adjustment.

Question 6: The Omnibus Budget Reconciliation Act of 1987 requires family-owned farming businesses to use the accrual method of accounting for tax purposes. The initial catch-up adjustment to change from the cash method to the accrual method is deferred and included in taxable income if the business ceases to be family-owned. It also is included in taxable income if gross receipts from farming activities in future years drop below certain 1987 levels. Does the deferral of the initial catch-up adjustment for that change in accounting method for tax purposes give rise to a temporary difference?

Answer: Yes. The entire amount of the catch-up adjustment is a temporary difference.

Question 7: State income taxes are deductible for U.S. federal income tax purposes. Does a deferred state income tax liability or asset give rise to a temporary difference for purposes of determining a deferred U.S. federal income tax liability or asset?

Answer: Yes. A deferred state income tax liability or asset gives rise to a temporary difference for purposes of determining deferred taxes for U.S. federal income tax purposes.

Recognition and Measurement

Question 8: The temporary difference for the "base-year tax reserve" of a savings and loan association is one of the exceptions to comprehensive recognition of deferred taxes under the guidance in ASC 740. If a deferred tax liability is not recognized for that temporary difference, should a savings and loan association anticipate future percentage-of-taxable-income (PTI) bad-debt deductions in determining the deferred tax liability for other types of temporary differences?

Answer: No. Deferred tax assets and liabilities for temporary differences are measured based on enacted tax rates expected to apply to taxable income when the deferred tax asset or liability is expected to be realized or settled. For the same reason that other special deductions may not be anticipated, it is not permissible to reduce a deferred tax liability by anticipating future PTI bad-debt reductions.

Question 9: An enterprise charged losses directly to contributed capital in a quasi-reorganization. At that time, the deferred tax asset for the enterprise's deductible temporary differences and carryforwards was offset by a valuation allowance. Part of those deductible temporary differences were related to losses that were included in determining income in prior years, and the remainder were attributable to losses that were charged directly to contributed capital. When recognized by reducing or eliminating the valuation allowance, how should the tax benefit of such deductible temporary differences and carryforwards be reported?

Answer: All unrecognized tax benefits of deductible temporary differences and carryforwards that existed at the time of a quasi-reorganization (except as provided in ASC 852-740-45-3 should be reported as a direct addition to contributed capital when recognized at a date after the quasi-reorganization. The benefit of an operating loss or tax credit carryforward that existed at the date of a quasi-reorganization should not be included in the determination of income of the "new" enterprise, regardless of whether they were charged to income before the quasi-reorganization or were charged directly to contributed capital as part of the quasi-reorganization. A charge to income is appropriate only if, subsequent to a quasi-reorganization, the enterprise determines that due to a change in circumstances it should recognize or increase a valuation allowance to reduce the tax benefits that were recognized in recording the quasi-reorganization.

Question 10: Some enterprises have credited a net gain directly to contributed capital at the date of a quasi-reorganization. Does the answer to Question 9 change for those enterprises?

Answer: No. The accounting for any subsequently recognized tax benefit of deductible temporary differences and carryforwards that exist at the time of a quasi-reorganization should not change based on whether gains were credited or losses charged directly to contributed capital.

Change in Tax Status

Question 11: What disclosure is required if a change in an enterprise's tax status becomes effective after year-end but before financial statements are issued?

Answer: This change should not be reflected in the financial statements of the previous year, but disclosure should include the change in the enterprise's tax status for the following year and the effects of that change, if material.

Question 12: Should an enterprise that changes from taxable C corporation status to nontaxable S corporation status eliminate its entire U.S. federal deferred tax liability?

Answer: The enterprise should continue to recognize a deferred tax liability to the extent that it would be subject to a corporate-level tax on net unrealized "built-in gains."

Illustration of Change in Tax Status

Company M's assets are as followed when its S corporation election becomes effective:

	Tax Basis	Reported Amount	Temporary Difference	Built-In Gain (Loss)
Marketable Securities	$100	$ 80	$(20)	$(8)
Inventory	50	100	50	20

If the enterprise has no tax loss or tax credit carryforwards available to offset the built-in gain and if marketable securities and inventory will both be sold in the same year, the $20 built-in gain on the inventory is offset by the $8 built-in loss on the marketable securities, and the $12 difference would be shown as a deferred tax liability.

Business Combinations

Questions 13-17a to c were nullified by the guidance in FAS-141(R).

Disclosure

Question 18: ASC 740 requires disclosure of the significant components of income tax expense attributable to continuing operations. Should the total of the amounts disclosed for the components of tax expense equal the amount of income tax expense that is reported in the statement of earnings? Should the amounts for current and deferred tax expense be disclosed before or after reduction for the tax benefit of operating loss carryforwards and tax credits?

Answer: The total of the amounts disclosed for the components of tax expense should be the amount of tax expense reported in the statement of earnings for continuing operations. Separate disclosure is required of (*a*) the tax benefit of operating loss carryforwards and (*b*) tax credits and tax credit carryforwards that were recognized.

Allocation of Tax Expense

Question 19: How should income tax expense be allocated between pretax income from continuing operations and other items when the enterprise has temporary differences?

Answer: The guidance in ASC 740 states that the amount of income tax expense or benefit allocated to continuing operations is the tax effect of pretax income or loss from continuing operations that occurred during the year (subject to certain adjustments). Income tax expense allocated between pretax income from continuing operations and other items should include deferred taxes.

Questions 20 and 21 are deleted because the effective date of FAS-109 has passed.

Tax-Planning Strategies

Question 25: The guidance in ASC 740 indicates that tax-planning strategies include elections for tax purposes. What are some examples of those elections?

Answer: Examples are as follows:

- Election to file a consolidated tax return
- Election to claim either a deduction or a tax credit for foreign taxes paid
- Election to forego carrying an operating loss back and only carry that loss forward

Question 26: An enterprise might identify several qualifying tax-planning strategies that would either reduce or eliminate the need for a valuation allowance for its deferred tax assets. May the enterprise recognize the effect of one strategy in the current year and postpone recognition of the effect of the other strategies to a later year?

Answer: No. The enterprise should recognize the effect of all tax-planning strategies that meet the criteria of ASC 740 in the current year.

Illustration of Multiple Tax Planning Strategies

Amber Co. has determined that its allowance on deferred tax assets should be $60,000, without regard to tax-planning strategies. The company has identified two income tax-planning strategies that would reduce its allowance on deferred tax assets by $10,000 (Strategy 1) and by $15,000 (Strategy 2), respectively. Both qualify as tax-planning strategies under FAS-109. Amber cannot recognize the effect of only Strategy 1 or only Strategy 2 but, rather, must recognize the impact of both and report an allowance on deferred tax assets of $35,000 [$60,000 − ($10,000 + $15,000)].

Question 27: Because the effects of known qualifying tax strategies must be recognized, is management required to make an extensive effort to identify all tax-planning strategies that meet the criteria for tax-planning strategies?

Answer: Management is required to make a reasonable effort to identify significant tax-planning strategies. If evidence indicates that other sources of taxable income will be adequate to eliminate the need for a valuation allowance, consideration of tax-planning strategies is not required.

Question 28: Under current U.S. federal income tax law, approval of a change from taxable C corporation status to nontaxable S status is automatic if the enterprise meets the criteria for S corporation status. If an enterprise meets those criteria but has not changed to S corporation status, would a strategy to change to nontaxable S corporation status be a qualifying tax-planning strategy that would permit an enterprise to not recognize deferred taxes?

Answer: No. The effect of a change in tax status should be recognized on the date when the change in tax status occurs.

ASC 740-10-25-39 through 25-40, 30-14 Accounting for Tax Credits Related to Dividend Payments in Accordance with ASC 740

BACKGROUND

In certain foreign jurisdictions, such as Germany, corporate income tax rates depend on whether the income is distributed to shareholders. In Germany, undistributed profits are taxed at a 45% rate, but distributed income is taxed at a 30% rate. If a corporation pays dividends from undistributed income that was taxed at the undistributed rate, it receives a tax credit or tax refund for the difference between (a) the tax calculated at the *undistributed rate* effective in the year the income was earned for tax purposes and (b) the tax calculated at the *distributed rate* effective in the year in which a dividend was paid. Germany also has an integrated tax system, under which shareholders are taxed on the pretax dividend and receive a credit for taxes previously paid by the corporation on that income. For example:

Corporate Tax before Distribution	
Taxable income	€ 500,000
Corporate tax (45%)	(225,000)
Retained earnings	275,000
Corporate Tax at Distribution	
Retained earnings	€ 275,000
Tax credit received on distribution [500,000 × (45% − 30%)]	75,000
Tax basis of dividend declared	350,000
Withholding tax (25%)	(87,500)
Cash distributed to shareholder	€ 262,500
Shareholder Taxation	
Cash received	€ 262,500
Tax withheld	87,500
	350,000
Add: Net corporate tax paid (30%)	150,000
Taxable income	500,000
Tax rate (maximum individual rate)	53%
Tax liability before credits	265,000
Tax credit for corporate tax	(150,000)
Credit for withholding tax	(87,500)
Net tax due	€ 27,500
Net cash to shareholder (262,500DM − 27,500DM)	€ 235,000

Because German companies are permitted to consider dividends declared from the current year's earnings and paid in a subsequent year in the tax provision, a blended tax rate between 45% and 30% is used. Some German companies also use a blended rate when calculating deferred tax assets and liabilities. Others use the undistributed rate and recognize the effect of the tax credit, which has no time limit, in the period in which dividends are paid. The effective tax rate for that year would be less than 30% to the extent that distributions are greater than earnings in that year.

> **OBSERVATION:** This guidance applies only to the accounting in the German entity's separate financial statements.

ACCOUNTING ISSUE

Should a corporate entity recognize in its separate financial statements a deferred tax asset for the tax benefit of future tax credits that will be realized when it distributes income that was previously taxed at the undistributed rate (thus measuring the tax effect of temporary differences at the distributed rate), or should the entity recognize the tax credit in the period in which it is realized on the tax return (thus measuring the tax effects of temporary differences at the undistributed tax rate)?

ACCOUNTING GUIDANCE

- A corporate entity paying dividends subject to a tax credit should *not* recognize a deferred tax asset for tax benefits related to future tax credits that it will realize when it distributes income that was previously taxed.
- The entity should reduce income tax expense in the period that these tax credits are included in the entity's tax return.

Consequently, the tax effects of temporary differences should be measured using the *undistributed* tax rate.

DISCUSSION

The approach supported is similar to the one discussed in ASC 740-10-25-37 for a special deduction, under which tax expense is recognized in the current period based on an estimate of the liability reported for tax purposes. The tax provision is reduced in the period in which the tax credit is realized for tax purposes. Proponents of this view argued that this approach avoids an overstatement of net assets by anticipating a refund that will occur only if earnings are distributed. The declaration and payment of dividends is the event that would trigger the recognition of a deferred tax asset in this Issue. Proponents also argued that because the company must distribute cash to realize the tax credits, a potential credit does not represent an asset that would be available to the entity's general creditors and that would be reported for an extended time period if the entity does not pay dividends. Another argument to support this view was that under FAS-109, deferred tax assets are recognized only for future deductible temporary differences and for tax credit and loss carryforwards; the tax credit in this Issue is not a basis difference or a carryforward.

> **OBSERVATION:** Under this guidance, entities with net operating loss carryforwards would recognize the deferred asset at the 45% undistributed rate.

ASC 740-10-25-41 Measurement in the Consolidated Financial Statements of a Parent of the Tax Effects Related to the Operations of a Foreign Subsidiary That Receives Tax Credits Related to Dividend Payments

OVERVIEW

Other guidance, which only applies to the accounting in the foreign entity's separate financial statements, states that a deferred tax asset should not be recognized for the tax benefits of future tax credits that will be realized when earnings taxed at the undistributed tax rate are subsequently distributed to shareholders. Thus, the tax effects of temporary differences would be measured at the undistributed tax rate in a foreign subsidiary's separate financial statements. This Issue applies to the accounting in the parent's consolidated financial statements.

ACCOUNTING ISSUE

Should the tax effects related to the operations of a foreign subsidiary eligible to receive a tax credit for dividends paid be measured based on the undistributed or distributed tax rate of the applicable foreign jurisdiction in the consolidated financial statements of a parent company that has not taken advantage of the exception in APB-23 for foreign unremitted earnings?

ACCOUNTING GUIDANCE

- The *distributed* rate should be used to measure a future tax credit that will be received when dividends are paid. The deferred tax effects related to a foreign subsidiary's operations should be measured at the distributed rate in a parent company's consolidated financial statements if the entity does not apply the exception for foreign unremitted earnings in ASC 740-30.

- The undistributed rate should be used in a parent company's consolidated financial statements to the extent that deferred taxes have not been provided for unremitted earnings as a result of the application of the exception in ASC 740-30.

DISCUSSION

Proponents of using the distributed rate in the parent's consolidated financial statements noted that, under this guidance, the transfer of cash is within the entity, while dividends discussed in other guidance would be paid to outside shareholders. An argument supporting the distributed rate was that a corporation's income will eventually be distributed to its shareholders for whose benefit it is earned. In addition, the tax credit is available to German corporations for an unlimited time once income has been taxed at the undistributed rate. When a dividend is distributed to the parent by a German subsidiary, the tax credit will be realized at the distributed rate. Some proponents of this view also analogized the distributed tax rate to the regular tax system and the undistributed tax rate to the alternative tax system as used in the discussion of the recognition of a deferred tax asset for alternative minimum tax credit carryforwards in ASC 740-10-25-3.

44,044 ASC 740—Income Taxes

ASC 840-30-35-48 through 35-52; ASC 740-10-25-43 Tax Reform Act of 1986: Issues Related to the Alternative Minimum Tax

BACKGROUND

Under the Tax Reform Act of 1986 (the Act), an entity computes its federal income tax liability based on the regular tax system or on the alternative minimum tax (AMT) system, whichever tax amount is greater. An entity may earn an AMT credit for tax paid under the AMT system that exceeds the amount that would have been paid under the regular tax system. An AMT credit can be carried forward indefinitely to reduce the regular tax in future years, but not below the AMT for that year.

ACCOUNTING ISSUES

- Should the AMT system be considered a separate but parallel tax system that can generate a credit for use in future years, or should the AMT amount paid in excess of the regular tax that results in an AMT credit be considered a prepayment of the regular tax in a future year?
- Should leveraged lease calculations consider the effect of the AMT on cash flows and, if so, how? (Discussed in Chapter 53, *ASC 840—Leases*.)

ACCOUNTING GUIDANCE

The AMT system should be considered a separate but parallel tax system that may result in a tax carryforward. Because the AMT credit can only be used to reduce regular tax in excess of AMT in a future year, it should not be considered a prepayment of the regular tax in a future year.

SUBSEQUENT DEVELOPMENT

The guidance in ASC 740-10-30-10 states that, for federal tax purposes, the applicable tax rate is the regular tax rate. The applicable tax rate in other jurisdictions is determined based on the tax law after considering any interaction between the two systems. A deferred tax asset is recognized for AMT carryforwards in accordance with the Statement's requirements for the computation of deferred tax assets and the provision of a valuation allowance.

DISCUSSION

The decision to treat the AMT as a separate tax system was based on the fact that the AMT system included many items considered to be "permanent" tax differences under the provisions of APB-11, which was the authoritative pronouncement on accounting for income taxes at the time this Issue was discussed. Some argued that because the AMT credit could be carried forward only to offset the regular tax in excess of the AMT in future years, its realizability was not assured and amounts that would otherwise be excluded from taxation would be taxed under the AMT system.

Under the guidance in ASC 740, the AMT credit is treated as a deferred tax asset that may require a valuation allowance. To simplify the calculation of deferred taxes, the recognition of deferred taxes for regular tax temporary differences at the enacted regular tax rate is required. Thus, an entity that can offset taxable differences with tax-deductible differences can realize the tax benefit at the regular tax rate. However, if an entity expects to be taxed indefinitely under the AMT system, has no reversals available, and must use regular tax-deductible differences against future taxable income, it may need to establish a valuation allowance to reduce its deferred tax asset to an amount that is realizable under the AMT system. In addition, under the provisions of ASC 740, an entity's deferred tax liability may build up beyond an amount that can be reversed, because deferred taxes continue to be provided on deferred tax liabilities at the regular rate, which exceeds the AMT rate. Nevertheless, an entity that continues paying taxes based on the AMT system will eventually have a deferred tax asset from AMT credit carryforwards sufficient to reduce the deferred tax liability to the AMT rate applied to AMT differences. Because of these anomalous results, some now believe that the AMT credit is a prepayment of regular taxes.

ASC 740-10-25-48 Effect of a Retroactive Change in Enacted Tax Rates That Is Included in Income from Continuing Operations

OVERVIEW

The Omnibus Budget Reconciliation Act of 1993 (OBRA) was enacted on August 10, 1993. OBRA increased the top corporate tax rate from 34% to 35% retroactively to January 1, 1993. ASC 740-10-35-4; 45-15 requires adjusting deferred tax liabilities and assets for the effect of a change in tax rates and including the adjustment in income from continuing operations in the period that includes the date the new tax law was enacted.

ACCOUNTING ISSUES

- If an enacted change in tax rates has a retroactive effective date, how should the tax effect on current and deferred tax assets and liabilities be measured on the date of enactment?

- How should the reported tax effect among items not included in income from continuing operations, such as discontinued operations, extraordinary items, cumulative effects of changes in accounting principles, and items charged or credited directly to shareholders' equity, be measured and recognized?

ACCOUNTING GUIDANCE

- The tax effect of a retroactive change in enacted tax rates on current and deferred tax assets and liabilities should be measured on the date of enactment (August 10, 1993), based on temporary differences and currently taxable income existing at the date of enactment. The cumulative tax effect should be included in income from continuing operations.

- An entity should measure the reported tax effect of items not included in income from continuing operations, such as discontinued operations, extraordinary items, cumulative effects of changes in accounting principles, and items charged or credited directly to shareholders' equity, that occurred during the current fiscal year but before the date of enactment based on the enacted rate at the time the transaction was recognized for financial reporting purposes. The tax effect of a retroactive change in enacted tax rates on current or deferred tax assets and liabilities related to such items should be included in income from continuing operations in the period in which the change was enacted.

Illustration Using Guidance in ASC 740-10-25-48

Income from January 1, 19X3, through August 9, 19X3

Pretax income from continuing operations	$5,000,000
Pretax income from extraordinary gain on June 30, 19X3	500,000
Total pretax income on August 9, 19X3	$5,500,000
Temporary differences	
Balance on January 1, 19X3	$8,000,000
Extraordinary gain on June 30, 19X3	500,000
Balance on August 10, 19X3	$8,500,000
Total 19X3 tax expense	
Current ($5,000,000 × .35)	$1,750,000
Deferred [($8,500,000 × .35) – ($8,000,000 × .34)]	255,000
Total 19X3 tax expense	$2,005,000
Allocation of 19X3 tax expense	
Continuing operations	
Current	$1,750,000
Rate change ($8,500,000 × .01)	85,000
Extraordinary item	
Tax effect on extraordinary gain ($500,000 × .34)	170,000
Total 19X3 tax expense	$2,005,000
Effect of change in rates enacted August 10, 19X3	
Increase in tax on income from continuing operations ($5,000,000 × .01)	$ 50,000
Increase in tax on balance of temporary differences on August 10, 19X3 ($8,500,000 × .01)	85,000
Adjustment included in continuing operations in period of enactment	$ 135,000
Tax adjustment allocated to extraordinary gain in period of enactment*	0

---

* The tax adjustment is included in the rate change on $8,500,000, which is allocated to continuing operations.

DISCUSSION

ASC 740-10-45-15 requires including the deferred tax effects of changes in tax laws or rates in income from continuing operations in the period that includes the enactment date. The EITF decided to measure the effect of a retroactive change in enacted tax rates on current and deferred tax assets and liabilities based on the balance of temporary differences at the date of enactment rather than on the balance at the beginning of the year, because they believed that such an approach conforms with the requirements of ASC 740-10-45-15. Proponents of this view also believed that remeasurement of items not included in income from continuing operations that originated before the enactment date using the newly enacted tax rates would be tantamount to backward tracing of tax rates and would violate the intent of ASC 740.

ASC 740-10-25-50, 25-51, 25-22 through 25-24, 52-55, S25-1, S99-3, 55-171 through 55-201, 55-203 through 55-204, 55-76 Accounting for Acquired Temporary Differences in Certain Purchase Transactions That Are Not Accounted for as Business Combinations

BACKGROUND

ASC 740-10-25-29 provides that a deferred tax liability or deferred tax asset be recognized for all temporary differences between the reported amount of an asset or liability and its tax basis. ASC 805-740-25-3 provides specific guidance for the accounting of deferred taxes in business combinations. ASC 740 provides that when the assigned values of assets and liabilities acquired in a purchase business combination differ from their tax bases, the acquiring entity should recognize a deferred tax liability or a deferred tax asset, or both, for those differences. Deferred tax assets and deferred tax liabilities recognized as a result of a purchase business combination are included in the calculation of the purchase price of the acquisition ASC 805-740-55-3, rather than in income of the period in which the combination occurred.

This Issue has been raised because ASC 740 does not provide guidance on how to account for a deferred tax asset or deferred tax liability that results from the purchase of a single asset that is *not* a business combination. The Issue applies to the following four types of transactions:

- A company imports an asset into a foreign jurisdiction. The asset costs $100 but its tax basis is reduced to $80 as a result of a penalty imposed by the jurisdiction on imported goods.

- A foreign jurisdiction is encouraging companies in certain industries to purchase certain kinds of equipment. A company purchases an asset that costs $100, but its tax basis has been increased to $150. The additional tax deduction cannot be recaptured on sale of the asset.

- A subsidiary of a U.S. company acquires a shell company that has no assets to take advantage of its net operating losses (NOLs). The NOLs are acquired at a discount from their undiscounted face value. For example, NOLs with a $5 million deferred tax benefit are acquired for $2 million.

- Corporate taxpayers in a foreign country can elect to step up the tax basis of certain fixed assets to fair value if they immediately pay the authorities 3% of the step-up. A company would make this election if it believes it's likely that it will use the additional deductions (at a 35% tax rate) to reduce future taxable income and the current payment is justified by the timing and amount of future tax savings.

ACCOUNTING ISSUES

- How should an entity account for the tax effect of the acquisition of assets not in a business combination if the acquisition cost and tax basis differ?

- How should an entity account for a net-tax benefit as a result of the purchase of future tax benefits from a nongovernmental third party that is not a taxing authority?
- How should an entity account for all direct transactions with a government acting as a taxing authority?

ACCOUNTING GUIDANCE

1. The carrying amount of an asset acquired individually, not in a business combination, should be adjusted for the tax effect resulting from the difference between the acquisition cost of the asset and its tax basis. The Task Force agreed that the asset's assigned value and the related deferred tax asset or liability should be recognized using the simultaneous equations method, which is illustrated in Question 15 of the FASB Special Report, *A Guide to Implementation of Statement 109 on Accounting for Income Taxes: Questions and Answers*. The guidance should be applied as follows:

    a. Recognize (1) a *financial asset* at its fair value, (2) an *acquired asset held for disposal* at fair value less cost to sell, and (3) deferred tax assets as required in ASC 740.

    b. Allocate the excess of amounts assigned to acquired assets over the amount paid pro rata to reduce the assigned values of acquired noncurrent assets, except those discussed in (a) above. If noncurrent assets have been reduced to zero, classify a remainder, if any, as a deferred credit, which is not a temporary difference under the guidance in ASC 740.

    c. Adjust the purchase price in accordance with the guidance in ASC 805-740-30-3, for a reduction in the acquiring company's valuation allowance directly related to the asset acquisition. After the acquisition, account for an acquired valuation allowance in accordance with the guidance in ASC 805-740-25-3 through 25-4; 45-2.

    d. Amortize to income tax expense deferred credits resulting from the application of the consensus in proportion to the tax benefits realized by recognizing those deferred credits, which should not be classified as deferred tax liabilities or offset against deferred tax assets.

    e. Subsequent to the acquisition, account for the effect of the adjustments as follows: (1) recognize in continuing operations as part of income tax expense, if it is more likely than not that some or all of the acquired deferred tax asset will not be realized, and (2) offset against income tax expense the proportionate share of any unamortized balance of the deferred credit.

    f. Account for income tax uncertainties that exist at the acquisition date in accordance with the guidance in ASC 740-30.

2. An entity purchasing future tax benefits from a nongovernmental third party should account for the net tax benefit using the same model as discussed above in the first consensus.

3. Recognize in income transactions directly between a taxpayer and a governmental entity acting in its capacity as a taxing authority, in a manner similar to the accounting for changes in tax laws, rates, or other tax elections under the guidance in ASC 740.

The Task Force noted that no deferred tax asset should be recognized for an increase in basis if the step-up in tax basis is related to previously nondeductible goodwill, except if the amount of newly deductible goodwill is more than the balance of the nondeductible goodwill.

In addition, the Task Force noted that the prohibition in ASC 740-10-25-3 against the recognition of a deferred tax asset for the difference between the basis of assets in the buyer's tax jurisdiction and the reported cost of those assets in the consolidated financial statements also applies to intercompany purchases of tax benefits by one member of a consolidated entity from another member.

SEC OBSERVER COMMENT

The SEC Observer reported that unless the SEC staff clearly understands the specific fact pattern, the staff would object if the consensus in this Issue were used to adjust the basis of acquired assets in situations other than those discussed in the following examples.

Illustrations of the Guidance on Accounting for Temporary Differences in Certain Purchases That Are Not Accounted for as Business Combinations

Example 1—Tax basis exceeds purchase price

A. A company purchases a building for $500,000 in a foreign jurisdiction that permits tax deductions to exceed the cost of the asset. The tax basis of the building is $600,000 and the tax rate is 40%. The additional tax deduction is not recaptured when the asset is sold.

The following simultaneous equations should be used to determine the amounts at which to recognize the building and the deferred tax asset:

FBB = Final Book Basis
CPP = Cash Purchase Price
DTA = Deferred Tax Asset

To determine the amount of the building's FBB:
FBB − (Tax Rate × (FBB − Tax Basis)) = CPP
FBB − (.40 × (FBB − $600,000)) = $500,000
FBB = $433,333

To determine the amount of DTA:
(Tax Basis − FBB) × Tax Rate = DTA
($600,000 − $433,333) × .40 = DTA
DTA = $66,667

The company would make the following entry for the transaction:

44,050 ASC 740—Income Taxes

Building	$433,333	
Deferred Tax Asset	66,667	
Cash		$500,000

B. The same situation as in A above, but the purchase price is $250,000 and the tax basis is $1,000,000.

Use the formulas above to calculate the FBB and DTA.

FBB = ($250,000)

Because FBB is a negative amount, zero is used for FBB in the second equation.

DTA = $400,000

When recording the transaction, the difference between the deferred tax asset and the amount of cash paid to acquire the building is recognized as a deferred credit as follows:

Building	$0	
Deferred tax asset	$400,000	
Deferred credit		$150,000
Cash		$250,000

C. In this example the acquisition of a financial asset results in a deferred credit. Company X acquires the stock of Company Y for $900,000. Company Y's principal asset is a marketable equity security with a fair value of $750,000 and a tax basis of $1,250,000. The tax rate is 40%. The acquisition of Company Y's stock is accounted for as an asset acquisition, not a business combination, because Company Y has no operations.

In recording this transaction, the acquired financial asset is recognized at its fair value and the deferred tax asset is calculated based on the guidance in ASC 740. A deferred credit is recognized for the difference between the total of the fair value of the stock plus the amount of the deferred asset and the amount paid for the stock.

Marketable equity security	$750,000	
Deferred tax asset ($500,000 × .40)	200,000	
Deferred credit		$ 50,000
Cash		900,000

D. In this example, Company Z acquires future tax benefits by purchasing the net operating loss carryforwards (NOLs) of Company P, which is a shell company without operations. The shell entity is acquired for $7 million, which is substantially less than the $15 million gross amount of the deferred tax asset for the NOLs. It is more likely than not that the deferred tax asset will be realized. The tax rate is 40%.

In recording the transaction, Company Z recognizes the deferred tax asset at its gross amount and records a deferred credit for the amount by which the deferred tax asset exceeds the amount paid.

Deferred tax asset	$15,000,000	
Deferred credit		$8,000,000

Cash		7,000,000

Example 2—Purchase price exceeds tax basis

A company in a foreign jurisdiction imports a machine, which costs $25,000. Its tax basis is reduced, however, to $20,000, because the jurisdiction imposes a 20% penalty on imported goods. A deferred tax liability has to be recognized for the temporary difference related to the machine. The tax rate is 40%.

The amount of the machine's final book basis (FBB) and the deferred tax liability (DTL) are calculated by the simultaneous equations used in Example 1.

FBB − .40 × (FBB − $20,000) = $25,000

FBB = $28,333

($28,333 − $20,000) .40 = DTL

DTL = $3,333

The company recognizes the following amount:

Machine	$28,333	
Deferred tax liability		$3,333
Cash		25,000

Example 3—A transaction with a governmental taxing authority

Under the tax laws of country X, Company A decides to step up the tax basis of fixed assets with a current tax basis of $4 million to their $8 million fair value. To do so, the company must pay the government $200,000, which is 5% of the $4 million step-up. The company believes that at its 40% tax rate, it is likely that it will be able to use the additional deductions from the stepped up tax basis of certain fixed assets, which would justify the $80,000 payment.

Company A would record the tax effects of the transaction as follows:

Deferred tax asset ($4 million × .4)	$1,600,000	
Deferred income tax benefit		$1,400,000
Cash		200,000

ASC 740-10-45-21; ASC 740-20-45-11 Accounting by a Company for the Income Tax Effects of Transactions among or with Its Shareholders under ASC 740

BACKGROUND

Under U.S. tax laws, the following transactions among shareholders or between a company and its shareholders may have tax consequences.

Transactions that result in a change in expectations about the future realization of deferred tax assets

If the ownership of more than 50% of a company's stock changes within a certain time period, the company may be prohibited from using an existing net operating loss (NOL) carryforward or the amount available to offset future income may be limited. Consequently, the NOL deferred tax asset would have to be written off or a valuation allowance, which was not previously required, would have to be recognized to reduce the deferred tax asset. The following are examples of such transactions:

- An investor purchases more than 50% of the shares in the open market and consolidates the company but does not use pushdown accounting for financial reporting purposes.
- The company converts debt into equity in a troubled debt restructuring.

Transactions that result in changes in tax bases of an entity's assets or liabilities for tax purposes

- One hundred percent of a company's shares are purchased by a privately held company. The company accounts for the transaction as a purchase business combination and consolidates the subsidiary, but because it is a private company it need not push down the fair value of the assets to the subsidiary. The company, however, adjusts the bases of the subsidiary's assets and liabilities for tax purposes.
- A company merges with another company and accounts for the business combination as a pooling of interests. The entity treats the transaction as a purchase of assets for tax purposes.

This Issue does not apply to transactions among or with a subsidiary's minority shareholders or to transactions with shareholders requiring a change in a company's tax status (for example, a change from a nontaxable S corporation to a taxable C corporation).

ACCOUNTING ISSUES

- Should an entity charge changes in the *valuation allowance* as a result of transactions among or with shareholders to the income statement or directly to equity?
- Should write-offs of deferred tax assets that result from transactions among or with shareholders be charged to the income statement or directly to equity?
- Should the tax effects of changes in the *tax bases of assets (and liabilities)* that result from transactions among or with shareholders be charged (or credited) to the income statement or directly to equity?
- Should a subsequent reduction in the valuation allowance that was initially established when deferred tax assets were created from changes in the tax bases of assets and liabilities in transactions among or with shareholders be credited to income or directly to equity?

ACCOUNTING GUIDANCE

- Changes in the *valuation allowance* caused by changes in expectations about the realization of deferred tax assets that result from transactions among or with shareholders should be included in the *income statement*.
- Write-offs of preexisting deferred tax assets that will not be realized that result from a transaction with or among an entity's shareholders should be included in the *income statement*.

The net effect is the same whether a deferred tax asset is eliminated or the valuation allowance is increased to equal 100% of the related deferred tax asset.

- The tax effects of all changes in the *tax bases of assets and liabilities* that result from transactions among or with shareholders should be included *in equity*. Also included in equity is the effect of a valuation allowance initially required on the recognition of deferred tax assets because of changes in the tax bases of assets and liabilities from transactions with or among shareholders.

- Changes in the valuation allowance initially required on the recognition of deferred tax assets that result from changes in the tax bases of assets and liabilities because of transactions with or among shareholders should be included in the *income statement* in subsequent periods.

DISCUSSION

This guidance was develop in response to requests for a framework that could be used to categorize the tax effects of transactions among shareholders and between a company and its shareholders in a consistent manner.

- Proponents of recognizing changes in the valuation allowance as a result of an entity's transactions with shareholders or among shareholders in the income statement argued that the model for intraperiod tax allocation in ASC 740 generally requires allocating the tax expense or benefit to income from continuing operations, unless the incremental portion of the tax expense or benefit is not directly related to continuing operations. Because there is no pretax charge or credit to equity for transactions among shareholders, the tax expense or benefit would not be allocated to equity under ASC 740. Further, they argued that changes in the valuation allowance as a result of an entity's transactions with shareholders are only indirectly related to the equity transaction, such as an initial public stock offering. The effects of the change should, therefore, also be included in the income statement.

- Proponents of this view believed that the treatment of a write-off of a deferred tax asset should be the same as that for an increase in the valuation allowance in Issue 1, because the end result is the same. In both cases, the company expects that a deferred tax asset will not be realized because of a transaction with or among shareholders.

- The rationale for charging equity with the tax effects of changes to the tax bases of assets and liabilities as a result of transactions with or among shareholders is that such transactions are similar to a taxable business combination accounted for as a pooling of interests, which is discussed in ASC 740-10-25-3, 25-18. It provides that the deferred tax consequences of temporary differences resulting from an increase in the tax basis of assets in the transaction be recognized in equity. Proponents of this view believe that a taxable pooling does not differ from other transactions among shareholders that result in a change in the tax bases of assets and liabilities.

- Proponents of this view also refer to ASC 740-10-25-3, 25-18, which requires that tax benefits resulting from increases in the tax bases of assets after the date of a taxable business combination should be recognized in the income statement.

ASC 740-10-45-18, 25-47 Adjustment Due to Effect of a Change in Tax Laws or Rates

Questions received by the FASB staff on proposed changes in tax rates, which were eventually enacted on August 10, 1993, retroactive to January 1, 1993 were addressed. The questions dealt with when such a change should be recognized, especially when a company is adopting a new accounting standard at the same time. In addition to referring to the requirements of ASC 740-10-35-4, the FASB staff stated that the effect of a change in tax rates should be recognized on the date it is enacted. Thus, if a company adopts a new accounting standard before the date of enactment, the cumulative effect of adopting that standard would not include the change in tax rates, which would be recognized in income from continuing operations in the period of enactment, even if the change in tax rates is retroactive to the date on which a new standard was adopted.

ASC 740-10-55-26, 55-140 through 55-144, 15-4, 05-5 Application of ASC 740 to a State Tax Based on the Greater of a Franchise Tax or an Income Tax

BACKGROUND

The state of Texas revised its corporate franchise tax in August 1991 to include a tax on income apportioned to Texas. The tax is based on federal taxable income and became effective January 1, 1992. The corporate tax is computed as follows:

- 0.25% of net taxable capital at the beginning of the year, *or*
- 4.5% of net earned surplus (a term used in the Texas tax code to refer to federal taxable income apportioned to Texas), whichever is greater.

ACCOUNTING ISSUE

What portion of the tax is based on income, and how should deferred taxes be calculated under ASC 740?

ACCOUNTING GUIDANCE

- The amount of computed Texas tax that exceeds the tax based on capital in a given year is considered an income tax. Under ASC 740, recognize a deferred tax liability for temporary differences that will reverse in future years in which annual taxable income is expected to be more than 5.5% (.25% of net taxable capital divided by 4.5% of taxable income) of expected net taxable capital. Companies this guidance should refer to ASC 740-10-55-138 for guidance on whether it is necessary to prepare a detailed analysis of the net reversals of temporary differences in each future year.
- Adjust the balance of a deferred tax liability or asset in the period of enactment for the effect of a change in tax law, and include the effect in income from continuing operations in that period. In this case, an adjustment was required in the first reporting period that included August 1991.

- Accrue the portion of the current tax liability that is based on income and charge to income in the period in which income is earned. Recognize the portion of the deferred tax liability that is related to temporary differences as of the balance sheet date for temporary differences existing as of that balance sheet date. The deferred tax liability or asset should be adjusted for the effect of changes in tax laws in the period in which the change is enacted with the effect included in income from continuing operations.

The Task Force's discussion implied that the recommended accounting would apply to other states with the same state tax structures.

DISCUSSION

Because it was unclear as to which portion of the tax under the Texas statute was based on income, the following approach was considered and supported: The portion related to income is equal to 4.5% of income that exceeds 5.5% (.05555) of capital (.0025/.045 = .05555). Deferred income taxes are calculated only on the excess.

This approach was supported, because it was similar to the approach used in AICPA Accounting Interpretation 24 of APB-11, which was issued in 1972 to address an Ohio corporate tax law that was based on capital and income, and that was similar to the Texas law. The Interpretation considered the portion of the tax related to income to be an additional tax, which should be accrued in the year the income was earned. Under this approach, deferred taxes should be recognized only on the amount that the tax on income exceeds the tax on capital.

The following illustration demonstrates how to apply the consensus under which only a portion of the state tax is considered an income tax and deferred taxes are recognized only for temporary differences that will reverse in future years in which net taxable income will exceed net taxable capital. To determine whether a deferred tax liability should be established, it is necessary to estimate net taxable capital and net taxable income in future years based on a consideration of enacted tax rates and future transactions.

Illustration of the Calculation of Texas State Tax and Deferred Tax Liability

- Company A is a Texas corporation whose business is conducted only in Texas.
- The company's net taxable income in 20X5 is $75,000, and net taxable income is expected to be $100,000 and $50,000 in 20X6 and 20X7, respectively.
- Company A has taxable temporary differences of $100,000 in 20X5 that are expected to reverse as follows: $75,000 in 20X6 and $25,000 in 20X7.
- Net taxable capital is $1,075,000 in 20X5 and is estimated to be $1,171,625 in 20X6 and $1,217,125 in 20X7.
- The following computation of the deferred tax liability for state franchise taxes at the end of 20X5 ignores the effects of federal income taxes.

State Franchise Tax—20X5

Tax based on net taxable capital (.0025 × $1,075,000)	= $2,687
Tax based on net taxable income (.045 × $75,000)	= $3,375

In 20X5, Company A's state franchise tax of $3,375 is based on net taxable income. Based on the consensus, that tax consists of the following components:

Tax related to net taxable capital (.0025 × $1,075,000)	$2,687
Tax related to net taxable income [$75,000 − (.05555 × $1,075,000) = .045 × $15,283]	688*
Total tax	$3,375

* If the franchise tax payable is based on net taxable income, a simpler method of determining the amount related to income is to calculate the difference between the tax based on net taxable capital and the tax based on net taxable income.

Income tax expense in 20×5 is $688, the amount related to net taxable income.

Estimated State Franchise Tax—20×6

Tax based on net taxable capital (.0025 × $1,171,625)	= $2,929
Tax based on net taxable income (.045 × $100,000)	= $4,500

The deferred tax liability on the $75,000 taxable temporary difference expected to reverse in 20X6 would be (.045 × $75,000) $3,375, but based on the consensus, the amount is limited to $1,571, the excess of net taxable income over net taxable capital ($4,500 X $2,929).

Estimated State Franchise Tax—20X7

Tax based on net taxable capital (.0025 × $1,217,125)	= $3,043
Tax based on net taxable income (.045 × $50,000)	= $2,250

No deferred tax liability is recognized for the $50,000 of temporary tax differences expected to reverse in 20X7, because the tax based on net taxable capital exceeds the tax based on net taxable income.

ASC 740-10-55-27 through 55-30, 55-146 through 55-148 Application of ASC 740 to the Tax Deduction on Qualified Production Activities Provided by the American Jobs Creation Act of 2004

BACKGROUND

Under the American Jobs Creation Act (the Job Act), which was signed into law on October 22, 2004, employers will be able to deduct up to 9% of (1) income from qualified production activities, as defined in the Job Act or (2) taxable income after the deduction for net operating loss carryforwards, if any, whichever is less. Up to 50% of W-2 wages paid by an employer qualify for the deduction. The FASB directed the FASB staff to provide guidance on the application of ASC 740 in accounting for this deduction.

QUESTION

Should the tax deduction related to income from qualified production activities be accounted for under ASC 740 as a special deduction or as a tax-rate reduction?

ACCOUNTING GUIDANCE

The FASB staff believes that the characteristics of the Job Act's deduction for qualified production activities are similar to the special deductions illustrated in ASC 740-10-25-37 because this deduction depends on the performance of specific activities and the level of wages in the future. Consequently, the deduction under the Job Act should be accounted for as a special deduction under the provisions of ASC 740. The FASB staff also noted that an entity should take this special deduction into account in (1) measuring deferred taxes if graduated taxes are a significant factor and (2) determining whether a valuation allowance is required in accordance with ASC 740-10-25-37.

ASC 740-10-55-50, 25-31 Temporary Differences Related to LIFO Inventory and Tax-to-Tax Differences

The following responses to inquiries related to LIFO temporary differences were discussed:

- A deferred tax liability should be recognized in accordance with FAS-109 for LIFO inventory temporary differences resulting from excess financial reporting basis over tax basis.
- A deferred tax liability should be recognized for LIFO inventory belonging to a parent company or its subsidiary even if that temporary difference is not "settled" because the subsidiary will be sold before that difference reverses.

Paragraph 72 of FAS-96 required recognition of a tax benefit for the difference between (1) the tax basis of a parent company in an acquired company's stock and (2) the acquired company tax basis of its net assets. Such differences are referred to as *tax-to-tax* differences. Although that requirement was eliminated in ASC 740, the FASB staff was asked whether recognition of a deferred tax asset for a tax-to-tax difference is *permitted*. The staff responded that under ASC 740, deferred tax assets may be recognized *only* for deductible temporary differences and carryforwards, which are book-tax differences.

ASC 740-10-55-51 Income Tax Consequences of Issuing Convertible Debt with a Beneficial Conversion Feature

OVERVIEW

Under the guidance in ASC 470-20, nondetachable conversion features of convertible securities are not accounted for separately. However, under previous guidance, a nondetachable conversion feature of a convertible debt security that is "in-the-money" should be accounted separately, because it is considered a beneficial conversion feature that is recognized and measured separately by allocating a portion of the proceeds equal to the intrinsic value of the conversion feature to additional paid-in capital. At the commitment date, as defined in EITF Issue 00-27, the intrinsic value of the beneficial conversion feature is calculated as the difference between the conversion price and the fair value of the common stock or other securities into which the security can be converted multiplied by the number of shares into which the security can be converted. A convertible security is recognized at par if no discount or premium is associated with it at issuance and a discount is recognized for the amount allocated to additional paid-in capital. A convertible instrument's debt discount should be accreted from the instrument's issuance date to a stated redemption date or through the earliest conversion date if the instrument does not have a stated redemption date as discussed in EITF Issue 00-27. Under the U.S. Federal Income Tax Code, a convertible debt security's tax basis equals the total proceeds received when the debt is issued.

ACCOUNTING ISSUES

1. Does the issuance of convertible debt with a beneficial conversion feature result in a basis difference when applying the guidance in ASC 740?

2. If issuance of convertible debt with a beneficial conversion feature results in a basis difference, is that difference a temporary difference under the guidance in ASC 740?

3. If issuance of convertible debt with a beneficial conversion feature results in a temporary difference under the guidance in ASC 740, should a deferred tax liability for the temporary difference of the convertible debt be recognized as an adjustment to additional paid-in capital or by recognizing a deferred charge by analogy to the accounting model in Example 4 of Issue 98-11 (Accounting for Acquired Temporary Differences in Certain Purchase Transactions That Are Not Accounted for as Business Combinations)?

EITF CONSENSUS

1. Convertible debt issued with a beneficial conversion feature results in a basis difference when the guidance in ASC 740 is applied. By recognizing a beneficial conversion feature, two separate instruments, a debt instrument and an equity instrument, are created for financial reporting purposes and are accounted for as a single debt instrument under the Federal Income Tax Code. As a result, the debt instrument's book basis and tax basis differ.

2. The basis difference resulting from the issuance of convertible debt with a beneficial conversion feature should be treated as a temporary difference under the guidance in ASC 740 This guidance is consistent with the definition of a temporary difference in ASC 740d because the amount recognized as a liability for the difference between the book basis and the tax basis of debt with a beneficial conversion feature becomes taxable when the liability's reported amount is settled.

3. Deferred taxes recognized for a temporary difference of debt with a beneficial conversion feature should be recognized as an adjustment of additional paid-in capital. The EITF noted that because additional paid-in capital was adjusted for the basis difference created when the beneficial conversion feature of the convertible debt was recognized, additional paid-in capital should be adjusted when the deferred tax liability caused by the basis difference is established in accordance with the guidance in ASC 740-20-45-11 that requires an adjustment to be made to "the related components of shareholders' equity."

ASC 740-10-55-53, 25-31 Intraperiod Tax Allocation of the Tax Effect of Pretax Income from Continuing Operations

In response to several inquiries about *intraperiod* tax allocation, the FASB staff stated at the July 1993 EITF meeting that ASC 740 generally requires determining the tax effect of pretax *income* from continuing operations without considering the tax effect of items not included in continuing operations. For example, an entity has income from continuing operations of $1,000 and a loss from discontinued operations of $1,000 in the current year. The entity also has a $2,000 net operating loss carryforward from a previous year. The deferred tax asset is zero, because it is offset by a valuation allowance that has not been reduced during the year. According to the FASB staff, tax expense from continuing operations should be offset by the loss carryforward with no tax benefit allocated to the loss from discontinued operations.

The staff noted, however, that the guidance in ASC 740-20-45-7 is an exception to the Statement's approach to intraperiod tax allocation. Under the approach discussed in that paragraph, items not included in income from continuing operations in the current year are considered, nevertheless, in calculating the amount of tax benefit that results from a *loss* from continuing operations and that should be allocated to continuing operations. The Board made that exception for consistency with the Statement's approach, under which the tax consequences of future taxable income are considered in evaluating whether deferred tax assets are realizable.

ASC 740-10-55-69, 55-70, 55-71 Classification of Payment Made to IRS to Retain Fiscal Year

BACKGROUND

The Revenue Act of 1987 changed the requirements of the Tax Reform Act of 1986 by permitting partnerships and S corporations to elect to either retain their fiscal year or adopt a calendar year for tax purposes. If an entity elects to retain its fiscal year, it is required to make one annual deposit that approximates the income tax the partners would have paid on the short-period income tax return had the entity adopted a calendar year.

The election and the deposit are made by the partnership or S Corporation rather than by the partners. The deposit is adjusted annually based on the entity's income in the previous year so the entity either makes a payment to the IRS or receives a refund.

ACCOUNTING ISSUE

Should an entity report the annual payment in the financial statements as a period expense, an asset in the form of a deposit, or as a debit to partners' equity?

ACCOUNTING GUIDANCE

The payment should be reported as an asset.

DISCUSSION

44,060 ASC 740—Income Taxes

The authoritative literature provides no specific guidance for the resolution of this issue, except for the definition and discussion of the characteristics of assets and expenses in CON-5 (Recognition and Measurement in Financial Statements of Business Enterprises) (not in ASC) and CON-6 (Elements of Financial Statements—A Replacement of FASB Concepts Statement No. 3) (not in ASC).

To support their view that the payment should not be reported as a debit to the partners' equity accounts, proponents argued that the payment was made on behalf of the entity so it could retain the fiscal year for tax purposes. In addition, the IRS does not associate the individual partners with the payment, which is not offset against their actual individual tax liabilities. The argument for recognizing the payment as an asset rather than as a current expense was based on the view that it will not be realized by the entity currently but only if the entity is liquidated, its income declines to zero, or it converts to a calendar year-end.

ASC 740-10-55-73 through 55-74, 15-4 Accounting for Tax Effects of Dividends in France in Accordance with ASC 740

BACKGROUND

To eliminate double taxation on dividends at the shareholder level, French shareholders who receive dividends from French corporations automatically receive a tax credit for taxes paid by the corporation under that country's integrated tax system. To achieve such integration, when a French corporation distributes dividends to its shareholders, it is required to pay a tax known as *precompte mobilier* (precompte), which is equal to the tax credit available to shareholders (50% of the dividend received) but is limited to the difference between the tax calculated by applying the regular corporate tax rate (currently, 33%) to the dividend declared and taxes already paid by the corporation on the income distributed to shareholders. However, taxes previously paid on income retained for five years or longer are not considered in this calculation. An example of a precompte calculation is as follows:

	Income Distributed within Five Years		Income Distributed after Five Years	
Corporate Taxation When Income Is Earned				
Taxable income		€600,000	Taxable income	€600,000
Corporate tax		(200,000)	Corporate tax	(200,000)
Available for dividends		€400,000	Available for dividends	€400,000
Corporate Taxation When Income Is Distributed				
Earnings to be distributed		€400,000	Earnings to be distributed	€400,000
Precompte*		0	Precompte*	(133,000)
Amount distributed		€400,000	Amount distributed	€267,000
Shareholder Taxation				
Cash dividend		€400,000	Cash dividend	€267,000
Imputed amount for corporate tax paid (50% of dividend)		200,000	Imputed amount for corporate tax paid (50% of dividend)	133,000
Taxable income		€600,000	Taxable income	€400,000
Shareholder tax rate**		60%	Shareholder tax rate**	60%
Tax liability before credit		360,000	Tax liability before credit	240,000

Income Distributed within Five Years		Income Distributed after Five Years	
Tax credit (50% of dividend)	(200,000)	Tax credit (50% of dividend)	(133,000)
Tax payable by shareholder	160,000	Tax payable by shareholder	107,000
Net dividend to shareholder		Net dividend to shareholder	
(€ 400,000 − € 160,000)	€ 240,000	(€ 267,000 − € 107,000)	€ 160,000

* Precompte paid by the corporation on distribution equals the regular corporate tax rate applicable to the amount distributed (€ € 400,000 × .33) less corporate taxes previously paid on that amount. The credit for previously paid corporate taxes is unavailable if earnings are not distributed within five years. The precompte is equal to zero in this example, because earnings are distributed within five years and the corporate rate on distributions is the same as the regular corporate tax previously paid on earnings.

** A 60% shareholder tax rate is assumed.

ACCOUNTING ISSUE

Should a distributing corporation record a tax assessed on dividends distributed to shareholders, such as the French precompte tax, as (*a*) an income tax recorded as tax expense or (*b*) a withholding tax for shareholders receiving dividends that would be recorded in equity and included in dividends paid?

EITF CONSENSUS

The EITF reached a consensus that a tax such as precompte is a withholding tax that should be included with the dividend and recorded in equity in the corporation's *separate* financial statements if both of the following conditions are met:

- The corporation is required to pay the tax only if a dividend is distributed to shareholders and the corporation's future income taxes are not reduced by that tax.

- Recipients of dividends receive (*a*) a credit for at least the amount of corporate taxes paid on amounts distributed that can be used to reduce taxes due, regardless of the recipient's tax status, or (*b*) a refund (if the shareholder's marginal tax rate is less than 33% or a foreign shareholder with ownership in excess of 5%-15% is from a country having a tax treaty with France).

DISCUSSION

The guidance is based on the arguments that the precompte is considered a withholding tax under the French tax system and that a corporation incurs this tax only when it distributes earnings. Although the precompte is equal to the tax credit available to shareholders to avoid double taxation, which is 50% of the dividend received, it cannot exceed the difference between the regular tax on the dividend paid and the amount previously paid by the corporation on that income. Thus, if a corporation is taxed at less than the 33% rate, the tax credit received by shareholders would be overstated. Through the precompte, the excess is withheld at the source, rather than by reducing the tax payer's credit. That approach treats all dividends in the same manner and is more convenient administratively. Another argument to support the view that the precompte is a withholding tax is that shareholders can receive a refund on overpayments of the tax.

This treatment would only be appropriate in the freestanding financial statements of a French company. In consolidation, the withholding tax could not be charged to equity, but would be recognized as an expense and charged to the subsidiary's retained earnings.

ASC 740-30: Other Considerations or Special Areas

ASC 740-30-25-10 Recognition of Deferred Tax Assets for a Parent Company's Excess Tax Basis in the Stock of a Subsidiary That Is Accounted for as a Discontinued Operation

OVERVIEW

A company decides to sell a subsidiary, which can be accounted for and reported as a discontinued operation. It is expected that the subsidiary's operations will break even between the date the company decides to dispose of the subsidiary (the measurement date) and the disposal date, and the company expects no pretax gain or loss on the disposal. Because the company's tax basis in the subsidiary's stock exceeds its basis in the subsidiary for financial reporting, the decision to sell the subsidiary makes it more likely than not that the deductible temporary difference will reverse in the near future and the company will realize the deferred tax asset.

ACCOUNTING ISSUE

Should the company recognize a deferred tax asset at the measurement date in accordance with the guidance in ASC 740-30-25-9?

ACCOUNTING GUIDANCE

A tax benefit should be recognized for the excess of the entity's outside tax basis over its financial reporting basis in the subsidiary in accordance with the guidance in ASC 740-30-25-9, when it becomes apparent that the temporary difference will reverse in the foreseeable future. this criterion should also be applied to situations in which the financial reporting basis exceeds the company's outside tax basis in its investment in the subsidiary by recognizing a deferred tax liability.

ASC 740-270: Interim Reporting

ASC 740-270-55-51 Accounting in Interim Periods for Changes in Income Tax Rates

BACKGROUND

Federal tax rates may change, raising questions about how a company with a fiscal year other than the calendar year should account for the change in interim periods.

STANDARDS

Question: How should a company with a fiscal year other than a calendar year account during interim periods for the reduction in the corporate tax rate resulting from the Revenue Act of 1978?

Answer: Under the guidance in ASC 740-270-55-50, the effects of a change in tax rate should be considered in a revised annual effective tax rate calculation in the same way that the change will be applied to the company's taxable income for the year. The revised annual tax rate would then be applied to pretax income for the year-to-date at the end of the current interim period.

CHAPTER 45
ASC 805—BUSINESS COMBINATIONS

CONTENTS

Part I: General Guidance	
ASC 805-10: Overall	45,002
Overview	45,002
Background	45,003
The Acquisition Method of Accounting for Business Combinations	45,003
Scope	45,003
The Acquisition Method	45,004
Identifying the Acquirer	45,004
Determining the Acquisition Date	45,004
Additional Guidance for Applying the Acquisition Method to Particular Types of Business Combinations	45,004
Measurement Period	45,005
Determining What Is Part of the Business Combination Transaction	45,006
Tax Issues Related to Business Combinations	45,006
Financial Statement Disclosures	45,007
General Information	45,007
Transactions Recognized Separately from the Business Combination	45,007
Special Disclosures for Public Companies	45,008
ASC 805-20: Identifiable Assets and Liabilities, and Any Noncontrolling Interest	45,008
Recognizing and Measuring the Identifiable Assets Acquired, the Liabilities Assumed, and Any Noncontrolling Interests in the Acquiree	45,008
Recognition Principle	45,008
Measurement Principle	45,009
Exception to the Recognition Principle	45,009
Exception to Both the Recognition and Measurement Principles	45,010
Exception to the Measurement Principle	45,010
Subsequent Measurement and Accounting	45,010
Reacquired Rights	45,011
Assets and Liabilities Arising from Contingencies	45,011
Indemnification Assets	45,011
Contingent Consideration	45,011
Financial Statement Disclosures Related to Contingencies	45,011
ASC 805-30: Goodwill or Gain from Bargain Purchase, Including Consideration Transferred	45,012
Recognizing and Measuring Goodwill or a Gain from a Bargain Purchase	45,012
Goodwill	45,012
Gain from a Bargain Purchase	45,012
Consideration Transferred	45,013
Financial Statement Disclosures Related to Goodwill	45,014

45,002 ASC 805—Business Combinations

Acquisition Method: Implementation Guidance	45,014
Types of Business Combinations	45,014
Asset Acquisition	45,014
Illustration of Asset Acquisition	45,014
Stock Acquisition	45,016
Illustration of Stock Acquisition	45,017
Disclosure of Certain Loss Contingencies	45,019
ASC 805-40 Reverse Acquisitions	45,019
Measuring Consideration	45,019
Non-Controlling Interest	45,019
Other Presentation Matters	45,019
ASC 805-50 Related Issues	45,020
Acquisition of Assets Rather than a Business	45,020
Transactions Between Entities under Common Control	45,020
New Basis of Accounting (Pushdown)	45,021
Important Notice for 2012	45,021
Part II: Interpretive Guidance	
ASC 805-10: Overall	45,022
ASC 805-10-35-1, 20-25-15A, 25-18A, 25-19 through 20B, 30-9 through 30-9A, 30-23, 35-3 through 35-4A, 50-1; ASC 805-30-35-1A	
Accounting for Assets Acquired and Liabilities Assumed in a Business Combination That Arise from Contingencies	45,022
ASC 805-10-50-2, 50-8 through 50-9, 55-49 through 50-50	
Disclosure of Supplementary Pro Forma Information for Business Combinations	45,024
ASC 805-20: Identifiable Assets and Liabilities, and Any Noncontrolling Interest	45,026
ASC 805-20-S30-1, S35-1, S99-3	
Use of the Residual Method to Value Acquired Assets Other Than Goodwill	45,026
ASC 805-50: Related Issues	45,027
ASC 805-50-05-7, 15-8,; 30-7 through 30-9 S30-2, S99-3	
Change of Accounting Basis in Master Limited Partnership Transactions	45,027
ASC 805-50-05-8, 15-8 through 15-9, 25-3, 25-13	
IRC Section 338 and Push-Down Accounting	45,028
ASC 805-50-S30-3, S99-4	
Changes of Ownership Resulting in a New Basis of Accounting	45,029
ASC 805-50-S55-1, S99-2	
Push Down Accounting	45,030

PART I: GENERAL GUIDANCE

ASC 805-10: OVERALL

OVERVIEW

A business combination occurs when two or more entities combine to form a single entity. An *asset combination* results when one company acquires the assets of one or more other companies, or when a new company is formed to acquire the assets of two or more existing companies. In an asset combination, the target companies cease to exist as operating entities and may be liquidated or become investment companies. An *acquisition of stock combination* occurs when one company acquires more than 50% of the outstanding voting common stock of one or more target companies, or when a new company is formed to acquire controlling interest in the outstanding voting common stock of two or more target companies.

In an acquisition method combination, the acquirer is required to measure the identifiable assets acquired, the liabilities assumed, and any noncontrolling interests in the acquiree at their acquisition-date fair values. Any excess of the fair value of the consideration given over the fair value of the net assets acquired is reported as goodwill. If the fair value of the consideration given is less than the fair market value of the net assets acquired, the resulting excess of fair value of acquired net assets over the cost of the acquired entity is recognized in earnings as a gain on the acquisition date. The operating statements for acquisition method combinations report combined results only for the period subsequent to the combination.

BACKGROUND

Business combinations are accounted for using the acquisition method of accounting. While the primary source of authoritative guidance on business combinations is ASC 805, other pronouncements also address issues related to business combinations. For example:

- ASC 740 (Income Taxes) requires that a liability or asset be recognized for the deferred tax consequences of differences between the assigned values and the tax bases of the assets and liabilities (other than nondeductible goodwill and leveraged leases) recognized in a purchase business combination.

- ASC 715 (Compensation—Retirement Benefits) requires that assets and liabilities recorded under the acquisition method include an asset or a liability representing the funded status of the plan.

THE ACQUISITION METHOD OF ACCOUNTING FOR BUSINESS COMBINATIONS

Scope

ASC 805 applies to any transaction or event in which an acquirer obtains control of one or more businesses. This includes combinations that are achieved without any consideration being transferred as well as to combinations involving mutual entities. ASC 805 does not apply to (ASC 805-10-15-4):

- The formation of a joint venture.
- The acquisition of an asset or a group of assets that does not constitute a business.
- A combination between entities or businesses under common control.

- A combination between not-for-profit organizations or the acquisition of a for-profit business by a not-for-profit organization.

The Acquisition Method

All business combinations subject to the requirements of ASC 805 are to be accounted for by the acquisition method. Application of the acquisition method requires the following (ASC 805-10-05-4)):

- Identifying the acquirer
- Determining the acquisition date
- Recognizing and measuring the identifiable assets acquired, the liabilities assumed, and any noncontrolling interests in the acquiree (discussed in ASC 805-20)
- Recognizing and measuring goodwill or a gain from a bargain purchase (discussed in ASC 805-30).

Identifying the Acquirer

ASC 805 defines the acquirer as the entity that obtains control of one or more businesses in the business combination.

ASC 805 also provides additional guidance for identifying the acquirer in a business combination in which a variable interest entity is acquired. The acquirer is always the primary beneficiary of the variable interest entity (ASC 805-10-25-5).

Determining the Acquisition Date

The acquirer must identify the acquisition date as the date on which it obtains control of the acquiree (ASC 805-10-25-6). This is usually the date on which the acquirer legally transfers the consideration for the combination, although in certain instances the acquirer may obtain control on an earlier or later date (ASC 805-10-25-7)).

Additional Guidance for Applying the Acquisition Method to Particular Types of Business Combinations

A Business Combination Achieved in Stages An acquirer may obtain control over another business in which it already owns a noncontrolling equity interest. ASC 805 refers to this as a *business combination achieved in stages*, but also as a step acquisition. In these cases, the acquirer must remeasure its previously held equity interest in the acquiree to reflect its acquisition-date fair value, with any resulting gain or loss recognized in earnings. The acquirer must also reclassify any changes in the value of its equity interest in the acquiree that it had recognized in previous reporting periods in other comprehensive income and include that amount in the calculation of gain or loss as of the acquisition date (ASC 805-10-25-10).

A Business Combination Achieved without a Transfer of Consideration As a result of the broader scope of ASC 805, the acquisition method of accounting for business combinations applies to those combinations that are achieved without a transfer of consideration by the acquirer. Examples of such combinations include (ASC 805-10-25-11):

 a. The acquiree repurchases a sufficient number of its own shares for an existing investor (the acquirer) to obtain control.
 b. Noncontrolling veto rights lapse that previously kept the acquirer from controlling an acquiree in which the acquirer held a majority voting interest.
 c. The acquirer and acquiree agree to combine their businesses by contract alone

Measurement Period

In some business combinations, the end of the reporting period occurs before the acquirer can complete the initial accounting for the combination. In these cases, the acquirer must report provisional amounts in its financial statements for those items for which the accounting is incomplete. ASC 805 provides a measurement period that allows the acquirer to obtain additional information that is needed to complete the accounting for the combination. This includes the information necessary to identify and measure the following as of the acquisition date (ASC 805-10-25-15):

 a. The identifiable assets acquired, liabilities assumed, and any noncontrolling interests in the acquiree
 b. The consideration transferred for the acquiree
 c. In a business combination achieved in stages, the equity interest in the acquiree previously held by the acquirer
 d. The resulting goodwill recognized for the business combination or the gain recognized on a bargain purchase.

If during the measurement period the acquirer obtains new information about facts and circumstances that existed at the acquisition date that, if known, would have affected the measurement of amounts recognized as of that date, the acquire must retrospectively adjust the provisional amounts that were recognized at the acquisition date. Further, the acquirer must recognize additional assets or liabilities if it obtains new information about facts or circumstances that existed as of the acquisition date and that, if known, would have resulted in the recognition of those assets and liabilities as of that date. The measurement period must not exceed one year and will end as soon as the acquirer receives the information it was seeking or learns that additional information is not obtainable (ASC 805-10-25-13, 14).

Measurement period adjustments are not included in earnings, but rather are recognized as an offset to goodwill. For example, if an acquirer recognizes an increase in the provisional amount recognized for an identifiable asset, there must be a corresponding decrease in goodwill. Adjustments made by the acquirer during the measurement period must be recognized as if the accounting for the business combination had been completed at the acquisition date. Thus, the acquirer must revise comparative information for prior periods in the financial statements as needed. After the measurement period ends, the accounting for a business combination shall only be revised by the acquirer to correct an error in accordance with the guidance on accounting changes (ASC 805-10-25-16, 17, 19).

Determining What Is Part of the Business Combination Transaction

In some cases, the acquirer and the acquiree may have preexisting or additional business arrangements that must be separated from the business combination. When applying the acquisition method to account for a business combination, the acquirer must recognize only the consideration transferred for the acquiree and the assets acquired and liabilities assumed in the exchange for the acquiree. All separate transactions must be accounted for in accordance with the relevant GAAP.

Transactions entered into before the business combination by the acquirer or primarily for the benefit of the acquirer or the combined entity, rather than primarily for the benefit of the acquiree, are likely to be separate transactions and not part of the business combination transaction. The following are examples of separate transactions that shall not be included as part of the business combination (ASC 805-10-25-21):

   a. A transaction that in effect settles preexisting relationships between the acquirer and acquiree
   b. A transaction that compensates employees or former owners of the acquiree for future services
   c. A transaction that reimburses the acquiree or its former owners for paying the acquirer's acquisition-related costs.

ASC 805 requires the acquirer to recognize acquisition-related costs as expenses in the periods in which the costs are incurred and the services are received. The costs to issue debt and equity securities are to be recognized in accordance with other relevant GAAP (ASC 805-10-25-23).

Tax Issues Related to Business Combinations

A deferred tax asset or liability is recognized as of the acquisition date for an acquired entity's taxable or deductible temporary differences or operating loss or tax credit carryforwards. Taxable or deductible temporary differences occur when there are differences between the tax bases and the recognized values of assets acquired and liabilities assumed in a business combination. The acquirer must assess the need for a valuation allowance related to any acquired deferred tax asset (ASC 805-740-25-3).

A change in a valuation allowance for an acquired entity's deferred tax asset that occurs during the measurement period and results from new information about fact and circumstances that existed at the acquisition date shall be recognized with a corresponding reduction to goodwill. Once goodwill is reduced to zero, any additional change in the valuation allowance shall be recognized as a bargain purchase. All other changes to the valuation allowance shall be reported as a reduction or increase to income tax expense (ASC 805-740-45-2).

Financial Statement Disclosures

General Information

The acquirer shall disclose the following information for each business combination that transpires during the current reporting period (ASC 805-10-50-2):

- The name and a description of the acquiree
- The acquisition date
- The percentage of voting stock acquired
- The primary reasons for the acquisition
- A description of how the acquirer obtained control of the acquiree
- The acquisition-date fair value of the total consideration transferred and of each class of consideration transferred (e.g., cash, equity interests, liabilities incurred)
- The amounts recognized as of the acquisition date for each major class of assets acquired and liabilities assumed
- The fair value of any noncontrolling interests in the acquiree at the acquisition date, including a description of how the fair value of the noncontrolling interests was measured
- For acquired receivables not subject to the requirements of ASC 310-30:
  — The fair value of the receivables
  — The gross contractual amounts receivable
  — The best estimate at the acquisition date of the expected uncollectible amount of the receivables
- In a bargain purchase:
  — The amount of gain recognized and the line item in the income statement in which the gain is recognized
  — A description of the reasons why the transaction resulted in a gain
- In a business combination achieved in stages:
  — The acquisition-date fair value of the equity interest in the acquiree held by the acquirer immediately before the acquisition date
  — The amount of gain or loss recognized as a result of remeasuring to fair value the equity interest in the acquiree held by the acquirer before the business combination, and the line item in the income statement in which that gain or loss is recognized

Transactions Recognized Separately from the Business Combination

The acquirer shall disclose the following information regarding transactions that are not part of the exchange for the acquiree, but rather are accounted for separately from the business combination (ASC 805-10-50-2):

- A description of each transaction
- How the acquirer accounted for each transaction

- The amounts recognized for each transaction and the line item in the financial statements in which each amount is recognized
- The method used to determine the settlement amount when the transaction is the effective settlement of a preexisting relationship
- The amount of acquisition-related costs, including the amount recognized as an expense and the line item(s) in the income statement in which those expenses are recognized
- The amount of issuance costs that are not recognized as an expense and a description of how they are recognized

Special Disclosures for Public Companies

If the acquirer is a public company, it shall disclose the following information (ASC 805-10-50-2):

- The amounts of revenue and earnings of the acquiree since the acquisition date included in the consolidated income statement for the reporting period
- If comparative financial statements are not presented, the revenue and earnings of the combined entity for the current reporting period as though the acquisition date for all business combinations that occurred during the year had been as of the beginning of the annual reporting period (supplemental pro forma information)
- If comparative financial statements are presented, the revenue and earnings of the combined entity as though the business combination(s) that occurred during the current year had occurred as of the beginning of the comparable prior annual reporting period (supplemental pro forma information)
- The nature and amount of any material, nonrecurring pro forma adjustments directly attributable to the business combination(s) included in the reported pro forma revenue and earnings (supplemental pro forma information)

ASC 805-20: IDENTIFIABLE ASSETS AND LIABILITIES, AND ANY NONCONTROLLING INTEREST

Recognizing and Measuring the Identifiable Assets Acquired, the Liabilities Assumed, and Any Noncontrolling Interests in the Acquiree

Recognition Principle

The acquirer must recognize, as of the acquisition date, the identifiable assets acquired, the liabilities assumed, and any noncontrolling interests in the acquiree separately from goodwill (ASC 805-20-25-1). To be recognized under the acquisition method, the assets acquired and liabilities assumed must meet the definitions of assets and liabilities in FASB Concepts Statement No. 6 (Elements of Financial Statements), at the acquisition date. For example, expected future costs for which the acquirer is not obligated at the acquisition date, such as relocation of acquiree's employees, are not liabilities at the acquisition date and, therefore, are not recognized when applying the acquisition method (ASC 805-20-25-2).

In some cases, the appropriate accounting treatment for a particular asset or liability depends on how the asset or liability has been classified or designated by the entity. ASC 805 requires the acquirer, at the acquisition date, to classify or designate the identifiable assets acquired and liabilities assumed as necessary to permit the subsequent application of other relevant GAAP. Some examples of these classifications and designations include (ASC 805-20-25-7):

- Classification of particular investments in securities as trading, available for sale, or held to maturity in accordance with ASC 320 (Investments—Debt and Equity Securities).

- Designation of a derivative instrument as a hedging instrument in accordance with ASC 815 (Derivatives and Hedging).

- Assessment of whether an embedded derivative is required to be separated from the host contract in accordance with ASC 815.

Measurement Principle

The acquirer is required to measure the identifiable assets acquired, the liabilities assumed, and any noncontrolling interests in the acquiree at their acquisition-date fair values (ASC 805-20-30-1). The acquirer will not recognize a separate valuation allowance for an asset that has related uncertainty regarding cash flows, because the effects of the cash flow uncertainty are included in the fair value measure (ASC 805-20-30-4). In some cases, the acquirer may not intend to use a particular acquired asset, or may intend to use the asset in a way other than its highest and best use. Nevertheless, the acquirer must measure the asset at fair value reflecting its highest and best use in accordance with ASC 820 (Fair Value Measurements and Disclosures), both initially and for purposes of subsequent impairment testing (ASC 805-20-30-6). This includes research and development assets that must be measured and recognized at their acquisition-date fair values.

Exception to the Recognition Principle

An exception to the recognition principle is made for assets and liabilities arising from contingencies. The acquirer **does not apply** the guidance in ASC 450 (Contingencies) in determining which assets and liabilities arising from contingencies to recognize as of the acquisition date. Rather, ASC 805 requires the acquirer to recognize as of the acquisition date all of the assets acquired and liabilities assumed that arise from *contractual contingencies*, measured at their acquisition-date fair values (ASC 805-20-25-19), par. 24a). For *non-contractual contingencies* the acquirer must assess whether it is **more likely than not** that as of the acquisition date the contingency gives rise to an asset or liability as defined in Concepts Statement No. 6, and will recognize the asset or liability at its acquisition-date fair value if that definition is met. If that definition is not met, the acquirer must account for the non-contractual contingency in accordance with other GAAP, including ASC 450 as appropriate (ASC 805-20-25-19).

Exceptions to Both the Recognition and Measurement Principles

Deferred tax assets and liabilities arising from the assets acquired and liabilities assumed in a business combination are to be recognized in accordance with ASC 740 (Income Taxes) (ASC 805-740-25-2). The acquirer shall also recognize a liability (or asset, if any) related to the acquiree's employee benefit plans in accordance with other relevant GAAP (ASC 805-20-25-22).

The acquiree may in some cases contractually indemnify the acquirer for the outcome of an asset or liability arising from a contingency. As a result, the acquirer obtains an indemnification asset, which shall be recognized at the same time the acquirer recognizes the indemnified item, measured on the same basis as the indemnified item (ASC 805-20-25-27).

Exceptions to the Measurement Principle

As part of a business combination, an acquirer may reacquire a right that it had previously granted to the acquiree. This may include, for example, the right to use the acquirer's trade name under a franchise agreement or a right to use certain of the acquirer's technology. A reacquired right is an identifiable intangible asset that is recognized by the acquirer separately from goodwill. The determination of the acquisition-date fair value of the reacquired right is based on the remaining term of the contract to which the reacquired right relates, even if market participants would consider potential contractual renewals in determining its fair value (ASC 805-20-30-20).

An acquirer may also recognize a liability or an equity instrument related to the replacement of an acquiree's share-based payment awards with share-based payment awards of the acquirer. In this case, the acquirer must measure the liability or equity instrument in accordance with ASC 718 (Compensation—Stock Compensation) (ASC 805-20-30-21).

Subsequent Measurement and Accounting

In general, the assets acquired, liabilities assumed or incurred, and equity instruments issued in a business combination shall be subsequently measured and accounted for by the acquirer in accordance with other applicable GAAP. However, ASC 805 provides specific guidance for the subsequent measurement and accounting for the following assets acquired, liabilities assumed or incurred, and equity instruments issued in a combination (ASC 805-10-35-1):

a. Reacquired rights

b. Assets and liabilities arising from contingencies recognized as of the acquisition date

c. Indemnification assets

d. Contingent consideration.

Reacquired Rights

A reacquired right recognized as an intangible asset as of the acquisition date must be amortized over the remaining contractual period of the contract in which the right was granted (ASC 805-20-35-2).

Assets and Liabilities Arising from Contingencies

An asset or liability arising from a contingency recognized as of the acquisition date, that would be in the scope of ASC 450 if not acquired or assumed in a business combination, shall continue to be recognized by the acquirer at its acquisition-date fair value unless new information is obtained about the possible outcome of the contingency. When new information is obtained, the acquirer must evaluate that information and measure an asset at the *lower* of its acquisition-date fair value or the best estimate of its future settlement amount, while a liability is measured at the *higher* of its acquisition-date fair value or the amount that would be recognized under ASC 450 (ASC 805-20-35-3). An asset or liability arising from a contingency shall only be derecognized by the acquirer when the contingency is resolved.

Indemnification Assets

The acquirer must subsequently measure an indemnification asset on the same basis as the indemnified liability or asset. If the indemnification asset is not measured at its fair value, the collectibility of the asset must be assessed. Indemnification assets shall only be derecognized by the acquirer when it collects the asset, sells it, or otherwise loses the right to it (ASC 805-20-35-4; 805-20-40-3).

Contingent Consideration

Some changes in the fair value of contingent consideration are measurement period adjustments and are accounted for in accordance with ASC 805-10. However, other changes in the fair value of contingent consideration result from events that occur after the acquisition date such as meetings a specified earnings target or reaching a specified share price. These changes are not measurement period adjustments, and the acquirer must account for them as follows (ASC 805-30-35-1):

  a. Contingent consideration classified as equity shall not be remeasured and its subsequent settlement shall be accounted for within equity.
  b. Contingent consideration classified as an asset or a liability is remeasured to fair value at each reporting date until the contingency is resolved. The changes in fair value are recognized in earnings unless the contingency involves a hedging instrument which is required by ASC 815 to recognize the changes in other comprehensive income.

Financial Statement Disclosures Related to Contingencies

The acquirer shall disclose the following information regarding contingencies:
- For contingent consideration arrangements (ASC 805-20-50-1):
  — The amount recognized as of the acquisition date

- A description of the arrangement and the basis for determining the amount of the payment
- An estimate of the range of outcomes (undiscounted) or, if a range cannot be estimated, that fact and the reasons why a range cannot be estimated.
• For assets and liabilities arising from contingencies (ASC 805-20-50-1):
  - The amounts recognized at the acquisition date or an explanation of why no amount was recognized
  - The nature of recognized and unrecognized contingencies
  - An estimate of the range of outcomes (undiscounted) for contingencies or, if a range cannot be estimated, that fact and the reasons why a range cannot be estimated.

ASC 805-30: GOODWILL OR GAIN FROM BARGAIN PURCHASE, INCLUDING CONSIDERATION TRANSFERRED

Recognizing and Measuring Goodwill or a Gain from a Bargain Purchase

Goodwill

The acquirer shall recognize goodwill as of the acquisition date, measured as the excess of (a) over (b) below (ASC 805-30-30-1):

a. The aggregate of:
   1. The consideration transferred, which is usually the acquisition-date fair value.
   2. The fair value of any noncontrolling interests in the acquiree
   3. In a business combination achieved in stages, the acquisition-date fair value of the acquirer's previously held equity interest in the acquiree
b. The net of the acquisition-date amounts of the identifiable assets acquired and the liabilities assumed.

In a business combination involving two mutual entities, the acquisition-date fair value of the acquiree's equity interests may be more readily measurable than the acquisition-date fair value of the acquirer's equity interests. If so, the acquirer shall use the acquisition-date fair value of the acquiree's equity interests in determining the amount of goodwill to be recognized. In a business combination in which no consideration is transferred, the acquirer must use a valuation technique to determine the acquisition-date fair value of the acquirer's interest in the acquiree. The value derived from this valuation technique is then used in place of the acquisition-date fair value of the consideration transferred when determining the amount of goodwill to be recognized (ASC 805-30-30-3).

Gain from a Bargain Purchase

Occasionally, an acquirer will make a bargain purchase, which is a business combination in which the amount of net assets acquired exceeds the value of the consideration transferred plus the fair value of any noncontrolling interests in the acquiree plus the fair value of the acquirer's previously held equity interest in the acquiree. ASC 805 requires the acquired assets and assumed liabilities to be recorded at their acquisition-date fair values with limited exceptions. This requirement results in the acquired assets and assumed liabilities being recognized at their fair value, while the amount of the bargain is recognized by the acquirer in earnings on the acquisition date (ASC 805-30-25-2).

However, before recognizing a gain from a bargain purchase, the acquirer is required by ASC 805 to reassess whether it has correctly identified all of the acquired assets and assumed liabilities, and to recognize any additional assets or liabilities that are discovered during this review. The acquirer must also review the procedures it used to measure the following amounts as of the acquisition date (ASC 805-30-30-5):

a. The identifiable assets acquired and liabilities assumed
b. The noncontrolling interests in the acquiree, if any
c. For a business combination achieved in stages, the acquirer's previously held equity interest in the acquiree
d. The consideration transferred.

Consideration Transferred

The consideration transferred in a business combination must be measured at fair value, and equals the sum of the acquisition-date fair values of the assets transferred by the acquirer, the liabilities incurred by the acquirer to former owners of the acquiree, and the equity interests issued by the acquirer. The consideration transferred may include assets and liabilities of the acquirer that have acquisition-date fair value that differ from their carrying amounts. If so, the acquirer must remeasure the transferred assets and liabilities to their fair values as of the acquisition date and recognize a gain or loss in earnings, unless the transferred assets and liabilities remain with the combined entity after the combination. In that case, the acquirer will continue to measure the transferred assets and liabilities at their carrying amounts immediately prior to the acquisition date and not recognize any gain or loss in earnings, since the acquirer controls the assets and liabilities both before and after the business combination (ASC 805-30-30-7, 8).

In some business combinations, the acquirer has an obligation to make additional payments based on the occurrence of future events (often called "contingent consideration"). Any such obligation must be recognized by the acquirer at its acquisition-date fair value as a part of the total consideration transferred (ASC 805-30-25-5). Another type of consideration is share-based payment awards which are awarded by the acquirer to replace awards held by employees of the acquiree. If the acquirer is obligated to issue these awards as a replacement for the acquiree's awards, then at least some, if not all, of the fair value of the acquirer's replacement awards are included in the amount of consideration transferred in the business combination (ASC 805-30-30-9). However, if the acquirer is not obligated to replace the acquiree awards but chooses to do so anyway, then all of the fair-value-based measure of the replacement awards must be recognized as compensation expense by the acquirer in the postcombination financial statements (ASC 805-30-30-10).

Financial Statement Disclosures Related to Goodwill

The acquirer shall disclose the following information regarding goodwill (ASC 805-30-50-1):

- A qualitative description of the factors that make up for the goodwill recognized. For example:
  - Expected synergies from combining the operations of the acquiree and the acquirer
  - Intangible assets that do not qualify for separate recognition
- The amount of goodwill that is expected to be deductible for tax purposes
- The amount of goodwill by reportable segment (assuming the entity is required to disclose segment information in accordance with ASC 280 (Segment Reporting))

ACQUISITION METHOD: IMPLEMENTATION GUIDANCE

Types of Business Combinations

A business combination may be accomplished in one of two ways. The acquiring company may purchase the assets (asset acquisition) of the target company. In this instance, normally the target company is liquidated and only one entity continues. Alternatively, the acquiring company may purchase more than 50% (up to 100%) of the outstanding voting common stock of the target company. In this instance, the financial statements of the two entities are consolidated in accordance with ASC 810.

Asset Acquisition

In an asset acquisition, entries are made to record the assets and assume the liabilities of the target company on the books of the acquiring company. These assets and liabilities are recorded at their acquisition-date fair values, with limited exceptions. If the purchase price exceeds the fair market value of the net assets, goodwill is recorded in the acquisition entry. If the fair market value of identifiable assets exceeds the purchase price, the resulting excess of fair value of acquired net assets over cost is recognized as a gain in earnings on the acquisition date (ASC 805-30-25-2).

Illustration of Asset Acquisition

On July 1, 20X8, S Company sold all its net assets and business to P Company for $430,000 cash. The following is S Company's balance sheet as of July 1, 20X8:

ASC 805—Business Combinations 45,015

Balance Sheet

Cash	$ 20,000
Accounts receivable	72,000
Allowance for doubtful accounts	(8,000)
Inventory	120,000
Plant and equipment (net)	260,000
Total assets	$464,000
Accounts payable	$ 60,000
Accrued expenses	5,000
Mortgage payable—plant	120,000
Common stock	200,000
Retained earnings	79,000
Total liabilities and equity	$464,000

Additional Information:

Confirmation of the accounts receivable revealed that $10,000 was uncollectible.

The physical inventory count was $138,000 (fair value).

The fair value of the plant and equipment was $340,000.

S Company has in-process research and development costs that have a fair value of $15,000.

The journal entry to record the investment on the books of P Company is:

Cash	$20,000	
Accounts receivable	62,000	
Inventory	138,000	
Plant & equipment	340,000	
In-process R&D	15,000	
Goodwill	40,000	
Accounts payable		$ 60,000
Accrued expenses		5,000
Mortgage payable		120,000
Cash		430,000

The computation of goodwill involved in the transaction is:

Computation of Goodwill

Assets (book value)	$ 464,000
Liabilities ($60,000 + $5,000 + $120,000)	(185,000)
Total net assets (book value)	$ 279,000
Adjustments to fair value:	
Additional uncollectibles	(2,000)
Increase in inventory	18,000
Increase in plant and equipment	80,000
In-process R&D	15,000
Adjusted net assets (fair value)	$ 390,000

Consideration transferred	$ 430,000
Adjusted net assets (fair value)	(390,000)
Goodwill	$ 40,000

Had the purchase price been only $365,000, the excess of fair value of acquired net assets over consideration transferred would have been computed as follows.

Adjusted net assets (fair value)	$ 390,000
Consideration transferred	(365,000)
Excess of fair value of acquired net assets over consideration transferred	$ 25,000

The $25,000 excess of fair value of acquired net assets over consideration transferred represents the "bargain" for this business combination that the acquirer must recognize in earnings as a gain on the acquisition date. The journal entry to record the investment on the books of P Company is:

Cash	$20,000	
Accounts receivable	62,000	
Inventory	138,000	
Plant & equipment	340,000	
In-process R&D	15,000	
Accounts payable		$ 60,000
Accrued expenses		5,000
Mortgage payable		120,000
Cash		365,000
Gain on bargain purchase		25,000

Stock Acquisition

In an acquisition of stock, entries are made to record the investment in the stock of the investee. An analysis of the difference between the underlying book value and the sum of the consideration transferred plus fair value of any noncontrolling interests is required to prepare consolidated financial statements for the parent and subsidiary to reflect the fair market value of the identifiable assets and goodwill as of the date of acquisition. Using data from the previous example in which the consideration transferred was $430,000, the only entry required to record the combination is:

Investment in S Company	$430,000	
Cash		$430,000

At the financial statement date, consolidated financial statements will be prepared that combine the assets and liabilities of the parent and subsidiary companies. At that time, the account "Investment in S Company" is eliminated from the statements along with the stockholders' equity in S Company. In addition, the identifiable assets of S Company are adjusted to fair market value and the goodwill of $40,000 is recorded in the consolidated balance sheet.

ASC 805—Business Combinations 45,017

Operating expenses, depreciation, and amortization of the combined entities are adjusted to reflect the revised asset values.

In a stock acquisition in which the acquirer purchases less than 100% of the outstanding voting common stock of the target company, the acquirer must recognize any noncontrolling interests at its fair value as of the acquisition date. Measuring the noncontrolling interests at its fair value results in the recognition of goodwill attributable to the noncontrolling interests in addition to the goodwill attributable to the acquirer. In the case of a bargain purchase, the recognition of the noncontrolling interests at its acquisition-date fair value may not result in any goodwill being recognized, but rather may reduce the amount of the bargain reported by the acquirer in its current income statement.

Illustration of Stock Acquisition

On July 1, 20X8, P Company acquires 90% of the equity interests of S Company for $540,000 cash. The following is S Company's balance sheet as of July 1, 20X8:

Balance Sheet

Cash	$ 40,000
Accounts receivable	65,000
Allowance for doubtful accounts	$ (5,000)
Inventory	175,000
Plant and equipment (net)	210,000
Total assets	$485,000
Accounts payable	$ 85,000
Accrued expenses	15,000
Common stock	260,000
Retained earnings	125,000
Total liabilities and equity	$485,000

Additional Information:

Confirmation of the accounts receivable revealed that $10,000 was uncollectible.

The physical inventory count was $230,000 (fair value).

The fair value of the plant and equipment was $275,000.

The fair value of the 10% noncontrolling interests in S Company is $60,000.

The journal entry to record the investment on the books of P Company is:

Investment in S Company	$540,000	
Cash		$540,000

P Company would record its acquisition of S Company in its consolidated financial statements as follows:

Cash	$40,000
Accounts receivable	55,000
Inventory	230,000

45,018   ASC 805—Business Combinations

Plant & equipment	275,000	
Goodwill	100,000	
Accounts payable		$ 85,000
Accrued expenses		15,000
Cash		540,000
Equity—noncontrolling interests in S Company		60,000

The computation of goodwill involved in the transaction is:

Computation of Goodwill

Assets (book value)	$ 485,000
Liabilities ($85,000 + $15,000)	(100,000)
Total net assets (book value)	$ 385,000
Adjustments to fair value:	
Additional uncollectibles	$(5,000)
Increase in inventory	55,000
Increase in plant and equipment	65,000
Adjusted net assets (fair value)	$ 500,000
Consideration transferred	$ 540,000
Fair value of noncontrolling interests in S Company	60,000
Adjusted net assets (fair value)	(500,000)
Goodwill	$ 100,000

Assume the former owners of S Company had to dispose of their investments in S Company by a specified date and did not have time to market S Company to multiple potential buyers. Therefore, the purchase price paid by P Company for its 90% ownership was only $425,000. In this case, the amount of gain on this bargain purchase that would be recognized by P Company in its income statement on the acquisition date is computed as follows.

Adjusted net assets (fair value)	$ 500,000
Consideration transferred	(425,000)
Fair value of noncontrolling interests in S Company	(60,000)
Excess of fair value of acquired net assets over consideration transferred plus noncontrolling interests	$ 15,000

The $15,000 excess of fair value of acquired net assets over consideration transferred plus noncontrolling interests represents the "bargain" for this business combination that the acquirer must recognize in earnings as a gain on the acquisition date. P Company would record its acquisition of S Company in its consolidated financial statements as follows:

Cash	$40,000	
Accounts receivable	55,000	
Inventory	230,000	
Plant & equipment	275,000	
Accounts payable		$ 85,000

Accrued expenses	15,000
Cash	425,000
Equity—noncontrolling interests in S Company	60,000
Gain on bargain purchase	15,000

DISCLOSURE OF CERTAIN LOSS CONTINGENCIES

ASC 805-40: REVERSE ACQUISITIONS

A reverse acquisition is an acquisition in which the entity that issues securities is identified as the acquire for accounting purposes based on guidance in 805-10-55-11 through 55-15. The entity whose equity interests are acquired must be the acquirer for accounting purposes for a transition to be considered a reverse acquisition.

Measuring Consideration

In a reverse acquisition, the accounting acquirer usually issues no consideration for the acquiree. Instead, the accounting acquiree usually issues its equity shares to the owners of the accounting acquirer. The acquisition-date fair value of the consideration transferred by the accounting acquirer for its interest in the accounting acquire is based on the number of equity interests the legal subsidiary would have had to issue to give the owners of the legal parent the same percentage interest in the combined entity that results from the reverse acquisition. (ASC 805-40-30-2)

Non-Controlling Interest

The assets and liabilities of the legal acquiree are measured and recognized in the consolidated financial statements at their precombination carrying amounts. Therefore, in a reverse acquisition the controlling interest reflects the noncontolling shareholders' proportionate interest in the precombination carrying amounts of the legal acquiree's net assets. This is true even though the noncontrolling interest in the other acquisition are measured at fair values at the acquisition date. (ASC 805-40-30-3)

Other Presentation Matters

Consolidated financial statement following a reverse acquisition are issued under the name of the legal parent (accounting acquiree) but described in notes to the financial statements as a continuation of the financial statements of the legal subsidiary (accounting acquirer) with the following adjustment. The legal acquirer's legal capital is adjusted to reflect the legal capital of the accounting acquiree. This adjustment is required to reflect the capital of the legal parent (accounting acquiree). Comparative-year information is retroactgively adjusted to reflect the legal capital of the legal parent (accounting acquiree). (ASC 805-40-45-1)

Information accompanying the financial post-refer-acquisition financial statements should disclose the following:

- The assets and liabilities of the legal subsidiary (accounting acquirer) recognized and measured at their precombination carrying amounts.
- The assets and liabilities of the legal parent (the accounting acquiree) recognized and measured as applicable with the guidance on business combinations.
- The retained earnings and other equity balances of the legal subsidiary (accounting acquirer) before the business combination.
- The amount recognized as issued equity interests in the consolidated financial statements determined by adding the issued equity interest of the legal subsidiary (accounting acquirer) outstanding immediately before the business combination to the fair value of the legal parent (accounting acquiree) in accordance with guidance applicable to business combinations.
- The noncontrolling interest's proportionate share of the legal subsidiary's (accounting acquirer's) precombination carrying amounts of retained earnings and other equity interests. (ASC 805-40-45-2)

ASC 805-50: RELATED ISSUES

Acquisition of Assets Rather Than a Business

Assets are usually acquired in exchange transactions that trigger the initial recognition of the assets acquired and liabilities assumed. If the consideration given in exchange for assets, or net assets, acquired is in the form of assets surrendered (e.g. cash), the assets surrender shall be derecognized at the date of the acquisitions. If the consideration given is in the form of liabilities incurred or equity interests issued, the liabilities incurred and equity interests issued are initially recognized at the date of acquisition. (ASC 805-50-25-1)

Assets are recognized based on their cost to the acquiring entity, which generally includes the transaction costs of the asset acquisition, and no gain or loss is recognized unless the fair value of the noncash assets given as consideration differs from the assets' carrying amounts on the acquiring entity's books. Asset acquisitions in which the consideration is given in cash are measured by the amount of cash paid, which generally includes the transactions costs of the asset acquisition. If the consideration given is not in the form of cash, measurement is based on either the cost, measured based on the fair value of the consideration give, or the fair value of the assets acquired, whichever is more reliably measured. (ASC 805-50-30-2)

Transactions Between Entities Under Common Control

In accounting for a transfer of assets or exchange of shares between entities under common control, the entity that receives the net assets or the equity interests initially recognizes the assets and liabilities transferred at the date of transfer. (ASC 805-50-25-2)

When accounting for a transfer of assets or exchange of shares between entities under common control, the entity that receives the net assets or the equity interest initially measures the recognized assets and liabilities transferred measured at their carrying amounts in the accounting of the transferring entity at the date of transfer. If the carrying amounts of the assets and liabilities transferred differ from the historical cost of the parent of the entities under common control (e.g., because pushdown accounting had not been applied), the financial statements of the receiving entity shall reflect the transferred assets and liabilities at the historical cost of the parent of the entities under common control. (ASC 805-50-30-5)

Financial statements of the receiving entity shall report results of operations for the period in which the transfer occurs as if the transfer had occurred at the beginning of the period, (ASC 805-50-45-2)

New Basis of Accounting (Pushdown)

Pushdown accounting is not required for entities that are not Securities and Exchange Commission registrants. (ASC 805-50-25-3)

Because of factors like the consideration of common ownership and changes in control, a new basis of accounting is not appropriate for the following transactions that create a master limited partnership:

- A rollup in which the general partner of the new master limited partnership was also the general partner of some or all of the predecessor limited partnerships and no cash is involved I the transactions.
- A dropdown in which the sponsor receives 1% of the units in the master limited partnership as the general partner and 24% of the units as a limited partner, the remaining 75% of the units are sold to the public, and a 2/3 vote of the limited partners is required to replace the general partner.
- A rollout.
- A reorganization. (ASC 805-50-30-7)

IMPORTANT NOTICE FOR 2012

As the 2012 *GAAP Guide* goes to press, the FASB has issued an Exposure Draft of a Proposed Statement of Financial Accounting Standards titled "Disclosure of Certain Loss Contingencies." The current FASB Technical Plan indicates that this project has been reassessed as a lower priority project, and thus, further action is not expected to be taken before December 2011.

The proposed standard would expand the disclosures about loss contingencies within the scope of ASC 450 and ASC 805, with limited exceptions. In addition, the proposed standard would: (1) expand the types of loss contingencies that require disclosure, (2) require the disclosure of certain quantitative and qualitative information related to the contingency, and (3) require a tabular reconciliation of recognized loss contingencies. Moreover, the proposed standard provides an exemption from certain disclosure items if making the disclosure would adversely affect the company in a dispute. The proposed standard does not change the criteria for recognizing and measuring contingencies articulated in ASC 450 and ASC 805.

The disclosures required under the proposed standard apply to: (1) loss contingencies recognized in a business combination, (2) loss contingencies under ASC 450 where a liability is recognized in the financial statements (i.e., the loss is both probable and reasonably estimable), and (3) loss contingencies under ASC 450 that are not recognized as a liability but where the probability of loss is more than remote. However, even if the probability of loss is remote, disclosure is required if the contingency exposes the entity to a potentially severe impact. Judgment will be necessary in deciding whether to disclose a contingency where the probability of loss is remote.

The entity is to provide quantitative information about the entity's exposure to loss, including the amount of the claim or assessment. The proposed standard requires numerous qualitative disclosures, and disclosures related to existing insurance and indemnification agreements. Finally, the entity must provide a tabular reconciliation of the liability for loss contingencies recognized in the statement of financial position from the beginning to the end of the year.

PART II: INTERPRETIVE GUIDANCE

ASC 805-10: Overall

ASC 805-10-35-1, 20-25-15A, 25-18A, 25-19 through 20B, 30-9 through 30-9A, 30-23, 35-3 through 35-4A, 50-1; ASC 805-30-35-1A Accounting for Assets Acquired and Liabilities Assumed in a Business Combination That Arise from Contingencies

BACKGROUND

Under the guidance in ASC 805 acquirer in a business combination must recognize the fair value on the acquisition date of all *contractual* contingencies and all *noncontractual* contingencies that more likely than not will result in an asset or liability, as defined in CON-6 (Elements of Financial Statements) (not in ASC). However, *noncontractual* contingencies that are *not* more than likely to result in an asset or a liability as of the acquisition date, would be accounted for in accordance with other U.S. generally accepted accounting principles (GAAP), including ASC 450.

In accordance with the guidance in ASC 805 such assets and liabilities would continue to be reported at their fair values as of the acquisition date until there is new information about the related contingency's possible outcome. At that time, the resulting liability would be measured at its fair value at acquisition or an amount based on the guidance in ASC 450, whichever is *lower*. An asset would be measured at its fair value at acquisition or at the best estimate of the amount at which it would be settled in the future. An acquirer would continue to report assets and liabilities that resulted from preacquisition contingencies until the related contingencies have been resolved.

Constituents raised issues related to the application of its guidance, which includes guidance to:

- Determine the fair value at acquisition of a contingency related to litigation;

ASC 805—Business Combinations

- Support the measurement and recognition of liabilities related to legal contingencies if supporting information is unavailable due to attorney-client privilege;
- Distinguish between contractual and noncontractual contingencies;
- Address a situation in which an acquiree that intends to settle a contingent liability out of court wants to recognize a loss contingency based on the guidance in ASC 450, but cannot do so because the liability does *not* meet the more-likely-than-not threshold for a noncontractual contingency, as required in ASC 805;
- Derecognize a liability that results from a contingency recognized as of the acquisition date;
- Disclose information in financial statements that is potentially prejudicial;
- Determine whether an acquiree's arrangements for contingent consideration assumed in a business combination should be accounted for in accordance with the guidance for contingent consideration or in accordance with guidance for the accounting of other assets and liabilities resulting from contingencies.

The following guidance amends the guidance in ASC 805 and clarifies its guidance on initial recognition and measurement, subsequent measurement and accounting, and disclosure of assets and liabilities that result from contingencies in business combinations.

ACCOUNTING GUIDANCE

Scope

The following guidance applies to all of a business combination's acquired assets and assumed liabilities that have resulted from contingencies that would be accounted for under the guidance in ASC 450. That is, in the same manner as contingencies that were *not* acquired or assumed in a business combination. The guidance in this pronouncement does *not* apply to assets or liabilities that result from contingencies for which there is specific accounting guidance in ASC 805).

Initial measurement and recognition

An asset acquired or a liability assumed in a business combination that has resulted from a contingency should be recognized at the acquisition date at its fair value if that amount can be determined during the measurement period, such as the fair value of an obligation under a warranty. If that fair value cannot be determined during the measurement period, the following two criteria must be met for such assets and liabilities to be recognized at the acquisition date based on the guidance in ASC 450 and in ASC 450, for the application of similar criteria in ASC 450-20-25-2:

- Based on information available *before* the end of the measurement period, it is probable that an asset existed and that a liability had been incurred at the acquisition date. This condition intended to imply that it is probable at the acquisition date that one or more future events will occur to confirm the existence of the recognized asset or liability.
- It is possible to reasonably estimate the amount of the asset or liability.

An asset or a liability resulting from a contingency should *not* be recognized as of the acquisition date if the criteria for measurement and recognition discussed above are *not* met at that date based on information available during the measurement period. After the acquisition date, assets and liabilities that result from contingencies that did *not* meet the criteria for recognition at the acquisition date should be accounted for *after* the acquisition date based on other applicable GAAP, including ASC 450, whichever is appropriate.

An acquirer should initially recognize at fair value an acquiree's arrangements for contingent consideration assumed in a business combination by applying the guidance in ASC 805 for such arrangements.

Subsequent measurement and accounting

Subsequent to an acquisition, an acquirer should:

- Measure and account for assets and liabilities that result from a contingency using a systematic and rational approach based on the nature of the contingency,

- Measure contingent consideration arrangements assumed from an acquiree in a business combination based on the guidance in ASC 805-30-35-1.

Disclosures

Information disclosed by an acquirer in a business combination should enable financial statement users to evaluate the nature of the business combination and how it affects the entity financially during the reporting period in which it occurs or after the reporting period but before financial statements are issued. An acquirer should disclose the following information in the notes to the financial statements about each business combination that occurs during a reporting period:

1. For assets and liabilities as a result of contingencies recognized at the acquisition date:

    a. Amounts recognized at the acquisition date and the basis used for recognition, that is, fair value or an amount based on the guidance in ASC 450.

    b. The nature of the contingencies.

2. For contingencies not recognized at the acquisition date, disclose information required in ASC 450, if the criteria for making those disclosures are met.

ASC 805-10-50-2, 50-8 through 50-9, 55-49 through 50-50 Disclosure of Supplementary Pro Forma Information for Business Combinations

OVERVIEW

Under the existing guidance in ASC 805-10-50-2(h), an acquirer that is a public entity is required to provide the following information:

- The amounts of revenue and earnings of an acquiree since the acquisition date included in the consolidated income statement for the reporting period;
- The revenue and earnings of the combined entity for the current reporting period as though the acquisition date for all business combinations that occurred during the year had been as of the beginning of the annual reporting period (supplemental pro forma information); and
- If comparative financial statements are presented, the revenue and earnings of the combined entity for the comparable prior reporting period as though the acquisition date for all business combinations that occurred during the current year had occurred as of the beginning of the comparable prior annual reporting period (supplemental pro forma information).

The Securities and Exchange Commission (SEC) also requires pro forma financial information to be included in a Form 8-K filing under the requirements of Article 11 of Regulation S-X. That information is intended to inform investors about how a transaction that has occurred in the current period might affect future financial statements by showing how it might have affected the historical financial statements had the transaction occurred at the beginning of a comparable prior period.

This Issue was discussed because the guidance in ASC 805-10-50-2(h)(2) and 50-2(h)(3) has been interpreted differently by preparers in practice. Some preparers have interpreted that guidance to mean that pro forma information should be prepared as if the business combination has occurred at the beginning of the current annual period and the beginning of the prior annual period. Others have interpreted the guidance to mean that pro forma information is required only as if the business combination had occurred at the beginning of the prior annual period.

ACCOUNTING ISSUE

How should a public entity prepare pro forma information in a business combination?

ACCOUNTING GUIDANCE

Scope

The following guidance applies to all public entities, as defined in ASC 805, that have entered into a material business combination or a series of immaterial business combinations that are material in their totality.

- A *public* entity that presents comparative financial statements is required to disclose pro forma information about the combined entity's revenue and earnings as if an acquisition that occurred during the current year had occurred as of the beginning of the comparable prior annual reporting period.
- To provide users of financial statements with additional useful information, the supplemental pro forma disclosures under ASC 805 are expanded to require a narrative description of the nature and amount of

material, nonrecurring pro forma adjustments directly as a result of a business combination.

Effective date and transition

Public entities should apply the guidance herein *prospectively* for business combinations with an acquisition date on or after the beginning of the first annual reporting period that begins on or after December 15, 2010, but early adoption is permitted.

ASC 805-20: Identifiable Assets and Liabilities, and Any Noncontrolling Interest

ASC 805-20-S30-1, S35-1, S99-3 Use of the Residual Method to Value Acquired Assets Other Than Goodwill

Under current guidance on accounting for business combinations in ASC 805-20-55-2, intangible assets that result from contractual or legal rights must be recognized separately from goodwill. The SEC Observer reported at the EITF's September 2004 meeting that, in some circumstances, SEC registrants have claimed that they are unable to value a legal or contractual right directly or separately from goodwill in a business combination because the asset's characteristics make it indistinguishable from goodwill. Examples are cellular/spectrum licenses and cable franchise agreements. Some of those entities have assigned a purchase price to all other identifiable assets and liabilities and have assigned the remaining residual amount to the "indistinguishable" intangible asset without recognizing goodwill or recognizing goodwill based on a technique other than that specified in ASC 805-30-30-1, 25-1.

Entities in the telecommunications, broadcasting, and cable industries have been using the residual method to value intangible assets. That method is similar to the allocation methods used to account for business combinations accounted for under the purchase method in APB-16 (Business Combinations), before that guidance was superseded by FAS-141 and later ASC 805 (FAS-141(R)). He stated that proponents of that approach claim that the residual method results in a value that approximates the value that would be arrived at under a direct value method or that, under the circumstances, it would be impracticable to use other methods. Some believe that the value obtained under the residual method for indistinguishable intangible assets is an acceptable surrogate for fair value because it is very difficult to determine fair value by using a direct value method. Entities that use the residual method to assign the purchase price to indistinguishable intangible assets often also use it to test for impairment.

SEC OBSERVER COMMENT

The SEC Observer stated that registrants must follow the guidance in 805-30-30-1 under which intangible assets meeting the criteria for recognition should be recognized at fair value. Goodwill differs from other recognized assets because it is specifically stated in ASC 805-30-30-1 that goodwill is the residual of the cost of an acquisition "over the net amounts assigned to assets acquired and liabilities assumed" and is, therefore, defined and measured as an excess. Other recognized intangible assets must be measured at fair value.

The SEC staff does not believe that it can be assumed that using the residual method to value intangible assets will result in amounts that represent the fair value of those assets. In addition, the fact that it is difficult to value certain intangible assets is not an excuse for not following the guidance in paragraphs ASC 805-20-55-2 through 45, under which the fair value of intangible assets must be determined separately from goodwill. In addition, the SEC Observer noted that some entities are valuing the same intangible assets by the direct value method. Consequently, entities should use a direct value method rather than the residual value method to determine the fair value of intangible assets other than goodwill. Further, impairment should be tested in accordance with the guidance in ASC 350.).

ASC 805-50: Related Issues

ASC 805-50-05-7, 15-8,; 30-7 through 30-9 S30-2, S99-3 Change of Accounting Basis in Master Limited Partnership Transactions

BACKGROUND

The enactment of the Tax Reform Act of 1986 resulted in the formation of an increasing number of Master Limited Partnerships (MLPs), which are partnerships whose interests are traded publicly. MLPs may be formed to realize the value of undervalued assets; to pass income and deductible losses through to its shareholders; to raise capital; to enable companies to sell, spin off, or liquidate operations; or to combine partnerships. They are generally formed from assets in existing businesses operated in the form of limited partnerships and in connection with a business in which the general partner is also involved.

The following are different methods of creating an MLP:

- In a *roll-up*, two or more legally separate limited partnerships are combined into one MLP.
- In a *drop-down*, units of a limited partnership that was formed with a sponsor's assets (usually a corporate entity) are sold to the public.
- In a *roll-out*, a sponsor places certain assets into a limited partnership and distributes its units to shareholders.
- In a *reorganization*, an entity is liquidated by transferring all of its assets to an MLP.

EFFECTS OF ASC 805 (FAS-141(R))

FAS-141, which superseded APB-16, applies to transactions in which all entities transfer net assets, or the owners of those entities transfer their equity interests to a newly formed entity in a transaction that is referred to as "roll-up." Its scope excludes, however, transfers of net assets or exchanges of equity interests between entities under common control. All the facts and circumstances should be analyzed to determine the nature of the transaction and the appropriate method of accounting for it.

FAS-141 has been replaced by ASC 805 (FAS-141(R)), which was issued in December 2007. Although, its scope continues the exclusion of transfers of net assets or exchanges of equity interests between entities under common control, guidance on the accounting for those transactions is included in Appendix D, "Continuing Authoritative Guidance," of the Statement.

ACCOUNTING ISSUES

1. Can new-basis accounting ever be used for the assets and liabilities of an MLP?
2. How should an MLP account for transaction costs in a roll-up?

ACCOUNTING GUIDANCE

1. A new basis is not appropriate in the following circumstances:

    a. The MLP's general partner in a roll-up was also the general partner of the predecessor limited partnerships, and no cash has been exchanged in the transaction.

    b. A sponsor in a drop-down receives 1% of the units of the MLP as its general partner and 24% of the units as a limited partner, with the remaining 75% of the units sold to the public. The general partner can be replaced by a two-thirds vote of the limited partners.

    c. An MLP is created as a roll-out.

    d. An MLP is created as a reorganization.

    In addition, the conclusion on a roll-up would not change even if the general partner was the general partner of only some of the predecessor limited partnerships. Task Force members noted that if a general partner of predecessor limited partnerships who will not be a general partner of the MLP receives MLP units in settlement of management contracts or for other services that will not carry over to the MLP, those units have the characteristics of compensation rather than equity, and should be accounted for as such by the MLP. The Task Force did not reach a consensus on situations in which new-basis accounting would be appropriate, but did not preclude the possibility.

2. A roll-up's transaction costs should be charged to expense.

SEC OBSERVER COMMENT

The SEC Observer announced that the SEC would not object to new-basis accounting in an MLP created as a drop-down to the extent of the percentage of change in ownership if (1) 80% or more of the MLP is sold to the public and (2) the limited partners can replace the general partner by a "reasonable" vote.

ASC 805-50-05-8, 15-8 through 15-9, 25-3, 25-13 IRC Section 338 and Push-Down Accounting

BACKGROUND

As a result of the Tax Equity and Fiscal Responsibility Act of 1982, an entity can step up an acquired company's tax basis by making such an election rather than changing its legal form through a liquidation, corporate reorganization, or statutory merger. In addition, some companies also have justified a "push down" of the acquiring company's basis to the subsidiary for financial reporting purposes.

One advantage of push-down accounting is that it conforms balances for both tax and financial reporting purposes.

ACCOUNTING ISSUES

- Should push-down accounting be required if (*a*) the acquired company is neither an SEC registrant nor a party to the transaction effecting the change in ownership, (*b*) a step-up in basis is elected, and (*c*) it is not essential to retain the old basis?
- If the acquiring company's basis for financial reporting is not pushed down to the financial statements of the acquired company, which one of the following methods is preferable for allocating the consolidated tax provision:
  — Modifying the intercorporate tax allocation agreement so that taxes are allocated to the acquired company using its preacquisition tax basis?
  — Crediting the tax benefit from the step-up in the acquired company's tax basis to its capital surplus when realized?
  — Crediting the tax benefit to the acquired company's income as a permanent difference when realized?

ACCOUNTING GUIDANCE

- Entities that are not SEC registrants are not required to use push-down accounting.
- Any one of the three methods may be used to allocate the consolidated tax provision, with appropriate disclosure.

SUBSEQUENT DEVELOPMENT

Although ASC 740-10-30-28, which was issued in February 1992, does not require a specific method of tax allocation for the separate financial statements of members of a group filing a consolidated tax return, it does require that the method of allocation be systematic, rational, and consistent with the principles established in the Statement. Those criteria are met if current and deferred taxes are allocated to members of the consolidated group as if they are separate tax payers. Footnote 10 notes that as a result of that method of allocation, the total of allocated amounts may not equal the consolidated amount.

ASC 805-50-S30-3, S99-4 Changes of Ownership Resulting in a New Basis of Accounting

OVERVIEW

Entity A has acquired the voting common stock of Entity B in a business combination accounted for as a purchase transaction. Under the guidance in ASC 805, Entity A is required to account for the assets and liabilities acquired in the transactions at their fair values. However, the accounting literature provides no guidance as to whether Entity B should report its assets and liabilities on the same basis as Entity A, thus adopting a "new basis of accounting."

ACCOUNTING ISSUES

1. At what level of change in ownership should an entity adopt a new basis of accounting to report its assets and liabilities?
2. How should the new basis of accounting be computed?
3. At what amount should minority interests be reported?

ACCOUNTING GUIDANCE

No conclusion was reached on those issues. However, the SEC Observer stated the view of the SEC staff.

SEC OBSERVER COMMENT

The SEC Observer stated that SEC registrants are required to adopt new-basis accounting only if virtually 100% of the stock has been acquired and there is no outstanding publicly held debt or preferred stock. The SEC Observer stated further that net assets (in a business combination) or long-lived assets transferred between companies under common control or between a parent and subsidiary should be reported at their historical cost in the subsidiary's separate financial statements.

DISCUSSION

Although the authoritative accounting literature does not provide guidance on this Issue, SEC SAB-54 (Application of Push-Down Basis of Accounting in Financial Statements of Subsidiaries Acquired by Purchase) provides guidance to SEC registrants. It requires the parent company's cost of acquiring a subsidiary to be "pushed down" to the subsidiary's separate financial statements if "substantially all" of the subsidiary's voting common stock has been acquired and the parent can control the form of ownership. SAB-54 encourages but does not require new-basis accounting if less than "substantially all" of a company's stock has been acquired or there is outstanding publicly held debt or preferred stock.

It was noted that the application of SAB-54 is inconsistent when less than 100% of a company is acquired or when there is a step acquisition.

ASC 805-50-S55-1, S99-2 Push Down Accounting

This SEC staff announcement discusses the staff's views regarding the facts and circumstances under which push down accounting should be applied. The staff's views on this matter can be found in Staff Accounting Bulletin (SAB) Topic 5.J (Push Down Basis of Accounting in Required in Certain Limited Circumstances), which states that push down accounting should be used in a purchase transaction in which an entity becomes substantially wholly owned. Application of that view is *required* if a company becomes substantially wholly owned, that is, *95% or more* of the company has been acquired, due to a series of related and anticipated transactions, unless the acquirer's ability to control the company's form of ownership is affected by the existence of outstanding public debt or preferred stock. Push down accounting is permitted if *80 to 95%* of the company has been acquired.

The staff believes that push down accounting should be applied in a subsidiary's financial statements, regardless of a minority interest sold to new investors, if a parent company has purchased all the minority interest of a majority-owned subsidiary in a single transaction or a series of related and anticipated transactions, and subsequently issues shares in the subsidiary to new investors. Further, push down accounting is required even if a subsidiary became wholly owned for a short time and there was a plan for the subsidiary to issue shares after it became wholly owned. Registrants should distinguish between transactions in which only a significant change in ownership occurs, such as in a recapitalization, which would not warrant the use of push down accounting, and those in which a company becomes substantially wholly owned.

The SEC staff believes that a company becomes substantially wholly owned in a single transaction or a series of transactions if a group of investors act together to acquire a company as if they are one investor and can control the company's form of ownership. That is, it is appropriate to combine the holdings of investors that both "mutually promote" the acquisition and "collaborate" on the investee's subsequent control (the collaborative group). Push down accounting applies in those circumstances. To determine whether an investor is part of that group, the SEC staff believes that a rebuttable presumption exists that investors who invest in a company at the same time or within a reasonably close time frame are part of the collaborative group. To rebut that presumption, the following are indicators that an investor is *not* part of a collaborative group:

1. Independence
    a. The investor is an entity with substantial capital and other operations of its own.
    b. The investor is independent of and unaffiliated with the other investors.
    c. The investor's investment in the investee does not depend on investments made by any other investor in the investee.
    d. The investor has no relationships with the other investors that are material to either party.
2. Risk of Ownership
    a. The investor invests at fair value.
    b. The investor uses its own resources to invest.
    c. The investor shares in the risks and rewards of ownership in the investee with the other owners in proportion to its class and amount of investment. Its upside rewards or downside risk are unlimited and the investor receives no other direct or indirect benefits from any other investor for making the investment.
    d. No other investor directly or indirectly provides or guarantees the investor's investment.
    e. The investor does not provide or guarantee any other investor's investment.
3. Promotion
    a. The investor did not ask others to invest in the investee.
4. Subsequent Collaboration

a. The investor can exercise its voting rights in all shareholder votes.
b. The investor has no special rights not given to the other investors, such as a guaranteed board seat.
c. The investor's right to sell its shares is unrestricted, except as required by securities laws or by what is reasonable or customary in individually negotiated investment transactions for closely held companies, such as the investee's right of first refusal on the investor's shares if a third party offers to purchase the shares.

The SEC staff believes that push down accounting also applies when several financial investors act together to acquire ownership interests in a company but no single investor obtains substantially all of the ownership interests even though there is a significant ownership change. In that type of scenario, the presumption that the investors acted as a collaborative group would not be overcome if:

- The investors negotiated their investments in the company at the same time, based on the same contract.
- The investors made their investments to achieve a broad strategic objective that they were pursuing together.
- The investors had several prior business relationships that were material to each of the investors.
- One of the investors does not share fully in the risks and rewards of ownership because of limited first-loss guarantees made by the other investors.
- The board of directors is not controlled by a single investor but as a result of bylaw amendments regarding board representation and voting, one of the investors can block board action. Therefore, the investors must collaborate on controlling the board.
- Each investor's ability to transfer its shares is restricted.

CHAPTER 46
ASC 808—COLLABORATIVE ARRANGEMENTS

CONTENTS

Interpretive Guidance	46,001
ASC 808 Collaborative Arrangements	46,001
ASC 808-10: Overall	46,001
ASC 808-10-10-1, 15-2 through 15-13, 45-1 through 45-5, 50-1, 55-1 through 55-19, 65-1	
Accounting for Collaborative Arrangements	46,001

INTERPRETIVE GUIDANCE

ASC 808 COLLABORATIVE ARRANGEMENTS

ASC 808-10: OVERALL

ASC 808-10-10-1, 15-2 through 15-13, 45-1 through 45-5, 50-1, 55-1 through 55-19, 65-1 Accounting for Collaborative Arrangements

BACKGROUND

The following discussion addresses the accounting for arrangements entered into by entities in a number of industries, such as the pharmaceutical, biotechnology, motion picture, software, and computer hardware industries, under which intellectual property is jointly developed and commercialized with other entities; usually, without creating a separate legal entity for that activity. All of the activities are conducted by the parties to the arrangement using their own employees and facilities. For example, one of the participants may be responsible for performing the research and development of a product while the other participant may be responsible for the product's commercialization. Because the accounting for such arrangements is diverse (i.e., arrangements may be accounted for on a gross basis or a net basis), accounting and disclosure guidance was developed to improve the comparability of financial statements.

    The following guidance applies to collaborative arrangements conducted by parties that participate in such arrangements without creating a separate legal entity for that purpose. This guidance is *not* limited to specific industries or to intellectual property. However, arrangements for which specific guidance exists under other current authoritative literature are excluded from the scope of this guidance and should be accounted for according to the existing guidance. In addition, the following guidance does *not* apply to arrangements that involve a financial investor.

ACCOUNTING GUIDANCE

Scope

A contractual arrangement under which the parties are involved in a joint operating activity and are exposed to significant risks and rewards that depend on the activity's ultimate success is referred to as a "collaborative arrangement." Although for the most part the activities of a collaborative arrangement under the scope of this guidance are *not* conducted through a separate legal entity created for that purpose, the existence of a specific legal entity for specific activities related to *part* of an arrangement or for a specific geographic location for part of an arrangement's activities would *not* exclude an arrangement from the definition of a *collaborative arrangement* in the ASC Glossary. However, the guidance in ASC 810, ASC 840-10-45-4, ASC 810-10-60-4, ASC 323-10, or other related literature should be applied to account for any part of a collaborative arrangement performed in a separate legal entity. The disclosure requirements under this guidance apply to the total arrangement, regardless of the parts that are conducted in a separate legal entity.

Participants should determine at the inception of an arrangement whether it is a collaborative arrangement based on the facts and circumstances at that time. However, a collaborative arrangement may begin at any time during an activity on which the participants have been collaborating. If the facts or circumstances of the participants' roles or their exposure to risks and rewards change, the arrangement should be reevaluated. Exercising an option is an example of a situation that might change a participant's role in a collaborative arrangement.

Joint Operating Activity

Participants in a collaborative arrangement may jointly develop and bring to market intellectual property, pharmaceutical products, software, computer hardware, or a motion picture. One participant may be primarily responsible for a specific activity or two or more participants may be jointly responsible for certain activities. Joint operating activities may include research and development, marketing, general and administrative activities, manufacturing, and distribution. A joint operation of a hospital is an example of a collaborative arrangement.

Active Participation

Active participation in a collaborative arrangement may consist of, but may not be limited to:

- Significant involvement in directing and carrying out joint activities;
- Participation on a steering committee or other means of oversight or governance; or
- Holding a contractual or other legal right to underlying intellectual property.

However, if an entity's only responsibility is to provide financial resources to a venture, that entity generally is *not* an active participant in a collaborative arrangement under the scope of this guidance.

Significant Risks and Rewards

To determine whether participants in a collaborative arrangement are exposed to significant risks and rewards that depend on a joint operating activity's commercial success, an arrangement's specific facts and circumstances, including, but not limited to, the arrangement's terms and conditions, should be considered. Based on an arrangement's terms and conditions, participants in an arrangement may *not* be exposed to *significant risks and rewards* if:

- Services are performed for fees at fair market value rates.
- A participant can leave an arrangement without cause and recover a significant portion or all of its cumulative economic participation to date.
- Only one participant receives an initial allocation of profits.
- The amount of a reward that a participant can receive is limited.

The following factors should be considered in an evaluation of risks and rewards:

- The stage of the endeavor's life cycle in which collaboration begins.
- The expected time period or financial commitment that participants will devote to the arrangement as it relates to an endeavor's total life span or expected value.

Consideration exchanged for a license related to intellectual property may *not* be an indicator that the participants are *not* exposed to risks or rewards on the ultimate success of their effort. Judgment is necessary to determine whether the participants are exposed to risks and rewards.

Income Statement Classification

Participants in a collaborative arrangement may report costs incurred and revenues generated from transactions with third parties in an appropriate line item in the participants' respective financial statements in accordance with the guidance in ASC 605-45-05-1, 05-2, 15-3 through 15-5, 45-1, 45-2, 45-4 through 45-14, 45-6 through 45-18, 50-1, 55-2, 55-3, 55-5, 55-6, 55-8, 55-9, 55-11 through 55-14, 55-16, 55-18, 55-20, 55-22, 55-24 through 55-25, 55-27 through 55-31, 55-33 through 55-34, 55-36 through 55-38, 55-40 through 55-45, Reporting Revenue Gross as a Principal versus Net as an Agent). Collaborative arrangements should *not* be accounted for using the equity method of accounting in ASC 505. A participant in a collaborative arrangement who is considered to be the principal participant in a specific revenue or cost transaction with a third party, should report that transaction on a gross basis in its financial statements based on the guidance in ASC 605-45.

The income statement description of payments between participants under a collaborative arrangement should be evaluated based on the arrangement's nature and contractual terms and the nature of each entity's business operations. If such payments fall under the scope of other authoritative literature, they should be accounted for under that guidance. Otherwise, the payments should be reported in the income statement based on an analogy to authoritative accounting literature, or if no appropriate analogy exists, the accounting policy selected should be applied in a reasonable, rational, and consistent manner.

Disclosure

Participants in a collaborative arrangement should disclose the following information in the initial reporting period and annually thereafter:

- The nature and purpose of collaborative arrangements.

- The entity's rights and obligations under a collaborative arrangement.
- The entity's accounting policy for collaborative arrangements.
- Income statement classification and amounts related to transactions as a result of the collaborative arrangement between participants for each period in which an income statement is presented.

Separate disclosure should be made about information related to collaborative arrangements that are significant individually.

CHAPTER 47
ASC 810—CONSOLIDATION

CONTENTS

Part I: General Guidance	47,003
ASC 810-10: Overall	47,003
Overview	47,003
Background	47,003
Majority-Owned Subsidiaries	47,003
Accounting and Reporting on Subsidiaries	47,004
Consolidation Issues	47,005
Combined Financial Statements	47,005
Comparative Financial Statements	47,005
Consolidation versus Equity Method	47,005
Consolidated Work Papers and Intercompany Transactions	47,006
Sales and Purchases	47,006
Receivables and Payables	47,006
Unrealized Profits in Inventory	47,006
Illustration of Profit in Inventory	47,007
Unrealized Profits in Long-Lived Assets	47,008
Illustration of Profit in Long-Lived Assets	47,008
Intercompany Bondholdings	47,009
Illustration of Intercompany Bonds	47,010
Illustration of Intercompany Bonds with Gain/Loss	47,010
Intercompany Dividends	47,012
Intercompany Stockholdings	47,012
Income Tax Considerations	47,012
Nature of Classification of the Noncontrolling Interest in the Consolidated Statement of Financial Position	47,012
Attributing Net Income and Comprehensive Income to the Parent and the Noncontrolling Interest	47,013
Changes in a Parent's Ownership Interest in a Subsidiary	47,013
Illustration of Changes in a Parent's Ownership Interest in a Subsidiary	47,014
Deconsolidation of a Subsidiary	47,015
Illustration of Gain or Loss on the Deconsolidation of a Subsidiary	47,016
Disclosures	47,017
Illustration of Computing Noncontrolling Interest and Consolidated Net Income	47,018
Variable Interest Entities	47,019
Key Definitions	47,020
Scope	47,020
Consolidation Criteria	47,022
Expected Losses and Expected Residual Returns	47,023

Variable Interests and Interests in Specified Assets	47,024
Consolidation Based on Variable Interests	47,024
Initial Measurement	47,026
Accounting after Initial Measurement	47,026
Disclosures Related to Variable Interest Entities	47,027
Part II: Interpretive Guidance	**47,029**
ASC 810-10: Overall	**47,029**
ASC 810-10-05-14 through 05-16, 15-18 through 15-22, 25-60 through 25-79, 25-81, 55-206 through 55-209; ASC 718-10-55-85A	
Consolidation of Entities Controlled by Contract	47,029
ASC 810-10-15-10, 25-1 through 25-8, 25-10 through 25-14, 55-1	
Investor's Accounting for an Investee When the Investor Has a Majority of the Voting Interest but the Noncontrolling Shareholder or Shareholders Have Certain Approval or Veto Rights	47,036
ASC 810-10-15-14, 25-21 through 25-29, 25-31 through 25-33, 25-35 through 25-36, 55-55 through 55-56, 55-58 through 55-86	
Determining the Variability to Be Considered	47,041
ASC 810-10-25-15; ASC 946-10-65-1	
Retention of Specialized Accounting for Investments in Consolidation	47,044
ASC 810-10-25-48 through 25-54, 55-87 through 55-89	
Implicit Variable Interests	47,044
ASC 810-10-25-58	
Reporting Variable Interests in Specified Assets of Variable Interest Entities as Separate Variable Interest Entities	47,046
ASC 810-10-40-1 through 40-2A; ASC 505-10-60-4	
Early Extinguishment of a Subsidiary's Mandatorily Redeemable Preferred Stock	47,046
ASC 810-10-45-13, 50-2	
Reporting a Change in (or the Elimination of) a Previously Existing Difference between the Fiscal Year-End of a Parent Company and That of a Consolidated Entity or between the Reporting Period of an Investor and That of an Equity Method Investee	47,047
ASC 810-10-55-2 through 55-4	
Elimination of Profits Resulting from Intercompany Transfers of LIFO Inventories	47,048
ASC 810-10-55-50 through 55-54	
Calculation of Expected Losses if There is no History, nor Future Expectation of, Net Losses	47,048
ASC 810-20: Control of Partnerships and Similar Entities	**47,050**
ASC 810-20-15-1 through 15-3, 25-1 through 25-20 45-1 55-1 through 55-16	
Determining Whether a General Partner, or the General Partners as a Group, Controls a Limited Partnership or Similar Entity When the Limited Partners Have Certain Rights	47,050
ASC 810-30: Research and Development Arrangements	**47,057**
ASC 810-30-15-2, 15-3, 25-1, 25-3; 30-1, 35-1, 45-1, 45-2, 55-1 through 55-4	
Accounting for Transactions with Elements of Research and Development Arrangements	47,057

PART I: GENERAL GUIDANCE

ASC 810-10: OVERALL

OVERVIEW

Consolidated financial statements represent the results of operations, statement of cash flows, and financial position of a single entity, even though multiple, separate legal entities are involved. Consolidated financial statements are presumed to present more meaningful information than separate financial statements and must be used in substantially all cases in which a parent directly or indirectly controls the majority voting interest (over 50%) of a subsidiary. Consolidated financial statements should not be used in those circumstances in which there is significant doubt concerning the parent's ability to control the subsidiary.

BACKGROUND

It is desirable to present comparative financial statements in annual reports, because such a presentation is likely to provide much more information than noncomparative statements. A consolidated financial statement presents the results of operations, statement of cash flows, and financial position of a single entity. With few exceptions, a parent company is to consolidate all of its majority-owned subsidiaries. A company must consolidate the assets, liabilities, revenues, and expenses of a variable interest entity if the company has a controlling financial interest in that entity. ASC 810 established accounting and reporting standards to ensure consistency in the reporting and disclosure of noncontrolling interests in consolidated financial statements, including the deconsolidation of a subsidiary. ASC 958 provides guidance on the application of ASC 810 for not-for-profit entities. ASC 810, changes the requirements for determining whether an entity is a variable interest entity, as well as the requirements for determining the primary beneficiary of a variable interest entity.

Retained earnings of a subsidiary at the date of acquisition are not treated as part of consolidated retained earnings (ASC 810-10-45-2). The retained earnings, other capital accounts, and contributed capital at the date of acquisition represent the book value that is eliminated in preparing consolidated statements.

A parent company should not exclude a majority-owned subsidiary from consolidation because it has a different fiscal year. For consolidation purposes, a subsidiary usually can prepare financial statements that correspond with its parent's fiscal period. If a subsidiary's fiscal year is within three months or less of its parent's fiscal year, it is acceptable to use those fiscal-year financial statements for consolidation purposes, provided that adequate disclosure is made of any material events occurring within the intervening period (ASC 810-10-45-12).

MAJORITY-OWNED SUBSIDIARIES

All investments in which a parent company has a controlling financial interest represented by the direct or indirect ownership of a majority voting interest (more than 50%) must be consolidated, except those in which significant doubt exists regarding the parent's ability to control the subsidiary. In addition, in some cases the existence of noncontrolling interests can prevent the owner of a more than 50% voting interest from having a controlling financial interest (ASC 810-10-15-3). For example, the majority owner may need the approval of the noncontrolling shareholder to control the operations or assets of the investee, or the noncontrolling shareholder may have veto rights over the actions of the majority owner, and these restrictions may be so substantive as to prevent the majority owner from having control (ASC 810-10-15-10).

> **PRACTICE POINTER:** In determining whether consolidated financial statements are required in a particular situation, a reasonable starting point is to assume that if majority ownership exists, consolidation is appropriate. For that point, consider those rare circumstances in which a majority ownership interest does exist but consolidation would not be appropriate. However, such circumstances are clearly intended to be exceptions to a policy of consolidation in most situations of majority ownership.

ASC 810 requires that the exchange restrictions or other governmental controls in a foreign subsidiary be so severe that they "cast significant doubt on the parent's ability to control the subsidiary." This amendment narrows the exception for a majority-owned foreign subsidiary from one that permits exclusion from consolidation of any or all foreign subsidiaries to one that effectively eliminates distinctions between foreign and domestic subsidiaries. Thus, a majority-owned subsidiary must be consolidated unless significant doubt exists regarding the parent's control of the subsidiary. ASC 830 contains special rules for translating foreign currency financial statements of foreign subsidiaries that operate in countries with highly inflationary economies.

> **PRACTICE POINTER:** ASC 810 comes close to requiring that all majority-owned subsidiaries be consolidated. A limited exception is a situation where control does not rest with the majority owner, as when a subsidiary is in legal reorganization or bankruptcy. ASC 323, on the other hand, is amended to eliminate the requirement that unconsolidated subsidiaries be accounted for by the equity method. In the rare instance indicated above, where (majority-owned) subsidiaries are not consolidated, the authoritative literature apparently does not specify a particular method of accounting, although the equity method may be judged the appropriate method to use in the circumstances.

ACCOUNTING AND REPORTING ON SUBSIDIARIES

The identifiable assets acquired, the liabilities assumed, and any non-controlling interests in the subsidiary must be measured at their acquisition-date fair values (ASC 805-20-30-1). Any excess of the fair market value of the consideration given over the fair market value of the net assets acquired is reported as goodwill (ASC 805-30-30-1). If the fair market value of the consideration given is less than the fair market value of the net assets acquired, the resulting excess of fair value of acquired net assets over the cost of the acquired entity is recognized in earnings as a gain on the acquisition date (ASC 805-30-25-2).

When a subsidiary is initially consolidated during the year, the consolidated financial statements shall include the subsidiary's revenues, expenses, gains, and losses only from the date the subsidiary is initially consolidated (ASC 810-10-45-4).

CONSOLIDATION ISSUES

Combined Financial Statements

Consolidated financial statements usually are justified on the basis that one of the consolidating entities exercises control over the affiliated group. When there is no such control, combined financial statements may be used to accomplish the same results. For example, a group of companies controlled by an individual shareholder, or a group of unconsolidated subsidiaries that could otherwise not be consolidated, should utilize combined financial statements. Combined financial statements are prepared on the same basis as consolidated financial statements, except that no company in the group has a controlling interest in the other (ASC 810-10-55-1B).

Comparative Financial Statements

Comparative financial statements reveal much more information than noncomparative statements and furnish useful data about differences in the results of operations for the periods involved or in the financial position at the comparison dates (ASC 205-10-45-1).

Consistency is a major factor in creating comparability. Prior-year amounts and classifications must be, in fact, comparable with the current period presented, and exceptions must be disclosed clearly (ASC 205-10-45-2, 4).

Consolidation versus Equity Method

The income and balance sheet effects of intercompany transactions are eliminated in equity method adjustments as well as in the financial statements of consolidated entities (ASC 810-10-45-1). In consolidated financial statements, the details of all entities to the consolidation are reported in full. In the equity method, the investment is shown as a single amount in the investor balance sheet, and earnings or losses generally are shown as a single amount in the income statement. This is the reason the equity method is frequently referred to as *one-line consolidation*.

PRACTICE POINTER: While their impact on reporting income is the same, the equity method and consolidation differ in the extent of detail each reflects in the financial statements. The authoritative literature clearly states that the equity method is not necessarily an appropriate alternative to consolidation, or vice versa. Generally, consolidation is appropriate where majority interest exists, and the equity method is appropriate where the investor has the ability to exert significant influence over the investee but lacks majority ownership.

Consolidated Work Papers and Intercompany Transactions

The preparation of consolidated financial statements is facilitated by the preparation of a consolidated statements worksheet. Traditionally, this worksheet was prepared by hand and the adjustments and eliminations required for consolidation were not posted to the books of the individual companies. Computerization of accounting processes, including the preparation of worksheets to assist in the preparation of consolidated financial statements, has modernized this process and all eliminations and adjustments are posted.

Following is a brief discussion of some of the most frequently encountered intercompany transactions.

Sales and Purchases

The gross amount of all intercompany sales and/or purchases is eliminated on the consolidated work papers. When the adjustment has already been made in the trial balance for ending inventory, the eliminating entry is made by debiting sales and crediting cost of sales. When no adjustment has been made for ending inventory, the eliminating entry is made by crediting the purchases account. In this latter case, a more straightforward approach is to make an adjusting entry establishing the cost of sales and then eliminating intercompany sales by crediting cost of sales.

Receivables and Payables

Intercompany receivables and payables include:

- Accounts receivable and accounts payable.
- Advances to and from affiliates.
- Notes receivable and notes payable.
- Interest receivable and interest payable.

The gross amounts of all intercompany receivables and payables are eliminated on the consolidated work papers. Care must be exercised when a receivable is discounted with one of the consolidated companies (no contingent liability). If the balance sheet reflects a discounted receivable with another affiliate, the amount must be eliminated by a debit to discounted receivables and a credit to receivables. If one affiliate discounts a receivable to another affiliate, who in turn discounts it to an outsider, a real contingent liability still exists, and must be shown on the consolidated balance sheet.

Unrealized Profits in Inventory

Regardless of any noncontrolling interests, all (100%) of any intercompany profit in ending inventory is eliminated on the consolidated workpapers. In addition, the cost of sales account must be adjusted for intercompany profit in beginning inventory arising from intercompany transactions in the previous year. If the adjustment for intercompany profits in inventories is not made, consolidated net income will be incorrect and consolidated ending inventory will be overstated.

Illustration of Profit in Inventory

P Company purchased $200,000 and $250,000 of merchandise in 20X8 and 20X9, respectively, from its subsidiary S at 25% above cost. As of December 31, 20X8, and 20X9, P had on hand $25,000 and $30,000 of merchandise purchased from S. The following is the computation of intercompany profits:

Computation of Intercompany Profits

Beginning inventory	$25,000	=	125%
Cost to S	(20,000)	=	(100%)
Intercompany profit	$ 5,000		25%
Ending inventory	$30,000	=	125%
Cost to S	(24,000)	=	(100%)
Intercompany profit	$ 6,000		25%

The adjustment is different for a consolidated balance sheet than for a consolidated income statement and balance sheet. If intercompany profit adjustments have not been recorded in equity method entries on P Company's books, for a consolidated balance sheet only the elimination entry is:

Retained earnings	6,000	
Inventory		6,000

Assuming no equity method adjustments are made, and a perpetual inventory system is used, for a consolidated income statement and balance sheet the following adjustments are necessary:

Sales	250,000	
Costs of sales		250,000

To eliminate intercompany sales.

Consolidated retained earnings	5,000	
Cost of sales		5,000

To reverse consolidated adjustment of 12/31/X8.

Cost of sales	6,000	
Inventory		6,000

To eliminate intercompany profit in ending inventory.

The adjustment to consolidated retained earnings is necessary because the intercompany profit was eliminated on the prior year's consolidated work papers. (Consolidated adjustments and eliminations are not posted to the books of the individual companies. Therefore, the beginning inventory for P still reflected the prior year's intercompany inventory profits from S.)

If merchandise containing an intercompany inventory profit is reduced from the purchase price to market value and the reduction is equal to, or more than, the actual intercompany inventory profit, no deferral of profit entry is required in consolidation. For example, if merchandise costing one affiliate $10,000 is sold to another affiliate for $12,000, who reduces it to market value of $11,000, the consolidated work paper adjustment for unrealized intercompany inventory profits should be only $1,000.

Noncontrolling interests do not affect the adjustment for unrealized intercompany profits in inventories. Consolidated net income and noncontrolling interests in the net income of a subsidiary are affected by the adjustment, however, because the reduction or increase in beginning or ending inventory of a partially owned subsidiary does affect the determination of net income.

Unrealized intercompany losses in inventory are accounted for in the same manner as unrealized profits, except that they have the opposite effect. Profits or losses on sales and/or purchases prior to an affiliation are not recognized as a consolidated adjustment.

Unrealized Profits in Long-Lived Assets

Regardless of any noncontrolling interests, all (100%) of any intercompany profits on the sale and/or purchase of long-lived assets between affiliates is eliminated on the consolidated workpapers.

When one affiliate constructs or sells a long-lived asset to another affiliate at a profit, the profit is eliminated on the consolidated work-papers. As with unrealized intercompany profits or losses in inventory, noncontrolling interests do not affect any consolidated adjustment for profits in intercompany sales of long-lived assets between affiliates. Net income of the subsidiary involved in the intercompany profit on a long-lived asset is affected by the adjustment, however, which in turn affects consolidated net income and noncontrolling interests.

If a nondepreciable asset is involved in an intercompany profit on a long-lived asset, the profit is eliminated by a debit to either retained earnings, in the case of an adjusted consolidated balance sheet, or to gain on sale, in the case of a consolidated income statement.

Depreciable assets require the same adjustment for intercompany profit as nondepreciable long-lived assets, and an adjustment must also be made for any depreciation recorded on the intercompany profit.

Illustration of Profit in Long-Lived Assets

S Company, an 80%-owned subsidiary, sells to P Company for $100,000 a piece of machinery that cost $80,000. The sale was made on July 1, 20X8, and consolidated statements are being prepared for December 31, 20X8. P Company depreciates machinery over ten years on a straight-line basis and records one-half year's depreciation on the purchased machinery.

The first entry eliminates the $20,000 of intercompany profit, as follows:

Gain on sale of machinery	20,000	
Machinery		20,000

Since P Company has recorded one-half year's depreciation on the machinery, the following additional entry is made:

Accumulated depreciation	1,000	
Depreciation expense		1,000

Because consolidated eliminations and adjustments are never posted to any books, additional entries are required in the following year. Assuming that intercompany profit adjustments were not made under the equity method on P Company's books, the following eliminations are needed:

Retained earnings—P Company	16,000	
Retained earnings—S Company	4,000	
Machinery		20,000

To eliminate intercompany profit on prior year's sale of machinery.

Accumulated depreciation	3,000	
Retained earnings—P Company		800
Retained earnings—S Company		200
Depreciation expense		2,000

To eliminate the $2,000 depreciation expense on intercompany profit on the sale of machinery and to eliminate the $1,000 depreciation expense for prior year's depreciation.

If the intercompany sale had been made from P Company to S Company, the retained earnings adjustments would have been made only to P Company's accounts.

The process of eliminating the depreciation expense on the intercompany profit on the sale of long-lived assets continues until the asset is fully depreciated. Thereafter, until the asset is disposed of or retired, adjustments are needed to the machinery and accumulated depreciation accounts. In the example, the following entry would be made every year on the consolidated work papers after the asset is fully depreciated and before it is disposed of or retired.

Accumulated depreciation	20,000	
Machinery		20,000

An affiliate that makes an intercompany profit on the sale of long-lived assets to another affiliate may pay income taxes on the gain. This occurs usually when the affiliated group does not file consolidated tax returns and the gain cannot be avoided for tax purposes. In such cases, the intercompany profit on the sale should be reduced by the related tax effects in computing the consolidated adjusting entry.

Intercompany Bondholdings

Intercompany bonds purchased by an affiliate are treated in the year of acquisition as though they have been retired. Any gain or loss is recognized in the consolidated income statement for the year of acquisition.

The amount of gain or loss on an intercompany bond purchase is the difference between the unamortized bond premium or discount on the books of the issuer and the amount of any purchase discount or premium.

47,010 ASC 810—Consolidation

An intercompany gain or loss on bonds does not occur when an affiliate makes the purchase directly from the affiliated issuer, because the selling price will be exactly equal to the cost.

Illustration of Intercompany Bonds

An affiliate purchases $20,000 face value 6% bonds from an affiliated issuer for $19,500.

On the affiliated investor's books the following entry is made:

Investment in bonds	19,500	
Cash		19,500

On the affiliated issuer's books the entry is:

Cash	19,500	
Discount on bonds payable	500	
Bonds payable		20,000

The consolidated elimination is:

Bonds payable	20,000	
Discount on bonds payable		500
Investment in bonds		19,500

An intercompany gain or loss on bonds does not occur when the purchase price is exactly the same as the carrying value on the books of the affiliated issuer.

The following conditions must exist for an affiliated investor to realize a gain or loss on intercompany bondholdings:

- The bonds are already outstanding.
- The bonds are purchased from outside the affiliated group.
- The price paid is different from the carrying value of the affiliated issuer.

Illustration of Intercompany Bonds with Gain/Loss

Company S acquires $50,000 of face amount 6% bonds from an outsider. These bonds were part of an original issue of $300,000 made by the parent of Company S. The purchase price was $45,000, and the bonds mature in four years and nine months (57 months). Interest is payable on June 30 and December 31, and the purchase was made on March 31.

The journal entry on the books of Company S to record the purchase is:

Investment in bonds	45,000	
Accrued interest receivable	750	
Cash		45,750

On the consolidated workpapers at the end of the year, the following entries are made:

Investment in bonds	5,000	
Gain on intercompany bondholdings		5,000

To adjust the investment in bonds to face amount and record the gain.		
Bonds payable—Co. P	50,000	
Investment in bonds—Co. S		50,000
To eliminate intercompany bondholdings.		
Interest income—Co. S	2,250	
Interest expense—Co. P		2,250
To eliminate intercompany interest on bonds that was actually paid.		
Interest income—Co. S	788	
Investment in bonds		788
To eliminate amortization of $5,000 discount on bonds recorded on Co. S's books. (9/57 of $5,000 = $788)		
Accrued interest payable	1,500	
Accrued interest receivable		1,500
To eliminate accrued interest payable on Dec. 31 by Co. P, and the accrued interest receivable on Dec. 31 by Co. S.		

This example contains all the possible adjustments except for an issuer's premium or discount. Assume the following additional information on the original issue:

Face amount	$300,000
Issued at 96	288,000
Date of issue	1/1/X1
Maturity date	1/1/Y0

Company S had purchased its $50,000 face amount when the issue had four years and nine months left to maturity.

On the parent company's books, this discount is being amortized over the life of the bond issue at the rate of $1,200 per year ($12,000 discount divided by 10 years). An adjustment is made on the consolidated workpapers to eliminate the portion of the unamortized bond discount existing at the date of purchase that is applicable to the $50,000 face amount purchased by Company S.

Total discount on issue	$12,000
1/6 applicable to Co. S's purchase	$ 2,000
Amount of discount per month ($2,000 divided by 120 months)	$ 16.67
Four years and nine months equal 57 months × $16.67	$ 950

The amount of unamortized bond discount on Co. P's books applicable to the $50,000 purchase made by Company S was $950 at the date of purchase. This $950 would have entered into the computation of the gain or loss on intercompany bondholdings. In the example, the gain or loss on intercompany bondholdings of $5,000 would have been reduced by $950 ($4,050) and the following additional consolidated elimination would have been made:

Gain or loss on intercompany bondholdings	950	
Unamortized bond discount		950

In addition, the amortization on the intercompany portion of the bond discount would be reversed in the consolidated worksheet (9 months × $16.67):

Unamortized bond discount	150	
Interest expense		150

Intercompany Dividends

Intercompany dividends are eliminated on the consolidated work-papers. Consolidated retained earnings should reflect the accumulated earnings of the consolidated group arising since acquisition that have not been distributed to the shareholders of, or capitalized by, the parent company. In the event that a subsidiary capitalizes earnings arising since acquisition by means of a stock dividend, or otherwise, a transfer to paid-in capital is not required in consolidating (ASC 810-10-45-9).

Intercompany Stockholdings

Shares of the parent held by a subsidiary should not be treated as outstanding stock in the consolidated balance sheet. Such shares are treated as "treasury stock" on the consolidated balance sheet and subtracted from consolidated stockholders' equity.

Income Tax Considerations

Income taxes are deferred on any intercompany profits where the asset still exists within the consolidated group (ASC 810-10-45-8). If consolidated tax returns are filed, however, no adjustment need be made for deferred income taxes, because intercompany profits are eliminated in computing the consolidated tax liability.

Nature of Classification of the Noncontrolling Interest in the Consolidated Statement of Financial Position

A noncontrolling interest is defined as as a portion of equity in a subsidiary that is not attributable to a parent company, and thus clarifies a noncontrolling interest in a subsidiary as part of the equity of the consolidated group (ASC 810-10-45-15). Furthermore, a noncontrolling interest is limited to a parent's ownership of a financial instrument issued by a subsidiary that is classified as equity in the subsidiary's financial statements. A financial instrument that is classified as a liability in the subsidiary's financial statements based on the guidance in other standards does not represent an ownership interest and, therefore, is not a noncontrolling interest (ASC 810-10-45-17).

Prior to ASC 810, there was limited guidance related to the classification and reporting of noncontrolling interests. This resulted in considerable diversity in practice with noncontrolling interests reported either as liabilities or in the mezzanine section between liabilities and equity. This diversity has been eliminated and comparability improved by requiring a noncontrolling interest to be reported in the consolidated statement of financial position within equity (net assets), separately from the parent's equity or net assets (ASC 810-10-45-16).

Attributing Net Income and Comprehensive Income to the Parent and the Noncontrolling Interest

Revenues, expenses, gains, losses, net income or loss, and other comprehensive income (and similar amounts reported by not-for-profit entities) attributable to the noncontrolling interest shall be included in the amount reported in consolidated net income (ASC 810-10-45-19). The amounts of consolidated net income attributable to the parent and to the noncontrolling interest also must be disclosed on the face of the consolidated statement of income.

ASC 958 modified how a subsidiary's losses are attributed to the parent and the noncontrolling interest in the unusual case in which losses attributable to the parent and the noncontrolling interest exceed their interests in the subsidiary's equity. Prior to ASC 958 such excess losses attributable to the noncontrolling interest were charged against the parent. Such excess losses attributable to the parent and the noncontrolling interest are now charged to those interests, respectively. In other words, the noncontrolling interest must continue to be attributed its share of losses even if doing so results in a deficit noncontrolling interest balance (ASC 810-10-45-21).

Changes in a Parent's Ownership Interest in a Subsidiary

ASC 958 established a single method of accounting for changes in a parent's ownership interest in a subsidiary when the parent retains its controlling financial interest in the subsidiary. Such a change in the parent's ownership interest in a subsidiary could include (ASC 810-10-45-22):

- the parent purchases additional ownership interests in its subsidiary,
- the parent sells some of its ownership interests in its subsidiary,
- the subsidiary reacquires some of its ownership interests, or
- the subsidiary issues additional ownership interests.

ASC 958 clarified that changes in a parent's ownership while retaining a controlling financial interest in the subsidiary must be accounted for as equity transactions, and, therefore, no gain or loss shall be recognized in consolidated net income or comprehensive income (changes in net assets). ASC 958 required the noncontrolling interest carrying amount to be adjusted to reflect the change in its ownership interest in the subsidiary, and any difference between the fair value of the consideration received or paid and the amount by which the noncontrolling interest is adjusted to be recognized in the equity (net assets) attributable to the parent (ASC 810-10-45-23). Similarly, if a change in a parent's ownership interest occurs in a subsidiary that has accumulated other comprehensive income, the carrying amount of accumulated other comprehensive income shall be adjusted to reflect the change in ownership interest with a corresponding charge or credit to the equity (net assets) attributable to the parent (ASC 810-10-45-24).

ASC 810-10 was amended by ASU 2010-02 in 2010 to clarify the scope of the decrease in ownership provisions of the subtopic and related guidance. Situations to which this guidance applies are the following:

1. A subsidiary or group of assets that is a business or nonprofit activity.
2. A subsidiary that is a business or nonprofit activity that is transferred to the equity method investee or joint venture.
3. An exchange of a group of assets that constitutes a business or nonprofit activity with a noncontrolling interest in an entity (including an equity method investee or joint venture).

The decrease in ownership guidance in ASC 810-10 does not apply to the following transactions if they involve businesses:

1. Sales of in substance real estate. (Entities should apply the sale of real estate guidance in ASC 360-20 (Property and Equipment) and 976-605 (Retail/Land) to these transactions.)
2. Conveyances of oil and gas mineral rights. (Entities should apply the mineral property conveyance and related transactions guidance in ASC 932-360 (Oil and Gas—Property, Plant, and Equipment) to these transactions.)

If a decrease in ownership occurs in a subsidiary that is not a business or nonprofit activity, the entity first must consider whether the substance of the transaction causing the decrease is addressed in other U.S. GAAP, such as transfers of financial assets, revenue recognition, exchanges of nonmonetary assets, sales of in substance real estate, or conveyances of oil and gas mineral rights, and apply the applicable guidance for those transactions. If no other guidance exists, ASC 810-10 applies.

Illustration of Changes in a Parent's Ownership Interest in a Subsidiary

Example 1

Subsidiary A has 50,000 shares of common stock outstanding, all of which are owned by its parent, ABC Co. The carrying amount of Subsidiary A's equity is $800,000. ABC Co. sells 10,000 of its shares in Subsidiary A to an unrelated entity for $200,000 in cash, reducing its ownership interest from 100 percent to 80 percent. That transaction is accounted for by recognizing a noncontrolling interest in the amount of $160,000 ($800,000 × 20 percent). The $40,000 excess of the cash received ($200,000) over the adjustment to the carrying amount of the noncontrolling interest ($160,000) is recognized as an increase in additional paid-in capital attributable to ABC Co. The sale of Subsidiary A's shares by ABC Co. is accounted for as an equity transaction in the consolidated financial statements as follows:

Cash	$200,000	
Noncontrolling interest		$ 160,000
Additional paid-in capital (ABC Co.)		40,000

Example 2

Subsidiary A has 50,000 shares of common stock outstanding. Of those shares, 45,000 are owned by its parent, ABC Co., and 5,000 are owned by other shareholders (a noncontrolling interest in Subsidiary A). The carrying amount of Subsidiary A's equity is $1,200,000. Of that amount, $1,080,000 is attributable to ABC Co., and $120,000 is a noncontrolling interest in Subsidiary A. Subsidiary A issues 10,000 previously unissued shares to a third party for $480,000 in cash, reducing ABC Co.'s ownership interest in Subsidiary A from 90 percent to 75 percent (45,000 shares owned by ABC Co. / 60,000 issued shares).

Even though the percentage of ABC Co.'s ownership interest in Subsidiary A is reduced when Subsidiary A issues additional shares to a third party, ABC Co.'s investment in Subsidiary A increases to $1,260,000, calculated as 75 percent of Subsidiary A's equity of $1,680,000 ($1,200,000 + $480,000). Therefore, ABC Co. recognizes a $180,000 increase in its investment in Subsidiary A ($1,260,000-$1,080,000) and a corresponding increase in its additional paid-in capital (that is, the additional paid-in capital attributable to ABC Co.). In addition, the noncontrolling interest is increased to $420,000, calculated as 25 percent of $1,680,000. The sale of additional shares by Subsidiary A is accounted for as an equity transaction in the consolidated financial statements as follows:

Cash	$480,000	
Noncontrolling interest		$ 300,000
Additional paid-in capital (ABC Co.)		180,000

Example 3

Subsidiary A has 50,000 shares of common stock outstanding. Of those shares, 40,000 are owned by its parent, ABC Co., and 10,000 are owned by other shareholders (a noncontrolling interest in Subsidiary A). The carrying amount of the noncontrolling interest is $240,000, which includes $20,000 of accumulated other comprehensive income. ABC Co. pays $150,000 in cash to purchase 5,000 shares held by the noncontrolling shareholders (50 percent of the noncontrolling interest), increasing its ownership interest from 80 percent to 90 percent. That transaction is recognized by reducing the carrying amount of the noncontrolling interest by $120,000 ($240,000 × 50 percent). The $30,000 excess of the cash paid ($150,000) over the adjustment to the carrying amount of the noncontrolling interest ($120,000) is recognized as a decrease in additional paid-in capital attributable to ABC Co. In addition, ABC Co.'s share of accumulated other comprehensive income is increased by $10,000 ($20,000 × 50 percent) through a corresponding decrease in additional paid-in capital attributable to ABC Co. The purchase of shares from the noncontrolling shareholders is accounted for as an equity transaction in the consolidated financial statements as follows:

Noncontrolling interest	$120,000	
Additional paid-in capital (ABC Co.)	40,000	
Accumulated other comprehensive income (ABC Co.)		$ 10,000
Cash		150,000

Deconsolidation of a Subsidiary

A parent is required to deconsolidate a subsidiary as of the date the parent ceases to have a controlling financial interest in the subsidiary. For example, the following events would result in the deconsolidation of a subsidiary (ASC 810-10-55-4A):

- A parent sells some or all of its ownership interest in the subsidiary, and as a result, the parent no longer has a controlling financial interest in the subsidiary
- A contractual agreement expires, and the parent's control of the subsidiary is dependent on that agreement
- The subsidiary issues additional shares, thereby reducing the parent's ownership interest in the subsidiary to a point that does not result in the parent having a controlling financial interest
- The subsidiary becomes under the control of a government, court, administrator, or regulator

When deconsolidating a subsidiary, the parent shall measure any noncontrolling interest it retains in the former subsidiary at its fair value and recognize a gain or loss in net income attributable to the parent, measured as the difference between:

a. The aggregate of:
   1. The fair value of any consideration received
   2. The fair value of any retained noncontrolling investment in the former subsidiary at the date the subsidiary is deconsolidated
   3. The carrying amount of any noncontrolling interest in the former subsidiary held by any party other than the former parent (including any accumulated other comprehensive income attributable to the noncontrolling interest) at the date the subsidiary is deconsolidated
b. The carrying amount of the former subsidiary's assets and liabilities

---

Illustration of Gain or Loss on the Deconsolidation of a Subsidiary

Sub Co. has 10,000 shares of common stock outstanding. Of those shares, 8,000 are owned by its parent, ABC Co., and 2,000 are owned by other shareholders (a noncontrolling interest in Sub Co.). The carrying amount of Sub Co.'s equity is $1,000,000. ABC Co. sells 4,000 of its shares in Sub Co. to an unrelated entity for $600,000 in cash, reducing its ownership interest from 80 percent to 40 percent. Therefore, ABC Co. no longer has a controlling interest in Sub Co., and would recognize a gain of $400,000 on the deconsolidation of Sub Co., calculated as follows:

Fair value of consideration received	$ 600,000
Fair value of retained noncontrolling investment in Sub Co.	600,000
Carrying amount of noncontrolling interest in Sub Co. held by parties other than ABC Co.	200,000
	$1,400,000
Less: carrying amount of Sub Co.'s net assets	− 1,000,000
Gain on deconsolidation of Sub Co.	$ 400,000

Note that ASC 310 does not apply to the deconsolidation of a subsidiary through a nonreciprocal transfer to owners, such as a spinoff. In this case, the guidance provided in APB-29 (Accounting for Nonmonetary Transactions) applies (ASC 810-10-40-5).

Disclosures

The consolidation policy should be disclosed fully on the financial statements or in footnotes thereto (ASC 810-10-50-1).

ASC 810 requires expanded disclosures in the consolidated financial statements that clearly identify and distinguish between the interests of the parent and the interests of the noncontrolling owners of a subsidiary. A parent with one or more less-than-wholly-owned subsidiaries shall disclose for each reporting period (ASC 810-10-50-1A):

- Separately, on the face of the consolidated financial statements, the amounts of consolidated net income and consolidated comprehensive income, including the amounts of each that are attributable to the parent and the noncontrolling interest
- Either in the notes or on the face of the consolidated income statement, amounts attributable to the parent for the following, if reported in the consolidated financial statements:
  — Income from continuing operations
  — Discontinued operations
  — Extraordinary items
- Either in the consolidated statement of changes in equity, if presented, or in the notes to the consolidated financial statements, a reconciliation at the beginning and the end of the period of the carrying amount of total equity (net assets), including the amounts attributable to the parent and to the noncontrolling interest. The reconciliation must separately disclose:
  — Net income
  — Transactions with owners acting in their capacity as owners, showing separately contributions from and distributions to owners
  — Each component of other comprehensive income
- In the notes to the consolidated financial statements, a separate schedule that shows the effects of any changes in a parent's ownership interest in a subsidiary on the equity attributable to the parent

Additional disclosures are required for a not-for-profit entity if it has one or more consolidated subsidiaries with noncontrolling interests. A schedule of changes in net assets attributable to the parent and the noncontrolling interests must appear either on the face of the financial statements or in the notes. The schedule reconciles the beginning and ending balances of the parent's controlling interest, as well as the beginning and ending balances for each class of net assets for which a noncontrolling interest exists. This schedule must include:

- A performance indicator (if the entity is subject to the AICPA Audit and Accounting Guide, *Health Care Organizations*)
- Discontinued operations

- Extraordinary items
- Changes in a subsidiary's ownership interests, including transactions with owners acting in their capacity as owners with contributions from and distributions to owners being shown separately
- The aggregate amount of all other changes in unrestricted net assets

If a subsidiary is deconsolidated, the parent is required to disclose (ASC 810-10-50-1B):

- The amount of any gain or loss recognized
- The portion of any gain or loss related to the remeasurement of any retained investment in the former subsidiary to its fair value
- The caption in the income statement in which the gain or loss is recognized unless separately presented on the face of the income statement (ASC 810-10-50-1B)
- The valuation technique used to measure the fair value of any retained investment in the former subsidiary or group of assets and information that enables users of its financial statements to assess the inputs used to develop the measurement
- The nature of continuing involvement with the subsidiary or entity acquiring the group of assets after it has been deconsolidated or derecognized
- Whether the transaction that resulted in the deconsolidation of the subsidiary or the derecognition of the group of assets was with a related party or whether the former subsidiary or entity acquiring the group of assets will be a related part after deconsolidation
- The valuation techniques used to measure an equity interest in an acquiree held by the entity immediately before the acquisition date in a business combination achieved in stages. (ASC 810-10-51-1B) (ASU 2010-02)

Illustration of Computing Noncontrolling Interest and Consolidated Net Income

Computing noncontrolling interests in a complex father-son-grandson affiliation may be demonstrated by using the following diagram (dollar amounts are income figures for the separate entities):

The computations of noncontrolling interests and consolidated net income follow:

	E	D	C	B	A
Net income	$60,000	$50,000	$80,000	$40,000	$100,000
75% to D	(45,000)	45,000			
		$95,000			
90% to A		(85,500)			85,500
85% to B			(68,000)	68,000	
				$108,000	

	E	D	C	B	A
80% to A				(86,400)	86,400
Noncontrolling interests	$15,000	$9,500	$12,000	$21,600	
Consolidated net income					$271,900

In a situation in which a subsidiary owns shares of the parent company, consolidated net income may be found algebraically, as the following depicts:

Company	Unconsolidated Income (excluding income from investees)	
A	$40,000	A, the parent, owns 80% of B
B	20,000	B owns 70% of C
C	10,000	C owns 20% of A

The figures and relationships can be put into algebraic form so as to compute *consolidated net income*.

Solving for A, we have:

Company A's income on an equity basis, which equals consolidated income, is determined by multiplying by the 80% interest outstanding (i.e., the remaining 20% is held within the consolidated entity):

$69,369 × 0.8 = $55,495 consolidated net income

The noncontolling interests in the two subsidiaries are determined as follows:

VARIABLE INTEREST ENTITIES

ASC 810 addresses consolidation by business enterprises of variable interest entities that have certain specified characteristics. If a business enterprise has a controlling financial interest in a variable interest entity, the assets, liabilities, and results of activities of that entity should be included in the consolidated financial statements of the business enterprise.

OBSERVATION: ASC 810 was issued because transactions involving variable interest entities have become increasingly common, and the authoritative accounting literature related to these transactions is fragmented and incomplete.

ASC 810 clarifies the accounting for certain entities in which equity investors do not have sufficient equity at risk for the entity to finance its activities without additional subordinated financial support or, as a group, the equity investors lack any one of the following characteristics that provide an enterprise with a controlling financial interest in a variable interest entity (ASC 810.10.05-8):

1. The power to direct the activities of an entity that most significantly impact the entity's economic performance

2. The obligation to absorb the expected losses of the entity
3. The right to receive the expected residual returns of the entity.

Consolidated financial statements usually are required for a fair presentation when one of the companies in the group directly or indirectly has a controlling financial interest in the other companies. The usual condition for a controlling financial interest is a majority voting interest. For certain types of entities, however, application of the majority voting interest requirement may not identify the party with a controlling interest because the control may be achieved through arrangements that do not involve voting interests (ASC 810-10-05-8).

Key Definitions

Variable interest in a variable interest entity refers to a contractual, ownership, or other pecuniary interest in an entity that changes with changes in the fair value of the entity's net assets excluding variable interests. Equity interests with or without voting rights are considered variable interests if the entity is a variable interest entity, only to the extent that the investment is at risk (ASC Glossary). In ASC 810, *entity* is used to refer to any legal structure used to conduct activities or hold assets. This includes corporations, partnerships, limited liability companies, grantor trusts, and other trusts (ASC 810-10-15-15).

PRACTICE POINTER: Examples of variable interests in a variable interest entity often include (1) equity investments that are at risk, (2) investments in subordinated beneficial interests, (3) investments in subordinated debt instruments, (4) guarantees, (5) written put options, (6) forward purchase and sale contracts, (7) derivatives and total return swaps that reduce the exposure of the entity to risks that cause variability, and (8) leases with a residual value guarantee and options to acquire leased assets at the lease's termination at specified prices (ASC 810-10-55).

Fees paid to a decision maker could be a variable interest, but if *all* of the following conditions are met, such fees would *not* be considered a variable interest: (1) the fees represent fair compensation for the services provided; (2) the fees are not subordinate to other operating liabilities; (3) in circumstances other than the first two, the decision maker (and its related parties) do not hold interests that would result in the decision maker absorbing more than a trivial amount of expected losses or receiving more than a trivial amount of expected returns; (4) the service arrangement does not include any unusual terms, conditions, or amounts; (5) the total amount of fees are expected to be insignificant relative to the total amount of the variable interest entity's economic performance; and (6) the fees are expected to absorb an insignificant amount of the variability associated with the entity's economic performance ASC 810-10-55.

Scope

ASC 810 applies to all entities except (1) not-for-profit (NFP) organizations, unless the NFP organization is used by a business enterprise to circumvent the provisions of ASC 810; (2) pension, other postretirement, and other postemployment benefit plans; and (3) separate accounts for life insurance enterprises.

Investment companies subject to SEC regulation S-X, Rule 6-03(c)(1) should not consolidate an entity unless that entity is also subject to the same SEC regulation (ASC 810-10-15-17).

In addition to the above exceptions contained in the original ASC 810, three more exceptions have been added. These exceptions pertain to situations in which the data needed to apply ASC 810-10-55 is unavailable, where the entity to be evaluated qualifies as a *business*, and where the entity to be evaluated is a governmental organization (ASC 810-10-15-17).

ASC 810 does not have to be applied to variable interest entities (or potential variable interest entities) created before December 31, 2003, if the reporting enterprise does not have the necessary information to (1) determine whether the entity is a variable interest entity, (2) determine whether the enterprise is the primary beneficiary of the variable interest entity, and (3) apply the consolidation provisions to a variable interest entity where the enterprise is the primary beneficiary. However, this exception is available only to those enterprises that lack the necessary information after making an *exhaustive effort* to obtain the needed information, and the exception lasts only as long as the needed information cannot be obtained (ASC 810-10-15-17).

PRACTICE POINTER: The FASB does not define what it means by an *exhaustive effort*. Therefore, companies and their auditors should exercise significant judgment in claiming a scope exception to (ASC 810-10-55) under this provision.

In most circumstances, an entity that qualifies as a *business* does not have to be evaluated by a reporting enterprise to determine whether it is a variable interest entity (ASC 810-10-15-17). The FASB defines a business as an integrated set of activities and assets that is capable of being conducted and managed for the purpose of providing a return in the form of dividends, lower costs, or other economic benefits directly to investors or other owners, members, or participants (ASC Glossary). However, if *one or more* of the following conditions exist, an entity that qualifies as a business must be evaluated by the reporting enterprise to determine whether the consolidation criteria apply (ASC 810-10-15-17):

- The reporting enterprise (or its related parties) designed or redesigned the entity (with the exception of operating joint ventures under joint control and franchisees).
- Substantially all of the entity's activities involve or are conducted on behalf of the reporting enterprise (or its related parties).
- The reporting enterprise (and its related parties) provide more than half of the entity's equity, subordinated debt, and other forms of subordinated financial support.
- The entity's primary activities are securitizations, asset-backed financings, or single-lessee leasing arrangements.

The consolidation criteria of ASC 810 generally are not applicable to governmental organizations or financing entities established by a governmental organization. The exception to this rule is if the governmental organization is used by a business enterprise to circumvent the provisions of ASC 810.

Finally, the provisions of ASC 810 are deferred for investment companies that *are not* subject to SEC Regulation S-X, Rule 6-03(c)(1), but rather are accounting for their investments in accordance with the AICPA Audit and Accounting Guide, *Audits of Investment Companies.*

Consolidation Criteria

An entity is subject to consolidation if *at least one* of the following three conditions exists, as a result of the manner in which the entity was originally structured (ASC 810-10-15-14):

1. The total equity investment at risk is not sufficient to permit the entity to finance its activities without additional subordinated financial support from any party, including equity holders (ASC 810-10-15-14). The total equity investment at risk:

   a. Includes only equity investments in the entity that participate significantly in profits and losses, even if those investments have no voting rights.

   b. Does *not* include equity interests that the entity issued in exchange for subordinated interests in other variable interest entities.

   c. Does *not* include amounts provided to the equity investor directly or indirectly by the entity or by other parties involved with the entity unless the provider is a parent, subsidiary, or affiliate of the investor that is required to be included in the same set of consolidated financial statements as the investor.

   d. Does *not* include amounts financed for the equity investor directly by the entity or by other parties involved with the entity unless that party is a parent, subsidiary, or affiliate of the investor that is required to be included in the same set of consolidated financial statements as the investor.

2. As a group, the holders of the equity investment at risk *lack any one* of the following characteristics (ASC 810-10-15-14):

   a. The power to direct the activities of an entity that most significantly impact the entity's economic performance through voting rights or similar rights. (The investors do not have that power through voting rights or similar rights if no owners hold voting rights or similar rights.)

   b. The obligation to absorb the expected losses of the entity. (The investors do not have that obligation if they are directly or indirectly protected from the expected losses or are guaranteed a return by the entity itself or by other parties involved with the entity.)

   c. The right to receive the expected residual returns of the entity. (The investors do not have that right if their returns are capped by the entity's governing documents or by arrangements with other variable interest holders or with the entity.)

3. Equity investors are considered to lack the direct or indirect ability to make decisions about an entity's activities if (ASC 810-10-15-14):
   a. The voting rights of some investors are not proportional to their rights to receive returns or absorb losses. In applying this requirement, the enterprise is to consider each party's obligations to absorb losses or receive returns related to all of each party's interests in the entity, not only to the equity investment at risk.
   b. Most of the entity's activities involve or are conducted for an investor that has disproportionately few voting rights.

A *variable interest entity* is an entity subject to ASC 810-10-55. *Variable interests* are the investments or other interests that will absorb portions of a variable interest entity's expected losses or receive portions of the entity's expected residual returns. The initial determination of whether an entity is a variable interest entity is made when an enterprise becomes involved with the entity, based on the circumstances on that date and including future changes that are required in existing governing documents and contractual arrangements (ASC 810-10-25-37). The initial determination of whether an entity is a variable interest entity is reconsidered only if one or more of the following occurs (ASC 810-10-35-4):

- The entity's governing documents or the contractual arrangements among the parties involved change and the change affects the characteristics or the adequacy of the entity's equity investment at risk.
- The equity investment or a portion thereof is returned to equity investors, and other interests become exposed to expected losses.
- The entity undertakes additional activities or acquires additional assets—beyond those envisioned when the entity was formed or at the most recent reconsideration event—that increase the entity's expected losses.
- An additional at-risk equity investment is received by the entity, or the entity's activities are changed in a manner as to reduce its expected losses.
- Circumstances change such that the holders of the equity investment at risk, as a group, lose the power to direct the activities that most significantly impact the entity's economic performance.

Expected Losses and Expected Residual Returns

Expected losses (expected residual returns) are a function of expected negative (positive) variability in the fair value of the entity's net assets, excluding variable interests (ASC Glossary).

PRACTICE POINTER: Variable interests held by the potential variable interest entity are excluded in computing expected losses (expected residual returns) because a variable interest is expected to absorb volatility and expected losses, rather than to create them.

An equity investment at risk of less than 10% of the entity's total assets is considered insufficient to permit the entity to finance its activities without subordinated financial support in addition to the equity investment, unless the equity investment can be demonstrated to be sufficient. ASC 810 establishes a hierarchy for evaluating the sufficiency of the equity investment: a qualitative assessment first; then a quantitative assessment if a conclusion about the adequacy of the equity investment at risk cannot be made after diligent effort; and finally, if neither analysis taken alone is conclusive, both the qualitative and quantitative analyses should be considered (ASC 810-10-25-45). The two qualitative factors that should be considered are whether (1) the entity has demonstrated that it can finance its activities without additional subordinated financial support (ASC 810-10-25-45) and (2) the entity has at least as much equity invested as other entities that hold only similar assets of similar quality in similar amounts and operate with no additional subordinated financial support (ASC 810-10-25-45). If the adequacy of the equity investment at risk cannot be determined based on the qualitative assessment, the one quantitative factor that should be considered is whether the amount of equity invested in the entity exceeds the estimate of the entity's expected losses based on reasonable quantitative evidence (ASC 810-10-25-45).

Some entities may require an equity investment at risk of greater than 10% of their assets to finance their activities, especially if they are involved in high-risk activities, hold high-risk assets, or have exposure to risks that are not reflected in the reported amounts of the entities' assets or liabilities (ASC 810-10-25-46).

Variable Interests and Interests in Specified Assets

A variable interest in specified assets of a variable interest entity is deemed to be a variable interest in the entity only if the fair value of the specified assets is more than half of the total fair value of the entity's assets or if the holder has another variable interest in the entity as a whole. The expected losses and expected residual returns applicable to variable interests in specified assets of a variable interest entity are deemed to be expected losses and expected residual returns of the entity only if that variable interest is deemed to be a variable interest in the entity. Expected losses related to variable interests in specified assets are not considered part of the expected losses of the entity for purposes of determining the adequacy of the equity at risk or identifying the primary beneficiary in the entity unless the specified assets constitute a majority of the assets of the entity (ASC 810-10-25-55).

An enterprise with a variable interest in specified assets of a variable interest entity shall treat a portion of the entity as a separate variable interest entity if the specified assets are essentially the only source of payment for specified liabilities or specified other interests. This requirement does not apply unless the entity has been determined to be a variable interest entity (ASC 810-10-25-57).

Consolidation Based on Variable Interests

An enterprise shall consolidate a variable interest entity when that enterprise has a variable interest (or combination thereof) that provides the enterprise with a controlling financial interest. The determination of a controlling financial interest includes an assessment of the characteristics of the enterprise's variable interest (including involvement of related parties) in the variable interest entity, as well as the involvement of other variable interest holders. An enterprise is considered to have a controlling financial interest in a variable interest entity if it has both (1) the power to direct the activities of the variable interest entity that are most important to the entity's economic performance and (2) the obligation to absorb losses and the right to receive benefits from the entity that could potentially be significant to the variable interest entity (ASC 810-10-05).

An enterprise is identified as the primary beneficiary of a variable interest entity if the enterprise is determined to have a controlling financial interest and, thus, is required to consolidate the variable interest entity. Ongoing reassessments are required of whether an enterprise is the primary beneficiary of a variable interest entity. Although more than one enterprise may share in the obligation to absorb losses and the right to receive benefits of the variable interest entity, only one enterprise, if any, will have the power to direct the activities that are most important to the variable interest entity's economic performance. Therefore, only one enterprise, if any, is expected to be identified as the primary beneficiary of a variable interest entity (ASC 810-10-050).

The determination of which enterprise, if any, has the power to direct the variable interest entity's most important activities requires judgment. For example, there may be kick-out rights and participating rights that are held by other parties. Kick-out rights are the ability to remove an enterprise with the power to direct the variable interest entity's most important activities, and participating rights are the ability to block the actions through which an enterprise would exercise such power. An enterprise's determination of whether it has the power to direct the most important activities of a variable interest entity is not affected by the existence of kick-out rights or participating rights held by other parties unless a single party (including its related parties) has the unilateral ability to exercise the kick-out rights or participating rights (ASC 810-10-25).

If an enterprise determines that the power to direct a variable interest entity's most important activities is shared among multiple unrelated parties such that no one party has such power, then no party shall be considered the primary beneficiary. Power is shared if decisions about those activities require the consent of each of the parties sharing power. If an enterprise concludes that power is not shared but that the activities that most significantly impact the variable interest entity's economic performance are directed by multiple unrelated parties and the nature of the activities that each party is directing is the same, then the party, if any, with the power over the majority of those activities shall be considered to have the power to direct the variable interest entity's most important activities (ASC 810-10-25).

PRACTICE POINTER: A related party includes not only those entities meeting the ASC 850 requirement but also those parties acting as de facto agents for the entity holding the variable interest. Examples of de facto agents of the enterprise include (1) a party that is dependent on the enterprise for the financing of its operations; (2) a party whose interest in the variable interest entity results from a contribution or loan from the enterprise; (3) an officer, director, or employee of the enterprise; (4) a party that cannot sell, transfer, or encumber its interest in the entity without the approval of the enterprise; and (5) a party that has a close business relationship (ASC 810-10-25-43). If two or more related parties would qualify as the primary beneficiary if their interests were combined, then the party within the related party group that is most closely associated with the variable interest entity is the primary beneficiary. Significant judgment must be exercised in making this determination (ASC 810-10-25-44).

Initial Measurement

The primary beneficiary of a variable interest entity that is under common control with the variable interest entity shall initially measure the assets, liabilities, and noncontrolling interests of a variable interest entity at the amounts at which they are carried in the accounts of the enterprise that controls the variable interest entity (ASC 810-10-30-1).

If the primary beneficiary and the variable interest entity are not under common control, then the initial measurement depends on whether or not the variable interest entity is a *business*. The initial consolidation of a variable interest entity that is a *business* is a business combination and shall be accounted for in accordance with the provisions of (ASC 810-10-30-3).

If the variable interest entity is not a business, then the primary beneficiary initially shall measure and recognize the assets (except goodwill) and liabilities of the variable interest entity in accordance with paragraphs 12-33 of ASC 805. However, the primary beneficiary of a variable interest entity shall initially measure assets and liabilities that it has transferred to that entity at the same amounts at which the assets and liabilities would have been measured had they not been transferred. No gain or loss is recognized on the transfer (ASC 810-10-30-3).

PRACTICE POINTER: This provision applies to transfers at, after, or shortly before the enterprise became the primary beneficiary (ASC 810-10-30-3).

The primary beneficiary shall recognize a gain or loss for the difference between (1) the fair value of any consideration paid, the fair value of any noncontrolling interests, and the reported amount of any previously held interests and (2) the net amount of the variable interest entity's identifiable assets and liabilities recognized and measured in accordance with the guidance in ASC 810. No goodwill shall be recognized if the variable interest entity is not a business (ASC 810-10-30-4).

Accounting after Initial Measurement

The principles of consolidated financial statements apply to the primary beneficiaries' accounting for consolidated variable interest entities. After initial measurement, accounting shall be as if the entity were consolidated based on voting interests. Any specialized accounting requirements applicable to the type of business of the variable interest entity shall be applied as they would for a consolidated subsidiary. Intercompany balances and transactions are eliminated. Fees and other sources of income or expense between a primary beneficiary and a consolidated variable interest entity are eliminated against the related expense or income of the variable interest entity. The effect of this elimination on net income or expense of the variable interest entity is attributed to the primary beneficiary in the consolidated financial statements. If an enterprise is required to deconsolidate a variable interest entity, the enterprise must follow the guidance for deconsolidating subsidiaries in ASC 810 (ASC 810-10-35-3).

Disclosures Related to Variable Interest Entities

The principal objectives of the disclosure requirements in ASC 810 are to provide financial statement users with an understanding of the following (ASC 810-10-50-8):

- The significant judgments and assumptions made by an enterprise in determining whether it must consolidate a variable interest entity
- The nature of restrictions on a consolidated variable interest entity's assets and on the settlement of its liabilities reported by an enterprise
- The nature of, and changes in, the risks associated with an enterprise's involvement with the variable interest entity
- How an enterprise's involvement with the variable interest entity affects enterprise's financial position, financial performance, and cash flows.

Disclosures may be reported in the aggregate for similar entities if separate reporting would not provide more useful information. An enterprise must disclose how similar entities are aggregated and must distinguish between variable interest entities that are consolidated and variable interest entities that are not consolidated because the enterprise is not the primary beneficiary but has a variable interest (ASC 810-10-50-9).

An enterprise that is a primary beneficiary of a variable interest entity or an enterprise that holds a variable interest in a variable interest entity but is not the entity's primary beneficiary must disclose the following (in addition to the disclosures required by other standards) (ASC 810-10-50-12):

- Its methodology for determining whether the enterprise is the primary beneficiary of a variable interest entity, including significant judgments and assumptions made
- If circumstances change such that the determination of whether to consolidate a variable interest entity has changed, the primary reasons for the change and the effect on the enterprise's financial statements
- Whether the enterprise has provided support to the variable interest entity that it was not required to provide, or whether the enterprise intends to provide such support, including:
  — The type and amount of support.
  — The reasons for proving the support

- Qualitative and quantitative information about the enterprise's involvement with the variable interest entity, including the nature, purpose, size, and activities of the variable interest entity, and how the entity is financed.

If the variable interest entity is a business, the primary beneficiary shall provide the disclosures required by ASC 805. If the variable interest entity is not a business, the primary beneficiary shall disclose the amount of gain or loss recognized on the initial consolidation of the variable interest entity. The primary beneficiary shall disclose the following (in addition to the disclosures required by other standards) (ASC 810-10-50-14):

- The carrying amounts and classification of the variable interest entity's assets and liabilities that are consolidated in the statement of financial position
- Lack of recourse if creditors of a consolidated variable interest entity have no recourse to the general credit of the primary beneficiary
- Terms of arrangements that could require the enterprise to provide financial support to the variable interest entity.

An enterprise that holds a significant variable interest in a variable interest entity but is not the primary beneficiary shall disclose the following (ASC 810-10-50-15):

- The carrying amounts and classification of the assets and liabilities in the enterprise's statement of financial position that relate to the enterprise's variable interest in the variable interest entity
- The enterprise's maximum exposure to loss as a result of its involvement with the variable interest entity
- A tabular comparison of the carrying amounts of the assets and liabilities and the enterprise's maximum exposure to loss
- Information about any liquidity arrangements, guarantees, and/or other commitments by third parties that may affect the fair value or risk of the enterprise's variable interest in the variable interest entity is encouraged
- If applicable, significant factors considered and judgments made in determining that the power to direct the most important economic activities of the variable interest entity is shared among multiple parties.

An enterprise that does not apply ASC 810 because the enterprise, after exhaustive effort, does not have the information necessary to (1) determine whether the entity is a variable interest entity, (2) determine whether the enterprise is the primary beneficiary of the variable interest entity, and (3) apply the consolidation provisions of ASC 810 to a variable interest entity where the enterprise is the primary beneficiary must make additional disclosures. These disclosures are as follows:

- The number of entities that ASC 810 is not being applied to and why the necessary information is not available.

- The nature, purpose, entity activities, size (if available), and the relation between the enterprise and entity or entities that ASC 810 is not applied to.
- The maximum amount of loss that the reporting enterprise is exposed to because of its involvement with the entity or entities.
- For all periods presented, the amount of income, expense, purchases, sales, or other activity measures between the reporting enterprise and the entity or entities. This information does not have to be disclosed for prior periods if it is unavailable.

PART II: INTERPRETIVE GUIDANCE

ASC 810-10: Overall

ASC 810-10-05-14 through 05-16, 15-18 through 15-22, 25-60 through 25-79, 25-81, 55-206 through 55-209; ASC 718-10-55-85A Consolidation of Entities Controlled by Contract

> **OBSERVATIONS:** The accounting guidance below applies only to physician practices that are *not* variable interest entities.

BACKGROUND

Changes in the delivery of medical services, such as the proliferation of health management organizations (HMOs) and preferred provider organizations (PPOs), have caused an increasing number of physician practices to enter into contractual arrangements, under which a physician practice management (PPM) entity acquires and manages the physician practice (medical entity) and may enter into employment and noncompete agreements with the physicians who become its employees. Because a PPM may be precluded from acquiring the physician practice's equity instruments for legal or business reasons (some states restrict ownership of medical practices to physicians), the PPM entity may acquire some or all of the physician practice's net assets, assume all of its contractual rights and responsibilities, and enter into a long-term management agreement with the physician owners to operate the physician practice in exchange for consideration. To reduce its exposure to malpractice suits, the PPM entity may acquire the physician practice's shares and transfer them to a physician shareholder of the PPM entity who has incorporated a nominally capitalized new medical practice and acts as a nominee shareholder of the PPM entity. The PPM entity can change the nominee at any time. The following are examples of such arrangements:

Company A—Existing physician practice

Company B—New physician practice

Company C—PPM entity

Company D—The PPM entity's subsidiary

Dr. Friendly—A physician who acts as nominee shareholder of Company C

47,030 ASC 810—Consolidation

- Physicians who are the shareholders of Company A exchange their shares in Company A for shares of Company C and also enter into a long-term management agreement with Company C. Because state law does not permit a non-physician-owned practice to enter into contractual arrangements between physicians and hospitals and between physicians and HMOs, the physicians form Company B concurrently with the merger and transfer their patient contracts to it. The physicians thus become the owners and employees of Company B under an employment contract with Company B.

- Company C creates a wholly owned subsidiary, Company D, which acquires all of Company A's net assets in exchange for some of its shares of voting common stock. At the same time, Company A enters into a long-term management agreement with Company D. The physicians who continue as the owners of Company A enter into new employment agreements with Company D.

- Company C issues shares to the shareholders of Company A, which simultaneously delivers the shares in Company A to Dr. Friendly and enter into a management agreement with Company C. The management agreement gives the rights to the residual interest in Company A to Company C, although the shares held by Dr. Friendly have only a nominal value. The physicians enter into employment agreements with the existing physician practice, which is now owned by Dr. Friendly.

This issue was raised for the following reasons:

- Although ASC 805 provides guidance on the accounting for combinations of business entities or their net assets, it does not address whether an ownership interest in an entity can be acquired by acquiring the target's tangible assets and entering into a long-term service agreement with the target, rather than by ownership of its outstanding equity instruments.

- Under the guidance in ASC 840-10-45-4 and ASC 810-10-60-4, entities are required to consolidate in their financial statements the financial statements of other entities in which they have a controlling financial interest as evidenced by a majority voting interest. That guidance states, however, that the majority owner may not always control the entity. In addition, the phrase *controlling financial interest* is not defined under that guidance, which also does not address the question of when a contract provides an entity with a controlling financial interest.

ACCOUNTING ISSUE

Can a PPM entity obtain a controlling financial interest (as discussed in ASC 840-10-45-4 and ASC 810-10-60-4) in a physician practice through a contractual management agreement without owning a majority of the physician practice's outstanding voting equity instruments?

SCOPE

The accounting guidance discussed below applies to contractual management relationships with both of the following characteristics:

1. Entities in the health care industry, such as practices of medicine, dentistry, veterinary science, and chiropractic medicine, which are collectively referred to here as physician practices.

2. Entities in which the PPM entity does not own a majority of the outstanding equity instruments of the physician practice, because the PPM entity is not permitted to own the equity instruments under the law or the PPM entity has chosen not to own them.

The accounting guidance that follows also may apply to entities in industries other than the health care industry if the circumstances are similar to those discussed here.

ACCOUNTING GUIDANCE

A PPM entity has a controlling financial interest in a physician practice through a contractual management agreement if the following requirements are met:

1. The term of the contractual arrangement between the PPM entity and the physician practice has the following characteristics:

2. It spans over the physician practice's remaining legal life or over a period of ten years or longer.

    a. The physician practice cannot terminate the agreement, except if the PPM entity commits gross negligence, fraud, other illegal acts, or declares bankruptcy.

3. The PPM entity's control is evidenced by its exclusive decision-making authority over both of the following:

    a. The physician practice's ongoing, major, or central operations, including the scope of services, patient acceptance policies and procedures, pricing, negotiation and execution of contracts, approval of operating and capital budgets, and issuance of debt in cases in which the physician practice uses debt financing as an ongoing, major, or primary source of financing, except for the authority to dispense medical services.

    b. Decisions related to (a) total compensation of the practice's licensed medical professionals, and (b) establishing and implementing guidelines for selecting, hiring, and firing those employees.

4. The PPM entity's financial interest in the physician practice must be significant and must meet both of the following requirements:

    a. The PPM entity has the unilateral ability to sell or transfer its financial interest.

    b. The PPM entity has the right to receive income from ongoing fees and the sale of its interest in the physician practice, based on the practice's operating performance and changes in its fair value.

The following requirements should be considered to determine whether a PPM entity controls a physician practice by contract:

Documentation of a Management Agreement

The management agreement between a PPM entity and a physician practice should be reviewed to determine whether it documents the existence of a controlling financial interest. If such documentation is available, it also should be reviewed to determine whether the requirements in the following accounting guidance are met, regardless of whether the parties are acting in accordance with the document's provisions.

If the existence of a controlling interest is not documented in the agreement, the relevant facts and circumstances (such as the legal rights and obligations of each party and the reasons for undocumented arrangements) should be evaluated to determine whether the requirements of the following accounting guidance have been met. For example, a controlling financial interest may be undocumented, because the shareholders of the physician practice have not transferred ownership of their outstanding equity interests to the PPM entity or its nominee. Documentation also may be unavailable in cases in which the PPM entity and the nominee own the shares collectively, because documentation may not seem necessary when there are no third-party physician practice owners.

Term of the Agreement

The term of the management agreement should be evaluated based on its substance, rather than on its form, by considering the original stated contract term and renewal or cancellation provisions. For example, the term of an arrangement that specifies an initial five-year term and that provides for a single five-year renewal option that can be exercised unilaterally by the PPM entity is considered to have an adequate term, because a contract that spans over an initial five-year term and a five-year renewal is effectively a ten-year contract.

The adequacy of the term generally should be based on the facts and circumstances of the specific arrangement. The requirement that the term of an arrangement be for at least ten years is intended to imply that the arrangement has an unlimited life. However, that requirement is not intended to apply to all consolidations. Specifically, in other situations involving consolidation, a ten-year term is not necessarily required for a relationship to be considered "other than temporary."

Control

1. Nominee shareholder situations
    a. *More than 50% ownership.* There is a rebuttable presumption that the physician practice is under the PPM entity's control, if the PPM entity's nominee shareholder or the PPM entity and the nominee shareholder *together* own a *majority* of the physician practice's outstanding voting equity instruments. That presumption may be rebutted, however, if the PPM entity does *not* have *exclusive authority* over the decisions that constitute the control requirement, because others, such as other physician practice shareholders and physicians employed by the physician practice, were granted decision-making rights by either (*a*) the PPM entity under the management agreement or through the nominee, or (*b*) by the physician practice under its corporate governance provisions. The presumption cannot be rebut-

ted if the PPM entity's exclusive decision-making authority is pursuant to a management agreement, the physician practice's corporate governance provisions, or obtained through its nominee.

  b. *Less than 50% ownership.* There is no presumption of control if a PPM entity's nominee shareholder or a PPM entity and a nominee together own less than a majority of a physician practice's outstanding voting equity instruments. In that case, a PPM entity must demonstrate that it meets the control requirements as a result of a combination of its rights under the management agreement, the power of its nominee shareholder, and the physician practice's provisions for corporate governance.

2. *Provisions for binding arbitration* The existence of a provision requiring binding arbitration to settle disagreements between a PPM entity and a physician practice without overriding a PPM entity's exclusive decision-making authority, such as disputes about the meaning of contract terms, does not necessarily indicate that the arrangement does not meet the requirement of control. In contrast, The control requirement is not met if binding arbitration can affect a PPM entity's exclusive decision-making authority.

3. *Powers limited by law* A PPM entity's exclusive decision-making authority over a matter is not precluded under the control requirement, if federal, state, or corresponding non-U.S. laws limit its powers or the discretion of any party over a particular decision. For example, a PPM entity's ability to control patient acceptance policies and procedures within the law is unaffected by "antidumping" statutes that prohibit physicians from refusing to treat certain types of patients.

4. *Scope of service decisions* A PPM entity is considered to have exclusive decision-making authority over the scope of a physician practice's services, if the PPM entity and the physician practice agree on the practice's range of medical disciplines, such as cardiology, neurology, or obstetrics, in the initial negotiations of the management agreement. If a PPM entity does not have exclusive decision-making authority over the initial and ongoing decisions about a practice's scope of services, the PPM entity does not control the physician practice. Scope-of-service decisions include those about the range of services to be provided within the selected disciplines.

5. *Physician cosigning provisions*

  a. *Perfunctory provisions.* A perfunctory provision requiring a PPM entity's physicians to sign contracts with the practice's customers, in addition to a PPM entity's execution of the contracts, does not affect a PPM entity's exclusive decision-making authority over the execution of customer contracts. A physician's signature is considered to be perfunctory, if the obligations under a contract are no greater than if only the PPM entity had signed a contract and if either of the following conditions is met:

(1) A physician is required to sign a contract under state law, or a payor on a contract requested a phy*sician's signature.*

(2) A management agreement or a physician's employment contract provides that a physician's approval is not needed to execute contracts negotiated by a PPM entity.

b. *Nonperfunctory provisions.* A physician's signature is *not* considered to be perfunctory and the first control requirement is not met if any one of the following exists:

(1) A PPM entity gave signatory authority to the physicians (other than a PPM entity's nominee shareholder).

(2) A physician's signature creates obligations in addition to those that would be incurred if only the PPM entity had signed a contract.

(3) The physicians can decide which customer contracts the PPM entity will execute (e.g., whether the physicians alone or together with the PPM entity decide the terms of an acceptable contract).

Financial Interest

A significant financial interest is not defined, so that what is significant is determined based on the facts and circumstances of the particular situation. The following guidance should be applied to determine whether a PPM arrangement or a similar contractual management arrangement meets the requirement of a controlling financial interest:

1. *Nominee shareholder situations*

    a. *Presumption of financial interest.* Without citing a PPM entity's current compliance with the financial interest requirement, there is a presumption that a PPM entity has a significant financial interest in a physician practice, if

    (1) A PPM entity's nominee shareholder or a PPM entity together with its nominee own a majority a physician practice's outstanding equity instruments, and

    (2) Based on a PPM entity's and its nominee shareholder's rights and obligations to others, such as other shareholders of the physician practice and the practice's employees, a PPM entity or its shareholder nominee can change the terms of the PPM entity's financial interest in the physician practice at its own discretion with or without nominal consideration.

    That presumption is rebutted only if a PPM entity is *no*t permitted to change the terms of its financial interest in a physician practice so that it meets the financial interest requirement, which would be very unlikely.

    b. *No presumption of financial interest.* There is no presumption that a PPM entity has a significant financial interest in a physician practice, if its nominee shareholder holds less than a majority of the physician practice's outstanding voting equity instruments. If so, a PPM entity would have to demonstrate that it has a significant financial interest, in accordance with the requirements discussed above, due to a combination of its rights under a management agreement and the powers of its nominee shareholder.

2. *Type and level of a PPM entity's participation in a practice's fair value*

   A PPM entity's financial interest in a physician practice gives it a right to share in a change, any, in the practice's fair value that must be economically similar to a shareholder's right. A change in a physician practice's fair value is composed of (a) a change in its current operating results and (b) an amount available only if the physician practice were to be sold or liquidated.

   A PPM entity must be able to share in both amounts, which must represent a significant portion of a change in the practice's total fair value. If a PPM entity's relationship with a physician practice ends before a sale or liquidation occurs, to me the requirement in (b) in the paragraph above, a PPM entity would need to have the right to share in a change in a physician practice's fair value during the period that the PPM entity was associated with the physician practice. To comply with that requirement, the calculation of ongoing fees and sales proceeds should be evaluated based on their substance rather than on their form. Judgment is required to determine whether the financial interest requirements are met for specific management fee structures.

Period in which consideration is recorded

A PPM entity's consideration to a physician practice for modifying its arrangement with a physician practice should be accounted for in the financial reporting period in which an arrangement has been modified and should be recognized under generally accepted accounting principles according to the nature of that consideration.

Share-based compensation—identifying a PPM entity's employees

Under the guidance in ASC 718-10-55-85A, employees of a physician practice that is consolidated by a PPM entity are considered to be the PPM entity's employees for the purpose of determining how to account for each employee's share-based payment compensation. Employees of a physician's practice that is not consolidated by a PPM entity are not considered to be the PPM entity's employees for that purpose.

SEC OBSERVER COMMENT

The SEC Observer stated that because no unique industry characteristics were identified in connection with the above guidance, it is not unique to physician practices. Therefore, the conclusions reached above may apply to arrangements in other industries in which one entity has a controlling financial interest in another entity through a contractual arrangement or a nominee structure. The SEC staff will consider the guidance the discussed above when evaluating the accounting for such arrangements.

ASC 810-10-15-10, 25-1 through 25-8, 25-10 through 25-14, 55-1 Investor's Accounting for an Investee When the Investor Has a Majority of the Voting Interest but the Noncontrolling Shareholder or Shareholders Have Certain Approval or Veto Rights

BACKGROUND

Under the guidance in ASC 810-15-10, an entity that holds a controlling financial interest in an investee, which is evidenced by ownership of a majority voting interest, is required to consolidate the investee in its financial statements. There are circumstances, however, under which noncontrolling shareholders are granted certain approval or veto rights, referred to as noncontrolling shareholder rights, that restrict the majority shareholders' powers to control an entity's operations or its assets.

The following guidance does *not* apply to the accounting by entities, such as investment companies, which are required under GAAP to present substantially all of their assets at fair value, including investments in controlled entities, and that report changes in value in a statement of net income or financial performance. Investments in noncorporate entities and variable interest entities (VIEs) also are outside the scope of this Issue.

ACCOUNTING ISSUES

1. Which rights held by noncontrolling shareholders overcome the presumption in ASC 840-10-45-4 that all majority-owned investments should be consolidated?

2. Does the extent of a majority shareholder's financial interest—50.1% versus 99.9%—affect the conclusion to Issue 1?

3. Would the conclusions in the above Issues apply in other circumstances under which a corporate investee would otherwise have been consolidated under the guidance in ASC 810-15-10?

ACCOUNTING GUIDANCE

Scope

The following guidance applies only to investments with majority voting interests in corporations or similar entities, such as limited liability companies that are equivalent to regular corporations as a result of their governing provisions. That guidance also should be used to evaluate the effect of noncontrolling shareholder approval or veto rights in other situations in which consolidation of an investee would normally be required under GAAP (e.g., a 49% ownership with 100% control of the board of directors).

OBSERVATION: The guidance in ASC 272-10-05-3, through 05-4; 323-30-15-4; 35-3, which provides guidance for determining whether a noncontrolling investment in an LLC should be accounted for by the cost or the equity method, does *not* affect the guidance in this Issue.

Framework for Evaluating the Rights of Noncontrolling Shareholders

Noncontrolling shareholders' rights should be evaluated based on the following framework when a noncontrolling interest is obtained and should be reassessed whenever the terms of those rights or their exercisability has been changed significantly:

1. Judgment, which depends on the facts and circumstances, should be used to determine whether a noncontrolling investor's rights overcome the presumption that an investor with a majority voting interest should consolidate an investee.

2. The facts and circumstances should be evaluated based on whether noncontrolling shareholders' rights, individually or in combination, provide the noncontrolling investors with effective participation in significant decisions made in the "ordinary course of business."

3. A noncontrolling investor that has *effective participation* can block significant decisions proposed by a majority investor. A noncontrolling investor's ability to block a majority investor from making the investee take a significant action in the ordinary course of business deprives the majority investor of the ability to control an investee.

All noncontrolling shareholders' rights are intended to protect the noncontrolling interests in an investee (protective rights). Such noncontrolling shareholders' rights do not overcome the presumption in ASC 840-10-45-4 that the majority shareholder should consolidate an investee. However, noncontrolling shareholders may have substantive rights (participating rights) that permit the noncontrolling shareholders to block certain actions proposed by the majority investor concerning an investee's financial and operating decisions made in the ordinary course of business. For the purpose of applying this guidance, decisions made *in the ordinary course of business* are defined as those normally made to deal with matters that are encountered in the current operations of a business. Although it may not necessarily be expected that the events or transactions requiring such decisions to be made will occur in the near term, it must be at least reasonably possible that events or transactions that require making such decisions will occur. This ordinary course of business definition *does not* apply to self-dealing transactions with controlling shareholders.

Participating rights enable noncontrolling shareholders to participate in significant decisions, because those holding a majority interest are prevented from making certain decisions in the ordinary course of business without the noncontrolling shareholders's agreement. The existence of noncontrolling shareholders' participating rights overcomes the presumption that a majority-owned investee should be consolidated by the majority owner.

Protective Rights

Contractual or legal rights that enable noncontrolling shareholders to block the following corporate actions are considered to be protective rights that would *not* overcome the presumption that a shareholder with a majority voting interest should consolidate an investee:

- Amendments to an investee's articles of incorporation

- Pricing of a majority owner's transactions with the investee and related self-dealing transactions
- An investee's liquidation or bankruptcy filing
- Acquisitions and dispositions of assets *not* expected to be undertaken in the ordinary course of business. Noncontrolling shareholders' rights related to acquisitions and dispositions made in the ordinary course of business are considered to be *participating* rights. Therefore, judgment based on the specific facts and circumstances should be used to determine whether such rights are substantive.
- Issuance or repurchase of equity interests

That list illustrates some, but not all, corporate actions that may be blocked as a result of a noncontrolling shareholder's protective rights.

Substantive Participating Rights

Contractual or legal rights that enable noncontrolling shareholders to effectively participate in the following corporate decisions are considered to be substantive participating rights that would overcome the presumption that a shareholder with a majority voting interest should consolidate an investee:

- Hiring, firing, *and* decisions related to the compensation of management implementing an investee's policies and procedures
- Operating *and* capital decisions, including operating and capital budgets that affect management's actions in the ordinary course of business

Those items illustrate some, but not all, substantive participating rights that may be granted to noncontrolling shareholders. They are considered to be participating rights, because in their entirety they permit noncontrolling shareholders to effectively participate in significant decisions required to conduct an investee's business activities in the ordinary course of business. It is necessary to consider the facts and circumstances in determining whether a noncontrolling investor's single right, such as the ability to prevent a majority investor from firing management responsible for implementing an investee's policies and procedures, should be considered in and of itself a substantive participating right. Nevertheless, the presumption that a majority investor should consolidate its investee would not be overcome by noncontrolling shareholders' rights that appear to be participating rights but that are not substantive individually. A determination whether a noncontrolling shareholder's right is a substantive participating right should *not* be based on the likelihood of whether a noncontrolling investor would exercise that right.

Determination of Noncontrolling Shareholders' Rights Based on Facts and Circumstances

Not all noncontrolling shareholders' rights that appear to be participating rights are substantive. The following factors should be considered in determining whether certain rights that enable noncontrolling shareholders to effectively participate in significant decisions made in an investee's ordinary course of business substantive participating rights:

ASC 810—Consolidation **47,039**

- *The significance of a majority owner's interest in an investee* The greater the difference between the noncontrolling shareholders' ownership interest and a majority's ownership interest in an investee, the more likely that the noncontrolling shareholders' rights are protective rights, not substantive rights. The greater the extent of the noncontrolling shareholders' interest in an investee, the greater the skepticism about a majority owner's ability to control an investee.

- *Whether corporate decisions are made by the shareholders or the board of directors, and the rights of each level* For matters that can be decided by a shareholders' vote, it is necessary to determine whether other shareholders, individually or as a whole, have substantive participating rights as a result of their ability to vote on matters submitted for a vote of the shareholders.

- *Whether relationships between the majority and noncontrolling shareholders are between related-parties, as defined in ASC 850-10,* For example, if noncontrolling shareholders are members of a majority shareholder's immediate family, it is likely that noncontrolling shareholders' rights would *not* overcome the presumption that a majority investor should consolidate an investee.

- *The significance of noncontrolling shareholders' rights to make operating or capital decisions in an entity's ordinary course of business* Noncontrolling shareholders' rights related to operating or capital decisions, such as the location of an investee's headquarters or the selection of its auditors, which do not significantly affect an investee's ordinary course of business are not considered to be substantive participating rights and would not. overcome the presumption that a majority investor should consolidate the investee,

- *The chance that significant decisions under noncontrolling shareholders' participating rights will occur* If there is only a remote possibility, which is defined in ASC 450 as a slight chance, that the noncontrolling shareholders' approval will be required in making certain decisions in the ordinary course of business, the presumption that the majority owner should consolidate an investee is not overcome.

- *The feasibility that a majority owner would exercise a contractual right to acquire the noncontrolling shareholders' interest in an investee at fair value or less* If a majority investor's acquisition of the noncontrolling shareholders' interest in an investee is prudent, feasible, and within the majority owner's control, it demonstrates that the noncontrolling shareholders' participating rights not substantive. However, that would not be true if the noncontrolling shareholders' control critical technology or are the entity's principal source of funding. A majority owner's call option on the noncontrolling shareholders' interest overrides the noncontrolling shareholders' rights to veto the majority shareholders' actions, but does not result in an additional ownership interest for a majority shareholder.

Implementation Guidance

The following implementation guidance is provided in addition to the factors discussed above to assist in evaluating whether noncontrolling shareholders' rights, individually or in combination, should be considered protective rights or substantive participating rights, which enable noncontrolling shareholders to be involved in significant decisions expected to be made in the ordinary course of business:

- Noncontrolling shareholders' rights to approve acquisitions or dispositions of assets that are expected to be made in the ordinary course of business may be substantive participating rights. The presumption that a majority investor should consolidate an investee would not be overcome by rights that affect acquisitions that are unrelated to an investee's existing business. Those rights are usually protective rights. Noncontrolling shareholders' rights to approve an investee's additional indebtedness to finance an acquisition not in the ordinary course of business would be considered a protective right.

- Noncontrolling shareholders' rights to approve the incurrence of additional debt should be evaluated based on existing facts and circumstances. If it is reasonably possible or probable that the noncontrolling shareholders' approval will be required to incur debt in the ordinary course of business, those rights would be considered a substantive participating right.

- Noncontrolling shareholders' rights to approve dividends or other distributions may be protective or participating and should be evaluated based on the facts and circumstances. Rights to block normal or expected dividend distributions may be substantive participating rights, whereas rights to block extraordinary dividends or distributions would be protective.

- Rights related to a specific action, such as leasing property, may be participating or protective and should be evaluated based on the specific facts and circumstances. If an investee could purchase instead of lease property without the noncontrolling shareholder's approval, the right to block a lease is not substantive.

- Rights related to negotiations of collective-bargaining agreements with unions may be participating or protective and should be evaluated based on the specific facts and circumstances. A noncontrolling shareholder's right to approve or veto a new or broader collective bargaining agreement is not substantive if an investee has no collective-bargaining agreement or the union does not represent a substantial number of an investee's employees.

- Determining whether a noncontrolling shareholder's right to block a majority owner's action is substantive requires consideration of the provisions in the shareholder agreement that state what happens if a noncontrolling investor has exercised its right. For example, if a shareholder agreement provides that if a noncontrolling shareholder blocks an operating budget's approval, the budget will default to the previous year's budget adjusted by inflation. If the investee is a mature company whose operating budgets do not vary significantly from one year to the next, the noncontrolling investor's right to block the budget's approval is not substantive and does not allow the noncontrolling investor to effectively participate.

- Noncontrolling shareholders' rights related to the initiation or resolution of a lawsuit may be participating or protective and should be evaluated based on the specific facts and circumstances. Such rights would be substantive participating rights if participating in law-suits is commonly a part of the entity's ordinary course of business, as it is for some insurance companies.

- If a noncontrolling investor has the right to block an investee's operating budget for a specified number of years, that right may be a substantive participating right during that specified time period, based on the facts and circumstances. However, if the noncontrolling investor's ability to exercise its right changes after that time period, for example, the right terminates, that right is no longer a substantive participating right from that date forward and the presumption that the majority investor should consolidate the investee can no longer be overcome.

ASC 810-10-15-14, 25-21 through 25-29, 25-31 through 25-33, 25-35 through 25-36, 55-55 through 55-56, 55-58 through 55-86 Determining Variability to Be Considered

BACKGROUND

Applying the guidance related to the accounting for a variable interest entity (VIE) in ASC 810-10-05-8 through 05-13, 15-13 through 15-17, 15-20, 25-37 through 25-38G, 25-42 through 25-44, 30-1 through 30-4, 30-7 through 30-9, 35-3 through 35-4, 45-25, 50-2AA through 50-4, 50-5A through 50-6, 50-9 through 50-10, 55-16 through 55-32, 55-37 through 55-89, 55-93 through 55-205, 69-30; ASC 323-10-45-4; ASC 712-10-60-2; ASC 715-10-60-3, 60-7; ASC 860-10-60-2; ASC 954-810-15-3, 45-2; ASC 958-810-15-4 requires determining the variability to be considered in order to establish (a) whether an entity is a VIE, (b) the interests in an entity that are variable interests, and (c) which party, if any, is a VIE's primary beneficiary. Calculations of expected losses, if any, and expected returns are affected by that variability.

Reporting entities are determining the variability to be considered in a variety of ways. Some reporting entities have been considering only variability caused by changes in cash flows under the *cash flow method*; others have been considering only variability caused by changes in fair value under the *fair value method*. Regardless of the method used, entities applying the guidance referred to above should reach the same conclusion as to whether an entity is a VIE and which interests should be considered variable interests. However, this is not always the case.

To protect certain equity and liability holders from exposure to (a) variability caused by certain assets and operations held by an entity or (b) divergence in the overall profile of an entity's assets and liabilities, reporting entities may enter into arrangements, such as derivative contracts that reduce or eliminate those types of variability. During the life of any entity, it may treat those arrangements as recorded or unrecorded assets or liabilities. Application of the cash flow method or the fair value method does not resolve the variety of opinions as to whether such arrangements should be treated as variable interests or should be considered *creators* of variability.

ACCOUNTING GUIDANCE

A VIE's design should be analyzed based on the following steps to determine its variability :

Step 1. Analyze the *nature* of an entity's risks.

Step 2. Determine (a) the *purpose* for which an entity was established and (b) the variability created by the risks identified in Step 1 that the entity has been designed to create and pass on to its interest holders, including all of an entity's potential variable interest holders (contractual, ownership, or other financial interests).

Once the variability to consider has been determined, the interests designed to absorb that variability may be identified. Although the cash flow and fair value methods are examples of methods that may be used to measure the amount of an entity's variability in the form of expected losses and expected residual returns, the FASB staff believes that such methods do *not* provide an appropriate means for determining which variability should be considered when accounting for VIEs.

In Step 1, risks that *cause* variability are considered. They include, but are not limited to, credit risk; interest rate risk, including prepayment risk, foreign currency exchange risk; commodity price risk; equity price risk; and operations risk.

In Step 2, which is intended to determine the *purpose* for which an entity was created and the variability it was designed to create and pass on to its interest holders, the relevant facts and circumstances that should be considered include, but are not limited to, the activities of the entity; the terms of contracts into which the entity has entered into; the nature of interests the entity has issued; the manner in which the interests were negotiated and marketed to potential investors; and the parties that participated in the design and redesign of an entity.

Assets are *not* variable interests. Rather, an entity's assets and operations *cause* variability, which is absorbed by the entity's liabilities and equity interests. Some contracts or arrangements appear to have the attributes of creating *and* absorbing variability because, at different times in an entity's life, they may be represented as assets or as liabilities that may or may not be recorded. As stated in ASC 810-10-55-19, a conclusion about whether a contract or arrangement *creates* or *absorbs* variability should be based on the arrangement's *role* in the entity's design, regardless of the arrangement's legal form or its classification as an asset or liability.

How to Determine Variability

A review of of the terms of contracts into which an entity has entered should include an analysis of other documents, such as the original documents prepared to establish the entity, governing documents, marketing materials, and other

ASC 810—Consolidation **47,043**

contractual arrangements into which the entity has entered and has provided to potential investors or other parties with which it is associated. To determine variability, the following should be considered:

- Whether the *terms of interests issued*, regardless of their legal form or accounting designation, transfer to the interest holders all or a portion of the risk or return, or both, of certain a legal entity's assets or operations. A transfer of variability to interest holders strongly indicates that the entity has been designed to create that variability and to pass it on to its interest holders.

- If a legal entity issues both senior interests and subordinated interests, whether *subordination* (i.e., the priority on claims to an entity's cash flows) is substantive, often affects the determination of which variability should be considered. Because expected losses generally are first absorbed by subordinated interests and then by senior interests, the latter have a higher credit rating and a lower interest rate than subordinated interests. The primary factor in determining whether a subordinated interest is substantive is the relationship of its amount to the legal entity's overall *expected* losses and residual returns. Absorption of variability by a substantively subordinated interest strongly indicates that the legal entity was designed to create such variability and pass it on to its interest holders. A subordinated interest that is considered equity-at-risk, as the term is used in ASC 810-10-15-14, may be considered substantive for the purpose of determining the variability that should be considered, even if it is not regarded to be sufficient under the guidance in ASC 810-10-15-14(a), and ASC 810-10-25-45.

- Periodic interest receipts or payment should be excluded from the variability to consider whether a legal entity was not *designed* to create and pass on interest rate risk associated with such interest receipts or payments to its interest holders. However, cash proceeds received from anticipated sales of fixed-rate investments in an actively managed portfolio or those held in a static pool that, by design, will be required to be sold before maturity to satisfy the legal entity's obligations also may vary as a result of interest rate fluctuations. That kind of variability strongly indicates that the legal entity was designed to create that variability and to pass it on to its interest holders.

The existence of the following two characteristics strongly indicates that a derivative instrument *creates* variability:

- The underlying is an observable market rate, price, index of prices or rates, or other market observable, which includes the occurrence or nonoccurrence of a specified market observable event.

- The derivative counterparty is *senior* in priority in relation to the entity's other interest holders.

An entity's design should be analyzed further to determine whether a derivative instrument having the two characteristics discussed above creates variability or is a variable interest if changes in the derivative instrument's fair value or cash flows are expected to offset all, or nearly all, of the risk or return, or both, related to a majority of an entity's assets, excluding the derivative instrument, or the entity's operations.

A qualitative analysis of an entity's design performed in accordance with this guidance and other accounting guidance for VIEs often will result in a conclusive determination of the variability that should be considered when accounting for a VIE—that is, the determination as to which interests are variable interests and the ultimate determination of which variable interest holder, if any, is the primary beneficiary.

ASC 810-10-25-15; ASC 946-10-65-1 Retention of Specialized Accounting for Investments in Consolidation

BACKGROUND

Some operating companies have subsidiaries that are venture capital investment companies, which provide financing to companies in various stages of development by investing in their securities. Venture capital investment companies generally follow the specialized accounting principles for investment companies and carry their investments at market value.

ACCOUNTING ISSUE

Should an operating company report the investments of its venture capital subsidiary in consolidated financial statements at market value based on the subsidiary's specialized accounting principles, or should the investments be reported in the same manner as the parent's investments?

ACCOUNTING GUIDANCE

A subsidiary's specialized industry accounting principles should be retained in consolidation if they are appropriate at the subsidiary's level.

ASC 810-10-25-48 through 25-54, 55-87 through 55-89 Implicit Variable Interests

OBSERVATION: The guidance below applies to public as well as nonpublic reporting entities. The circumstances discussed are common in leasing arrangements among related parties and in other types of arrangements that involve related and unrelated parties.

BACKGROUND

There has been diversity in practice in accounting for situations in which a reporting entity, Entity A, has an interest in or other involvement that is *not* a variable interest with Entity B, which is a variable interest entity (VIE) or a potential VIE. In addition, Entity C, which is *not* a VIE, is a related party to Entity A that also has a variable interest in Entity B. Questions have been raised as to whether the reporting entity (Entity A) should consider whether an *implicit* variable interest has been created between it and the VIE (Entity B). A reporting entity's interest in or other financial involvement with a VIE may be in the form of a lessee under a leasing arrangement, as a party to a supply contract, service contract, derivative contract, or in other forms of involvement.

An *implicit* variable interest is an indirect financial interest in an entity that changes as a result of changes in the fair value of the entity's net assets, not including variable interests. Such variable interests may result from transactions with related parties and other parties. *Explicit* variable interests in an entity *directly* absorb or receive the entity's variability, while *implicit* variable interests act the same as explicit variable interests but they absorb or receive variability *indirectly* from the entity.

The question addressed is whether a reporting entity should consider if it has an *implicit* variable interest in a VIE or a potential VIE under specific conditions. Information about implicit and explicit variable interests is necessary in the application of the accounting guidance for VIEs in ASC 810-10-05-8 through 05-13; 15-13 through 15-17; 15-20 through 25-38G; 25-42 through 25-44; 30-1 through 30-4; 30-7 through 30-9; 35-3 through 35-4; 45-25; 50-2AA through 50-4, 50-5A through 50-6; 50-9 through 50-10; 55-16 through 55-32; 55-37 through 55-89, 55-93 through 55-205, because it may affect (*a*) whether a potential VIE should be considered to be a VIE, (*b*) the calculation of expected losses and residual returns, and (*c*) which party, if any, is a VIE's primary beneficiary.

ACCOUNTING GUIDANCE

Question: Should a reporting entity consider whether it has an *implicit* variable interest in a VIE or potential VIE under the following conditions:

- A reporting entity has an interest in, or other involvement with, a VIE or potential VIE that is *not* considered a variable interest in the VIE under the *explicit* terms of the reporting entity's interest in or involvement with the VIE. Therefore, the entity has *no* explicit variable interest in the VIE. Further, without considering related party relationships, the reporting entity would have *no* implicit variable interest in the entity.
- The reporting entity's related party has a variable interest in the same entity.

Answer: A reporting entity should consider whether it has an *implicit* variable interest in a VIE or potential VIE based on all the facts and circumstances when the reporting entity determines whether it may absorb the VIE's or a potential VIE's variability. If a reporting entity determines that it holds an implicit variable interest in a VIE and it is a related party, as defined in ASC 810-10-25-43, to other holders of variable interests in an entity, it should determine whether it is the VIE's primary beneficiary based on the guidance in ASC 810-10-25-44. That is, a party within a related party group that is most closely associated with a VIE is deemed to be the *primary* beneficiary, if a single party holding the total implicit and explicit variable interests that are held by the reporting entity and its related parties would be identified as the primary beneficiary under those circumstances. Judgment based on all the facts and circumstances is required to determine which party in a related party group is most closely associated with a VIE. The factors stated in ASC 810-10-25-44 that should be considered include (*a*) whether a principal-agency relationship exists between parties in a related party group; (*b*) the VIE's relationship to and significance of its activities with parties in a related party group; (*c*) exposure to a VIE's expected variability; and (*d*) a VIE's design.

47,046 ASC 810—Consolidation

If a reporting entity that holds an implicit variable interest in a VIE is not the primary beneficiary, the entity should disclose the information required in ASC 810-10-50-4.

ASC 810-10-25-58 Reporting Variable Interests in Specified Assets of Variable Interest Entities as Separate Variable Interest Entities

Question: Should a variable interest entity (Entity A) treat a specified asset (or a group of assets) and a related liability that is secured only by the specified asset or group of assets as a separate variable interest entity (Entity B), as discussed in the ASC 810-10-25-57, if other parties have rights or obligations related to the specified asset or to residual cash flows from the specified asset?

Answer: A separate variable interest entity does not exist under the circumstances discussed above. Entity B should be treated as a separate variable interest entity for accounting purposes only if all of its assets, liabilities, and equity are separate from those of Entity A and can be identified separately. Under those circumstances, Entity A would not be able to use returns on Entity B's assets and Entity B would not be able to use Entity A's assets to settle its liabilities.

ASC 810-10-40-1 through 40-2A; ASC 505-10-60-4 Early Extinguishment of a Subsidiary's Mandatorily Redeemable Preferred Stock

> **OBSERVATION:** Under the guidance in ASC 480, Distinguishing Liabilities from Equity, a financial instrument that is mandatorily redeemable at a specified or determinable date, or on the occurrence of a certain event, should be accounted for as a liability, except if a redemption occurs when a reporting entity is being liquidated or terminated. Consequently, that guidance nullifies the guidance in this Issue related to mandatorily redeemable preferred stock. In addition, under the guidance in ASC 480, amounts paid to holders of those contracts in excess of the initial amount at which they were measured should be accounted for as an interest cost rather than as a charge to a noncontrolling interest in the entity. The guidance in this Issue continues to apply to a financial instrument with a redemption feature that is *not* considered a mandatorily redeemable financial instrument under the guidance in ASC 480.

BACKGROUND

Company X acquires Company Z in a purchase business combination. Subsequent to the business combination, Company Z issues mandatorily redeemable preferred stock with a fixed dividend and no voting rights. The carrying amount of that stock is $75 million. Eighteen months after the redeemable stock is issued, its market value declines. Company X purchases the subsidiary's redeemable preferred stock for $60 million on the open market and holds it until it is due to be redeemed.

ACCOUNTING ISSUE

How should Company X account for the purchase of its wholly owned subsidiary's mandatorily redeemable preferred stock?

ACCOUNTING GUIDANCE

The company should treat the acquisition of the subsidiary's mandatorily redeemable preferred stock as a capital transaction. Thus, the company should recognize no gain or loss from the acquisition in its consolidated financial statements.

ASC 810-10-45-13, 50-2 Reporting a Change in (or the Elimination of) a Previously Existing Difference between the Fiscal Year-End of a Parent Company and That of a Consolidated Entity or between the Reporting Period of an Investor and That of an Equity Method Investee

OVERVIEW

Under the guidance in the ASC 810, *Consolidations* and ASC 323, *Investments—Equity Method and Joint Ventures,* a parent company's reporting year-end is permitted to be different from that of a consolidated entity's year-end for the purpose of consolidating the entity's operations; and an investor's reporting year-end is permitted to be different from its equity-method investee's year-end for the purpose of recognizing a change in an equity investment's net assets. Parent companies and investors that want to obtain financial results that are more consistent with, or the same as, their respective entity's results have asked for guidance on how to account for a change in or an elimination of a previously existing difference (lag period) in a consolidated entity's or equity method investee's reporting year-end.

SCOPE

This guidance applies to all entities that change or eliminate an existing difference between a parent company's reporting year-end and that of a consolidated entity or that of an investor and its equity method investee. This guidance does *not* apply if a parent company changes its fiscal year-end.

ACCOUNTING ISSUE

How should a parent company recognize the effect of a change to or the elimination of an existing difference between a parent company's reporting period and a consolidated entity's reporting period or between an investor's reporting period and an equity-method investee's reporting period?

ACCOUNTING GUIDANCE

A change or elimination of an existing difference between a parent company's reporting period and that of an entity consolidated in its financial statements or between an investor's reporting period and the reporting period of an equity method investee should be accounted for in a parent company's or an investor's financial statements as a change in accounting principle in accordance with the guidance in ASC 250-10-05, 10-15, 10-45, 10-50, 10-55, 10-60. That guidance is on the view that a change to or elimination of a lag period is a change in accounting principle. Although voluntary changes under the guidance in ASC 250, *Accounting Changes and Error Corrections,* are required to be reported retrospectively, according to the guidance in ASC 250-10-45-9 through 45-10, retrospective application is *not* required if applying the effects of a change in accordance with that guidance would be impracticable.

DISCLOSURE

The information required under the guidance in ASC 250-10-50 for a change in accounting principle should be disclosed.

ASC 810-10-55-2 through 55-4; ASC 810-10-55-2 through 55-4 Elimination of Profits Resulting from Intercompany Transfers of LIFO Inventories

BACKGROUND

This guidance was issued as a reminder concerning inventory transfers between or from LIFO pools, either within a company or between a reporting entity's subsidiaries or divisions. A LIFO liquidation or decrement occurs when the number of units (or total base year cost if the dollar-value LIFO method is used) in a LIFO pool is less at the end of the year than at the beginning of the year, causing prior-year costs, rather than current-year costs, to be charged to current-year income.

ACCOUNTING STANDARDS

According to the guidance in ASC 810-10-1, the purpose of consolidated financial statements is to present the results of operations and the financial position of a parent company and its subsidiaries as if the group were a single company. Intercompany profits on assets remaining within a group should be eliminated in the preparation of consolidated financial statements so that the results of operations and financial position are not affected by inventory transfers within a reporting entity. Inventory transferred between or from LIFO pools may cause LIFO inventory liquidations that could affect the amount of intercompany profit to be eliminated.

Different approaches are used to eliminate such profit in the preparation of consolidated financial statements. Each reporting entity should adopt an approach that, if consistently applied, defers reporting intercompany profits from transfers within a reporting entity until those profits are realized by the reporting entity through sales outside the consolidated group of entities. The approach selected should be one that is suited to the reporting entity's circumstances.

ASC 810-10-55-50 through 55-54 Calculation of Expected Losses if There is no History, nor Future Expectation of, Net Losses

Question: Should an entity be accounted for as a variable interest entity if it has no history of net losses and expects to continue to be profitable in the foreseeable future?

Answer: An entity should be treated as a variable interest entity under those circumstances because even entities that expect to be profitable will have expected losses. The term "expected losses" is used to refer to negative variability in the fair value of a variable interest entity's net assets, without its variable interests, and does *not* apply to the expected amount of variability of its net income or loss. A variable interest entity's expected losses are defined in ASC 810-10-20, *Glossary*, as the expected negative variability in the fair value of the entity's net assets without the variable interests, not an expected amount of variability in net income or loss.

Example: Entity A is formed on January 1, 200X, to purchase a building that is financed with 95% debt and 5% equity. If Entity A does not make the required debt payments, its lenders have recourse only to the building. On the same day, Entity A leases the building to Entity B under a five-year market-rate lease that includes a guarantee of a portion of the building's residual value. The present value of the minimum lease payments, including the residual value guarantee, is less than 90% of the building's fair value. No other entities have interests in Entity A. The appropriate discount rate is assumed to be 5%.

In accordance with the definitions of expected losses and expected residual returns in ASC 810-10-20 *Glossary,* the entity's estimated annual results in the above example include estimated cash flows and the estimated fair value of Entity A's assets that will be distributed to variable interest holders instead of cash, regardless of cash flows or flows of other assets to and from variable interests. The guarantee constitutes a variable interest in Entity A, because it is an interest in assets with a fair value that is more than half of the total fair value of Company A's assets. Consequently, losses absorbed by the residual value guarantee are Company A's losses and are included in the results used to calculate expected losses. To simplify the calculation, it is assumed that (*a*) the estimated results, which include both cash flows and changes in the fair value of Company A's net assets, and related probabilities are the same each year of the five-year lease and (*b*) the carrying value of the building at the end of the lease is its fair value.

The illustration below demonstrates the calculation at January 1, 200X, of the expected results identified as a variable interest at the inception of the guarantee. It is assumed that the fair value of the expected result will be equal to the sum of the present values of probability-weighted estimated annual results for the five-year lease term, without the effects of the residual value guarantee. A variation in the estimated results, if any, as compared to the expected result, is a change in the value of the entity's net assets, without the variable interests, from the value of those net assets on the calculation date.

Illustration of Expected Results at Inception of Guarantee Identified as Variable Interest (amounts in thousands)

Estimated Annual Results[a]	Probability	Expected Annual Results	Fair Value of Expected Five-Year Results[b]
$(10,000)	5.0%	$(500)	$(2,165)
(5,000)	10.0	(500)	(2,165)
0	20.0	0	0
10,000	50.0	5,000	21,648
50,000	15.0	7,500	32,471
	100.0	$11,500	$49,789

(a) Estimated annual results include estimated cash flow, excluding cash flow or flows of other assets to and from variable interests, and the estimated fair value of Company A's assets to be distributed to holders of variable interests instead of cash.

(b) It is assumed that the fair value of expected five-year results is the sum of the present values of the expected results for each year in the five-year period. In the present value calculations to determine the fair value of the five-year expected results, the expected annual results are treated as level annuities because to simplify the calculation it is assumed that the annual estimated results and probabilities are the same for each year of the five-year period.

The illustration below demonstrates the calculation of expected losses as the negative variability from the fair value of the expected results. It shows that an estimated annual result of $0 and one of $10,000 can contribute to expected losses even though neither is a negative amount, because a company's value will be less relative to its value based on the expected results if a positive estimated result is less than the expected results. The calculation of an expected loss shows that the expected loss is the fair value of the probability-weighted negative variation from the expected results. Expected losses include all negative variations.

Illustration of Calculation of Expected Losses as Negative Variability from Fair Value of Expected Results (amounts in thousands)

Estimated Annual Result	Present Value of Estimated Five-Year Result(a)	Positive Fair Value of Expected Five-Year Results (from above)	(Negative) Variation Expected from Value	Probability	Expected Losses	Residual Returns
$(10,000)	$(43,294)	$49,789	$(93,083)	5.0%	$(4,654)	
(5,000)	(21,648)	49,789	(71,437)	10.0	(7,144)	
0	0	49,789	(49,789)	20.0	(9,958)	
10,000	43,294	49,789	(6,495)	50.0	(3,247)	
50,000	216,473	49,789	166,684	15.0		25,003
				100.0%	$(25,003)	$25,003

(a) The estimated annual results are treated as level annuities in calculating the present value of the estimated five-year results because, in order to simplify the calculation, it is assumed that the annual estimated results are the same for each year of the five-year periods.

ASC 810-20: Control of Partnerships and Similar Entities

ASC 810-20-15-1 through 15-3, 25-1 through 25-20 45-1 55-1 through 55-16 **Determining Whether a General Partner, or the General Partners as a Group, Controls a Limited Partnership or Similar Entity When the Limited Partners Have Certain Rights**

BACKGROUND

ASC 810—Consolidation **47,051**

This question was considered, because preparers of financial statements and auditors were asking for guidance on how to determine whether a partnership should be consolidated in the financial statements of the partners. Practice has been to analogize to the guidance in ASC 970-323, which provides specific guidance on investments in real estate ventures that may include investments in corporate joint ventures, general partnerships, limited partnerships, and undivided interests. The guidance in ASC 970-323-25-8 provides that "a controlling investor should account for its investment under the principles of accounting applicable to investments in subsidiaries" (i.e., by consolidating the limited partnership). The guidance in ASC 970-810-25-1 through 25-2, however, provides that the guidance in ASC 970-323-25-8 applies only "if the substance of the partnership or other agreements provides for control by the general partners." The presumption of the general partner's control in ASC 970-323 may be affected by *important* rights held by the *limited* partners, such as the right to replace the general partner(s) and approve the sale, refinancing, or acquisition of the partnership's major assets.

Although there is little authoritative guidance for determining whether rights held by limited partners are important rights, the issuance of certain pronouncements has affected the consolidation of partnerships. In ASC 810-10-15-10; 25-1 through 25-8, 25-10 through 25-14, 55-1, which specifically excluded noncorporate entities, the concept of *participating rights* was introduced in the guidance requiring that the rights of *noncontrolling* shareholders be analyzed based on whether those rights enable the noncontrolling shareholders, individually or in total, to participate in significant decisions made in an entity's ordinary course of business. That is, if the noncontrolling shareholders can veto significant decisions made by an investor holding a majority voting interest, the majority investor does *not* have control.

The guidance in ASC 810-10-05-8 through 05-13, 15-13 through 15-17, 25-20 through 25-38G 25-42 through 25-44; 25-48 through 25-54, 30-1 through 30-4, 30-7 through 30-9, 35-3 through 35-4, 45-25, 50-2AA through 50-4, 50-5A through 50-6, 50-9 through 50-10, 55-16 through 55-32, 55-37 through 55-89, 55-93 through 55-205, which applies to entities that are *not* controlled through voting interests or those in which equity investors do *not* have residual economic risks, provides guidance for a consolidation model that is based on the concept of economic risks and rewards. It does *not*, however, provide guidance for partnerships, which are considered voting interest entities, regarding what *important rights* held by the limited partners would preclude a general partner from consolidating a partnership.

ACCOUNTING ISSUE

When does a general partner, or when do the general partners as a group, control a limited partnership or a similar entity if the limited partners have certain rights?

ACCOUNTING GUIDANCE

SCOPE

ASC 810—Consolidation

The scope of this Issue is limited to limited partnerships or similar entities, such as limited liability companies that function like limited partnerships as a result of their governing provisions but which are *not* variable interest entities accounted for under the guidance in. ASC 810-10-05-8 through 05-13, 15-13 through 15-17, 25-20 through 25-38G, 25-42 through 25-44, 25-48 through 25-54, 30-1 through 30-4, 30-7 through 30-9, 35-3 through 35-4, 45-25, 50-2AA through 50-4, 50-5A through 50-6, 50-9 through 50-10, 55-16 through 55-32, 55-37 through 55-89, 55-93 through 55-205. The guidance in this Issue applies to general partners that are required to account for their investments in a limited partnership in accordance with the guidance in ASC 810-20 and ASC 840-10-45-4; ASC 810-10-60-4. Limited partnerships with multiple general partners should determine, based on an analysis of the relevant facts and circumstance, which general partner, if any, controls the partnership and, therefore, should consolidate the limited partnership in its financial statements.

The guidance in this Issue *does not*:

- Apply to entities required under generally accepted accounting principles (GAAP) to carry their investments in limited partnerships at fair value and to report changes in the investments' fair value in their statements of operations or financial performance.
- Affect the guidance in ASC 323-30-25-1; ASC 910-810-45-1; ASC 930-810-45-1; ASC 932-810-45-1; ASC 810-10-45-14, regarding when general partners should consolidate their investments in limited partnership by the pro rata consolidation method.
- Apply if *no* individual general partner in a group of general partners controls a limited partnership.

Although this Issue does not provide guidance on which general partner in a group of general partners should consolidate an investment in a limited partnership, the concepts discussed may help in determining which general partner controls a partnership—for example, whether other general partners' combined rights and those of the limited partners prevail over the conclusion that a single partner controls the limited partnership.

The following framework should be used by a limited partnership's general partners to determine whether they control the limited partnership:

Presumption of control. The presumption is that a limited partnership's general partners control a limited partnership regardless of their ownership interests in the partnership. To address comments regarding the relevance of a financial statement presentation in which a general partner consolidates a limited partnership in its financial statements even though its interest in that partnership is insignificant, reference was made to the existence of alternative financial statement presentations and disclosures, such as consolidating financial statements or separating classification of the limited partnership's assets and liabilities on the face of the balance sheet.

A decision whether the limited partners' rights should prevail over the presumption of the general partners' control should be based on the facts and circumstances of the particular situation. The general partners do *not* control a

ASC 810—Consolidation **47,053**

limited partnership if the limited partners have *either* of the following rights, which are referred to as kick-out rights:

- A substantive right to liquidate the limited partnership or to remove the general partners without cause, referred to as *kick-out rights*, or
- Substantive participating rights.

Substantive kick-out rights The relevant facts and circumstances must be considered to determine whether kick-out rights are substantive. Kick-out rights with *both* of the following characteristics are considered to be substantive:

- A single partner, a simple majority, or a lower percentage of the *limited partner* voting interests held by parties *other than* the general partners, entities under common control with the general partners, and other parties acting on behalf of the general partners can exercise those rights. The following are examples of a simple majority that would qualify for a substantive kick-out right:
  — Two out of three limited partners with equal voting interests and no relationship to the general partners vote for the removal of a general partner under a limited partnership agreement that requires a vote of any individual limited partner or a vote of two of the limited partners for the removal of a general partner.
  — Two limited partners who hold equal voting interests in a limited partnership vote to remove a general partner under a limited partnership agreement that requires a vote of both limited partners or the vote of an individual limited partner.
  — A vote of 101 out of 200 limited partners with equal voting interests and no relationship to the general partners vote for the removal of a general partner under a limited partnership agreement that requires a vote of less than 102 of the limited partners for the removal of a general partner.

  A kick-out right could be considered to be substantive even if a limited partnership agreement requires *more* than a simple majority (supermajority) of the voting interests of the limited partners' to exercise its kick-out right. That would be the case if a simple majority of the limited partners' voting interests would result in a vote for the removal of the general partner(s) under every combination of those voting interests. For example, a vote for the removal of a general partner by any two out of three limited partners with *equal* voting interests under an agreement that requires a vote of 66.6% of the voting interests to exercise the limited partners' kick-out rights would represent a simple majority that meets the requirements for a substantive kick-out right. In the following example there are three limited partners with the following voting interests: Limited Partner A has a 30% voting interest and Limited Partners B and C each have a 35% voting interest. A vote of at least 66.6% of the voting interests of the limited partners is required to overcome the presumption that the general partners control the limited partnership. A combination of the votes of limited partners B and C would be a simple majority of

70% of the voting interests that would meet the 66.6% threshold. Although, a combination of the votes of limited partner A and limited partner B *or* limited partner C also would be a simple majority of the partners' voting interests, their total voting interests of 65% would *not* meet the agreement's required 66.6% threshold to remove a general partner. Therefore, the limited partners' kick-out rights in this example would *not* be considered to be substantive, because the votes of the limited partners in *all* combinations did *not* meet the required percentage to remove a general partner.

— All of the facts and circumstances should be considered in determining whether other parties, including but not limited to parties defined as related parties in ASC 850-10-05-2 through 05-5, 10-1, 15-3 through 15-4, 50-1, 50-3 through 50-6; ASC 958-810-60-2, 60-8; ASC 958-20-50-1 may be acting on behalf of the general partners when exercising their voting rights as limited partners. Those considerations also apply in determining whether a single limited partner has the ability to remove a general partner.

- There are no significant barriers to prevent limited partners with kick-out rights to exercise those rights if they choose to do so. The following are examples of such barriers:
   — Conditions making it unlikely that kick-out rights will be exercised, such as a limit on the time during which they can be exercised.
   — Disincentives to dissolution of the partnership or removal of the general partner in the form of financial penalties or operational barriers.
   — Inability to replace general partners because of a lack of qualified candidates or inadequate compensation to attract candidates.
   — No provision in the limited partnership agreement or the applicable laws or regulations for an explicit and reasonable means by which the limited partners can call for and conduct a vote to exercise their kick-out rights.
   — Inability of the limited partners holding kick-out rights to obtain the necessary information to exercise those rights.

A limited partner's right to withdraw from a limited partnership is *not* a kick-out right. Therefore, the presumption that the general partners control a limited partnership would prevail if the limited partners have a unilateral right to withdraw from a partnership *without* dissolving or liquidating the entire limited partnership. To be considered a potential kick-out right, however, the requirement to dissolve or liquidate a limited partnership if a limited partner(s) withdraws need not be contractual.

Each general partner should account for its investment in a limited partnership by the equity method in accordance with the guidance in ASC 323 if the presumption that the general partners' control of the limited partnership has been overcome, because the limited partners' kick out rights are substantive based on the previous discussion.

Substantive participating rights Limited partners that have substantive participating rights can participate in significant decisions made in the ordinary course of conducting a limited partnership's business operations. That is, the limited partners participate in making certain of the limited partnership's financial and operating decisions. Participating rights providing the limited partners with the right to block or approve decisions made by the general partners are considered to be substantive Although the general partners are unable to act without the limited partners' agreement, the limited partners' participation does *not* require the ability to initiate an action.

Participating rights granted to limited partners by contract or by law which enable limited partners to participate in the following activities—which are illustrative and not all-inclusive—should be considered to be substantive and would overcome the presumption that the general partners control the limited partnership:

- Selecting, terminating, and setting the compensation of management responsible for implementing the limited partnership's policies and procedures.
- Establishing the limited partnership's operating and capital decisions, including budgets, in the ordinary course of business.

Those participating rights are substantive, because they allow the limited partners to actively participate in decisions made in a limited partnership's ordinary course of business and are significant in directing and carrying out a limited partnership's activities. Individual rights should be evaluated based on the facts and circumstances to determine whether they are substantive participating rights independent of other rights. Rights that appear to be participating rights but are *not* deemed to be substantive by themselves *do not* overcome the presumption that the general partners control a limited partnership. The probability that a limited partner will use the power to veto a general partners' decisions should *not* be considered in evaluating whether a limited partner's participation right is substantive.

The following factors should be considered to determine whether participating rights are substantive rights providing limited partners with the ability to participate in significant decisions in a limited partnership's ordinary course of business:

- The level at which decisions affecting the limited partnership are made under an agreement, i.e., whether decisions are made by the general partners or the limited partnership as a whole and whether the limited partners have substantive participation rights individually or as a whole as a result of their ability to vote on matters presented for a vote of the limited partnership. Whether matters that can be voted on by the limited partners or the partnership as a whole are substantive should be based on the relevant facts and circumstances.
- Consideration of relationships between the general partners and limited partners that have the characteristics of related party transactions under the guidance in ASC 850-10-05-2 through 05-5, 10-1, 153 through 15-4,

50-1, 50-3 through 50-6; ASC 958-810-60-2, 60-8; ASC 958-20-50-1. In determining whether the limited partners' participating rights are substantive, for example, if a limited partner is a member of a general partner's family, the presumption of the general partner's control probably would *not* be overcome.

- Whether rights to vote on operating or capital decisions *not* significant to the ordinary course of a limited partnership's business are substantive participating rights. Such rights are *not* substantive participating rights and would *not* overcome the presumption of the general partners' control. Examples include the ability to vote on the location of a limited partnership's headquarters or the selection of its auditors.

- The likelihood that the limited partners will ever exercise their right to participate in certain significant decisions expected to be made in certain business activities in the ordinary course of business. The presumption that the general partners control a limited partnership would *not* be overcome if that likelihood is remote.

- The feasibility of the general partners' contractual right to buy out the limited partners in the limited partnership for fair value or less. If the general partners' buyout would be prudent, feasible, and substantially within the general partners' control, that buyout right indicates that the limited partners' participating right is *not* substantive. For the purpose of this discussion, the existence of such call options cancels the limited partners' participating rights required to approve or veto the general partners' actions to create an additional ownership interest for the general partners. It would *not* be prudent, feasible, and substantially within the general partners' control to buy out the limited partners, however, if the limited partners control important technology needed by the limited partnership or if the limited partnership depends on the limited partners for funding.

Each general partner should account for its investment in a limited partnership by the equity method if the presumption that the general partners' control of the limited partnership has been overcome, because the limited partners' participation rights are substantive based on the previous discussion.

Protective rights Limited partners' ability to block the following actions, among others, are considered to be protective rights that would *not* overcome the presumption that the general partners control a limited partnership:

- Amendments to the limited partnership agreement.
- Pricing on transactions between the general partners and the limited partnership and related self-dealing transactions.
- The limited partnership's liquidation initiated by the general partners or a decision to put the limited partnership into bankruptcy or receivership.
- Acquisitions and dispositions of assets not in the ordinary course of business.
- Issuance or repurchase of limited partnership interests.

Initial and Continuing Assessment of Limited Partners' Rights

Limited partners' rights and their effect on the presumption that the general partners control a limited partnership should be evaluated when an investor first becomes a general partner and reassessed at each following reporting period for which a general partner prepares financial statements.

ASC 810-30: Research and Development Arrangements

ASC 810-30-15-2, 15-3, 25-1, 25-3; 30-1, 35-1, 45-1, 45-2, 55-1 through 55-4
Accounting for Transactions with Elements of Research and Development Arrangements

BACKGROUND

The following guidance applies only to certain new transactions, such as the one in this example. A Sponsor capitalizes a *wholly owned* subsidiary (Newco) with $110 million in cash and the right to technology developed by the Sponsor, which has no book value, in exchange for shares in Class A and Class B common stock in Newco, which have a nominal fair value. Simultaneously, the Sponsor and Newco enter into agreements that include a *development contract* and a *purchase option.* Thereafter, the Sponsor distributes the Class A common shares in Newco, which have a fair value of $80 million, to its shareholders. The Sponsor continues to hold all of the Class B common shares that give the Sponsor no financial interest and no voting interest except for certain blocking rights. Newco, which has no employees—except for a CEO—and has only nominal office facilities, is required to spend all of the cash contributed by the Sponsor on R&D, which will be performed by the Sponsor under a cost plus 10% development contract with Newco. The Sponsor will be paid $55 million for each of two years, at the end of which all of the cash will have been expended.

The Sponsor has the right to exercise the option to purchase all of Newco's Class A common shares at any time during the term of the development contract at a price that approximates the fair value of the shares. During that two-year period, Newco is not permitted to change the Sponsor's rights under the purchase option without the Sponsor's previous approval. Newco also is prohibited from merging, liquidating, selling a substantial portion of its assets, or amending its certificate of incorporation to change the purchase option, Newco's authorized capitalization, or the certificate of incorporation's provisions regarding Newco's board of directors without the Sponsor's previous approval.

The following guidance does not apply to: (a) arrangements in which funds are provided by third parties, because those arrangements generally would be accounted for under the guidance in ASC 730, *Research and Development,* and (b) special-purpose entities that must be consolidated under the guidance for variable interest entities (VIE's) under the guidance in ASC 810-10.

Under the provisions of ASC 730, an entity should account for an R&D arrangement that gives it the right to the results of R&D funded partially or entirely by others based on the nature of the obligation incurred under that arrangement. An entity that must repay funds provided by others, regardless of the results of the R&D, is required to estimate and recognize that liability.

However, if the financial risk related to the R&D has been transferred to that entity, because its obligation to repay funds provided by others depends totally on whether the R&D's results have a future economic benefit, the entity would account for its obligation as a contract to perform R&D for others.

ACCOUNTING ISSUE

How should a Sponsor account for a research and development arrangement under the scope of this Issue?

ACCOUNTING GUIDANCE

- A Sponsor should account for an R&D arrangement under the scope of this guidance as follows:

  — On distribution of Newco's Class A common stock, reclassify cash contributed to Newco as restricted cash and recognize R&D expense as those activities are performed.

  — Account for the distribution of the Class A common stock as a dividend to the Sponsor's common stockholders.

  — Calculate the amount of the dividend based on the fair value of Newco's Class A common stock and recognize the transaction when the Sponsor distributes the stock to its stockholders.

  — Present Newco's Class A common stock as a noncontrolling interest in the Sponsor, classified in equity separate from the parent's equity.

- In determining the amount of net income or earnings available to the Sponsor's common stockholders for the EPS calculation, the Sponsor should *not* allocate any portion of R&D expense to Newco's Class A common stock. It was noted that the accounting result under this guidance is in essence the same as it would be in consolidation with the incurred R&D costs allocated to Newco's Class B common stock held by the Sponsor, because the value of the Class A common stock is related to the value of the purchase option, *not* to the Sponsor's original funding of the arrangement

- The Sponsor should account for a purchase option, if any, as follows:

  — *Purchase option is exercised* Account for the exercise of the option to acquire the Class A common stock like an acquisition of a noncontrolling interest by allocating the excess of the option's exercise price over its carrying amount to the assets acquired (in-process or completed R&D) and liabilities assumed, if any.

  — *Purchase option is* not *exercised* If an option expires, reclassify Newco's Class A common stock to additional paid-in capital as an adjustment to the initial dividend.

CHAPTER 48
ASC 815—DERIVATIVES AND HEDGING

CONTENTS

Part I: General Guidance	48,003
Overview	48,003
Background	48,003
ASC 815-10: Overall	48,004
Accounting for Derivative Instruments and Hedging	48,004
Activities	48,004
Definition of a Derivative and Scope Issues	48,004
General Disclosures	48,006
Reporting Cash Flows of Derivative Instruments That Contain Financing Elements	48,008
ASC 815-15: Embedded Derivatives	48,008
Embedded Derivatives	48,008
ASC 815-20: Hedging—General	48,010
Recognition and Measurement of Derivatives	48,010
Derivatives Designated in Hedging Relationships	48,011
Fair Value Hedges	48,011
Cash Flow Hedges	48,012
ASC 815-25: Fair Value Hedges	48,014
Accounting for Fair Value Hedges	48,014
Fair Value Hedge Disclosures	48,014
ASC 815-30: Cash Flow Hedges	48,015
Accounting for Cash Flow Hedges	48,015
Cash Flow Hedge Disclosures	48,015
Reporting Changes in Components of Comprehensive Income	48,016
ASC 815-35: Net Investment Hedges	48,016
Foreign Currency Hedges	48,016
Offsetting Derivative Assets and Liabilities	48,017
Financial Instruments	48,017
Important Notice for 2012	48,017
Part II: Interpretive Guidance	48,018
ASC 815-10: Overall	48,018
ASC 815-10-15-58, 55-45; ASC 815-15-15-9, 15-11, 25-8; ASC 460-10-50-4 through 50-6	
Disclosures about Credit Derivatives and Certain Guarantees: An Amendment of ASC 815 and ASC 460	48,018
ASC 815-10-15-141 through 15-142, 25-17, 30-5, 35-5, 50-9; ASC 320-10-55-5	
Accounting for Forward Contracts and Purchased Options to Acquire Securities Covered by ASC 320	48,020
ASC 815-10-45-2	

Offsetting Foreign Currency Swaps	48,025
ASC 815-10-45-9; ASC 932-330-35-1	
Issues Involved in Accounting for Derivative Contracts Held for Trading Purposes and Contracts Involved in Energy Trading and Risk Management Activities	48,025
ASC 815-10-45-10, 55-46 through 55-48	
Accounting for Options Granted to Employees in Unrestricted, Publicly Traded Shares of an Unrelated Entity	48,027
ASC 815-10-55-62	
Reporting Realized Gains and Losses on Derivative Instruments That Are Subject to ASC 815, and Not "Held for Trading Purposes" as Defined in ASC 815-10-45-9; ASC 932-330-35-1	48,028
ASC 815-10-S99-3	
Determining the Nature of a Host Contract Related to a Hybrid Financial Instrument Issued in the Form of a Share under ASC 815	48,028
ASC 815-15: Embedded Derivatives	48,029
ASC 815-15-35-4, 40-1 through 40-2, 40-4, 50-3; ASC 470-20-25-16	
Issuer's Accounting for a Previously Bifurcated Conversion Option in a Convertible Debt Instrument When the Conversion Option No Longer Meets the Bifurcation Criteria in ASC 815	48,029
ASC 815-20: Hedging—General	48,031
ASC 815-20-25-3	
Documentation of Methods Used to Measure Hedge Ineffectiveness under ASC 815	48,031
ASC 815-25: Fair Value Hedges	48,031
ASC 815-25-35-14, 55-52; ASC 815-30-35-45	
Effect of Derivative Gains and Losses on the Capitalization of Interest	48,031
ASC 815-40: Contracts in Entity's Own Equity	48,032
ASC 815-40-05-1 through 05-4, 05-10 through 05-12, 25-1 through 25-5, 25-7 through 25-20, 25-22 through 25-24, 25-26 through 25-35, 25-37 through 25-40, 30-1, 35-1 through 35-2, 35-6, 35-8 through 35-13, 40-1 through 40-2, 50-1 through 50-5, 55-1 through 55-18; ASC 815-10-1578, 55-52, 15-25-15; ASC 460-10-60-14; ASC 480-10-55-63; ASC 505-10-60-5	
Accounting for Derivative Financial Instruments Indexed to, and Potentially Settled in, a Company's Own Stock	48,032
ASC 815-40-15-5 through 15-8, 55-26 through 55-48; ASC 815-10-65-3; ASC 718-10-60-1B	
Determining Whether an Instrument (or Embedded Features) Is Indexed to an Entity's Own Stock	48,052
ASC 815-40-25-41 through 42	
The Meaning of "Conventional Convertible Instrument" in EITF Issue No. 00-19, "Accounting for Derivative Financial Instruments Indexed to, and Potentially Settled in, an Entity's Own Stock"	48,056
ASC 815-45: Weather Derivatives	48,057
ASC 815-45-15-2, 25-1, 25-5, 25-6, 30-1 through 3A, 35-1 through 35-2, 35-4, 35-7, 55-1 through 55-8, 55-10, through 55-11, 50-1; ASC 460-10-60-15	
Accounting for Weather Derivatives	48,057

PART I: GENERAL GUIDANCE

OVERVIEW

Other chapters within this *Guide* discuss pronouncements that specifically address other types of financial instruments. For ease of reference, the table below summarizes current accounting pronouncements related to financial instruments; relevant discussions of these topics can be found in the specific chapters covering these ASC pronouncements.

Pronouncement	Title
ASC 210	Balance Sheet
ASC 310	Receivables
ASC 320	Investments—Debt and Equity Securities
ASC 460	Guarantees
ASC 470	Debt
ASC 480	Distinguishing Liabilities from Equity
ASC 505	Equity
ASC 810	Consolidation
ASC 835	Interest
ASC 860	Transfers and Servicing

OBSERVATIONS: The accounting for financial instruments has become increasingly complex in recent years. Readers also should refer to CCH's *Financial Instruments* for comprehensive accounting guidance for each major type of financial instrument or transaction. Practitioners who encounter these areas should seek the assistance of experts in analyzing the applicable accounting literature.

BACKGROUND

Significant financial innovation and the rapid development of complex financial instruments prompted the FASB to undertake an involved and lengthy project to develop guidance for financial instruments in 1986. Many financial instruments were described as *off-balance-sheet* instruments because they failed to meet one or more of the criteria for recognition. Before addressing the difficult recognition and measurement issues associated with financial instruments, the FASB developed guidance to improve disclosures surrounding financial instruments.

The FASB issued considerable guidance in the early and mid-1990s that addressed the recognition and measurement of financial instruments. A significant milestone in the FASB's financial instrument project was reached in 1998 with the issuance of guidance on accounting for derivative instruments and hedging activities. This guidance was the result of extensive discussion and debate by the FASB on the subject of accounting for derivative instruments; it overhauled the fragmented preexisting accounting model for derivative instruments by establishing recognition and measurement standards for all derivatives, regardless of their use, based on fair value. For guidance on the disclosure of information about the fair value of financial instruments, see Chapter 50, *ASC 825—Financial Instruments*.

ASC 815-10: OVERALL

ACCOUNTING FOR DERIVATIVE INSTRUMENTS AND HEDGING ACTIVITIES

ASC 815 establishes accounting and reporting standards for derivative instruments, including derivative instruments that are embedded in other contracts, and hedging activities. The guidance in ASC 815 is based on the following fundamental principles (ASC 815-10-10-1):

- Derivative instruments represent rights or obligations that meet the definitions of assets and liabilities and, therefore, should be reported in the financial statements.
- Fair value is the most relevant measure for financial instruments and the only relevant measure for derivative instruments.
- Only items that are assets or liabilities should be reported as such in the financial statements.
- Special accounting for items designated as being hedged should be provided only for qualifying items. One aspect of qualification is an assessment of the expectation of effective offsetting changes in fair value or cash flows during the term of the hedge for the risk being hedged.

Definition of a Derivative and Scope Issues

A derivative instrument is defined as a financial instrument or other contract with all of the following characteristics:

- It has (1) one or more underlyings and (2) one or more notional amounts or payment provisions, or both. (An *underlying* is a specified interest rate, security price, commodity price, foreign exchange rate, index of prices or rates or other variable including the occurrence or nonoccurrence of a specified event. A *notional amount* is a number of currency units, shares, bushels, pounds, or other unit specified in the contract.) The interaction of the underlying and notional amount determine the amount of the settlement and, in some cases, whether or not a settlement is required;
- It requires no initial investment or an initial investment that is smaller than would be required for other types of contracts that would be expected to have a similar response to changes in market factors; and
- Its terms require or permit net settlement, it can be readily settled net by a means outside the contract, or it provides for delivery of an asset that puts the recipient in a position not substantially different from net settlement (ASC 815-10-15-83).

ASC 815 contains a number of exceptions to the definition of a derivative. Some of the scope exceptions were granted because the FASB recognized established accounting models already existed for certain instruments that would meet the definition of a derivative. Other scope exceptions were granted in order to simplify application of the standard. The following is a partial list of those scope exceptions (ASC 815-10-15-13):

- "Regular-way" security trades (i.e., security trades that require delivery of an existing security within a timeframe established by regulations in the marketplace or exchange in which the transaction is executed), if they cannot be net settled; purchases and sales of "when-issued" securities or other securities that do not yet exist that meet certain specified conditions; and all security trades that are required to be recognized on a trade-date basis by other GAAP
- Normal purchases and normal sales (i.e., contracts that provide for the purchase or sale of something other than a financial instrument or derivative instrument that will be delivered in quantities expected to be used or sold by the reporting entity over a reasonable period in the normal course of business)
- Certain insurance contracts
- Certain financial guarantee contracts
- Certain contracts that are not traded on an exchange
- Derivatives that serve as impediments to sales accounting
- Investments in life insurance (in specific circumstances)
- Certain investment contracts (in specific circumstances)
- Loan commitments for origination of any type of loan that are held by a potential borrower
- Loan commitments issued to originate mortgage loans that will be classified as held for investment under ASC 948 (Financial Services—Mortgage Banking) (however, loan commitments issued to originate mortgage loans that will be classified as held for sale under ASC 948 are subject to ASC 815)
- Contracts issued or held by the reporting entity that are both indexed to the entity's own stock and classified in stockholders' equity
- Contracts issued by the entity in connection with stock-based compensation arrangements (should be analyzed to determine if subject to ASC 815)
- Contracts between a buyer and a seller to enter into a business combination at a future date
- Forward purchase contracts for the reporting entity's shares that require physical settlement that are covered by ASC 480-10-30-3, 4, 5; ASC 480-10-35-3; ASC 480-10-45-3

A contract that qualifies for a scope exception under ASC 815 should be accounted for in accordance with relevant GAAP.

PRACTICE POINTER: The definition of a derivative and the scope exceptions in ASC 815 are complicated and highly interpretive. Practitioners encountering complex instruments that may be subject to ASC 815 should seek the advice of experts in the area of accounting for derivatives.

General Disclosures

An entity with derivative instruments shall disclose information to allow financial statement users to understand how and why the entity uses the derivative instruments as well as how the derivative instruments are accounted for and how they affect the entity's financial position, financial performance, and cash flows. An entity that holds or issues derivative instruments must make the following disclosures (ASC 815-10-50-1, 2):

- Objectives for holding or issuing the instruments
- The context needed to understand these objectives
- The entity's strategies for achieving these objectives
- Information about these instruments in the context of each instrument's primary underlying risk exposure (e.g., interest rate, credit, foreign exchange rate, overall price)
- Distinction between those instruments used for risk management purposes and those used for other purposes
- Information that allows users of its financial statements to understand the volume of its derivative activity
- For instruments designated as hedging instruments, a distinction between derivative instruments designated as fair value hedges, cash flow hedges, or hedges of the foreign currency exposure of a net investment in a foreign operation
- For instruments not designated as hedging instruments, the purpose of the derivative activity

ASC 815 requires the following quantitative disclosures for all derivative instruments and nonderivative instruments that qualify as hedging instruments (ASC 815-10-50-4A, 4B, 4C):

- The location and fair value amounts of derivative instruments reported in the statement of financial position
  - Fair value shall be presented on a gross basis even when the derivative instruments qualify for net presentation in accordance with ASC 210-20 (Balance Sheet—Offsetting)
  - Fair value amounts shall be presented as separate asset and liability values segregated between derivatives that are designated and qualify as hedging instruments and those that are not. Within these two broad categories, fair values amounts shall be presented separately by type of derivative contract (e.g., interest rate contracts, foreign exchange contracts, commodity contracts)
  - The disclosure shall identify the line item(s) in the statement of financial position in which the fair value amounts are included

- The location and amount of gains and losses on derivative instruments and related hedged items reported in the statement of financial performance, or when applicable the statement of financial position (e.g., gains and losses initially recognized in other comprehensive income). Gains and losses must be presented separately for:
  - Fair value hedges and related hedged items
  - The effective portion of gains and losses in cash flow hedges and net investment hedges that was recognized in other comprehensive income during the current period
  - The effective portion of gains and losses in cash flow hedges and net investment hedges recorded in accumulated other comprehensive income during the term of the hedging relationship and reclassified into earnings during the current period
  - The portion of gains and losses in cash flow hedges and net investment hedges representing:
    - The amount of the hedges' ineffectiveness
    - The amount, if any, excluded from the assessment of hedge effectiveness
  - Derivative instruments not designated or qualifying as hedging instruments

The quantitative disclosures listed above must be presented by type of derivative contract and in tabular format except for the information required for fair value hedges and their related hedged items, which can be disclosed in either a tabular or nontabular format.

Derivative instruments often include contingent features that can result in an immediate payment to a counterparty or a posting of additional collateral on an agreement that is in a liability position. ASC 815 requires disclosures about credit-risk-related contingent features that could affect an entity's liquidity. Specifically, an entity must disclose (ASC 815-10-50-4H):

- The existence and nature of credit-risk-related contingent features and the circumstances that would trigger these features in derivative instruments that are in a net liability position at the end of the reporting period
- The aggregate fair value amounts of derivative instruments that contain credit-risk-related contingent features and are in a net liability position at the end of the reporting period
- The aggregate fair value of assets already posted as collateral at the end of the reporting period and:
  - The aggregate fair value of additional assets that would be required to be posted as collateral if the contingent features were triggered
  - The aggregate fair value of assets needed to settle the instruments immediately if the contingent features were triggered

Disclosures about derivative instruments are typically scattered throughout multiple footnotes to the financial statements, which can make them difficult to understand and follow. ASC 815 requires an entity to cross-reference from the derivative footnote to any other footnotes in which derivative-related information is disclosed (ASC 815-10-50-4I).

Reporting Cash Flows of Derivative Instruments That Contain Financing Elements

An instrument accounted for as a derivative under ASC 815 that at its inception includes off-market terms, requires an up-front cash payment, or both, often contains a financing element. If a significant financing element is present at inception, other than a financing element inherently included in an at-the-market derivative instrument with no prepayments, then the borrower shall report all cash inflows and outflows associated with that derivative instrument as a financing activity as described in ASC 230 (Statement of Cash Flows) (ASC 815-10-45-11, 12).

ASC 815-15: EMBEDDED DERIVATIVES

EMBEDDED DERIVATIVES

Contracts that do not in their entirety meet the definition of a derivative instrument (e.g., bonds, insurance policies, leases) may contain embedded derivative instruments as a result of implicit or explicit terms that affect some or all of the cash flows or the value of other exchanges required by the contract in a manner that makes them similar to a derivative instrument.

ASC 815 also applies to interests in securitized financial assets. That is, an entity must now evaluate whether an interest in securitized financial assets contains an embedded derivative (ASC 815-10-15-11).

Interest-only and principal-only strips are not subject to the provisions of ASC 815-10 if the interest-only or principal-only strips represent the rights to receive only a specified proportion of the contractual interest cash flows or contractual principal cash flows of a particular debt instrument and do not include any terms not in the original debt instrument. This exemption applies if some portion of the interest or principal cash flows is stripped to provide compensation to either a servicer or to the entity that stripped the debt instrument. However, this exemption does not apply if a portion of the interest or principal cash flows are stripped to guarantee payments, to pay for servicing in excess of adequate compensation, or for any other purpose (ASC 815-10-15-72, 73).

Other than the limited exemption provided above, a holder of an interest in a securitized financial asset must determine whether the interest represents a freestanding derivative or whether it contains an embedded derivative. The analysis requires the entity to understand the contractual terms of the interest in the securitized financial assets. The entity must analyze the nature and amounts of assets, liabilities, and other financial instruments that comprise the entire securitization transaction. The holder of an interest in securitized financial assets must understand the interest's payoff structure and its payment priority to determine whether the instrument contains an embedded derivative (ASC 815-15-25-11, 12, 13). An embedded derivative must be separated from the host contract and accounted for as a derivative instrument assuming the following conditions are met (ASC 815-15-25-1):

- The economic characteristics and risks of the embedded derivative instrument are not clearly and closely related to the economic characteristics of the host contract.
- The hybrid instrument that embodies the embedded derivative instrument and the host contract is not remeasured at fair value under otherwise applicable generally accepted accounting principles.
- A separate instrument with the same terms as the embedded instrument would be a derivative subject to the requirements of ASC 815.

PRACTICE POINTER: ASC 815 contains implementation guidance and illustrations related to the assessment of whether an embedded derivative is considered clearly and closely related to a host contract. For a more in-depth discussion of the application of ASC 815 and related interpretations to instruments with embedded derivatives, see CCH's *Financial Instruments*.

Under ASC 815, entities are permitted, but not required, to irrevocably elect to measure financial instruments with an embedded derivative at fair value. Rather than bifurcating the instrument with the embedded derivative accounted for at fair value and the host contract accounted for separately under whatever GAAP requirements pertain to that instrument, the entire instrument can be accounted for at fair value (ASC 815-15-25-4). However, a hybrid financial instrument that is not bifurcated between the embedded derivative and the underlying host, but rather is accounted for as one combined instrument at fair value, *cannot* be designated as a hedging instrument (ASC 815-20-25-71(a)(3)).

The hybrid financial instrument can be either an asset or a liability, and it can either have been issued by or acquired by the entity. The election as to whether to record a hybrid financial instrument at fair value can be made on an instrument-by-instrument basis. Once an entity chooses to measure a hybrid financial instrument at fair value, it cannot change this measurement basis for that particular instrument in the future. Changes in the fair value of the hybrid financial instrument are recognized in earnings as they occur (ASC 815-15-25-5).

An entity that chooses to measure a hybrid financial instrument at fair value must support the decision with concurrent documentation. Alternatively, an entity can have a policy to automatically elect to measure hybrid financial instruments at fair value, but any such preexisting policy must be documented (ASC 815-15-25-5).

At the inception of a hybrid financial instrument, the transaction price and the instrument's fair value would normally be the same. However, in some circumstances, the transaction price may differ from the instrument's fair value. In these situations, the difference between the transaction price and fair value can only be recognized in earnings if the entity chooses the fair value election and if fair value is determined by a quoted market price in an active market, comparison to other observable current market transactions, and a valuation technique that uses observable market data.

As clarified by ASC 815, the requirements in ASC 815-10-15-11 and ASC 815-15-25 do not apply to a transfer of credit risk that is only in the form of subordination of one financial instrument to another. However, only the embedded credit derivative feature created by the subordination is exempt from these requirements. Other embedded credit derivative features are subject to these requirements even if their effects are allocated to interests in tranches of securitized financial instruments in accordance with those subordination provisions (ASC 815-15-15-9).

Entities may have some hybrid financial instruments measured at fair value under ASC 815 and other hybrid financial instruments measured using another measurement attribute. Hybrid financial instruments with different measurement bases must be separately grouped and presented on the balance sheet. The entity can include separate line items on the balance sheet for the fair-value/non-fair-value carrying amounts or combine the amounts, with parenthetical disclosure, on the face of the balance sheet, of the fair value amount included in the combined total (ASC 815-15-45-1).

Entities that choose to measure hybrid financial instruments at fair value under ASC 815 must provide information to allow users to understand the effect of changes in fair value on earnings (ASC 815-15-50-2).

ASC 815-20: HEDGING—GENERAL

RECOGNITION AND MEASUREMENT OF DERIVATIVES

ASC 815 requires the recognition of all derivatives (both assets and liabilities) in the statement of financial position and the recognition of their measurement at fair value. In accordance with ASC 815, each derivative instrument is classified in one of the following four categories: (1) no hedge designation, (2) fair value hedge, (3) cash flow hedge, and (4) foreign currency hedge. Changes in the fair value of derivative instruments in each category are accounted for as indicated in the following table (ASC 815-20-35-1):

Derivative Designation	*Accounting for Changes in Fair Value*
No hedge designation	Included in current income
Fair value hedge	Included in current net income (with the offsetting gain or loss on the hedged item attributable to the risk being hedged)
Cash flow hedge	Included in other comprehensive income (outside net income)
Foreign currency hedge of a net investment in a foreign operation	Included in comprehensive income (outside of net income) as part of the cumulative translation adjustment

Derivatives Designated in Hedging Relationships

Fair Value Hedges

Certain instruments are designated as hedging the exposure to changes in the fair value of an asset or liability or an identified portion thereof that is attributed to a particular risk. A fair value hedge must meet all of the following criteria:

- At the inception of the hedge, there is formal documentation of the hedging relationship and the entity's risk management objective and strategy for undertaking the hedge. This must include identification of *(a)* the hedged instrument, *(b)* the hedged item, *(c)* the nature of the risk being hedged, and *(d)* how the hedging instrument's effectiveness in offsetting the exposure to changes in the fair value of the hedged item will be assessed (ASC 815-20-25-3).

- Both at the inception of the hedge and on an ongoing basis, the hedging relationship is expected to be highly effective in achieving offsetting changes in fair value attributed to the hedged risk during the period that the hedge is designated. An assessment is required whenever financial statements or earnings are reported, and at least every three months (ASC 815-20-25-75).

- If a written option is designated as hedging a recognized asset or liability or an unrecognized firm commitment, the combination of the hedged item and the written option provides at least as much potential for gains as the exposure to losses from changes in the combined fair values (ASC 815-20-25-94).

An asset or liability is eligible for designation as a hedged item in a fair value hedge if all of the following criteria are met (ASC 815-20-25-12):

- The hedged item is specifically identified as either all or a specified portion of a recognized asset or a recognized liability or an unrecognized firm commitment. The hedged item is a single asset or liability (or specified portion thereof) or is a portfolio of similar assets or a portfolio of similar liabilities (or a specified portion thereof).

- The hedged item presents an exposure to changes in fair value attributable to the hedged risk that could affect reported earnings. (The reference to affecting reported earnings does not apply to an entity that does not report earnings as a separate caption in a statement of financial performance, such as a not-for-profit organization.)

- The hedged item is not *(a)* an asset or liability that is remeasured with the changes in fair value attributable to the hedged risk reported currently in earnings, *(b)* an investment accounted for by the equity method, *(c)* a noncontrolling interest in one or more consolidated subsidiaries, *(d)* an equity investment in a consolidated subsidiary, *(e)* a firm commitment either to enter into a business combination or to acquire or dispose of a subsidiary, a noncontrolling interest, or an equity method investee, or *(f)* an equity instrument issued by the entity and classified as stockholders' equity in the statement of financial position.

- If the hedged item is all or a portion of a debt security that is classified as held-to-maturity in accordance with ASC 320 (Investments—Debt and Equity Securities), the designated risk being hedged is the risk of changes in its fair value attributable to credit risk, foreign exchange risk, or both. If the hedged item is an option component of a held-to-maturity security that permits its prepayment, the designated risk being hedged is the risk of changes in the entire fair value of that option component.
- If the hedged item is a nonfinancial asset or liability other than a recognized loan servicing right or a nonfinancial firm commitment with financial components, the designated risk being hedged is the risk of changes in the fair value of the entire hedged asset or liability.
- If the hedged item is a financial asset or liability, a recognized loan servicing right, or a nonfinancial firm commitment with financial components, the designated risk being hedged is (*a*) the risk of changes in the overall fair value of the entire hedged item, (*b*) the risk of changes in its fair value attributable to changes in the designated benchmark interest rate (i.e., interest rate risk), (*c*) the risk of changes in its fair value attributable to changes in the related foreign currency exchange risk (i.e., foreign exchange risk), or (*d*) the risk of changes in its fair value attributable to both changes in the obligor's creditworthiness and changes in spread over the benchmark interest rate with respect to the hedged item's credit section at inception (i.e., credit risk).

Cash Flow Hedges

A derivative instrument may be designated as hedging the exposure to variability in expected future cash flows attributed to a particular risk. That exposure may be associated with an existing recognized asset or liability (e.g., variable rate debt) or a forecasted transaction (e.g., a forecasted purchase or sale). Designated hedging instruments and hedged items or transactions qualify for cash flow hedge accounting if all of the following criteria are met:

- At the inception of the hedge, there is formal documentation of the hedging relationship and the entity's risk management objective and strategy for undertaking the hedge. This must include identification of (*a*) the hedging instrument, (*b*) the hedged transaction, (*c*) the nature of the risk being hedged, and (*d*) how the hedging instrument's effectiveness hedges the risk to the hedged transaction's variability in cash flows attributable to the hedged risk will be assessed (ASC 815-20-25-3).
- Both at the inception of the hedge and on an ongoing basis, the hedging relationship is expected to be highly effective in achieving offsetting cash flows attributable to the hedged risk during the term of the hedge. An assessment is required when financial statements or earnings are reported, and at least every three months (ASC 815-20-25-75).
- If a written option is designated as hedging the variability in cash flows for a recognized asset or liability, the combination of the hedged item and the written option provides at least as much potential for favorable cash flows as the exposure to unfavorable cash flows (ASC 815-20-25-94).

- If a hedging instrument is used to modify the interest receipts or payments associated with a recognized financial asset or liability from one variable rate to another variable rate, the hedging instrument must be a link between an existing designated asset with variable cash flows and an existing designated liability with variable cash flows and must be highly effective in achieving offsetting cash flows (ASC 815-20-25-50).

A forecasted transaction is eligible for designation as a hedged transaction in a cash flow hedge if all of the following additional criteria are met (ASC 815-20-25-15):

- The forecasted transaction is specifically identified as a single transaction or a group of individual transactions. If a group, the individual transactions within the group must share the same risk exposure that is being hedged.
- The occurrence of the forecasted transaction is probable.
- The forecasted transaction is with a party external to the reporting entity.
- The forecasted transaction is not the acquisition of an asset or incurrence of a liability that will subsequently be remeasured with changes in fair value attributed to the hedged risk reported currently in earnings.
- If the variable cash flows of the forecasted transaction relate to a debt security that is classified as held-to-maturity under ASC 320, the risk being hedged is the risk of changes in its cash flows attributable to credit risk, foreign exchange risk, or both.
- The forecasted transaction does not involve a business combination subject to the provisions of ASC 805 (Business Combinations), or a combination of not-for-profit entities subject to the provisions of ASC 958 (Not-for-Profit Entities), and is not a transaction involving *(a)* a parent company's interest in consolidated subsidiaries, *(b)* a noncontrolling interest in a consolidated subsidiary, *(c)* an equity-method investment, or *(d)* an entity's own equity instruments.
- If the hedged transaction is the forecasted purchase or sale of a nonfinancial asset, the designated risk being hedged is *(a)* the risk of changes in the functional-currency-equivalent cash flows attributable to changes in the related foreign currency exchange rates, or *(b)* the risk of changes in the cash flows relating to all changes in the purchase price or sales price of the asset, regardless of whether that price and the related cash flows are stated in the entity's functional currency or a foreign currency.
- If the hedged transaction is the forecasted purchase or sale of a financial asset or liability, the interest payments on that financial asset or liability, or the variable cash inflow or outflow of an existing financial asset or liability, the designated risk being hedged is *(a)* the overall risk of changes in the hedged cash flows related to the asset or liability, *(b)* the risk of changes in its cash flows attributable to changes in the designated benchmark interest rates, *(c)* the risk of changes in the functional- currency-equivalent cash flows attributable to changes in the related foreign currency exchange rates, or *(d)* the risk of changes in cash flows attributable

to default, changes in the obligor's creditworthiness, and changes in the spread over the benchmark interest rate.

ASC 815-25: FAIR VALUE HEDGES

Accounting for Fair Value Hedges

Changes in the fair value of derivative instruments that qualify as fair value hedges are recognized currently in earnings. The gain or loss on the hedged item attributable to the hedged risk adjusts the carrying amount of the hedged item and is recognized currently in earnings (ASC 815-25-35-1).

OBSERVATIONS: Although ASC 815 generally requires accounting for derivative instruments at fair value, those qualifying as fair value hedges are the only types of hedges for which the change in value is included currently in determining net income. This accounting distinguishes fair value hedges from cash flow hedges and foreign currency hedges and can be expected to result in some volatility in reported income.

An entity shall discontinue prospectively accounting for a fair value hedge if *any* of the following occurs (ASC 815-25-40-1):

- Any criterion of a fair value hedge, or hedged item, is no longer met.
- The derivative expires, or is sold, terminated, or exercised.
- The entity removes the designation of the fair value hedge.

An asset or liability that is designated as a fair value hedge is subject to the applicable GAAP requirement for assessment of impairment (asset) or recognition of an increased obligation (liability) (ASC 815-25-35-10).

Fair Value Hedge Disclosures

The following disclosures are required for derivative instruments, as well as nonderivative instruments that may give rise to foreign currency transaction gains or losses under ASC 830-20 that have been designated and qualify as fair value hedging instruments (ASC 815-25-50-1):

- The net gain or loss recognized in earnings during the period representing:
  - The amount of the hedges' ineffectiveness.
  - The component of the derivative instruments' gain or loss, if any, excluded from the assessment of hedge effectiveness.
- The amount of net gain or loss recognized in earnings when a hedged firm commitment no longer qualifies as a fair value hedge.

ASC 815-30: CASH FLOW HEDGES

Accounting for Cash Flow Hedges

The effective portion of the gain or loss (i.e., change in fair value) on a derivative designated as a cash flow hedge is reported in other comprehensive income (outside net income). The ineffective portion is reported in earnings. Amounts in accumulated other comprehensive income are reclassified into earnings (net income) in the same period in which the hedged forecasted transaction affects earnings (ASC 815-30-35-3).

OBSERVATIONS: Changes in the fair value of cash flow hedges are not included currently in determining net income as they are with fair value hedges. Rather, they are included in "other comprehensive income," outside the determination of net income.

An entity shall discontinue prospectively accounting for cash flow hedges as specified above if *any* of the following occurs (ASC 815-30-40-1):

- Any criterion for a cash flow hedge, or the hedged forecasted transaction is no longer met.
- The derivative expires, or is sold, terminated, or exercised.
- The entity removes the designation of the cash flow hedge.

If cash flow hedge accounting is discontinued, the accumulated amount in other comprehensive income remains and is reclassified into earnings when the hedged forecasted transaction affects earnings. Existing GAAP for impairment of an asset or recognition of an increased liability apply to the asset or liability that gives rise to the variable cash flows that were designated in the cash flow hedge (ASC 815-30-35-42).

Cash Flow Hedge Disclosures

The following disclosures are required for derivatives that have been designated and qualify as cash flow hedging instruments and the related hedged transactions (ASC 815-30-50-1):

- A description of the transactions or other events that will result in the reclassification into earnings of gains or losses that are reported in accumulated other comprehensive income and the estimated net amount of the existing gains or losses at the reporting date that is expected to be reclassified into earnings within the next 12 months.
- The maximum length of time over which the entity is hedging its exposure to the variability in future cash flows for forecasted transactions excluding those forecasted transactions related to the payment of variable interest on existing financial instruments.
- The amount of gains and losses reclassified into earnings as a result of the discontinuance of cash flow hedges, because it is probable that the origi-

nal forecasted transactions will not occur by the end of the originally specified time period.

Reporting Changes in Components of Comprehensive Income

Changes in components of comprehensive income are the following:

- Within other comprehensive income, entities must display a separate classification of the net gain or loss on derivative instruments designated and qualifying as cash flow hedging instruments that are reported in comprehensive income (ASC 815-30-45-1)
- As part of the disclosure of accumulated other comprehensive income in accordance with ASC 220 (Comprehensive Income), entities must disclose the beginning and ending accumulated derivative gain or loss, the related net change associated with current period hedging transactions, and the net amount of any reclassification into earnings (ASC 815-30-50-2)

ASC 815-35: NET INVESTMENT HEDGES

Foreign Currency Hedges

If the hedged item is denominated in a foreign currency, ASC 815 indicates that an entity may designate the following types of hedges as hedges of foreign currency exposure:

- A fair value hedge of an unrecognized firm commitment or a recognized asset or liability (including an available-for-sale security)
- A cash flow hedge of a forecasted transaction, an unrecognized firm commitment, the forecasted functional-currency equivalent cash flows associated with a recognized asset or liability, or a forecasted intercompany transaction
- A hedge of a net investment in a foreign operation

Foreign currency fair value hedges and cash flows hedges are generally subject to the fair value and cash flow hedge accounting requirements, respectively, covered earlier.

The change in fair value of a derivative instrument that qualifies as a hedge of net investment of a foreign operation is reported in other comprehensive income (outside net income) as part of the cumulative translation adjustment in accordance with ASC 830 (Foreign Currency Matters) (ASC 815-35-35-1).

OBSERVATIONS: Foreign currency hedges build on the guidance for fair value and cash flow hedges presented earlier, and (for foreign currency hedges of net investments in foreign operations) on accounting for the cumulative translation adjustment requirements of ASC 830. If a foreign currency hedge satisfies the ASC 815 criteria as a fair value or cash flow hedge, it is treated accordingly. If the foreign currency hedge is a hedge of net investment in a foreign operation, it is treated as a part of the cumulative translation adjustment. In this latter case, changes in fair value are included in other comprehensive income (much like a cash flow hedge), and are included in the cumulative translation adjustment rather than separately disclosed.

OFFSETTING DERIVATIVE ASSETS AND LIABILITIES

Offsetting of assets and liabilities in the balance sheet is improper except when the right of setoff exists. ASC 210-20 (Balance Sheet—Offsetting) establishes four criteria that must be satisfied to in turn establish a valid right of setoff. Generally, for an asset and liability to be offset and displayed as a net position, all four of the following criteria must be satisfied (ASC 210-20-45-1):

1. Each party owes the other party determinable amounts.
2. The reporting party has the right to set off the amount payable, by contract or other agreement, with the amount receivable.
3. The reporting entity intends to net settle.
4. The right of setoff is enforceable at law.

The chapter in this *Guide* covering ASC 210 discusses the guidance related to offsetting of assets and liabilities in greater detail.

An exception to the general offsetting rule exists for derivative contracts executed with the same counterparty under a master netting agreement. A master netting agreement is a contractual agreement entered into by two parties to multiple contracts that provides for the net settlement of all contracts covered by the agreement in the event of default under any one contract. For such derivative contracts, assets and liabilities may be offset and presented as a net amount even if the reporting entity does not meet the requirement in ASC 210 that the reporting entity has the intent to net settle. Offsetting derivative assets and liabilities under this exception is an election and the reporting entity must apply the election consistently.

FINANCIAL INSTRUMENTS

IMPORTANT NOTICE FOR 2012

As CCH's 2012 *GAAP Guide* goes to press, the FASB has outstanding an Exposure Draft of an Accounting Standards Update (ASU) (Accounting for Financial Instruments and Revisions to the Accounting for Derivative Instruments and Hedging Activities) that may have an important impact on the preparation of financial statements in the future.

This proposed ASU simplifies and improves financial reporting for financial instruments by developing a consistent, comprehensive framework for classifying financial instruments. Under this proposed ASU, most financial instruments would be measured at fair value in the statement of financial position each reporting period, while certain qualifying financial instruments would be measured at amortized cost or at a remeasured value specific to that type of instrument (e.g., core deposit liabilities). The proposed ASU recognizes that for certain financial instruments measured at fair value with qualifying changes in fair value recognized in other comprehensive income, financial statement users may benefit from both fair value and amortized cost information. Therefore, it requires both fair value and amortized cost information for these financial instruments to be presented on the face of financial statements by presenting the amortized cost, any allowance for credit losses on financial assets, any other accumulated amounts needed to reconcile amortized cost to fair value, and fair value. Proposed guidance for additional disclosures related to financial instruments is also included in this proposed ASU.

The proposed ASU removes the existing "probable" threshold for recognizing impairments on loans and proposes a common approach to providing for credit losses on loans and debt instruments. This proposed ASU also provides guidance related to the recognition of interest income on debt instruments that will provide a better reflection of a financial instrument's interest yield. The proposed ASU also makes changes to the requirements to qualify for hedge accounting. The proposed guidance replaces the highly complex, quantitative-based hedging requirements with more qualitative-based assessments that make it easier to qualify for hedge accounting and should result in the economic effects of hedging being reported more consistently over multiple reporting periods. Finally, the proposed ASU provides new guidance regarding the criteria used to determine if an investee should be accounted for under the equity method.

The effective date for this proposed ASU will be determined when the final ASU is issued. However, this proposed ASU does include a deferral provision that will permit nonpublic entities with less than $1 billion in total consolidated assets to defer the adoption of the guidance in this ASU for four years. Earlier adoption of this ASU is prohibited.

PART II: INTERPRETIVE GUIDANCE

ASC 815-10: Overall

ASC 815-10-15-58, 55-45; ASC 815-15-15-9, 15-11, 25-8; ASC 460-10-50-4 through 50-6 Disclosures about Credit Derivatives and Certain Guarantees: An Amendment of ASC 815 and ASC 460

BACKGROUND

As a result of the expansion of the market in credit derivatives, concerns have been raised that the information about derivative instruments and certain guarantees presented in financial reports do not include an adequate discussion of how potential unfavorable changes in credit risk would affect a reporting entity's financial position, financial performance, and the cash flows of sellers of credit derivatives and certain guarantees. As a result of the issuance of this guidance, (a) the guidance in ASC 815 has been amended to require that sellers of credit derivatives make such disclosures, including information about derivatives embedded in hybrid instruments, and (b) the guidance in ASC 460-10-05-1, 05-2, 10-1, 15-4 through 15-7, 15-9, 15-10, 25-1 through 25-4, 30-1 through 30-4, 35-1 through 35-2, 35-4, 50-2, 50-4 through 50-6, 50-8, 55-2 through 55-3, 55-5 through 55-9, 55-12 through 55-13, 55-15 through 55-18, 55-20 through 55-24, 55-28 through 55-29; ASC 840-10-25-34, 60-2, is amended to require an additional disclosure about the current status of a guarantee's payment and/or performance risk.

ACCOUNTING GUIDANCE

Scope

This pronouncement provides guidance for disclosures about credit derivatives accounted for under the guidance in ASC 815, hybrid instruments that have embedded credit derivatives, and guarantees accounted for under the scope of ASC 460-10.

> A credit derivative is defined under this guidance as follows:
>
> A credit derivative is a derivative instrument (a) in which one or more of its underlyings are related to the credit risk of a specified entity (or a group of entities) or an index based on the credit risk of a group of entities and (b) that exposes a seller to potential loss from credit-risk-related events specified in the contract.

The following guidance applies to credit derivatives, which include credit default swaps, credit spread options, and credit index products, among others. The amendment to ASC 815 also applies to hybrid instruments that have embedded credit derivatives, such as credit-linked notes.

Amendment to Disclosure Requirements of ASC 815

The following guidance applies to sellers of credit derivatives that are defined as "a party that assume financial risk." That party, which is sometimes called a *writer of a contract*, might be "a guarantor in a guarantee-type contract, and any party that provides the credit protection in an option-type contract, a credit default swap, or any other credit derivative contract." ASC 815 is amended to require that sellers of credit derivatives disclose information about their credit derivatives and hybrid instruments that have embedded credit derivatives so that users of financial statements can evaluate the possible effect of those financial instruments on their sellers' financial position, financial performance, and cash flows.

A seller of a credit derivative is required to disclose the following information in its balance sheet about each credit derivative or group of similar credit derivatives, even if there is only a remote likelihood that the seller will have to make any payments under the credit derivative. Disclosures for groups of similar derivatives may be presented by (1) separating the information by major types of contracts, such as single-name credit default swaps, traded indexes, other portfolio products, and swaptions, and (2) further separating the information into additional subgroups for major types of referenced/underlying asset classes, such as corporate debt, sovereign debt, and structured finance. The following information should be disclosed:

   a. The nature of the credit derivative, including its approximate term; the reason for entering into it; events or circumstance under which a seller would have to perform under a credit derivative; the balance sheet date of the payment/performance risk of a credit derivative, which could be based on either credit ratings issued by an external source or current internal groupings that the seller uses to manage its risk, and if so, how those internal groupings are determined and used to manage risk.

b. The maximum potential amount of undiscounted future payments that a seller could be required to make under a credit derivative that would not be reduced by the effect of amounts, if any, that may possibly be recovered under provisions in the credit derivative providing for recourse or collateralization (see (d) below). If the maximum potential payments under a credit derivative's terms are unlimited, that fact should be disclosed. In addition, a seller that is unable to estimate the maximum potential amount of future payments under a contract should disclose the reasons for the inability to estimate that amount.

c. A credit derivative's fair value as of the balance sheet date.

d. The nature of (1) recourse provisions, if any, that would enable a seller to recover payments made under a credit derivative from a third party, and (2) assets, if any, held as collateral or by a third party that a seller can obtain and liquidate to recover all or a portion of an amount that would be paid under a credit derivative if a payment is triggered by the occurrence of a specified event or condition. If possible, a seller should estimate the approximate portion of the maximum potential amount under a credit derivative that would be expected to be covered by proceeds from the liquidation of those assets. A seller of credit protection should consider the effect of purchased credit protection with identical underlyings in estimating potential recoveries.

A seller of credit derivatives that are embedded in hybrid instruments should disclose the required information for the total hybrid instruments, not solely for the embedded credit derivatives.

Amendment to Disclosure Requirement of ASC 460

The disclosures required under this guidance are substantially similar to those for guarantors under the guidance in ASC 460-10-50-4, except for the disclosure about the current status of the payment/performance risk of the credit derivative. Therefore, ASC 460-10-50-4 is amended by to require that the current status of a payment/performance risk of a guarantee be disclosed so that similar disclosures will be made for instruments with similar risks and rewards. That is, a guarantor that uses internal groupings to manage its risk is also required to disclose how those groupings are determined and used to manage risk.

ASC 815-10-15-141 through 15-142, 25-17, 30-5, 35-5, 50-9; ASC 320-10-55-5 Accounting for Forward Contracts and Purchased Options to Acquire Securities Covered by ASC 320

BACKGROUND

An entity enters into forward contracts or purchased options to acquire securities that will be accounted for under the guidance in ASC 320. The forward contracts, purchased options, and underlying securities are denominated in the same currency as the entity's functional currency. A period of time elapses between the date the forward contracts are entered into or the options are purchased and the acquisition date of the underlying securities. This guidance applies only to transactions that involve physical settlement of the securities.

ACCOUNTING ISSUE

How should an entity account for forward contracts and purchased options having no intrinsic value at acquisition that are entered into to purchase securities that will be accounted for under the guidance in ASC 320 during the time the forward contract or option is outstanding and when the securities are acquired?

ACCOUNTING GUIDANCE

An entity entering into forward contracts and purchased options with no intrinsic value at acquisition in order to acquire securities that will be accounted for under the guidance in ASC 320 should designate the forward contracts or options at inception as held-to-maturity, available-for-sale, or trading securities and account for them based on the guidance for the applicable category in ASC 320. Those forward and option contracts should not be used as hedging instruments.

OBSERVATIONS: The forward contracts and purchased options discussed above would meet the definition of a derivative in ASC 815 if the asset to which the underlying to the derivative contract is convertible to cash. Contracts that permit net settlement would be accounted for in the same manner. Forward contracts and purchased options that are derivatives should be recognized as assets or liabilities and accounted for at fair value in accordance with the guidance in ASC 815.

An entity's accounting policy for the premium paid to acquire an option classified as held-to-maturity or available-for-sale should be disclosed.

After inception, the guidance should be applied to the three categories of securities as follows:

1. **Held-to-maturity**
    a. Recognize *no* changes in the fair value of the forward contract or purchased option; recognize a loss in earnings, however, if a decline in the fair value of the underlying securities is other than temporary.
    b. Record debt securities purchased under a forward contract at the forward contract price on the settlement date.
    c. Record debt securities purchased by exercising an option at the option strike price plus the option premium's remaining carrying amount, if any.
    d. Record a debt security purchased in the market at its market price plus the option premium's remaining carrying amount, if any, if the option to purchase the security expired worthless.
    e. If a purchased option expires worthless, an entity's intent to hold other debt securities to maturity would be called into question if the entity does not purchase the same securities in the market. Further, if

the entity does not take delivery under a forward contract, its intent also would be questionable.

2. **Available-for-sale**

   a. Recognize changes in the fair value of a forward contract or purchased option as part of the ASC 320 separate component of shareholders' equity as they occur; recognize a loss in earnings, however, if a decline in the fair value of the underlying securities is other than temporary.

   b. Record securities purchased under a forward contract at their fair values on the settlement date.

   c. Record securities purchased by exercising an option at the option strike price plus the fair value of the option at the exercise date.

   d. Record the purchase of the same security in the market at its market price plus the option premium's remaining carrying amount, if any, if the option to purchase a security expired worthless.

3. **Trading**

   a. Recognize changes in the fair value of a forward contract or purchased option in earnings as they occur.

   b. Record securities purchased under a forward contract or by exercising an option at the fair value of the securities at the settlement date.

OBSERVATIONS: Because ASC 220 requires that unrealized gains and losses on available-for-sale securities be reported in other comprehensive income, changes in the fair value of forward contracts or purchased options would be reported in that manner. Accumulated changes in value continue to be reported in a separate component of equity.

DISCUSSION

The guidance follows the *trade date accounting approach* used in ASC 320 under which the effect of a transaction is recognized when it occurs. That is, unrealized gains or losses are recognized when incurred rather than when a security is recorded—as would be the case under a settlement approach.

Illustration of Accounting for Forward Contracts and Purchased Options to Acquire Securities Covered by ASC 320

Example 1

On December 1, 20X5, Rolling Ridge Realty Corp., an entity with a 12/31 year-end, entered into a forward purchase contract to purchase a debt security on February 28, 20X6, at $5,000. The forward purchase contract has no cost. Assume that on December 31, 20X5, the fair value of the debt security declined to $4,500, but the decline is *not* considered to be other than temporary. The fair value of the debt security was $4,000 on the settlement date. The entity should account for the transaction as follows if the debt security is classified as (*a*) held-to-maturity, (*b*) available-for-sale, or (*c*) trading:

(a) Held-to-maturity

December 1, 20X5

A forward contract having no cost is not recognized.

December 31, 20X5

A change in the fair value of the forward contract is not recognized.

February 29, 20X6

The debt security is recognized at the forward contract price on the settlement date.

Debt security	$5,000	
Payable		$5,000

(b) Available-for-sale

December 1, 20X5

A forward contract having no cost is not recognized.

December 31, 20X5

A decline in the fair value of the forward contract is recognized in a separate component of equity and also is reported in comprehensive income in the financial statements.

Equity (separate component)	$500	
Payable		$500

February 29, 20X6

A debt security purchased under a forward contract is recognized at the fair value of the underlying security at the settlement date.

Debt security	$4,000	
Loss on forward contract	1,000	
Payable		$4,500
Equity (separate component)		500

(c) Trading

December 1, 20X5

A forward contract having no cost is not recognized.

December 31, 20X5

A decline in the fair value of the forward contract is recognized in earnings.

Loss on forward contract	$500	
Payable		$500

February 29, 20X6

A debt security purchased under a forward contract is recognized at the fair value of the security on the settlement date.

Debt security	$4,000	
Loss on forward contract	500	
Payable		$4,500

Example 2

On December 1, 20X5, Rolling Ridge Realty Corp., an entity with a 12/31 year-end, purchases an option at a $50 premium to purchase a debt security at $5,000. The option, which has no intrinsic value at acquisition, expires on February 29, 20X6. Assume that the price of the debt security and the fair value of the option are as follows: (a) $5,100 and $100, respectively, on December 31, 20X5, and (b) $5,200 and $200, respectively, on February 29, 20X6, the settlement date.

The entity should account for the transaction as follows if the debt security is classified as (a) held-to-maturity, (b) available-for-sale, or (c) trading:

(a) Held-to-maturity

December 1, 20X5

The cost of the option is recognized as an asset.

Option	$50	
Cash		$50

December 31, 20X5

A change in the fair value of the option is not recognized.

February 29, 20X6

On the settlement date, the debt security is recognized at the strike price plus the cost of the option.

Debt security	$5,050	
Payable		$5,000
Option		50

(b) Available-for-sale

December 1, 20X5

The cost of the option is recognized as an asset.

Option	$50	
Cash		$50

December 31, 20X5

An unrealized increase in the fair value of the option is recognized in a separate component of equity and also is reported in comprehensive income in the financial statements.

Option	$50	
Equity (separate component)		$50

February 29, 20X6

On settlement, the debt security is recognized at the option strike price plus the fair value of the option on the exercise date.

Debt security	$5,200	
Equity (separate component)	50	
Payable		$5,000
Option		100
Gain on option		150

(c) Trading

December 1, 20X5

The option is recognized as an asset.

Option	$50	
Cash		$50

December 31, 20X5

An increase in the fair value of the option is recognized in earnings.

Option	$50	
Gain on option		$50

February 29, 20X6

On settlement, the debt security is recognized at its fair value.

Debt security	$5,200	
Payable		$5,000
Option		100
Gain on option		100

ASC 815-10-45-2 Offsetting Foreign Currency Swaps

BACKGROUND

An entity has entered into a debt agreement with principal and interest payable in a foreign currency. The entity's functional currency is the U.S. dollar. To avoid fluctuations in the value of the debt resulting from changes in exchange rates, the entity enters into a currency swap contract under which periodically it will receive foreign currency equivalent to its principal and interest payments on the debt (which is denominated in the foreign currency) for which the entity will pay a stipulated amount in U.S. dollars. The swap thus creates a foreign currency receivable and a U.S. dollar payable. If the terms of the swap contract require settlement only of the net change in the contract value, the entity calculates and recognizes that amount at each balance sheet date. Some believe, as a result of these transactions, the U.S. dollar debt replaces the foreign currency debt.

ACCOUNTING ISSUE

How should the effect of a change in exchange rates on a foreign currency swap contract be displayed in the balance sheet?

ACCOUNTING GUIDANCE

The effect of a change in exchange rates (the difference between the accrued receivable and payable) on a foreign currency swap should *not* be netted against foreign currency debt, because a swap and debt are unrelated transactions without the legal right of setoff in ASC 220.

ASC 815-10-45-9; ASC 932-330-35-1 Issues Involved in Accounting for Derivative Contracts Held for Trading Purposes and Contracts Involved in Energy Trading and Risk Management Activities

BACKGROUND

The following guidance was developed because some have questioned whether companies should be permitted to report unrealized gains or losses at the *inception* of energy trading contracts if *no* quoted market prices or other current market transactions with similar terms and counterparties exist. The FASB staff believes that the guidance related to dealer profit indicates that quoted market prices or information about other market conditions is *required* to recognize unrealized gains or losses at the inception of a contract. In addition, the there were questions about the application of the guidance on disclosures in ASC 235-10-05-3 through 05-4; 50-1 through 50-6 and ASC 205-20-55-80, 55-81; 275-10-05-2 through 05-8; 10-1; 15-3 through 15-6; 50-1, 50-2, 50-4, 50-6 through 50-21, 50-23; 55-1 through 55-19; 60-3; 330-10-55-8 through 55-13; 410-30-55-8 through 55-13; 450-20-50-2; 55-36, 55-37; 460-10-55-27; 605-35-55-3 through 55-10; 740-10-55-219 through 55-222; 932-360-55-15 through 15-19; 958-205-60-1; 605-55-70; 985-20-55-24 through 5-29 applies to energy trading contracts and to suggest additional disclosures.

ACCOUNTING ISSUES

1. Should gains and losses on energy trading contracts be reported gross or net in the income statement?

2. Is recognition of unrealized gains and losses at the inception of an energy trading contract appropriate if no quoted market prices or current market transactions for contracts with similar terms exist?

3. What information should companies be required to disclose about energy trading activities?

ACCOUNTING GUIDANCE

1. Realized and unrealized gains or losses should be presented on a *net* basis for *all* securities accounted for as *derivatives* under the provisions of ASC 815 that are part of a trading activity or held for trading purposes. To clarify the meaning of *trading purposes,* the FASB staff observed that whether derivatives are held for trading purposes depends on an issuer's or holder's intent as discussed in ASC 320-10-25-1—that is, whether the instruments are bought and sold frequently to produce profits on short-term price differences. It was noted that other commodity derivatives, such as gold, are presented net in the financial statements.

SUBSEQUENT DEVELOPMENTS

- The following is a clarification regarding the determination of fair value when a quoted market price is unavailable. The FASB staff believes that the price used in a transaction is the best information available on which to estimate the fair value of a transaction at the inception of an arrangement if there are *no* (a) *quoted* market prices in an active market, (b) *observable* prices of other current market transactions, or (c) other *observable data* to use in making a valuation. Consequently, unrealized gains or losses should be recognized on derivative instruments only if the fair value of an instrument can be obtained from quoted market prices in active markets, from observable evidence of comparable market transactions, or based on valuation techniques using observable market data.

- Mark-to-market accounting for energy trading contracts that are not derivative instruments under the guidance in ASC 815 is prohibited. In addition, gains and losses on all derivative instruments under the guidance in ASC 815 that are held for trading purposes should be presented *net* in the income statement, regardless of the method of settlement. Some have questioned whether the guidance regarding the meaning of *trading purposes* in the context of that guidance contradicts the hedge criteria in ASC 815 so that a derivative held for trading purposes could not be designated as a hedge. The FASB staff reported that the clarification regarding the meaning of *trading purposes* was not intended to limit the designation of a derivative as a hedge under the provisions of ASC 815. Therefore, a derivative held for trading purposes may be designated *prospectively* as a hedge if it meets all the related requirements in ASC 815.

> **OBSERVATIONS:** Derivatives and other financial instruments accounted for under the guidance in ASC 815 should be measured at fair value on initial recognition and in subsequent periods under the guidance in ASC 820-10. The provisions of ASC 820-10 should be applied *retrospectively* in the year in which that guidance is first applied to a financial instrument that was measured at fair value when initially recognized under the provisions of ASC 815 using the transaction price in accordance with the FASB staff's guidance.

SEC OBSERVER COMMENT

The SEC Observer stated that the guidance prohibiting mark-to-market accounting for energy trading contracts that are not derivatives also applies to brokers and dealers in securities, because the guidance applicable to those entities does not provide for specialized accounting in that area.

The SEC Observer also reminded registrants about the required disclosures in Item 303 of Regulations S-K and S-B, which addresses the requirements for Management's Discussion and Analysis, and the guidance in Financial Reporting Release (FRR) 61.

ASC 815-10-45-10, 55-46 through 55-48 Accounting for Options Granted to Employees in Unrestricted, Publicly Traded Shares of an Unrelated Entity

BACKGROUND

This guidance addresses how an employer that grants to its employees stock option awards in the publicly traded shares of an unrelated entity should account for those awards.

ACCOUNTING ISSUE

How should an employer account for stock option awards issued to employees in unrestricted, publicly traded shares of an unrelated entity?

ACCOUNTING GUIDANCE

- Option awards granted to employees in the stock of an unrelated entity that require employees to remain employed for a specified time period and specify the exercise price meet the definition of a derivative in ASC 815 that should be accounted for at its fair value at inception. Subsequent changes in the derivative's fair value should be included in determining net income. The options should continue to be accounted for as a derivative after the award has vested.
- Before an award has vested, an employer should present changes in an option award's fair value as *compensation* expense in the income statement.

After an award has vested, an employer may present changes in an option award's fair value elsewhere in the income statement.

ASC 815-10-55-62 Reporting Realized Gains and Losses on Derivative Instruments That Are Subject to ASC 815 and Not "Held for Trading Purposes" as Defined in ASC 815-10-45-9; ASC 932-330-35-1

BACKGROUND

During its discussion of the guidance in ASC 815-10-45-9; ASC 932-330-35-1 (Involved in Energy Trading and Risk Management Activities), the EITF reached a consensus that *all* derivatives instruments held for trading purposes that are accounted for under the provisions of ASC 815 should be reported *net* in the income statement, regardless of whether or not they are settled physically.

ACCOUNTING ISSUE

Should realized gains and losses on contracts *not* held for trading purposes (as defined in ASC 932-330-35-1; 815-10-45-9) that are accounted for as derivatives under the guidance in ASC 815 be reported gross or net in the income statement, regardless whether the derivative is designated as a hedging instrument?

ACCOUNTING GUIDANCE

- Judgment based on the facts and circumstances, considering the context of the entity's various activities rather than solely on the terms of the contract, should be used to determine whether realized gains and losses on *physically* settled derivative contracts *not* held for trading purposes should be reported in the income statement gross or net; and
- The economic substance of the transaction, the guidance in ASC 845-10 for nonmonetary exchanges, and the gross versus net reporting indicators in ASC 605-45-05-1, 05-2; 15-3 through 15-5; 45-1, 45-2, 45-4 through 45-14, 45-6 through 45-18; 50-1; 55-2, 55-3, 55-5, 55-6, 55-8, 55-9, 55-11 through 55-14, 55-16, 55-18, 55-20, 55-22, 55-24, 55-25, 55-27 through 55-31, 55-33, 55-34, 55-36 through 55-38, 55-40 through 55-45, should also be considered in that decision.

ASC 815-10-S99-3 Determining the Nature of a Host Contract Related to a Hybrid Financial Instrument Issued in the Form of a Share under ASC 815

The following is the position of the SEC staff related to an entity's determination whether a host contract related to a hybrid financial instrument issued in the form of a share is considered to be a debt instrument or an equity instrument when an embedded derivative is evaluated under the guidance in ASC 815-15-25-1.

SCOPE

This announcement applies only to the determination stated above. It is *not* intended to address when an embedded derivative (or multiple embedded derivatives) should be separated from the host contract under the guidance in ASC 815 or the accounting under ASC 815 if a separation is required. ASC 815 provides guidance on such matters.

ACCOUNTING GUIDANCE

The SEC staff believes that in accordance with the guidance in ASC 815-15-25-1 (1), an entity should consider the host instrument's economic characteristics and risks in determining whether a host contract related to a hybrid financial instrument issued in the form of a share is considered to be a debt instrument or an equity instrument. When evaluating the features of an embedded derivative under the guidance in ASC 815-15-25-1a, the economic characteristics and risks of the host contract should be considered based on *all* of the hybrid instrument's stated or implied substantive terms and features. Although a host contract's economic characteristics and risks should *not* be determined based on whether a single term or feature does or does not exist, a single term or feature may be considered more significant. Judgment based on an evaluation of *all* of the relevant terms and features is required to determine whether the host contract in this situation should be considered a debt instrument or an equity instrument.

ASC 815-15: Embedded Derivatives

ASC 815-15-35-4, 40-1 through 40-2, 40-4, 50-3; ASC 470-20-25-16 Issuer's Accounting for a Previously Bifurcated Conversion Option in a Convertible Debt Instrument When the Conversion Option No Longer Meets the Bifurcation Criteria in ASC 815

BACKGROUND

Under the guidance in ASC 815, convertible debt with an embedded conversion option must be bifurcated to separate the conversion option from its host contract and accounted for separately as a derivative if the three conditions discussed in ASC 815-15-25-1 are met. Because under the guidance in ASC 815 an entity must reassess in each reporting period whether an embedded conversion option meets the conditions for bifurcation, sometimes an embedded conversion option that has been separated from its host contract no longer meets the conditions for separate accounting as a derivative. This Issue was undertaken because opinions vary as to how to account for the change. Some believe that the change should be recognized by combining the liability related to the derivative with the liability on the debt instrument. Proponents of this view believe that a premium resulting from the change should be amortized over the remaining term of the debt. Others reclassify the carrying value of the liability on the derivative and combine it with the liability on the debt instrument only as long as the future amortization of a premium that results from the transaction does *not* result in a negative effective yield.

ACCOUNTING ISSUE

How should an issuer account for a previously bifurcated conversion option in a convertible debt instrument if that conversion option no longer meets the criteria for bifurcation in ASC 815?

ACCOUNTING GUIDANCE

- An issuer should reclassify the carrying amount of a liability related to an embedded conversion option in a convertible debt instrument that had been bifurcated but that no longer meets the criteria for bifurcation in FAS-133 to shareholders' equity at its fair value on the date the liability is reclassified. Amortization of a debt discount, if any, recognized when a conversion option was originally bifurcated from a convertible debt instrument should continue.

- An issuer should immediately recognize as interest expense the unamortized amount of a discount, if any, which remains at the conversion date, if a holder exercises a conversion option whose carrying amount had been reclassified to shareholders' equity under the guidance in this Issue.

- If a convertible debt instrument with a conversion option whose carrying amount had been reclassified to shareholders' equity according to the guidance in this Issue is extinguished for cash or other assets before its stated maturity date, the issuer should allocate the reacquisition price as follows: (a) allocate to equity the portion that equals the fair value of the conversion option at the extinguishment date, and (b) allocate the remaining amount to the debt extinguishment to determine the amount of a gain or loss.

This consensus is *not* inconsistent with the guidance in ASC 470-20-05-2 through 05-6; 25-2, 25-3, 25-10 through 25-13; 30-1, 30-2; 505-10-60-3, because *(a)* the instrument was bifurcated initially in accordance with the guidance in ASC 815, and *(b)* the guidance in ASC 470-20 applies to convertible debt instruments only at issuance, not to subsequent changes.

DISCLOSURE

Issuers should disclose the following information for the period in which an embedded conversion option that was previously accounted for as a derivative under the guidance in ASC 815 no longer meets the criteria for bifurcation:

- A description of the principal changes as a result of which an embedded conversion option is no longer required to be bifurcated under the guidance in FAS-133.

- The amount of a liability that is reclassified to stockholders' equity.

ASC 815-20: Hedging—General

ASC 815-20-25-3 Documentation of the Methods Used to Measure Hedge Ineffectiveness under ASC 815

This announcement clarifies the guidance in ASC 815 related to the required documentation at the beginning of fair value, cash flow, and net investment hedges. According to the FASB staff, the guidance in ASC 815-20-25-3 and ASC 815-30-35-11 through 35-32, 55-91 through 55-93 requires formal documentation, at the beginning of a hedge, about the hedging relationship, and the entity's risk management objective for entering into the hedge. The following information is required:

- The hedging instrument
- The hedged item or transaction
- The nature of the hedged risk
- The method used to retrospectively and prospectively evaluate whether the hedging instrument will be effective
- The method to be used to measure hedge ineffectiveness (including when the change in fair value method discussed in Issue G7 of the Implementation Guide is used).

ASC 815-25: Fair Value Hedges

ASC 815-25-35-14, 55-52; ASC 815-30-35-45 Effect of Derivative Gains and Losses on the Capitalization of Interest

BACKGROUND

According to the guidance in ASC 835-20, the purpose of capitalizing interest costs of an acquired asset is to measure cost of interest incurred to finance the asset acquisition that would otherwise not have been incurred. Under that guidance, interest that is eligible for capitalization on qualified assets includes interest on borrowings and obligations with explicit interest rates, interest imputed in accordance with the guidance in ASC 835-30 on certain types of payables, and interest on capital leases. If the specific interest on a new borrowing can be associated with the eligible portion of the asset, that rate should be used for interest capitalization purposes. Otherwise, a weighted average of the rates on borrowings is applied to expenditures not related to specific new borrowings. Interest capitalization during a period is limited to the amount of interest incurred during the period.

This Issue has been raised because there is diversity in practice when the guidance in ASC 835-20 is applied in connection with the guidance in ASC 815 to interest costs in a fair value hedge accounting model.

ACCOUNTING ISSUE

Should the interest rate used to capitalize interest costs according with the guidance in ASC 835-20 on the historical cost of certain assets be the effective yield after gains and losses have been recognized on the effective portion of a derivative instrument that qualifies as a fair value hedge of fixed interest rate debt or should the original effective interest rate on that debt be used?

ACCOUNTING GUIDANCE

An entity that elects to begin amortizing adjustments of the carrying amount of a hedged liability under the guidance in ASC 815-25-55-66 should include those amounts in interest costs used to determine the capitalization rate under the guidance in ASC 835-20. Interest costs related to the ineffective portion of a fair value hedge should *not* be included in the capitalization rate.

In the example in ASC 815-25-55-46, 55-48, the entity decides to immediately begin amortizing the adjustments of the carrying amount of the fixed rate debt while the hedge is still in place. If the entity in that example recognizes as interest expense the fair value change attributed to the passage of time, the amounts recognized as expenses in ASC 815-25-55-48 would be eligible for capitalization under the guidance in ASC 835-20.

Under the guidance in ASC 815, a gain or loss on the hedging instrument in a cash flow hedge is not permitted to be capitalized as a basis adjustment of the qualifying assets. Under the guidance in ASC 815-30-35-3, 35-4, 35-7, 35-38 through 35-41, amounts accumulated in other comprehensive income must be reclassified into earnings in the period in which the forecasted transaction affects earnings. Because an asset's depreciable life coincides with the amortization period of the capitalized interest on the debt, the FASB staff believes that amounts accumulated in comprehensive income that are related to a cash flow hedge of the fluctuations in the variable interest rate on a specific borrowing associated with an asset under construction for which interest costs are capitalized as a cost of that asset should be reclassified into earnings over the depreciable life of the constructed asset.

ASC 815-40: Contracts in Entity's Own Equity

ASC 815-40-05-1 through 05-4, 05-10 through 05-12, 25-1 through 25-5, 25-7 through 25-20, 25-22 through 25-24, 25-26 through 25-35, 25-37 through 25-40, 30-1, 35-1 through 35-2, 35-6, 35-8 through 35-13, 40-1 through 40-2, 50-1 through 50-5, 55-1 through 55-18; ASC 815-10-1578, 55-52, 15-25-15; ASC 460-10-60-14; ASC 480-10-55-63; ASC 505-10-60-5 Accounting for Derivative Financial Instruments Indexed to, and Potentially Settled in, a Company's Own Stock

BACKGROUND

OBSERVATIONS: ASC 480-10 (FAS-150) provides guidance for issuers on the classification and measurement of financial instruments with the characteristics of both liabilities and equity. Financial instruments under the scope of the Statement must be classified as liabilities or as assets in some situations.

The guidance in this Issue has been *partially nullified* as follows:
- Free-standing instruments under the scope of ASC 480-10 (FAS-150), such as forward purchase contracts, written put options, and certain other

ASC 815—Derivatives and Hedging **48,033**

instruments that can be settled with the issuer's equity shares, must be classified as liabilities and measured in accordance with that guidance.

- Nonpublic entities are no longer permitted to classify proceeds from put warrants as equity. In accordance with the provisions ASC 480-10, a liability should be recognized for a put warrant that includes an obligation to repurchase an issuer's equity shares, or one that is indexed to such an obligation, which requires or may require a transfer of assets. Put warrants that include an obligation to issue a variable number of shares if the value of that obligation is primarily based on (*a*) a fixed sum of money at inception, (*b*) variations based on something different than the fair value of the issuer's shares, or (*c*) variations inversely related to changes in the fair value of the issuer's equity shares are also included under the scope of ASC 480-10 Put warrants *not* under the scope of ASC 480-10 should be accounted for under the guidance in this Issue. (See ASC 480-10-55-29 through 55-32; 40-42 through 40-52 for additional guidance on put warrants.)

- The guidance in ASC 480-10 (FAS-150) *nullifies* the requirement under this Issue (which is analogous to the SEC's guidance in ASR-268) that public companies account as temporary equity for the cash redemption amounts of obligations to deliver cash in exchange for the entity's own shares in physical settlements of freestanding financial instruments classified as equity. Such amounts should be classified as liabilities under the guidance in ASC 480-10 (FAS-150) and measured at their fair value or at the present value of the redemption amount, unless the Statement requires a different valuation or other accounting guidance applies.

- The guidance in this Issue continues to apply when financial instruments embedded in other financial instruments that are *not* derivatives in their entirety are evaluated for bifurcation under ASC 815 (FAS-133), such as written put options embedded in nonderivative host contracts, because the guidance in ASC 480-10 (FAS-150) does *not* apply to such financial instruments. That is, an embedded written option that would have been classified in equity under this Issue before the guidance in ASC 480-10 (FAS-150) was issued would continue to be considered an equity instrument when evaluating whether an embedded derivative could be bifurcated under the guidance in ASC 815-15-25-1 (paragraph 12 of FAS-133).

An entity may enter into contracts that are indexed to and settled in its own stock for various economic reasons, for example, to hedge share dilution from existing written call options, to hedge the effect of existing written option positions on earnings, to hedge planned future purchases of treasury stock, to hedge a planned future issuance of shares, or to hedge the cost of a business combination. The following are such contracts:

- *Forward sale contract* A contract requiring an entity to sell a specific number of its shares of stock at a specific price on a specific future date. For example, an entity enters into a contract to sell 500 shares of its common stock at $50 per share on June 30, 20X8. The entity has a loss if the market price of the stock is more than $50 per share on that date.

Conversely, the entity has a gain if the market price of the stock is less than $50 per share on that date.

- *Forward purchase contract* A contract requiring an entity to purchase a specific number of shares of its stock at a specific price on a specific future date. For example, an entity enters into a contract to purchase 500 shares of its common stock at $50 per share on June 30, 20X8. The entity has a gain if the market price of the stock is more than $50 per share on that date. Conversely, the entity has a loss if the market price of the stock is less than $50 per share on that date.

- *Purchased put option* A contract giving an entity a right to, but not requiring it to, sell a specific number of its shares of stock at a specific price on a specific future date. For example, an entity may purchase a right to sell 500 shares of its common stock at $50 per share on June 30, 20X8. The entity has a gain if the market price of the stock is less than $50 per share on that date. The contract is worthless if the market price of the stock is more than $50 per share on that date because the entity would not exercise the option if it can sell shares for more elsewhere.

- *Purchased call option* A contract giving an entity the right to, but not requiring it to, buy a specific number of its shares of stock at a specific price on a specific future date. For example, an entity may purchase a right to buy 500 shares of its common stock at $50 per share on June 30, 20X8. The entity has a gain if the market price of the stock is more than $50 per share on that date. The contract is worthless if the market price of the stock is less than $50 per share on that date because the entity would not exercise the option if it can buy shares for less elsewhere.

- *Written put option* A contract sold by an entity giving the holder the right, but not the obligation, to sell to the entity a specific number of the entity's shares of stock at a specific price on a specific future date. For example, an entity may sell put options giving the holder the right to sell to the entity 500 shares of its commons tock at $50 per share on June 30, 20X8. If the market price is less than $50, the option will expire unexercised because the holder can buy the shares for less on the open market. The entity's gain will be limited to the option premium received.

- *Written call option (and warrant)* A contract sold by an entity giving the holder the right, but not the obligation, to purchase a specific number of the entity's shares of common stock at a specific price on a specific future date. For example, an entity may sell a call option giving the holder the right to purchase 500 shares of the entity's common stock at $50 per share on June 30, 20X8. If the market price is less than $50 per share on that date, the option will expire unexercised, because the holder can purchase the shares for less on the option market. The entity's gain will be limited to the option premium. If the market price is more than $50 on that date, the holder will exercise the option and the entity will have a loss.

Such contracts may be settled as follows:

- *Physical settlement* The buyer delivers the full stated amount of cash and the seller delivers the full stated number of shares.

- *Net share settlement* The party incurring a loss delivers to the party realizing a gain shares equal to the current fair value of the gain.
- *Net cash settlement* The party incurring a loss pays cash to the party realizing a gain in an amount equal to the gain; no shares are exchanged.

The contracts may be freestanding, that is, they are entered into separately from the entity's other financial instruments or equity transactions, or they are entered into with another action, but the contract can be detached legally and exercised separately. Although such contracts may be embedded, that is, be an integral part of a debt security (see ASC 480-10-55-29 through 55-32; 40-42 through 40-52 for an example of such a security), the contracts discussed in this Issue are freestanding.

The EITF discussed the initial recognition of written put options in Issue 87-31, which is codified in this Issue. Under that consensus, proceeds received on the sale of written put options were recognized as equity transactions. Changes in the market value of the options were not recognized. Although the consensus in Issue 87-31 did not specify the method of settlement, it is clear that the Task Force expected such transactions would be settled in shares, not in net cash nor based on a choice of settlement in cash or shares. The consensus analogized the transactions to those contemplated under SEC Accounting Series Release (ASR) No. 268 (Presentation in Financial Statements of "Redeemable Preferred Stock"), thus requiring public companies to transfer from permanent equity to temporary equity an amount equal to the redemption price of the common stock, regardless of whether the put options can be exercised immediately or are "in the money" when issued. Under that consensus, permanent equity would not be adjusted until the options are redeemed, exercised, or expire.

Although ASC 470-20 (APB-14), and Issue 86-35 (codified in this Issue), provided guidance on accounting for free-standing written call options or warrants on an entity's own stock, they did not specifically address the accounting for freestanding written call options or warrants that must be settled in either net shares or net cash or that permit the entity to choose the method of settlement.

ACCOUNTING ISSUE

How should an entity classify and measure freestanding contracts that are indexed to, and potentially settled in, the entity's own stock?

EITF CONSENSUS

The Framework for Accounting (the Model)

Scope

The EITF developed a framework of accounting ("the Model"), which only applies to freestanding derivative financial instruments that are indexed to and settled in an entity's own stock, such as forward contracts, options, and warrants.

The Model does *not* apply to the accounting for:

- A derivative or a financial instrument if the derivative is embedded in the financial instrument and cannot be detached from it

- Contracts issued to compensate employees or to acquire goods and services from nonemployees *before* performance has occurred (the Issue does apply after performance has occurred)
- Contracts indexed to and settled in a consolidated subsidiary's stock (see Issues 00-4 and 00-6)

Initial and Subsequent Balance Sheet Classification and Measurement

Under the Model, freestanding contracts that are indexed to, and potentially settled in, an entity's own stock are classified in the balance sheet based on the concept that contracts that must be settled in net cash are assets or liabilities, and that contracts that must be settled in shares are equity instruments. (See the Observation in a discussion of Issue 00-6 under "EITF CONSENSUS.") It is assumed under the Model that if given a choice between settlement in shares or in cash, an entity would choose to settle a contract in its own stock in shares or in net shares, whereas the counterparty would choose to settle the same contract in cash or in net cash. The Model does not apply, however, if the settlement alternatives do not have the same economic value or if one of the settlement alternatives is fixed or has caps or floors. If this is the case, the accounting is based on the instrument's (or combination of instruments') economic substance. If the number of shares an entity is required to deliver under a contract is limited in accordance with a net-share settlement alternative, the Model applies even though the settlement alternatives may have different economic values.

Freestanding contracts are measured initially at fair value. At each subsequent balance sheet date before settlement, they are accounted for based on the initial classification and the required or assumed settlement method. For example, if a contract that is classified as an equity instrument gives the entity a choice between net share settlement or physical settlement requiring the entity to deliver cash, it is assumed that the entity would choose to settle the contract in net shares. Conversely, it is assumed that given the choice, the counterparty would require the entity to settle the contract by physical delivery of cash.

The contracts are classified based on their economic substance and measured as follows:

1. Contracts Classified as Equity Instruments

   a. *Contracts that require physical settlement in shares or settlement in net shares* Reported in *permanent* equity (see the following discussion on equity instruments classified as temporary equity) and measured initially at fair value. Fair value is not adjusted for subsequent changes for contracts classified in equity.

   b. *Contracts under which the entity can choose to settle in (a) its own shares (physical settlement in shares or net share settlement) or in net cash or (b) in net shares or by physical settlement requiring the entity to deliver cash* Reported in *permanent* equity and measured initially at fair value, which is not adjusted for subsequent changes. Amounts paid or received for contracts settled in cash are included in contributed capital.

c. ASR 268 provides guidance by analogy to *public* companies for the transactions discussed in this Issue. Consequently, for the following contracts, which are generally reported in permanent equity, public companies must transfer to *temporary equity* an amount equal to the cash redemption amount in a physical settlement:

  (1) Contracts under which physical settlement in cash is required (for example, the entity must buy back its share from the holder of a written put option)

  (2) Contracts under which the entity chooses settlement in net cash or by physical settlement requiring the entity to deliver cash

  (3) Contracts under which the counterparty can choose to settle in net shares or by physical settlement requiring the entity to deliver cash

2. Contracts Classified as Assets or Liabilities

  a. *Contracts that must be settled in net cash* Measured initially and subsequently at fair value.

  b. *Contracts under which a counterparty can choose to settle in net cash or in shares (physical settlement or in net shares)* Measured initially and at fair value.

Gains and losses on contracts classified as assets or liabilities are reported in income and disclosed in the financial statements. Gains or losses continue to be included in income even if the contract is ultimately settled in shares.

DISCUSSION

- Those who believe that contracts requiring physical settlement in shares should be classified in equity argue that classifying such contracts as assets or liabilities, and thus including gains and losses in income, would be inconsistent with the guidance in ASC 225-10-15-3; 45-1; 225-20-05-1; 250-10-05-5; 45-22, 45-24, 45-28; 50-8 through 50-9; 505-10-25-2 (APB-9) and that in ASC 310-10-45-14; 505-10-45-1 through 45-2; and 850-10-60-4 (EITF Issue 85-1). Such classification also would be inconsistent with the guidance in ASR-268 (Presentation Financial Statements of "Redeemable Preferred Stocks"), which requires an entity to transfer an amount that equals the contracted purchase price of the stock under financial instruments (such as forward purchase contracts and purchased call options) from permanent equity to temporary equity. In addition, a transaction settled in the entity's shares was considered to be a classic equity transaction.

- The Task Force agreed that because contracts in which an *entity* chooses whether to settle the obligation with the entity's shares or in cash are under the entity's control, such contracts should be accounted for as equity transactions.

- Contracts that require net cash settlement should be classified as assets or liabilities because the right to receive or pay cash is a future economic benefit or future economic sacrifice that meets the definition of an asset or a liability in CON-6 (Elements of Financial Statements) (not in ASC). In addition, because no shares are exchanged, the transaction does not have the characteristics of an equity transaction, even if the amount of cash to be exchanged is indexed to the price of the entity's stock.

- Contracts giving the counterparty the right to demand payment in cash or in shares should be recognized as an asset or a liability because the transaction is not under the entity's control. For example, a liability may be incurred if the counterparty demands a cash settlement when a forward contract is in a loss position.

- Proponents of the view that gains and losses on contracts recognized as assets or liabilities should be recognized currently in income argue that ASC 250-10-45-22; 225-10-45-1 (paragraph 17 of APB-9, *Reporting the Results of Operations*) requires that treatment. They believe that because the entity does not transfer its shares, the transaction does not qualify for the exemption in ASC 505-10-25-2 (paragraph 28 of APB-9), which states that charges or credits resulting from transactions in the entity's capital stock may be excluded from the determination of net income. This is analogous to the view of the majority of the EITF in Issue 86-28 (nullified by FAS-133), that is, that an increase in a contingent payment should be recognized as an expense.

Additional Requirements for Equity Classification

The guidance in ASC 815-10-15-74; 815-15-25-1(paragraphs 11(a) and 12(c) of FAS-133) provides that embedded derivatives indexed to a reporting entity's *own* stock and classified in stockholders' equity should *not* be considered to be derivatives for the purposes of ASC 815 (FAS-133), even if they were freestanding. The EITF reached a consensus that the additional requirements for equity classification discussed in this section do *not* apply under the provisions of ASC 815 (FAS-133) when evaluating whether derivative financial instruments, such as forward contracts, options, or warrants, indexed to an entity's own stock that are embedded in a *debt* instrument would be classified in stockholders' equity if they were freestanding.

The Task Force also reached a consensus that the requirements in this Issue used to determine whether an embedded derivative indexed to an entity's own stock should be classified in stockholders' equity if it were freestanding do not apply to *conventional convertible debt instruments* if the value of the conversion option can be realized only when the holder exercises that option and receives all of the proceeds in a fixed number of shares or in an equivalent amount of cash, at the issuer's option. Issuers should apply the requirements of this Issue, however, when evaluating whether other embedded derivatives are equity instruments not covered under the scope of ASC 815 (FAS-133).

Equity derivative contracts that include a provision under which an entity could be required to settle a contract in net cash should be accounted for as an asset or liability under the Model, *not* as the issuer's equity.

SEC registrants should classify equity contracts as temporary equity in accordance with the SEC's Accounting Series Release (ASR) No. 268 (Presentation in Financial Statements of "Redeemable Preferred Stocks") if the contract includes a provision that could require the issuer to pay cash to the counterparty in a *physical settlement* for the issuer's shares. A contract that permits the counterparty to require a *net cash settlement* should be classified as an *asset* or *liability*. This consensus does *not* require an evaluation of the likelihood that an event causing a cash settlement (net cash or physical) would occur. However, the potential outcome need not be considered when the provisions of ASR-268 are applied if cash payment is required only in the case of the issuer's final liquidation.

A derivative indexed to, and potentially settled in, a company's own stock should be classified in equity *only* if all of the following conditions are met:

- The entity is permitted to settle the contract in registered or unregistered shares.
- The entity has enough authorized but unissued shares available to settle the contract, after considering all of its other commitments that may require issuing stock during the period the contract is outstanding.
- The contract specifically limits the number of shares to be delivered in a share settlement, even if the contract terminates when the stock price is at a stated trigger price.
- The contract does not require the entity to post collateral for any reason.
- The issuer is not required to pay cash to the counterparty if the counterparty has sold the shares initially delivered to it and the proceeds are less than the total amount due.
- The counterparty's rights under a contract are no greater than those of the underlying stock's shareholders.

An entity may be required under a contract's provisions to settle in net shares or to physically deliver cash and receive its own shares, such as in a forward purchase contract or a written put option. Therefore, an entity that does not control settlement in net shares under the above conditions or the Issues discussed below would continue to account for the contract as an equity instrument. SEC registrants, however, would be required to transfer to temporary equity the amount due in cash on settlement.

The conditions discussed above apply to the following guidance:

- A contract that requires an issuer to settle by delivering only registered shares in a net-share or physical settlement, or cash in a net-cash settlement, should be accounted for as an *asset or liability*, because (*a*) events or actions necessary to deliver registered shares are *not* within the entity's control and (*b*) under the model discussed above, it is assumed that the entity will be required to settle in net cash.
- Delivery of unregistered shares in a *private placement* is within an entity's control if during the six months before the classification assessment date, the entity did not file a statement with the SEC that was later withdrawn (a failed registration statement). However, if the entity did have a failed registration during the previous six months, there should be a legal determination as to whether the entity can deliver unregistered shares in a

settlement in shares or in net shares. An entity, therefore, should classify a contract as permanent equity if the entity (*a*) has not had a failed registration statement, (*b*) is permitted under the contract to deliver unregistered shares to settle a contract in net shares, and (*c*) meets other conditions in this Issue.

- Settlement in shares or net shares is *not* within an entity's control if the shareholders' approval is required to increase the number of authorized shares for such settlement. To control settlement, an entity must determine whether it will have a sufficient number of authorized and unissued shares at the date on which a contract's classification is determined. To make this determination, an entity should compare (*a*) the number of authorized but unissued shares, less the number of shares the entity could be required to deliver during the contract period to satisfy existing commitments, with (*b*) the maximum number of shares that the entity could be required to deliver in a net-share or physical settlement under the contract. An entity controls settlement in shares if the number of shares in (*a*) is greater than the number of shares in (*b*) and meets the entity conditions above. If settlement is *not* under the entity's control, the contract should be classified as an *asset* or *liability*.

- If the number of shares an entity may need to settle a contract cannot be determined at the classification date, net-share settlement is *not* under the entity's control because the entity cannot determine whether it has sufficient authorized shares for settlement. If a contract limits the number of shares delivered at the contract's expiration in a net-share settlement, the entity *can* determine whether such settlement is within its control by comparing the maximum number of shares needed with the available authorized but unissued shares. That comparison would determine whether a sufficient number of shares are available to settle a contract in net shares after delivering shares to satisfy other existing commitments as well as for top-off or make-whole provisions discussed below.

- A derivative contract must be classified as an *asset* or *liability* if net-share settlement is permitted, but net-cash settlement is *required* if an entity does not make timely SEC filings because doing so is not within the entity's control.

- If a contract requires net-cash settlement on the occurrence of an event that results in a change of control, the contract should be classified as an *asset* or *liability*, because the occurrence of such an event would not be under the entity's control. However, classification in permanent equity would be acceptable if, under a contract's change of control provision, the counterparty can receive or deliver on settlement the same form of consideration as to the shareholders of the security underlying the contract. For example, the counterparty to the contract and the shareholders would both receive cash in the transaction. Further, a contract's classification would not be affected if it includes a provision related to a change in control that specifies that if all stockholders receive the acquiring entity's stock, the contract will be indexed to the purchaser's stock (or the issuer's in a business combination accounted for as a pooling of interests).

- A contract that grants a counterparty the rights of a creditor in case the entity declares bankruptcy should *not* be classified as equity, unless the contract includes a statement that the counterparty's rights are not senior to the claims of the common shareholders of the underlying stock in case of bankruptcy. However, equity classification would be permitted for a contract that requires net-cash settlement in case of bankruptcy if it is possible to demonstrate that the counterparty's claims in bankruptcy could be settled in net shares or would not have a higher rank in bankruptcy than those of the underlying stock's common shareholders.
- Equity classification is permitted if a contract requires net-cash settlement in case of nationalization, because the counterparty and the underlying stock's common shareholders, who would receive cash as compensation for the expropriated assets, would receive the same form of compensation.
- *Top-off* or *make-whole* provisions are sometimes included in contracts to reimburse a counterparty for losses incurred, or to transfer to the entity gains the counterparty recognized on the difference between the value of the contract at the settlement date and the value the counterparty realized in a sale of the securities after the settlement date. A contract that includes such a provision may be classified as equity only if (*a*) the provision can be settled in net shares and (*b*) the maximum number of shares that could be delivered is fixed and is less than the number of available authorized shares after meeting other commitments settled in shares.
- Equity classification is *not* permitted if a contract includes a provision requiring an issuer to post collateral if certain events occur (e.g., a drop in the price of the underlying stock), because the requirement to post collateral is not consistent with the concept of equity. However, equity classification is permitted if the equity securities to be delivered under a contract are placed in trust.

Contract Reclassification

A contract's classification should be reassessed at each balance sheet date. If necessary, a contract should be reclassified as of the date on which an event causing a change in classification has occurred. Contracts may be reclassified an unlimited number of times.

A contract's change in classification should be accounted for as follows:

- A change in the fair value of a contract that is reclassified from permanent or temporary equity to an asset or liability classification should be accounted for as an adjustment to stockholders' equity for the period between the date of the contract's last classification as equity to the date of reclassification to an asset or a liability. In addition, after a contract is reclassified from permanent or temporary equity to an asset or a liability, all changes in the contract's fair value should be recognized in income.

- Conversely, gains or losses recognized in accounting for the fair value of a contract that has been properly classified as an asset or a liability should not be reversed if the contract is reclassified to equity.
- If the total notional amount of a contract that can be partially settled in net shares can no longer be classified in permanent equity, the portion that could be settled in net shares as of the balance sheet date would continue to be classified in permanent equity while the other portion would be reclassified in temporary equity, or as an asset or liability, as appropriate.

If more than one of an entity's derivative contracts may be partially settled, and some or all of those contracts are *required* to be partially settled, different methods can be used to determine which contracts, or portions thereof, should be reclassified.

Determining how to partially reclassify such contracts is an accounting policy decision that should be disclosed in accordance with ASC 235-10-05-3 through 05-4, 50-1 through 50-6. However, the reclassification method should be systematic, rational, and consistent. Under acceptable methods, an entity might (*a*) partially reclassify all contracts proportionately, (*b*) reclassify contracts with the *earliest inception* date first, (*c*) reclassify contracts with the *earliest maturity* date first, (*d*) reclassify contracts with the *latest inception* date first, or (*e*) reclassify contracts with the *latest maturity* date first.

Disclosures

The following disclosures required under the guidance in ASC 505-10-15-1, 50-3 through 50-5, 50-11; ASC 470-10-50-5 apply to *all* contracts under the scope of this Issue:

- For an option or forward contract indexed to the issuer's equity, disclose the forward rate, option strike price, number of issuer's shares to which the contract is indexed, the settlement date or dates of the contract, and whether the issuer accounts for the contract as an asset, a liability, or equity.
- For contracts with terms that *state* alternative settlement methods, disclose the alternatives, including who controls the alternatives and the *maximum* number of shares that *could be required to be issued* to settle a contract with net shares. Under the guidance in ASC 505-10-15-1; 50-3 through 50-5, 50-11; 470-10-50-5 additional disclosures about actual issuances and settlements that occurred during the accounting period also are required.
- For contracts that *do not* state a fixed or determinable maximum number of shares that may be required to be issued, disclose the fact that an infinite number of shares potentially could be issued to settle the contract.
- Disclose the contract's current fair value for each settlement alternative, denominated in monetary amounts or number of shares, and the effect of changes in the price of the issuer's equity instruments on settlement amounts.
- For equity instruments under this Issue that are classified as temporary equity, disclose the amount of redemption requirements, by issue or combined for all issues, that are redeemable at fixed or determinable

prices on fixed or determinable dates in each of the five years after the date of the latest balance sheet presented.

- For contracts classified as assets or liabilities that meet the definition of a derivative under the guidance in ASC 815, disclose information regarding the objective for holding or issuing those instruments based on the guidance in ASC 815-10-50-1 through 50-5, as well as the disclosures required in ASC 815-30-50-1, regarding fair value hedges, cash flow hedges, and hedges of net investments in foreign operations.

Issuers should disclose information about contract reclassifications in or out of equity during the life of an instrument, the reason for reclassification, and the effect on the issuer's financial statements. In addition, the entity's accounting policy regarding the method used to partially reclassify contracts under this Issue should be disclosed in accordance with the guidance in ASC 235-10-50-1 through 50-6.

Application Guidance for Specific Instruments

The following guidance represents the Task Force's consensus positions on the application of the Model to the following types of freestanding derivative financial instruments that are indexed to, and potentially settled in, an entity's own stock.

1. Forward Sale Contracts, Written Call Options or Warrants, and Purchased Put Options

BACKGROUND

An entity enters into a contract to sell a specific number of its shares of common stock to the holder at a specified price on a specified future date. The contract may be settled by delivery of shares to the counterparty (physical settlement), in net shares, in net cash, or based on the entity's or counterparty's choice of settlement method.

ACCOUNTING GUIDANCE

Based on the Model, the contracts are accounted for as follows:

- *Contracts requiring physical settlement in shares or settlement in net shares* The contracts are *equity* instruments recognized in permanent equity and measured initially at fair value. Fair value is not adjusted for subsequent events.
- *Contracts requiring net cash settlement* The contracts are reported as *assets* or *liabilities* and measured initially and subsequently at fair value. Subsequent changes in fair value, if any, are reported in income and disclosed in the financial statements.
- *Contracts giving the entity the choice of settlement method*
  — Settlement in net shares or by physical settlement in shares. The contracts are *equity* instruments recognized in permanent equity and measured initially at fair value, which is not adjusted for subsequent changes.

— Settlement in net shares or net cash, or settlement in net cash or physical settlement in shares. The contracts are *equity* instruments reported in permanent equity and measured initially at fair value, which is not adjusted for subsequent changes. If cash is paid or received in a net cash settlement, that amount is reported in contributed capital.

- *Contracts giving the counterparty the choice of settlement method*
  — Settlement in net shares or by physical settlement in shares. The contracts are *equity* instruments reported in permanent equity and measured initially at fair value, which is not adjusted for subsequent changes.
  — Settlement in net shares or net cash, or settlement in net cash or physical settlement in shares. The contracts are reported as *assets* or *liabilities* and measured initially and subsequently at fair value. Subsequent changes in fair value, if any, are reported in earnings and disclosed in the financial statements. Gains or losses are included in income and disclosed in the financial statements, even if the contract is ultimately settled in shares.

Illustration of the Accounting for a Purchased Put Option Indexed to, and Potentially Settled in, an Entity's Own Stock

On 7/15/X5, Preston Company (a public entity with a 12/31 year-end) purchases a put option that is indexed to 100 common shares of the entity's own stock at $25 per share, when the fair value of the stock is $25 per share. The option expires on 10/13/X5. The option premium is $150. Assume that the price of each common share and the fair value of the option are $23 and $225 on 9/30/X5. The price of each share of common stock on 10/13/X5, the settlement date, is $20. Under the following two scenarios, Preston accounts for the contract at each date as follows: (a) 7/15/X5, (b) 9/30/X5, and (c) 10/13/X5.

Scenario 1: The entity can choose to settle in net shares or net cash

(a) At initiation of the contract—7/15/X5

Because the entity can choose the method of settlement, the indexed option is an equity transaction.

Additional paid-in capital	$150	
Cash		$150

(b) At interim dates—9/30/X5

Contracts recorded as equity transactions are not adjusted to fair value at interim dates.

(c) At settlement—10/13/X5

The entity chooses to settle in net cash. Because the price per share is $20 on the settlement date, the option is worth $500 [($25 - $20) × 100]. The counterparty pays the entity $500 to settle the contract.

Cash	$500	
Additional paid-in capital		$500

Scenario 2: The counterparty can choose to settle in net cash or in net shares

(a) At initiation of the contract—7/15/X5

Because the counterparty decides on the method of settlement, the indexed option is recognized as an asset.

Indexed option	$150	
Cash		$150

(b) At interim dates—9/30/X5

The per share price has increased to $23. The entity reduces the carrying amount of the option to its fair value of $225 and recognizes a loss of $105 ($330 - $225).

Loss on indexed option	$105	
Indexed option		$105

(c) At settlement—10/13/X5

The counterparty chooses to settle in net shares. Because the price per share is $20 on the settlement date—$5 less than the reference price of $25—the option is worth $500. The entity, therefore, had a total gain recognized on settlement is $275 ($500 less the $225 recorded amount of the option).

Treasury stock	$500	
Indexed option		$225
Gain on indexed option		275

SUBSEQUENT DEVELOPMENT

SEC registrants that have entered into forward equity sales transactions after May 1, 1998, should classify those transactions as debt. Such transactions combine the issuance of common stock with a forward contract that requires the issuer to give the holder a guaranteed return.

2. Written Put Options and Forward Purchase Contracts

BACKGROUND

An entity enters into a contract under which it agrees to purchase a specified number of the entity's shares of common stock at a specified price on a specified future date. The contract may be settled by physical settlement, in net shares, in net cash, or the issuing entity or the counterparty may have the right to choose the settlement method. (This discussion also applies to shareholder rights (SHARPs) issued by an entity to its shareholders, which give them the right to sell a specified number of common shares to the entity for cash.)

ACCOUNTING GUIDANCE

Based on the Model, the contracts are accounted for as follows:

- *Contracts requiring physical settlement in cash* The contracts are *equity* instruments reported in permanent equity, but because the option writer is required to settle the contract in cash, *public* companies must transfer to temporary equity an amount equal to the redemption amount. The instruments are measured initially at fair value without subsequent adjustment for changes in fair value.

- *Contracts requiring net share settlement* The contracts are equity instruments reported in permanent equity and measured initially at fair value, without subsequent adjustment for changes in fair value.
- *Contracts requiring net cash settlement* The contracts are *liabilities* that are measured initially at fair value and adjusted for changes in fair value, which are reported in earnings and disclosed in the financial statements.
- *Contracts giving the entity the choice of settlement method*
  — Settlement in net shares or physical settlement in cash, or settlement in net shares or net cash. The contracts are equity instruments that are reported in permanent equity. The instruments are measured initially at fair value without subsequent adjustment for changes in fair value. Cash paid or received in a physical settlement in cash or a net cash settlement is recognized in contributed capital. (It is assumed that the entity will settle in net shares.)
  — Settlement in net cash or by physical settlement in cash. The contracts are *equity* instruments that are reported in permanent equity, but because the option writer is required to settle the contract in cash, *public* companies must transfer to temporary equity an amount equal to the redemption amount. The instruments are measured initially at fair value without subsequent adjustment for changes in fair value. If the contract is ultimately settled in net cash or in net shares, the amount reported in temporary equity is transferred and reported as an addition to permanent equity.
- *Contracts giving the counterparty the choice of settlement method*
- Settlement in net cash or by physical settlement in cash. The contracts are *equity* instruments that are reported in permanent equity, but because the option writer is required to settle the contract in cash, *public* companies must transfer to temporary equity an amount equal to the redemption amount. The instruments are measured initially at fair value without subsequent adjustment for changes in fair value. If the contract is ultimately settled in net cash or in net shares, the amount reported in temporary equity is transferred and reported as an addition to permanent equity.
- Settlement in net cash or net shares, or in net cash or physical settlement in cash. The contracts are liabilities that should be measured at fair value and adjusted for changes in fair value. Gains or losses are included in earnings and disclosed in the financial statements, even if the contract is ultimately settled in shares.

OBSERVATIONS: Under the provisions of ASC 460-10-05-1, 05-2,-,10-1, 15-4 through 15-7, 15-9, 15-10; 25-1 through 25-4, 30-1 through 30-4, 35-1 through 35-2, 35-4, 50-2, 50-4 through 50-6, 50-8, 55-2 through 55-3, 55-5 through 55-9, 55-12 through 55-13, 55-15 through 55-18, 55-20 through 55-24,

55-28, 55-29; ASC 840-10-25-34; ASC 840-10-60-2, guarantors are required to recognize a liability at the inception of a guarantee for the obligation assumed. Contracts under the guidance in this Issue that also meet the definition of a guarantee in ASC 460, such as physically settled written puts, are initially valued at fair value, as required in ASC 460. Although the accounting is *not* affected, the guarantee should be disclosed under the requirements in ASC 460.

DISCUSSION

- A written put option or forward purchase contract that requires settlement in net cash is a liability because it represents an obligation to sacrifice assets in the future. Proponents of this view argued that the transaction should not be recognized in equity because no shares will be exchanged. They also referred to the treatment of purchased options or purchased forward contracts settled in cash. Recognition of gains or losses is based on the view that such recognition is required by ASC 250-10-45-22; ASC 225-10-45-1 for items treated as assets or liabilities and is consistent with the Model.

- A written put option that permits the *counterparty* to choose the settlement method should also be recognized as a liability, because the entity cannot control whether it will be required to transfer cash to the counterparty. Proponents of this approach also referred to the treatment of purchased put options and purchased forward contracts when the counterparty can choose the method of settlement. Recognition of a gain or loss is based on the view that such recognition is required by ASC 250-10-45-22; ASC 225-10-45-1 for items treated as assets or liabilities and is consistent with the Model.

- Written put options giving the entity the choice of settlement method should be accounted for as equity transactions because the entity can choose to settle the option in shares of stock rather than in cash.

Illustration of the Accounting for the Sale of Written Put Options on an Issuer's Stock That Require or Permit Cash Settlement

On 12/15/X5, Preston Company (a public entity with a 12/31 year-end) sells a put option that is indexed to 100 common shares of the entity's own stock at a price of $25 per share when the fair value of the stock is $25 per share. The option expires on 3/14/X6. The option premium is $150. Assume that the price of each common share and the fair value of the option is as follows: *(a)* $22 and $330, respectively, on 12/31/X5. The price of each share of common stock on 3/14/X6, the settlement date, is $20.

Under the following two scenarios, Preston accounts for the contract as follows at each date: (a) 12/15/X5, (b) 12/31/X5, and (c) 3/14/X6.

Scenario 1: The entity can choose to settle in net cash or by physical settlement in cash.

(a) At initiation of the contract—12/15/X5

Because the entity chooses the method of settlement, the indexed option is treated as an equity transaction.

Cash	$150	
Additional paid-in capital		$150

Because the entity's stock is publicly traded, the entity must transfer to temporary equity an amount equal to 100 shares at the settlement price.

Additional paid-in capital	$2,500	
Cost of settling put options		$2,500

(b) At year-end—12/31/X5 (interim date)

Contracts recorded as equity transactions are not adjusted to fair value at interim dates.

(c) At settlement of the contract in net shares—3/14/X6

Because the price per share is $20 on the settlement date, the option contract is worth $500 [($25 - $20) × 100]. The entity chooses to settle in net cash and pays the counterparty $500 to settle the contract.

Cost of settling put options	$2,500	
Additional paid-in capital		$2,000
Cash		500

Scenario 2: The counterparty can choose to settle in net cash or in net shares

(a) At initiation of the contract—12/15/X5

Because the counterparty can choose to settle in net cash or net shares, the option is treated as a liability.

Cash	$150	
Indexed option contract payable		$150

(b) At year-end—12/31/X5 (interim date)

The per share price of $22 is $3 less than the $25 per share price on settlement. The entity adjusts the liability to the option's fair value of $330 and recognizes a loss of $180.

Loss on indexed option contract	$180	
Indexed option contract payable		$180

(c) At settlement—3/14/X6

The counterparty chooses to settle in net shares. Because the price per share is $20 on the settlement date—$5 less than the reference price of $25—the option is worth $500. The entity, therefore, has a total loss of $350 on the contract ($500 less $150 premium). The entity settles the contract by delivering 25 shares ($500/$20) to the counterparty to settle the contract. The loss recognized on settlement is $275 ($500 less the $225 recorded liability).

Loss on indexed option contract	$275	
Indexed Option payable	225	
Treasury shares		$500

3. Purchased Call Option

BACKGROUND

An entity purchases a call option giving it the right, but not the obligation, to purchase from the option's seller a specific number of the entity's shares of common stock at a specified price on a specified future date. The contract may be settled by physical settlement, in net shares, in net cash, or based on the settlement method chosen by the entity or the counterparty.

ACCOUNTING GUIDANCE

Purchased call options are accounted for the same as forward sale contracts, written call options or warrants, and purchased put options as previously discussed.

4. Detachable Stock Purchase Warrants

BACKGROUND

An entity issues senior subordinated notes with a detachable warrant giving the holder the right to purchase 5,000 shares of the issuer's stock for $50 per share at any time and the right to require the entity to repurchase all or some of the warrants for at least $1,000 per share several months after the notes mature in about five years.

ACCOUNTING GUIDANCE

The issuer should account for the notes as follows:

- The proceeds should be allocated between the liability for the debt and the warrant. The resulting discount should be amortized over the term of the notes in accordance with the guidance in ASC 835-30.

- The warrants are considered to be, in substance, a debt instrument and are accounted for as a liability, because the alternatives for settling the warrants do not have the same economic value. The put gives the holder a guaranteed return in cash (5,000 shares × $1,000 = $5,000,000) that significantly exceeds the value of the share settlement (5,000 shares × $ 50 = $ 250,000) without the put at the date of issuance.

DISCUSSION

This Issue deals with the balance sheet classification of a detachable stock purchase warrant with a put option at a fixed price. Under the provisions of ASC 470-20-05-2 through 05-6; 25-2 through 25-3, 25-10 through 25-11, 25-13; 30-1 through 30-2; and 505-10-60-3, the proceeds would be allocated between the debt and the warrant. However, the treatment of the warrant as a liability is more appropriate because, based on the economics of the transaction, it is probable that it will be put to the issuer at the fixed price, which substantially exceeds the price of the stock.

5. Put Warrants

BACKGROUND

Put warrants, which generally are issued with debt instruments, combine the characteristics of warrants and put options. They are detachable from the debt and can be exercised under specified conditions by (a) using the warrant feature to acquire the issuer's stock at a specified price, (b) using the put feature to receive cash from the issuer, or (c) using both the warrant and put features to acquire stock and receive cash from the issuer. The put feature may be exercisable only for a specified time period and may expire under certain conditions. The put feature is canceled if the warrant is exercised and, likewise, exercising the put feature cancels the warrant feature. APB-14 requires that a portion of the proceeds from the issuance of debt with detachable warrants be allocated to the warrants.

ACCOUNTING GUIDANCE

Public companies should report the proceeds from the issuance of put warrants as liabilities because the counterparty has the choice of settling the contract in cash or in shares. In subsequent periods, the put warrants are measured at fair value; changes in fair value are reported in earnings.

6. Contracts with Multiple Settlement Alternatives

- Account as *equity instruments* for contracts under the Model if the contract has several alternatives under which the issuer is required to *receive* net cash when the contract is in a *gain* position, but is required to choose between *paying* in net cash or in net stock when the contract is in a *loss* position.

This guidance does not apply if a contract is primarily a purchased option under which the amount of cash that could be received when the contract is in a gain position would significantly exceed the amount that could be paid when the contract is in a *loss* position—for example, if the amount of loss is contractually limited to a small amount. Such contracts should be accounted for as assets or liabilities.

Account as *assets* or *liabilities* for contracts under the Model, if the contract has several alternatives under which an issuer is required to *pay* net cash when the contract is in a *loss* position, but is required to choose between receiving net cash or net stock when the contract is in a *gain* position.

7. Earnings per Share

The guidance in ASC 480-10-05-1 through 05-6, 10-10-1, 15-3 through 15-5, 15-7 through 15-10, 25-1 through 25-2, 25-4 through 25-15, 30-1 through 30-7, 35-3 through 35-5, 45-1 through 45-4, 50-1 through 50-4, 55-1 through 55-12, 55-14 through 55-28, 55-34 through 55-41, 55-64; ASC 835-10-60-13; ASC 260-10-45-70A amends the guidance in ASC 260 for forward-purchase contracts that must be physically settled by repurchasing a fixed number of the issuer's equity shares of common stock for cash. Diluted earnings per share can no longer be computed by the reverse treasury stock method for those contracts. Therefore, common shares subject to the forward-purchase contracts should be excluded from the calculation of basic and diluted earnings per share (EPS).

BACKGROUND

An entity sells put options that are publicly traded and expire two years from the date of issuance. The puts obligate the entity to purchase from the holder one share of the entity's stock at a fixed price, which is lower than the market price of the entity's stock at the date of issuance. The entity may repurchase the puts in the open market at any time during the redemption period.

ACCOUNTING ISSUE

Although none of the issues specifically addresses the calculation of EPS, one of the Task Force's consensus positions provides related guidance.

ACCOUNTING GUIDANCE

an issuer should use the reverse treasury stock method to calculate the potential dilutive effect of put options having a higher exercise price than the market price of the stock ("in the money") during the reporting period. Under the reverse treasury stock method, the number of additional shares to be included in the calculation of EPS is equal to the number of shares the entity must issue for cash at the current market price to satisfy the put obligation minus the number of shares repurchased from the holder of the puts.

To calculate the *dilutive* effect of written put options and similar contracts when the contract's exercise price *exceeds* its market price during the reporting period (the contract is in the money), the *average* market price of the contract *during the period* should be used in calculating the incremental number of shares that would have to be issued to obtain the cash to satisfy a *put* obligation under the reverse treasury method.

OBSERVATIONS: It is assumed that company shares will be issued if the entity can choose the settlement method. However, that presumption may be overcome if the entity has a stated policy that requires contracts to be settled in cash or has historically settled contracts wholly or partially in cash. If the counterparty can choose the settlement method, the more dilutive method should be used in computing EPS.

DISCUSSION

The treasury stock method discussed in ASC 260-10-45-23 is used to calculate the incremental number of shares to be issued for options under which the holder can purchase an entity's stock at less than its market price. This calculation assumes that the entity receives cash, satisfies a portion of its obligation by repurchasing an equivalent number of shares in the open market, and satisfies the remainder of the obligation by issuing stock. The guidance requires using the *reverse treasury stock method* in ASC 260-10-45-35, under which it is assumed that the entity (1) finances the cash payment to the holder of the put option by issuing new shares at the market price (in this case, a lower price than the amount at which the put will be exercised), and (2) sells the shares obtained by redeeming the put options at the market price for cash. The difference between (1) and (2) is the *incremental number of shares,* for example:

Number of puts outstanding	$1,000
Exercise price	$50
Market price at 12/31/X4	$40
Shares to be sold to satisfy puts ($50,000/$40)	1,250

Less: Treasury shares obtained from satisfaction of put options	1,000
Incremental shares	250

ASC 815-40-15-5 through 15-8, 55-26 through 55-48; ASC 815-10-65-3; ASC 718-10-60-1B Determining Whether an Instrument (or Embedded Features) Is Indexed to an Entity's Own Stock

BACKGROUND

Under the guidance in ASC 815-10-15-74, a freestanding contract, such as a stock purchase warrant, that is (1) indexed to its own stock *and* (2) classified in an entity's balance sheet as equity is *not* considered to be a derivative.

Although under the guidance in ASC 815-15-25-1, a derivative instrument embedded in a host contract must be separated and accounted for separately as a derivative, under the guidance in ASC 815-15-25-1, an embedded instrument's terms must be the same as those of the host instrument in order for that instrument to be accounted for separately as a derivative. Therefore, an embedded derivative that meets the exception in ASC 815-10-15-74 would *not* be separated from its host instrument and accounted for as a derivative.

The purpose of this discussion is to develop guidance on how to determine whether an instrument or an embedded feature is indexed to an entity's own stock, which is the first part of the exception in ASC 815-10-15-74. However, the second requirement in ASC 815-10-15-74 (i.e., whether an instrument or an embedded feature that has the characteristics of a derivative, as discussed in ASC 815-10-15-83, 15-85, 15-88 through 15-89, 15-92 through 15-96, 15-99 through 15-100, 15-110, 15-119 through 15-120, 15-128, ASC 440-10-60-10, is classified in an entity's stockholder's equity or would be classified that way if it were a freestanding instrument) is not addressed because other authoritative accounting guidance, including that in ASC 460-10-60-14; ASC 480-10-55-63; ASC 505-10-60-5; ASC 815-10-15-78, 55-52, 15-25-15, 40-05-1 through 05-4, 05-10, 05-11 through05-12; 25-1 through 25-5, 25-7 through 25-20, 25-22 through 25-24, 25-26 through 25-35, 25-37 through 25-40, 30-1, 35-1 through 35-2, 35-6, 35-8 through 35-13, 40-1 through 40-2, 50-1 through 50-5, 55-1 through 55-18 and ASC 815-40-25-4 through 25-42 address that question.

The purpose of this guidance is to help users to evaluate whether certain freestanding instruments that do *not* have all of the characteristics of a derivative under the guidance in ASC 815, but are potentially settled in an entity's own equity shares, should be accounted for under the guidance in ASC 460-10-60-14; ASC 480-10-55-63; ASC 505-10-60-5; ASC 815-10-15-78, 55-52; ASC 815-15-25-15; ASC 815-40-05-1 through 05-4, 05-10 through 05-12; 25-1 through 25-5, 25-7 through 25-20, 25-22 through 25-24, 25-26 through 25-35, 25-37 through 25-40, 30-1, 35-1 through 35-2, 35-6, 35-8 through 35-13, 40-1 through 40-2, 50-1 through 50-5, 55-1 through 55-18. For example, a physically settled forward contract to issue an entity's own equity shares for cash does *not* meet the net settlement characteristic of a derivative discussed in ASC 815-10-15-83, 15-85, 15-88 through 15-89, 15-92 through 15-96, 15-99 through 15-100, 15-110, 15-119 through 15-120, 15-128, ASC 440-10-60-10 if the underlying equity shares are *not* readily convertible to cash. However, if that forward contract is *not* considered to be indexed to an entity's own stock, the contract would *not* be accounted for under the guidance in ASC 460-10-60-14; ASC 480-10-55-63; ASC 505-10-60-5; ASC 815-10-15-78, 55-52; ASC 815-15-25-15; ASC 815-40-05-1 through 05-4, 05-10 through 05-12, 25-1 through 25-5, 25-7 through 25-20, 25-22 through 25-24, 25-26 through 25-35, 25-37 through 25-40, 30-1, 35-1 through 35-2, 35-6, 35-8 through 35-13, 40-1 through 40-2, 50-1 through 50-5, 55-1 through 55-18, which applies only to instruments indexed to, and potentially settled in, an issuer's own stock.

The following guidance should be applied to a unit of accounting based on the requirements in other U.S. generally accepted accounting principles (GAAP). That is, an issuer that had issued two freestanding financial instruments should apply the guidance in this Issue separately to each instrument if that treatment is required under other GAAP. However, an issuer that had issued two freestanding financial instruments would apply this guidance to a *single combined* financial instrument if under other GAAP, the two instruments must be *linked* and accounted for as one financial instrument.

ACCOUNTING GUIDANCE

Scope

The following guidance applies to: (1) freestanding financial instruments or embedded features with all of the characteristics of derivatives in ASC 815-10-15-83, 15-85, 15-88 through 15-89, 15-92 through 15-96, 15-99 through 15-100, 15-110, 15-119 through 15-120, 15-128, ASC 440-10-60-10 when determining whether those instruments qualify for the first part of the scope exception in ASC 815-10-15-74 and (2) freestanding financial instruments that are potentially settled in an entity's own stock, regardless of whether they have all of the characteristics of a derivative in ASC 815-10-15-83, 15-85, 15-88 through 15-89, 15-92 through 15-96, 15-99 through 15-100, 15-110, 15-119 through 15-120, 15-128, ASC 440-10-60-10, when determining whether an instrument should be accounted for under the guidance in ASC 460-10-60-14; ASC 480-10-55-63; ASC 505-10-60-5; ASC 815-10-15-78, 55-52; ASC 815-15-25-15; ASC 815-40-05-1 through 05-4, 05-10 through 05-12; 25-1 through 25-5, 25-7 through 25-20, 25-22 through 25-24, 25-26 through 25-35, 25-37 through 25-40, 30-1, 35-1 through 35-2, 35-6, 35-8 through 35-13, 40-1 through 40-2, 50-1 through 50-5, 55-1 through 55-18.

This guidance does *not* apply to share-based payment awards under the scope of ASC 718, when determining whether those instruments are classified as liability awards or equity awards under the guidance in ASC 718. However, because equity-linked financial instruments issued to investors in order to establish a market-based measure of the fair value of employee options at the grant date are *not* covered under the guidance in ASC 718, the guidance in this Issue applies when determining whether an instrument or an embedded feature: (1) is indexed to an entity's own stock; or (2) should be accounted for under the guidance in ASC 460-10-60-14; ASC 480-10-55-63; ASC 505-10-60-5; ASC 815-10-15-78, 55-52; ASC 815-15-25-15; ASC 815-40-05-1 through 05-4, 05-1 through 05-12; 25-1 through 25-5, 25-7 through 25-20, 25-22 through 25-24, 25-26 through 25-35, 25-37 through 25-40, 30-1, 35-1 through 35-2, 35-6, 35-8 through 35-13, 40-1 through 40-2; 50-1 through 50-5; 55-1 through 55-18.

Accounting Issue

How should an entity determine whether an equity-linked financial instrument or an embedded feature is indexed to the entity's own stock?

Recognition

For accounting purposes, the financial instruments discussed in this Issue are always considered to have been issued, except when parties to a business combination exchange contingently exercisable options (i.e., lock-up options) to purchase the other entity's equity securities at favorable prices in order to encourage a merger's completion. Under the terms of such options, if a specified event interferes with a merger's completion, it may trigger the exercise of those options. However, such options are *not* exercised and expire if a merger is completed as planned. For accounting purposes, lock-up options are *not* considered to have been issued. The guidance in this paragraph applies to both the issuer and the holder of instruments under the scope of this Issue.

An "exercise contingency," as the term is used in this Issue, is a provision that gives the right to an entity or its counterparty to exercise an equity-linked financial instrument or an embedded feature based on changes in an "underlying," which is defined in ASC 815 as a specific interest rate, security price, commodity price, foreign exchange rate, index of prices or rates, or other variable, such as a requirement that a specific event should or should *not* occur. For example, an instrument may include a provision that accelerates an entity's or counterparty's ability to exercise an instrument or a provision that extends the time period during which an entity or its counterparty can exercise an instrument. Both are exercise contingencies. An exercise contingency that would result in an adjustment to an instrument's strike price or to the number of shares used to calculate the amount of a settlement should be evaluated under Step 1 (below) and the potential adjustment of the settlement amount should be evaluated under Step 2 (below).

The following two-step approach should be used to determine whether an equity-linked financial instrument or an embedded feature is indexed to an entity's own stock:

- *Step 1.* Evaluate the instrument's contingent exercise provisions, if any. A financial instrument or an embedded feature that is subject to an exercise contingency may be considered to be indexed to an entity's own stock if the index triggering the instrument's contingent exercise provisions is *not* based on: (1) an observable market, except for the market for the issuer's stock, if applicable; or (2) an observable index, except for one that is calculated or measured exclusively by referring to the issuer's own operations, such as its sales revenues; earnings before interest, taxes, depreciation, and amortization (EBITDA); net income; or total equity. Proceed to Step 2 if (as a result of the evaluation in Step 1) an instrument is *not* prohibited from being considered to be indexed to an entity's own stock.

- *Step 2.* Evaluate the instrument's settlement provisions. An instrument should be considered to be indexed to an entity's own stock if the amount of the settlement will be equal to the difference between the fair value of a *fixed* number of the entity's equity shares and a *fixed* monetary amount or a *fixed* amount of a debt instrument issued by the entity. For example, an issued share option that gives a counterparty the right to buy a *fixed* number of the issuer's shares for a *fixed* price or for a *fixed* stated principal amount of a bond to be issued by the entity should be considered to be indexed to the issuing entity's own stock.

If an instrument's strike price or the number of shares used to calculate the amount to settle may be adjusted under an instrument's provisions, they are *not* fixed—regardless of the probability that an adjustment will occur or whether an adjustment is under the entity's control. However, an instrument or an embedded feature whose strike price or number of shares used to calculate the settlement amount are *not* fixed may still be considered to be indexed to an entity's own stock if inputs to the fair value of a "fixed-for-fixed" forward or option on equity shares are the only variables that could affect the amount of a settlement, which is equal to the difference between the price of a *fixed* number of equity shares and a *fixed* strike price. Such fair value inputs may include an entity's stock price and additional variables, such as: (1) the instrument's strike price; (2) its terms; (3) expected dividends or other dilutive activities; (3) stock borrow cost; (4) interest rates; (5) stock price volatility; (6) an entity's credit spread; and (7) an entity's ability to maintain a standard hedge position in the underlying shares. The determination and adjustments of the settlement amount, including a determination of an entity's ability to maintain a standard hedge position must be commercially reasonable.

Nevertheless, an instrument or an embedded feature should *not* be considered to be indexed to an entity's own stock if the *calculation* of the amount at which a fixed-for-fixed option or forward on equity shares would be settled: (1) is affected by variables that are *not* pertinent to the option's or forward contract's pricing; (2) include variables other than those used to determine the forward's or option's fair value; or (3) includes a feature, such as a leverage factor, that increases the instrument's exposure to the additional variables related to fair value inputs discussed above in a manner that is inconsistent with a fixed-for-fixed forward or option on equity shares.

The following two types of provisions related to equity-linked financial instruments also should *not* prevent an instrument from being considered to be indexed to an entity's own stock:

1. Provisions permitting adjustments that would neutralize the effects of events that may cause stock price irregularities. For example, provisions that adjust a financial instrument's terms to offset a net gain or loss incurred by an instrument's holder as a result of differences between changes in: (1) the fair value of an equity-linked instrument; and (2) the fair value of an offsetting hedge position in the underlying shares caused by a merger announcement or a similar event.

2. Provisions that enable an entity to unilaterally modify a financial instrument's terms at any time, as long as that modification benefits the counterparty. An issuer's ability to reduce the conversion price of a

convertible debt instrument at anytime to induce conversion is an example of such a provision.

Strike Price Denominated in a Foreign Currency

An issuer of an equity-linked financial instrument having a strike price denominated in a functional currency that differs from the issuer's is exposed to changes in currency exchange rates. If the strike price of an equity-linked financial instrument is valued in a currency other than the issuer's functional currency, including a conversion option that is embedded in a convertible debt instrument valued in a currency other than the issuer's functional currency, an equity-linked financial instrument would *not* be considered to be indexed to the issuing entity's own stock. However, the currency in which the underlying shares trade does *not* affect the determination of whether an equity-linked instrument is indexed to an entity's own stock.

ASC 815-40-25-41 through 42 The Meaning of "Conventional Convertible Instrument" in EITF Issue No. 00-19, "Accounting for Derivative Financial Instruments Indexed to, and Potentially Settled in, an Entity's Own Stock"

BACKGROUND

ASC 815-10-15-74 provides that contracts issued or held by a reporting entity should *not* be considered to be derivative instruments if they are (*a*) indexed to that entity's *own* stock and (*b*) reported in the entity's balance sheet in stockholders' equity. In ASC 460-10-60-14; ASC 480-10-55-63; ASC 505-10-60-5; ASC 815-10-15-78, 55-52; ASC 815-15-25-15; ASC 815-40-05-1 through 50-4, 05-10 through 05-12, 25-1 through 25-5, 25-7 through 25-20, 25-22 through 25-24, 25-26 through 25-35, 25-37 through 25-40, 30-1, 35-1 through 35-2, 35-4 through 35-6, 35-8 through 35-13, 40-1 through 40-2, 50-1 through 50-5, 55-1 through 55-18, which applies only to *freestanding* derivatives such as forward contracts, options, and warrants, the guidance is provided for determining whether an embedded derivative would be classified in stockholders' equity in accordance with the guidance in ASC 815-10-15-74 if it were freestanding. However, that guidance provides that a *conventional convertible debt instrument* should be exempted from the evaluation of whether it contains an embedded derivative indexed to the entity's own stock that would require bifurcation if the holder of that debt instrument can realize the value of the conversion option only by exercising the option and receiving the proceeds, at the issuer's discretion, in a fixed number of shares or an equivalent amount of cash.

Because the guidance in ASC 460-10-60-14; ASC 480-10-55-63; ASC 505-10-60-5; ASC 815-10-15-78, 55-52; ASC 815-15-25-15; ASC 815-40-05-1 through 50-4, 05-10 through 05-12; 25-1 through 25-5, 25-7 through 25-20, 25-22 through 25-24, 25-26 through 25-35, 25-37 through 25-40, 30-1, 35-1 through 35-2, 35-4 through 35-6, 35-8 through 35-13, 40-1 through 40-2, 50-1 through 50-5, 55-1 through 55-18 does not specifically define the term *conventional convertible debt*, there has been diversity in practice in determining which convertible debt instruments qualify for the exemption.

ACCOUNTING ISSUE

Should the exemption for applying the Accounting Model discussed in paragraphs 12 to 32 of Issue 00-19 for "conventional convertible debt instruments" be deleted from the Issue or clarified?

ACCOUNTING GUIDANCE:

- The exemption for conventional convertible debt instruments should be *retained*.

- A convertible debt instrument should be considered to be *conventional* for the purpose of applying the guidance in ASC 460-10-60-14; ASC 480-10-55-63; ASC 505-10-60-5; ASC 815-10-15-78, 55-52; ASC 815-15-25-15; ASC 815-40-05-1 through 05-4, 05-10 through 05-12, 25-1 through 25-5, 25-7 through 25-20, 25-22 through 25-24, 25-26 through 25-35, 25-37 through 25-40, 30-1; 35-1, 35-2, 35-4 through 35-6, 35-8 through 35-13, 40-1 through 40-2; 50-1 through 50-5, 55-1 through 55-18 if the holder has an option under the debt instrument's provisions to convert it into a fixed number of shares or an equivalent amount of cash at the issuer's discretion based on the passage of time or the occurrence of a contingent event. The existence of a standard antidilution provision does *not* prohibit the conversion of an instrument into a fixed number of shares.

- Convertible preferred stock having a mandatory redemption date may qualify for the exemption provided in Issue 00-19 (see ASC references above) for conventional convertible debt if the instrument's economic characteristics are more similar to debt than equity.

The applicable information required in ASC 505-10-15-1, 50-3 to 50-5, 50-11, should be disclosed for instruments under the scope of this Issue.

ASC 815-45: Weather Derivatives

ASC 815-45-15-2, 25-1, 25-5, 25-6, 30-1 through 3A, 35-1 through 35-2, 35-4, 35-7, 55-1 through 55-8, 55-10, through 55-11, 50-1; ASC 460-10-60-15 Accounting for Weather Derivatives

BACKGROUND

Weather derivative contracts, which are contracts indexed to climactic or geological variables, are new types of derivatives seen in the market. An increasing number of entities are entering into such contracts for a number of business reasons. Current accounting practices are diverse, because it is unclear whether the contracts should be accounted for under accrual accounting, settlement accounting, or insurance accounting. Some believe that changes in the fair value of those contracts should be recognized in earnings at each reporting date.

Under the guidance in ASC 815, contracts that are not traded on an exchange are not covered by the Statement if they are settled based on a climactic or geological variable or another physical variable. However, if derivatives settled based on a physical variable eventually become exchange-traded, they will be covered under the guidance in ASC 815

Contracts written by insurance companies to compensate their holders for an insurable event that causes the holder to incur a liability or that adversely affects the value of a specific asset or liability for which the holder is at risk are *not* covered by the scope of this Issue.

ACCOUNTING ISSUES

1. How should an entity account for a weather derivative that is nonexchange-traded or forward-based (risk is two-directional)?
2. How should an entity account for a purchased weather derivative that is nonexchange-traded and option-based (risk is one-directional)?
3. How should an entity account for a written weather derivative that is nonexchange-traded and option-based?

ACCOUNTING GUIDANCE

1. Use the *intrinsic value method* to account for nonexchange-traded, forward-based weather derivatives that are entered into for nontrading purposes. Under that method, the value of the derivative is computed as follows: (*a*) determine the difference between the expected results of an allocation of the cumulative strike price at inception and the actual results during the period; (*b*) multiply that amount by the contract price, such as dollars per heating degree day; (*c*) allocate the cumulative strike price based on information from external statistical sources, such as the National Weather Service, to individual periods within the contract's term based on a reasonable expectation at the inception of the term of normal or expected experience under the contract. At interim periods, calculate the intrinsic value of the contract based on the cumulative difference between actual experience and the allocation through that date. The allocation of the cumulative strike price at inception should *not* be adjusted when actual results are known.

2. Amortize the premium paid or due on a nonexchange-traded, option-based weather derivative purchased for nontrading purposes to expense in a rational and systematic manner. Measure the contract at interim balance-sheet dates using the intrinsic value method as discussed above.

3. Account for all weather derivatives entered into for trading or speculative purposes at *fair value* and report subsequent fair value changes in period earnings.

4. Under this Issue, entering into weather derivative contracts for the purpose of earning a profit on an exposure to changes in climactic or geological conditions indicates that an entity may be involved in trading or speculative activities. Judgment based on the relevant facts and circumstances must be used in evaluating whether or when an entity's involvement in weather derivative contracts should be considered a trading or speculative activity. That evaluation should consider the entity's various activities rather than merely considering the terms of the contract. The entity's intent for entering into weather derivative contracts is another consideration. The following factors or indicators should be considered in evaluating whether an operation's (subsidiary,

division, or unit) weather derivative contracts are entered into for trading or speculative purposes. Affirmative answers to the questions in Category A are strong indicators that the operation is not engaged in trading activities. Although affirmative answers only to the questions in Category B may indicate that the operation is engaged in trading activities, negative answers to any or all of the questions in either category may not by themselves indicate that the operation is not engaged in trading activities. All available information should be used to reach a conclusion:

a. Fundamental indicators

   (1) Is the operation's primary business exposed to weather related risk covered by the contracts held?

   (2) Is the volume of weather derivative contracts reasonable in relation to the operation's primary business?

   (3) Is the contract's change in value expected to move in a direction that would mitigate or offset the risk of the underlying exposure?

   (4) Does the operation price the contract offers or trades based on externally developed price models?

b. Secondary indicators—management and controls

   (1) Are compensation or performance measures or both related to short-term profits on weather derivative contracts?

   (2) Do internal communications discuss the operation's business activities in terms of the operation's trading strategy?

   (3) Does the operation's business name include the term *trading*?

   (4) Are the operation's employees referred to as *traders*?

   (5) Are net market positions determined regularly?

   (6) Is the operation's infrastructure segregated by back office processing functions and front office trading function as in a trading operation or an investment bank?

   (7) Is the operation's infrastructure equipped to determine price and other risks on a real-time basis?

   (8) Does the operation manage its activities on a portfolio or book basis?

Although it is easier to determine whether an operation is engaged in trading activities when those activities are segregated within the organization or by legal entity, only the portion of an operation that is determined to be engaged in trading activities, based on an evaluation of the indicators discussed above, should be required to account for its activities at fair value. Entities whose trading activities are not segregated from their other activities should identify their trading and nontrading contracts at inception using the above indicators.

Because weather derivative contracts under the scope of this Issue are financial instruments, entities that enter into such contracts should make the required disclosures for financial instruments in ASC 825-10-50-2A, 50-3 through 50-4, 50-8 through 50-23, 50-26; 55-3 through 55-5.

> **OBSERVATIONS:** Under the guidance in ASC 460, at the inception of a guarantee, a guarantor is required to recognize a liability for the obligation assumed by issuing the guarantee. Weather derivatives are option-based contracts under which the party receiving the guarantee is paid based on whether a specific event related to the weather does or does not occur at a specified location within a specified time period, such as 20 inches of snow in New York City during the first week of February. Under the guidance in ASC 460, which requires that payments be based on a change in an underlying related to an asset or liability of the party to whom the guarantee was given, a weather derivative is *not* a guarantee, because an event related to the weather is not an asset or liability of the party to whom the guarantee was given.

SEC OBSERVER COMMENT

> The SEC Observer stated that because weather derivative contracts under the scope of this guidance are financial instruments, the SEC staff believes that registrants should make the disclosures about those contracts required in Item 305 of SEC Regulation S-K, if applicable.

CHAPTER 49
ASC 820—FAIR VALUE MEASUREMENT

CONTENTS

Part I: General Guidance	49,002
ASC 820-10: Overall	49,002
Overview	49,002
Background	49,002
Fair Value Measurement	49,002
Scope	49,003
Measurement	49,003
Principal or Most Advantageous Market	49,004
Illustration of Determining the Highest and Best Use of an Asset	49,005
Market Participants	49,005
Application to Nonfinancial Assets	49,005
Application to Liabilities and Instruments Included Within Shareholders' Equity	49,006
Application to Financial Assets and Financial Liabilities with Offsetting Positions	49,008
Fair Value at Initial Recognition	49,008
Illustration of Using Observable Market Inputs in the Most Advantageous Market	49,009
Valuation Techniques	49,009
Illustration of Use of Multiple Techniques to Estimate Fair Value	49,010
Fair Value Hierarchy	49,011
Fair Value Given a Decline in the Volume or Level of Activity	49,012
Transactions that Are Not Orderly	49,012
Illustration of Using a Level 2 Input to Estimate Fair Value	49,013
Disclosures	49,013
Part II: Interpretive Guidance	49,016
ASC 820-10: Overall	49,016
ASC 820-10-05-3, 55-23C through 55-23D, 25-1 through 25-2, 50-4A, 55-8 through 55-9	
Determining Fair Value When the Volume and Level of Activity for the Asset or Liability Have Significantly Decreased and Identifying Transactions That Are Not Orderly	49,016
ASC 820-10-35-54C through 35-54M, 65-8	
Determining Fair Value When the Volume and Level of Activity for the Asset or Liability Have Significantly Decreased	49,017

GENERAL GUIDANCE

ASC 820-10: OVERALL

OVERVIEW

The early years of the 21st century have introduced a new era in which fair value measurement is gradually replacing historical cost as the primary measurement approach for certain assets and liabilities. Evidence suggests that fair value measurement and reporting will be extended to a wide range of balance sheet items as experience with developing and auditing fair value information becomes more widespread.

The Codification has two primary Topics on fair value: ASC 820 (Fair Value Measurement) and ASC 825 (Financial Instruments). For a discussion of the fair value option for financial assets and liabilities, see the Chapter 50, *ASC 825—Financial Instruments*. In addition, fair value is currently required in accounting for a wide range of financial instruments under other FASB standards. Guidance related to financial reporting and changing prices was issued in 1979 during a period of the highest inflation in the United States in recent history. That guidance, which required companies that met a specified size criterion to report supplemental information on current value basis, was later eliminated as a requirement owing to a reduction in inflation and the belief that the information required was of limited value to users of financial statements. This guidance is technically still in effect, although application of it is on a voluntary basis and rarely, if ever, implemented. For coverage of this guidance, see Chapter 10, *ASC 255—Changing Prices*.

BACKGROUND

For many years, historical cost was the primary basis by which assets and liabilities were accounted. The advantage of historical cost over alternative measurement methods was primarily due to its objectivity. That is, the cost of an item at its origin (i.e., its historical cost) to the reporting entity was generally believed to be more readily determined by objective means than were other measures of value, such as current replacement cost, current exit or sales price, or fair value. Notable exceptions were situations in which the historical cost exceeded the current value of an item, leading to the application of the lower of cost or market for inventories and some investments. More recently, however, standards have been developed that require an assessment of the impairment of value where evidence suggests that an item's current worth is less than its recorded amount.

FAIR VALUE MEASUREMENT

ASC 820 defines fair value, establishes a framework for measuring fair value in generally accepted accounting principles, and requires disclosures about fair value measurements. Fair value is based on market prices or market inputs; fair value is not based on entity-specific measurements. The objective of fair value measurement is to estimate the price at which an asset could be sold, or a liability settled, in an orderly transaction between market participants at the measurement date (i.e., fair value measures exit prices) (ASC 820-10-05-1B).

When available, fair value should be determined by referring to market prices for identical assets and liabilities. If market prices are not available, fair value is to be estimated using a valuation technique that maximizes the use of relevant observable market inputs and minimizes the use of unobservable market inputs. Assumptions used in determining fair value should be consistent with the assumptions that market participants would use (ASC 820-10-05-1C).

Scope

The guidance in ASC 820 applies in situations where other accounting pronouncements require or permit fair value measurements with the following exceptions:

- ASC 820 does not apply under accounting principles that address share-based payment transactions, such as ASC 718 (Compensation—Stock Compensation) and ASC 505-50 (Equity—Equity-Based Payments to Non-Employees) (ASC 820-10-15-2).
- ASC 820 does not eliminate the practicability exceptions to fair value measurements that are included in accounting pronouncements within the scope of ASC 820 (ASC 820-10-15-3).

In addition, ASC 820 does not apply under accounting pronouncements that require or permit measurements that are similar to fair value but that are not intended to measure fair value (e.g., ASC 330 (Inventory)) (ASC 820-10-15-2). The guidance in ASC 820 also does not apply for purposes of lease classification or measurement (ASC 820-10-15-2).

Measurement

Fair value is the price that would be received to sell an asset or paid to transfer a liability in an orderly transaction between market participants at the measurement date (ASC 820-10-35-2). In determining the fair value of an asset or liability, the characteristics of the asset or liability should be considered if these characteristics would be considered by the market. Examples of potentially relevant characteristics are the condition and location of the asset, as well as any restrictions on the sale or use of the asset (ASC 820-10-35-2B).

The asset or liability may be a standalone asset or liability or a group of assets or liabilities, depending on its unit of account (ASC 820-10-35-2D). The unit of account determines what is being measured by reference to the level at which the asset or liability is aggregated for purposes of applying other ASC topics that require or permit fair value measurement (ASC 820-10-35-2E).

Fair value measurement assumes that the asset or liability is exchanged in an orderly transaction between market participants to sell the asset or transfer the liability at the measurement date under current market conditions. The term "orderly transaction" refers to a transaction that assumes exposure to the market for a period prior to the measurement date to allow for market activities that are usual and customary for transactions involving such assets or liabilities. It is not a forced transaction. The objective of a fair value measurement is to determine the price that would be received to sell the asset or paid to transfer the liability at the measurement date (referred to as the exit price) (ASC 820-10-35-3).

> **PRACTICE POINTER:** The Securities and Exchange Commission's Division of Corporate Finance indicates that actual market prices are relevant in determining fair value even when the market is less liquid than its historical norm (i.e., reduced trading volume). However, actual market prices should not be used in determining fair value if they reflect a forced liquidation or distress sale.

Principal or Most Advantageous Market

A fair value measurement assumes that the transaction to sell the asset or transfer the liability occurs in the principal market for the asset or liability or, in the absence of a principal market, the most advantageous market for the asset or liability (ASC 820-10-35-5). The principal market is the market in which the reporting entity would normally sell the asset or transfer the liability. The most advantageous market is the market in which the reporting entity would sell the asset or transfer the liability at a price that maximizes the amount that would be received for the asset or minimizes the amount that would be paid to transfer the liability. An exhaustive search does not have to be performed to identify the principal or most advantageous market (ASC 820-10-35-5A). However, the reporting entity must have access to the principal (or most advantageous) market at the measurement date. Since different entities have access to different markets, the principal (or most advantageous market) for a particular asset or liability may differ across entities (ASC 820-10-35-6A). Although a reporting entity must have access to the principal (or most advantageous) market, the entity does not need to be able to sell the asset or transfer the liability on the measurement date in order to estimate fair value using the principal (or most advantageous) market (ASC 820-10-35-6B).

> **OBSERVATION:** Assuming a principal market (i.e., market with the greatest volume of activity for the asset or liability), fair value is determined by reference to the price in that market even if the price in another market is more advantageous for the company (ASC 820-10-35-6).

The price in the principal or most advantageous market used to measure the fair value of the asset or liability should not be adjusted for transaction costs. Transaction costs represent the incremental direct costs to sell the asset or transfer the liability in the principal or most advantageous market for the asset or liability. These costs are not an attribute of the asset or liability. Transaction costs do not include the costs that would be incurred to transport the asset or liability to its principal or most advantageous market. The price in the principal or most advantageous market used to measure the fair value of the asset or liability shall be adjusted for the costs that would be incurred to transport the asset or liability to its principal or most advantageous market (ASC 820-10-35-9B, 9C).

OBSERVATION: In some cases, there may not be a market price available for the asset or liability on the measurement date. In this case, the reporting entity must still assume that a transaction to sell the asset or transfer the liability could take place. A reporting entity will have to determine fair value using a model when market prices do not exist (ASC 820-10-35-6C).

Illustration of Determining the Highest and Best Use of an Asset

Hogan Company (Hogan) has recently acquired land in a business combination. The land hosts a manufacturing facility. Similar parcels of land have recently been sold and converted to residential use. Hogan determines that it could sell its land for residential use. The fair value of the manufacturing operation is $2.5 million. It would cost Hogan $500,000 to demolish the manufacturing operation and to otherwise convert the land to a vacant site suitable for residential development. The value of a vacant site if sold for such a development is $2.7 million. The fair value of the land if used to host the manufacturing operation (i.e., in-use value), $2.5 million, exceeds the fair value of the land if readied and sold for residential development (i.e., in-exchange value), $2.2 million (i.e., $2.7 million − 0.5 million). Therefore, the highest and best use of the land is its in-use value, $2.5 million.

Market Participants

Market participants are buyers and sellers in the principal or most advantageous market for the asset or liability that meet the following criteria:

- They are independent of the reporting entity.
- They are knowledgeable, having a reasonable understanding about the asset or liability and the transaction based on all available information.
- They are able to transact for the asset or liability.
- They are willing to transact for the asset or liability (i.e., willing, but not forced or otherwise compelled to do so).

The fair value of the asset or liability is determined based on the assumptions market participants would use in pricing the asset or liability, assuming that market participants will act in their own best interests. In developing the assumptions, the reporting entity is not required to identify specific market participants. Rather, it should identify characteristics that distinguish market participants generally, considering factors specific to the asset or liability, the principal or most advantageous market for the asset or liability, and market participants with whom the reporting entity would transact in that market (ASC 820-10-35-9).

Application to Nonfinancial Assets

A fair value measurement assumes the highest and best use of the nonfinancial asset by market participants, considering the use of the asset that is physically possible, legally permissible, and financially feasible at the measurement date.

The highest and best use of the nonfinancial asset determines the valuation premise that is used to measure the fair value of the asset (ASC 820-10-35-10A, 10B).

> **OBSERVATION:** The reporting entity's current use of a nonfinancial asset is assumed to be the asset's highest and best use absent evidence to the contrary (ASC 820-10-35-10C).

In-Use Assets The highest and best use of the nonfinancial asset is in use if the asset would provide maximum value to market participants principally in combination with other assets or with other assets and liabilities. In this instance, the fair value of the nonfinancial asset is determined based on the price that would be received in a current transaction to sell the asset assuming that the asset would be used with other assets or with other assets and liabilities and that the assets would be available to market participants (ASC 820-10-35-10E).

> **OBSERVATION:** If a nonfinancial asset's highest and best use is in-use, the assumption is that other market participants already own the other assets and liabilities that the asset to be measured is used in combination with (ASC 820-10-35-11A).

An entity must measure the fair value of a nonfinancial asset at its highest and best use, from the perspective of market participants, even if the reporting entity doesn't plan to use the asset in that manner (ASC 820-10-35-10D).

Standalone Assets A nonfinancial asset might provide maximum value to market participants if the asset is used on a standalone basis. In this instance, the fair value of the nonfinancial asset is measured based on the price that would be received in a current transaction to sell the nonfinancial asset standalone (ASC 820-10-35-10E).

Application to Liabilities and Instruments Included Within Shareholders' Equity

Fair value measurement assumes that the liability or instrument included within shareholders' equity (e.g., equity instruments issued as consideration in a business combination) is transferred to a market participant at the measurement date and that the nonperformance risk related to the liability is the same before and after its transfer. Nonperformance risk refers to the risk that the obligation will not be fulfilled and affects the value at which the liability is transferred. The fair value of the liability shall reflect the nonperformance risk relating to that liability. The credit risk of the reporting entity is one factor in determining the nonperformance risk. Nonperformance risk should be the same after the assumed transfer as it was before the transfer (ASC 820-10-35-16, 17, 18). Some liabilities include a third-party credit enhancement (e.g., credit default insurance, other guarantees, etc.). When that third-party enhancement is accounted for separately, it should not be considered in determining the fair value of the liability (ASC 820-10-35-18A).

A fair value measurement assumes that a liability is exchanged in an orderly transaction between market participants. However, most liabilities have contractual or legal restrictions that prevent the liabilities from being transferred, although some liabilities are traded in the marketplace as assets. If a quoted market price for an identical liability exists, then that price would represent a Level 1 measurement. However, if no such quoted price exists for an identical liability, a reporting entity must measure fair value using one or more of the following techniques (ASC 820-10-35-16B, 16BB):

- A valuation technique that uses:
  - The quoted price in an active market of an identical item when that item is held by another entity as an asset
  - The quoted price in a non-active market of an identical item when that item is held by another entity as an asset
  - Quoted prices for similar liabilities or similar liabilities when traded as assets
  - A valuation technique—for example, an income approach that would be used to value the item if it was held as an asset

When the fair value of a liability or instrument included within shareholders' equity is measured using the quoted price of the liability or shareholders' equity instrument when traded as an asset, the quoted price of the asset must not be adjusted for the effect of a restriction preventing its sale. However, the quoted price must be adjusted for any factors that are specific to the asset but are not applicable to the fair value measurement of the liability or shareholders' equity instrument. For example, a reporting entity must consider whether the quoted price of the asset should be adjusted if the quoted price for the asset relates to a similar (but not identical) liability or shareholders' equity instrument traded as an asset, or if the unit of account for the asset is not the same as for the liability or shareholders' equity instrument (ASC 820-10-35-16D).

There are some liabilities and shareholders' equity instruments without a readily determinable market value and where the identical item is not held by another party as an asset (e.g., an asset retirement obligation). In this case, fair value is determined using a valuation technique from the perspective of a market participant that owes the liability or has issued the claim on equity (ASC 820-10-35-16H). For example, the present value of a liability in this case would include estimates of future cash outflows to settle the liability and the compensation that the market participant would require to assume the obligation. The compensation required to assume the obligation includes payment both for assuming the obligation given that resources can be used for other purposes, and includes a premium for the risk that the actual cash outflows will exceed the expected cash outflows (ASC 820-10-35-16J). In adjusting for risk, either future cash outflows can be increased or the discount rate used to determine present value can be reduced, but not both (ASC 820-10-35-16L).

49,008 ASC 820—Fair Value Measurement

Application to Financial Assets and Financial Liabilities with Offsetting Positions

Generally, the fair value of financial instruments is to be measured at the level of the individual asset or liability (i.e., the fair values of assets and liabilities are presented gross and are not netted). Some entities hold groups of financial assets and liabilities that are exposed to common risks. These common risks might be interest rate risk, currency risk, or credit risk. An entity might manage its exposure to these types of risks on a net basis, rather than on a group basis. When an entity manages its exposure to market and credit risk on a net basis, the entity can determine the fair value of the net position—either the price that would be received for selling a net asset position, or the price that would be paid to transfer a net liability position. However, this exception to the normal guidance in ASC 820 is only available when the risks to be offset are substantially the same (ASC 820-10-35-18D, 18J). The reporting entity must make an accounting policy decision to avail itself of the exception which allows certain financial instruments to be measured on a net basis rather than on a gross basis (ASC 820-10-35-18G).

> **OBSERVATION:** The exception that allows certain financial instruments to be measured on a net rather than a gross basis only applies to fair value measurements involving derivatives and hedges (ASC 815) or involving financial instruments (ASC 825) (ASC 820-10-35-18H).

Although an entity may be able to measure fair value on a net basis given the guidance in the preceding paragraph, the exception does not pertain to financial statement presentation. That is, financial instruments may need to be presented on a gross basis in the financial statements even though they are measured on a net basis (ASC 820-10-35-18F).

Fair Value at Initial Recognition

When an asset is acquired or a liability assumed in an exchange, the transaction price represents the price paid to acquire the asset or received to assume the liability. In contrast, the fair value of the asset or liability represents the price that would be received to sell the asset or paid to transfer the liability (i.e., an exit price) (ASC 820-10-30-2).

In many cases, the transaction price equals the exit price and, therefore, represents the fair value of the asset or liability at initial recognition. In determining whether a transaction price represents the fair value of the asset or liability at initial recognition, the reporting entity must consider factors specific to the transaction and to the specific asset or liability. Examples of situations in which the transaction price might not represent the fair value of an asset or liability at initial recognition are when:

- The transaction is between related parties.
- The transaction occurs under duress or the seller is forced to accept the price in the transaction.

- The unit of account represented by the transaction price is different from the unit of account of the asset or liability measured at fair value (e.g., the asset is one element in the transaction that includes multiple elements).
- The market in which the transaction occurs is different from the market in which the reporting entity would sell the asset or transfer the liability. (ASC 820-10-30-3A).

Illustration of Using Observable Market Inputs in the Most Advantageous Market

Daves Incorporated (Daves) owns 50,000 shares of the common stock of Fauver Company (Fauver). The stock of Fauver is traded on two different markets, A and B. The price of Fauver on A is $17 per share and transaction costs are $2. The price of Fauver on B is $16 per share and transaction costs are $0.50. Neither market is the principal market for Fauver. Because neither market is the principal market, fair value is determined using the market that maximizes the amount that would be received after considering transaction costs. The net amount received on Market A would be $15 and it would be $15.50 on Market B. Therefore, the fair value of Fauver stock is determined using the price in that market—$16. Note that although transaction costs are considered in determining the most advantageous market, these costs are not considered in determining the fair value of the asset.

Valuation Techniques

Valuation techniques are classified in ASC 820 in three categories: (1) market approach; (2) income approach; and (3) cost approach. Following are brief descriptions of each approach.

Market approach The market approach uses prices and other relevant information generated by market transactions involving identical or comparable assets or liabilities. These approaches often use market multiples derived from a set of comparables. Multiples might lie in ranges with a different multiple for each comparable. The selection of where within the range the appropriate multiple falls requires judgment. Matrix pricing is a valuation technique that is consistent with the market approach.

Income approach The income approach uses valuation techniques to convert future amounts to a single present amount. The measurement is based on the value indicated by current market expectations about those future amounts. Examples include present value techniques, option pricing models, such as the Black-Scholes-Merton formula, and a binomial model.

Cost approach The cost approach is based on the amount that currently would be required to replace the service capacity of an asset (sometimes referred to as current replacement cost). The price that would be received for the asset is determined on the basis of the cost to a buyer to acquire or construct a substitute asset of comparable utility, adjusted for obsolescence.

Valuation techniques that are appropriate in the circumstances and for which sufficient data are available shall be used to measure fair value. A combination of valuation techniques may be appropriate, and valuation techniques used to measure fair value shall be applied consistently. A change in the valuation technique or its application is appropriate if the change results in a measurement that is equally or more representative of fair value in the circumstance. Revisions from a change in the valuation technique or its application are accounted for as changes in accounting estimate in accordance with ASC 250 (Accounting Changes and Error Corrections).

The term "inputs" refers to the assumptions that market participants use in pricing the asset or liability. Observable inputs reflect the assumptions market participants would use in pricing the asset or liability based on market data obtained from sources independent of the reporting entity. Unobservable inputs reflect the reporting entity's own assumptions about the assumptions market participants would use in pricing the asset or liability developed on the basis of the best information available in the circumstances. Valuation techniques should maximize the use of observable inputs and minimize the use of unobservable inputs (ASC 820-10-35-24, 25-26, 36).

Premiums or discounts in determining fair value are not to be considered when a quoted price in an active market is available. However, if a quoted price in an active market is not available, premiums or discounts are to be considered in determining fair value if they would be considered by market participants in pricing the asset or liability. Any premium or discount considered needs to be related to the underlying asset or liability—for example, a control premium would be considered. Conversely, features that describe an entity's asset holding—for example, the size of the reporting entity's ownership stake in another entity's equity securities (sometimes referred to as a blockage factor)—is not to be considered in determining fair value (ASC 820-10-35-36B).

Illustration of Use of Multiple Techniques to Estimate Fair Value

Cochran Incorporated (Cochran) completes a business acquisition on July 1, 20X8. Among the assets acquired is an internally developed, custom software program that is licensed to external customers. Cochran must estimate the fair value of this software program in assigning the purchase price to the individual assets and liabilities acquired. Cochran determines that the asset has a higher value in use than in exchange. Cochran cannot determine the fair value of the asset using a market approach because transactions for comparable software assets are not available given the customized nature of the software. Cochran estimates the fair value of the software using both the income and cost approach. Cochran applies the income approach by determining the present value of expected license fees over the software's useful life; the estimated fair value using this approach is $7 million. The cost of writing a substitute software program of comparable utility is $5 million. Because the software program was developed using proprietary information, Cochran concludes that it is not possible to directly replace the existing program. Therefore, Cochran estimates the fair value of the software program as $7 million.

Fair Value Hierarchy

ASC 820 contains a fair value hierarchy that is intended to increase consistency and comparability in fair value measurements and related disclosures. This hierarchy prioritizes the inputs to valuation techniques used to measure fair value into three levels: Level 1 (highest priority), Level 2, and Level 3 (lowest priority):

1. Quoted Market Prices in Active Markets (Level 1):
   a. Level 1 inputs are quoted market prices in active markets for identical assets or liabilities that are accessible at the measurement date.
   b. An active market for the asset or liability is a market in which transactions for the asset or liability occur with sufficient frequency and volume to provide pricing information on an ongoing basis.
   c. A quoted market price in an active market provides the most reliable evidence of fair value and should be used whenever available.
   d. For liabilities, a quoted price in an active market for the identical liability is a Level 1 input. A quoted price for the identical liability when traded as an asset is also a Level 1 input if no adjustments are required to the quoted price of the asset. Any adjustment required to the quoted price of the asset will result in a lower level measurement.
2. Other Than Quoted Market Inputs (Level 2):
   a. Level 2 inputs are from other than quoted market prices included in Level 1 that are observable for the asset or liability, either directly or indirectly.
   b. Level 2 inputs include the following:
      (1) Quoted market prices of similar assets or liabilities in active markets;
      (2) Quoted market prices for identical or similar assets or liabilities in markets that are not active;
      (3) Inputs other than quoted prices that are observable for the asset or liability (e.g., interest rates and yield curves observable at commonly quoted intervals, volatilities, prepayment speeds, loss severities, credit spreads, and default rates); and
      (4) Inputs that are derived principally from or corroborated by observable market data by correlation or other means.
3. Unobservable Inputs (Level 3):
   a. Level 3 inputs are unobservable and shall be used to measure fair value to the extent that observable inputs are not available.
   b. Unobservable inputs are allowed in situations where there is little, if any, market activity for the asset or liability at the measurement date.
   c. Unobservable inputs reflect the assumptions that market participants would use in pricing the asset or liability.

d. Unobservable inputs shall be developed based on the best information available under the circumstances. The entity is not required to consider all possible efforts to obtain information about market participant assumptions, but the entity shall not ignore information about market participant assumptions that is reasonably available without undue cost and effort.

If a fair value measurement is based on bid and ask prices, the price within the bid-ask spread that is most representative of fair value in the circumstances shall be used to measure fair value (ASC 820-10-35-39, 40-56).

OBSERVATION: In some cases both observable and unobservable inputs may be used to estimate fair value. When the use of an unobservable input has a significant effect on the fair value estimate, the measurement would be categorized as having been made within Level 3 of the fair value hierarchy (ASC 820-10-35-38A).

Fair Value Given a Decline in the Volume or Level of Activity

The fair value of an asset or liability may be affected when there is a significant decline in the volume or level of activity for the asset or liability. Items to consider in evaluating the significance of any decline in the volume or level of activity include: (1) the number of recent transactions; (2) whether price quotations are based on current information; (3) wide variations in price quotations, either compared to the past or across different market makers; (4) indices that historically were correlated with fair value measurements are no longer highly correlated; (5) a significant increase in implied liquidity risk premiums or yields; (6) a wide bid-ask spread or a significant increase in the bid-ask spread; (7) a significant decrease in new issuances of securities; and (8) a lack of information about transactions in principal-to-principal markets (ASC 820-10-35-54C).

A significant decrease in the volume or level of activity does not automatically indicate that market prices do not represent fair value or that transactions in the market are not orderly. However, if the entity determines that the transaction (market) price does not represent fair value, an adjustment to the entity's fair value determination must be made. Moreover, any such adjustment may be significant to the entity's estimate of fair value. Generally, a reduction in the volume or level of activity in a market indicates heightened risk. As a result, in determining fair value, the risk premium that would be assessed by market participants needs to be considered in determining fair value (ASC 820-10-35-54E). When there is a significant decline in the volume or level of activity, the entity may want to use multiple valuation techniques in determining fair value (ASC 820-10-35-54F).

Transactions that Are Not Orderly

Just because the volume or level of activity for an asset or liability has declined does not automatically indicate that transactions are not orderly. Indicators that a transaction may not be orderly include: (1) the asset or liability was exposed to the market for too short a time before the financial statement date to adequately market the asset or liability, (2) the seller only marketed the asset or liability to a single buyer, (3) the seller is distressed, (4) the seller was forced to sell by a regulator or to meet legal requirements, (5) the transaction price differs greatly from the prices of other recent transactions (ASC 820-10-35-54I).

If the transaction is not orderly, very little weight should be placed on the transaction in determining fair value. If the entity cannot determine whether the transaction was orderly, the transaction price is one input in determining fair value but it would receive less weight than when the transaction is known to have been orderly. The entity does not have to undertake exhaustive efforts to determine if the transaction is orderly; however, the entity cannot ignore evidence that is reasonably available (ASC 820-10-35-54J).

OBSERVATION: An entity can use quoted prices provided by third parties (e.g., pricing services and brokers) in determining fair value. However, these third parties must determine fair value in accordance with the guidance in ASC 820 (ASC 820-10-35-54L). Moreover, not all quotes from third parties are created equal—binding offers should be afforded greater weight in determining fair value than indicative prices (ASC 820-10-35-54M).

Illustration of Using a Level 2 Input to Estimate Fair Value

King Company (King) acquires a recently developed and unoccupied office building. King needs to estimate the fair value of the building in assigning the purchase price to the individual assets and liabilities acquired. As the building is new and has not yet been occupied, King cannot determine the fair value of the building using a Level 1 input—a quoted price in an active market for the identical asset. However, it can determine a fair value for the building using a Level 2 input. King determines the price per square foot received in rent for similar buildings in similar locations based on actual transactions. Using this price per square foot, King can determine the likely rental income the building will generate and thereby estimate the fair value of the building using an income approach.

Disclosures

For assets and liabilities that are measured at fair value on a *recurring basis* in periods subsequent to initial recognition, the reporting entity shall disclose information that helps users of the financial statements to assess the valuation techniques and inputs used to develop the fair value measurements. For recurring fair value measurement using significant unobservable inputs (Level 3), the effect of the measurements on earnings (or changes in net assets) or other comprehensive income for the period shall be disclosed (ASC 820-10-50-1). In deciding whether this disclosure objective is met, the reporting entity shall consider: (1) how detailed its disclosures need to be, (2) which disclosures to emphasize, (3) the appropriate level of aggregation vs. disaggregation, and (4) whether users need additional information to be able to properly evaluate the quantitative information disclosed (ASC 820-10-50-1A).

> **PRACTICE POINTER:** If the required disclosures are insufficient to meet the reporting objectives outlined in ASC 820-10-50-1, the entity needs to disclose additional information to ensure that the reporting objectives are met (ASC 820-10-50-1A).

To meet these requirements, the following information, at a minimum, is required to be disclosed for each class of assets and liabilities measured at fair value in the statement of financial position after initial recognition (ASC 820-10-50-2):

- The fair value measurement at the end of the reporting period, for both recurring and nonrecurring fair value measurements. The reasons for any nonrecurring fair value measurements need to be disclosed (e.g., a long-lived asset held for sale measured at fair value less cost to sell).
- The level within the fair value hierarchy in which the fair value measurement in its entirety falls, segregating the fair value measurement using quoted prices in active markets (Level 1), significant other observable inputs (Level 2), and significant unobservable inputs (Level 3), separately for both recurring and nonrecurring fair value measurements. For assets and liabilities measured at fair value on a recurring basis and held at the end of the reporting period, the amounts of significant transfers between Level 1 and Level 2 of the fair value hierarchy and the reasons for the transfers. These disclosures must separately identify significant transfers into each level from transfers out of each level. These disclosures are not required for nonpublic entities (ASC 820-10-50-2F).
- A description of the valuation techniques and inputs to determine fair value for recurring and nonrecurring fair value measurements categorized within Level 2 or 3 of the hierarchy. In addition, any change in the valuation technique, and the reason therefor, needs to be disclosed.
- Quantitative information about significant unobservable inputs for fair value measurements determined using Level 3 of the hierarchy.
- For recurring fair value measurements based on Level 3 of the hierarchy, a reconciliation as of the beginning and ending balances, separately presenting changes during the period from each of the following:
  - Total gains or losses for the period recognized in earnings (or changes in net assets), and the line item of where those gains or losses are included in earnings (or changes in net assets);
  - Total gains or losses for the period recognized in other comprehensive income, and the line item of where those gains and losses are included in other comprehensive income.
  - Purchases, sales, issues, and settlements (each type disclosed separately); and

- Transfers in and/or out of Level 3 and the reasons for those transfers. These disclosures must separately identify significant transfers into Level 3 from transfers out of Level 3. A reporting entity must disclose and consistently follow its policy for determining which transfers are significant and when those transfers between levels are recognized. A reporting entity's policy as to the timing of recognizing transfers must be the same for transfers into Level 3 as that for transfers out of Level 3. The timing of this recognition could be, for example: (1) the actual date of the event or change in circumstances that caused the transfer, (2) the beginning of the reporting period, or (3) the end of the reporting period (ASC 820-10-50-2C).

- For recurring fair value measurements based on Level 3 of the hierarchy, the amount of the total gains or losses for the period included in earnings (or changes in net assets) that is attributable to the change in unrealized gains or losses relating to those assets and liabilities held at the end of the reporting period and the line item of where those unrealized gains or losses are reported in the statement of income (or activities).

- For recurring and nonrecurring fair value measurements based on Level 3 of the hierarchy, a description of the valuation processes used by the entity. For recurring fair value measurements based on Level 3 of the hierarchy, a description of how sensitive the fair value measurement is to changes in unobservable inputs if a change in those inputs might result in a significant change in the fair value measurement. In addition, if other unobservable inputs interrelate with other highly-sensitive unobservable inputs, these interrelationships and their possible effects must be disclosed. These disclosures are not required for nonpublic entities (ASC 820-10-50-2F).

- For recurring and nonrecurring fair value measurements, disclose if the highest and best use of a nonfinancial asset differs from its current use, and explain why a nonfinancial asset is being used in a manner different from its highest and best use.

An entity must determine the appropriate classes of assets and liabilities—these classes determine the relevant groupings for which fair value information is reported. In determining the appropriate classes of assets and liabilities, the entity is to consider: (1) nature, characteristics, and risks of the assets and liabilities; and (2) the level of the hierarchy used to determine fair value (ASC 820-10-50-2B).

PRACTICE POINTER: Determining the appropriate classes of assets and liabilities for which to disclose fair value information requires judgment. Notwithstanding this fact, the number of classes of assets and liabilities disclosed when fair value is determined using Level 3 of the hierarchy is likely to be greater due to the greater degree of uncertainty and subjectivity associated with Level 3 measurements (ASC 820-10-50-2B).

The fair value of certain assets and liabilities may be required to be disclosed but the asset or liability may not be measured at fair value in the financial statements. In that case, limited disclosures are required for public companies. However, public companies are not required to disclose information about significant unobservable inputs (ASC 820-10-50-2E). No disclosures are required for nonpublic companies (ASC 820-10-50-2F).

For derivative assets and liabilities, an entity must present both of the following (ASC 820-10-50-3):

- The fair value disclosures required by ASC 820-10-50-2(a) through (bb) on a gross basis.
- The reconciliation disclosure required by ASC 820-10-50-2(c) through (d) on either a gross or a net basis.

PRACTICE POINTER: If a liability is measured at fair value, and if the liability has an inseparable credit enhancement issued by a third party, the entity shall disclose the existence of the third-party credit enhancement (ASC 820-10-50-4).

The quantitative disclosures required by ASC 820 are required to be presented using a tabular format (ASC 820-10-50-8). In addition, a change in the valuation technique used to determine fair value is not considered a change in accounting estimate under ASC 250 (ASC 820-10-50-7).

PART II: INTERPRETIVE GUIDANCE

ASC 820-10: Overall

ASC 820-10-05-3, 55-23C through 55-23D, 25-1 through 25-2, 50-4A, 55-8 through 55-9 Issuer's Accounting for Liabilities Measured at Fair Value with a Third-Party Credit Enhancement

BACKGROUND

Issuers of debt securities sometimes issue their securities combined with a financial guarantee made by an unrelated third party (i.e., a credit enhancement), which the issuer purchases to guarantee its credit obligations. The guarantee gives investors additional assurance that the debt will be paid by the issuer or the guarantor and usually enables the issuer to: (1) pay a lower interest rate on the debt securities; (2) receive higher proceeds; or (3) both.

Generally, if an issuer that has issued debt securities with a credit enhancement defaults on its debt, the issuer is *not* released from its obligation, because the issuer is required to reimburse the guarantor for payments made to investors. Consequently, if an issuer of debt securities defaults on its obligation, that obligation still exists but the investor has been paid by a different creditor.

Under the guidance in ASC 825, which was effective for fiscal years that began after November 15, 2007, an entity is permitted to measure its financial assets and liabilities at fair value depending on certain requirements. Therefore, an entity is permitted to measure the liability discussed below at fair value. In addition, under the guidance in ASC 825 requires entities to disclose the fair value of all financial instruments (with some exceptions). Because under the guidance in ASC 820, the fair value of a liability must include the risk that an obligation will *not* be satisfied, some have questioned whether a debt instrument that includes an *inseparable* credit enhancement should be accounted for as one unit of accounting or as two if the debt instrument is measured at fair value.

ACCOUNTING ISSUE

Should a debt instrument that includes an *inseparable* credit enhancement be accounted for as one unit of accounting or as two if the debt instrument is measured at fair value?

SCOPE

The guidance in this Issue applies to the accounting for a debt instrument measured at fair value that is issued with a contractual guarantee from a third party (i.e., credit enhancement) that cannot be separated from the debt instrument. It does *not* apply to the accounting for guarantees, such as deposit insurance, provided by a government or a government agency.

ACCOUNTING GUIDANCE

Measurement

An issuer's fair value measurement of its liability for a debt instrument issued with a credit enhancement purchased from an unrelated third party should *not* include the effect of the credit enhancement in the liability's fair value measurement, which is not the issuer's asset but was purchased by the issuer for the investor's benefit. By purchasing a credit enhancement, an issuer transfers its debt obligation from the investor to the guarantor. Proceeds received by the issuer from an investor who has purchased the liability with the credit enhancement should be allocated to the premium paid for the credit enhancement and to the issued liability.

Disclosure

An issuer should disclose the existence of a credit enhancement on its issued debt that the issuer purchased from an unrelated third party.

ASC 820-10-35-54C through 35-54M, 65-8 Determining Fair Value When the Volume and Level of Activity for the Asset or Liability Have Significantly Decreased

OBSERVATION: Previous guidance on this matter has been revised to conform with the guidance in Accounting Standards Update (ASU) No. 2011-04, *Fair Value Measurement (Topic 820): Amendments to Achieve Common Fair Value Measurement and Disclosure Requirements in U.S. GAAP and IFRSs,* which should be applied *prospectively* and is effective as follows: (a) For public entities, for interim periods that begin after December 15, 2011, and (b) For nonpublic entities, for annual periods that begin after December 15, 2011. Early application is permitted for nonpublic entities, but only for interim periods that begin after December 15, 2011. A change that results from a revised valuation technique or its application should be accounted for as a change in an accounting estimate in accordance with the guidance in ASC 250-1-45-17. A change, if any, in a valuation technique and related inputs should be disclosed by providing the amount of the total effect, in the period in which the guidance is adopted.

BACKGROUND

With the issuance of the guidance in ASC 820 in September 2006, the FASB established a single definition of fair value and a framework for measuring fair value under U.S. generally accepted accounting principles (GAAP) for the purpose of increased consistency and comparability of fair value measurements. The following guidance was issued, because constituents asked for additional guidance on determining when a market for a financial asset is no longer active and whether a transaction is not orderly.

The following guidance supersedes the guidance in ASC 820-10-35-51A through 35-51H.

ACCOUNTING GUIDANCE

To determine whether there has been a significant decrease in the volume and level of activity for an asset or liability, a reporting entity should evaluate, the significance and relevance of the following factors, among others, based on the available evidence:

- Few recent transactions;
- Price quotations based on outdated information;
- Substantial variance in price quotations either over time or among market makers;
- Lack of correlation between indices and recent indications of the fair value of assets and liabilities that previously were highly correlated;
- Based on all available market data about credit and other nonperformance risk for an asset or liability, a significant increase in implied liquidity risk premiums, yields, or performance indicators (e.g., delinquency rates or loss severities) for observed transactions or quoted prices as compared to a reporting entity's estimate of expected cash flows;
- Wide bid-ask spread or significant increase in bid-ask spread;
- Significant decline or lack of a market for new issuances (i.e., a primary market) for an asset or liability or similar assets or liabilities; and
- Limited public information available (e.g., for transactions in a principal-to-principal market).

A reporting entity that concludes that the volume and level of activity for an asset or liability has significantly decreased in comparison to normal market activity for that asset or liability should perform further analysis of the transactions or quoted prices. A decrease in the volume or level of activity may not by itself indicate that a transaction price or quoted price does not represent fair value or that a transaction in that market is not orderly. However, if a reporting entity determines that a transaction price or quoted price does not represent fair value, the transaction prices or quoted prices need adjustment if the reporting entity uses that information to measure fair value and that adjustment may be significant to the entire fair value measurement. Significant adjustments to fair value estimates also may be necessary if the price of a similar asset requires significant adjustment for comparability to the asset being measured or if a price is out-of-date.

No guidance is provided in this discussion on how to make significant adjustments to transactions or quoted prices in the process of estimating fair value. Valuation techniques used to measure fair value are discussed in ASC 820-10-35-24 through 35-27 and 55-3A through 55-3G.) Regardless of the valuation technique used, risk adjustments should be included, including a risk premium, which represents the amount that market participants would require to compensate them for uncertainty inherent in an asset's or liability's cash flows. A risk adjustment should represent an orderly transaction between market participants at the measurement date under current market conditions.

Using a different valuation technique or multiple techniques may be appropriate if there has been a significant decrease in the volume of an asset's or liability's activity. A range of fair value estimates may result when multiple valuation techniques are used to estimate fair value. The reasonableness of the range of fair values should be considered with the objective of determining the amount in the range that best represents the fair value of an asset or liability under the existing conditions. Further analysis may be required if a wide range of fair value estimates results from the use of multiple valuation techniques.

The objective of a fair value measurement does *not* change, regardless of the circumstances or the valuation techniques used. Under the guidance in ASC 820-10-35-54G:

> Fair value is the price that would be received to sell an asset or paid to transfer a liability in an orderly transaction (that is, not a forced liquidation or distressed sale) between market participants at the measurement date under current market conditions.

Estimating the price at which willing market participants would enter into a transaction considering the conditions that exist at the measurement date if there has been a significant decrease in the volume and level of activity for an asset or liability depends on the facts and circumstances and requires using significant judgment. It is irrelevant in estimating fair value whether a reporting entity intends to hold an asset or to settle a liability, because under the guidance in ASC 820-10-35-54H "[f]air value is a market-based measurement, not an entity-specific measurement."

The fact that there has been a significant decrease in the volume and level of activity for an asset or liability should not lead to a presumption that all transactions are distressed or forced (i.e., not orderly). The following circumstances, among others, may indicate that a transaction is *not* orderly:

- The lack of an adequate period of market exposure before the measurement date to carry out the usual and customary marketing activities for transactions related to such assets or liabilities under current market conditions.

- The asset or liability was marketed only to one market participant during the usual and customary marketing period.
- The seller is in or close to bankruptcy or receivership, or the sale was forced to meet regulatory or legal requirements.
- The transaction price is outside the range of fair value estimates in comparison to other recent transactions for the same or similar asset or liability.
- The seller was forced to sell because of regulatory or legal requirements.

To determine whether a transaction is orderly, an entity should evaluate the circumstances based on the weight of the evidence.

If there has been a significant decrease in the volume or level of activity for an asset or liability, an entity should consider the following guidance in its determination of whether a transaction is or is not orderly:

- Little, if any, significance, as compared to other indicators of fair value, should be placed on a transaction price in an entity's estimate of fair value or market risk premiums if the weight of the evidence indicates that the transaction is *not* orderly.
- A transaction price should be considered in an entity's estimate of fair value or market risk premiums if there is significant evidence to indicate that a transaction is orderly. The importance of a transaction price as compared to other indicators of fair value depends on the facts and circumstance, such as the volume of the transaction, comparability of the transaction to the asset or liability being measured at fair value, and the period of time between the transaction and the measurement date.
- An entity should consider a transaction price in estimating fair value or market risk premiums even if the information is insufficient to indicate whether the transaction was orderly. However, that transaction price should *not* be used as the only or primary basis for making that estimate. Less significance should be placed on transactions for which the reporting entity has insufficient information to reach a conclusion about whether the transaction is orderly in comparison to other known orderly transactions.

Although a reporting entity should *not* ignore information that is easily accessible at a reasonable cost, it need not make all possible efforts to determine whether a transaction is orderly. If a reporting entity is a party to a transaction, it is expected to have sufficient evidence as to whether a transaction is orderly.

Under the guidance in ASC 820, fair value may be estimated by using quoted prices from third parties, such as pricing services or brokers, if a reporting entity finds that those amounts were determined in accordance with the guidance in ASC 820. However, if there is a significant decrease in the volume or level of activity for an asset or liability, the reporting entity needs to evaluate whether the information is based on current orderly transactions or on a valuation technique that represents the assumptions of market participants, including assumptions about risk. Less significance should be placed on quoted prices that are not related to transactions. In addition, the nature of a quote (i.e., whether it is an indicative price or a binding offer) should be considered in determining the significance of available evidence. Binding offers should be considered to be more significant.

CHAPTER 50
ASC 825—FINANCIAL INSTRUMENTS

CONTENTS

Part I: General Guidance	50,001
ASC 825-10: Overall	50,001
Overview	50,001
Fair Value Option for Financial Assets and Liabilities	50,002
Eligibility	50,002
Election Dates	50,003
Applying the Fair Value Option	50,004
Disclosure of Information about Fair Value of Financial Instruments	50,004
Disclosures about Concentrations of Credit Risk	50,007
Encouraged Disclosures about Market Risk of All Financial Instruments	50,008
Situations Not Covered by ASC 825	50,008
Applying the Fair Value Option to Not-for-Profit Organizations	50,009
Optional Disclosures by Nonpublic Entities	50,009
Estimating Fair Value	50,010
Part II: Interpretive Guidance	50,011
ASC 825-10 Overall	50,011
ASC 825-10-50-2A through 50-3, 50-8, 50-10 through 50-12; ASC 320-10-35-26; ASC 270-10-50-1(m)	
Interim Disclosures about Fair Value of Financial Instruments	50,011
ASC 825-10-55-1 through 55-2; ASC 310-10-50-25	
Terms of Loan Products That May Give Rise to a Concentration of Credit Risk	50,012
ASC 825-20: Registration Payment Arrangements	50,015
ASC 825-20-05-1 15-1 through 15-5, 25-2 through 25-3, 30-1, 30-4 through 30-5, 35-1, 50-1 through 50-2, 55-2 through 55-8, 55-10 through 55-14; ASC 815-10-25-16; ASC 815-40-25-21, 25-43; ASC 470-20-30-23	
Accounting for Registration Payment Arrangements	50,015

PART I: GENERAL GUIDANCE

ASC 820-10: OVERALL

OVERVIEW

ASC 825 defines the term "financial instrument" as cash, evidence of an ownership interest in an entity, or a contract that both (ASC Glossary):

- Imposes on one entity a contractual obligation (1) to deliver cash or another financial instrument to a second entity or (2) to exchange other financial instruments on potentially unfavorable terms with the second entity

- Conveys to the second entity a contractual right (1) to receive cash or another financial instrument from the first entity or (2) to exchange other financial instruments on potentially favorable terms with the first entity

The Codification contains various Topics that provide guidance on accounting for different financial instruments. This chapter focuses on principles governing only fair value disclosures for all financial instruments. The term *fair value* is defined as the price that would be received to sell the instrument in an orderly transaction between market participants at the measurement date (ASC Glossary).

ASC 825 requires disclosure of fair value information about financial instruments, whether or not those instruments are recognized in the financial statements, with certain exceptions. It applies to all entities. It does not change requirements for recognition, measurement, or classification of financial instruments in financial statements (ASC 825-10-50-8).

FAIR VALUE OPTION FOR FINANCIAL ASSETS AND LIABILITIES

ASC 825 provides companies with an option to report selected financial assets and liabilities at fair value. This is hereafter referred to as the "fair value option." The fair value option reduces both the complexity in accounting for financial instruments and the volatility in earnings caused by measuring related assets and liabilities differently. ASC 825 contains presentation and disclosure requirements that are designed to facilitate comparisons between companies that choose different measurement attributes for similar types of assets and liabilities.

ASC 825 requires companies to provide additional information that is intended to help investors and other users of financial statements to more easily understand the effects on reported earnings of the company's choice to use fair value. It also requires companies to display the fair value of those assets and liabilities for which the company has chosen to use fair value in the primary financial statements.

ASC 825 permits all entities to elect to measure eligible items at fair value. Under this standard, a business entity shall report unrealized gains and losses at each subsequent reporting date. Upfront costs and fees related to items for which the fair value option is elected are recognized in earnings as incurred and are not deferred.

Eligibility

The following items are eligible to be accounted for by ASC 825:
- A recognized financial asset or liability (with certain specified exceptions).
- A firm commitment that would otherwise not be recognized at inception and that involves only financial instruments.
- A written loan commitment.
- The rights and obligations under an insurance contract that is not a financial instrument but whose terms permit the insurer to settle by paying a third party to provide those goods or services.

- The rights and obligations under a warranty that is not a financial instrument but whose terms permit the warrantor to settle by paying a third party to provide those goods or services.
- A host of financial instruments resulting from the separation of an embedded nonfinancial derivative instrument from a nonfinancial hybrid instrument under ASC 815-15-25-1 (ASC 825-10-15-4).

On the other hand, the following are *not* eligible for ASC 825 accounting:

- An investment in a subsidiary that the entity is required to consolidate.
- An interest in a variable interest entity that the entity is required to consolidate.
- Employers' and plans' obligations for pension benefits, other postretirement benefits, postemployment benefits, employee stock options and stock purchase plans, and other forms of deferred compensation.
- Financial assets and financial liabilities recognized under leases.
- Deposit liabilities, withdrawable on demand, of banks, savings and loan associations, credit unions, and other similar depository institutions.
- Financial instruments that, in whole or in part, are classified by the issuer as a component of stockholders' equity (ASC 825-10-15-5).

Election Dates

The choice of whether to elect the fair value option is made on each eligible item's election date, which is when one of the following occurs (ASC 825-10-25-4):

- The entity first recognizes the eligible item.
- The entity enters into an eligible firm commitment.
- Financial assets that have been reported at fair value with unrealized gains and losses included in earnings because of specialized accounting principles cease to qualify for that specialized accounting.
- The accounting treatment for an investment in another entity changes because (1) the investment becomes subject to the equity method of accounting; or (2) the investor ceases to consolidate a subsidiary or variable interest entity but retains an interest.
- An event that requires an eligible item to be measured at fair value at the time of the event but does not require fair value measurement at each subsequent reporting date (excluding the recognition of impairment under lower-of-cost-or-market accounting or other-than-temporary impairment).

Some additional events that require the remeasurement of eligible items at fair value, initial recognition of eligible items, or both, and thereby create an election date for the fair value option are (1) business combinations; (2) consolidation or deconsolidation of a subsidiary or variable interest entity; and (3) significant modifications of debt (ASC 825-10-25-5).

Applying the Fair Value Option

The fair value option may be elected for a single eligible item without electing it for other identical items with the following exceptions:

- If multiple advances are made to one borrower pursuant to a single contract, and the individual advances lose their identity as a part of a larger loan balance, the fair value option must be applied only to the larger balance and not to each advance individually.
- If the fair value option is applied to an investment that would otherwise be accounted for by the equity method, it is applied to all of the investor's financial interests in the same entity that are eligible items.
- If the fair value option is applied to an eligible insurance or reinsurance contract, it shall be applied to all claims and obligations under the contract.
- If the fair value option is elected for an insurance contract for which integrated or unintegrated contract features or coverages are issued, the fair value option must also be applied to those features or coverages (ASC 825-10-25-7).

The fair value option is not required to be applied to all instruments issued or acquired in a single transaction. A financial instrument that is legally a single contract may not be separated into parts for the purposes of applying the fair value option. In contrast, a loan syndication arrangement may result in multiple loans to the same borrower by different lenders, each of which is a separate instrument for which the fair value option may be elected or not elected. An investor in an equity security may elect the fair value option for its entire investment in that security, including any fractional shares issued by the investee (ASC 825-10-25-10, 11-12).

In the statement of financial position, entities shall report assets and liabilities that are presented by the fair value option in a manner that separates those reported fair values from the carrying amounts of similar assets and liabilities measured using another measurement attribute in either of the following ways:

- Present the aggregate of fair value and non-fair-value amounts in the same line item and parenthetically disclose the amount measured at fair value included in that aggregate amount; or
- Present two separate line items to display fair value and non-fair-value carrying amounts (ASC 825-10-45-2).

In the statement of cash flows, receipts and cash payments related to items measured at fair value are classified according to their nature and purpose as required by ASC 230 (Statement of Cash Flows) (ASC 825-10-45-3).

DISCLOSURE OF INFORMATION ABOUT FAIR VALUE OF FINANCIAL INSTRUMENTS

General Disclosure Requirements

ASC 825 includes extensive disclosures in the financial statements. The primary objectives of these disclosures are to facilitate comparisons between (1) entities that choose different measurement attributes for similar assets and liabilities; and (2) assets and liabilities in the financial statements of an entity that selects different measurement attributes for similar assets and liabilities.

As of each date for which a statement of financial position is presented, the following information is required to be disclosed:

1. Management's reason for electing a fair value option for each eligible item or for a group of eligible items

2. If the fair value option is elected for some, but not all, eligible items within a group:

    a. A description of those items and the reason for partial election

    b. Information to enable users to understand how the group of similar items relates to individual line items on the statement of financial position

3. For each line item in the statement of financial position that includes an item or items for which the fair value option has been elected:

    a. Information to enable users to understand how each line item in the statement of financial position relates to major categories of assets and liabilities presented in accordance with the fair value disclosure requirements in ASC 820

    b. The aggregate carrying amount of items included in each line item in the statement of financial position that are not eligible for the fair value option

4. The difference between the aggregate fair value and the aggregate unpaid principal balance of:

    a. Loans and long-term receivables that have contractual principal amounts and for which the fair value option has been elected

    b. Long-term debt instruments that have contractual principal amounts and for which the fair value option has been elected

5. For loans held as assets for which the fair value option has been elected:

    a. The aggregate fair value of loans that are 90 days or more past due

    b. If the entity's policy is to recognize interest income separately from other changes in fair value, the aggregate fair value of loans in nonaccrual status

    c. The difference between the aggregate fair value and the aggregate unpaid principal balance for loans that are 90 days or more past due, in nonaccrual status, or both

6. For investments that would have been accounted for under the equity method if the entity had not chosen the fair value option, the information required by ASC 323-10-50-3 with certain specified exclusions (ASC 825-10-50-28).

For each period for which an interim or annual income statement is presented, the following information is required:

1. For each line item in the statement of financial position, the amounts of gains and losses from fair value changes included in earnings during the period and in which line item in the income statement those items are reported
2. A description of how interest and dividends are measured and where they are reported in the income statement
3. For loans and other receivable held as assets:
    a. The estimated amount of gains or losses included in earnings during the period attributable to changes in instrument-specific credit risk
    b. How the gains or losses attributed to changes in instrument-specific credit risk were determined
4. For liabilities with fair values that have been significantly affected during the reporting period by changes in the instrument-specific credit risk:
    a. The estimated amount of gains and losses from fair value changes included in earnings that are attributed to changes in the instrument-specific credit risk
    b. Qualitative information about the reasons for those changes
    c. How the gains and losses attributed to changes in instrument-specific credit risk were determined (ASC 825-10-50-30).

Other disclosure requirements are as follows:

1. In annual periods only, an entity shall disclose the methods and significant assumptions used to estimate the fair value of items for which the fair value option has been elected.
2. If an entity elects the fair value option at the time of the events described in ASC 825-10-25-4(d) and 4(e) (see explanation below), the following information is required:
    a. Qualitative information about the nature of the event
    b. Quantitative information by line item in the statement of financial position indicating which line items in the income statement include the effect on earnings of initially electing the fair value option for an item (ASC 825-10-50-31, 32).

    ASC 825-10-25-4(d) and 4(e) permit the fair value option to be elected when the accounting treatment of an investment changes because of either of the following: the investment becomes subject to the equity method of accounting; or the investor ceases to consolidate a subsidiary or variable interest entity but retains an interest. ASC 825-10-25-5 also indicates that a business combination, consolidation or deconsolidation of a subsidiary, and significant modifications of debt are options that would trigger this disclosure.
3. An entity shall disclose, either in the body of the financial statements or in the accompanying notes, the fair value of financial instruments for which it is practicable to estimate that value. An entity also shall disclose the method(s) and significant assumptions used to estimate the fair

value of financial instruments. For financial instruments recognized at fair value in the statement of financial position, the disclosure requirements of ASC 820 (Fair Value Measurements and Disclosures) also apply (ASC 825-10-50-10).

OBSERVATION: ASC 825 indicates that fair value information disclosed in the notes shall be presented with the related carrying value in a form that makes it clear whether the fair value and the carrying value represent assets or liabilities and how the carrying amounts relate to information reported in the statement of financial position. If disclosure of fair value information is in more than one note, one of the notes must include a summary table that contains cross-referenced locations(s) of the remaining disclosures (ASC 825-10-50-10, 11, 12).

4. In estimating the fair value of deposit liabilities, a financial entity shall not take into account the value of its long-term relationships with depositors, commonly known as core deposit intangibles, which are separate intangible assets, not financial instruments. For deposit liabilities with no defined maturities, the fair value to be disclosed is the amount payable on demand at the reporting date. An entity is not prohibited from disclosing separately the estimated fair value of any of its nonfinancial intangible and tangible assets and nonfinancial liabilities (ASC 942-470-50-1).

5. For trade receivables and payables, no disclosure is required under ASC 825 when the carrying amount approximates fair value (ASC 310-10-50-26).

6. In disclosing the fair value of a financial instrument, amounts of instruments shall not be netted, even if the instruments are of the same class or otherwise related except as permitted by ASC 210.

7. If it is not practicable for an entity to estimate the fair value of a financial instrument, or a class of financial instruments, the entity shall disclose information pertinent to estimating the fair value, such as the carrying amount, effective interest rate, and maturity, and provide an explanation of why it is not practicable to estimate fair value (ASC 825-10-50-16).

Disclosures about Concentrations of Credit Risk

An entity shall disclose all significant credit risks from all financial instruments. Group concentrations of credit risk exist if a number of counterparties are engaged in similar activities and have similar economic characteristics that would cause their ability to meet contractual obligations to be affected in a similar way by changes in economic or other conditions (ASC 825-10-50-20). Following is information required to be disclosed about each significant concentration of credit risk (ASC 825-10-50-21):

- Information about the shared activity, region, or economic characteristic that identifies the concentration

- The maximum amount of loss due to credit risk (i.e., the loss that would result to parties to the financial instrument if the parties failed completely to perform and any security proved to be of no value)
- The entity's policy of requiring collateral to support financial instruments subject to credit risk, information about the entity's access to the collateral, and the nature and a brief description of collateral
- The entity's policy of entering into master netting arrangements to mitigate credit risk of financial instruments, information about the arrangements for which the entity is a party, and a description of the terms of those agreements.

Encouraged Disclosures about Market Risk of All Financial Instruments

Entities are encouraged, but not required, to disclose quantitative information about the market risks of financial instruments that are consistent with the way it manages or adjusts those risks (ASC 825-10-50-23).

Methods of disclosure are expected to vary among reporting entities. Possible ways of disclosing this information include (ASC 825-10-50-23):

- Details about current positions and activity during the period
- The hypothetical effects on comprehensive income or net income of possible changes in market value
- A gap analysis of interest rate repricing or maturity dates
- The duration of the financial instruments
- The entity's value at risk from derivatives and from other positions at the end of the reporting period and the average value of the risk during the period.

Situations Not Covered by ASC 825

While ASC 825 is intended to require disclosure of fair value information about a wide spectrum of financial instruments, a number of instruments and other items are exempt. These exemptions fall into three categories (ASC 825-10-50-8):

- Items subject to reporting and disclosure requirements of other authoritative pronouncements (e.g., pensions, extinguished debt, insurance contracts other than financial guarantees and investment contracts, leases, and equity method investments). ASC 825 does not change existing disclosure requirements for these items.
- Other items explained in terms of certain definitional problems that the FASB was unable to resolve at the time (e.g., insurance contracts other than those mentioned above, lease contracts, warranty obligations, and unconditional purchase obligations that may have both financial and nonfinancial components). The FASB believes that definitional and valuation difficulties for these contracts and obligations require further consideration before decisions can be made about the appropriateness of fair value disclosure requirements.

- The ASC 825 disclosures are intended to apply only to financial assets and liabilities, thereby excluding items such as noncontrolling interests in consolidated subsidiaries and an entity's own equity instruments included in stockholders' equity.

Applying the Fair Value Option to Not-for-Profit Organizations

The following modifications are required in applying the fair value option to not-for-profit organizations:

1. References throughout ASC 825 to the income statement are replaced with references to the statement of activities, statement of changes in net assets, or statement of operations. Similarly, references to earnings are replaced with references to changes in net assets.
2. Health care organizations subject to the AICPA Audit and Accounting Guide, *Health Care Organizations*, shall report unrealized gains and losses on items for which the fair value option has been elected within the performance indicator or a part of discontinued operations, as appropriate.
3. Certain disclosure requirements (presented in ASC 825-10-50-30) apply not only with respect to the effect on performance indicators or other measures of operations, if presented, but also with respect to the effect on the change in each of the net asset classes (unrestricted, temporarily restricted, and permanently restricted), as appropriate (ASC 825-10-15-7).

Optional Disclosures for Nonpublic Entities

ASC 825 makes the fair value disclosures optional for entities meeting the following criteria (ASC 825-10-50-3):

1. The entity is a nonpublic entity.
2. The entity is small enough that it comes under the size criterion of less than $100 million of total assets on the date of the financial statements.
3. The entity has no instrument that, in whole or in part, is accounted for as a derivative under ASC 815, other than commitments related to the origination of mortgage loans to be held for sale, during the reporting period.

OBSERVATION: Public accountants serving smaller nonpublic entities convinced the FASB that the practicability provisions of ASC 825 were useful in reducing the costs of compliance, but a cost is still incurred simply to document compliance, even if the fair value information is deemed to be not practicable.

The FASB observed that smaller nonpublic entities are less likely than larger entities to engage in complex financial transactions. These smaller entities' financial assets tend to consist of traded securities, investments in other closely held entities, and balances with related parties. Their financial liabilities tend to be trade payables and variable-rate and fixed-rate loans. The FASB also observed that the types of financial instruments commonly held by smaller nonpublic entities, such as trade receivables and payables and variable rate

50,010 ASC 825—Financial Instruments

instruments, already are carried at amounts that approximate fair value, or that information about fair values already is required by other authoritative pronouncements, such as ASC 320 (Investments—Debt and Equity Securities) and ASC 958 (Not-for-Profit Entities). Taken together, these mutually reinforcing observations led the FASB to conclude that the ASC 825 disclosure requirements should be optional for smaller nonpublic companies.

Estimating Fair Value

One of the greatest challenges in applying ASC 825 is estimating the fair value of financial instruments. ASC 825 establishes a framework for measuring fair value and discusses alternative valuation techniques that can be used to measure fair value.

> **PRACTICE POINTER:** An important dimension of ASC 825 is the latitude that entities have in deciding whether applying procedures to measure fair value is "practicable." *Practicable* means that an entity can estimate fair value without incurring excessive costs. It is a dynamic concept—what is practicable in one year may not be in another. Cost considerations are important in judging practicability and may affect the precision of the estimate, leading to determination of fair value for a class of financial instruments, an entire portfolio (rather than individual instruments), or a subset of a portfolio. Whatever is practicable to determine must be disclosed. The burden of this decision rests on the reporting entity and its auditor; if the decision is made that determining fair value is not practicable, reasons for not disclosing the information must be given. The explanation will normally be found in notes to the financial statement (ASC 825-10-50-17).

IMPORTANT NOTICE FOR 2012

As CCH's 2012 *GAAP Guide* goes to press, the FASB has outstanding an Exposure Draft of an Accounting Standards Update (ASU) (Accounting for Financial Instruments and Revisions to the Accounting for Derivative Instruments and Hedging Activities) that may have an important impact on the preparation of financial statements in the future.

This proposed ASU simplifies and improves financial reporting for financial instruments by developing a consistent, comprehensive framework for classifying financial instruments. Under this proposed ASU, most financial instruments would be measured at fair value in the statement of financial position each reporting period, while certain qualifying financial instruments would be measured at amortized cost or at a remeasured value specific to that type of instrument (e.g., core deposit liabilities). The proposed ASU recognizes that for certain financial instruments measured at fair value with qualifying changes in fair value recognized in other comprehensive income, financial statement users may benefit from both fair value and amortized cost information. Therefore, it requires both fair value and amortized cost information for these financial instruments to be presented on the face of financial statements by presenting the amortized cost, any allowance for credit losses on financial assets, any other accumulated amounts needed to reconcile amortized cost to fair value, and fair value. Proposed guidance for additional disclosures related to financial instruments is also included in this proposed ASU.

The proposed ASU removes the existing "probable" threshold for recognizing impairments on loans and proposes a common approach to providing for credit losses on loans and debt instruments. This proposed ASU also provides guidance related to the recognition of interest income on debt instruments that will provide a better reflection of a financial instrument's interest yield. The proposed ASU also makes changes to the requirements to qualify for hedge accounting. The proposed guidance replaces the highly complex, quantitative-based hedging requirements with more qualitative-based assessments that make it easier to qualify for hedge accounting and should result in the economic effects of hedging being reported more consistently over multiple reporting periods. Finally, the proposed ASU provides new guidance regarding the criteria used to determine if an investee should be accounted for under the equity method.

The effective date for this proposed ASU will be determined when the final ASU is issued. However, this proposed ASU does include a deferral provision that will permit nonpublic entities with less than $1 billion in total consolidated assets to defer the adoption of the guidance in this ASU for four years. Earlier adoption of this ASU is prohibited.

PART II: INTERPRETIVE GUIDANCE

ASC 825-10: Overall

ASC 825-10-50-2A through 50-3, 50-8, 50-10 through 50-12; ASC 320-10-35-26; ASC 270-10-50-1(m) Interim Disclosures about Fair Value of Financial Instruments

BACKGROUND

The following was issued to address the concerns of constituents regarding a lack of comparability between the financial statements of entities that report the values of their financial instruments based on different measurement attributes, for example, at fair value or at amortized cost. Although the FASB and the International Accounting Standards Board (IASB) had undertaken a joint project to address the recognition and measurement of financial instruments, the FASB decided that the clarity and quality of financial information in financial statements would be improved if reporting entities disclose the information about fair value more frequently. In addition, the FASB believes that such disclosures about fair value would stimulate the discussion between financial statement users and preparers regarding the current valuations of financial instruments.

This guidance amends the guidance in ASC 825 by requiring that publicly traded companies disclose information about the fair value of financial instruments for interim periods in addition to those in their annual financial statements. The guidance in ASC 270 is also amended to require that the disclosures be made in summarized financial information at interim reporting periods.

ACCOUNTING GUIDANCE

ASC 825—Financial Instruments

Scope

The following guidance applies to all financial instruments under the scope of ASC 825 that are held by publicly traded companies, as defined in ASC 270.

Amendment to Disclosure Requirements of ASC 825 and AS260C

Disclosures about the fair value of a publicly traded company's financial instruments, if it is practicable to estimate that value, should be included in the body and the accompanying notes of an entity's summarized financial information issued for interim periods and its financial statements issued for annual periods.

As required in ASC 825), the disclosures should be made, regardless of whether the financial instruments are recognized in the entity's balance sheet. The manner in which information about the fair value and carrying amount of financial instruments is disclosed in the notes to the financial statements should be unambiguous as to whether the instruments are assets or liabilities and should clarify how the carrying amounts are related to the information reported on the balance sheet.

- The methods and significant assumptions used to estimate the fair value of financial instruments should be disclosed and should describe changes in methods and significant assumptions, if any, made during the period.

ASC 825-10-55-1 through 55-2; ASC 310-10-50-25 Terms of Loan Products That May Give Rise to a Concentration of Credit Risk

BACKGROUND

The following guidance was issued in response to questions from constituents and as a result of discussions with the staff of the SEC and with regulators of financial institutions. Those questions are related to loan products that have contractual terms and features that may cause the originator, holder, investor, guarantor, or servicer of the loan to experience a greater exposure to nonpayment or realization. The following terms or loan features may increase credit risk:

- The ability to defer principal repayment or to make payments that are smaller than interest accrual and result in negative amortization
- High loan-to-value ratio
- Using the same collateral for multiple loans that result in a high loan-to-value ratio when combined
- Adjustable-rate mortgages (option ARMs) under which a borrower may choose to pay a different amount each month for a specified period of the loan term but eventually may be subject to future increases in repayments that exceed increases solely from increased market interest rates—for example, if a loan to reach a maximum limit for accrual of principal because of negative amortization
- A below market interest rate during the initial period of a loan term that may increase significantly thereafter
- Interest-only loans

Information about credit losses on loans that have reduced payment requirements in the early part of the loans' terms may not be known to creditors until a loan's payment terms change. This delays a creditor's ability to determine that a loss accrual should be recognized and a loan loss allowance should be established under the guidance in ASC 450 and ASC 310-10-30-2, 35-13 through 35-14, 35-16 through 35-22, 35-24 through 35-29, 35-32, 35-34, 35-37, 35-39; 45-5 through 45-6; 50-12 through 50-13, 50-15, 50-19; ASC 310-40-35-8 through 35-9, 35-12, 50-2 through 50-3.

Loan products with initial payment requirements for amounts less than or equal to the contractual interest, such as option ARMs, negative amortizing, deferred interest, or interest-only loans, can increase the loan-to-value ratio and reduce a borrower's equity. A borrower's contractually required repayments on such loans may increase in the future as a result of increases in interest rates, a step-up from the initial interest rate, or required amortization of the principal amount. The borrower's ability to repay a loan may be affected by those payment increases and may lead to default and losses. The risk of loss on loans with high loan-to-value ratios that are based on appreciation of the collateral may increase if the expected appreciation does not occur.

The purpose of this guidance is to emphasize the requirement to assess the adequacy of disclosures for secured and unsecured loans and how changes in market and economic conditions affect the adequacy of those disclosures.

ACCOUNTING GUIDANCE

Question 1: Under what circumstances, if any, do the terms of loan products cause a *concentration of credit risk* as the term is used in ASC 825-10-50-2A through 50-3, 50-8 through 50-23, 55-3 through 55-5, 60-1; ASC 942-470-50-1; ASC 310-10-50-26; ASC 958-320-50-4?

Answer: A reporting entity's *concentration of credit risk* may be caused by the terms of certain loan products, either as individual products or as a group of products with similar features. Under the guidance in ASC 958-320-50-4; ASC 825-10-50-20 through 50-21, disclosures are required about each significant concentration, including "information about the (shared) activity, region, or economic characteristic that identifies the concentration." Shared characteristics that may be used to determine significant concentrations may include, but are not limited to:

- Borrowers subject to significant increases in payments
- Loan terms permitting negative amortization
- Loans with high loan-to-value ratios

Judgment should be used in determining whether a loan's terms cause a concentration of credit risk.

Under the guidance in ASC 825-10-50-23, entities are encouraged to disclose "quantitative information about the market risks of financial instruments that is consistent with the way it manages or adjusts those risks." In addition, entities may disclose information about how their underwriting procedures deal with controlling credit risk that may occur as a result of future payment increases on loans.

Question 2: What disclosures or other accounting considerations apply for entities that originate, hold, guarantee, service, or invest in loan products whose terms may give rise to a concentration of credit risk?

Answer: Disclosures in addition to those required in Question 1 should be considered. The type of disclosures and their extent should be influenced by the type of entity making the disclosures and how significant the loan products are to the reporting entity. Under the guidance in ASC 275-10-50-1, disclosure is required about the existence of risks and uncertainties as of the date of the financial statements in the following areas:

- Nature of operations
- Estimates used in preparing the financial statements
- Certain significant estimates
- Current exposure as a result of certain concentrations

The contractual terms of certain loan products cause entities to be vulnerable to risks and uncertainties in one or more of those areas. Under the guidance in ASC 275-10-50-18, revenue concentrations from particular products should be disclosed. Disclosure of other concentrations is required if they meet the following requirements in ASC 275-20-50-16:

- A concentration that exists at the date of the financial statements
- The entity is exposed to the risk of a near-term severe impact as a result of that concentration
- There is at least a reasonable possibility that the events that could cause the severe impact will occur in the near term

Disclosure about a possible change in estimate is required under ASC 275-10-50-8 if information available before the issuance of financial statements suggests both that "it is at least reasonably possible that the estimate of the effect on the financial statements of a condition, situation, or set of circumstances that existed at the date of the financial statements will change in the near term because of one or more future confirming events" and "the effect of the change would be material to the financial statements."

If significant, noncash interest income recognized as a result of negative amortization that is added to the principal balance of an outstanding loan before it is received in cash should be included in the reconciliation of an entity's net income to net cash flows from operating activities under the provisions of ASC 230.

An entity should consider whether the principal risk characteristics of a recognized servicing asset related to loan products with terms that may cause a concentration of credit risk would result in a separate stratum when impairment is determined. Disclosure of the risk characteristics used to stratify recognized servicing assets for the measurement of impairment is required under the provisions of ASC 860, as amended by ASC 860-10-40-5 through 40-6A. Originators and servicers that have provided guarantees on those loan products also should consider the specific risk characteristics when they estimate the guarantees' fair value. Each product's characteristics should be considered when estimating the fair value of loan products than an entity classifies a held for sale and when fair value is determined for the disclosures required under ASC 825-10-50-2A through 50-3, 50-8 through 50-23, 55-3 through 55-5, 60-1; ASC 942-470-50-1; ASC 310-10-50-26, ASC 958-320-50-4.

Entities are reminded that interest income must be recognized by the interest method as discussed in ASC 310. If, during the term of a loan, the loan's stated interest rate increases so that interest accrued under the interest method in early periods would exceed interest at the stated rate, interest income should *not* be recognized if the net investment in the loan would increase to such an extent that it would exceed the amount at which the borrower could settle the obligation. The guidance in ASC 310-20-35-18 and the related implementation guidance should be applied if interest income is recognized on loans with interest rates that increase during the term of the loan, such as loans with a reduced initial interest rate.

SEC Rules and Regulations, such as Item 303 of Regulation S-K (Management's Discussion and Analysis of Financial Conditions and Results of Operations), may require public entities to make additional disclosures. Additional disclosures also may be required of banks and bank holding companies that are subject to the requirements of SEC Regulation S-X, rule 9-03, and SEC Industry Guide 3.

ASC 825-20: Registration Payment Arrangements

ASC 825-20-05-1 15-1 through 15-5, 25-2 through 25-3, 30-1, 30-4 through 30-5, 35-1, 50-1 through 50-2, 55-2 through 55-8, 55-10 through 55-14; ASC 815-10-25-16; ASC 815-40-25-21, 25-43; ASC 470-20-30-23 Accounting for Registration Payment Arrangements

BACKGROUND

An entity may issue equity shares, warrants, or debt instruments that are conditional on a *registration payment arrangement,* which has the following characteristics:

- The agreement states that the issuer agrees to try to use its "best efforts" or apply "commercially reasonable efforts" to (*a*) file a registration statement for the resale of specified financial instruments or equity shares that will be issued when specified financial instruments are exercised or converted and to have the Securities and Exchange Commission (SEC) or another securities regulator (if the registration statement is filed in a foreign jurisdiction) declare the registration statement effective within a specified grace period, and (*b*) to maintain the registration statement's effectiveness for a specified time period or indefinitely.

- The issuer must transfer consideration, which may be significant, to the counterparty if the issuer fails to take those actions within the grace period or the registration statement's effectiveness is not maintained. The consideration may be required to be transferred in a lump sum of cash or in periodic cash payments, equity instruments, or as adjustments to the financial instrument conditional to the registration payment arrangement.

This guidance addresses the accounting under such arrangements for financial instruments that are accounted for under the guidance in ASC 460-10-60-14; ASC 480-10-55-63; ASC 505-10-60-5; ASC 815-10-15-78, 55-52; ASC 815-15-25-15; 40-05-1 through 05-4, 05-10 through 05-11,05-12, 25-1 through 25-5, 25-7 through 25-20, 25-22 through 25-24, 25-26 through 25-35; 25-37 through 25-40, 30-1, 35-1 through 35-2, 35-6, 35-8 through 35-13, 40-1, 40-2, 50-1 through 50-5, 55-1 through 55-18.

ACCOUNTING GUIDANCE

The following guidance applies to:

- Issuers' accounting for registration payment arrangements having the characteristics discussed in the Overview, regardless of whether the arrangement is included as a provision of a financial instrument or other agreement or is issued as a separate agreement.
- Arrangements under which an issuer is required to obtain or maintain a listing on a stock exchange, instead of, or in addition to, obtaining or maintaining an effective registration statement, as long as the registration payment arrangement has the characteristics discussed in the Overview.

This guidance does *not* apply to:

- Contracts that are *not* registration payment arrangements that have the characteristics discussed in the Overview, such as a building contract with a provision that requires a contractor to obtain a certificate of occupancy by a specific date or pay a penalty every month until it is obtained.
- Arrangements requiring registration or listing of convertible debt instruments or convertible preferred stock if the form of consideration that would be transferred to a counterparty is an adjustment to the conversion ratio. (See ASC 470-20-05-7 through 05-08, 25-4 through 25-5; 30-3, 30-6, 30-8, 30-10, 30-15; 35-2 through 35-3, 35-7, 40-2 through 40-3, 55-30 through 55-33, 55-35 through 55-38, 55-45 through 55-48, 55-50 through 55-52, 55-54 through 55-54A, 55-56 through 55-58, 55-60 through 55-60A, 55-62 through 55-66, 55-69; ASC 505-10-50-8 ("Accounting for Convertible Securities with Beneficial Conversion Features or Contingently Adjustable Conversion Ratios") and ASC 260-10-50-1; ASC 470-20-25-8, 25-9, 25-20, 30-1, 30-5, 30-7, 30-9 through 30-10, 30-12 through 30-13, 30-16 through 30-21, 35-1, 35-4, 35-7 through 35-10, 40-1, 40-4, 45-1, 55-11 through 55-12, 55-14 through 55-17, 55-19 through 55-21, 55-23 through 55-24, 55-26 through 55-27; ASC 505-10-50-7 (for accounting guidance.)
- Arrangements in which an observable market, other than the market for the issuer's stock, or an observable index must be consulted to determine the amount of consideration that should be transferred to a counterparty, for example, if consideration transferred to a counterparty when an issuer cannot obtain an effective registration statement is determined based on the price of a commodity.

- Arrangements in which the financial instrument or instruments conditional on the registration payment arrangement are settled when consideration is transferred, for example, if a warrant can be put to the issuer when an effective registration statement is not declared within the grace period for the resale of equity shares that would be issued when the warrant is exercised.

Recognition and Measurement

The following recognition and measurement guidance is provided:

- A contingent obligation to make future payments or to transfer consideration in another manner under a registration payment arrangement should be recognized and measured *separately* in accordance with the guidance in ASC 450 and ASC 450-20.

- A financial instrument conditional on a registration payment arrangement should be recognized and measured in accordance with other guidance in generally accepted accounting principles, such as ASC 835-30, ASC 815, and ASC 825-20-05-1, 15-1 through 15-5, 25-2 through 25-3, 30-1, 30-4 through 30-5, 35-1, 50-1 through 50-2, 55-2 through 55-8, 55-10 through 55-14; ASC 815-10-25-16; ASC 815-40-25-21, 25-43; ASC 470-20-30-23 without considering the contingent obligation to transfer consideration under a registration payment arrangement. In other words, the registration payment arrangement should be recognized and measured separately from the financial instrument conditional on the arrangement.

- A contingent liability under a registration payment arrangement should be included in the allocation of proceeds for a related financing transaction in accordance with the measurement guidance in ASC 450 if it is *probable* that consideration under a registration payment arrangement will be transferred. The guidance in other applicable GAAP should be applied to allocate the remaining proceeds to financial instruments issued along with the registration payment arrangement. For example, after a liability for a registration payment arrangement has been recognized and measured under the guidance in ASC 450, the remaining proceeds of a debt instrument and a warrant classified as equity that are issued along with the registration payment arrangement would be allocated based on their relative fair values of the debt and the warrant under the guidance in ASC 470-20-25-2, 25-3. Under this allocation method, a financial instrument issued along with a registration payment arrangement might initially be measured at a discount to its principal amount. To determine whether a convertible instrument includes a beneficial conversion feature under the guidance in ASC 470-20-05-7 through 05-08, 25-4 through 25-5, 30-3, 30-6, 30-8, 30-10, 30-15, 35-2 through 35-3, 35-7, 40-2 through 40-3, 55-30 through 55-33, 55-35 through 55-38, 55-45-through 55-48, 55-50 through 55-52, 55-54 through 55-54A, 55-56 through 55-58, 55-60 through 55-60A, 55-62 through 55-66, 55-69; ASC 505-10-50-8 and ASC 260-10-50-1; ASC 470-20-25-8 through 25-9, 25-20, 30-1, 30-5, 30-7, 30-9, through 30-10, 30-12 through 30-13, 30-16 through 30-21, 35-1, 35-4, 35-7 through 35-10, 40-1, 40-4, 45-1, 55-11 through 55-12, 55-14 through 55-17, 55-19 through 55-21,

50,018 ASC 825—Financial Instruments

55-23 through 55-24, 55-26 through 55-27; ASC 505-10-50-7, an entity should use the effective conversion price based on the proceeds allocated to the convertible instrument to calculate the embedded conversion option's intrinsic value, if any.

- If it becomes probable that consideration will be transferred under a registration payment arrangement or if the amount of a previously recognized contingent liability increases or decreases in a subsequent period, the initial recognition of the contingent liability or the change in the amount of a previously recognized contingent liability should be recognized as income.
- An issuer's share price at the reporting date should be used to measure a contingent liability under ASC 450, if:
  - The entity would be required to deliver shares under a registration payment arrangement,
  - It is probable that consideration will be transferred, and
  - It is possible to reasonably estimate the number of shares that will be delivered.

DISCLOSURES

In addition to the required disclosures under other applicable GAAP, an issuer of a registration payment arrangement is required to disclose the following information about each registration payment arrangement or each group of similar arrangements, even if there is only a *remote* likelihood that the issuer will be required to transfer consideration under an arrangement:

- The features of a registration payment arrangement, including its term, the financial instrument conditional on the arrangement, and the events or circumstances under which an issuer would be required to transfer consideration.
- Settlement alternatives, if any, stated in a registration payment arrangement, including the party controlling the settlement alternatives.
- The maximum potential undiscounted amount of consideration that an issuer would be required to transfer under a registration payment arrangement, including the maximum number of shares that may be required to be issued or, if applicable, that the potential amount of the consideration to be transferred is *unlimited*.
- The current carrying amount of an issuer's liability under a registration payment arrangement and the income statement classification of gains or losses, if any, as a result of changes in that liability's carrying amount.

AMENDMENTS TO OTHER PRONOUNCEMENTS

This following guidance is amended:

- ASC 815-10-15-82. The following guidance has been added:

  Registration payment arrangements. Registration payment arrangements within the scope of are not subject to the requirements of this Statement. The exception in this subparagraph applies to both (a) the issuer that accounts for the arrangement pursuant to the guidance in ASC 825-20-05-1 15-1 through 15-5, 25-2 through 25-3, 30-1, 30-4 through 30-5, 35-1, 50-1 through 50-2, 55-2 through 55-8, 55-10 through 55-14; ASC 815-10-25-16; ASC 815-40-25-21, 25-43; ASC 470-20-30-23 and (b) the counterparty.

- ASC 480-10-15-7 the following guidance has been added:

  This Statement does not apply to registration payment arrangements within the scope of ASC 825-20-05-1 15-1 through 15-5, 25-2 through 25-3, 30-1, 30-4 through 30-5, 35-1, 50-1 through 50-2, 55-2 through 55-8, 55-10 through 55-14; ASC 815-10-25-16; ASC 815-40-25-21, 25-43; ASC 470-20-30-23.

- ASC 460-10-15-7 The following guidance has been added: A registration payment arrangement within the scope of the guidance in ASC 825-20-05-1 15-1 through 15-5, 25-2 through 25-3, 30-1, 30-4 through 30-5, 35-1, 50-1 through 50-2, 55-2 through 55-8, 55-10 through 55-14; ASC 815-10-25-16; ASC 815-40-25-21, 25-43; ASC 470-20-30-23.

CHAPTER 51
ASC 830—FOREIGN CURRENCY MATTERS

CONTENTS

Part I: General Guidance	51,002
Overview	51,002
Background	51,002
ASC 830-10: Overall	51,004
Translation Objectives	51,004
Functional Currency	51,004
Cash Flow Indicators	51,005
Sales Price Indicators	51,005
Sales Market Indicators	51,006
Expense Indicators	51,006
Financing Indicators	51,006
Intercompany Transactions	51,006
Remeasuring Financial Statements to the Functional Currency	51,007
Translation of Foreign Operations—Highly Inflationary Economies	51,009
ASC 830-20: Foreign Currency Transactions	51,010
Foreign Currency Transactions	51,010
Illustration of Foreign Currency Transaction	51,010
Deferred Foreign Currency Transactions	51,011
Deferred Taxes	51,012
Foreign Currency Transaction Disclosures	51,013
ASC 830-30: Translation of Financial Statements	51,013
Translation of Foreign Currency Statements	51,013
Illustration of Foreign Currency Translation When Euro Is Functional Currency	51,015
Illustration of Foreign Currency Translation When U.S. Dollar Is Functional Currency	51,015
Realization of Separate Component of Stockholders' Equity	51,016
Elimination of Intercompany Profits	51,016
Exchange Rates	51,016
Financial Statement Translation Disclosures	51,017
Illustration of How an Enterprise Determines the Beginning Balance of the Separate Component of Stockholders' Equity	51,017
Part II: Interpretive Guidance	51,017
ASC 830-10: Overall	51,017
ASC 830-10-45-1 through 45-5, 55-13 through 55-14	
Accounting for a Change in Functional Currency When an Economy Ceases to Be Considered Highly Inflationary	51,017
ASC 830-10-45-10, 45-16	

51,002   ASC 830—Foreign Currency Matters

Accounting for a Change in Functional Currency and Deferred Taxes When an Economy Becomes Highly Inflationary	51,020
ASC 830-10-45-12; 55-24 through 55-26	
Determining a Highly Inflationary Economy under ASC 830	51,020
ASC 830-20: Foreign Currency Transactions	51,021
ASC 320-10-35-36 through 35-37; 830-20-35-6 through 35-7	
Accounting for the Effects of Changes in Foreign Currency Exchange Rates on Foreign-Currency-Denominated Available-for-Sale Debt Securities	51,021
ASC 830-20-55-1 through 55-3	
Foreign Debt-for-Equity Swaps	51,022
ASC 830-30: Translation of Financial Statements	51,024
ASC 830-30-45-13 through 45-15	
Application of ASC 830 to an Investment Being Evaluated for Impairment That Will Be Disposed Of	51,024
ASC 830-30-55-1	
Foreign Currency Translation—Selection of Exchange Rate When Trading Is Temporarily Suspended	51,025
ASC 830-740: Income Taxes	51,025
ASC 830-740-25-4 through 25-5. 30-1 through 30-,2, 55-1 through 55-3	
Application of ASC 740 in Foreign Financial Statements Restated for General Price-Level Changes	51,025
ASC 830-740-25-6 through 25-8; 740-30-25-17	
Application of ASC 740 to Basis Differences within Foreign Subsidiaries That Meet the Indefinite Reversal Criterion of ASC 740-30	51,027

PART I: GENERAL GUIDANCE

OVERVIEW

There are two primary areas in accounting for foreign operations:

1. Translation of foreign currency financial statements for purposes of consolidation, combination, or reporting on the equity method (one-line consolidation)
2. Accounting and reporting of foreign currency transactions, including forward exchange contracts

BACKGROUND

Business transactions and foreign operations that are recorded in a foreign currency must be restated in U.S. dollars in accordance with generally accepted accounting principles.

Transactions occur at various dates and exchange rates tend to fluctuate considerably. Before an attempt is made to translate the records of a foreign operation, the records should be in conformity with GAAP. In addition, if the foreign statements have any accounts stated in a currency other than their own, they must be converted into the foreign statement's currency before translation into U.S. dollars or any other reporting currency.

A brief summary of ASC 830 follows:
- Foreign currency financial statements must be in conformity with GAAP before they are translated.
- Assets, liabilities, and operations of an entity must be expressed in the functional currency of the entity. The functional currency of an entity is the currency of the primary economic environment in which the entity operates.
- The current rate of exchange is used to translate the assets and liabilities of a foreign entity from its functional currency into the reporting currency.
  — The weighted-average exchange rate for the period is used to translate revenue, expenses, and gains and losses of a foreign entity from its functional currency to the reporting currency.
  — The current rate of exchange is used to translate changes in financial position other than those items found in the income statement, which are translated at the weighted average exchange rate for the period.
- Gain or loss on the translation of foreign currency financial statements is not recognized in current net income but is reported as a separate component of stockholders' equity. If remeasurement from the recording currency to the functional currency is necessary prior to translation, however, gain or loss on remeasurement is recognized in current net income.
- The amounts accumulated in the separate component of stockholders' equity are realized on the sale or substantially complete liquidation of the investment in the foreign entity.
- The financial statements of a foreign entity in a country that has had cumulative inflation of approximately 100% or more over a three-year period (highly inflationary) must be remeasured into the functional currency of the reporting entity.
- A foreign currency transaction is one that requires settlement in a currency other than the functional currency of the reporting entity.
- Gains or losses from foreign currency transactions are recognized in current net income, except for:
  — Gain or loss on a designated and effective economic hedge of a net investment in a foreign entity
  — Gain or loss on certain long-term intercompany foreign currency transactions
  — Gain or loss on a designated and effective economic hedge of a firm, identifiable, foreign currency commitment that meets certain conditions
- Taxable foreign exchange gains or losses that do not appear in the same period in taxable income and either (*a*) financial accounting income (books) or (*b*) a separate component of stockholders' equity (books) are temporary differences for which deferred taxes must be provided in accordance with existing GAAP.
- Certain specific disclosures are required by ASC 830.

> **OBSERVATION:** ASC 815 (Derivatives and Hedging) addresses accounting for freestanding foreign currency derivatives and certain foreign currency derivatives embedded in other instruments. ASC 830 does not address accounting for derivative instruments.

ASC 830-10: OVERALL

TRANSLATION OBJECTIVES

ASC 830 establishes accounting and reporting standards for (*a*) foreign currency transactions and (*b*) translation of foreign currency financial statements that are included by consolidation, combination, or the equity method in a parent company's financial statements. Foreign financial statements must conform to U.S. generally accepted accounting principles before they can be translated into dollars (ASC 830-10-10-1). Translation of financial statements for any other purpose is beyond the scope of ASC 830 (ASC 830-10-15-3).

> **OBSERVATION:** If the functional currency of a foreign operation is the same as that of its parent, there is no need for translation. A translation adjustment occurs only if the foreign operation's functional currency is a functional currency different from that of its parent.

An important objective in translating foreign currency is to preserve the financial results and relationships that are expressed in the foreign currency. This is accomplished by using the *functional currency* of the foreign entity. The functional currency is then translated into the *reporting currency* of the reporting entity. ASC 830 assumes that the reporting currency for an enterprise is U.S. dollars. The reporting currency may be a currency other than U.S. dollars, however.

> **OBSERVATION:** The ultimate objective of translating foreign transactions and financial statements is to produce the same results that each individual underlying transaction would have produced on the date it occurred, if it had then been recorded in the reporting currency.

FUNCTIONAL CURRENCY

ASC 830 requires that the assets, liabilities, and operations of an entity be measured in terms of the functional currency of that entity. The functional currency is the currency of the primary economic environment in which an entity generates and expends cash. The functional currency generally is the currency of the country in which the entity is located (ASC 830-10-45-2).

> **OBSERVATION:** In some instances, two levels of translation are required. For example, if a foreign entity's books of record are kept in Euros and the

functional currency is the British pound, the books of record are remeasured into British pounds before the financial statements are translated into the currency of the reporting entity. Any translation gain or loss from Euros to British pounds is included in the remeasured net income. If the functional currency of the foreign entity is the Euro, only translation to the reporting currency is necessary. If the functional currency of the foreign entity is that of the reporting entity, only remeasurement from Euros to the reporting currency is required.

For the purposes of determining functional currency under ASC 830, foreign operations may be separated into two models. The first model is the self-contained foreign operation, located in a particular country, whose daily operations are not dependent on the economic environment of the parent's functional currency. This type of foreign operation primarily generates and expends local currency; the net cash flows that it produces in local currency may be reinvested, or converted and distributed to its parent company. The functional currency for this type of foreign operation is its local (domestic) currency.

The second model of foreign operation usually is a direct and integral component or extension of the parent company's operation. Financing usually is in U.S. dollars and frequently is supplied by the parent. The purchase and sale of assets usually are made in U.S. dollars. In other words, the daily operations of this type of foreign operation are dependent on the economic environment of the parent's currency. In addition, the changes in the foreign operation's individual assets and liabilities directly affect the cash flow of the parent company. The functional currency for this type of foreign operation is the U.S. dollar.

In the event that the facts in a given situation do not clearly identify the functional currency, the determination rests on the judgment of management. The FASB has developed guidelines based on certain indicators discussed below that should be considered in determining the functional currency of a foreign operation (ASC 830-10-55-5).

Cash Flow Indicators

The foreign operation's cash flows are mostly in foreign currency that does not directly affect the parent company's cash flows. Under these circumstances, the functional currency is the local currency.

The foreign operation's cash flows directly affect the parent company's cash flows on a current basis and usually are available for remittance through intercompany account settlement. Under these circumstances, the functional currency is the parent company's currency.

Sales Price Indicators

The foreign operation's sales prices for its products are primarily determined (on a short-term basis) by local competition or local government regulation, and not by exchange rate changes. Under these circumstances, the functional currency is the local currency.

The foreign operation's sales prices for its products are mostly responsive (on a short-term basis) to exchange rate changes, such as worldwide competition and prices. Under these circumstances, the functional currency is the parent company's currency.

Sales Market Indicators

The foreign operation has an active local sales market for its products, although there also may be significant amounts of exports. Under these circumstances, the functional currency is the local currency.

The foreign operation's sales market is mostly in the parent's country, or sales contracts are mostly made in the parent company's currency. Under these circumstances, the functional currency is the parent company's currency.

Expense Indicators

The foreign operation's costs of production (e.g., labor or material) or service are mostly local costs, although there also may be imports from other countries. Under these circumstances, the functional currency is the local currency.

The foreign operation's costs of production or service, on a continuing basis, are primarily costs for components obtained from the parent's country. Under these circumstances, the functional currency is the parent company's currency.

Financing Indicators

Financing for the foreign operation is in local currency, and funds generated by the foreign operation are sufficient to service debt obligations. Under these circumstances, the functional currency is the local currency.

Financing for the foreign operation is provided by the parent company or is obtained in U.S. dollars. Funds generated by the foreign operation are insufficient to service its debt. Under these circumstances, the functional currency is the parent company's currency.

Intercompany Transactions

There is little interrelationship between the operations of the foreign entity and the parent company, except for competitive advantages, such as trademarks, patents, etc. Intercompany transactions are of a low volume. Under these circumstances, the functional currency is the local currency.

There is an extensive interrelationship between the operations of the foreign entity and the parent company. Intercompany transactions are numerous. Under these circumstances, the functional currency is the parent company's currency.

The functional currency of a foreign entity must be used consistently from one fiscal year to another, unless significant changes in economic facts and circumstances dictate a change (ASC 830-10-45-7).

> **PRACTICE POINTER:** Once an entity determines its functional currency, the entity should not change that determination unless significant changes in economic facts and circumstances indicate that the functional currency has changed. If there is a change in the functional currency of a foreign entity, that

change is accounted for as a change in accounting estimate. Thus, the change is accounted for in the period of the change and/or future periods (prospectively).

If a change in functional currency occurs, do not remove the translation adjustments for prior periods from the separate component of stockholders' equity. Thus, the translated amounts of nonmonetary assets at the end of the period prior to the change in functional currency become the accounting basis for subsequent periods (ASC 830-10-45-10).

REMEASURING FINANCIAL STATEMENTS TO THE FUNCTIONAL CURRENCY

The following is a brief review of the translation provisions of ASC 830 for the remeasurement process from the recording currency to the functional currency, prior to translation from the functional currency to the reporting currency. (For further explanation, see the observation under the "Functional Currency" section, above.)

Two categories of exchange rates are used in remeasuring financial statements. Historical exchange rates are those that existed at the time of the transaction, and the current exchange rate is the rate that is current at the date of remeasurement.

Monetary assets and liabilities are those that are fixed in amount, such as cash, accounts receivable, and most liabilities. Monetary assets and liabilities are translated at the current rate of exchange. All other assets, liabilities, and stockholders' equity are remeasured by reference to the following four money price exchanges based on the type of market and time:

1. *Past purchase exchange*—the historical or acquisition cost, because it is based on the actual past purchase price
2. *Current purchase exchange*—the replacement cost, because it is measured by the current purchase price of a similar resource
3. *Current sale exchange*—the market price, because it is based on the current selling price of the resource
4. *Future exchange*—the present value of future net money receipts, discounted cash flow, or the discounted net realizable value, because it is based on a future resource

All other assets, liabilities, and stockholders' equity are remeasured based on the four money price exchanges, as follows:

- Accounts based on past purchase exchanges (historical or acquisition cost) are remeasured at historical exchange rates.
- Accounts based on current purchase, current sale, and future exchanges are remeasured at the current exchange rate.

Revenue and expense transactions are remeasured at the average exchange rate for the period, except those expenses related to assets and liabilities, which are remeasured at historical exchange rates. For example, depreciation and amortization are remeasured at historical exchange rates, the rate that existed at the time the underlying related asset was acquired.

51,008 ASC 830—Foreign Currency Matters

The following is a list of assets, liabilities, and stockholders' equity items and their corresponding remeasurement rates under per ASC 830:

	Remeasurement Rates	
	Current	Historical
Cash (in almost all forms)	X	
Marketable securities—at cost		X
Marketable securities—at market	X	
Accounts and notes receivable	X	
Allowance for receivables	X	
Inventories—at cost		X
Inventories—at market, net realizable value, selling price	X	
Inventories—under fixed contract price	X	
Prepaid expenses		X
Refundable deposits	X	
Advances to subsidiaries	X	
Fixed assets		X
Accumulated depreciation		X
Cash surrender value—life insurance	X	
Intangible assets (all)		X
Accounts and notes payable	X	
Accrued expenses	X	
Accrued losses on firm commitments	X	
Taxes payable	X	
All long-term liabilities	X	
Unamortized premium or discount on long-term liabilities	X	
Obligations under warranties		X
Deferred income		X
Capital stock		X
Retained earnings		X
Noncontrolling interests		X

Revenue and expenses not related to any balance sheet items are remeasured at the average currency exchange rate for the period. The average may be based on a daily, weekly, monthly, or quarterly basis or on the weighted-average rate for the period, which will probably result in a more meaningful conversion. Revenue and expense items that are related to a balance sheet account, such as deferred income, depreciation, and beginning and ending inventories, are remeasured at the same exchange rate as the related balance sheet item.

In remeasuring the lower-of-cost-or-market rule, the remeasured historical cost is compared to the remeasured market, and whichever is lower in functional currency is used. This may require a write-down in the functional currency from cost to market, which was not required in the foreign currency financial statements. On the other hand, if market was used on the foreign statements and in remeasuring to the functional currency market exceeds historical cost, the write-down to market on the foreign statements will have to be reversed before remeasuring, which would then be done at the historical rate. Once inventory has been written down to market in remeasured functional currency statements, the resulting carrying amount is used in future translations until the inventory is sold or a further write-down is necessary. This same procedure is used for assets, other than inventory, that may have to be written down from historical cost.

> **OBSERVATION:** The reason for the above procedure in applying the lower-of-cost-or-market rule in remeasuring foreign financial statements is that exchange gains and losses are a consequence of remeasurement and not of applying the lower-of-cost-or-market rule. This means that remeasured market is equal to replacement cost (market) in the foreign currency remeasured at the current exchange rate, except that:
>
> - Remeasured market cannot exceed net realizable value in foreign currency translated at the current exchange rate.
> - Remeasured market cannot be less than (1) above, reduced by an approximate normal profit translated at the current exchange rate.

For remeasurement purposes, the current exchange rate is the one in effect as of the balance sheet date of the foreign statements. Therefore, if the parent company's financial statements are at a date different from the date(s) of its foreign operation(s), the exchange rate in effect at the date of the foreign subsidiary's balance sheet is used for remeasurement and translation purposes.

Any translation adjustment arising from the remeasurement process is included in remeasured net income. In other words, any gain or loss resulting from the remeasurement process that is required by ASC 830 is included in net income in the remeasured financial statements (ASC 830-10-45-17).

After the foreign entity's financial statements are remeasured in the functional currency, they are ready for translation. If the functional currency of a foreign entity is the U.S dollar and the reporting currency of the parent is also the U.S. dollar, there will be no translation adjustment.

TRANSLATION OF FOREIGN OPERATIONS—HIGHLY INFLATIONARY ECONOMIES

ASC 830 defines a highly inflationary economy as one in which the cumulative inflation over a three-year consecutive period approximates 100%. In other words, the inflation rate in an economy must be rising at the rate of about 30 to 35% per year for three consecutive years to be classified as highly inflationary.

For the purposes of ASC 830, a foreign entity in a highly inflationary economy does not have a functional currency. The functional currency of the reporting entity is used as the functional currency of the foreign entity in a highly inflationary economy. Thus, the financial statements for a foreign entity in a highly inflationary economy are remeasured into the functional currency of the reporting entity. The remeasurement process required by ASC 830 is the same as that required for a foreign entity's financial statements that are not expressed in the functional currency (ASC 830-10-45-11).

> **OBSERVATION:** Apparently, exchange adjustments resulting from the remeasurement process for foreign entities in highly inflationary economies are included in the determination of remeasured net income, rather than reported as a separate component of stockholders' equity.

The International Monetary Fund (IMF) publishes monthly statistics on international inflation rates. After the financial statements of a foreign entity in a highly inflationary economy are expressed in the functional currency of the reporting entity, they are ready for translation. Since the financial statements are now expressed in the reporting currency, however, there will be no translation adjustment.

ASC 830-20: FOREIGN CURRENCY TRANSACTIONS

FOREIGN CURRENCY TRANSACTIONS

A foreign currency transaction is one that requires settlement in a currency other than the functional currency of the reporting entity. Generally, gains and losses on foreign currency transactions are recognized in current net income (ASC 830-20-40-1). The following transactions, however, may require different treatment:

- Gain or loss resulting from a foreign currency transaction that is designated as an economic hedge of a net investment in a foreign entity
- Gain or loss resulting from intercompany foreign currency transactions of a capital nature or long-term financing nature, between an investor and investee where the investee entity is consolidated, combined, or accounted for by the equity method by the investor
- Forward exchange contracts

If the exchange rate changes between the time a purchase or sale is contracted for and the time actual payment is made, a foreign exchange gain or loss results.

Illustration of Foreign Currency Transaction

Alex Co. purchased goods for 100,000 pesos when the exchange rate was 10 pesos to a dollar. The journal entry in dollars is:

Purchases	10,000	
Accounts payable		10,000

Assuming that when the goods are paid for, the exchange rate is 12:1, the journal entry in dollars is:

Accounts payable	10,000	
Cash		8,333
Foreign exchange gain		1,667

At a 12:1 exchange rate, the $8,333 can purchase 100,000 pesos. The difference between the $8,333 and the original recorded liability of $10,000 is a foreign exchange gain. If payment is made when the exchange rate is less than 10 pesos to a dollar, a foreign exchange loss would result.

For example, if the exchange rate when the payment is made in only eight pesos to one dollar, a loss of $2,500 would result because $12,500 would be required to satisfy the payable of 100,000 pesos. In this case, the entry to record the payment would be:

Accounts payable	10,000	
Foreign exchange loss	2,500	
Cash		12,500

A foreign exchange gain or loss is computed at each balance sheet date on all recorded foreign transactions that have not been settled. The difference between the exchange rate that could have been used to settle the transaction at the date it occurred, and the exchange rate that can be used to settle the transaction at a subsequent balance sheet date, is the gain or loss recognized in current net income. Generally, the current exchange rate is the rate that is used to settle a transaction on the date it occurs, or on a subsequent balance sheet date (ASC 830-20-25-1).

Deferred Foreign Currency Transactions

Certain gains and losses on forward exchange contracts and certain types of foreign currency transactions are not included in current net income but are either (*a*) reported in the separate component of stockholders' equity, along with translation adjustments, or (*b*) included in the overall gain or loss of the related foreign currency transaction. These deferred gains and losses may be classified as follows (ASC 830-20-35-3):

- Gain or loss on a designated and effective economic hedge of a net investment in a foreign entity
- Gain or loss on certain long-term intercompany foreign currency transactions
- Gain or loss on a designated and effective economic hedge of a firm, identifiable, foreign currency commitment

The accounting required by ASC 830 commences with the designation date of the transaction (ASC 830-20-35-3).

OBSERVATION: As an example of a foreign currency transaction intended to be an economic hedge of a net investment in a foreign entity, take the case of a U.S. parent company with a net investment in a Greek subsidiary that borrows Greek currency in the amount of its net investment in the Greek subsidiary.

The U.S. company designates the loan as an economic hedge of its net investment in the Greek subsidiary. In other words, the U.S. parent computes its net investment in the foreign currency of its foreign subsidiary and then borrows the same amount of foreign currency as the amount of its net investment. In this event, if the net investment in the foreign subsidiary declines because of a change in exchange rates, the change is made up in the foreign currency loan. The U.S. company can buy a larger amount of the subsidiary's foreign currency with fewer U.S. dollars. When the net investment in the foreign subsidiary and the loan in the foreign currency of the foreign subsidiary are both translated into U.S. dollars, the change in the net investment in the foreign subsidiary (an asset) should be approximately equal to the change in the foreign currency loan, except for taxes, if any. Thus, the foreign currency loan acts as a hedge against any increase or decrease in the net foreign investment that is attributable to a change in the exchange rate.

ASC 830 requires that both translated amounts be recorded and reported in a separate component of stockholders' equity. If the translated amount of the foreign currency loan (after taxes, if any) exceeds the translated amount of the net investment in the foreign subsidiary that was hedged, however, the gain or loss that is allocable to the excess must be included in net income, and not recorded and reported as a separate component of stockholders' equity.

Gains or losses on intercompany foreign currency transactions of a capital or long-term nature are not included in current net income, but are reported in the separate component of stockholders' equity, along with translation adjustments. The entities involved in the intercompany foreign currency transactions reported in this manner must be consolidated, combined, or accounted for by the equity method. Gain or loss on intercompany foreign currency transactions that are not of a permanent nature are included in net income (ASC 830-20-35-3).

Accounting for a gain or loss on a foreign currency transaction that is intended to hedge an identifiable foreign currency commitment is addressed by ASC 815 (Derivative and Hedging). An example is an agreement to purchase or sell equipment.

Deferred Taxes

ASC 830 requires that deferred taxes be recognized on taxable foreign currency transactions and taxable translation adjustments of foreign currency financial statements, regardless of whether the exchange gain or loss is charged to current net income or recorded and reported as a separate component of stockholders' equity. Thus, all taxable foreign exchange gains or losses that do not appear in the same period in taxable income and either (*a*) financial accounting income or (*b*) the separate component of stockholders' equity are temporary differences, for which deferred taxes must be provided (ASC 830-20-05-3). The amount of the deferred taxes should be determined in accordance with existing GAAP (ASC 830-30-45-21).

OBSERVATION: Historically, there has been a presumption in GAAP that all undistributed earnings of a subsidiary (domestic or foreign) would eventually be transferred to the parent company. Hence, GAAP have always considered undistributed income from foreign and domestic subsidiaries to be a temporary difference, requiring a provision for deferred income taxes. ASC 740 (Income Taxes) does not require deferred taxes to be provided for the excess of the book basis over the tax basis of an investment in a foreign subsidiary, if the excess is considered to be relatively permanent. An important reason that such an excess might exist is undistributed income from foreign subsidiaries. ASC 740 indicates:

A deferred tax liability is not recognized for the following types of temporary differences, unless it is apparent that those temporary differences will reverse in the foreseeable future:

In the basis for conclusions of ASC 740, the FASB states that the hypothetical nature of the tax allocation calculations for undistributed income from foreign subsidiaries "introduces significant implementation issues." Thus, tax allocation is not required for undistributed income of foreign subsidiaries that is essentially permanent in nature or for any other difference between the book basis and tax basis of investments of permanent nature.

Intraperiod income tax allocation is also required in the preparation of financial statements. The total income tax expense for a period should be allocated properly to (*a*) income before extraordinary items, (*b*) extraordinary items, (*c*) adjustments of prior periods, and (*d*) direct entries to other stockholders' equity accounts. Therefore, the portion of income tax expense for a period that is attributable to items in the separate component of stockholders' equity is allocated to the separate component of stockholders' equity, and does not appear as an increase or decrease of income tax expense for the period. In other words, deferred taxes related to items in the separate component of stockholders' equity account are charged or credited to the separate component of stockholders' equity account (ASC 830-20-45-5). The illustration at the end of the chapter demonstrates this concept.

OBSERVATION: All aspects of income tax allocation are complicated, and these provisions of ASC 830 require careful application to the specific facts of each situation. In particular, intercompany transactions of a long-term nature and the discontinuation of a foreign operation may present peculiar problems.

Foreign Currency Transaction Disclosures

The aggregate transaction gain or loss that is included in determining net income for the period, including gain or loss on forward exchange contracts, shall be disclosed in the financial statements or notes thereto (ASC 830-20-45-1).

Disclosure of exchange rate changes and related effects on foreign currency transactions that occur subsequent to the balance sheet date should be disclosed, if the effects are material. No adjustment should be made to the financial statements for exchange rate changes that occur subsequent to the balance sheet date (ASC 830-20-50-2; 830-20-35-8).

ASC 830-30: TRANSLATION OF FINANCIAL STATEMENTS

TRANSLATION OF FOREIGN CURRENCY STATEMENTS

The translation of foreign currency financial statements to the functional currency of the reporting entity does not produce realized exchange gains or losses. Instead, the gains or losses are considered unrealized and are recorded and reported as a separate component of stockholders' equity (ASC 830-30-45-12).

> **OBSERVATION:** Although ASC 830 generally requires translation using the current exchange rate, not all financial statement elements are converted at this rate. For example, common stock, paid-in capital, donated capital, retained earnings, and similar items are not translated at the current exchange rate. Translation of these elements of the financial statements is made as follows:
>
> *Capital accounts* are translated at their historical exchange rates when the capital stock was issued, or at the historical exchange rate when the capital stock was acquired.
>
> *Retained earnings* are translated at the translated amount at the end of the prior period, plus the translated amount of net income for the current period, less the translated amount of any dividends declared during the current period.

Assets and liabilities are translated from the foreign entity's functional currency to the reporting entity's functional currency using the current exchange rate at the balance sheet date of the foreign entity (ASC 830-30-45-3). If a current exchange rate is not available at the balance sheet date of the foreign entity being translated, the first exchange rate available after the balance sheet date is used (ASC 830-20-30-2).

Revenue, expenses, and gains and losses are translated from the foreign entity's functional currency to produce the approximate results that would have occurred if each transaction had been translated using the exchange rate in effect on the date that the transaction was recognized. Since the separate translation of every transaction is impractical, an appropriate weighted-average exchange rate for the period should be used (ASC 830-30-45-3; 830-10-55-10).

Gains or losses on the translation of foreign currency financial statements for the purposes of consolidation, combination, or reporting on the equity method are not included in current net income. All adjustments resulting from the translation of foreign currency financial statements are recorded and reported as a separate component of stockholders' equity. These adjustments are treated as unrealized gains and losses, similar to unrealized gains and losses of available-for-sale securities (ASC 320 [Investments—Debt and Equity Securities]).

To summarize, the translation process embodied in ASC 830 includes the following steps:

1. Financial statements must be in conformity with U.S. GAAP prior to translation.
2. The functional currency of the foreign entity is determined.
3. The financial statements are expressed in the functional currency of the foreign entity. Remeasurement of the financial statements into the functional currency may be necessary. Gains or losses from remeasurement are included in remeasured current net income.
4. If the foreign entity operates in a country with a highly inflationary economy, its financial statements are remeasured into the functional currency of the reporting entity.

5. The functional currency financial statements of the foreign entity are translated into the functional currency of the reporting entity using the current rate of exchange method. Gains or losses from translation are not included in current net income.

Illustration of Foreign Currency Translation When Euro Is Functional Currency

On December 31, 20X8, Gardial Inc. (a U.S. company) created a 100%-owned subsidiary in Prague, investing $15,000,000 in equity at that time when the direct exchange rate was $1.20. Gardial used this investment to purchase $13,200,000 of fixed assets on that date. The direct exchange rates were $1.30 at December 31, 20X9, and $1.25 for 20X9 as an average. No dividends were declared or paid in 20X9.

During 20Y0, the dollar strengthened so that the direct exchange rate at December 31, 20Y0, was $1.26. The average rate for 20Y0 was $1.28. Cash dividends of €1,000 were declared and paid on November 29, 20Y0, when the direct exchange rate was $1.27.

Assume that (1) the subsidiary is a self-contained foreign operation that uses the euro as its functional currency, (2) the statements have already been adjusted so that they conform to U.S. GAAP, (3) all intercompany adjustments have been made, and (4) all sales, costs, and expenses occurred evenly throughout the year.

Illustration of Foreign Currency Translation When U.S. Dollar Is Functional Currency

Assume the same monetary facts as in the previous illustration. In addition, all ending inventory existing on December 31, 20X9, was purchased when the exchange rate was $1.29, and all ending inventory existing on December 31, 20Y0, was purchased when the exchange rate was $1.27. Also, the ending inventory cost was always below market. All fixed assets were acquired in prior years when the direct exchange rate was $1.20, and no fixed assets were retired in 20X9 or 20Y0.

Also assume that (1) the subsidiary is a direct and integral component of the parent company's operation and uses the U.S. dollar as its functional currency, (2) the statements have already been adjusted so that they conform to U.S. GAAP, (3) all intercompany adjustments have been made, and (4) all sales, costs, and expenses occurred evenly throughout the year.

OBSERVATION: Total assets and total equity are both slightly higher under the current translation method than under the monetary/nonmonetary translation method. This difference is the result of using historical exchange rates for inventory and fixed assets rather than the current rate. Thus, under certain circumstances, these two methods can produce significantly different reporting results.

REALIZATION OF SEPARATE COMPONENT OF STOCKHOLDERS' EQUITY

Upon part, complete, or substantially complete sale or upon complete liquidation of an investment in a foreign entity, a *pro rata* portion of the accumulated translation adjustments attributable to that foreign entity, which has been recorded as a separate component of stockholders' equity, is included in determining the gain or loss on the sale or other disposition of that foreign investment (ASC 830-30-40-2). Thus, if an enterprise sells a 50% ownership interest in a foreign investment, 50% of the accumulated translation adjustments related to that foreign investment is included in determining the gain or loss on the sale of the interest.

OBSERVATION: Any required provision for the permanent impairment of a foreign investment is determined before translation and consolidation. Apparently, this means that the amounts accumulated in the separate component of stockholders' equity for a specific foreign investment are not included in determining whether the investment has become permanently impaired.

ELIMINATION OF INTERCOMPANY PROFITS

The exchange rate to be used to eliminate intercompany profits is the rate that existed on the date of the intercompany transaction. The use of approximations and/or averages is permitted as long as they are reasonable (ASC 830-30-45-10).

OBSERVATION: Intercompany profits occur on the date of sale or transfer. Thus, the exchange rate on the date of sale or transfer is used to determine the amount of intercompany profit to be eliminated.

EXCHANGE RATES

The balance sheet date of the foreign entity that is consolidated, combined, or accounted for by the equity method is used for translation purposes, if different from the balance sheet date of the reporting entity. Thus, the current exchange rate for the translation of foreign currency financial statements is the rate in effect on the balance sheet date of the foreign entity that is being translated (ASC 830-30-45-8). If a current exchange rate is not available at the foreign entity's balance sheet date, the first exchange rate available after the balance sheet date is used. The current rate used for the above translations is the rate applicable to currency conversion for the purpose of dividend remittances (ASC 830-30-45-6).

Conditions may exist when it will be prudent to exclude a foreign entity from financial statements that are consolidated, combined, or accounted for by the equity method. Disruption of a foreign operation caused by internal strife or severe exchange restrictions may make it impossible to compute meaningful exchange rates. Under these circumstances, earnings of a foreign operation should be included only to the extent that cash has been received in unrestricted funds. Disclosure should be made of any foreign subsidiary or investment that is excluded from the financial statements of the parent or investor. This may be accomplished by separate supplemental statements or a summary describing the important facts and information.

Financial Statement Translation Disclosures

An analysis of the changes in the separate component of stockholders' equity account for cumulative translation adjustments for the period shall be disclosed in either (*a*) a separate financial statement or (*b*) notes to the financial statements, or (*c*) be included as part of a stockholders' equity or a similar statement. The following is the minimum information that must be disclosed in the analysis (ASC 830-30-45-20).

- Beginning and ending cumulative balances
- The aggregate increase or decrease for the period from translation adjustments and gains and losses from (*a*) hedges of a net investment in a foreign entity and (*b*) long-term intercompany transactions (ASC 815 specifies additional disclosures for instruments designated as hedges of the foreign currency exposure of a net investment in a foreign operation.)
- The amount of income taxes for the period allocated to translation adjustments
- The amount of translation adjustment transferred to net income during the period as a result of a sale or complete or substantially complete liquidation of a foreign investment

---

Illustration of How an Enterprise Determines the Beginning Balance of the Separate Component of Stockholders' Equity

---

PART II: INTERPRETIVE GUIDANCE

ASC 830-10: Overall

ASC 830-10-45-1 through 45-5, 55-13 through 55-14 Accounting for a Change in Functional Currency When an Economy Ceases to Be Considered Highly Inflationary

BACKGROUND

Company A has a subsidiary operating in an economy that was considered highly inflationary during the previous five years. A *highly inflationary economy* is defined in ASC 830 (FAS-52) as one that has experienced a cumulative inflation rate of 100% or more for the most recent three-year period. In accordance with the guidance in ASC 830, the subsidiary used Company A's reporting currency rather than the local (foreign) currency as its functional currency. Based on the criteria in ASC 830, except for the inflationary environment, the subsidiary would have used the local currency as its functional currency. In 20X6, the inflation rate had declined sufficiently that the cumulative rate for the three most recent years was less than 100%; the economy was no longer considered highly inflationary. Accordingly, Company A decided to use the local currency as the subsidiary's functional currency.

> **OBSERVATION:** When the local currency is not the functional currency, the subsidiary's statements must be **remeasured** into the functional currency using **current** exchange rates for monetary items and **historical** exchange rates (exchange rate at acquisition) for nonmonetary items. When the local currency is also the functional currency, all assets and liabilities are **translated** at current exchange rates.

ACCOUNTING ISSUE

How should an entity account for a change in a subsidiary's functional currency from the reporting currency to the local currency solely because the economy in which the subsidiary operates is no longer considered to be highly inflationary?

ACCOUNTING GUIDANCE

The EITF reached a consensus in ASC 830-10-45-9 through 45-10, which provides guidance on the treatment of a change in functional currency from the reporting currency to the local currency, does not apply to situations in which the functional currency changes solely because the economy has ceased to be highly inflationary. The functional currency bases of nonmonetary assets and liabilities should be restated at the date of change by translating reporting currency amounts into the local currency at their current exchange rates. Those translated amounts become the new accounting bases for the nonmonetary assets and liabilities in the entity's new functional currency (the local currency).

The difference between the new accounting bases in the functional currency and their tax bases in that currency is considered a temporary difference under ASC 740. The guidance in ASC 830-740-25-2; 45-2 addresses how related deferred taxes should be recognized.)

DISCUSSION

The issue arose because in cases in which the local currency becomes the functional currency, the bases of nonmonetary assets and liabilities must be established in the new functional currency (local currency). Those functional currency bases are then translated into the reporting currency at current rates in accordance with ASC 830. The following two methods were suggested for determining the bases of nonmonetary assets and liabilities in the newly established functional currency:

Method 1 The historical bases in the *local currency* become the functional currency bases for nonmonetary items.

Method 2 Historical bases in the *reporting currency* are translated into the local currency at current rates to establish the new functional currency bases for nonmonetary items. (This method was adopted.)

Illustration of Two Methods Considered for Determining New Functional Currency Bases of Nonmonetary Items

- Company A's Subsidiary F operated in a highly inflationary economy from 1/1/X1 to 12/31/X5.
- On 1/1/X2, Subsidiary F purchased equipment costing LC10,000 (local currency) with a useful life of 20 years.
- On 1/1/X6, the economy in which Subsidiary F operated ceased to be considered highly inflationary. As of this date, under the consensus, a new functional currency basis needs to be established.
- The exchange rates used in this illustration are as follows:

1/1/X2	$1 = LC2
1/1/X6	$1 = LC10
19X6 average	$1 = LC11
12/31/X6	$1 = LC12

On 12/31/X5, the equipment has a net book value of LC8,000 (LC10,000 less accumulated depreciation of LC2,000) in Subsidiary F's financial statements. The equipment is presented in Company A's financial statements at a net book value of $4,000 [$5,000 original remeasured cost (LC10,000 × $1/LC2) less $1,000 accumulated depreciation].

Effect of Using Methods 1 and 2

Method 1

Net book value in local currency	LC8,000
Current exchange rate	LC10 to $1
Translation at current rate—New reporting currency basis	$800
Prior reporting currency basis	$4,000
Cumulative translation adjustment	$3,200

Method 2 (Adopted in the Consensus)

Reporting currency basis	$4,000
Translation back to local currency at current rate	LC10 to $1
New local currency basis	LC40,000

Comparison of Methods

	Method 1	Method 2
Local currency basis	LC8,000	LC40,000
Reporting currency basis	$800	$4,000
Prior reporting currency basis	$4,000	$4,000
Adjustment to cumulative Translation adjustments account	$3,200	0

Effect on 20X6 Earnings

	Method 1	Method 2
Book value 1/1/X6	$800	$4,000
20X6 depreciation expense		
Functional currency basis	LC8,000	LC40,000
Remaining useful life	16 years	16 years
Depreciation in LC	500	2,500
Average exchange rate	LC11 to $1	LC11 to $1

Effect on 20X6 Earnings
Depreciation expense $45 $227
Book value 12/31/X6 $755 $3,773

The principal argument for Method 2 was that it is stated in the discussion in ASC 830 that financial information presented in the local currency of a highly inflationary economy is not meaningful, because the local currency is too unstable to provide a reliable measurement of an entity's financial position and results of operations. Accordingly, the reporting currency provides a better basis for establishing the new measurement basis of nonmonetary assets and liabilities. In the same vein, opponents to Method 1 argued that using the historical local currency basis would deem the local currency a reliable measuring unit during a highly inflationary period, thus reintroducing the effects of inflation and negating the intent of ASC 830.

ASC 830-10-45-10, 45-16 Accounting for a Change in Functional Currency and Deferred Taxes When an Economy Becomes Highly Inflationary

The FASB staff announced that a change in the functional currency of an economy that is determined to be highly inflationary in accordance with the provisions in ASC 830 should be accounted for based on the guidance in ASC 830-10-45-9, 45-10. According to that guidance "translation adjustments for prior periods should not be removed from equity and the translated amounts for nonmonetary assets at the end of the prior period become the accounting basis for those assets in the period of the change and subsequent periods."

The FASB staff also announced its view on the recognition of deferred tax benefits when the functional currency changes to that of the reporting entity. Under the guidance in ASC 740-10-25-3, recognition of deferred tax benefits is not permitted for assets and liabilities indexed for tax purposes, if those assets are remeasured into the reporting currency using historical exchange rates. Consequently, no deferred tax benefits should be recognized as a result of tax indexing that occurs after a functional currency becomes the reporting currency until those benefits are realized on the tax return. Nevertheless, deferred tax benefits that are recognized before the functional currency changes to the reporting currency should be eliminated only when the related indexed amounts are realized as deductions for tax purposes.

ASC 830-10-45-12; 55-24 through 55-26 Determining a Highly Inflationary Economy under ASC 830

The FASB staff made an announcement interpreting the guidance in ASC 830 on how to determine whether an economy is highly inflationary. It is stated in ASC 830-10-45-11 that an economy is highly inflationary if its cumulative inflation rate is 100% or more over a three-year period. The role of judgment in making that determination is discussed in ASC 830-10-45-13.

The FASB staff believes that an economy should always be considered highly inflationary if the cumulative inflation rate for the previous three-year period exceeds 100%. However, the staff gave the following examples in which historical trends and other factors would be considered to determine whether an economy is highly inflationary if the cumulative inflation rate is *less* than 100%:

- An economy would continue being considered highly inflationary if it was so in the past, even though its cumulative three-year inflation rate is close to but less than 100% as a result of a decrease in the rate during the last one or two years, unless evidence suggests that the drop is not temporary.
- An economy that was highly inflationary in the prior year should *not* be considered highly inflationary in the current year, if its cumulative three-year inflation rate is close to but less than 100%, even though the inflation rate was very high in one isolated year, which was atypical in comparison to the economy's historical inflation rates and the rate in the current year.

ASC 830-20: Foreign Currency Transactions

ASC 320-10-35-36 through 35-37; 830-20-35-6 through 35-7 Accounting for the Effects of Changes in Foreign Currency Exchange Rates on Foreign-Currency-Denominated Available-for-Sale Debt Securities

BACKGROUND

The *available-for-sale*(AFS) category of securities was established in ASC 320-10. Unrealized holding gains or losses on securities in that category are reported in a separate component of stockholders' equity and recognized in income when realized.

This Issue addresses the accounting for available-for-sale securities denominated in a foreign currency. Under the guidance in ASC 830-20-35-1, foreign currency transaction gains or losses occur when *monetary* assets and liabilities are denominated in a currency other than the entity's functional currency and the exchange rate between the currencies changes. Some have questioned whether available-for-sale debt securities should be considered to be non-monetary with no recognition of gains and losses on remeasurement, because such securities, which are not held to maturity, are carried at fair value, so their amounts are not fixed. Gains or losses on hedges of net investments in foreign entities and hedges of identifiable foreign currency commitments also are exempted from recognition in earnings under the guidance in ASC 830-20-35(a).

A change in the fair value of available-for-sale (AFS) debt securities denominated in a foreign currency consists of the following two components: (*a*) a change in the market price of the security in the local currency as a result of such factors as changes in interest rates and credit risk and (*b*) a change in exchange rates between the local currency and the entity's functional currency.

ACCOUNTING ISSUE

Should both components of a change in the fair value of available-for-sale debt securities be reported in a separate component of stockholders' equity, or should the component related to the change in exchange rates (component b) be reported in earnings as a foreign currency transaction gain or loss, with changes due to other factors (component a) reported in stockholders' equity?

ACCOUNTING GUIDANCE

Entities should report both components of a change in the fair value of foreign-currency-denominated available-for-sale debt securities in other comprehensive income in accordance with the guidance in ASC 220.

Based on the guidance in ASC 320, changes in market interest rates and foreign exchange rates since acquisition should be considered when determining whether an AFS debt security denominated in a foreign currency has experienced an other-than-temporary impairment.

EFFECT OF ASC 815

The guidance in Issue 1 is not affected by the guidance in ASC 815, which applies only to AFS debt securities that are designated in fair value hedging relationships. A gain or loss on a currency derivative in a fair value hedge of an AFS security is reported in earnings under the guidance in ASC 815, instead of in other comprehensive income as required under this guidance, together with the gain or loss on the AFS security related to changes in the foreign currency's exchange value.

Illustration of a Change in Market Value of an Available-for-Sale Debt Security Denominated in a Foreign Currency

On 7/1/X6, a company whose functional currency is the U.S. dollar acquires a debt security denominated in a foreign currency (FC) and classifies it as available for sale. How would the company compute the change in market value at 9/30/X6?

At 7/1/X6

- Purchase price = FC500
- Exchange rate = $2.50 per FC1
- Historical cost basis = $1,250

At 9/30/X6

- Fair market value = FC600
- Exchange rate = $2.00 per FC1
- U.S. dollar fair market value = $1,200

Components of the Change in Market Value at 9/30/X6

(a) *Change in market value* Change in fair market value at historical exchange rate

(FC600 − FC500) × $2.50 $250

(b) *Effect of exchange rates* Current fair market value less historical cost basis plus change in fair market value at historical exchange rates

(FC600 × $2.00) − ($1,250 + $250)   (300)
Net effect   ($ 50)

ASC 830-20-55-1 through 55-3 Foreign Debt-for-Equity Swaps
OVERVIEW

In a foreign debt-for-equity swap, a U.S. company that has a subsidiary in Mexico purchases a U.S. dollar-denominated loan in the secondary market at less than the loan's face amount. The loan is due from the Mexican government or an entity operating in Mexico. The company in turn enters into an agreement to sell the loan to the Mexican government for an amount denominated in Mexican pesos that exceeds the amount the company paid for the loan. Under the agreement, which is designed to keep the pesos within Mexico's economy, the company must invest the proceeds in its subsidiary, which is required to use the proceeds for a specified purpose, such as capital expenditures. When the Mexican government purchases the loan, it transmits the pesos directly to the subsidiary, which issues capital stock to the U.S. parent. The agreement restricts the U.S. parent from redeeming the shares, receiving dividends on those shares, or selling the shares within Mexico for a stated period of time. For example, a U.S. company purchases a loan with remaining principal of $15 million for $7.5 million. The Mexican government purchases the loan from the company for $11 million in pesos translated at the official exchange rate, which the company invests in its Mexican subsidiary and receives stock.

ACCOUNTING ISSUE

How should the U.S. company report in its consolidated financial statements the difference between the amount paid to purchase the dollar-denominated loan and the local currency proceeds from the sale of the loan invested in its foreign subsidiary?

ACCOUNTING GUIDANCE

Note: ASC 805 provides guidance on accounting for a bargain purchase, which was previously referred to as negative goodwill.

The excess proceeds in local currency from the sale of a loan translated at the official exchange rate over the cost to purchase the loan should be reported as follows in the parent company's consolidated financial statements:

- Reduce the basis of long-lived assets acquired or constructed under the agreement.
- Reduce the carrying amounts of existing long-lived assets other than goodwill by a corresponding amount, if the agreement does not specifically require the acquisition or construction of long-lived assets, or if the excess is greater than the cost of such assets.

The excess should be applied first to fixed assets with the longest remaining lives until they have been reduced to zero. A remainder, if any, after the carrying amounts of all fixed assets have been reduced to zero should be reported as a bargain purchase as required in ASC 805-30.

This guidance applies to a debt-to-equity swap of a foreign branch that has (1) an accumulated deficit and no significant assets or liabilities other than the local currency debt, and (2) used the proceeds from the foreign debt-for-equity currency swap to extinguish the debt. The excess should be reported as a bargain purchase as required in ASC 805-30.

DISCUSSION

Because the excess in a foreign debt-for-equity swap does not result from a change in exchange rates, it does not meet the criteria to be reported as a transaction gain or loss or a translation adjustment under the provisions of ASC 830. The issue here was whether the U.S. company should report the excess of the proceeds invested in the subsidiary over the purchase price of the loan in income in its consolidated financial statements. Proponents of the consensus argued that because the foreign government required the company to invest the total proceeds in the subsidiary and restricted its use of the proceeds, the earnings process was not complete. Any excess that cannot be identified with assets is accounted for similarly to an unallocated excess in a purchase method business combination, which would be reported as a bargain purchase.

ASC 830-30: Translation of Financial Statements

ASC 830-30-45-13 through 45-15 Application of ASC 830 to an Investment Being Evaluated for Impairment That Will Be Disposed Of

BACKGROUND

Under the provisions of ASC 830, translation adjustments that result when a foreign entity's financial statements are translated into a parent company's or an investor's reporting currency are reported separately from the entity's earnings in other comprehensive income. Foreign currency translation adjustments (CTA) that are accumulated in other comprehensive income are reclassified to income only when they are realized if the investment in the foreign entity is sold or is substantially or completely liquidated. This Issue does not apply to foreign investments that are held for use or to transactions related to foreign investments in which CTA will not be reclassified when the transaction is consummated.

ACCOUNTING ISSUES

1. Should an entity include CTA in the carrying amount of its investment in evaluating the impairment of an *equity* method investment in a foreign entity that has committed to a plan to dispose of an investment that will result in the reclassification of CTA to earnings?

2. Should an entity include CTA in the carrying amount of its investment in evaluating the impairment of a *consolidated* investment in a foreign entity that has committed to a plan to dispose of an investment that will result in the reclassification of CTA to earnings?

3. Should an entity that has committed to a plan to dispose of a net investment in a foreign operation (accounted for as an equity investment or as a consolidated subsidiary) include the portion of CTA representing a gain or a loss from an effective hedge of that net investment in the carrying amount of the investment when evaluating the investment for impairment?

ACCOUNTING GUIDANCE

When the impairment of a foreign investment is evaluated, an entity that has committed to a plan to dispose of an equity method investment in a foreign operation or a consolidated foreign subsidiary should *include* in the investment's carrying amount (1) foreign currency translation adjustments that will be reclassified to earnings on the foreign entity's disposal and (2) the portion of CTA related to a gain or loss from an effective hedge of the entity's net investment in the foreign operation.

ASC 830-30-55-1 Foreign Currency Translation—Selection of Exchange Rate When Trading Is Temporarily Suspended

The FASB staff discussed an inquiry from a U.S. company, which had a significant subsidiary in Israel, about the appropriate exchange rate for translating financial statements at year-end. In this case, foreign currency trading was suspended between December 30, 1988, and January 2, 1989. The Israeli government had announced on December 30 that the Israeli shekel, which traded at 1.68 shekel to $1 on December 29, would be devalued on January 2. Although trading resumed on January 2, the new exchange rate of 1.81 shekel to $1 was not established until January 3, 1989. The issue was how to select an exchange rate for year-end reporting when trading is temporarily suspended.

The FASB staff announced that, based on the guidance in ASC 830-30-45-9, the exchange rate on January 3, 1989, would be appropriate for translating the year-end financial statements. ASC 830-30-45-9 states that "[i]f exchangeability between two currencies is *temporarily* lacking at the transaction date or balance sheet date, the first subsequent rate at which exchanges could be made shall be used for purposes of this Statement."[Emphasis added.] The FASB staff noted that the SEC staff agrees with that guidance.

ASC 830-740: Income Taxes

ASC 830-740-25-4 through 25-5, 30-1 through 30-2, 55-1 through 55-3 Application of ASC 740 in Foreign Financial Statements Restated for General Price-Level Changes

BACKGROUND

Company M, which is located in a country with a highly inflationary economy, prepares price-level-adjusted financial statements in accordance with U.S. GAAP that present changes in the local currency's general purchasing power. In addition, the tax bases of Company M's assets and liabilities are indexed to consider the effects of inflation. Because the adjustments may not be the same for tax and financial statement purposes, the financial reporting and tax bases of assets and liabilities may differ.

Under the guidance in ASC 840, the difference between an asset and liability's financial reporting basis and tax basis is a temporary difference that generally requires the provision of deferred taxes. However, ASC 740-10-25-3 prohibits recognizing a deferred tax liability or asset for differences related to the bases of assets or liabilities that are remeasured under the provisions of ASC 830 from the local currency used in the country in which the entity operates to the functional currency at historical exchange rates and that result from changes in exchange rates or from indexing for tax purposes. ASC 740 states that to do so would result in recognition of deferred taxes on exchange gains or losses not recognized for financial reporting purposes.

Because of that prohibition in paragraph ASC 740-10-25-3, it was unclear whether deferred taxes should be provided for differences in the bases of assets and liabilities that occur as a result of tax indexing when comprehensive, general price-level-adjusted financial statements are prepared using the guidance in APB-3.

ACCOUNTING ISSUES

1. Should paragraph ASC 740-10-25-3 apply to temporary differences between the bases of assets and liabilities for financial reporting in general price-level-adjusted financial statements and their indexed tax bases?
2. If paragraph ASC 740-10-25-3 does not apply, how should deferred income tax expense or benefit for the year be determined?

ACCOUNTING GUIDANCE

1. The guidance in ASC 740-10-25-3 should not apply to general price-level-adjusted financial statements. Temporary differences in financial statements restated for general price-level changes using end-of-current-year units of purchasing power should be calculated based on the difference between the indexed tax basis amounts of assets and liabilities and the related amounts reported in general price-level-adjusted financial statements.
2. The deferred tax expense or benefit should be calculated as the difference between (*a*) the deferred tax asset or liability reported at the end of the current year based on the above calculation and (*b*) the deferred tax asset or liability reported at the end of the prior year remeasured in end-of-current-year units of purchasing power. Remeasurement of deferred tax assets and liabilities at the end of the prior year should be reported with the remeasurement of all other assets and liabilities as a restatement of beginning equity.

Illustration Using EITF Issue 93-9 Consensus

Assumptions

- Company M has land that was purchased in 20X0 for FC10,000 (local currency).
- The general price-level-adjusted financial reporting amount of the land at December 31, 20X4, is CFC48,384 (current purchasing power units).
- The indexed basis for tax purposes at December 31, 20X4, is CFC36,456.
- The enacted tax rate is 50%.
- Company M has a taxable temporary difference of CFC11,928 (CFC48,384 − CFC36,456) at December 31, 20X4.
- The related deferred tax liability in current purchasing power units at December 31, 20X4, is CFC5,964 (CFC11,928 × .5).

- During 20X5, general price levels increased by 40% and indexing for tax purposes was 30%.
- The following is the calculation of the deferred tax liability and deferred tax expense at December 31, 20X5:

	20X5
Land—financial reporting basis (CFC48,384 × 1.4)	CFC67,738
Land—tax basis (CFC36,456 × 1.3)	CFC47,393
Taxable temporary difference	CFC20,345
Tax rate	× .5
Deferred tax liability, end of year	CFC10,173
Deferred tax liability restated, at beginning of year (CFC5,964 × 1.4)	CFC 8,350
Deferred tax expense for 20X5	CFC 1,823

Company M should report CFC2,386 (CFC8,350 − CFC5,964) as a restatement of beginning equity for 20X5.

ASC 830-740-25-6 through 25-8; 740-30-25-17 Application of ASC 740 to Basis Differences within Foreign Subsidiaries That Meet the Indefinite Reversal Criterion of ASC 740-30

OVERVIEW

Under the guidance in ASC 740 and ASC 740-30, entities do not recognize a deferred tax liability on temporary differences related to the financial reporting and tax bases of investments in foreign subsidiaries or foreign joint ventures that are not expected to reverse in the foreseeable future. Such differences are referred to as outside basis differences. However, forcign subsidiaries may have other temporary differences, referred to as inside basis differences that also may not reverse in the foreseeable future.

In this particular situation, an Italian subsidiary of a U.S. company uses the Italian lira as its functional currency. The tax basis of the company's fixed assets has been increased to compensate for the effects of inflation, and an equivalent amount has been credited to an account referred to as "revaluation surplus," which is a component of equity established for tax purposes. That amount becomes taxable only if the Italian entity is liquidated or if earnings associated with the revaluation surplus are distributed. Because that amount would not be taxable if the asset is sold, the tax related to the surplus may be deferred indefinitely. However, for discussion purposes, it was assumed that there was no strategy within the entity's control under which it could avoid triggering the tax on the revaluation surplus if it were to realize the carrying amounts of its assets and transfer the net assets to its shareholders.

ACCOUNTING ISSUES

1. Should the indefinite reversal criterion in APB-23, as amended by FAS-109, apply only to outside basis differences, or should it also apply to the revaluation surplus related to inside basis differences of foreign

subsidiaries in the consolidated financial statements of the U.S. parent and its foreign subsidiaries?

2. If the indefinite reversal criterion does not apply to inside basis differences, how should the provisions of ASC 740 be applied?

ACCOUNTING GUIDANCE

1. The indefinite reversal criterion in ASC 740-30, does not apply to a revaluation surplus related to *inside* basis differences of foreign subsidiaries. A deferred tax liability should be provided on the balance of the revaluation surplus. This guidance was analogized to the guidance in ASC 740-10-05-10, which discusses temporary differences that have balances only on the income tax balance sheet and that cannot be related to specific assets or liabilities in the financial statements. Deferred taxes are nevertheless provided for such differences, which will result in taxable or deductible amounts in the future. Similarly, based on Italian law, a revaluation surplus related to inside basis differences will be taxable in the future and thus qualifies as a temporary difference, even though it is a component of equity for tax purposes. In addition, the guidance in ASC 740-10-25-3 specifically limits the indefinite reversal criterion in ASC 740-30 to the situations discussed in that paragraph and prohibits applying it by analogy to other types of temporary differences.

2. Entities should recognize a deferred tax liability for inside basis differences that originated in fiscal years beginning *after* December 15, 1992. Therefore, recognition of a deferred tax liability is not required for existing inside basis differences that originated in fiscal years beginning *before* December 16, 1992 and for which no deferred tax liability was recognized on adoption of the guidance in ASC 740. However, the information required in ASC 942-740-50-1 should be disclosed in those situations.

CHAPTER 52
ASC 835—INTEREST

CONTENTS

Part I: General Guidance	
ASC 835-10: Overall	52,002
Overview	52,002
Background	52,002
ASC 835-20: Capitalization of Interest	52,003
Qualifying Assets	52,003
Acquisition Period	52,003
Intended Use	52,004
Computing Interest Cost to Be Capitalized	52,004
Average Accumulated Investment	52,005
Illustration of Computing Average Accumulated Investment	52,005
Identification of Interest Rates	52,005
Illustration of Calculating Weighted-Average Interest Rate	52,006
Capitalization Period	52,007
Special Applications	52,007
Equity Method Investments	52,007
Tax-Exempt Borrowings and Gifts and Grants	52,008
Capitalization Period	52,008
Amount of Capitalized Interest Cost	52,008
External Restriction Requirement	52,009
Disposition of Capitalized Interest	52,009
Disclosure Requirements	52,009
Illustration of the Application of ASC 835	52,009
ASC 835-30: Imputation of Interest	52,012
Circumstances Requiring Imputed Interest	52,012
Applying ASC 835-30 Principles	52,013
Determining Present Value	52,013
Figure 52-1: Circumstances Indicating a Need to Impute Interest	52,013
Discount and Premium	52,014
Disclosure	52,014
Illustration of Interest Imputed and Accounted for on a Noninterest-Bearing Note	52,014
Illustration of Recording a Note with an Unreasonable Rate of Interest	52,015
Part II: Interpretive Guidance	
ASC 835-30 Imputation of Interest	52,016
ASC 835-30-55-2	
Required Use of Interest Method in Recognizing Interest Income	52,016

PART I: GENERAL GUIDANCE

ASC 835-10: OVERALL

OVERVIEW

Under certain conditions, interest is capitalized as part of the acquisition cost of an asset. Interest is capitalized only during the period of time required to complete and prepare the asset for its intended use, which may be either *sale or use within the business*. Capitalization of interest is based on the principle that a better measure of acquisition cost is achieved when certain interest costs are capitalized. This results in a better matching of revenue and costs in future periods.

Business transactions may involve the exchange of cash or other assets for a note or other instrument. When the interest rate on the instrument is consistent with the market rate at the time of the transaction, the face amount of the instrument is assumed to be equal to the value of the other asset(s) exchanged. An interest rate that is different from the prevailing market rate, however, implies that the face amount of the instrument may not equal the value of the other asset(s) exchanged. In this case, it may be necessary to impute interest that is not stated as part of the instrument, or to recognize interest at a rate other than that stated in the instrument.

BACKGROUND

The basis of accounting for depreciable fixed assets is cost, including all normal expenditures of readying an asset for use are capitalized as part of acquisition cost. Unnecessary expenditures that do not add to the utility of the asset should be charged to expense.

ASC 835 covers the promulgated GAAP on the capitalization of interest costs on certain qualifying assets that are undergoing activities to prepare them for their intended use. ASC 835 requires that the same materiality tests applied by regular GAAP be applied to the materiality of capitalizing interest cost.

ASC 835 applies to the capitalization of interest cost on equity funds, loans, and advances made by investors to certain investees that are accounted for by the equity method as described in ASC 323 (Investments—Equity Method and Joint Ventures).

ASC 835 provides special treatment in capitalizing interest costs on qualifying assets that are acquired with (*a*) the proceeds of tax-exempt borrowings and (*b*) gifts or grants that are restricted for the sole purpose of acquiring a specific asset.

OBSERVATION: The basis of capitalizing certain interest costs is that the cost of an asset should include all costs necessary to bring the asset to the condition and location for its intended use. The requirements of ASC 835 to capitalize interest cost may result in a lack of comparability among reporting entities, depending on their method of financing major asset acquisitions. For example, Company A and Company B both acquire an identical asset for $10 million that requires three years to complete for its intended use. Company A pays cash, and at the end of three years, the total cost of the asset is $10 million. In addition, assume that Company A also had net income of $2 million a year for each of the three years and had no interest expense. Assume also that Company B had $1.5 million net income for each of the three years after deducting $500,000 of interest expense per year. If Company B qualifies for capitalized interest costs under ASC 835, it would reflect $2 million per year net income and not show any interest expense. On the balance sheet of Company B at the end of three years, the identical asset would appear at a cost of $11.5 million. Future depreciation charges will vary between the two companies by a total of $1.5 million. Although the interest cost may be necessary to Company B, it does not add to the utility of the asset.

ASC 835 is also the main source of GAAP on imputing interest on receivables and payables. However, ASC 830 excludes receivables and payables under the following conditions (ASC 835-30-15-3):

1. They arise in the ordinary course of business and are due in approximately one year or less.
2. Their repayment will be applied to the purchase price of the property, goods, or services to which they relate rather than requiring a transfer of cash.
3. They represent security or retainage deposits.
4. They arise in the ordinary course of business of a lending institution.
5. They arise from transactions between a parent and its subsidiaries, or between subsidiaries of a common parent.
6. Their interest rate is determined by a governmental agency.

Receivables and payables that are not specifically excluded from the provisions of ASC 835 and that are contractual rights to receive or pay money at a fixed or determinable date must be recorded at their present value if (*a*) the interest rate is not stated or (*b*) the stated interest rate is unreasonable (ASC 310-10-30-6).

OBSERVATION: This is an application of the basic principle of substance over form in that the substance of the instrument (interest-bearing), rather than the form of the instrument (noninterest-bearing or bearing interest at an unreasonable rate), becomes the basis for recording.

ASC 835-20: CAPITALIZATION OF INTEREST

QUALIFYING ASSETS

Acquisition Period

Interest cost must be capitalized for all assets that require an *acquisition period* to get them ready for their intended use. *Acquisition period* is defined as the period commencing with the first expenditure for a qualifying asset and ending when the asset is substantially complete and ready for its intended use. Thus, before interest costs can be capitalized, expenditures must have been made for the qualifying asset, providing an investment base on which to compute interest, and activities that are required to get the asset ready for its intended use must actually be in progress (ASC 835-20-15-2).

The usual rules of materiality embodied in GAAP must be followed in determining the materiality for the capitalization of interest costs. Thus, in applying the provisions of ASC 835, all the usual materiality tests used in applying other promulgated GAAP should also be used in determining the materiality for capitalization of interest costs.

Intended Use

Capitalization of interest cost is applicable for assets that require an acquisition period to prepare them for their intended use. Assets to which capitalized interest must be allocated include both (1) assets acquired for a company's own use and (2) assets acquired for sale in the ordinary course of business (ASC 835-20-15-5). Thus, inventory items that require a long time to produce, such as a real estate development, qualify for capitalization of interest costs. However, interest costs are not capitalized for inventories that are routinely produced in large quantities on a repetitive basis (ASC 835-20-15-6).

OBSERVATION: The FASB concluded that the benefit of capitalizing interest costs on inventories that are routinely produced in large quantities does not justify the cost. Thus, interest costs should not be capitalized for inventories that are routinely produced in large quantities.

Capitalization of interest cost is not permitted (*a*) for assets that are ready for their intended use or that are actually being used in the earning activities of a business and (*b*) for assets that are not being used in the earning activities of a business and that are not undergoing the activities required to get them ready for use (ASC 835-20-15-6).

COMPUTING INTEREST COST TO BE CAPITALIZED

The amount of interest cost that may be capitalized for any accounting period may not exceed the actual interest cost (from any source) that is incurred by an enterprise during that same accounting period (ASC 835-20-30-6). In addition to interest paid and/or accrued on debt instruments, interest imputed in accordance with ASC 835-30 (Imputation of Interest) and interest recognized on capital leases in accordance with ASC 840 (Leases) are available for capitalization. ASC 835 specifically prohibits imputing interest costs on any equity funds. In consolidated financial statements, this limitation on the maximum amount of interest cost that may be capitalized in a period should be applied on a consolidated basis.

OBSERVATION: ASC 715 (Compensation—Retirement Benefits) requires that the interest cost component of net periodic pension cost shall not be considered to be interest for purposes of applying ASC 835.

Similarly, the interest cost component of postretirement benefit cost shall not be considered interest for purposes of applying ASC 835.

PRACTICE POINTER: A logical starting point for applying ASC 835 and related pronouncements is to determine the total amount of interest that was incurred and that is available for capitalization as a cost of a qualifying asset. If a company incurs little or no qualifying interest on debt instruments, interest imputed in accordance with ASC 835-30, or interest on capital leases, the requirement to capitalize interest may not be effective, even though the company may have invested in assets that would otherwise require interest capitalization.

Average Accumulated Investment

To compute the amount of interest cost to be capitalized for a particular accounting period, the average accumulated investment in a qualifying asset during that period must be determined. To determine the average accumulated investment, each expenditure must be *weighted* for the time it was outstanding during the particular accounting period.

Illustration of Computing Average Accumulated Investment

In the acquisition of a qualifying asset, a calendar year company expends $225,000 on January 1, 20X8; $360,000 on March 1, 20X8; and $180,000 on November 1, 20X8. The average accumulated investment for 20X8 is computed as follows:

Amount of Expenditure	Period from Expenditure to End of Year	Average Investment
$225,000	12 months (12/12)	$225,000
360,000	10 months (10/12)	300,000
180,000	2 months (2/12)	30,000
$765,000		$555,000

Identification of Interest Rates

If a specific borrowing is made to acquire the qualifying asset, the interest rate incurred on that borrowing may be used to determine the amount of interest costs to be capitalized. That interest rate is applied to the average accumulated investment for the period to calculate the amount of capitalized interest cost on the qualifying asset. Capitalized interest cost on average accumulated investments in excess of the amount of the specific borrowing is calculated by the use of the weighted-average interest rate incurred on other borrowings outstanding during the period (ASC 835-20-30-3).

If no specific borrowing is made to acquire the qualifying asset, the weighted-average interest rate incurred on other borrowings outstanding during the period is used to determine the amount of interest cost to be capitalized. The weighted-average interest rate is applied to the average accumulated investment for the period to calculate the amount of capitalized interest cost on the qualifying asset. Judgment may be required to identify and select the appropriate specific borrowings that should be used in determining the weighted-average interest rate. The objective should be to obtain a reasonable cost of financing for the qualifying asset that could have been avoided if the asset had not been acquired (ASC 835-20-30-4).

PRACTICE POINTER: In determining the weighted average interest rate for purposes of capitalizing interest, take care not to overlook interest that is available for capitalization even though it has another specific purpose. For example, a company might have interest on mortgage debt on buildings and plant assets. Unless that interest already is being capitalized into a different asset under ASC 835, it is available for capitalization despite the fact that it was incurred specifically to finance the acquisition of a different asset.

Progress payments received from the buyer of a qualifying asset are deducted in the computation of the average amount of accumulated expenditures during a period. Nonetheless, the determination of the average amount of accumulated expenditures for a period may be reasonably estimated (ASC 835-20-30-5).

Illustration of Calculating Weighted-Average Interest Rate

A company has the following three debt issues outstanding during a year in which interest must be capitalized as part of the cost of plant assets:

$1,000,000 par value, 8% interest rate

$1,500,000 par value, 9% interest rate

$1,200,000 par value, 10% interest rate

The weighted-average interest rate is computed as follows:

$1,000,000 × 8%	=	$80,000
1,500,000 × 9%	=	135,000
1,800,000 × 10%	=	180,000
$4,300,000	=	$395,000
$395,000/$4,300,000	=	9.19%

Interest available for capitalization is $395,000. Assuming none of the debt issues relates directly to the asset for which interest is being capitalized, interest is charged to the cost of the asset at a 9.19% interest rate applied to the average investment made on the asset during the year. If, instead, one of the debt issues relates directly to the asset for which interest is being capitalized, interest may be charged at the interest rate applicable to that debt issue on the investment equal

ASC 835—Interest **52,007**

to the amount of that debt. Interest on any remaining investment is calculated at the weighted-average interest rate for the remaining debt.

Capitalization Period

The interest capitalization period starts when three conditions are met (ASC 835-20-25-3):

7. Expenditures have occurred.
8. Activities necessary to prepare the asset (including administrative activities before construction) have begun.
9. Interest cost has been incurred.

Interest is not capitalized during delays or interruptions initially by the entity, except for brief interruptions, that occur during the acquisition or development stage of the qualifying asset. However, interest continues to be capitalized during externally imposed delays or interruptions (e.g., strikes) (ASC 835-20-25-4).

When the qualifying asset is substantially complete and ready for its intended use, the capitalization of interest ceases. The qualifying asset may be completed in independent parts (i.e., the parts can be used separately from the rest of the project, like units in a condominium) or in dependent parts (i.e., parts that, although complete, cannot be used until other parts are finished, like subassemblies of a machine). Interest capitalization ceases for an independent part when it is substantially complete and ready for its intended use. For dependent parts of a qualifying asset, however, interest capitalization does not stop until all dependent parts are substantially complete and ready for their intended use (ASC 835-20-25-5).

SPECIAL APPLICATIONS

Equity Method Investments

An investor's qualifying assets, for the purposes of capitalizing interest costs under ASC 835, include equity funds, loans, and advances made to investees accounted for by the equity method. Thus, an investor must capitalize interest costs on such qualifying assets if, during that period, the investee is undergoing activities necessary to start its planned principal operations and such activities include the use of funds to acquire qualifying assets for its operations. The investor does not capitalize any interest costs on or after the date that the investee actually begins its planned principal operations.

> **PRACTICE POINTER:** The term *planned principal operations* has the same meaning as used in ASC 915 (Development Stage Entities). Under the provisions of ASC 915, a development stage company is one that devotes substantially all of its efforts to establishing a new business and (*a*) planned principal operations have not commenced or (*b*) planned principal operations have commenced, but there has been no significant revenue therefrom.

For the purposes of applying the above guidance, the term *investor* means both the parent company and all consolidated subsidiaries. Thus, all qualifying assets of a parent company and its consolidated subsidiaries that appear in the consolidated balance sheet are subject to the interest capitalization provisions of ASC 835. Capitalization of interest cost in the investee's separate financial statements is unaffected by this guidance.

Capitalized interest costs on an investment accounted for by the equity method are included in the carrying amount of the investment. Up to the date on which the planned principal operations of the investee begin, the investor's carrying amount of the investment, which includes capitalized interest costs (if any), may exceed the underlying equity in the investment. If the investor cannot relate the excess carrying amount of the investment to specific identifiable assets of the investee, the difference is considered goodwill (ASC 323-10-35-34).

Any interest cost capitalized is not changed in restating financial statements of prior periods. Thus, if an unconsolidated investee is subsequently consolidated in the investor's financial statements as a result of increased ownership or a voluntary change by the reporting entity, interest costs capitalized are not changed if restatement of financial statements is necessary.

Tax-Exempt Borrowings and Gifts and Grants

Under the provisions of ASC 835, capitalized interest cost for a qualifying asset is determined by applying either a specific interest rate or a weighted-average interest rate to the average accumulated expenditures during a particular period for the qualifying asset. An underlying premise in ASC 835 is that borrowings usually cannot be identified with specific qualifying assets. The financing policies of most enterprises are planned to meet general funding objectives, and the identification of specific borrowings with specific assets is considered highly subjective.

GAAP concludes that different circumstances are involved in the acquisition of a qualifying asset with tax-exempt borrowings, such as industrial revenue bonds and pollution control bonds. The tax-exempt borrowings, temporary interest income on unused funds, and construction expenditures for the qualifying asset are so integrated that they must be accounted for as a single transaction (ASC 835-20-30-10). Thus, capitalization of interest cost for any portion of a qualifying asset that is acquired with tax-exempt borrowings is required, as follows (ASC 835-20-30-11).

Capitalization Period

Interest cost is capitalized from the date of the tax-exempt borrowings to the date that the qualifying asset is ready for its intended use.

Amount of Capitalized Interest Cost

The amount of capitalized interest cost allowable is equal to the total actual interest cost on the tax-exempt borrowing, less any interest income earned on temporary investments of the tax exempt funds. The net cost of interest on the tax-exempt borrowing is capitalized and added to the acquisition cost of the related qualifying asset (ASC 835-20-30-11).

External Restriction Requirement

The above guidance only applies when the qualifying asset is financed by taxexempt borrowing, in which the use of the borrowed funds is restricted to acquiring the assets or servicing the related debt. The restriction must be *external*, that is, imposed by law, contract, or other authority outside the enterprise that borrows the funds. This guidance does not permit the capitalization of interest cost on any portion of a qualifying asset that is acquired with a gift or grant that is restricted to the acquisition of the specified qualifying asset. Restricted interest income on temporary investment of funds is considered an addition to the restricted gift or grant.

> **OBSERVATION:** No interest cost should be capitalized on qualifying assets acquired by restricted gifts or grants, because there is no economic cost of financing involved in acquiring an asset with a gift or grant. In addition, any interest earned on temporary investment of funds from a gift or grant is, in substance, part of the gift or grant.

Disposition of Capitalized Interest

If capitalized interest costs are added to the overall cost of an asset, the total cost of the asset, including capitalized interest, may exceed the net realizable or other lower value of the asset that is required by GAAP. In this event, ASC 835 requires that the provision to reduce the asset cost to the lower value required by GAAP be increased. Thus, the total asset cost, including capitalized interest, less the provision, will equal the lower value for the asset that is required by GAAP (ASC 835-20-25-7).

Capitalized interest costs become an integral part of the acquisition costs of an asset and should be accounted for as such in the event of disposal of the asset (ASC 835-20-40-1).

DISCLOSURE REQUIREMENTS

The total amount of interest costs incurred and charged to expense during the period and the amount of interest costs, if any, which has been capitalized during the period, should be disclosed in the financial statements or notes thereto (ASC 835-20-50-1).

Illustration of the Application of ASC 835

On January 1, 20X8, Poll Powerhouse borrowed $300,000 from its bank at an annual rate of 12%. The principal amount plus interest is due on January 1, 20Y0. The funds from this loan are specifically designated for the construction of a new plant facility. On February 1, 20X8, Poll paid $15,000 for architects' fees and for fees for filing a project application with the state government.

52,010 ASC 835—Interest

On March 1, 20X8, Poll received state approval for the project and began construction. The following summarizes the costs incurred on this project.

20X8

February 1 (architects' and filing fees)	$ 15,000
April 1	150,000
September 1	60,000

20X9

January 1	1,000
March 1	360,000
November 1	180,000
Total Project Cost	$766,000

The $1,000 is a miscellaneous cost and was expensed in 20X9, since it was determined by Poll to be immaterial.

The following schedule summarizes the additional borrowings of Poll as of December 31, 20X9:

Borrowing Date	Amount	Maturity Date	Annual Interest Rate
Mar. 1, 20X8	$1,000,000	Feb. 28, 20Y0	13%
Oct. 1, 20X9	$ 500,000	Sept. 30, 20Y1	14%

From February 1, 20X9, to March 31, 20X9, a major strike of construction workers occurred, halting all construction activity during this period.

In August 20X9, Poll voluntarily halted construction for the entire month because the chief executive officer did not want construction to continue without her supervision during her scheduled vacation.

Calculation of Interest

Poll's new plant facility is a qualifying asset under the provisions of ASC 835 and is subject to interest capitalization. The interest capitalization period begins on the first date that an expenditure is made by Poll, which was for architects' fees, February 1, 20X8.

To compute the interest capitalization for 20X8, the average accumulated expenditures for 20X8 are first calculated as follows:

Amount of Expenditure	Period from Expenditure to End of Year	Average Investment
$ 15,000	11 months (11/12)	$ 13,750
150,000	9 months (9/12)	112,500
60,000	4 months (4/12)	20,000
$225,000		$146,250

Next, the average investment amounts are multiplied by the interest rate on the borrowing (12%). This rate is used because Poll has specifically associated the borrowing with the construction of the new plant facility, and the average accumulated investment ($146,250) do not exceed the amount of the borrowing ($300,000). Therefore, the interest capitalized for 20X8 is computed as follows:

Average accumulated investment	$146,250
Interest rate	12%
Capitalizable interest cost—20X8	$17,550

Since Poll incurred $144,333 of interest costs [($300,000 × 12%) + ($1,000,000 × 13% × 10/12)], the full $17,550 must be capitalized.

The investment in the asset for 20X8 ($225,000 + $17,550 capitalized interest = $242,550) is included as part of the base to compute 20X9 capitalizable interest cost. One further adjustment is necessary to calculate the average accumulated expenditures for 20X9. The plant facility was completed on December 31, 20X9, but there were two interruptions in construction in 20X9. Interest is capitalized during delays or interruptions that are externally imposed, or during delays inherent in acquiring the qualifying asset. However, interest is not capitalized during delays or interruptions that are caused internally by an enterprise, unless they are brief. Thus, in this problem, interest capitalization continues during the externally imposed strike. However, interest capitalization ceases during August 20X9, because the CEO's vacation is a voluntary interruption.

The average accumulated investment for 20X9 is computed as follows:

Amount of Expenditure	Period from Expenditure to End of Year, Less One Month of Interruption	Average Investment
$242,550	11 months (11/12)	$222,338
360,000	9 months (9/12)	270,000
180,000	2 months (2/12)	30,000
$782,550		$522,338

Note: The $180,000 was expended on November 1, 20X9, after the interruption, so no adjustment need be made to the average expenditure of $30,000 for the interruption.

The $1,000 miscellaneous cost is not included, since Poll decided that this amount was immaterial and expensed it.

If the average accumulated investment for the qualifying asset exceeds the amount of the specific borrowing made to construct the asset, the capitalization rate applicable to the excess is the weighted-average interest rate incurred on other borrowings. In this problem, the computation of the excess investment over the original loan amount is as follows:

Average investment through December 31, 20X9	$522,338
Less: Amount of original loan	300,000
Excess investment	$222,338

Thus, in 20X9, interest on $222,338 of the $522,338 average investment is capitalized using the weighted-average borrowing rate, whereas interest on the balance of $300,000 is capitalized using the interest rate on the original loan made specifically to acquire the qualifying asset. The weighted-average rate on the other borrowings is computed as follows:

ASC 835—Interest

Amount	Weighted Amount	Rate	Annual Interest
$1,000,000	$1,000,000	13%	$130,000
500,000	125,000 (3 mos.)	14%	$17,500
$1,500,000	$1,125,000		$147,500

$$\frac{\$147,500}{\$1,125,000} = 13.11\% \text{ weighted-average interest rate.}$$

The interest cost to be capitalized for 20X9 is computed as follows:

$300,000	×	12.00%	=	$36,000
222,338	×	13.11%	=	29,149
$522,338				$65,149

Since Poll incurred $183,500 [($300,000 × 12%) + ($1,000,000 × 13%) + ($500,000 × 14% × 3/12)] of interest, the full $65,149 is capitalizable as part of the acquisition cost of the asset in 20X9.

The total interest capitalized on the asset is $82,699 ($17,550 in 20X8 plus $65,149 in 20X9). The total asset cost at the end of 20X9 is as follows:

Expenditures other than interest	$765,000
Interest cost capitalized	$82,699
	$847,699

OBSERVATION: In this illustration, interest capitalized in 20X9 was based on an investment amount from 20X8 that included the amount of interest capitalized in 20X8. The authors have not found specific authoritative guidance that supports the inclusion of previously capitalized interest in the investment base, but believes this is consistent with the inclusion of interest in other situations and is logical in the circumstances.

ASC 835-30: Imputation of Interest

CIRCUMSTANCES REQUIRING IMPUTED INTEREST

A note issued or received in a noncash transaction contains two elements to be valued: (1) the principal amount for the property, goods, or services exchanged and (2) an interest factor for the use of funds over the period of the note. These types of notes must be recorded at their present value. Any difference between the face amount of the note and its present value is a discount or premium that is amortized over the life of the note.

PRACTICE POINTER: The interest rate on a note that results from a business transaction entered into at arm's length is generally presumed to be fair. If no interest is stated or if the interest stated appears unreasonable, however, record the substance of the transaction. Further, if rights or privileges are attached to the note, evaluate them separately.

For example, a beer distributor lends $5,000 for two years at no interest to a customer who wishes to purchase bar equipment. There is a tacit agreement that the customer will buy the distributor's products. In this event, a present value must be established for the note receivable, and the difference between the face of the note ($5,000) and its present value must be considered an additional cost of doing business for the beer distributor.

Circumstances requiring interest to be imputed as specified in ASC 835 are summarized in Figure 835-1.

The present value techniques used in ASC 835 should not be applied to estimates of a contractual property or other obligations that are assumed in connection with a sale of property, goods, or services such as an estimated warranty for product performance.

OBSERVATION: Interest that is imputed on certain receivables and payables in accordance with ASC 835-30 is eligible for capitalization under the provisions of ASC 835-20 (Capitalization of Interest).

APPLYING ASC 835-30 PRINCIPLES

Determining Present Value

There is no predetermined formula for determining an appropriate interest rate. *However, the objective is to approximate what the rate would have been, using the same terms and conditions, if it had been negotiated by an independent lender.* The following factors should be considered (ASC 835-30-25-12):

- Credit rating of the borrower
- Restrictive covenants or collateral involved
- Prevailing market rates
- Rate at which the debtor can borrow funds

The appropriate interest rate depends on a combination of the above factors.

Figure 52-1: Circumstances Indicating a Need to Impute Interest

PRACTICE POINTER: In determining an appropriate interest rate for purposes of imputing interest for the purchaser in a transaction, a starting point might be the most recent borrowing rate. The more recent the borrowing, the more appropriate that rate may be. Even if the borrowing rate is recent, however, give consideration to the impact that the additional debt from the earlier borrowing would likely have on the company's next borrowing. The size of the transaction for which interest is being imputed relative to other outstanding debt also may be an important factor in determining an appropriate rate.

Discount and Premium

The difference between the present value and the face amount of the receivable or the payable represents the amount of premium or discount. A discount exists if the present value of the total cash flow of the note (face amount plus stated interest), using the appropriate rate of interest, is *less* than the face amount of the note. A premium exists if the present value of the total proceeds of the note (face amount plus stated interest), using the appropriate rate of interest, is *more* than the face amount of the note.

The premium or discount is amortized over the life of the note, using a constant rate on any outstanding balance. This method is called the *interest method* and is illustrated at the end of this chapter (ASC 835-30-35-2).

The premium or discount that arises from the use of present values on cash and noncash transactions is inseparable from the related asset or liability. Therefore, premiums and discounts are added to or deducted from their related asset or liability in the balance sheet. Discounts or premiums resulting from imputing interest are not classified as deferred charges or credits (ASC 835-30-45-1A).

Disclosure

A description of the receivable or payable, the effective interest rate, and the face amount of the note should be disclosed in the financial statements or notes thereto. Issue costs are reported separately in the balance sheet as deferred charges (ASC 835-30-45-2, 3)

Illustration of Interest Imputed and Accounted for on a Noninterest-Bearing Note

A manufacturer sells a machine for $10,000 and accepts a $10,000 note receivable bearing no interest for five years; 10% is an appropriate interest rate. The initial journal entry would be:

Note receivable	10,000.00	
Sales (present value at 10%)		6,209.00
Unamortized discount on note		3,791.00

The manufacturer records the note at its face amount but records the sale at the present value of the note because that is the value of the note today. The difference between the face amount of the note and its present value is recorded as *unamortized discount on note*.

The *interest method* is used to produce a constant rate, which is applied to any outstanding balance. In the above example, the present value of $6,209 was recorded for the $10,000 sale using the appropriate interest rate of 10% for the five-year term of the note. The difference between the $10,000 sale and its present value of $6,209 is $3,791, which was recorded as unamortized discount on note. The 10% rate, when applied to each annual outstanding balance for the same five years, will result in amortization of the discount on the note, as follows:

ASC 835—Interest **52,015**

		Amortization of Discount on the Note
Original balance	$ 6,209.00	$3,791.00
Year 1, 10%	620.90	(620.90)
Remaining balance	$ 6,829.90	$3,170.10
Year 2, 10%	682.99	(682.99)
Remaining balance	$ 7,512.89	$2,487.11
Year 3, 10%	751.29	(751.29)
Remaining balance	$ 8,264.18	$1,735.82
Year 4, 10%	826.42	(826.42)
Remaining balance	$ 9,090.60	$ 909.40
Year 5, to clear accounts	909.40	(909.40)
Remaining balance	$10,000.00	$-0-

Following are the journal entries to record imputed interest at the end of each year and the final collection of the note.

End of 1st year:
Unamortized discount on note	620.90	
Interest income		620.90

End of 2nd year:
Unamortized discount on note	682.99	
Interest income		682.99

End of 3rd year:
Unamortized discount on note	751.29	
Interest income		751.29

End of 4th year:
Unamortized discount on note	826.42	
Interest income		826.42

End of 5th year:
Unamortized discount on note	909.40	
Interest income		909.40
Cash	10,000.00	
Note receivable		10,000.00

Illustration of Recording a Note with an Unreasonable Rate of Interest

A company purchases a $10,000 machine and issues for payment a $10,000 four-year note bearing 2% compound interest per year; 10% is considered an appropriate rate of interest. The entire amount due, including all interest, is payable at the maturity date of the note. The initial journal entry is:

Machine (present value of $10,824 @ 10% for 4 periods)	7,393	
Unamortized discount on note	3,431	

Note payable		10,000
Deferred interest payable		824
First year:		
Interest expense	739	
Unamortized discount on note (10% on $7,393)		739
Second year:		
Interest expense	813	
Unamortized discount on note [10% on ($7,393 + $739)]		813
Third year:		
Interest expense	895	
Unamortized discount on note [10% on ($7,393 + $739 + $813)]		895
Fourth year:		
Interest expense	984	
Unamortized discount on note [10% on ($7,393 + $739 + $813 + $895)]		984

In the fourth year, when the note and the 2% interest are paid, the following journal entry is made:

Note payable	$10,000	
Deferred interest payable	824	
Cash		$10,824

The future amount of the note is $10,824 ($10,000 × 1.0824, which compounds the 2% for four periods). The company records a note payable ($10,000) and the deferred interest ($824). The machine is recorded at the present value of this amount ($7,393), determined by discounting the $10,824 at 10% (the reasonable interest rate) for four years. This is because today the $10,824 is worth only $7,393, which is the amount at which the sale is recorded. The difference between the total amount due in four years ($10,824) and its present value ($7,393) is deferred interest ($3,431) for the use of the seller's funds and is amortized by the interest method over the term of the note.

PART II: INTERPRETIVE GUIDANCE

ASC 835-30 IMPUTATION OF INTEREST

ASC 835-30-55-2 Required Use of Interest Method in Recognizing Interest Income

Because ASC 310-20 discusses the application of the interest method to nonrefundable loan fees and costs, not to interest income, some have questioned whether the interest method must be used to determine interest income. Using the interest method to recognize interest income is required under GAAP. Alternative methods, such as the rule of 78s, sum of the years' digits, and straight-line methods, should *not* be used to impute interest unless the results do not differ materially from those based on the interest method.

CHAPTER 53
ASC 840—LEASES

CONTENTS

Part I: General Guidance	
ASC 840-10: Overall	53,005
Overview	53,005
Background	53,007
Terminology	53,007
Capital Lease	53,007
Sales-Type Lease	53,008
Direct Financing Lease	53,008
Fair Value	53,008
Fair Rental	53,008
Related Parties	53,008
Executory Costs	53,009
Bargain Purchase Option	53,009
Bargain Renewal Option	53,009
Estimated Economic Life	53,009
Estimated Residual Value	53,009
Unguaranteed Residual Value	53,009
Incremental Borrowing Rate	53,009
Lease Inception	53,009
Interest Rate Implicit in the Lease	53,009
Initial Direct Costs	53,010
Contingent Rentals	53,010
Lease Term	53,011
Noncancelable Lease Term	53,011
Penalty	53,011
Minimum Lease Payments	53,011
Lease Classification	53,013
Lessees	53,013
Lessors	53,014
Changing a Provision of a Lease	53,014
Leases Involving Real Estate	53,014
Review of Classification of Leases by Lessees	53,015
Leases Involving Land Only	53,015
Leases Involving Land and Building(s)	53,016
Leases That Meet Criterion 1 or Criterion 2	53,016
Fair Value of the Land Is Less Than 25% of the Total Fair Value of the Leased Property at the Inception of the Lease	53,017
Fair Value of the Land Is 25% or More of the Total Fair Value of the Leased Property at the Inception of the Lease	53,017
Leases Involving Land, Building(s), and Equipment	53,018
Leases Involving Only Part of a Building(s)	53,018

Lessee	53,018
Lessor	53,019
Other Lease Accounting Issues	53,019
Subleases and Similar Transactions	53,019
Leases Involving Governmental Units	53,021
Related Party Leases	53,021
Leveraged Leases	53,022
Lessor's Existing Asset in a Leveraged Lease	53,023
General Disclosures	53,023
ASC 840-20: Operating Leases	53,023
Operating Leases	53,023
Accounting and Reporting by the Lessee	53,023
Contingent Rental Expense	53,024
Scheduled Rent Increases or Decreases	53,024
Leasehold Improvements	53,024
Rent Holidays	53,025
Accounting and Reporting by Lessors	53,027
Contingent Rental Income	53,028
Lease Sale or Assignment to Third Parties	53,028
Financial Statement Disclosures	53,029
Illustration of Lessee's Financial Statement Disclosure	53,029
Illustration of Lessor's Financial Statement Disclosure	53,030
ASC 840-30: Capital Leases	53,031
Capital Leases	53,031
Accounting and Reporting by Lessees	53,031
Initial Recording	53,031
Leases with Escalation Clauses	53,031
Amortization	53,033
Interest Expense: Interest Method	53,034
Illustration of Interest Method	53,034
Change in Lease Terms	53,034
Termination of a Lease	53,035
Illustration of Capital Lease (Lessee)	53,035
Accounting and Reporting by Lessors	53,037
Recording Sales-Type Leases	53,037
Recording Direct Financing Leases	53,038
Balance Sheet Classification	53,039
Annual Review of Residual Values	53,039
Accounting for Lease Changes	53,039
Termination of a Lease	53,040
Financial Statement Disclosure	53,040
Illustration of Lessee's Financial Statement Disclosure	53,041
Illustration of Lessor's Financial Statement Disclosure	53,042
Lease Modifications	53,043
Refunding of Tax-Exempt Debt	
Figure 53-1: Classification of a Lease as a Capital or Operating Lease	53,045
Other Lease Accounting Issues	53,046

Leverage Leases	**53,046**
Business Combinations	**53,047**
ASC 840-40: Sale-Leaseback Transactions	**53,048**
Sale-Leaseback Transactions	**53,048**
Non-Real Estate	**53,048**
Substantially All or Minor	**53,048**
More Than Minor but Less Than Substantially All	**53,049**
Profit Recognition Other Than by the Full Accrual Method	**53,050**
Real Estate	**53,050**
Criteria for Sale-Leaseback Accounting	**53,051**
Adequate Initial and Continuing Investment by the Purchaser-Lessor	**53,051**
Terms of the Sale-Leaseback Transaction	**53,051**
Continuing Involvement	**53,052**
Financial Statement Presentation	**53,053**
Wrap Lease Transactions	**53,053**
Illustration of Wrap Lease Transactions	**53,054**
Part II: Interpretive Guidance	
ASC 840-10: Overall	**53,055**
ASC 840-10-05-7 through 05-8, 25-12 through 25-13, 25-14; ASC 840-40-15-2, 25-13; ASC 958-840-55-4; ASC 450-20-60-16; 460-10-60-23	
Implementation Issues in Accounting for Lease Transactions, Including Those Involving Special-Purpose Entities	**53,055**
ASC 840-10-05-9A through 05-9C, 25-39A through 25-39B, 35-9A	
Accounting by Lessees for Maintenance Deposits under Lease Agreements	**53,057**
ASC 840-10-15-3 through 15-6, 15-10 through 15-20, 35-2 through 35-3, 55-26, 55-30 through 55-37; ASC 840-20-25-9, 25-22, 40-2, 40-6; ASC 840-30-25-4, 30-5, 40-2 through 40-3, 40-6; ASC 440-10-25-1, 25-3; ASC 815-10-15-79	
Determining Whether an Arrangement Is a Lease	**53,058**
ASC 840-10-15-20; ASC 815-10-15-80 through 15-81; ASC 460-10-60-20	
The Impact of the Requirements of ASC 815 on Residual Value Guarantees in Connection with a Lease	**53,062**
ASC 840-10-25-3	
Fiscal Funding Clauses in Lease Agreements	**53,063**
ASC 840 ASC 840-10-25-46, 25-48 through 25-50	
Lessors' Evaluation of Whether Leases of Certain Integral Equipment Meet the Ownership Transfer Requirements of ASC 840	**53,063**
ASC 840-10-25-6 ; ASC 840-20-25-8, 25-12 through 25-13, 30-1, 35-1; ASC 840-40-55-42 through 55-47; ASC 958-810-25-9, 55-7 through 55-16; ASC 958-840-55-2 through 55-3; ASC 460-10-60-24	
Implementation Issues in Accounting for Leasing Transactions	**53,064**
ASC 840-10-25-10 through 25-11, 25-53, 50-3; ASC 460-10-55-23A	
Tax Indemnifications in Lease Agreements	**53,067**
ASC 840-10-25-21 through 25-22; ASC 460-10-60-19	
Allocation of Residual Value or First-Loss Guarantee to Minimum Lease Payments in Leases Involving Land and Building(s)	**53,068**
ASC 840-10-25-35, 40-1, 50-5; ASC 450-20-60-15; ASC 450-30-60-5	
Accounting for Contingent Rent	**53,069**

53,004   ASC 840—Leases

ASC 840-10-35-6 through 35-9; ASC 805-20-35-6
    Determining the Amortization Period for Leasehold Improvements Purchased after Lease Inception or Acquired in a Business Combination   53,071

ASC 840-10-45-2 through 45-3
    Applicability of ASC 840 to Current Value Financial Statements   53,072

ASC 840-10-55-12 through 55-25; ASC 460-10-55-17, 60-22; ASC 605-50-60-1
    Sales with a Guaranteed Minimum Resale Amount   53,073

ASC, *Glossary—Incremental Borrowing Rate*
    Interest Rate Used in Calculating the Present Value of Minimum Lease Payments   53,076

ASC 840-20: Operating Leases   53,076

ASC 840-20-25-2
    Accounting for Operating Leases with Scheduled Rent Increases   53,076

ASC 840-20-25-3 through 25-7, 55-1 through 55-3; ASC 840-10-55-45 through 55-46; ASC 840-30-55-14, 55-19 through 55-20; ASC 840-40-55-17 through 55-21
    Issues Relating to Accounting for Leases   53,077

ASC 840-20-25-10 through 25-11, 45-1
    Accounting for Rental Costs Incurred during a Construction Period   53,080

ASC 840-20-25-14 through 25-15; ASC 840-30-35-13
    Accounting for Loss on a Sublease Not Involving the Disposal of a Segment   53,080

ASC 840-30: Capital Leases   53,081

ASC 840-30-35-25
    Upward Adjustment of Guaranteed Residual Values   53,081

ASC 840-30-35-41, 50-6
    Effect of a Change in Income Tax Rate on the Accounting for Leveraged Leases   53,081

ASC 840-30-35-48 through 35-52; ASC 740-10-25-43
    Issues Related to the Alternative Minimum Tax   53,082

ASC 840-30-S35-1, S99-2
    Effect of a Change in Tax Law or Rates on Leveraged Leases   53,083

ASC 840-30-55-15 through 55-16
    Leveraged Leases: Real Estate Leases and Sale-Leaseback Transactions, Delayed Equity Contributions by Lessors   53,084

ASC 840-40: Sale-Leaseback Transactions

ASC 840-40-05-5, 15-5, 25-4, 35-3, 55-2 through 55-16, S55-2, S99-2 ASC 460-10-60-28 through 60-31
    The Effect of Lessee Involvement in Asset Construction   53,085

ASC 840-40-15-2
    Application of the Guidance in ASC 840-40-55-2 through 55-16 and ASC 840-10-25-25 to Entities That Enter into Leases with Governmental Entities   53,089

ASC 840-40-25-14; ASC 460-10-60-33
    Impact of an Uncollateralized Irrevocable Letter of Credit on a Real Estate Sale-Leaseback Transaction   53,090

ASC 840-40-25-15 through 25-16; ASC 460-10-60-26 through 60-27

Unsecured Guarantee by Parent of Subsidiary's Lease Payments in a Sale-Leaseback Transaction	53,091
ASC 840-40-25-18, 55-48	
Sale-Leaseback Transactions with Continuing Involvement	53,092
ASC 840-40-30-5 through 30-6	
Consideration of Executory Costs in Sale-Leaseback Transactions	53,092
ASC 840-40-55-22 through 55-24	
Accounting for the Sale and Leaseback of an Asset That Is Leased to Another Party	53,093
ASC 840-40-55-26 through 55-28; ASC 460-10-55-17, 60-32	
Deferred Profit on Sale-Leaseback Transaction with Lessee Guarantee of Residual Value	53,094
ASC 840-40-55-29 through 55-34	
Accounting for Cross Border Tax Benefit Leases	53,096
ASC 840-40-55-37 through 55-41	
Accounting for the Sale of Property Subject to the Seller's Preexisting Lease	53,097

PART I: GENERAL GUIDANCE

ASC 840-10: OVERALL

OVERVIEW

A *lease* is an agreement that conveys the right to use property, usually for a specified period. Leases typically involve two parties: the owner of the property (lessor) and the party contracting to use the property (lessee). Because of certain tax, cash flow, and other advantages, leases have become an important alternative to the outright purchase of property by which companies (lessees) acquire the resources needed to operate.

Leases include agreements that, while not nominally referred to as leases, have the characteristic of transferring the right to use property (e.g., heat supply contracts), and agreements that transfer the right to use property even though the contractor may be required to provide substantial services in connection with the operation or maintenance of the assets (ASC 840-10-15-8).

The term *lease*, as used in promulgated GAAP, does *not* include the following (ASC 840-10-15-10, 15):

- Agreements that are contracts for services that do not transfer the right to use property from one contracting party to another
- Agreements that concern the right to explore for or exploit natural resources such as oil, gas, minerals, and timber
- Agreements that represent licensing agreements for items such as motion picture films, plays, manuscripts, patents, and copyrights

A central accounting issue associated with leases is the identification of those leases that are treated appropriately as sales of the property by lessors and as purchases of the property by lessees (*capital leases*). Those leases that are not identified as capital leases are called *operating leases* and are not treated as sales by lessors and as purchases by lessees. Rather, they are treated on a prospective basis as a series of cash flows from the lessee to the lessor.

Following is a brief overview of GAAP for leases.

A lease is an agreement that conveys the right to use assets (tangible or intangible) for a stated period. A lease that transfers substantially all the benefits and risks inherent in the ownership of property is called a *capital lease*. Such a lease is accounted for by the lessee as the acquisition of an asset and the incurrence of a liability. The lessor accounts for such a lease as a sale (sales-type lease) or financing (direct financing lease). All other leases are referred to as *operating leases*.

If the leased property is yet to be constructed or acquired by the lessor at the inception of the lease, the lessor's criterion pertaining to "no important uncertainties of unreimbursable costs yet to be incurred by the lessor" is applied at the date that construction of the property is completed or the property is acquired. Any increases in the minimum lease payments that have occurred during the preacquisition or preconstruction period as a result of an escalation clause are to be considered in determining the fair value of the leased property at the inception of the lease. The amount that can be recorded by the lessor for the residual value of leased property is limited to an amount not greater than the estimate as of the inception of the lease.

A lessor is required to classify a renewal or an extension of a sales-type or direct financing lease as a sales-type lease if the lease would otherwise qualify as a sales-type lease and the renewal or extension occurs at or near the end of the lease term. Otherwise, ASC 840 prohibits the classification of a renewal or extension of a sales-type or direct financing lease as a sales-type lease at any other time during the lease term.

The appropriate accounting for sale-leaseback transactions depends on the percentage amount of the property that the seller-lessee leases back (substantially all of the property, a minor portion of the property, or more than a minor portion of the property but less than substantially all) and whether the lease is classified as a capital lease or an operating lease.

ASC 840 defines *contingent rentals* as those that cannot be determined at the inception of the lease because they depend on future factors or events. Rental payments based on future sales volume, future machine hours, future interest rates, and future price indexes are examples of contingent rentals. Contingent rentals can either increase or decrease lease payments.

ASC 310 establishes accounting and reporting standards for nonrefundable fees and costs associated with lending, committing to lend, or purchasing a loan or group of loans. Under ASC 310, direct loan origination fees and costs, including initial direct costs incurred by a lessor in negotiating and consummating a lease, are offset against each other and the net amount is deferred and recognized over the life of the loan as an adjustment to the yield on the loan. The provisions of ASC 310 apply to all types of loans, including debt securities, and to all types of lenders, including banks, thrift institutions, insurance companies, mortgage bankers, and other financial and nonfinancial institutions. However, ASC 310 does not apply to nonrefundable fees and costs that are associated with originating or acquiring loans which are carried at market value.

ASC 840 defines *penalty* and *lease term* for all leasing transactions. In addition, it specifies the appropriate accounting for a seller-lessee in a sale-leaseback transaction involving real estate, including real estate with equipment, such as manufacturing facilities, power plants, furnished office buildings, etc. It also establishes the appropriate accounting for a sale-leaseback transaction in which property improvements or integral equipment is sold to a purchaser-lessor and leased back by the seller-lessee who retains the ownership of the underlying land. Finally, it provides the appropriate accounting for sale-leaseback transactions involving real estate with equipment that include separate sale and leaseback agreements for the real estate and the equipment (*a*) with the same entity or related parties and (*b*) that are consummated at or near the same time, suggesting that they were negotiated as a package.

BACKGROUND

Some lease agreements are such that an asset and a related liability should be reported on the balance sheet of the lessee enterprise. The distinction is one of *substance over form* when the transaction actually *transfers substantially all the benefits and risks inherent in the ownership of the property.*

Established in GAAP are criteria to determine whether a lease transaction is in substance a transfer of the incidents of ownership. If, *at its inception*, a lease meets one or more of the following four criteria, the lease is classified as a capital lease (ASC 840-10-25-1):

1. By the end of the lease term, ownership of the leased property is transferred to the lessee.
2. The lease contains a bargain purchase option.
3. The lease term is substantially (75% or more) equal to the estimated useful life of the leased property.
4. At the inception of the lease, the present value of the minimum lease payments, with certain adjustments, is 90% or more of the fair value of the leased property.

These criteria are examined in more detail later in this chapter.

TERMINOLOGY

The authoritative literature includes many terms that are important for an understanding of lease accounting. Several of these terms are explained below.

Capital Lease

A capital lease transfers the benefits and risks inherent in the ownership of the property to the lessee, who accounts for the lease as an acquisition of an asset and the incurrence of a liability (ASC 840-10-25-1).

Sales-Type Lease

A sales-type lease is a type of capital lease that results in a manufacturer's or dealer's profit or loss to the lessor and transfers substantially all the benefits and risks inherent in the ownership of the leased property to the lessee; in addition, (*a*) the minimum lease payments are reasonably predictable of collection and (*b*) no important uncertainties exist regarding costs to be incurred by the lessor under the terms of the lease (ASC 840-10-25-43).

In a sales-type lease, the *fair value* of the leased property at the inception of the lease differs from the cost or carrying amount because a manufacturer's or dealer's profit or loss exists. Fair value usually is the *normal selling price* of the property.

Direct Financing Lease

A direct financing lease is a type of capital lease that does *not* result in a manufacturer's or dealer's profit or loss to the lessor, but does transfer substantially all the benefits and risks inherent in the ownership of the leased property to the lessee; in addition, (*a*) the minimum lease payments are reasonably predictable of collection and (*b*) no important uncertainties exist regarding costs to be incurred by the lessor under the terms of the lease (ASC 840-10-25-43).

Separately identifying sales-type and direct financing leases is an accounting issue for the lessor only, who accounts for the two types of capital leases differently, as described later in this chapter. Both types of leases transfer substantially all the benefits and risks inherent in the ownership of the leased property to the lessee, who records the transaction as a *capital lease.*

Fair Value

Fair value is the price for which the leased property could be sold between unrelated parties in an arm's-length transaction at the measurement date (ASC 840-10-55-43).

For the manufacturer or dealer, fair value usually is the normal selling price less trade or volume discounts. Fair value may be less than the normal selling price, however, and sometimes less than the cost of the property.

For others, fair value usually is cost less trade or volume discounts. Fair value may be less than cost, however, especially in circumstances in which a long period elapses between the acquisition of the property by the lessor and the inception of a lease.

Fair Rental

Fair rental is the rental rate for similar property under similar lease terms and conditions.

Related Parties

Related parties are one or more entities subject to the significant influence over the operating and financial policies of another entity (ASC 840-10-55-27).

Executory Costs

Executory costs are items such as insurance, maintenance, and taxes paid in connection with the leased property (ASC 840-10-25-5).

Bargain Purchase Option

A bargain purchase option is a lessee's option to purchase the leased property at a sufficiently low price that makes the exercise of the option relatively certain (ASC 840-10-25-1).

Bargain Renewal Option

A bargain renewal option is a lessee's option to renew the lease at a sufficiently low rental that makes the exercise of the option relatively certain (ASC Glossary).

Estimated Economic Life

Estimated economic life is the estimated remaining useful life of the property for the purpose for which it was intended, regardless of the term of the lease (ASC 840-10-25-1).

Estimated Residual Value

Estimated residual value is the estimated fair value of the leased property at the end of the lease term. The estimated residual value shall not exceed the amount estimated at the inception of the lease except for the effect of any increases that result during the construction or preacquisition period, because of escalation provisions in the lease (ASC Glossary).

Unguaranteed Residual Value

Unguaranteed residual value is the estimated fair value of the leased property at the end of the lease term that is not guaranteed by either the lessee or a third party unrelated to the lessor. A guarantee by a third party related to the lessee is considered a lessee guarantee (ASC Glossary).

Incremental Borrowing Rate

The lessee's incremental borrowing rate is the rate of interest that the lessee would have had to pay at the inception of the lease to borrow the funds, on similar terms, to purchase the leased property (ASC Glossary).

Lease Inception

The inception of the lease is the date of the lease agreement *or* the date of a written commitment signed by the parties involved that sets forth the principal provisions of the lease transaction. A written commitment that does not contain all of the principal provisions of the lease transaction does not establish the inception date (ASC Glossary).

Interest Rate Implicit in the Lease

The interest rate implicit in the lease is the rate that, when applied to certain items (enumerated below), results in an aggregate present value equal to the fair value of the leased property at the beginning of the lease term, less any investment credit expected to be realized and retained by the lessor. The discount rate is applied to (a) the minimum lease payments, excluding executory costs such as insurance, maintenance, and taxes (including any profit thereon) that are paid by the lessor and (b) the estimated fair value of the property at the end of the lease term, exclusive of any portion guaranteed by either the lessee or a third party unrelated to the lessor (unguaranteed residual value) (ASC Glossary).

Initial Direct Costs

The definition of *initial direct costs* is as follows (ASC 840-20-25-17):

> *Initial direct costs.** Only those costs incurred by the lessor that are (a) costs to originate a lease incurred in transactions with independent third parties that (i) result directly from and are essential to acquire that lease and (ii) would not have been incurred had that leasing transaction not occurred and (b) certain costs directly related to specified activities performed by the lessor for that lease. Those activities are: evaluating the prospective lessee's financial condition; evaluating and recording guarantees, collateral, and other security arrangements; negotiating lease terms; preparing and processing lease documents; and closing the transaction. The costs directly related to those activities shall include only that portion of the employees' total compensation and payroll-related fringe benefits directly related to time spent performing those activities for that lease and other costs related to those activities that would not have been incurred but for that lease. Initial direct costs shall not include costs related to activities performed by the lessor for advertising, soliciting potential lessees, servicing existing leases, and other ancillary activities related to establishing and monitoring credit policies, supervision, and administration. Initial direct costs shall not include administrative costs, rent, depreciation, any other occupancy and equipment costs, and employees' compensation and fringe benefits related to activities described in the previous sentence, unsuccessful origination efforts, and idle time.

In determining the net amount of initial direct costs in a leasing transaction under ASC 840, a lessor shall apply the provisions of ASC 310 relating to loan origination fees, commitment fees, and direct loan origination costs of completed loans. Initial direct costs are accounted for by lessors as part of the investment in a direct financing lease.

> **OBSERVATION:** The recognition of a portion of the unearned income at the inception of a lease transaction to offset initial direct costs is not permitted (ASC 310-20-35-2).

Contingent Rentals

Contingent rentals are those that cannot be determined at the inception of the lease because they depend on future factors or events. Rental payments based on future sales volume, future machine hours, future interest rates, and future price indexes are examples of contingent rentals. Contingent rentals can either increase or decrease lease payments (ASC Glossary).

---

* Initial direct cost shall be offset by nonrefundable fees that are yield adjustments.

Increases in minimum lease payments that occur during the preacquisition or construction period as a result of an escalation clause in the lease are not considered contingent rentals (ASC Glossary).

Lease Term

The lease term includes all of the following (ASC Glossary):

- Any fixed noncancelable term
- Any period covered by a bargain renewal option
- Any period in which penalties are imposed in an amount that at the inception of the lease reasonably assures the renewal of the lease by the lessee
- Any period covered by ordinary renewal options during which a guarantee by the lessee of the lessor's debt that is directly or indirectly related to the leased property is expected to be in effect or a loan from the lessee to the lessor that is directly or indirectly related to the leased property is expected to be outstanding

    Note: The phrase *indirectly related to the leased property* is used to cover situations that in substance are guarantees of the lessor's debt or loans to the lessor by the lessee that are related to the leased property, but are structured in such a manner that they do not represent a direct guarantee or loan.

- Any period covered by ordinary renewal options preceding the date on which a bargain purchase option is exercisable
- Any period representing renewals or extensions of the lease at the lessor's option

A lease term does not extend beyond the date a bargain purchase option becomes exercisable.

Noncancelable Lease Term

A noncancelable lease term is a provision in a lease agreement that specifies that the lease may be canceled only (*a*) on some remote contingency, (*b*) with permission of the lessor, or (*c*) if the lessee enters into a new lease with the same lessor (ASC Glossary).

Penalty

The term *penalty* refers to any outside factor or provision of the lease agreement that does or can impose on the lessee the requirement to disburse cash, incur or assume a liability, perform services, surrender or transfer an asset or rights to an asset or otherwise forego an economic benefit, or suffer an economic detriment (ASC 840-10-25-6):

MINIMUM LEASE PAYMENTS

Normal minimum lease payments for the lessee include (ASC 840-10-25-6):

- The minimum rent called for during the lease term

- Any payment or guarantee that the lessee must make or is required to make concerning the leased property at the end of the lease term (residual value), including:
  — Any amount stated to purchase the leased property
  — Any amount stated to make up any deficiency from a specified minimum
  — Any amount payable for failure to renew or extend the lease at the expiration of the lease term

When a lease contains a *bargain purchase option,* the minimum lease payments include only (*a*) the *minimum rental payments over the lease term* and (*b*) *the payment required to exercise the bargain purchase option.*

The following are excluded in determining minimum lease payments (ASC 840-10-25-5):

- A guarantee by the lessee to pay the lessor's debt on the leased property
- The lessee's obligation (separate from the rental payments) to pay executory costs (insurance, taxes, etc.) in connection with the leased property
- Contingent rentals (ASC Glossary)

OBSERVATION: Guidance on lessee guarantee of the residual value of the leased property is as follows:

- A guarantee by a lessee to make up a residual value deficiency caused by damage, extraordinary wear and tear, or excessive usage is similar to a contingent rental, since the amount is not determinable at the inception of the lease. Therefore, this type of lessee guarantee does not constitute a lessee guarantee of residual value for purposes of computing the lessee's minimum lease payments (ASC 840-10-25-9).
- A lessee's guarantee to make up a residual value deficiency at the end of a lease term is limited to the specified maximum deficiency called for by the lease (ASC 840-10-55-9).
- Unless the lessor explicitly releases the lessee, a guarantee of residual value by an unrelated third party for the benefit of the lessor does not release the obligation of the lessee. Therefore, such a guarantee by an unrelated third party shall not be used to reduce the lessee's minimum lease payments. Costs incurred in connection with a guarantee by an unrelated third party are considered executory costs and are not included in computing the lessee's minimum lease payments (ASC 840-10-55-10).

The minimum lease payments to a lessor are the sum of (ASC 840-10-25-7):

- The minimum lease payments under the lease terms
- Any guarantee by a third party, unrelated to the lessee and lessor, of the residual value or rental payments beyond the lease term, providing such guarantor is financially capable of discharging the potential obligation

LEASE CLASSIFICATION

Lessees

If one or more of the following four criteria is present at the inception of a lease, it is classified as a capital lease by the lessee (ASC 840-10-25-1, 29):

1. Ownership of the property is transferred to the lessee by the end of the lease term.
2. The lease contains a bargain purchase option.
3. The lease term, at inception, is substantially (75% or more) equal to the estimated economic life of the leased property, including earlier years of use. (*Exception:* This criterion cannot be used for a lease that begins within the last 25% of the original estimated economic life of the leased property. *Example:* A jet aircraft that has an estimated economic life of 25 years is leased for five successive five-year leases. If the first four five-year leases were classified as operating leases, the last five-year lease cannot be classified as a capital lease, because the lease would commence within the last 25% of the estimated economic life of the property and would fall under this exception.)
4. The present value of the minimum lease payments at the beginning of the lease term, excluding executory costs and profits thereon to be paid by the lessor, is 90% or more of the fair value of the property at the inception of the lease, less any investment tax credit retained and expected to be realized by the lessor. (*Exception:* This criterion cannot be used for a lease that begins within the last 25% of the original estimated economic life of the leased property.)

A lessee's incremental borrowing rate is used to determine the present value of the minimum lease payments, except that the lessor's implicit rate of interest is used if it is known and it is lower (ASC 840-10-25-30).

PRACTICE POINTER: While the criteria for identifying a capital lease appear very specific, significant professional judgment must be exercised in implementing them. For example:

- Except in the simplest cases, determining the lease term may involve judgment.
- Several of the criteria include terms that require judgment when they are applied to a specific lease. These include "bargain purchase option," "estimated useful life of the property," and "fair value of the property."
- The lease term and the present value of minimum lease payments criteria are not available for leases that begin within the last 25% of the asset's estimated useful life, which is subject to judgment.
- Determining the minimum lease payments for the lessee may require use of that party's incremental borrowing rate, which may involve judgment.

Lessors

If, at inception, a lease meets any one (or more) of the four criteria indicating that substantially all the benefits and risks of ownership have been transferred to the lessee, and it *meets both the following conditions,* the lease is classified by the lessor as a sales-type or direct financing lease, whichever is appropriate:

- *Collection of the minimum lease payments is reasonably predictable.* A receivable resulting from a lease subject to an estimate of uncollectibility based on experience is not precluded from being classified as either a sales-type or a direct financing lease.

- *No important uncertainties exist for unreimbursable costs yet to be incurred by the lessor under the lease.* Important uncertainties include extensive warranties and material commitments beyond normal practice. *Executory costs,* such as insurance, maintenance, and taxes, are not considered important uncertainties (ASC 840-10-25-42).

   Note: In the event the leased property is not acquired or constructed before the inception of the lease, this condition is not applied until such time as the leased property is acquired or constructed by the lessor (ASC 840-10-25-42).

In applying the fourth basic capitalization criterion—the present value of the lease equals or exceeds 90% of the fair value of the property—a *lessor* computes the present value of the minimum lease payments, using the interest rate *implicit in the lease* (ASC 840-10-25-41).

A lease involving real estate is not classified by the lessor as a salestype lease unless the title to the leased property is transferred to the lessee at or shortly after the end of the lease term.

Classification of a lease as a capital or operating lease is summarized in Figure 53-1.

CHANGING A PROVISION OF A LEASE

If a change in a provision of a lease results in a different lease classification at the inception of the lease because it meets different criteria, a new lease agreement is created that must be reclassified according to its different criteria. Renewal, extension, or a new lease under which the lessee continues to use the same property is not considered a change in a lease provision (ASC 840-10-35-4).

Any action that extends the lease term, except to void a residual guarantee, or a penalty for failure to renew the lease at the end of the lease term, is considered a new lease agreement that is classified according to the different criteria (ASC 840-10-35-4).

Changes in estimates or circumstances do not cause a reclassification.

LEASES INVOLVING REAL ESTATE

Leases involving real estate are categorized as follows:

- Land only
- Land and building(s)

- Land, building(s), and equipment
- Only part of a building(s)

Review of Classification of Leases by Lessees

A review of the classifications of leases by lessees is necessary because accounting for leases involving real estate depends primarily on the criteria for classifying leases.

If one or more of the following four criteria are present at the inception of a lease, it is classified as a capital lease by the lessee:

1. Ownership of the property is transferred to the lessee by the end of the lease term.
2. The lease contains a bargain purchase option.
3. The lease term, at inception, is substantially (75% or more) equal to the estimated economic life of the leased property, including earlier years of use. (*Exception:* This criterion cannot be used for a lease that begins within the last 25% of the original estimated economic life of the leased property.)
4. The present value of the minimum lease payments at the beginning of the lease term, excluding executory costs and profits thereon to be paid by the lessor, is 90% or more of the fair value of the property at the inception of the lease, less any investment tax credit retained and expected to be realized by the lessor. (*Exception:* This criterion cannot be used for a lease that begins within the last 25% of the original estimated economic life of the leased property.)

These criteria are referred to by number in the following discussion.

Leases Involving Land Only

A *lessee* accounts for a lease involving land only as a capital lease if either criterion 1 or criterion 2 is met. All other leases involving land only are classified as operating leases by the lessee.

A *lessor* classifies a lease involving land only as a sales-type lease and accounts for the transaction as a sale under the provisions of ASC 360, if the lease gives rise to a manufacturer's or dealer's profit (or loss) and criterion 1 is met. A lessor classifies a lease involving land only as a direct financing lease or a leveraged lease, whichever is applicable, if the lease does not give rise to a manufacturer's or dealer's profit (or loss), criterion 1 is met, and (*a*) the collection of the minimum lease payments is reasonably predictable and (*b*) no important uncertainties exist regarding costs yet to be incurred by the lessor under the lease. A lessor classifies a lease involving land only as a direct financing lease, a leveraged lease, or an operating lease, whichever is applicable, if criterion 2 is met, and (*a*) the collection of the minimum lease payments is reasonably predictable and (*b*) no important uncertainties exist regarding costs yet to be incurred by the lessor under the lease. All other leases involving land only are classified as operating leases by the lessor.

PRACTICE POINTER: The criteria for recognition of a sale under ASC 360 (Property, Plant, and Equipment) are quite similar to the additional criteria that must be met by lessors under ASC 840 in order for the lease to qualify as a capital lease. That is, under ASC 360, two criteria must be met in order for profit to be recognized in full at the time of the sale: (1) the sales price is reasonably predictable of collection and (2) the lessor of the land is not obligated to perform significant activities under the terms of the lease (ASC 360-20-40-3). Collectibility is assessed by evaluating the adequacy of the lessee's initial and continuing investment (ASC 360-20-40-4). For land to be developed within (after) two years of the sale, the lessee's initial investment should be at least 20% (25%) of the land's sales value (ASC 360-20-55-2). The lessee's continuing investment must be at least an amount equal to the level annual payment required to liquidate the unpaid balance (both interest and principal) over no more than 20 years for a lease involving land (ASC 360-20-40-19).

Leases Involving Land and Building(s)

Leases involving land and building(s) may be categorized as follows:

- Leases that meet criterion 1 or criterion 2
- Leases in which the fair value of the land is less than 25% of the total fair value of the leased property at the inception of the lease
- Leases in which the fair value of the land is 25% or more of the total fair value of the leased property at the inception of the lease

Leases That Meet Criterion 1 or Criterion 2

Leases that meet either criterion 1 or criterion 2 are accounted for as follows:

- *Lessee* The present value of the minimum lease payments, less executory costs and profits thereon (to be paid by the lessor), is allocated between the land and building(s) in proportion to their fair value at the inception of the lease. The present value assigned to the building(s) is amortized in accordance with the lessee's normal depreciation policy (ASC 840-10-25-38).
- *Lessor* If a lease gives rise to a manufacturer's or dealer's profit (or loss) and criterion 1 is met, a lessor classifies a lease involving land and building(s) as a sales-type lease and accounts for the transaction as a sale under the provisions of ASC 360. If a lease does not give rise to a manufacturer's or dealer's profit (or loss) and criterion 1 is met, a lessor classifies a lease involving land and building(s) as a direct financing lease or a leveraged lease, whichever is applicable, providing that (*a*) collection of the minimum lease payments are reasonably predictable and (*b*) no important uncertainties exist regarding costs yet to be incurred by the lessor under the lease (ASC 840-10-25-61).

  If a lease gives rise to a manufacturer's or dealer's profit (or loss) and criterion 2 is met, a lessor classifies a lease involving land and building(s) as an operating lease. If the lease does not give rise to a manufacturer's or dealer's profit (or loss) and criterion 2 is met, a lessor classifies a lease involving land and building(s) as a direct financing lease or a leveraged lease, whichever is applicable, providing that (*a*) collection of the minimum lease payments is reasonably predictable and (*b*) no important uncertainties exist regarding costs yet to be incurred by the lessor under the lease (ASC 840-10-25-62).

All other leases involving land and building(s) are classified as operating leases by the lessor.

Fair Value of the Land Is Less Than 25% of the Total Fair Value of the Leased Property at the Inception of the Lease

When applying criteria 3 and 4, both the lessee and the lessor consider the land and building(s) as a single unit, and the estimated economic life of the building(s) is the estimated economic life of the single unit. This type of lease is accounted for as follows:

- *Lessee* The land and building(s) are accounted for as a single capitalized asset and amortized in accordance with the lessee's normal depreciation policy over the lease term if either criterion 3 or criterion 4 is met (ASC 840-10-25-38).
- *Lessor* If a lease gives rise to a manufacturer's or dealer's profit (or loss) and criterion 3 or criterion 4 is met, a lessor classifies a lease involving land and building(s), in which the fair value of the land is less than 25% of the total fair value of the leased property at the inception of the lease as an operating lease. If the lease does not give rise to a manufacturer's or dealer's profit (or loss) and criterion 3 or criterion 4 is met, a lessor classifies a lease involving land and building(s) in which the fair value of the land is less than 25% of the total fair value of the leased property at the inception of the lease as a direct financing lease or a leveraged lease, whichever is applicable, providing that (*a*) collection of the minimum lease payments is reasonably predictable and (*b*) no important uncertainties exist regarding costs yet to be incurred by the lessor under the lease. All other leases involving land and building(s) are classified as operating leases by the lessor (ASC 840-10-25-63, 64, 65).

Fair Value of the Land Is 25% or More of the Total Fair Value of the Leased Property at the Inception of the Lease

When applying criteria 3 and 4, both the lessee and the lessor shall consider the land and building(s) separately. To determine the separate values of the land and building(s), the lessee's incremental borrowing rate is applied to the fair value of the land to determine the annual minimum lease payments applicable to the land. The balance of the minimum lease payments remaining is attributed to the building(s). This type of lease is accounted for as follows (ASC 840-10-25-66, 67):

- *Lessee* The building(s) portion is accounted for as a capital lease and amortized in accordance with the lessee's normal depreciation policy over the lease term if the building(s) portion meets either criterion 3 or criterion 4. The land portion is accounted for separately as an operating lease.

- *Lessor* If a lease gives rise to a manufacturer's or dealer's profit (or loss) and criterion 3 or criterion 4 is met, a lessor classifies a lease involving land and building(s) in which the fair value of the land is 25% or more of the total fair value of the leased property at the inception of the lease as an operating lease. If the lease does not give rise to a manufacturer's or dealer's profit (or loss) and criterion 3 or 4 is met, a lessor shall classify the building(s) portion of a lease in which the fair value of the land is 25% or more of the total fair value of the leased property at the inception of the lease as a direct financing lease or a leveraged lease, whichever is applicable, providing that (*a*) collection of the minimum lease payments is reasonably predictable and (*b*) no important uncertainties exist regarding costs yet to be incurred by the lessor under the lease. The land portion is accounted for separately as an operating lease.

All other leases involving land and building(s) are classified as operating leases by the lessor.

Leases Involving Land, Building(s), and Equipment

Equipment values, if material, should not be commingled with real estate values in leases. The minimum lease payments attributed to the equipment shall, if necessary, be estimated appropriately and stated separately. The criteria for the classification of leases are applied separately to the equipment to determine proper accountability (ASC 840-10-25-19, 20).

Leases Involving Only Part of a Building(s)

If the cost and fair value of a lease involving only part of a building(s) can be determined objectively, the lease classification and accounting are the same as for any other land and building(s) lease. An independent appraisal of the leased property or replacement cost can be made as a basis for the objective determination of fair value (ASC 840-10-25-23). In the event that cost and fair value cannot be determined objectively, leases involving only part of a building(s) are classified and accounted for as follows (ASC 840-10-25-39, 69):

Lessee

The lessee classifies the lease only in accordance with criterion 3 as follows: The lease term, at inception, is substantially (75% or more) equal to the estimated economic life of the leased property, including earlier years of use. (*Exception*: This particular criterion cannot be used for a lease that begins within the last 25% of the original estimated economic life of the leased property.)

In applying the above criterion, the estimated economic life of the building(s) in which the leased premises are located is used.

In the event the above criterion is met, the leased property is capitalized as a single unit and amortized in accordance with the lessee's normal depreciation policy over the lease term. In all other cases, the lease is classified as an operating lease.

Lessor

In all cases in which the cost and fair value are indeterminable, the lessor accounts for the lease as an operating lease.

OTHER LEASE ACCOUNTING ISSUES

Subleases and Similar Transactions

Unless the original lease agreement is replaced by a new agreement, the original lessor continues to account for the lease as before (ASC 840-10-35-10).

A termination of a lease is recognized by a lessor in the income of the period in which termination occurs, as follows (ASC 840-10-40-3):

- The remaining net investment is eliminated from the accounts.
- The leased property is recorded as an asset using the lower of the (*a*) original cost, (*b*) present value at termination, or (*c*) present carrying amount at termination.

When an original lessee subleases property, the new lessee is either (1) substituted under the *original* lease agreement or (2) substituted through a new lease agreement. In either case, the original lessee is relieved of the primary obligation under the original lease. The accounting for the termination of the original lease agreement depends on whether the original lease was for property other than real estate or whether it was for real estate.

If the original lease was a capital lease for property other than real estate, the termination of the lease agreement is accounted for as follows

- Remove the asset and liability pertaining to the capital lease from the books.
- Recognize a gain or loss for the difference between the lease asset and lease liability, and consider any consideration received or paid upon lease termination in computing the gain or loss.
- If the original lessee remains secondarily liable, recognize this guarantee obligation under the provisions specified in ASC 860 (Transfers and Servicing).

If the original lease was a capital lease for real estate, the termination of the lease agreement is accounted for as follows.

- The lease asset and liability are to be removed from the books if the ASC 360 criteria for sale recognition are met.
- If the ASC 360 sales criteria are met, treatment of (1) the lease asset and liability, (2) any consideration received or paid, and (3) any guarantees are all accounted for as immediately above (the same as if the original lease was a capital lease for property other than real estate).
- Any gain should be recognized by the full accrual method if the ASC 360 criteria for the use of this method are met; otherwise, gain should be recognized using one of the other revenue recognition methods discussed in ASC 360 (installment, cost recovery, deposit, or reduced-profit methods).

- Any loss is recognized immediately.

Finally, the original lessee is to recognize its guarantee obligation (per ASC 860) if it remains secondarily liable on a lease that was originally classified as an operating lease.

When a lessee subleases leased property, the original lease continues and a simultaneous new lease is created in which the lessee becomes a sublessor. The results are that the original lessee is both a lessee in the original lease and, at the same time, a sublessor in the new lease. In situations like this, the original lease continues to be accounted for as if nothing happened, but the new lease is classified and accounted for separately.

If an original lessee is not relieved of the primary obligation under an original lease, the transaction is accounted for by the original lessee-sublessor as follows (ASC 840-30-35-12):

- If the criterion for the original lease was criterion (1) (ownership of the property is transferred before the end of the lease term) or (2) (lease contains a bargain purchase option), the new lease is classified based on its own new criteria. If the new lease qualifies for capitalization, it is accounted for as a sales-type or a direct financing lease, whichever is appropriate, and the unamortized balance of the asset under the original lease is treated as the cost of the leased property to the sublessor (original lessee).

  In the event that the new lease does not qualify for capitalization, it is treated as an operating lease.

- If the criterion for the original lease was criterion (3) (lease term is substantially—75% or more—equal to the estimated economic life of the leased property at the inception of the lease) or (4) (present value of the minimum lease payments—excluding executory costs—is 90% or more of the fair value at inception), the new lease is capitalized only if it meets criterion (3) and (*a*) the collection of the minimum lease payments is reasonably predictable and (*b*) no important uncertainties exist regarding costs yet to be incurred by the lessor under the lease. If the new lease meets the criteria above, it is accounted for as a direct financing lease, with the amortized balance of the asset under the original lease as the cost of the leased property.

  If the new lease does not meet the specific conditions above, it is accounted for as an operating lease.

In any event, if the original lease is an operating lease, the sublease also is accounted for as an operating lease (ASC 840-20-25-14).

Even though the sublessor (original lessee) remains primarily obligated under an original lease, a loss may be recognized on a sublease. The loss is measured as the difference between the unamortized cost of the leased property (net carrying amount) and the present value of the minimum lease payments which will be received under the terms of the sublease.

ASC 360 provides guidance on the accounting treatment of long-term leases (including related sublease revenue) terminated as part of the disposal of a component of a business entity. ASC 360 requires that the assets in the component of the business entity being disposed of be carried at the lower of the asset's carrying amount or fair value less cost to sell. Although explicit guidance on this topic no longer appears in the literature, the authors believe that the fair value of the component of the business entity to be disposed of will be (implicitly) reduced by the present value of future rental receipts to be paid on the original lease in excess of the present value of future rental receipts that will be collected on the operating sublease.

Leases Involving Governmental Units

Leases with governmental units usually lack fair values, have indeterminable economic lives, and cannot provide for transfer of ownership. These special provisions usually prevent their classification as any other than operating leases (ASC 840-10-25-25).

Leases involving governmental units, however, are subject to the same criteria as any other lease unless all of the following conditions exist; and in that event, these leases are classified as operating leases (ASC 840-10-25-25):

- A governmental unit or authority owns the leased property.
- The leased property is operated by or on behalf of a governmental unit or authority and is part of a larger facility, such as an airport.
- The leased property cannot be moved to another location because it is a permanent structure or part of a permanent structure.
- Any governmental unit or authority can terminate the lease agreement at any time under the terms of the lease agreement, existing statutes, or regulations.
- Ownership is not transferred to the lessee and the lessee cannot purchase the leased property.
- Equivalent property in the same area as the leased property cannot be purchased or leased from anyone else.

Related Party Leases

Except in cases in which the substance of a lease transaction indicates clearly that the terms and conditions have been significantly influenced by the related parties, related party leases are classified and accounted for as if the parties were unrelated (ASC 840-10-25-26).

It is important to note that, generally, a subsidiary whose principal business activity is leasing property to its parent must be consolidated with the parent's financial statements (ASC 840-10-45-1).

OBSERVATION: Specific financial statement disclosures pertaining to related parties are required by ASC 850 (Related Party Disclosures).

Leveraged Leases

A lessee classifies and accounts for *leveraged* leases in the same manner as *nonleveraged* leases. *Only a lessor* must classify and account for leveraged leases in the specific manner prescribed herein (ASC 840-10-25-33).

ASC 840 defines a *leveraged lease* as a lease having all the following characteristics (ASC 840-10-25-43):

- A leveraged lease meets the definition of a *direct financing lease* as follows:

    A direct financing lease is a lease that does not result in a manufacturer's or dealer's profit or loss because the fair value of the leased property at the inception of the lease is the same as the cost or carrying amount. In a direct financing lease, substantially all the benefits and risks inherent in the ownership of the leased property are transferred to the lessee. In addition, the following requirements must be met:

    — The minimum lease payments are reasonably predictable of collection.

    — No important uncertainties exist regarding costs to be incurred by the lessor under the terms of the lease.

- It involves at least three parties: (*a*) a lessee, (*b*) a lessor, and (*c*) a long-term creditor. (**Note:** The lessor is sometimes referred to as the *equity participant*.)

- The financing is sufficient to provide the lessor with substantial leverage in the transaction and is nonrecourse as to the general credit of the lessor.

- Once the lessor's net investment is completed, it declines in the early years and rises in later years before being liquidated. These fluctuations in the lessor's net investment can occur more than once in the lease term.

PRACTICE POINTER: Leveraged leases are complex contracts that meet very specific criteria. Accounting for leveraged leases is unique in certain ways (e.g., offsetting assets and liabilities) and, therefore, determining whether a given lease is a leveraged lease is particularly important. A lease must meet *all* of the following specific criteria (taken from the definition of a leveraged lease) to be accounted for as a leveraged lease:

---

1. The lease is a direct financing lease.
2. The lease involves three parties rather than the normal two.
3. The lease provides the lessor with substantial leverage.
4. The pattern of the lessor's investment declines then rises.

    Only when all four of these criteria are met is the lease subject to leveraged lease accounting.

If the investment tax credit is accounted for as provided herein and a lease meets the preceding definition, it is classified and accounted for as a leveraged lease (ASC 840-10-25-43).

Lessor's Existing Asset in a Leveraged Lease

Only a direct financing lease may qualify as a leveraged lease (ASC 840-10-25-43). One of the requirements of a direct financing lease is that it may not result in a manufacturer's or dealer's profit or loss. It is difficult for an existing asset of a lessor to qualify for leveraged lease accounting because the carrying amount (cost less accumulated depreciation) of an asset previously placed in service is not likely to be the same as its fair value. An existing asset of a lessor may qualify for leveraged lease accounting, however, if its carrying amount is equal to its fair value, without any write-down or other adjustment to its fair value.

GENERAL DISCLOSURES

General disclosures: A general description of the lessee's leasing arrangements, including (*a*) basis of contingent rental payments; (*b*) terms of renewals, purchase options, and escalation clauses; and (*c*) restrictions imposed by lease agreements, such as additional debt, dividends, and leasing limitations, must be disclosed (ASC 840-10-50-2).

General disclosures for leases of lessors whose significant business activity is leasing: a general description of the lessor's leasing arrangements (ASC 840-10-50-4).

ASC 840-20: OPERATING LEASES

OPERATING LEASES

Accounting and Reporting by the Lessee

Leases that do not qualify as capital leases in accordance with the provisions of ASC 840 are classified as operating leases. The cost of property covering an operating lease is included in the lessor's balance sheet as property, plant, and equipment. ASC 840 requires that rental income and expense relating to an operating lease be recognized over the periods in which the lessee derives benefit from the physical usage of the leased property. Thus, rental expense is recognized over the lease term on a straight-line basis, unless some other systematic and rational basis is more representative of the time pattern in which the benefits of the leased property are derived by the lessee (ASC 840-20-25-1).

PRACTICE POINTER: Use care when implementing accounting standards for sales-type leases involving real estate. A lessor shall not classify a lease involving real estate as a sales-type lease unless title to the leased property is transferred to the lessee at or shortly after the end of the lease term. As a result, a lessor may be required to classify a lease involving real estate as an operating lease, instead of a sales-type lease, because the lease agreement does not provide for the transfer of the leased property to the lessee by the end of the lease term. In this event, the lessor must recognize a loss at the inception of an operating lease involving real estate if the fair value of the leased property is less than its cost or carrying amount, whichever is applicable. The amount of loss is equal to the difference between the fair value of the leased property and its cost or carrying amount at the inception of the lease.

Contingent Rental Expense

Some operating lease agreements provide for rental increases or decreases based on one or more future conditions, such as future sales volume, future machine hours, future interest rates, or future price indexes. These types of rental increases or decreases are classified as *contingent rentals*. Contingent rentals are defined as those that cannot be determined at the inception of the lease because they depend on future conditions or events. A lessee's contingent rental payments are deducted as an expense in the period in which they arise.

Scheduled Rent Increases or Decreases

To accommodate the lessee, a lessor may structure an operating lease agreement to provide for smaller rental payments in the early years of the lease and higher rental payments toward the end of the lease. *Example:* A six-year operating lease agreement may provide for rental payments of $1,000 per month for the first two years; $1,500 per month for the next two years; and $2,000 per month for the last two years; for a total rental payment of $108,000 for the six years. Under this circumstance, ASC 840 requires that the $108,000 total rental payments be amortized over the six-year lease term on a straight-line basis. The monthly amortization for the first two years of the lease term is $1,500, even though only $1,000 per month is paid by the lessee under the terms of the lease (ASC 840-20-25-1).

> **OBSERVATION:** A reasonable argument can be made that in the early years of the above type of lease agreement, the lessee receives not only the use of the leased property, but also the temporary use of cash, equal to the excess of the fair rental value of the leased property over the actual rental payments. Theoretically, to recognize the economic substance of this lease transaction, both the lessee and the lessor should record imputed interest on the difference between the actual amount of rental payments and the computed amount of level rental payments. ASC 840, however, precludes the use of the time value of money as a factor in recognizing rentals under operating leases.

Leasehold Improvements

Leasehold improvements in an operating lease should be amortized by the lessee over the shorter of the economic life of the improvement or the lease term. An assumption of lease renewal where a renewal option exists is appropriate only when the renewal has been determined to be "reasonably assured," as that term is contemplated in ASC 840.

Leasehold improvements made by a lessee that are funded by landlord incentives or allowances under an operating lease should be recorded by the lessee as leasehold improvement assets and should be amortized over a term consistent with the above-stated guidance. The incentives should be recorded as deferred rent and amortized as reductions to lease expense over the lease term. It is inappropriate to net the deferred rent against the leasehold improvements. Further, the statement of cash flows should reflect cash received from the lessor that is accounted for as a lease incentive within operating activities and the acquisition of leasehold improvements for cash within investing activities.

Rent Holidays

Rent holidays in an operating lease should be recognized by the lessee on a straight-line basis over the lease term (including any rent holiday period), unless another systematic and rational allocation is more representative of the time pattern in which leased property is physically employed.

Illustration of Lessee's Financial Statement Disclosure

Lessee's Balance Sheet
(in thousands)

	December 31 20X6	December 31 20X5
Assets:		
Leased property:		
Capital leases, less accumulated amortization (Note:____)	$ 2,200	$ 1,600
Liabilities:		
Current:		
Obligations under capital leases (Note:____)	$ 365	$ 340
Noncurrent:		
Obligations under capital leases (Note:____)	$ 1,368	$ 1,260

Capital Leases
Gross Assets and
Accumulated Amortization
(in thousands)

	December 31 20X6	December 31 20X5
Type of Property		
Manufacturing plants	$ 1,500	$ 1,100
Retail stores	1,200	840
Other	300	210
Total	$ 3,000	$ 2,150
Less: Accumulated amortization	800	550
Capital leases, net	$ 2,200	$ 1,600

Capital Leases
Minimum Future Lease Payments and Present Values of the Net Minimum Lease Payments
(in thousands)

Year Ended December 31	
20X7	$ 406
20X8	1,232
20X9	160
20Y0	125
20Y1	100
After 20Y1	450
Total minimum lease payments	$ 2,473
Less: Executory costs (estimated)	250
Net minimum lease payments	$ 2,223
Less: Imputed interest	490
Present value of net minimum lease payments	$ 1,733

In addition to the foregoing statements and schedules, footnotes describing minimum sublease income and contingent rentals should be included, if required.

Operating Leases
Schedule of Minimum Future Rental Payments
(in thousands)

Year Ended December 31	
20X7	$ 815
20X8	2,400
20X9	320
20Y0	250
20Y1	200
After 20Y0	900
Total minimum future rental payments	$ 4,885

In addition to the above information on operating leases, a note should be included describing minimum sublease income due in the future under noncancelable subleases.

Operating Leases
Composition of Total Rental Expense
(in thousands)

	December 31	
	20X6	20X5
Minimum rentals	$1,100	$1,050
Contingent rentals	100	125
Less: Sublease rental income	(200)	(150)
Total rental expense, net	$1,000	$1,025

Note: The above schedule of total rental expense excludes leases with terms of one month or less that were not renewed.

In addition to the foregoing information on capital and operating leases, a footnote describing the general disclosure policy for the lessee's leases should be included, containing (a) general leasing arrangements, (b) basis of contingent rental payments, (c) terms of renewals, purchase options, and escalation clauses, and (d) restrictions imposed by lease agreements, such as additional debt, dividends, and leasing limitations.

Accounting and Reporting by Lessors

Leases that do not qualify as capital leases in accordance with the provisions of ASC 840 are classified as operating leases. The cost of the property leased to the lessee is included in the lessor's balance sheet as property, plant, and equipment. The lessor's income statement will normally include the expenses of the leased property (unless it is a net lease), such as depreciation, maintenance, taxes, insurance, and other related items. Material initial direct costs (those directly related to the negotiation and consummation of the lease) are deferred and allocated to income over the lease term (ASC 840-20-45-2; 840-20-25-16).

ASC 840 requires that rental income from an operating lease be amortized over the periods in which the lessor's benefits in the leased property are depleted. Thus, rental income is amortized over the lease term on a straight-line basis, unless some other systematic and rational basis is more representative of the time pattern in which the benefits of the leased property are depleted (ASC 840-20-25-1).

ASC 840 requires that a lease involving real estate not be classified by the lessor as a sales-type lease unless title to the leased property is transferred to the lessee at or shortly after the end of the lease term. As a result, an enterprise may be required to classify a lease involving real estate as an operating lease, instead of a sales-type lease, because the lease agreement does not provide for the transfer of the leased property to the lessee by the end of the lease term. In this event, the lessor recognizes a loss at the inception of an operating lease involving real estate if the fair value of the leased property is less than its cost or carrying amount, whichever is applicable. The amount of loss is equal to the difference between the fair value of the leased property and its cost or carrying amount at the inception of the lease.

Contingent Rental Income

Contingent rental income is defined as that which cannot be determined at the inception of the lease because it depends on future conditions or events. A lessor's contingent rental income is accrued in the period in which it arises (ASC Glossary).

Lease Sale or Assignment to Third Parties

Sale or assignment of a sales-type or a direct financing lease does not negate the original accounting treatment. The transfer of minimum lease payments under a sales-type or direct financing lease are accounted for in accordance with ASC 860 (Transfers and Servicing). The accounting for transfers of residual values depends on whether the residual value is guaranteed. If the residual value is guaranteed, its transfer is accounted for in accordance with ASC 860. Transfers of unguaranteed residual values are not subject to the guidance in ASC 860.

Frequently, a sale of property *subject to an operating lease* is complicated by some type of indemnification agreement by the seller. The seller may guarantee that the property will remain leased or may agree to reacquire the property if the tenant does not pay the specified rent. These types of transactions cannot be accounted for as a sale because of the substantial risk assumed by the seller. The principle of *substance over form* must be applied to such situations and treated accordingly. Examples of *substantial risk* on the part of the seller are (ASC 840-20-40-3):

- Agreements to reacquire the property or lease.
- Agreements to substitute another existing lease.
- Agreements to use "best efforts" to secure a replacement buyer or lessee.

Examples of *nonsubstantial risk* situations on the part of the seller are (ASC 840-20-40-4):

- Execution of a remarketing agreement that includes a fee for the seller.
- Situations in which the seller does not give priority to the releasing or other disposition of the property owned by a third party.

If a sale to a third-party purchaser is not recorded as a sale because of the substantial risk factor assumed by the seller, it is accounted for as a *borrowing*. The proceeds from the "sale" are recorded as an obligation on the books of the seller. Rental payments made by the lessee under the operating lease are recorded as revenue to the seller, even if the rentals are paid to the third party. Each rental payment shall consist of imputed interest, and the balance of the payment shall be applied as a reduction of the obligation. Any sale or assignment of lease payments under an operating lease is accounted for as a borrowing (ASC 840-20-35-4).

Financial Statement Disclosures

The following financial statement disclosures are required for all operating leases of lessees having noncancelable lease terms in excess of one year (ASC 840-20-50-1, 2):

- Minimum future rental payments in total and for each of the next five years
- Minimum sublease income due in future periods under noncancelable subleases
- Schedule of total rental expense showing the composition by minimum rentals, contingent rentals, and sublease income (excluding leases with terms of a month or less that were not renewed)

Following is an illustration of a lessee's financial statement disclosures for operating leases (using assumed numbers).

Illustration of Lessee's Financial Statement Disclosure

Operating Leases
Schedule of Minimum Future Rental Payments
(in thousands)

Year Ended December 31	
20X7	$ 815
20X8	2,400
20X9	320
20Y0	250
20Y1	200
After 20Y1	900
Total minimum future rental payments	$ 4,885

In addition to the above information on operating leases, a note should be included describing minimum sublease income due in the future under noncancelable subleases.

Operating Leases
Schedule of Minimum Future Rental Payments
(in thousands)

	December 31	
	20X6	20X5
Minimum Rentals	$1,100	$1,050
Contingent Rentals	100	125
Less: Sublease rental income	(200)	(150)
Total rental expense, net	$1,000	$1,025

Note: The above schedule of total rental expense excludes leases with terms of one month or less that were not renewed.

53,030 ASC 840—Leases

In addition to the foregoing information, a footnote describing the general disclosure policy for the lessee's leases should be included, containing (a) general leasing arrangements, (b) basis of contingent rental payments, (c) terms of renewals, purchase options, and escalation clauses, and (d) restrictions imposed by lease agreements, such as additional debt, dividends, and leasing limitations.

The following financial statement disclosures are required for operating leases for lessors whose significant business activity is leasing (ASC 840-20-50-4):

- A schedule of the investment in property on operating leases, and property held for lease, by major categories, less accumulated depreciation, as of each balance sheet presented

- A schedule of future minimum rentals on noncancelable operating leases, in total and for each of the next five years

- The amount of contingent rentals included in each income statement presented

Following is an illustration of a lessor's financial statement disclosures for operating leases (using assumed numbers).

Illustration of Lessor's Financial Statement Disclosure

Lessor's Balance Sheet
(in thousands)

	December 31	
	20X6	20X5
Noncurrent assets:		
Property on operating leases and property held for leases (net of accumulated depreciation of $450 and $400 for 20X6 and 20X5, respectively) (Note:_____)	$1,800	$1,600

Schedule of Investment in Property on Operating Leases and Property Held for Lease (by Major Class Categories)
(in thousands)

Data-processing equipment	$ 900
Transportation equipment	700
Construction equipment	400
Other	200
Total	$2,200
Less: Accumulated depreciation	400
Net investment	$1,800

Schedule of Future Minimum Rentals on Noncancelable Operating Leases
(in thousands)

Year Ended December 31	
20X7	$ 200
20X8	175
20X9	165
20Y0	125
20Y1	110
After 20Y1	200
Total future minimum rentals	$ 975

A footnote should be included for contingent rentals.

ASC 840-30: CAPITAL LEASES

CAPITAL LEASES

Accounting and Reporting by Lessees

Initial Recording

The lessee records a capital lease as an asset and a corresponding liability. The initial recording value of a lease is the *lesser* of the fair value of the leased property or the present value of the minimum lease payments, excluding any portion representing executory costs and profit thereon to be paid by the lessor. Fair value is determined as of the inception of the lease, and the present value of the minimum lease payments is computed at the beginning of the lease term. The inception of the lease and the beginning of the lease term are not necessarily the same dates (ASC 840-30-25-1; 840-30-30-1).

Because the lessee's minimum lease payments *exclude* a lessee's obligation to pay executory costs, executory costs paid by the lessee are expensed as paid or appropriately accrued. If such costs are included in the rental payments and are not identified separately (which is the most likely case), an estimate of the amount is necessary.

A lessee's incremental borrowing rate is used to determine the present value of the minimum lease payments unless the lessor's implicit rate of interest is known and is lower (ASC 840-10-25-31).

Leases with Escalation Clauses

In lease agreements or written commitments in which the leased property is to be acquired or constructed by the lessor, there may be a provision for the escalation of the minimum lease payments during the construction or preacquisition period. Usually, the escalation is based on increased costs of acquisition or construction of the leased property. A provision to escalate the minimum lease payments during the construction or preacquisition period can also be based on other measures of cost or value, including general price-level changes or changes in the consumer price index.

The relationship between the total amount of minimum lease payments and the fair value of a lease is such that when one increases so does the other. For example, assume that the total minimum lease payments of a particular lease are $100,000 payable in five equal annual installments, and the fair value of the same lease is $350,000. If the minimum lease payments are increased 20% to $120,000, it is likely that the fair value of the lease will increase correspondingly, because the lease is then worth more to an investor.

Increases in the minimum lease payments that occur during the preacquisition or construction period as a result of an escalation clause be considered in determining the fair value of the leased property at the inception of the lease for the purposes of the initial recording of the lease transaction by the lessee, or where fair value is used as a basis of allocation.

The initial recording value of a lease transaction by the lessee, which is required by ASC 840, is the lesser of the fair value of the leased property or the present value of the minimum lease payments. For leases that contain escalation clauses, fair value includes the effects of any escalation clauses.

OBSERVATION: The question arises as to when leases of this type should be recorded on the books of the lessee. The initial recording should be made only after the effects of the escalation clause on the fair value of the leased property are determined. Otherwise, ASC 840 is silent in all respects as to when the lease transaction should be recorded. In the case of significant amounts of leases, it appears illogical to wait several years to record the transaction. If this is the only viable alternative, however, full disclosure of all pertinent facts pertaining to the lease agreement or commitment should be made in a prominent footnote.

The other alternative is to record these types of lease transactions immediately at the inception of the lease, utilizing whatever information is available and subsequently adjusting the recorded amounts when the effects of the escalation clauses are known. This alternative does not appear to be viable because of the difficulties mentioned in the following paragraphs.

The last-enumerated criterion in ASC 840 for capitalizing a lease is when the present value of the minimum lease payments is 90% or more of the fair value of the leased property at the inception of the lease. When this criterion is considered for capitalizing a lease in conjunction with the alternative of recording lease transactions at the inception of the lease and then subsequently adjusting the recorded amounts when the effects of the escalation clauses become known, the following problems arise, which are not addressed by ASC 840.

- If we assume that ASC 840 requires that the fair value of leases with escalation clauses be determined at a future date, what fair value should be used to determine whether the lease is or is not a capital lease in accordance with the criterion of whether the present value of the minimum lease payments is 90% or more of the fair value of the leased property at the inception of the lease?

- What if a lease of this type is capitalized in accordance with the criterion that the present value of the minimum lease payments is 90% or more of the fair value at inception of the lease, and subsequently, as a result of the escalation clause, the present value becomes less than 90% of the fair value, so that the lease should not have been capitalized?

- Suppose a lease with an escalation clause is properly classified as an operating lease at inception of the lease and subsequently, as a result of the escalation clause, the lease qualifies as a capital lease.

The above are just a few of the complications that could arise in applying the provisions relating to escalation clauses to lease transactions.

ASC 840 also permits increases in the estimated residual value (see definition) that occur as a result of escalation provisions in leases in which the leased property is to be acquired or constructed by the lessor. For example, if the estimated residual value is 10% of the fair value at the inception of a lease and during the construction or preacquisition period of the leased property the effects of the escalation clause increase the fair value, then the estimated residual value also is allowed to increase above the amount that was estimated at the date of the inception of the lease.

Amortization

The asset recorded under a capital lease is amortized in a manner consistent with the lessee's normal depreciation policy for other owned assets. The period for amortization is either (*a*) the estimated economic life or (*b*) the lease term, depending on which criterion was used to classify the lease. If the criterion used is either of the first two criteria (ownership of the property is transferred to the lessee by the end of the lease term or the lease contains a bargain purchase option), the asset is amortized over its estimated economic life. In all other cases, the asset is amortized over the lease term. Any *estimated residual value* is deducted from the asset to determine the amortizable base (ASC 840-30-35-1).

PRACTICE POINTER: Determining the appropriate amortization period for capital leases is an important issue where the lease term is significantly less than the expected useful life of the asset. A simple rule of thumb is simply to determine which party to the lease is expected to have use of the property during the period between the end of the lease period and the end of the expected life of the asset. If the lease is capitalized by the first or second capitalization criteria (transfer of title and bargain purchase option), the underlying assumption is that the lessee will become the legal owner of the asset by the end of the lease term and will have use of it for the remainder of the asset's expected life. Thus, the estimated life of the asset is the logical period of amortization. On the other hand, an assumption of the transfer of legal title does not underlie the lease if it is capitalized because of the third or fourth criteria (lease term and the present value of minimum lease payments). In either of these circumstances, the lease term is the logical period for amortization of the leased asset. Generally, if the same lease satisfies one or both of the first two criteria and one or both of the second criteria, use the expected life of the asset as the period of amortization.

ASC 840—Leases

Interest Expense: Interest Method

The interest method, sometimes referred to as the *effective interest method*, is used to produce a constant rate of interest on the remaining lease liability. A portion of each minimum lease payment is allocated to interest expense and/or amortization, and the balance is applied to reduce the lease liability. Any *residual guarantee(s)* by the lessee or penalty payments are automatically taken into consideration by using the interest method and will result in a balance at the end of the lease term equal to the amount of the guarantee or penalty payments at that date (ASC 840-30-35-6, 7, 8).

Illustration of Interest Method

Jones Company leases a tractor-trailer for $8,000 per year on a noncancelable five-year lease. The yearly lease payment is due at the beginning of the year. Jones guarantees to the lessor that the tractor-trailer will have a residual value of at least $5,000 at the end of the lease term.

Assume that a 12% interest rate is used.

Present value of $8,000 payments for five years at 12% =	$32,299*
Present value of $5,000 guaranteed residual value in five years at 12% =	2,837**
Total asset and lease obligation	$35,136

* $8,000 × 4.03735
** $5,000 × .56743

A schedule of interest expense, amortization, and reduction of the lease obligation of $35,136 to the $5,000 residual guarantee using the interest method follows:

Book Value Lease Obligation Beginning of Year	Rental Payment/ Reduction in Lease Obligation	Outstanding Balance During Year	Interest @ 12%	Book Value Lease Obligation End of Year
$35,136	$8,000	$27,136	$3,256	$30,392
30,392	8,000	22,392	2,687	25,079
25,079	8,000	17,079	2,049	19,129
19,129	8,000	11,129	1,335	12,464
12,464	8,000	4,464	536	5,000

Change in Lease Terms

If a guarantee or penalty is rendered inoperative because of a renewal or other extension of the *lease term*, or if a new lease is consummated in which the lessee continues to lease the same property, an adjustment must be made to the asset and lease obligation for the difference between the present values of the old and the revised agreements. In these cases, the present value of the future minimum lease payments under the new or revised agreement is computed using the original rate of interest on the initial lease (ASC 840-30-35-8).

Other lease changes are accounted for as follows (ASC 840-30-35-19):

- If a lease change results in revised minimum lease payments, but also is classified as a capital lease, an adjustment is made to the asset and lease obligation for the difference between the present values of the old and the new or revised agreement. The present value of the future minimum lease payments under the new or revised agreement is computed using the original rate of interest used on the initial lease.

- A capital lease may be modified in such a way that the new lease agreement is treated as an operating lease. ASC 840 required that the lease asset and obligation (liability) be removed from the accounts and any resulting gain or loss be recognized in determining current period income. The new lease agreement was accounted for as an operating lease (ASC 840-30-35-20).

   The FASB concluded that the economic effects of the above transaction are similar to those of a sale-leaseback. However, ASC 840 does not require sale-leaseback accounting. Sale-leaseback accounting is required when a capital lease is modified such that the revised lease agreement is classified as an operating lease.

- A renewal, extension, or new lease under which the lessee continues to use the same property, except when a guarantee or penalty is rendered inoperative (see above), is accounted for as follows:

   — *Renewal or extension classified as a capital lease:* An adjustment is made for the difference between the original and revised present values, using the original discount rate.

   — *Renewal or extension classified as an operating lease:* The existing lease continues to be accounted for as a capital lease to the end of its lease term, and the renewal or extension is accounted for as an operating lease.

When leased property under a capital lease is purchased by the lessee, it is accounted for as a renewal or extension of a capital lease. Thus, any difference between the carrying amount and the purchase price on the date of purchase is treated as an adjustment of the carrying amount of the property (ASC 840-30-35-14).

Termination of a Lease

Gain or loss, if any, is recognized on the termination of a capital lease, and the asset and lease liability is removed from the books (ASC 840-30-40-1).

Illustration of Capital Lease (Lessee)

Paine Corporation leases a computer under a noncancelable five-year lease for annual rental payments of $10,000. The yearly lease payment is due at the beginning of the year. The fair value of the computer at the inception of the lease is $40,373, and the incremental borrowing rate of Paine is 10%. There are no executory costs. The annual rent of $10,000 is considered a fair rental as opposed to a bargain rental. The estimated economic life of the computer is ten years.

Classification of Lease

A review is made of the criteria involved in the provisions of the lease to determine its classification.

1. Criterion (1) is not met, because there is no transfer of the ownership of the leased property before the end of the lease term.
2. Criterion (2) is not met, because the lease does not contain a bargain purchase option.
3. Criterion (3) is not met, because the lease term (five years) is not equal to 75% or more of the estimated economic life (10 years) of the leased property. (*Note:* There are no other provisions affecting the lease term other than the five-year noncancelable term.)
4. Criterion (4) is met, because the present value ($41,699) of the minimum lease payments, excluding executory costs and profits thereon paid by the lessor, is 90% or more of the fair value ($40,373 × .9 = $36,336) of the leased property. [*Note:* The present value of the lease is $41,699, computed as follows:$10,000 × 4.16987, the present value factor for an annuity due, 5 periods, 10%.]

Paine Corporation should record the transaction as a capital lease.

Accounting for the Lease

The initial recording value of the leased property, at the beginning of the lease term, is the lesser of the fair value of the leased property or the present value of the minimum lease payments, excluding any portion that represents executory costs and profit thereon to be paid by the lessor.

The discount rate used by the lessee to find the present value of the minimum lease payments is its incremental borrowing rate of 10%, unless the lessee has knowledge of the lessor's implicit interest rate in the lease, and that rate is lower.

The lessor's interest rate implicit in the lease in this example is 12%. As a rule, the interest rate implicit in the lease is equal to the discount rate that, when applied to the minimum lease payments of $10,000 per year for five years and, if any, the unguaranteed residual value of the leased property, results in a present value equal to the fair value of the leased property at the inception of the lease. (For simplicity, this definition excludes any unusual factors that a lessor might recognize in determining its rate of return.)

This means that Paine must use its incremental borrowing rate of 10% to discount the minimum lease payments to their present value, which is $41,699.

The initial recording value of the leased property is the lesser of the fair value of the leased property at inception or the present value of the minimum lease payments using the lower interest rate. Therefore, the $40,373 fair value is less than the minimum lease payments of $41,699 (computed by using the lower incremental borrowing rate) and is used to initially record the lease, as follows:

Lease property, capital leases	40,373	
Obligations, capital leases		40,373

Amortization by Lessee

The asset(s) recorded under a capital lease is amortized in a manner consistent with the lessee's normal depreciation policy for other owned assets. The period for amortization is either (a) the estimated economic life or (b) the lease term, depending on which criterion was used to classify the lease. If the criterion used to classify the lease as a capital lease was either criterion (1) (ownership of the property is transferred to the lessee by the end of the lease term) or criterion (2) (lease contains a bargain purchase option), the asset is amortized over its economic life. In all other cases, the asset is amortized over the lease term. Any residual value is deducted from the asset to determine the amortizable base.

Because the Paine Corporation's lease qualified under criterion (4) (present value of the minimum lease payments, excluding executory costs and profit thereon paid by the lessor, is 90% or more of the fair value of the leased property), the amortization period is over the lease term.

A schedule of amortization, interest expense, and lease obligation payments for Paine Corporation's computer lease, using the interest method, follows:

Book Value Lease Obligation Beginning of Year	Rental Payment/ Reduction in Lease Obligation	Outstanding Balance During Year	Interest @ 12%	Book Value Lease Obligation End of Year
$40,373	$10,000	$30,373	$3,645	$34,018
34,018	10,000	24,018	2,882	26,900
26,900	10,000	16,900	2,028	18,928
18,928	10,000	8,928	1,072	10,000
10,000	10,000	-0-	-0-	-0-

Note: The interest rate used is 12%, which is the interest rate implicit in the lease.

Accounting and Reporting by Lessors

Leases are classified for the lessor as either (a) sales-type, (b) direct financing, or (c) operating. Both sales-type and direct financing are forms of capital leases.

Sales-type leases usually are used by sellers of property to increase the marketability of expensive assets. The occurrence of a manufacturer's or dealer's profit or loss generally is present in a sales-type lease.

Direct financing leases do not give rise to a manufacturer's or dealer's profit or loss, and the fair value usually is the cost or the carrying amount of the property.

Recording Sales-Type Leases

The lessor's *gross investment* in the lease is the sum of (a) the minimum lease payments to be received less any executory costs and profit thereon to be paid by the lessor and (b) any unguaranteed residual value accruing to the benefit of the lessor (this is the estimated fair value of the leased property at the end of the lease term, which is not guaranteed). (**Note:** If the residual value is guaranteed, it is included in the minimum lease payments) (ASC 840-30-30-6).

The estimated residual value used to compute the unguaranteed residual value accruing to the benefit of the lessor shall not exceed the amount estimated at the inception of the lease (ASC 840-30-30-6).

Using the interest rate implicit in the lease, the lessor's gross investment in the lease is discounted to its present value. The present value of the lessor's gross investment in the lease represents the sales price of the property that is included in income for the period. (**Note:** When using the interest rate implicit in the lease, the present value will always be equal to the fair value) (ASC 840-30-30-10).

The cost or carrying amount of the property sold plus any initial direct costs (costs incurred by the lessor to negotiate and consummate the lease, such as legal fees and commissions), less the present value of the unguaranteed residual value (if any) accruing to the benefit of the lessor is charged against income in the period in which the corresponding sale is recorded (ASC 840-30-25-6).

The difference between the lessor's gross investment in the lease and the sales price of the property is recorded as unearned income, which is amortized to income over the lease term by the interest method. The unearned income is included in the balance sheet as a deduction from the related gross investment, which results in the net investment in the lease (ASC 840-30-30-98; 840-30-35-22).

A lease involving real estate is not classified by the lessor as a sales-type lease unless the title to the leased property is transferred to the lessee at or shortly after the end of the lease term.

Recording Direct Financing Leases

The lessor's *gross investment* in the lease is computed, which is equal to the sum of (*a*) the minimum lease payments to be received by the lessor, less any executory costs and profit thereon to be paid by the lessor, and (*b*) any unguaranteed residual value accruing to the benefit of the lessor (this is the estimated fair value of the lease property at the end of the lease term, which is not guaranteed). If the residual value is guaranteed, it is included in the minimum lease payments.

Under ASC 310, loan origination fees and direct loan origination costs, including initial direct costs incurred by the lessor in negotiating and consummating the lease, are offset against each other and the resulting net amount is deferred and recognized over the life of the loan as an adjustment to the yield on the loan (ASC 310-20-30-2; 310-20-35-2).

The difference between the lessor's gross investment in the lease and the cost or carrying amount of the leased property, if different, is recorded as unearned income, which is amortized to income over the lease term by the interest method. The unearned income is included in the balance sheet as a deduction from the related gross investment, which results in the net investment in the lease.

OBSERVATION: The practice of recognizing a portion of the unearned income at the inception of the lease to offset initial direct costs is no longer acceptable (ASC 310-20-25-2).

Balance Sheet Classification

The resulting net investment in both sales-type and direct financing leases is subject to the same treatment as other assets in classifying as current or noncurrent.

Annual Review of Residual Values

The unguaranteed residual values of both sales-type and direct financing leases should be reviewed at least annually to determine whether a decline, other than temporary, has occurred in their estimated values. If a decline is not temporary, the accounting for the transaction should be revised using the new estimate, and the resulting loss should be recognized in the period that the change is made. *Upward adjustments are not allowed* (ASC 840-30-35-25).

Accounting for Lease Changes

The definition of *lease term* includes any periods in which penalties are imposed in an amount that reasonably assures the renewal of the lease by the lessee. The definition of *minimum lease payments* includes any payments or guarantees that the lessee is required to make concerning the leased property, including any amount (*a*) to purchase the leased property, (*b*) to make up any deficiency from a specified minimum, and (*c*) for failure to renew or extend the lease at the expiration of the lease term. Guarantees and penalties such as these usually are canceled and become inoperative in the event the lease is renewed or extended or a new lease for the same property is consummated.

If a sales-type or direct financing lease contains a residual guarantee or a penalty for failure to renew and is rendered inoperative as a result of a lease renewal or other extension of the lease term, or if a new lease is consummated in which the lessee continues to lease the same property, an adjustment must be made to the unearned income account for the difference between the present values of the old and the revised agreements. The present value of the future minimum lease payments under the new agreement is computed by using the original rate of interest used for the initial lease (ASC 840-30-35-23).

In sales-type and direct financing leases that do not contain residual guarantees or penalties for failure to renew, an adjustment is made to account for lease changes, renewals, or other extensions, including a new lease in which the lessee continues to lease the same property. If the classification of the lease remains unchanged or is classified as a direct financing lease and the amount of the remaining minimum lease payments is changed, an adjustment is made to unearned income to account for the difference between the present values of the old and the new agreements (ASC 840-30-35-30). If a new classification results in a sales-type lease, it is classified and treated as a direct financing lease, unless the transaction occurs within the last few months of the original lease, in which case it is classified as a sales-type lease.

If the classification of a lease is changed to an operating lease, the accounting treatment depends upon whether the operating lease starts immediately or at the end of the existing lease. If the operating lease starts immediately, the remaining net investment is eliminated from the accounts and the leased property is recorded as an asset using the lower of (a) original cost, (b) present fair value, or (c) present carrying amount. The difference between the remaining net investment and the new recorded value of the asset is charged to income in the period of change (ASC 840-30-40-6).

If the operating lease starts at the end of the existing lease, the existing lease continues to be accounted for as a sales-type or direct financing lease until the new operating lease commences, at which time the accounting treatment is the same as if the operating lease started immediately. Renewals and extensions usually commence at the end of the original sales-type or direct financing lease. Under these circumstances there should not be any remaining investment to eliminate from the books and the leased property is not recorded as an asset (ASC 840-30-35-28).

Termination of a Lease

Termination of a lease is recognized in the income of the period in which the termination occurs by the following journal entries (ASC 840-30-40-7).

- The remaining net investment is eliminated from the accounts.
- The leased property is recorded as an asset using the lower of the (a) original cost, (b) present fair value, or (c) present carrying amount.

Financial Statement Disclosure

Assets, accumulated amortization, and liabilities from capital leases are reported separately in the balance sheet by the lessee and classified as current or noncurrent in the same manner as other assets and liabilities (ASC 840-30-45-1, 2, 3).

The lessee must clearly disclose current amortization charges to income, along with the following additional information (ASC 840-30-50-1):

- Gross assets as of each balance sheet date presented, in aggregate and by major property categories (this information may be combined with comparable owned assets)
- Minimum future lease payments in total and for each of the next five years, showing deductions for executory costs, including any profit thereon, and the amount of imputed interest to reduce the net minimum lease payments to present values
- Minimum sublease income due in future periods under noncancelable subleases
- Total contingent rentals actually incurred for each period for which an income statement is presented

Following is an illustration of a lessee's financial statement disclosures for capital leases (using assumed numbers).

Illustration of Lessee's Financial Statement Disclosure

Lessor's Balance Sheet
(in thousands)

	December 31	
	20X6	20X5
Assets:		
Leased property:		
Capital leases, less accumulated amortization (Note:____)	$2,200	$1,600
Liabilities:		
Current:		
Obligations under capital leases (Note:____)	$365	$340
Noncurrent:		
Obligations under capital leases (Note:____)	$1,368	$1,260

Capital Leases
Gross Assets and Accumulated Amortization
(in thousands)

	December 31	
	20X6	20X5
Type of Property		
Manufacturing plants	$1,500	$1,100
Retail stores	1,200	840
Other	300	210
Total	$3,000	$2,150
Less: Accumulated amortization	800	550
Capital leases, net	$2,200	$1,600

Capital Leases
Minimum Future Lease Payments and Present Values
of the Net Minimum Lease Payments
(in thousands)

Year Ended December 31	
20X7	$ 406
20X8	1,232
20X9	160
20Y0	125
20Y1	100
After 20Y1	450
Total future minimum rentals	$ 2,473
Less: Executory costs (estimated)	250
Net minimum lease payments	$2,223

53,042   ASC 840—Leases

Year Ended December 31

Less: Imputed interest	490
Present value of net minimum lease payments	$1,733

In addition to the foregoing statements and schedules, footnotes describing minimum sublease income and contingent rentals should be included, if required.

The following financial statement disclosures are required by lessors whose *significant business activity is leasing* (not including *leveraged* leasing) for sales-type and direct financing leases (ASC 840-30-50-4):

- A schedule of the components of the *net investment* in leases, as of each balance sheet date, including:

    - Future minimum lease payments, with separate deductions for executory costs and the allowance for uncollectibles

    - Unguaranteed residual values accruing to the benefit of the lessor

    - Initial direct costs (direct financing leases only)

    - Unearned income

- A schedule of the minimum lease payments, in total and for the next five years

- Contingent rentals included in income

Following is an illlustration of a lessor's financial statement disclosures for capital losses (using assumed numbers).

Illustration of Lessor's Financial Statement Disclosure

Lessor's Balance Sheet
(in thousands)

	December 31	
	20X6	20X5
Assets:		
Current assets:		
Net investment in sales-type and direct financing leases (Note:)	$208	$200
Noncurrent assets:		
Net investment in sales-type and direct financing leases (Note:)	$972	$830

Schedule of Components—Net Investment in Leases Sales-Type and Direct Financing Leases
(in thousands)

	20X6	20X5
Total minimum lease payments receivable	$1,450	$1,250
Less: Estimated executory costs, including profit thereon	150	125
Minimum lease payments	$1,300	$1,125
Less: Allowance for uncollectibles	65	60
Net minimum lease payments receivable	$1,235	$1,065
Add: Estimated unguaranteed residual values of leased properties	240	215
	$1,475	$1,280
Less: Unearned income	295	250
Net investment in sales-type and direct financing leases	$1,180	$1,030

A footnote should be included for contingent rentals.

Schedule of Minimum Lease Payments
(in thousands)

Year Ended December 31

20X7	$ 260
20X8	195
20X9	156
20Y0	132
20Y1	125
After 20Y1	432
Total minimum lease payments receivable, net of executory costs	$1,300

LEASE MODIFICATIONS

Under the provisions of ASC 840, a capital lease may be modified in such a way that the new lease agreement is treated as an operating lease. ASC 840 requires that the lease asset and obligation (liability) be removed from the accounts and any resulting gain or loss be recognized in determining current period income. The new lease agreement is accounted for as an operating lease.

The FASB concluded that the economic effects of the above transaction are similar to those of a sale-leaseback accounting when a capital lease is modified such that the revised lease agreement is classified as an operating lease.

Refunding of Tax-Exempt Debt

If a change in a lease occurs as a result of a refunding by the lessor of tax-exempt debt and (*a*) the lessee receives the economic advantages of the refunding and (*b*) the revised lease qualifies and is classified either as a capital lease by the lessee or as a direct financing lease by the lessor, the change in the lease shall be accounted for on the basis of whether or not an extinguishment of debt has occurred, as follows (ASC 840-30-35-10).

ASC 840—Leases **53,045**

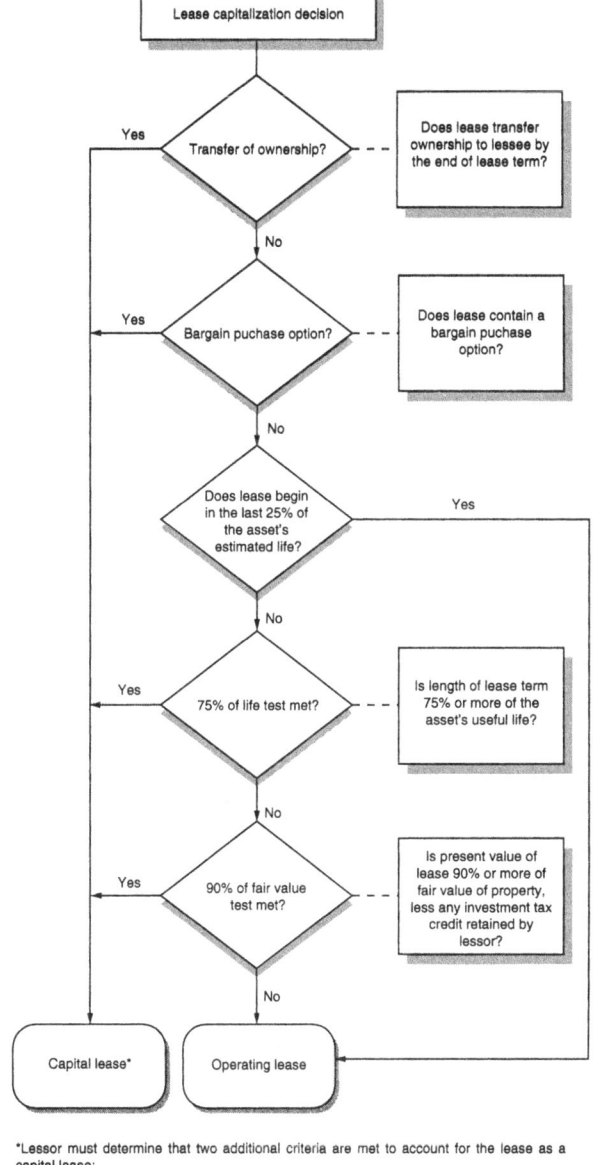

Figure 53-1: Classification of a Lease as a Capital or Operating Lease.

```
                    ┌──────────────────────────┐
                    │ Lease capitalization decision │
                    └──────────────┬───────────┘
                                   │
                                   ▼
          Yes              ╱ Transfer of ownership? ╲ - - - Does lease transfer
       ◄──────────────────                                  ownership to lessee by
                                                            the end of lease term?
                                   │ No
                                   ▼
          Yes              ╱ Bargain puchase option? ╲ - - - Does lease contain a
       ◄──────────────────                                   bargain puchase
                                                             option?
                                   │ No
                                   ▼
                          ╱ Does lease begin  ╲              Yes
                          ╱ in the last 25% of ╲ ─────────────────────┐
                          ╲ the asset's        ╱
                          ╲ estimated life?   ╱
                                   │ No                              │
                                   ▼                                 │
          Yes              ╱ 75% of life test met? ╲ - - - Is length of lease term
       ◄──────────────────                                  75% or more of the
                                                            asset's useful life?
                                   │ No                              │
                                   ▼                                 │
                                                          Is present value of
          Yes              ╱ 90% of fair value ╲ - - -    lease 90% or more of
       ◄──────────────────   test met?                    fair value of property,
                                                          less any investment tax
                                                          credit retained by
                                                          lessor?
                                   │ No                              │
                                   ▼                                 ▼
                    ┌──────────────┐              ┌──────────────┐
                    │ Capital lease*│              │Operating lease│
                    └──────────────┘              └──────────────┘
```

*Lessor must determine that two additional criteria are met to account for the lease as a capital lease:

1. Collection of minimum lease payments is reasonably predictable.
2. No important uncertainties exist for unreimbursable costs to be incurred by the lessor.

- Accounted for as an extinguishment of debt:
  — The lessee adjusts the lease obligation to the present value of the future minimum lease payments under the revised agreement, using

the effective interest rate of the new lease agreement. Any gain or loss is treated as a gain or loss on an early extinguishment of debt.
- The lessor adjusts the balance of the minimum lease payments receivable and the gross investment in the lease (if affected) for the difference between the present values of the old and new or revised agreement. Any gain or loss is recognized in the current period.
- Not accounted for as an extinguishment of debt:
  - The lessee accrues any costs connected with the refunding that are obligated to be reimbursed to the lessor. The interest method is used to amortize the costs over the period from the date of the refunding to the call date of the debt to be refunded.
  - The lessor recognizes as revenue any reimbursements to be received from the lessee for costs paid related to the debt to be refunded over the period from the date of the refunding to the call date of the debt to be refunded.

OTHER LEASE ACCOUNTING ISSUES

Leveraged Leases

The initial and continuing investment of the lessor in a leveraged lease is recorded *net* of the nonrecourse debt, as follows (ASC 840-30-30-14) (FAS-13, par. 43).

- Rentals receivable, net of that portion applicable to principal and interest on the nonrecourse debt
- A receivable for the amount of the investment tax credit to be realized on the transaction
- The estimated residual value of the leased property
- Unearned and deferred income consisting of (*a*) the estimated pretax lease income or loss, after deducting initial direct costs of negotiating and consummating the lease transaction, that remains to be allocated to income over the lease term and (*b*) the investment tax credit that remains to be allocated to income over the lease term

The investment in a leveraged lease, less applicable deferred taxes, represents the lessor's net investment for purposes of computing periodic net income from the leveraged lease (ASC 840-30-35-33) (FAS-13, par. 43). The following method is used to compute periodic net income (ASC 840-30-35-33) (FAS-13, par. 44):

- A projected cash flow analysis is prepared for the lease term.
- The rate of return on net investment in the years it is positive is computed (usually by trial and error).
- Every year the net investment is increased or decreased by the difference between the net cash flow and the amount of income recognized, if any.

The amount of net income that is recognized each year consists of (ASC 840-30-35-44) (FAS-13, par. 44):

- Pretax lease income or loss (allocated from the unearned income portion of the net investment)
- Investment tax credit (allocated from the deferred income portion of the net investment)
- The tax effect of the pretax lease income or loss recognized (which is reflected in tax expense for the year)

Any tax effect on the difference between pretax accounting income or loss and taxable income or loss is charged or credited to deferred taxes.

All the important assumptions affecting the estimated net income from the leveraged lease, including any estimated residual values, should be reviewed at least annually.

If, at the inception or at any time during the lease, the projected net cash receipts over the initial or remaining lease term are less than the lessor's initial or current investment, the resulting loss is immediately recognized (ASC 840-30-25-9) (FAS-13, par. 45).

Upward adjustments of the estimated residual value are not permitted (ASC 840-30-35-40) (FAS-13, par. 46).

The lessor's financial statement disclosure for leveraged leases shall include the amount of deferred taxes stated separately. When leveraged leasing is a significant part of the lessor's business activity, a schedule of the components of the net investment in leveraged leases shall be disclosed fully in the footnotes to the financial statements (ASC 840-30-45-5) (FAS-13, par. 47).

Business Combinations

A business combination (or a combination of not-for-profit entities), in itself does not affect the classification of a lease. If as a result of a business combination, however, a lease is revised or modified to the extent that under ASC 840 it is considered a new agreement, it is reclassified based on its revision or modification. Ordinarily, a lease retains its previous classification under ASC 840 and is accounted for in the same manner as it was prior to the combination.

The acquiring company in a business combination accounts for a leveraged lease by assigning a fair value (present value, net of tax) to the net investment in a leveraged lease based on the remaining future cash flows with appropriate recognition for any future estimated tax effects. After the fair value (present value, net of tax) of the net investment is determined, it is allocated to net rentals receivable, estimated residual value, and unearned income. Thereafter, a company accounts for the leveraged lease by allocating the periodic cash flow between the net investment and the lease income (ASC 840-30-30-15; 840-30-25-10).

In a business combination in which an acquired lease has not been conformed to ASC 840, the acquiring company classifies such a lease to conform retroactively to ASC 840.

ASC 840-40: SALE-LEASEBACK TRANSACTIONS

SALE-LEASEBACK TRANSACTIONS

A sale-leaseback is a transaction in which an owner sells property and then leases back part or all of the same property. Such an owner is referred to as the seller-lessee. The purchaser-lessor is the party who purchases the property and leases back the same property to the seller-lessee.

Non-Real Estate

Profit or loss on the sale is the amount that would have been recognized on the sale by the seller-lessee, assuming there was no leaseback.

Recognition of profit or loss from the sale-leaseback by the seller-lessee is determined by the degree of rights in the remaining use of the property the seller-lessee retains, as follows:

- Substantially all
- Minor
- More than minor but less than substantially all

Substantially All or Minor

Under the terms of the lease, the seller-lessee may have a *minor* portion or *substantially all* of the rights to the remaining use of the property. This is determined by the present value of a total *reasonable rental* for the rights to the remaining use of the property retained by the seller-lessee. The seller-lessee has transferred *substantially all* of the rights to the remaining use of the property to the purchaserlessor if the present value of the total *reasonable rental* under the terms of the lease is 10% or less of the fair value of the property sold at the inception of the lease. The seller-lessee has transferred a *minor* portion of the remaining rights to the purchaser-lessor if the terms of the leaseback include the entire property sold and qualify as a capital lease under ASC 840.

OBSERVATION: ASC 840 does not define *reasonable rental* or *fair value*. However, it defines *fair value* as the price the leased property could be sold for between unrelated parties in an arm's length transaction. ASC 840 defines *fair rental* as the rental rate for similar property under similar lease terms and conditions.

Whether the lease is recorded as a capital lease or an operating lease, any profit or loss on the sale by the seller-lessee must be deferred and amortized as follows:

- *Capital lease* For a capital lease, the deferred profit or loss on the sale is amortized in proportion to the amortization of the leased property.

- *Operating lease* For an operating lease, the deferred profit or loss on the sale is amortized in proportion to the gross rental charged to expense over the lease term.

  Whether a capital lease or an operating lease, if the leased asset is land only, the amortization of the deferred profit or loss on the sale must be on a straight-line basis over the lease term.

  If the seller-lessee retains the rights to a *minor* portion of the remaining use in the property, the seller-lessee accounts for the sale and leaseback as two independent transactions based on their separate terms. The lease must provide for a reasonable amount of rent, however, considering prevailing market conditions at the inception of the lease. The seller-lessee must increase or decrease the profit or loss on the sale by an amount, if any, which brings the total rental for the leased property to a reasonable amount. Any amount created by this adjustment is amortized, as follows:

- *Capital lease* For a capital lease, the deferred or accrued amount is amortized in proportion to the amortization of the leased property.
- *Operating lease* For an operating lease, the deferred or accrued amount is amortized in proportion to the gross rental charged to expense over the lease term.

  Whether a capital lease or an operating lease, if the leased asset is land only, the amortization of the deferred or accrued amount must be on a straight-line basis over the lease term.

PRACTICE POINTER: If the total rental on the lease is less than a reasonable amount compared to prevailing market conditions at the inception of the lease, increase a profit on the sale and decrease a loss on the sale.

For an operating lease, the journal entry is a debit to prepaid rent and a credit to profit or loss. Amortize the prepaid rent in an amount that increases the periodic rental expense over the lease term to a reasonable amount. Conversely, if the total rental on the lease is more than a reasonable amount compared to prevailing market conditions at the inception of the lease, decrease a profit on the sale and increase a loss on the sale. The journal entry is a debit to profit or loss and a credit to deferred rent. Amortize the deferred rent in an amount that decreases the periodic rental expense over the lease term to a reasonable amount.

For a capital lease, make no debit to prepaid rent or credit to deferred rent. Instead, the debit or credit increases or decreases the amount that is recorded for the leased property. Then, amortize the leased property in the usual manner.

More Than Minor but Less Than Substantially All

If the seller-lessee retains the rights to more than minor but less than substantially all of the remaining use in the property, the seller-lessee shall recognize any excess profit (not losses) determined at the date of sale as follows:

- *Capital lease* The excess profit (if any) on a sale-leaseback transaction is equal to the amount of profit that exceeds the seller-lessee's recorded amount of the property as determined under the provisions of ASC 840 (the lesser of the fair value of the leased property or the present value of the minimum lease payments). For example, if the seller-lessee's recorded amount of the sale-leaseback property is $100,000 as determined under the provisions of ASC 840, and the amount of profit on the sale-leaseback transaction is $120,000, the excess profit that is recognized by the seller-lessee is $20,000. The balance of the profit ($100,000) is deferred and amortized in proportion to the amortization of the leased property.

- *Operating lease* The excess profit (if any) on a sale-leaseback transaction is equal to the amount of profit that exceeds the present value of the minimum lease payments over the term of the lease. The amount of profit on the sale-leaseback transaction that is not recognized at the date of the sale is deferred and amortized over the lease term in proportion to the gross rentals charged to expense.

Whether a capital lease or an operating lease, if the leased property is land only, the amortization of the deferred profit (if any) must be on a straight-line basis over the lease term.

Profit Recognition Other Than by the Full Accrual Method

A sale-leaseback transaction must qualify under the provisions of ASC 840 and under most of the provisions of ASC 360 before the full amount of the profit on the sale portion of the transaction can be recognized by the sale-leaseback accounting method (full accrual method).

When one (or more) of the criteria for recognizing the full amount of profit on the sale portion of a sale-leaseback transaction is not met, an alternative method of recognizing revenue from the sale must be used. The alternative method selected may be required by ASC 360 or may be a matter of professional judgment. The four accounting methods recommended by ASC 360 are (1) the deposit method, (2) the cost-recovery method, (3) the installment sales method, and (4) the reduced profit method. (The four alternative methods are discussed earlier in this chapter.)

The collectibility of the receivable should be evaluated periodically. When it becomes apparent that the seller's receivable is reasonably assured of being collected, the seller should change to the full accrual accounting method. (Change to the full accrual method is discussed thoroughly earlier in this chapter.)

Real Estate

Standards of accounting for sale-leaseback transactions involving real estate include transactions including real estate with equipment, such as a manufacturing facility, power plant, and an office building with furniture and fixtures. A sale-leaseback transaction involving real estate with equipment includes any sale-leaseback transaction in which the equipment and the real estate are sold and leased back as a package without regard to the relative value of the equipment and real estate elements of the transaction.

Criteria for Sale-Leaseback Accounting

Sale-leaseback accounting shall be used by a lessor-lessee only if the transaction meets all of the following criteria (ASC 840-40-25-9):

- The leaseback is a normal leaseback (see discussion below).
- Payment terms and provisions adequately demonstrate the buyer-lessor's initial and continuing investment in the property.
- Payment terms and provisions transfer all of the other risks and rewards of ownership as demonstrated by the absence of any continuing involvement by the seller-lessee.

A *normal leaseback* is one in which the seller-lessee actively uses substantially all of the property in consideration for payment of rent, including contingent rentals that are based on the future operations of the seller-lessee. The phrase "actively uses the property" refers to the use of the property during the lease term in the seller-lessee's trade or business, provided that subleasing of the property is minor. The term "minor" means that the present value of the sublease is not more than 10% of the fair value of the asset sold. Active use of the property may involve providing services where the occupancy of the property is generally transient or short-term and is integral to the ancillary services being provided. Ancillary services may include, but are not limited to, housekeeping inventory control, entertainment, bookkeeping, and food services. For example, the use of property by a seller-lessee engaged in the hotel or bonded warehouse business or the operation of a golf course or parking lot is considered active use.

Adequate Initial and Continuing Investment by the Purchaser-Lessor

To qualify for sale-leaseback accounting under ASC 840, the purchaser-lessor's initial and continuing investment in the property must be adequate as prescribed by ASC 360. In determining whether the purchaser's minimum initial investment is adequate under the provisions of ASC 360, the sales value of the property is used and not the stated sales price that appears in the sales contract.

In addition to an adequate initial investment, ASC 360 requires that the purchaser maintain a continuing investment in the property by increasing the investment each year. The purchaser's total indebtedness for the purchase price of the property must be reduced each year in equal amounts that will extinguish the entire indebtedness (interest and principal) over a specified maximum period. The specified maximum period for land transactions is 20 years. The specified maximum period for all other real estate transactions is no more than that offered at the time of sale for first mortgages by independent financial institutions.

Terms of the Sale-Leaseback Transaction

Terms of the sale-leaseback transaction that are substantially different from terms that an independent third-party would accept represent an exchange of some stated or unstated rights or privileges. Those rights or privileges are considered in evaluating the seller-lessor's continuing involvement (described below). Those terms or conditions include, but are not limited to, the sales price, interest rate, and other terms of any loan from the seller-lessee to the buyer-lessor (ASC 840-40-25-10). The fair value of the property used in making that evaluation is based on objective evidence, such as an independent third-party appraisal or recent sales of comparable property.

Continuing Involvement

A sale-leaseback transaction that does not qualify for sale-leaseback accounting because of continuing involvement by the seller-lessee other than a normal leaseback shall account for the transaction by the deposit method or the financing method, whichever is appropriate. Two examples of continuing involvement that are frequently found in sale-leaseback transactions are:

- The seller-lessee has an obligation or an option to repurchase the property so that the buyer-lessor can compel the seller- lessee to repurchase the property.
- The seller-lessee guarantees the buyer-lessor's investment or a return on that investment for a limited or extended period of time.

Other provisions or conditions that represent guarantees and that do not transfer all of the risks of ownership and that constitute continuing involvement for purposes of these standards include:

- The seller-lessee is required to pay the buyer-lessor at the end of the lease term a decline in the fair value of the property below the estimated residual value on some basis other than excess wear and tear of the property.
- The seller-lessee provides nonrecourse financing to the buyer-lessor for any portion of the sales proceeds or provides recourse financing in which the only recourse is to the leased asset.
- The seller-lessee is not relieved of the obligation under any existing debt related to the property.
- The seller-lessee provides collateral on behalf of the buyer-lessor other than the property directly involved in the sale-leaseback transaction, the seller-lessee or a related party guarantees the buyer-lessor's debt, or a related party to the seller-lessee guarantees a return of or on the buyer-lessor's investment.
- The seller-lessee's rental payment is contingent on some predetermined or determinable level of future operations by the buyer-lessor.

Examples of provisions or conditions that are considered continuing involvement for purposes of determining proper accounting for sale-leaseback transactions of real estate are as follows:

- The seller-lessee enters into a sale-leaseback transaction involving property improvements or integral equipment without leasing the underlying land to the buyer-lessor.
- The buyer-lessor is obligated to share with the seller-lessee any portion of the appreciation on the property.

- Any other provision or circumstance that allows the seller-lessee to participate in any future profits of the buyer-lessor or the appreciation of the leased property.

Financial Statement Presentation

In addition to disclosure requirements presented earlier for leases in general, the financial statements of a seller-lessee shall include a description of the terms of sale-leaseback transactions, including future commitments, obligations, provisions, or circumstances that require or result in the seller-lessee's continuing involvement (ASC 840-40-50-1).

The financial statements of a seller-lessee that has accounted for a sale-leaseback transaction by the deposit method or as a financing shall disclose the following information (ASC 840-40-50-2):

- The obligation for future minimum lease payments as of the date of the latest balance sheet presented in the aggregate and for each of the five succeeding fiscal years.
- The total minimum sublease rentals, if any, to be received in the future under noncancelable subleases in the aggregate for each of the five succeeding fiscal years.

OBSERVATION: Additional guidance concerning profit recognition and sale-leaseback transactions involving real estate can be found in Appendix G, *ASC 970—Real Estate.*

WRAP LEASE TRANSACTIONS

In a wrap lease transaction, a lessor leases equipment to a lessee and obtains nonrecourse financing from a financial institution using the lease receivable and the asset as collateral. The lessor sells the asset subject to the lease and the nonrecourse financing to a third-party investor and then leases the asset back. Thus, the original lessor remains the principal lessor, who continues to service the lease. The transaction with the third-party investor may or may not occur at the same time that the original lease is executed with the original equipment user. As a matter of fact, it is not unusual in a wrap lease transaction for the subsequent nonrecourse financing or sale to a third party to occur up to six months after the original lease agreement is executed.

In exchange for the sale of the asset to a third-party investor, the lessor may receive a combination of cash, a note, an interest in the residual value of the leased asset, and certain other rights or contingent rights, such as the right to remarket the asset at the end of the lease term. Depending on the terms of the specific transaction, (*a*) the lessor may or may not be liable for the leaseback payments if the primary lessee defaults, (*b*) the lessor may or may not receive a fee for servicing the lease, (*c*) payments under the leaseback may or may not approximate collections under the note, and (*d*) the terms of the leaseback may or may not correspond with the terms of the original equipment lease.

53,054 ASC 840—Leases

Under sale-leaseback accounting, the sale portion of a sale-leaseback transaction is recorded as a sale by the seller-lessee. The property sold and all of its related liabilities are eliminated from the seller-lessee's balance sheet. Gain or loss on the sale portion of the sale-leaseback transaction is recognized by the seller-lessee. The lease portion of the sale-leaseback transaction should be classified as a capital lease or an operating lease.

The purchaser-lessor records a sale-leaseback transaction as a purchase and a direct financing lease if the lease portion of the sale-leaseback meets the criteria of a capital lease under ASC 840. Otherwise, the purchaser-lessor records the transaction as a purchase and an operating lease (ASC 840-40-25-8).

In reporting a wrap lease transaction, an enterprise's statement of financial position should include (a) the amount of the retained residual interest in the leased property, (b) the amount of the gross sublease receivable, (c) the amount of the nonrecourse third-party debt, (d) the amount of the leaseback obligation, and (e) the amount of the note receivable from the investor.

Illustration of Wrap Lease Transactions

Assume that a lessor leases an asset with an undepreciated cost of $1,000 to a lessee for five years at $19.12 a month. The residual value of the leased asset at the end of the lease term is estimated to be $164.53 and the interest rate implicit in the lease is 10%. The lessor would classify the lease as a direct financing lease under the provisions of ASC 840 and record the following journal entry:

Lease receivable (60 × $19.12)	1,147.20	
Residual value of leased asset	164.53	
Asset		1,000.00
Unearned income—lease receivable		247.20
Unearned income—residual		64.53

Note: For financial reporting purposes, ASC 840 requires that the lease receivable and residual value of the leased asset be combined and reported as the gross investment in the lease. In addition, the unearned income amounts must also be combined.

Using the lease receivable and the asset as collateral, the lessor enters into a nonrecourse financing arrangement with a financial institution for $900.00 (the present value of the $19.12 monthly lease payment for 60 months discounted at 10%) at a rate of 10%. The lessor would record the following journal entry to reflect the liability for the nonrecourse debt:

Cash	900.00	
Nonrecourse debt		900.00

The lessor then sells the asset subject to the lease and the nonrecourse debt to a group of equity partners and leases the asset back for five years at $19.12 a month (for simplicity, assume that the lease, the nonrecourse financing, and the sale to the equity partners occur at the same time). The lessor is now the lessee-sublessor and remains the obligor with the financial institution that financed the nonrecourse debt. In return for the asset, the lessor receives the following:

1. Cash of $50, representing the sale of 50% of the residual value of the leased asset
2. An additional $103.66 in cash, representing the transfer of tax benefits
3. A note receivable for $900.00 bearing interest at 10% with 60 monthly payments of $19.12 (60 payments at $19.12 represent a gross note of $1,147.20 and unearned income of $247.20)
4. The right to receive a fee of $82.27 for remarketing the asset at the end of the initial lease term (the present value of an $82.27 payment 60 months in the future discounted at 10% equals $50.00)
5. In addition, the lessor retains a 50% interest in the proceeds of the residual value of the leased asset at the end of the lease term5.

PART II: INTERPRETIVE GUIDANCE

ASC 840-10: Overall

ASC 840-10-05-7 through 05-8, 25-12 through 25-13, 25-14; ASC 840-40-15-2, 25-13; ASC 958-840-55-4; ASC 450-20-60-16; 460-10-60-23 Implementation Issues in Accounting for Lease Transactions

OVERVIEW

The following guidance addresses questions related to a lessee's balance sheet classification of leases that (1) require a lessee to accept responsibility for certain risks that normally are the responsibility of the property's legal owner, such as environmental contamination that occurred before the inception of the lease, or (2) include default covenants for nonperformance—for example, if a lessee does not maintain certain financial ratios. Under such provisions, lessor may have the right to require a lessee to acquire the property or to pay the lessor.

Questions 1 and 2 apply to all leasing transactions.

OBSERVATION: Under the provisions of ASC 460, a guarantor is required to recognize a liability for an obligation assumed by issuing a guarantee. Guidance also is provided on appropriate disclosures that should be made by a guarantor. If a guarantee or indemnification included in an *operating lease* meets any of the characteristics in ASC 460-10-15-4, a lessee may be required to recognize a liability at the inception of a lease. The disclosure requirement in ASC 450 also would apply to the guarantee. Capital leases accounted for under the guidance in ASC 840 are excluded from the scope of that guidance.

Under the guidance in ASC 810-10 consolidation of variable interest entities by an entity that absorbs a majority of a variable interest entity's expected losses or has the right to receive a greater part of the variable interest entity's expected residual returns or both is required.

Lessee's Responsibility for Environmental Risk
BACKGROUND

Under the provisions of a certain leases, a lessee may be required to indemnify the lessor or the lessor's lender against loss or damage from the lessee's environmental contamination during the term of the lease and for environmental contamination that occurred before the inception of the lease. Alternatively, a lessee may be required to acquire the property.

ACCOUNTING ISSUE

How should a lease with such provisions be classified in a lessee's balance sheet?

ACCOUNTING GUIDANCE

- Lease provisions requiring indemnification for a lessee's environmental contamination during the term of the lease do *not* affect a lessee's balance sheet classification of the lease.
- If a lessee is required under the terms of a lease to indemnify the lessor or its lender for environmental contamination that existed before the lease term, the lessee should at the inception of the lease term evaluate the likelihood of a loss (without recoveries from third parties) based on enacted environmental laws and existing regulations and policies and whether the lessee may be considered the owner of the property.
  - If the likelihood of a loss is remote, the lease's classification would be unaffected;
  - If the likelihood of a loss is at least reasonably possible the lessee should account for the lease in accordance with the sale-leaseback provisions under the guidance in ASC 840-40 as if the lessee had purchased, sold, and leased back the property.

DISCUSSION

If a lessee agrees to pay for remediation of environmental contamination that occurred before the term of a lease, the lessee is taking on a risk of ownership of a property, which is beyond the responsibility of a lessee. The lessee reflects that additional risk by classifying the lease as a capital rather than as an operating lease.

Non-Performance-Related Default Covenants

OVERVIEW

If a lease contains default provisions unrelated to the lessee's use of the property, such as financial covenants that require the lessee to maintain certain financial ratios, the lessee may be required to make a payment to the lessor or acquire the property to remedy a default.

ACCOUNTING ISSUE

How should a lessee classify a lease containing a default provision that is unrelated to the lessee's performance on the lease?

EITF CONSENSUS

1. The classification of a lease containing a default provision is unaffected if it meets *all* the following conditions:
    a. The default covenant is customary in financing arrangements.

      b. The occurrence of default can be determined objectively (acceleration clauses would not meet this condition).
      c. Default would be determined based on specific criteria that apply only to the lessee and its operations.
      d. Based on the facts and circumstances existing at the inception of the lease, it is reasonable to assume that a default will not occur.

      Recent trends in a lessee's operations should be considered in applying condition (d) above. If one of the above conditions is absent, the lessee should include the maximum required payment under the default covenant in the amount of minimum lease payments when applying the guidance in ASC 840-10-25-1(d).

2. A lease with a default provision that is part of a sale-leaseback transaction and thus covered by the provisions of ASC 840-40 should be accounted for by the deposit method or as a financing transaction based on the guidance in ASC 360, regardless of whether all the conditions in (1) above are met. This is so because a default remedy that allows a buyer--lessor to require the seller-lessee to acquire the property violates the continuing involvement criteria in ASC 840-40. That default remedy is equivalent to a purchase option under which the seller-lessee can compel the buyer-lessor to sell back the property, for example, by missing scheduled lease payments to the lessor.

ASC 840-10-05-9A through 05-9C, 25-39A through 25-39B, 35-9A Accounting by Lessees for Maintenance Deposits under Lease Agreements

BACKGROUND

Under the terms of certain agreements for leased *equipment*, a lessee is required to repair and maintain the leased asset during the lease term. To protect a lessor if a lessee does *not* properly maintain the leased equipment, some lease agreements include a requirement that the lessee give the lessor a deposit, which is commonly referred to as a "maintenance reserve" or "supplemental rent." Usually, the deposit is calculated based on a performance measure, such as the number of hours a leased asset has been used. Under the terms of the lease, the lessor must use the deposit to reimburse the lessee, up to the amount of the deposit, for costs incurred for maintenance activities that the lessee is contractually obligated to perform under the lease agreement.

    If at the end of the lease term of some agreements, the deposit exceeds the total cumulative cost of maintaining the equipment over the lease term, the lessor is required to return the remainder of the deposit to the lessee. Lessees generally account for such refundable maintenance deposits as deposits. However, under the terms of other lease agreements, at the end of the lease term, the lessor is permitted to retain an excess of a deposit, if any, over the lessee's maintenance expenditures if the lessee has not performed the required maintenance activities. There is diversity in practice in the way that lessees account for the portion of a deposit that has *not* been refunded.

Under some contracts, the lessee is required to return the leased asset in a certain condition at the end of the lease term. In that case, a lessee should consult other generally accepted accounting principles (GAAP) to determine when and whether to recognize a liability related to that requirement.

ACCOUNTING ISSUE

How should lessees account for maintenance deposits?

ACCOUNTING GUIDANCE

Scope

The following guidance addresses a lessee's accounting for a maintenance deposit under an arrangement providing that the remainder of the deposit will be refunded only if the lessee has performed specified maintenance activities. The guidance does *not* apply to a lessee's payments to a lessor that are *not* substantively and contractually related to the maintenance of a leased asset.

Recognition

At the inception of a lease, a lessee that determines that it is *less than probable* (as defined in paragraph 25 of CON-6 (Elements of Financial Statements—a Replacement of FASB Concepts Statement No. 3 (incorporating an amendment of FASB Concepts Statement No. 2)) (not in the Codification) that the lessor will return to the lessee the total amount of payments as a reimbursement of maintenance activities, the lessee should consider that fact in determining the portion of each payment that is not accounted for under the scope of this guidance. Lessees should account for maintenance deposits under the scope of this guidance as deposit assets. After the inception of a lease agreement, a lessee should continue to evaluate the probability that the lessor will return the deposit to the lessee through reimbursements for the costs of maintenance activities incurred by the lessee. A lessee should recognize a deposit as additional expense if it is determined that it is less than probable that the lessor will return the deposit. A lessee should expense or capitalize the cost of maintenance activities when the underlying maintenance is performed in accordance with its accounting policy for maintenance activities.

ASC 840-10-15-3 through 15-6, 15-10 through 15-20, 35-2 through 35-3, 55-26, 55-30 through 55-37; ASC 840-20-25-9, 25-22, 40-2, 40-6; ASC 840-30-25-4, 30-5, 40-2 through 40-3, 40-6; ASC 440-10-25-1, 25-3; ASC 815-10-15-79 Determining Whether an Arrangement Is a Lease

BACKGROUND

Determining whether an arrangement contains a lease that should be accounted for under the guidance in ASC 840 should be based on the substance of an arrangement. Under the definition of a lease in the ASC Glossary, a lease is an agreement under which the *right to use* property, plant, or equipment transfers from one party to another, usually for a stated period of time. The following guidance should be used to determine whether an arrangement contains a lease under the guidance in ASC 840.

ACCOUNTING ISSUE

How should an entity determine whether an arrangement is a lease that should be accounted for under the guidance in ASC 840?

ACCOUNTING GUIDANCE

Application Guidance

The determination as to whether or not an arrangement includes a lease, which is accounted for under the guidance in ASC 840, should be made based on the facts and circumstances in accordance with the following application guidance at the time an entity enters into an arrangement:

1. An arrangement transfers the *right to use* property, plant, or equipment if a purchaser/lessee has the right to control how the property, plant, or equipment is used. A right to use has been transferred if a purchaser/lessee is able to, or has the right to do, any one of the following:

    a. Operate the property, plant, or equipment or instruct others to do so at will during the time the purchaser/lessee obtains and controls more than a minor amount of the property, plant, or equipment's output or other function,

    b. Control physical access and obtain and control more than a minor amount of the property, plant, or equipment's output or other function, or

    c. Take the output produced or other function of the property, plant, or equipment during the term of the arrangement and if, based on the facts or circumstances, it is a remote possibility that other parties will take more than a minor amount of the output or other function of the property, plant, or equipment. The price paid per unit of output does not equal the current market price per unit at the time the output is delivered.

2. Under the guidance in ASC 840, the phrase *property, plant, and equipment* refers only to land and *depreciable* assets. Therefore, any inventory, as well as minerals, precious metals, or other natural resources—all of which are *not* depreciable assets—cannot be subject to a lease under the definition of a lease. Similarly, intangible assets, such as motion picture film licensing rights and rights to minerals, precious metals, or other resources, which are amortized or depleted but not depreciated, would *not* qualify for lease accounting.

3. Although an arrangement may explicitly refer to a transfer of specific property, plant, or equipment, it contains a lease only if the transferred property, plant, or equipment—*not* other available property, plant, or equipment—is used to fulfill the purpose of the arrangement.

4. An arrangement qualifies as a lease even if the property, plant, or equipment is *not* explicitly identified, if the owner/seller owns or leases only one asset with which the obligation can be fulfilled and it is not possible for the owner/seller to fulfill its obligation with alternative property, plant, or equipment.

5. Lease accounting is permitted (*a*) if an owner/seller has the right to substitute other property, plant, or equipment because the owner/seller has a warranty obligation under the arrangement, (*b*) until a substitution occurs, if an owner/seller has an obligation or the ability, which may be contingent, to substitute other property, plant, or equipment for any reason on or after a specified date.

Reevaluating an Arrangement

1. The judgment that an arrangement is a lease, which was made when entering into the arrangement, should be reevaluated, only under the following circumstances:

    a. *Contractual terms change* The arrangement should be reevaluated under the application guidance in this Issue unless a change is due to a renewal or extension of the arrangement.

    b. *A renewal option or an extension of the arrangement is exercised* Only the renewal or extension period of an arrangement should be reevaluated if the original terms of an arrangement are not modified. The accounting for the remaining term of the arrangement should not be modified. Exercising a renewal option included in the *lease term*, as defined in the ASC Glossary, is *not* considered a renewal that requires a reevaluation of a lease.

    c. *Dependence on specific property, plant, or equipment exists* An arrangement should be reevaluated to determine whether it contains a lease *prospectively* if there is a change in the position as to whether or not fulfillment depends on specified property, plant, or equipment.

    d. *There is a physical change of specific property, plant, or equipment* An arrangement should be reevaluated to determine whether it includes a lease prospectively if a physical change in specified property, plant, or equipment occurs. For example, replacement of a machine specified in the original arrangement with one that has a higher or lower production capacity would require a reevaluation. However, a physical change of property, plant, or equipment that does not affect the productivity of the property, plant, or equipment specified in the original arrangement does not require such a reevaluation.

2. The following guidance should be applied to account for an arrangement if its classification, or that of a portion of the arrangement, changes, because a modification or another change in the arrangement discussed previously causes the arrangement to be classified as a lease or ends its classification as a lease:

    a. *A supply arrangement becomes an operating lease for a Purchaser/Lessee* A recognized asset for a purchase contract, such as a prepaid asset or a derivative instrument, should be considered part of minimum lease payments and recognized initially as prepaid rent. A recognized liability for a purchase contract, such as a payable or a derivative, should be considered a reduction of minimum lease payments and recognized initially as a lease payable.

b. *A supply arrangement becomes an operating lease for a Seller/Lessor* A recognized liability for a sales contract, such as deferred revenue or a derivative instrument, should be part of minimum lease payments and recognized initially as deferred rent. A recognized asset, if any, for a sales contract, such as a receivable or a derivative instrument, should be considered a *reduction* of minimum lease payments and recognized initially as a lease receivable if the asset can be recovered from future receipts.

c. *A supply arrangement is no longer an operating lease but becomes a capital lease for a Purchaser/Lessee* A recognized asset or liability for the purchase contract, such as a prepaid asset, a payable, or a derivative instrument should be included in the basis of the leased asset or lease obligation.

d. *A supply arrangement becomes a sales-type lease for a Seller/Lessor* If the criteria for treatment as a sale in ASC 840-10-25-42 or other applicable literature, such as ASC 360, are met, (i) the property, plant, or equipment should be derecognized, and (ii) an asset or liability for a supply arrangement, if any, should be recognized in earnings as an adjustment of minimum lease payments. Otherwise, (i) a recognized asset or liability for the supply arrangement, if any, should be considered as a reduction of, or part of, minimum lease payments, and (ii) a lease should be recognized in accordance with the guidance in ASC 840.

e. *A supply arrangement is no longer an operating lease for a Purchaser/Lessee* Previously recognized prepaid rent or rent payable, if any, should be recognized initially as an asset or a liability related to the purchase contract.

f. *A supply arrangement is no longer an operating lease for a Seller/Lessor* Previously recognized deferred rent or rent receivable, if any, should be recognized initially as a liability or an asset related to the sales contract, subject to a recoverability test.

g. *A supply arrangement is no longer a capital lease for a Purchaser/Lessee*, Leased property, plant, or equipment that is real estate, including integral equipment, should be derecognized based on the guidance in ASC 360-20. Leased property, plant, or equipment, and the related lease obligation, other than real estate, including integral equipment, also should be derecognized. Before a sale is recognized, an asset subject to a capital lease should be evaluated for impairment under the guidance in ASC 360-10 The terms of the changes in the arrangement that cause a reevaluation of the lease arrangement must be considered in that evaluation. After an asset is reduced for impairment, if any, the difference between the capital lease asset and the obligation, if any, is recognized initially as an asset or a liability associated with the supply arrangement.

h. *A direct-financing, or sales-type lease becomes a supply arrangement for a Seller/Lessor* The remaining net investment should be removed from the accounts with the leased asset being recognized at the lower of its (1) original cost, (2) current fair value, or (3) current carrying amount. The net adjustment should be charged to income in the period in which the change is made. The lessor should account for a new lease entered into thereafter as an operating lease.

Multiple-Element Arrangements That Include a Lease

A purchaser and a supplier to a lease element of an arrangement should apply the classification, recognition, measurement, and disclosure requirements of ASC 840 if an arrangement includes a lease and related executory costs as well as other nonlease elements. Elements of an arrangement not under the scope of ASC 840 should be accounted for in accordance with other applicable GAAP. When the guidance in ASC 840 is applied, payments and other consideration required under an arrangement should be separated at the inception of an arrangement or when it is reevaluated into (*a*) payments for the lease, including related executory costs and profits, and (*b*) payments for other services based on their relative fair value in accordance with the guidance in ASC 605-25-15-3A(b).

ASC 840-10-15-20; ASC 815-10-15-80 through 15-81; ASC 460-10-60-20 The Impact of the Requirements of ASC 815 on Residual Value Guarantees in Connection with a Lease

BACKGROUND

The following guidance is the result of an attempt to resolves a scope overlap between the guidance ASC 815, *Derivatives and Hedging*, and ASC 840, *Leases*, related to the accounting for residual value guarantees (*a*) for transactions accounted for under the guidance in ASC 840, (*b*) that meet the definition of a derivative in ASC 815, and (*c*) that are either not explicitly excluded from the scope of ASC 815 or do not meet one of its scope exceptions. Although the guidance in ASC 815 did not amend the guidance in ASC 840, ASC 815 does not explicitly exclude residual value guarantees included in lease transactions, except as provided in ASC 815-10-15. The scope overlap does not apply, however, to third-party guarantors' accounting for obligations related to residual guarantees or to contracts not accounted for under the scope of the guidance in ASC 840

ACCOUNTING ISSUES

1. How should the scope overlap between ASC 840 and ASC 815 related to residual value guarantees be resolved?

2. Should third-party residual value guarantors account for residual value guarantees under the requirements in ASC 815?

ACCOUNTING GUIDANCE

1. Residual value guarantees subject to the guidance in ASC 840 are not subject to the guidance in ASC 815-10.

2. Third-party residual value guarantors should consider the guidance in ASC 815-10 for *all* residual value guarantees provided to determine whether those guarantees are derivatives and whether they qualify for one of the scope exceptions in ASC 815.

OBSERVATION: Under the provisions of ASC 460, *Guarantees*, a guarantor is required to recognize a liability for an obligation assumed by issuing a guarantee. ASC 460 also provides guidance on appropriate disclosures that should be made by a guarantor. However, residual value guarantees related to capital leases accounted for under the guidance in ASC 840 are excluded from the scope of ASC 460. In addition, residual value guarantees accounted for as derivative instruments under the guidance in ASC 815 also are exempted from the initial measurement and recognition requirements in ASC 460 and are only subject to the disclosure requirements in ASC 460. However, the initial recognition, initial measurement, and disclosure requirements in ASC 460 would apply to the guarantees discussed under the accounting guidance above.

ASC 840-10-25-3 Fiscal Funding Clauses in Lease Agreements

BACKGROUND

Fiscal funding clauses are frequently found in lease agreements in which the lessee is a governmental entity. The clause generally provides for the lease to be cancelable if the legislature or other funding authority does not appropriate the funds necessary for the governmental unit to fulfill its obligations under the lease agreement.

ACCOUNTING GUIDANCE

Question: What effect, if any, does the existence of a fiscal funding clause in a lease agreement have on the classification of a lease under the guidance in ASC 840?

Answer: The existence of a fiscal funding agreement in a lease requires making an assessment of the likelihood that the lease will be canceled by exercising the fiscal funding clause agreement. If the likelihood that the agreement will be exercised is remote, the lease should be considered to be noncancelable. If the probability is considered other than remote, the lease is considered cancelable and, therefore, is classified as an operating lease.

PRACTICE POINTER: The term *remote* is used in this guidance in the same manner as in ASC 450 (i.e., the chance of the future event or events occurring is slight).

ASC 840 ASC 840-10-25-46, 25-48 through 25-50 Lessors' Evaluation of Whether Leases of Certain Integral Equipment Meet the Ownership Transfer Requirements of ASC 840

BACKGROUND

The guidance in ASC 360-20-15-2 through 15-4, 15-10, 55-4 through 55-5 provides that lease transactions involving integral equipment, as defined under that guidance, are considered to be leases of real estate. Under the guidance in ASC 840-10-25-1, classification as a sales type lease requires that *ownership* of the property be transferred to the lessee by the end of the lease term.

Article 2 of the Uniform Commercial Code (UCC) provides guidelines to be used in determining whether title to personal property has passed. However, unlike transfers of real property, which are recorded in accordance with state law as evidence that ownership has been transferred, there is no system under which title to personal property is recorded. Consequently, questions have been raised about how to provide evidence of a transfer of ownership in integral equipment (without a transfer of the real property) to a lessee by the end of the lease term.

ACCOUNTING ISSUES

- Should integral equipment under a lease be evaluated as real estate in accordance with the guidance in ASC 840?
- If so, how should the requirement in ASC 840-10-25-1(a) regarding the transfer of ownership be evaluated if there is no statutory registration system for leased integral equipment?

ACCOUNTING GUIDANCE

- Equipment subject to a lease that is attached to real property (integral equipment) should be evaluated as real estate using the guidance in ASC 840.
- Without the existence of a statutory system of title registration to integral equipment, the requirement in ASC 840-10-25-1(a) that ownership to equipment be transferred to a lessee by the end of the lease term is met if, under the lease agreement, the lessor is required to deliver the necessary documents (including a bill of sale, if applicable) that will release the integral equipment from the lease and will transfer ownership of the equipment to the lessee. The requirement in ASC 840-10-25-1(a) would also be met if an agreement requires a nominal payment on the transfer of ownership. However, the requirement in ASC 840-10-25-1(a) would *not* be met if a lease agreement states that a transfer of ownership to the lesse would not occur if the lessee chooses not to pay the specified fee, regardless of the amount, because that requirement would be considered a *purchase option*.

ASC 840-10-25-6 ; ASC 840-20-25-8, 25-12 through 25-13, 30-1, 35-1; ASC 840-40-55-42 through 55-47; ASC 958-810-25-9, 55-7 through 55-16; ASC 958-840-55-2 through 55-3; ASC 460-10-60-24 Implementation Issues in Accounting for Leasing Transactions

Lessee Payments Made before the Beginning of the Lease Term

BACKGROUND

Lessees may sometimes be required to make payments (known as construction period lease payments) to the lessor before construction is completed and the lease term has begun in build-to-suit transactions.

ACCOUNTING ISSUES

1. Should construction period lease payments be included in the minimum lease payments when applying the 90% of fair value recovery test specified in ASC 840-10-25-1?

2. How should a lessee account for such payments if the lease is classified as an operating lease?

ACCOUNTING GUIDANCE

1. Payments made before the lease term begins should be considered to be part of the minimum lease payments, and they should be included in the 90% test at their future value at the beginning of the lease term. The interest rate used to compute the future value of payments to be made before the beginning of the lease term should be the same as that used to discount lease payments to be made during the lease term.

2. If a lease is classified as an operating lease, lease payments made before the lease term begins should be accounted for as prepaid rent and included in total rent costs, which generally should be allocated on a straight-line basis over the term of the lease, in accordance with the guidance in ASC 840-20-25-3 through 25-7, 55-1 through 55-3; ASC 840-10-55-45 through 55-46; ASC 840-30-55-14, 55-19 through 55-20; ASC 840-40-55-17 through 55-21.

Fees Paid to an SPE's Owners

BACKGROUND

Under some lease agreements, a lessee is required to pay an SPE's owner certain fees, which are referred to as structuring or administrative fees, for arranging the lease.

ACCOUNTING ISSUE

How should the lessee and the SPE account for structuring or administrative fees paid to the SPE's owner of record?

ACCOUNTING GUIDANCE

A lessee should include such fees in the minimum lease payments—but not in the fair value of the property—for the purpose of applying the 90% test in paragraph ASC 840-10-25-1.

Costs Incurred by Lessees before Entering into a Lease

BACKGROUND

In build-to-suit lease transactions, a lessee sometimes incurs certain development costs before entering into a lease with a developer-lessor.

The costs may be soft costs, such as architectural fees and zoning fees, or hard costs, such as site preparation and construction costs.

ACCOUNTING ISSUE

What kinds of costs (and in what amount) can a lessee incur before entering a lease agreement without being considered the owner of the property and therefore subject to the requirements of ASC 840-40 for sale-leaseback transactions?

ACCOUNTING GUIDANCE

A lessee that begins construction activities should recognize construction in progress as an asset and account for it under the guidance in ASC 840-40, as discussed below. Construction activities are deemed to have begun if any of the following activities have occurred:

- The lessee has begun construction (broken ground).
- The lessee has incurred hard costs, whether those costs are insignificant or not to the fair value of the property to be constructed.
- The lessee has incurred soft costs that amount to more than 10% of the expected fair value of the leased property. In a build-to-suit lease, soft costs would include the fair value of the lessee's option to acquire real property that is transferred to the securitization entity. Off-balance-sheet purchase commitments at market would not be included, however.

DISCUSSION

A lessee that is involved in more than an insignificant aspect of the construction process and has incurred hard costs or significant soft costs on a project assumes the risks of ownership.

Accounting under the Guidance in ASC 840-40 for Construction-in-Process Transferred to a Lessor

BACKGROUND

A lessee begins construction activities, as discussed above, and subsequently transfers the property to a lessor in a transaction deemed to be within the scope of ASC 840-40-05-9 through 05-10, 15-4, 15-9 through 15-10, 25-9 through 25-14, 25-17, 50-1 through 50-2, 55-36, 55-49 through 55-77; ASC 980-840-25-1 through 25-3, 35-1 through 35-2.

ACCOUNTING ISSUE

How should the lessee apply the provisions of ASC 840-40 to the transaction?

ACCOUNTING GUIDANCE

The transaction would be evaluated as a sale-leaseback under the provisions of ASC 840-40, because the lessee is considered the owner of the project. The lessee should account for the property as follows:

- Recognize a sale and profit or loss if the transaction qualifies as a sale under the guidance in ASC 360 and 840-40.
- Continue reporting construction-in-progress as an asset and recognize proceeds received from the lessor as a liability; if the transaction does *not* qualify for sale-leaseback accounting, the lessee would:
  — Report additional amounts spent by the lessor on construction as construction-in-progress and as a liability to the lessor.
  — Depreciate the property after the property is placed in service and account for the lease payments as debt service on the liability.

Interest-only Payments

BACKGROUND

Rental payments on real estate leases that involve a securitization entity often consist of the total interest on the securitization entity's debt plus a return on the securitization entity's equity. The lessee also frequently guarantees that the value of the property will be a specified amount at the end of the lease term. The lease is classified as an operating lease, because the present value of the minimum lease payments, including the maximum deficiency under the residual value guarantee that the lessee is required to pay, does not meet the 90% test under the guidance in ASC 840-10-25-1.

ACCOUNTING ISSUE

How should a lessee account for an interest-only lease that otherwise qualifies as an operating lease?

ACCOUNTING GUIDANCE

In accordance with the guidance in ASC 460-10-30-2(b), a guarantor-lessee should recognize the fair value of a residual value guarantee at the inception of the lease even though the likelihood that a deficiency will occur is *not* probable at that time. A lessee should recognize rent expense on a straight-line basis, in accordance with the guidance in ASC 840-20-25-1. Payments related to a deficiency would not be included in that calculation until it becomes probable that the value of the property at the end of the lease term will be less than the guaranteed amount (even though the maximum deficiency under the residual value guarantee is included in minimum lease payments for the 90% test). When a deficiency becomes probable, the lessee should accrue the amount of the expected deficiency and recognize it on a straight-line basis over the remainder of the lease term. The deficiency must be accrued even if the lessee expects to exercise a purchase or renewal option at the end of the lease term.

ASC 840-10-25-10 through 25-11, 25-53, 50-3; ASC 460-10-55-23A Tax Indemnifications in Lease Agreements

BACKGROUND

Some lessors include tax indemnification clauses in lease agreements that would require a lessee to indemnify the lessor, on an after-tax basis, for tax benefits that may be lost as a result of changes in tax laws.

ACCOUNTING ISSUE

Should lessors and lessees account for tax indemnification payments as (1) contingent rent, (2) replacement of tax benefits, (3) ratably as income/expense, or (4) a revision of the lease?

ACCOUNTING GUIDANCE

Although tax indemnification payments may appear to meet the definition of a contingent rental in ASC 840, they are not the type of payments normally expected to occur under continuing rent provisions. Because they can be closely associated with specific aspects of the tax law, such payments should be accounted for in a manner that recognizes that association. The transaction should not affect the lease's original classification.

Lessors should recognize tax indemnification payments related to tax effects, other than the investment tax credit, in income based on a lease's classification as follows:

   a. Capital lease—Adjust the lessor's investment.

53,068   ASC 840—Leases

b. Operating lease—Recognize ratably over the lease term.

Under the guidance in ASC 460-10-25-4, a lessee (guarantor) should recognize a liability at the inception of a lease for a tax indemnification to a lessor. The liability should be measured in accordance with the guidance in ASC 460-10-30-2 at the fair value of the lessee's obligation under the tax indemnification agreement.

Lessees should make the disclosures about guarantees required under the guidance in ASC 460-10-50-4.

DISCUSSION

The decision to account for tax indemnification payments as a replacement of tax benefits is based on the view that this approach is consistent with the economics of the transaction and allows the parties to continue accounting for a lease without revising the agreement.

ASC 840-10-25-21 through 25-22; ASC 460-10-60-19 Allocation of Residual Value or First-Loss Guarantee to Minimum Lease Payments in Leases Involving Land and Building(s)

BACKGROUND

Real estate leases for land and buildings often include a clause guaranteeing the property's residual value (guarantee) that transfers some risks to a lessee and ensures that a lessor will receive an appropriate return of and on the investment in the property. Under the guidance in ASC 840-10-55-15 a guarantee must be included in minimum lease payments in determining whether to classify a lease as an operating or as a capital lease.

A lease should be classified as a capital lease if any of the following criteria ASC 840-10-25-1 are met:

1. Ownership of the property is transferred to the lessee by the end of the lease term.
2. The lease contains a bargain purchase option.
3. The lease term is 75% or more of the estimated economic life of the leased property.
4. The present value of minimum lease payments (as defined) is 90% or more of the estimated fair value of the leased property.

ASC 840 distinguishes between real estate leases involving only land and those that involve land and buildings for the purpose of lease classification. Under the guidance in ASC 840-10-25-55 through 55-59, which applies to leases of land only a lease is classified as a capital lease if it meets one of the above criteria. Thus, a guarantee, which is a component of minimum lease payments and is considered in the calculation in ASC 840-10-25-1(d), is excluded from the calculation in determining the lease classification of land.

Under the provisions of ASC 840-10-25-38, a lease involving land and buildings should be classified and accounted for as a capital lease if either criterion (*a*) or criterion (*b*) is met. If neither of those criteria is met, and the fair value of the land is less than 25% of the total value of the leased property at inception of the lease, ASC 840-10-25-38(b)(1) provides that the land and building be considered as a unit and treated essentially the same as a building.

However, if the fair value of the land is greater than 25% of the total fair value of the property at inception of the lease, paragraph ASC 840-10-25-38(b)(2) requires that the land and building be evaluated *separately* in applying the guidance ASC 840-10-25-1(c) to determine whether to classify the building as an operating or capital lease. Because a guarantee is not considered in the classification of land only, as discussed above, a literal interpretation of paragraph ASC 840-10-25-38(b)(2) would include a guarantee solely in minimum lease payments attributed to the building in this separate evaluation.

Some have questioned that interpretation of the treatment of a guarantee in an economic environment in which land may no longer retain its value. A literal interpretation of paragraph ASC 840-10-25-38(b)(2) often provides anomalous results. For example, if a guarantee equals or exceeds a building's fair value, a separate evaluation of the land and building may indicate that the lessee should classify the lease on the building as a capital lease; an evaluation of the land and building as a unit would result in an operating lease classification. Consequently, alternative methods have been used in practice.

ACCOUNTING ISSUE

How should a residual value guarantee be treated when applying the criterion in ASC 840-10-25-1(d) to a real estate lease involving land and a building if the fair value of the land is 25% or more of the total fair value of the leased property?

ACCOUNTING GUIDANCE

A literal interpretation of ASC 840-10-25-38(b)(2) should be followed. Thus, the lessee and the lessor should determine the amount of annual minimum lease payments to be attributed to the portion of the lease related to the land by multiplying the fair value of the land by the lessee's incremental borrowing rate. The remaining minimum lease payments, including the full amount of the guarantee, should be attributed to the portion of the lease related to the building.

OBSERVATION: The embedded guarantee discussed in this Issue is not a derivative under the guidance in ASC 815.

DISCUSSION

Under the model followed in ASC 840, the value of land does not depreciate and therefore does not require a guarantee.

ASC 840-10-25-35, 40-1, 50-5; ASC 450-20-60-15; ASC 450-30-60-5 Accounting for Contingent Rent

BACKGROUND

Under some lease agreements, a lessee may be required to pay the lessor a contingent amount in addition to a fixed monthly rental payment. Contingent rental payments are usually related to the lessee's use of the property and may be based on machine hours of use or on sales volume during the lease term. For example, a manufacturer may be required to pay contingent rent of $1 per machine hour over 600,000 machine hours per year. *Contingent rental* is defined in the ASC Glossary as "[t]he increases or decreases in lease payments that result from changes occurring after lease inception in the factors (other than the passage of time) on which lease payments are based . . . ."

Some lessors and lessees were accruing amounts related to contingent rent in interim periods based on estimates of the final amount while others waited for recognition until the actual amount was determined.

ACCOUNTING ISSUES

5. How should a *lessor* account in interim periods for contingent rental revenue that is based on future specified targets to be met by the lessee during the lessor's fiscal year?

6. How should a *lessee* account in interim periods for contingent rental expense that is based on future specified targets to be met during the lessee's fiscal year?

ACCOUNTING GUIDANCE

A lessee should recognize contingent rental expense in annual periods and interim periods before having reached specified targets that trigger contingent rental expense if it is *probable* that the target will be reached. If at any time thereafter it becomes probable that a specified target will *not* be reached, the lessee should reverse the expense into income.

A lessor should disclose its accounting policy for contingent rental income. A lessor accrues contingent rental income before the lessee has achieved the specified target and achievement of the target is probable, should disclose the effect of the contingent rental income on its rental income as if the lessor's accounting policy were to defer that income until the lessee has met the specified target.

SUBSEQUENT DEVELOPMENT

The SEC staff has issued SAB-101 (Revenue Recognition in Financial Statements), which applies to the accounting by lessors. It provides that contingent rental income *accrues* when changes in the factors on which contingent lease payments are based actually occur (for example, when a lessee's sales volume reaches an amount that triggers contingent rental income). Because it is inappropriate to recognize revenue based on a probability that an event will occur, registrants should recognize contingent rental income only in the period in which the contingency is resolved.

Illustration of a Lessee's Recognition of Contingent Rental Expense in Interim Periods

Barr Stationary and Supplies, Inc., a retail store, has a 3/31 year-end. The company has entered into a three-year lease at a new location beginning 1/1/X8. The lease specifies a monthly rental of $10,000. In addition, at the end of each year during the term of the lease, the company is obligated to pay the lessor an additional $1,000 rent for each month the company's revenues were equal to or exceeded $50,000 and if the company's total annual sales revenues during that year of the lease were at least $600,000 or more. During the past three years, Barr's monthly revenues ranged between $50,000 and $60,000.

Barr moved into its new location on 2/15/X8. Revenues during January 20X8 were $35,000. Revenues during February were $35,000. Because it was not probable that Barr would meet its monthly target in March, no contingent rental income was accrued for the last quarter of 20X8. Therefore, Barr will accrue contingent rent expense in interim periods beginning in the first quarter of fiscal 20X9.

ASC 840-10-35-6 through 35-9; ASC 805-20-35-6 Determining the Amortization Period for Leasehold Improvements Purchased After Lease Inception or Acquired in a Business Combination

OVERVIEW

A *lease term* is defined in the ASC Glossary as a predetermined period of time during which a lessee cannot cancel a lease as well as periods of time covered by bargain renewal options or periods during which renewal is reasonably assured because the lessee would incur a large penalty if the lease is not renewed. The guidance in ASC 840-30-35-1 states that assets, such as leasehold improvements, under capital leases that do *not* transfer ownership of those assets to a lessee and do not contain a bargain renewal option should be amortized over the assets' useful life or a period limited to the term of a lease, whichever is shorter. Although the amortization of leasehold improvements under capital leases was not discussed in ASC 840, practitioners analogized to the guidance in ASC 840-30-35-1 for operating leases, because as in capital leases, a lessee would not control the use of leasehold improvements if there is no assurance that the lease will be renewed.

Some practitioners questioned whether the amortization period of leasehold improvements acquired a period of time after a lease term begins can extend beyond the lease term. The guidance in ASC 840-10-35-4 provides that the term of a lease for purposes of lease classification cannot be changed unless (*a*) a lease's provisions are modified so that the lease is considered a new agreement or (*b*) a lease is extended or renewed beyond the existing lease term.

The same question was raised regarding the amortization of leasehold improvements acquired as a result of the assumption of existing lease agreements in a business combination, i.e., whether leasehold improvements acquired in a business combination can be amortized over a period that extends beyond the term determined at the inception of a lease by the acquired entity. Under the guidance in paragraphs ASC 840-10-35-5, the acquiring entity is required to retain the lease classification used by the acquired entity, unless one of the conditions in ASC 840-10-35-4 has been met.

ACCOUNTING ISSUES

1. What period should be the amortization period for leasehold improvements acquired in a business combination?

2. What period should be the amortization period for leasehold improvements in operating leases that were *not* considered at the beginning of a lease term but purchased a significant period of time after the inception of a lease?

EITF CONSENSUS

The EITF reached the following consensus positions:

1. Under the guidance in ASC 805-20-35-6, leasehold improvements acquired in a business combination or an acquisition by a not-for-profit entity should be amortized over (*a*) the useful life of the assets or (*b*) a term that includes required lease periods and renewals that are considered to be "reasonably assured," as defined in the definition of a "lease term" in the ASC Glossary, at the acquisition date, whichever is shorter.

2. Leasehold improvements in operating leases *not* considered at or near the beginning of a lease and placed in service a significant period of time after a lease's inception should be amortized over (*a*) the assets' useful life or (*b*) a term that includes required lease periods and renewals that are considered to be "reasonably assured," under the definition of a "lease term" in the ASC Glossary, at the date the leasehold improvements are purchased, whichever is shorter.

The guidance above does not apply to preexisting leasehold improvements and should not be used to justify a reevaluation of the amortization period of preexisting leasehold improvements for additional renewal periods when new leasehold improvements that were not considered before are placed into service significantly after the beginning of a lease term.

That guidance also does not address the amortization of intangible assets that may be recognized in a business combination or an acquisition by a not-for-profit entity for a lease's favorable or unfavorable terms

ASC 840-10-45-2 through 45-3 Applicability of ASC 840 to Current Value Financial Statements

BACKGROUND

The following guidance was provided as a result of uncertainty concerning the applicability of ASC 840 in current value financial statements.

ACCOUNTING GUIDANCE

Question: Are financial statements prepared on a current value basis subject to the provisions of ASC 840?

Answer: A lessor should classify a lease in financial statements that are prepared on a current value basis as a sales-type or direct financing lease, as appropriate, if it meets any of the criteria in ASC 840-10-25-1 and both of the criteria in ASC 840-10-25-42. In subsequent periods, the lessor should adjust its investment in the lease payments receivable on the lease based on the valuation technique used to prepare its current value financial statements.

ASC 840-10-55-12 through 55-25; ASC 460-10-55-17, 60-22; ASC 605-50-60-1
Sales with a Guaranteed Minimum Resale Amount

BACKGROUND

Some manufacturers selling equipment to end users offer an incentive program, under which the manufacturer contractually guarantees the purchaser a minimum resale value on disposition of the equipment, which has an expected useful life of several years. If the equipment meets certain conditions, such as no excess wear and tear, manufacturers may guarantee the resale price in one of two ways: the equipment will be reacquired at a guaranteed price at specified times periods, or the purchaser will be paid for any difference between the proceeds received on the sale of the equipment at the guaranteed minimum resale value. The purchaser is not required, however, to resell the asset to the manufacturer under the incentive program.

Although equipment dealers may be involved in those transactions, the manufacturer is the party responsible for the resale value guarantee. Manufacturers using such programs have been recognizing revenue on the sale of the equipment to independent dealers and have considered the resale protection as a sales incentive. They have recorded the estimated cost of the incentive as a sales discount in the period in which the equipment is sold to the dealer based on historical data, such as amounts realized on resale at auction.

ACCOUNTING ISSUE

Should manufacturers recognize a sale on equipment sold to purchasers with a resale value guarantee?

ACCOUNTING GUIDANCE

- A manufacturer should not recognize a sale on a transfer of equipment if purchasers receive a resale value guarantee.
- The transaction should be accounted for as a lease, based on the guidance in ASC 840.
- The difference between the proceeds on the initial transfer of equipment to a purchaser (the selling price) and the manufacturer's residual value guarantee at the first date on which the purchaser can exercise the guarantee should be used as the amount of minimum lease payments in determining whether the lease should be classified as an operating or as a sales-type lease.

A manufacturer should account for a transfer of equipment under an operating lease as follows:

- Record a liability for the net proceeds received when the equipment is transferred.
- Reduce the liability on a pro rata basis to the guaranteed amount on the first date on which the buyer can exercise the guarantee, and credit revenue for corresponding amounts.
- Continue reducing the liability in a similar manner if a buyer decides to use the equipment beyond the first exercise date.

- Report the equipment in the balance sheet and depreciate it based on the entity's customary depreciation policy.
- Account for potential impairment of the equipment based on the guidance in ASC 360-10.
- Account for a buyer's exercise of the resale value guarantee as follows:
  — If a buyer exercises the resale value guarantee by selling the equipment to another party, (a) reduce the liability by any amount paid to the purchaser, (b) remove the undepreciated carrying amount of the equipment and any remaining liability from the balance sheet, and (c) include the amounts in (a) and (b) in determining income for the period in which the buyer sells the equipment.
  — If a buyer exercises the resale value guarantee by selling the equipment back to the manufacturer at the guaranteed amount, (a) reduce the liability by the amount paid to the purchaser and (b) include remaining liability, if any, in determining income for the period in which the guarantee is exercised.

OBSERVATION: ASC 460, which requires a guarantor to recognize the fair value of a liability at the inception of a guarantee, does *not* affect the guidance. Because a manufacturer continues to carry the residual value of equipment (which is guaranteed) as an asset, the guarantee does *not* meet the characteristics in ASC 460-10-15-4 and is not under the scope of the guidance in ASC 460.

DISCUSSION

The FASB staff and the SEC staff both believed that the transactions discussed above should be accounted for under the guidance in ASC 840, because the manufacturer has retained the risk of reselling the equipment. In effect, the purchaser has the right to use the equipment for a predetermined period of time without the risk of resale at the end of that period.

Illustration of Revenue Recognition on Sales with a Guaranteed Minimum Resale Value

On June 1, 20X4, ABC Motor Co. enters into an agreement with Affordable Auto Rental Co. under which ABC sells ten automobiles to Affordable for $15,000 cash per automobile. ABC conditionally guarantees Affordable either (a) a maximum resale value (residual value guarantee) of $7,500 per automobile sold back to ABC starting on December 1, 20X5, the first exercise date (subject to wear and tear), or (b) the difference between the residual value guarantee and the amount Affordable receives in a sale to an unrelated party. ABC's inventory cost of each automobile is $12,000. ABC, which accounts for the transaction as an operating lease under the consensus in EITF Issue 95-1, depreciates the automobiles over an estimated economic life of five years on a straight-line basis. The company has a November 30th year-end.

Under the two scenarios below, ABC should account for the transaction initially, during the term of the lease, and when Affordable exercises the residual value guarantee as follows:

Scenario 1 On December 1, 20X5, Affordable sells nine automobiles (one was destroyed in a fire) to another party for $60,000 and exercises ABC's residual value guarantee for the nine automobiles.

Scenario 2 On December 1, 20X5, Affordable exercises the residual value guarantee by selling nine automobiles back to ABC.

At June 1, 20X4—Date of Transfer with Residual Value Guarantee.

Under both scenarios, ABC recognizes the leased automobiles as an asset at its inventory cost and recognizes a liability (deferred revenue) for the net proceeds it received from Affordable on the transfer. (Net proceeds are assumed to be the cash payment received.)

Cash	$150,000	
Leased automobiles	120,000	
Deferred revenue		$150,000
Inventory—automobiles		120,000

At November 30, 20X4

Under both scenarios, ABC reduces the residual value guarantee by a proportionate amount and recognizes a corresponding amount of revenue [$75,000 × (6/18)]. Six months of depreciation is recognized for the automobiles [$120,000 × (6/60)].

Deferred revenue	$25,000	
Depreciation expense	12,000	
Revenue		$25,000
Accumulated depreciation		12,000

At November 30, 20X5

Under both scenarios, ABC reduces the residual value guarantee by a proportionate amount and recognizes a corresponding amount of revenue [$75,000 × (12/18)]. Six months of depreciation is recognized for the automobiles [$120,000 × (12/60)].

Deferred revenue	$50,000	
Depreciation expense	24,000	
Revenue		$50,000
Accumulated depreciation		24,000

Scenario 1: Exercise of the Residual Value Guarantee

On December 1, 20X5, Affordable sells nine automobiles to an unrelated party for $60,000 and exercises the residual value guarantee. ABC pays Affordable $7,500 (the difference between the guaranteed amount of $67,500 for nine automobiles and $60,000). ABC removes the remaining residual value guarantee and the undepreciated carrying amount of the asset from its balance sheet and uses those amounts to determine income for the quarter ending February 29, 20X6.

Deferred revenue	$75,000	
Accumulated depreciation	36,000	

Cost of sales—automobiles	84,000	
Sale—automobiles		$ 67,500
Leased automobiles		120,000
Cash		7,500

Scenario 2: Exercise of the Residual Value Guarantee

On December 1, 20X5, Affordable exercises the residual value guarantee by selling nine automobiles back to ABC. ABC pays Affordable $67,500 and credits revenue for the amount of the remaining residual value guarantee after the payment.

Deferred revenue	$75,000	
Cash		$67,500
Revenue		$7,500

ASC *Glossary—Incremental Borrowing Rate* Interest Rate Used in Calculating the Present Value of Minimum Lease Payments

BACKGROUND

Under the guidance in ASC 840, a lessee is required to use its incremental borrowing rate (or the lessor's implicit interest rate in certain circumstances) to calculate the minimum lease payments on a lease. The *incremental borrowing rate* is defined as the interest rate that a lessee would have incurred over a similar term to borrow funds it required to purchase a leased asset.

ACCOUNTING GUIDANCE

Question: Is a lessee permitted to use its secured borrowing rate to calculate the present value of minimum lease payments in accordance with the guidance in ASC 840?

Answer: The definition of the *incremental borrowing rate* in the ASC's *Glossary* states that does a lessee is not preclude from using a secured borrowing rate as its incremental borrowing rate "if that rate is determinable, reasonable, and consistent with the financing that would have been used in the particular circumstances."

ASC 840-20: Operating Leases

ASC 840-20-25-2: Accounting for Operating Leases with Scheduled Rent Increases

BACKGROUND

The guidance in ASC 840 specifies that rent income generally should be recognized by lessors and lessees as it becomes receivable or payable. If rental payments vary from a straight-line pattern, the income or expense should be recognized on a straight-line basis, unless another systematic and rational method is more representative of the time pattern in which a benefit from the use of an asset was diminished (lessor) or received (lessee). It has been suggested that, under certain circumstances, rentals should be recognized on a basis that is neither straight-line nor representative of the time pattern of an asset's physical use. Examples of situations in which another pattern of recognition might be appropriate are (*a*) rent reductions in the early periods to induce a lessee to sign a lease and (*b*) scheduled rent increases that anticipate inflation.

ACCOUNTING GUIDANCE

Question: If an operating lease includes a scheduled rent increase, is it ever permissable for lessees and lessors to recognize rent expense or income on a basis other than straight-line?

Answer: The following guidance in ASC 840-20-25-2 differentiates between scheduled rent increases that depend on future events from contingent rentals:

- Scheduled rent increases that do not depend on future events. The effects of scheduled rent increases, which are included in the calculation of minimum lease payments, should be recognized on a straight-line basis over the lease term, unless some other systematic and rational allocation basis is more representative of the time pattern in which a leased property is used. Factors such as the time value of money, anticipated inflation, and expected future revenues to allocate scheduled rent increases are inappropriate, because they do not relate to the time pattern of the physical use of the leased asset. These factors may affect the amount of rent, however, if they affect the amount of contingent rentals that are not part of the minimum lease payment amount.

Contingent rentals. Iincreases or decreases in the amount of rental depend on the occurrence of future events, such as changes in sales volume, inflation, or property taxes, are considered to be contingent rentals, which affect the measurement of the amount of income or expense accrued under the guidance in ASC 840-10-25-4. The accounting for contingent rentals should reflect the different circumstances if the lessee and the lessor agree to implement scheduled rent increases that will eliminate the risk of variable payments inherent in contingent rentals.

ASC 840-20-25-3 through 25-7, 55-1 through 55-3; ASC 840-10-55-45 through 55-46; ASC 840-30-55-14, 55-19 through 55-20; ASC 840-40-55-17 through 55-21
Issues Relating to Accounting for Leases

BACKGROUND

The guidance below responds to five questions related to the following issues in lease accounting:

- Time pattern of the physical use of the property in an operating lease
- Lease incentives in an operating lease
- Applicability of leveraged lease accounting to a lessor's existing assets
- Money-over-money lease transactions
- Wrap lease transactions

ACCOUNTING GUIDANCE

53,078   ASC 840—Leases

Question 1: Under the guidance in ASC 840, how should a lessee and a lessor recognize a lessee's rental payment obligation for an operating lease that includes scheduled rent increases designed to accommodate the lessee's projected physical use of a leased property?

Answer: Both the lessee and the lessor should recognize those lease payments as follows:

- If rent escalates in contemplation of a lessee's physical use of a leased property, but the lessee takes possession of or controls the physical use of the property at the beginning of the lease term, the lessee should recognize all rental payments, including the escalated rental payments, as rental expense and the lessor should recognize revenue on a straight-line basis. Under this guidance, the right to control the use of a leased property is treated the same as the physical use of a property. Consequently, the extent to which a property is used does not affect the recognition of rental expense or revenue.

- If rent is escalated under a master leasing agreement because a lessee gains access to and control over additional leased property at the time of the escalation, (a) the lessee should consider the escalated rents as additional rental expense and (b) the lessor should consider the escalated rents as additional revenue, attributable to the additional leased property. The lessee and the lessor should recognize the escalated rental payments in proportion to the additional property's relative fair value.

Illustration of an Operating Lease with Scheduled Rent Increases

Reeve & Sons is a construction company. Reeve leases a number of pieces of heavy equipment on 1/1/20X4 by entering into a ten-year operating lease. The fair value of this equipment is $600,000 at lease inception, and the yearly lease payment is $50,000. In addition, Reeve's yearly lease payment will increase to $100,000 on 1/1/20X9. On 1/1/20X9, Reeve will also gain access to and control over additional leased property. This additional leased property has a fair value of $300,000 on 1/1/20X4.

Reeve will recognize rental expense of approximately $58,333 during the years 20X4-20X8, and approximately $91,667 during the years 20X9-20Y3. These amounts are computed as follows:

Absolute (relative) fair value of equipment Reeve gains access to on 1/1/20X4	$600,000 (66.67%)
Absolute (relative) fair value of equipment Reeve gains access to on 1/1/20X9	$300,000 (33.33%)
Total lease payments over the ten-year lease	$750,000 [($50,000 × 5) + ($100,000 × 5)]
Portion of $100K annual lease payment from X9-Y3 attributable to the additional leased property	$33,334 ($100K × .3333, rounded)
Total lease payments attributable to the additional leased property	$167,667 ($33,334 × 5, rounded)
Total lease payments attributable to the original leased property	$583,333 [$750K - $167.667K]

Portion of lease payment attributable to original leased property, X4-Y3	$58,333 ($583,333 / 10)
Lease expense recognized, X4-X8	$58,333
Lease expense recognized, X9×Y3	$91,667 ($58,333 + $33,334)

Question 2: For operating leases that include an incentive for a lessee to sign (e.g., up-front cash payment to the lessee), should the lessee or lessor ever recognize rental expense or revenue other than on a straight-line basis?

Answer: Incentive payments to a lessee represent reductions in a lessee's rent expense and a lessor's rental revenue that should be recognized by both on a straight-line basis over the lease term.

Question 3: To be classified as a direct financing lease, the cost or carrying amount of the asset, if different, must be the same as its fair value at the inception of the lease. For a lease to qualify for leveraged lease accounting, the lease must be a direct financing lease. How should a lessor apply those requirements to a lease on an asset that the lessor has owned and previously had placed in service?

Answer: The carrying amount of an asset previously placed in service may not be significantly different from its fair value, but the two are not likely to be the same. Therefore, leveraged lease accounting is not appropriate, except if the lessor acquired the asset to be leased. If a lessir's existing asset's carrying amount is the same as its fair value before a writedown, the asset could qualify for leveraged lease accounting. However, any write-down to an existing asset's fair value in contemplation of leasing the asset precludes the transaction from being accounted for as a leveraged lease.

Question 4: An entity manufactures or purchases an asset, leases the asset to a lessee, and obtains nonrecourse financing in excess of the asset's cost by using the leased asset and the future lease rentals as collateral (referred to as a money-over-money lease transaction). Should an entity ever recognize a gain on a transaction in which cash received plus the present value of any estimated retained residual exceeds the carrying amount of the leased asset at the beginning of the lease term? If not, how should a lessor account for that transaction?

Answer: Other than recognizing a manufacturer's or dealer's profit in a sales-type lease, an entity should never recognize the proceeds from a borrowing in a money-over-money lease as income at the beginning of the lease term. The entity should account for the transaction as (1) the manufacture or purchase of an asset; (2) the leasing of the asset under an operating, direct financing, or sales-type lease; and (3) the borrowing of funds. The asset and the liability for the nonrecourse financing should *not* be offset in the entity's balance sheet unless a legal right of setoff exists.

Question 5: A lessor purchases an asset, leases it to a lessee, obtains nonrecourse financing using the lease rentals or the lease rentals and the asset as collateral, sells the asset and the nonrecourse debt to a third-party investor, and leases the asset back while remaining the principal lessor under the original lease (referred to as a wrap-lease transaction). How should an entity account for that kind of transaction?

Answer: If the leased asset is real estate, the guidance in ASC 840-40 applies to a sale-leaseback transaction. If the property is not real estate, an entity should account for that kind of transaction as a sale-leaseback transaction in accordance with the guidance in ASC 840-40-25-2 through 25-3, 25-8, 30-1 through 30-3, and 35-1 through 35-2, and the lease to the end user should be accounted for as a sublease under the guidance in ASC 840-10-35-10.

ASC 840-20-25-10 through 25-11, 45-1 Accounting for Rental Costs Incurred during a Construction Period

Under some operating leases for land and buildings, a lessee may be able to control the leased property even *before* beginning its operations or beginning to pay rent under a lease's terms. A lessee usually uses a leased asset during that period to construct an asset, such as leasehold improvements. A lessee begins its operations *after* construction is completed and it is then that the lessee begins paying rent under the lease's terms. However, under some leases, a lessee may be required to begin paying rent as soon as the lessee controls the property.

Under the guidance in ASC 840-10-55-45 through 55-46; 840-20-25-3 through 25-7, 55-1 through 55-3; ASC 840-30-55-14, 55-19 through 55-20; and ASC 840-40-55-17 through 55-21, Issues Relating to Accounting for Leases, which is discussed above, rental costs related to operating leases are required to be allocated on a straight-line basis over the term of a lease beginning on the date that a lessee is given control of a leased property, in accordance with the guidance in ASC 840-20-25-2, Accounting for Operating Leases with Scheduled Rent Increases, which is also discussed above. For example, a lessee enters into an operating lease on January 1, 200X, and is given control of the leased property on that date for the purpose of constructing leasehold improvements. The lessee expects to begin its operations on July 1, 200X, and, therefore, must begin paying rent on that date. In that case, the lessee would begin *allocating* rental costs on January 1, 200X, on a straight-line basis over the term of the lease.

The question addressed here is whether a lessee is permitted to *capitalize* rental costs related to ground and building operating leases that are incurred during a construction period.

ACCOUNTING GUIDANCE

A lessee's right to use a leased asset during the construction period or thereafter does *not* differ. Therefore, rental costs incurred on ground or building operating leases during and after the construction period should be accounted for in the same the same manner (i.e., they should be recognized as rental expense and included in income from continuing operations). Rental costs should be allocated over the lease term based on the guidance in ASC 840-20-25-1 through 25-2, discussed above. However, this guidance does *not* affect the application of the maximum guarantee test discussed in ASC 840-40-55-2.

ASC 840-20-25-14 through 25-15; ASC 840-30-35-13 Accounting for Loss on a Sublease Not Involving the Disposal of a Segment

BACKGROUND

The general principle of recognizing a loss on transactions is well established, and extends to contracts that are expected to result in a loss. The following guidance addresses the recognition of a loss on a lease contract.

ACCOUNTING GUIDANCE

Question: Should a loss on a sublease not involving a disposal of a segment be recognized, and how is that loss determined?

Answer: If costs such as executory costs and either amortization of a leased asset or rental payments expected to be incurred on an operating sublease exceed anticipated revenue on a sublease, the sublessor should recognize a loss. Similarly, a loss should be recognized on a direct financing sublease if the carrying amount of the investment in the sublease exceeds (1) the total of rentals expected to be received and (2) the property's estimated residual value. An exception to that requirement exists if as sublessor, the original lessee's l tax benefits from the transaction are sufficient to offset that loss.

ASC 840-30: Capital Leases

ASC 840-30-35-25 Upward Adjustment of Guaranteed Residual Values

BACKGROUND

Under the guidance in ASC 840, a lessor is required to periodically review the estimated residual value of sales-type, direct-financing, and leveraged leases. However, under the guidance in ASC 840, an upward adjustment of residual values is prohibited.

ACCOUNTING GUIDANCE

Question: Does the prohibition of upward adjustments of estimated residual values in ASC 840 also apply to upward adjustments that result from renegotiations of the guaranteed portions of residual values?

Answer: The prohibitions against upward adjustments of residual values of leased assets under the guidance in ASC 840 also apply to the guaranteed portion of residual values.

ASC 840-30-35-41, 50-6 Effect of a Change in Income Tax Rate on the Accounting for Leveraged Leases

BACKGROUND

When an important assumption changes, a recalculation of the rate of return and allocation of income from the inception of the lease is required under the guidance in ASC 840. A change in the recalculated balances of net investment is recognized as a gain or loss in the year in which the assumption changes.

ACCOUNTING GUIDANCE

Question: What effect, if any, does a change in income tax rate have on the accounting for leveraged leases under the guidance in ASC 840?

Answer: A lessor's income tax rate is an important assumption in accounting for a leveraged lease. Accordingly, the effect of a change in income tax rate should be recognized in the first accounting period ending on or after the date on which the legislation affecting the change becomes law. If such a change results in a significant variation in the normal relationship between income tax expense and pretax accounting income, the reasons for that variation should be disclosed if they are not otherwise apparent, in accordance with the guidance in ASC 740-10-50-12 through 50-14.

ASC 840-30-35-48 through 35-52; ASC 740-10-25-43 Issues Related to the Alternative Minimum Tax

BACKGROUND

Under the Tax Reform Act of 1986 (the Act), an entity computes its federal income tax liability based on the regular tax system or on the alternative minimum tax (AMT) system, whichever tax amount is greater. An entity may earn an AMT credit for tax paid under the AMT system that exceeds the amount that would have been paid under the regular tax system. An AMT credit can be carried forward indefinitely to reduce the regular tax in future years, but not below the AMT in the current year.

ACCOUNTING ISSUE

Should leveraged lease calculations consider the effect of the AMT on cash flows and if so, how?

ACCOUNTING GUIDANCE

An entity's leveraged lease tax computations should include assumptions about the effect of the AMT by considering the entity's overall tax position. Under the guidance in ASC 840-30-35-38 through 35-40 entities with leveraged leases are required to evaluate important assumptions that affect total net income from the lease at least annually. If total after-tax net income changes as a result of a change in tax assumptions, the lessor should:

- Recalculate the rate of return on the leveraged lease from inception,
- Adjust accounts that constitute the lessor's net investment, *and*
- Recognize a gain or loss in the year in which an assumption is changed.

However, if an entity's tax position changes frequently between the AMT and the regular tax, such a recomputation is not required unless there is an indication that the original assumptions about total after-tax income are no longer valid. In that case, the entity should revise the leveraged lease computations in any period in which total net income from the leveraged lease changes because of the effect of the AMT on the lease's cash flows.

According to the guidance in ASC 840-30-35-33 through 35-35, a lessor is required to allocate income from a leveraged lease among years in which the net investment in the leveraged lease is positive based on projected after-tax cash flows at the inception of the lease. Important assumptions in a leveraged lease calculation include a lessor's income tax rate and the amount of taxes paid or tax benefits received. A difference, if any, between AMT depreciation and tax depreciation assumed in a leveraged lease calculation or between income recognition for financial reporting and AMT income could—depending on a lessor's overall tax situation—result in AMT or utilization of AMT credits. An AMT payment or use of an AMT credit could change total cash flows from the leveraged lease and affect the lessor's income recognition.

ASC 840-30-S35-1, S99-2 Effect of a Change in Tax Law or Rates on Leveraged Leases

BACKGROUND

Under the guidance in ASC 840-30-35-38 and 35-39 if there is a change in an important assumption, an entity is required to recalculate its total net income from a leveraged lease as well as the rate of return and the income allocation to years in which the investment had a positive balance from the inception of the lease. Because the tax rate is considered an important assumption, lessors under leveraged leases are required to recalculate such leases and recognize an adjustment as a result of a change in corporate tax rates.

ACCOUNTING ISSUE

How should a lessor under a leveraged lease calculate and recognize an adjustment, if any, as a result of a change in tax rates?

ACCOUNTING GUIDANCE

Under the requirements in ASC 840-30-35-38 through 35-39, a lessor should:

- Recalculate all components of a leveraged lease from the inception of the lease based on the revised *after-tax* cash flows resulting from a change in tax law, including revised tax rates and the repeal of the investment tax credit.
- Include the difference between the originally recognized amount and recalculated amounts in income in the year in which the tax law is enacted.

SEC OBSERVER COMMENT

The SEC Observer noted that the ratio of earnings to fixed charges as calculated may be distorted as result of the recommended accounting. For example, a favorable after-tax effect might consist of an unfavorable adjustment to pretax income that is more than offset by a favorable adjustment to income tax expense. If so, notwithstanding the overall favorable effect, there would be a negative effect on the ratio as calculated based on the instructions to Item 503(d) of Regulation S-K, because the "earnings" component of the ratio is based on pretax income.

The SEC Observer also stated that the SEC staff expects registrants to report the cumulative effect on pretax income and income tax expense, if material, as separate line items in the income statement. The SEC staff would not object if registrants exclude an unfavorable pretax adjustment from the "earnings" component of the ratio if the *aftertax* effect is favorable and (1) the exclusion is adequately identified and explained in all the disclosures related to the ratio and (2) there is supplemental disclosure of the ratio as calculated in accordance with the applicable instructions.

> **OBSERVATION:** See the guidance in, Issues Related to the Alternative Minimum Tax, in Chapter 44, Income Taxes.

ASC 840-30-55-15 through 55-16 Leveraged Leases: Real Estate Leases and Sale-Leaseback Transactions, Delayed Equity Contributions by Lessors

BACKGROUND

Lessors finance leveraged leases of real estate and equipment with debt that is nonrecourse to the general credit of the lessor as required under guidance in ASC 840-10-25-43(c)(3). Rental payments in leveraged lease transactions usually are equal to or greater than payments to service the nonrecourse debt. Depreciation deductions in typical leveraged lease transactions exceed the net amount of rental income and interest expense and provide lessors with tax savings during the early periods of the lease term. Lessors thus recover equity investments quickly. Excess cash accumulated in the middle periods of a leveraged lease's term is used in later periods to pay for taxes due on amounts deferred in earlier periods.

When this question was discussed in 1985, some leveraged lease transactions were being structured so that the lessee began making payments from one to two years after the inception of a lease, thus obligating the lessor to make up the deficiency between rent payments and debt service during that period. In such cases, the lessor agreed, in the lease agreement or in a separate binding agreement, to service the nonrecourse debt with equity contributions limited to a specific amount during the period. Such contributions, which are referred to as *delayed equity investments,* were limited to the specified amount and could be measured at the inception of the lease. Although the debt was nonrecourse to the lessor, long-term creditors frequently had recourse to the lessor's general credit for debt service contributions.

ACCOUNTING ISSUES

The following are issues related to accounting for delayed equity contributions by lessors:

1. Does paragraph ASC 840-10-25-43(c)(3) preclude leveraged lease accounting if a delayed equity investment is considered to be recourse debt?
2. If leveraged lease accounting is not precluded, should a lessor recognize a liability for a delayed equity investment at the inception of a lease?

ACCOUNTING GUIDANCE

- Leveraged lease accounting is not precluded if a delayed equity investment is considered to be recourse debt, because such debt does not contradict the notion of nonrecourse debt under under the guidance in ASC 840-10-25-43(c)(3).
- A lessor should recognize a liability for the present value of the obligation at the inception of the lease. The liability increases a lessor's net investment on which the lessor's pattern of income recognition is based. Al-

though an increase in the net investment would result in additional income, the accrual of interest on the liability would offset that amount.

DISCUSSION

A delayed equity investment is part of a lessor's initial investment and does not differ in substance from debt incurred to finance the initial investment. Although a lessor uses such contributions to service the debt, the agreement limits a lessor's payments, which are measurable at the inception of a lease. Further, based on the economics of the transaction, leveraged lease accounting should not be precluded if the substantial leverage criterion in ASC 840-10-25-43(c)(3) has been met and the transaction conforms with the investment phases stipulated in ASC 840-10-25-43(d).

ASC 840-40: Sale-Leaseback Transactions

ASC 840-40-05-5, 15-5, 25-4, 35-3, 55-2 through 55-16, S55-2, S99-2 ASC 460-10-60-28 through 60-31 The Effect of Lessee Involvement in Asset Construction

BACKGROUND

The following guidance addresses the effect of a lessee's involvement in the construction of an asset by discussing a build-to-suit lease transaction in which a lessee is actively involved with an asset's construction and may assume some or all of the construction risk. The property may be owned by a developer, a Real Estate Investment Trust (REIT), or an institutional investor. Frequently, a securitization entity is established to hold the real estate and becomes the owner-lessor of the property. The SPE's activities include constructing, owning, and leasing the land and buildings to a lessee.

Although a lessee may be actively involved in the asset's construction by entering into an agreement with the owner-lessor to act as the construction manager or general contractor, the owner-lessor retains title to the land and improvements during construction and during the lease period. Sometimes, an affiliate of a lessee enters into a fixed-price construction contract to perform those duties. The lessee leases the property from the owner-lessor when construction is completed. Some have questioned whether a lessee is, in substance, the owner of a project rather than an agent for the owner-lessor if the lessee assumes some or all of the following obligations during the construction period:

- Makes lease payments before construction is completed
- Guarantees construction debt or provides financing, directly or indirectly
- Assumes primary or secondary obligation on construction contracts
- Acts as an agent for the owner-lessor in the construction, financing, or sale of the asset
- Acts as a developer or in the capacity of a general contractor
- Assumes the obligation to purchase the asset if construction is not completed by a specific date
- Assumes the obligation to fund cost overruns

Although the discussion below refers to the construction of a build-to-suit real estate project, the accounting guidance applies to all projects involving the construction of an asset, such as a project to build or lease a ship. However, the guidance would *not* apply if a lessee's (or a party that has an option to become a lessee) maximum obligation, including guaranteed residual values, is only a minor amount, as defined in ASC 840-40, relative to the asset's fair value.

ACCOUNTING ISSUE

How should an entity involved in the construction of an asset that it plans to lease when completed determine whether it should be considered the asset's owner while the asset is under construction?

OBSERVATION: See the guidance in "Accounting for Rental Costs Incurred during a Construction Period," discussed above under ASC 840-20 Operating Leases.

ACCOUNTING GUIDANCE

1. A lessee that has *substantially* all of the construction period risks should be considered the owner of a real estate project during the construction period and should follow the guidance in ASC 840-40. A 90% *maximum guarantee test* similar to the recovery-of-investment test discussed in ASC 840-10-25-1(d) should be used to evaluate whether a lessee has substantially all of the risks during the construction period. All payments associated with the construction project that a lessee is obligated to or can be required to make are included in the lessee's maximum guarantee.

    The following are some items that should be included in a lessee's maximum guarantee, unless modified by other guidance:

    a. Lease payments on a "date certain" lease that must be made whether or not the project is complete;

    b. Construction financing guarantees, which can only be made to the owner-lessor as specified in ASC 840-4055-15(d);

    c. Existing equity investments in the owner-lessor or in a party related to the owner-lessor or an obligation to make such investments;

    d. Existing loans or advances (or an obligation to makes loans or advances) to the owner-lessor or a party related to the owner-lessor;

    e. Payments made in the capacity of developer, general contractor, or construction manager or agent that are reimbursed more infrequently than normal or customary in the real estate construction industry for transactions with parties not involved in the project in any other capacity;

    f. Payments as the primary or secondary obligor for project costs under construction contracts;

    g. Obligations as a result of the lessee's activities in the capacity of developer or general contractor;

ASC 840—Leases **53,087**

h. An obligation to purchase the real estate project under any circumstances;

i. An obligation to pay for construction cost overruns;

j. An obligation to pay to the lessor, or on behalf of the lessor, rent or fees, such as transaction costs, during the construction period;

k. Payments that may be made for indemnities or guarantees to the owner-lessor.

A lessee is considered to have substantially all of the construction period risks and to be the owner of the real estate project during the construction period, if it is determined at the inception of the lease or the date on which the parties agree to the terms of the construction arrangement, whichever is earlier, that the lessee could be required, under the governing documents, to pay at least 90% of the project's total costs (other than the costs of land acquisition) under any circumstances at any time during the construction period.

Although the evaluation of whether the lessee is the owner of the construction project should be made only once, it is necessary to determine whether, at each point during the construction period, the *sum* of the following *two* amounts is *less* than 90% of the total costs incurred on the project to date, other than the costs of acquiring the land:

1. The accreted value of the lessee's previous payments, if any; and

2. The present value of the maximum amount the lessee can be required to pay as of that point in time, regardless of whether construction is complete.

If the test is not met, a lessee is considered to be the real estate project's owner during construction. The lessee also is permitted to provide guarantees in an amount that does not exceed the acquisition cost of the land, but any unused portion of that guarantee may not be used to cover a shortfall in the guarantee of total project costs. To accrete and discount the cash flows in this calculation, the lessee should use (*a*) the interest rate used to discount the lease payments for lease classification purposes, if it is known, or (*b*) the construction borrowing rate. The probability that a lessee will be required to make such payments is *not* considered in the maximum guarantee test.

2. A lessee would be considered the owner of a real estate project even if the present value of the maximum guarantee is *less than 90%* of the project's total costs under the following conditions:

 a. The lessee or any party related to the lessee associated with the construction project makes or is required to make on behalf of the lessee an equity investment in the owner-lessor that would be considered to be in substance an investment in real estate according ASC 976-10-15-4, which includes examples of equity investments that are in substance real estate. Based on the guidance in ASC 840-40-55-45, the fair value of an option to acquire real property transferred by a lessee to a lessor would be considered a soft cost that a lessee incurred before entering into a lease agreement. A lessee's loans, such as those discussed in ASC 310-10 regarding Acquisition, Development, and Construction Arrangements, made during the construction period, which in substance are an investment in the real estate project, would be another indicator that a lessee is a real estate project's owner during the construction period,

b. The lessee must pay directly, instead of through rent payments under the lease, for project costs other than

   (1) Costs reimbursed under a contract (as discussed under the first consensus above),

   (2) Preexisting environmental risks with a remote risk of loss, or

   (3) Costs of normal tenant improvements, except for the following:

      (a) Costs of structural elements, even if those costs were incurred specifically for the lessee

      (b) Equipment that would be a necessary improvement for any lessee, such as the costs of elevators, air conditioning systems, or electrical wiring

      (c) Amounts included in the project's original budget that the owner-lessor agreed to pay for on the date the contract was negotiated, regardless of the character of those costs

c. The lessee indemnifies the owner-lessor or its lenders for preexisting environmental risks for which the risk of loss is more than remote. (See the guidance in ASC 840-10- 25-12 through 25-13.)

d. Except as permitted in (c), the lessee provides indemnities or guarantees to parties other than the owner-lessor or agrees to indemnify the owner-lessor for costs as a result of claims for damages made by third parties, but not for claims made by third parties as a result of the lessee's own actions or lack of action while possessing or controlling the construction project. (See the discussion in ASC 840-40-55-9(d) on the maximum guarantee test, which should include any indemnification of or guarantee to the owner-lessor against third-party claims related to completion of construction.) For example, a lessee is not permitted to provide indemnities or guarantees for acts not under the lessee's control, such as condemnation proceedings or casualties.) A lessee who acts in the capacity of a general contractor is responsible for the actions or failure to act of its subcontractors.

e. The lessee takes title to the real estate during the construction period or provides supplies or other materials used in the construction other than those purchased after the lease term began (or the date of the construction agreement, whichever is earlier) that can be reimbursed as discussed above. Materials provided by the lessee are considered "hard costs," which are discussed in ASC 840-40-55-42.

f. The lessee (i) owns the land but does not lease it, or (ii) leases the land but does not sublease it (or provides an equivalent interest in the land, such as a long-term easement) to the owner-lessor before construction begins. A lessee's sale of the land to the owner-lessor must occur before construction begins. If that transaction occurs and the lessee subsequently leases the land back with improvements, the sale of the land would be accounted for under the requirements of ASC 840-40, even if that guidance would not apply to the lease or the improvements under this guidance.

3. A lessee involved in the transactions discussed above should defer its profit, if any, realized during construction—for example, from rental income received under a ground lease or from fees for construction or development services—and amortize it to income based on the guidance in ASC 840-40-55-26 through 55-28.

4. This guidance should be used to determine whether an entity is the owner of a project during the construction period if the entity has an option to or is required to lease the asset after construction is completed.

SEC OBSERVER COMMENT

The SEC Observer stated that the SEC staff believes that a lessee's loan to a lessor should be treated as an Acquisition, Development, and Costruction (ADC) arrangement under the scope of AICPA Practice Bulletin (PB) No. 1, Exhibit I, if the lessee can participate in expected residual profit. The staff further believes that a lessee that has an option to purchase a leased asset at a fixed price would be considered to be entitled to participate in expected residual profit. Under the the guidance in ASC 310-25-27(a), a loan is, in substance, an investment if the lessee is expected to receive more than 50% of the residual profit. Under the guidamce in ASC 310-10-25-27(b), the classification of the loan depends on the circumstances if the lender/lessee receives 50% or less of the residual profit. Under the guidance in ASC 310-10-25-20(b), a borrower that has a substantial investment in a project not funded by a lender may classify the borrowing as a loan. To determine whether a borrower has a sufficient equity investment, the SEC staff will apply the guidance in ASC 360-20-55-1 through 55-2. A lessee would also be considered the owner of a real estate project if the lessor is a special-purpose entity and the lease gives the lessee a fixed-price option to purchase the property or a remarketing agreement under which the lessee would be entitledt o the majority of the sales proceeds in excess of the leased asset's original cost.

ASC 840-40-15-2 Application of the Guidance in ASC 840-40-55-2 through 55-16 and ASC 840-10-25-25 to Entities That Enter into Leases with Governmental Entities

BACKGROUND

As discussed in ASC 840-40-05-5, 15-5, 25-4, 35-3, 55-2 through 55-16, S55-2, S99-2 ASC 460-10-60-28 through 60-31, The Effect of Lessee Involvement in Asset Construction, above, a lessee who is involved with a property during the construction period may be considered the owner of the property for financial reporting purposes depending on the circumstances. For example, a lessee that guarantees the construction debt during the construction period is automatically deemed to be the owner of the property.

Although that guidance was initially intended to apply to the private sector, some have questioned whether it also should apply to projects involving major real estate improvements funded by governmental entities, such as airports and other transit facilities. A governmental entity generally finances such projects by issuing tax-exempt bonds that are repaid from rental payments made by lessees. A lessee, such as an airline, is usually the general contractor of the project and is reimbursed by the bond trustee for costs incurred during the project.

Some believe that depending on the arrangement, a lessee involved in the construction of such a project may be required to account for the property under the guidance in ASC 840-40-55-2 through 55-16. Some projects may be accounted for as financings or as deposits, because they do not qualify for lease accounting under the guidance in ASC 840-40, Sale-Leaseback Transactions. However, under the guidance in ASC 840-10-25-25 leases meeting certain criteria must be accounted for as operating leases.

ACCOUNTING ISSUE

Should projects that involve the construction and lease of properties owned by governmental entities that would be accounted for as operating leases under the provisions in ASC 840-10-25-25 (FIN-23) be excluded from the scope of the guidance in ASC 840-40-05-5, 15-5, 25-4, 35-3, 55-2 through 55-16, S55-2, S99-2 ASC 460-10-60-28 through 60-31, The Effect of Lessee Involvement in Asset Construction?

ACCOUNTING GUIDANCE

Government-owned properties under construction that will be leased by others after completion should be included under the scope of ASC 840-40-05-5, 15-5, 25-4, 35-3, 55-2 through 55-16, S55-2, S99-2 ASC 460-10-60-28 through 60-31, The Effect of Lessee Involvement in Asset Construction. That is, a lessee that has substantially all of the risk during the construction period, as defined that guidance, should be considered the property's owner for accounting purposes. The guidance in ASC 840-40 would apply to a subsequent sale-leaseback transaction.

ASC 840-40-25-14; ASC 460-10-60-33 Impact of an Uncollateralized Irrevocable Letter of Credit on a Real Estate Sale-Leaseback Transaction;)

BACKGROUND

A buyer-lessor may require a seller-lessee to provide an irrevocable letter of credit to secure all or a portion of the lease payments in connection with a sale-leaseback of real estate. If a seller-lessee pledges assets as collateral for a letter of credit, sale-leaseback accounting for the transaction is precluded under the guidance in ASC 840-40, because there is a continuing involvement. It is unclear, however, whether an *uncollateralized* letter of credit would constitute continuing involvement.

ACCOUNTING ISSUE

Does the existence of an uncollateralized, irrevocable letter of credit preclude sale-leaseback accounting for a transaction that otherwise would qualify?

ACCOUNTING GUIDANCE

Sale-leaseback accounting is not precluded if an uncollateralized, irrevocable letter of credit is provided, because that kind of guarantee is not a form of continuing involvement under the guidance in ASC 840-40-25-14(d). Although a lessee is not precluded from accounting for a transaction as a sale-leaseback under the that guidance while providing an independent third-party guarantee of the lease payments, such transactions should be analyzed carefully to ensure that they are uncollateralized in form and substance. For example, a financial institution's right to offset amounts on deposit against payments on a letter of credit would be considered to be a form of collateral and, therefore, a continuing involvement that would preclude sale-leaseback accounting.

DISCUSSION

The following arguments were made in support of sale-leaseback accounting:

- An uncollateralized letter of credit does not increase the lessee's commitment beyond the obligation to pay rent. It is not a guarantee of return of the buyer's investment.
- A buyer-lessor could achieve almost the same protection by purchasing a surety bond to secure the lease payments. The lessee would not be involved in that transaction and sale-leaseback accounting would not be precluded. If an equivalent level of security could be achieved without a seller-lessee's consent, the seller-lessee would not be providing additional collateral or a guarantee by obtaining an uncollateralized letter of credit.
- Letters of credit and lease guarantees are only promises to pay obligations under a lease agreement. If a seller-lessee has provided a letter of credit and subsequently defaults on the lease payments, the seller-lessee has the same unsecured obligation, but to another party.

ASC 840-40-25-15 through 25-16; ASC 460-10-60-26 through 60-27 Unsecured Guarantee by Parent of Subsidiary's Lease Payments in a Sale-Leaseback Transaction

BACKGROUND

A wholly owned subsidiary enters into a sale-leaseback transaction for a building. In connection with the sale-leaseback, the buyer-lessor requires the subsidiary's parent to guarantee the subsidiary's obligations under the lease. Under the guidance in ASC 840-40-25-12 through 25-14 the use of sale-leaseback accounting is prohibited if there is continuing involvement with a real estate property other than a normal leaseback involving the active use of the property by the seller-lessee. A guarantee is one example of continuing involvement mentioned in ASC 840-40, Sale-Leaseback Transactions. Except for the lease guarantee, the transaction meets all the requirements for sale-leaseback accounting under the guidance in ASC 840-40.

ACCOUNTING ISSUE

If one member of a consolidated group guarantees another member's lease payments in a sale-leaseback of real estate, can the transaction be accounted for as a sale-leaseback in the seller-lessee's separate financial statements and in the entity's consolidated financial statements?

ACCOUNTING GUIDANCE

The following guidance addresses the effect on sale-leaseback accounting if one member of a consolidated group provides an unsecured guarantee of a lease obligation incurred by another member of the consolidated group:

- Sale-leaseback accounting is *not* precluded in the consolidated financial statements if one member of a consolidated group guarantees the lease payments of another member of that group. This conclusion is based on the rationale that an entity's unsecured guarantee of its own lease does not provide a lessor with additional collateral, except if the lessee declares bankruptcy. Thus, such a guarantee does not constitute a continuing involvement that would preclude sale-leaseback treatment under the guidance in ASC 840-40.

- Sale-leaseback accounting *is precluded*, however, in a seller-lessee's separate financial statements, because an unsecured guarantee of the seller-lessee's lease payments by another member of the consolidated group provides the buyer-lessor with additional collateral that reduces its risk of loss and thus constitutes a form of continuing involvement.

ASC 840-40-25-18, 55-48 Sale-Leaseback Transactions with Continuing Involvement

The following guidance is a response to questions on the accounting for sale-leaseback transactions in which a seller has a continuing involvement with the property:

- Sale-leaseback accounting is *precluded* in transactions in which a seller retains a partial ownership in a property.

- Sale-leaseback accounting is *precluded* if a seller-lessee can require the buyer-lessor to refinance debt related to the property and pass the interest savings to the seller-lessee in the form of reduced leaseback payments. Sale-leaseback accounting is *permitted,* however, if leaseback payments, which are considered contingent rentals under the provisions of ASC 840-40, change because they are indexed to an interest rate.

ASC 840-40-30-5 through 30-6 Consideration of Executory Costs in Sale-Leaseback Transactions

BACKGROUND

Executory costs on a lease include such items as maintenance, insurance, and taxes. Those costs may be included in each rental payment, paid separately by a seller-lessee, or paid by a buyer-lessor and billed to the seller-lessee.

Although minimum lease payments, as defined in ASC 840-10-25-6, include executory costs but exclude such costs if they are paid separately, minimum lease payments exclude executory costs in certain lease calculations. For example, executory costs are excluded from minimum lease payments when determining lease classification or in accounting for capital, sales-type, or direct financing leases.

Under the guidance in ASC 840-40-25-4 through 25-5, 35-4, 55-79 through 55-80, 55-82 through 55-84, 55-86 through 55-88, 55-90 through 55-92, 55-94, profit equal to the present value of minimum lease payments in certain sale-leaseback transactions should be deferred. That guidance is silent, however, on whether executory costs should be included or excluded from minimum lease payments when making that calculation.

ACCOUNTING ISSUE

Should the calculation of profit to be deferred on a sale-leaseback transaction include or exclude executory costs?

ACCOUNTING GUIDANCE

Executory costs should be excluded from the calculation of deferred profit on a sale-leaseback transaction, regardless of how executory costs are paid or whether a lease is a capital or operating lease.

ASC 840-40-55-22 through 55-24 Accounting for the Sale and Leaseback of an Asset That Is Leased to Another Party

BACKGROUND

Company A sells equipment to Company B and then leases it back from Company B. The sale and leaseback of the asset is subject to an operating lease and is intended to be leased by Company A to another entity under an operating lease. Company A has thus become a seller, lessee, and sublessor. The question here addresses the accounting treatment of a sale-leaseback transaction in which a seller-lessee retains substantial risks of ownership in a property through the terms of a leaseback.

ACCOUNTING ISSUE

Should a sale-leaseback transaction in which a seller-lessee retains substantial risks of ownership in personal property through a leaseback be accounted for as a borrowing or as a sale-leaseback transaction, if personal property not under the scope of the real estate guidance in ASC 840-40 is subject to an operating lease, is subleased, or is intended to be subleased by a seller-lessee to a third party at the time of a sale?

ACCOUNTING GUIDANCE

A seller-lessee should account for the transaction described above as a sale-leaseback in accordance with the guidance ASC 840-40-25-2 through 25-3, 30-1 through 30-3, and 35-1 through 35-2. Thus, a seller-lessee should recognize a sale, remove the asset from the balance sheet, and classify the leaseback in accordance with the guidance in ASC 840-10-25-43. A gain, if any, on the transaction should be recognized or deferred and amortized in accordance with the guidance in ASC 840-40-25-3.

DISCUSSION

53,094 ASC 840—Leases

The guidance in ASC 840-20-40-3 states that "the sale of property subject to an operating lease, or of property that is leased by or intended to be leased by the third-party purchaser to another party, shall not be treated as a sale if the seller or any party related to the seller retains substantial risks of ownership of the leased property. A seller may by various arrangements assure recovery of the investment by the third-party purchaser in some operating lease transactions and thus retain substantial risks in connection with the property." The question discussed above was raised because it was unclear whether and how the provisions of ASC 840-20-40-3 through 40-4 apply to sale-leaseback transactions that include assets under an operating lease or that are intended to be subleased by a seller-lessee to another party.

Under one view, the provisions of ASC 840-20-40-3 through 40-4 and of ASC 840-40-25-2 through 25-3 do not apply to the same transactions. That is, transactions that do not qualify as sale-leasebacks under the definition in ASC 840-40-25-2 fall under the provisions of ASC 840-20-40-3 through 40-4 and are accounted for as borrowings in accordance with the provisions of ASC 840-20-35-4. ASC 840-40-25-3 would apply to the accounting for transactions that qualify as sale-leaseback transactions. This view, referred to as the "mutually exclusive" approach, represented predominant practice.

Under a second view, referred to as the "sequential approach," the provisions of ASC 840-20-40-3 through 40-4 and 25-2 through 25-3 do apply to the same transactions. Following this approach, the provisions of a sale-leaseback agreement of property subject to an operating lease or intended to be subleased to an unrelated party after a sale-leaseback are evaluated to determine whether the transaction qualifies for sales recognition under the provisions of ASC 840-20-40-3 through 40-4. Transactions that do not are accounted for as borrowings under the guidance in ASC 840-20-35-4.

Although unstated, the accounting guidance provided above indicates support for the mutually exclusive approach, which applies only the provisions of ASC 840-40-25-2 through 25-3 in accounting for a sale-leaseback transaction of property other than real estate that is subject to an operating lease or a sublease of the property.

ASC 840-40-55-26 through 55-28; ASC 460-10-55-17, 60-32 Deferred Profit on Sale-Leaseback Transaction with Lessee Guarantee of Residual Value

BACKGROUND

A seller-lessee in a sale-leaseback transaction guarantees to a buyer-lessor that a property's residual value will be a stated amount at the end of the lease term. The lease agreement stipulates that the seller-lessee will indemnify the buyer-lessor for a deficiency, if any, in the property's residual value up to a specified amount. The lease does not meet any of the criteria for a capital lease in ASC 840-10-25-1. Hence, it is classified as an operating lease. More than a minor portion of the property, but less than substantially all of it, is covered by the leaseback.

ACCOUNTING ISSUES

If a residual value guarantee affects the determination of profit on a sale-leaseback transaction in accordance with the guidance in ASC 840-40-25-4 through 25-5, 35-4, 55-79 through 55-80, 55-82 through 55-84, 55-86 through 55-88, 55-90 through 55-92, 55-94, should a seller-lessee use the gross amount or the present value of the guarantee in making that calculation?

ACCOUNTING GUIDANCE

A seller-lessee should defer profit equal to the present value of the periodic rents plus the *gross* amount of the residual value guarantee at the date of sale and should account for the components as follows:

- Defer profit equal to the gross amount of the guarantee until the guarantee is resolved at the end of the lease term.

- Amortize profit equal to the present value of the periodic rents in proportion to total gross rental expense over the lease term.

OBSERVATION: This guidance applies only to sale-leasebacks *other than* real estate. Under the provisions in ASC 360 that are related to real estate, sale-leaseback accounting would be precluded if a seller-lessee has any kind of continuing involvement with the property, such as a guarantee of the buyer's investment.

Illustration of Calculation of Profit at the Sale Date and Amortization of Deferred Profit

Assumptions	
Sales price of property	$150,000
Seller's basis in the property	$ 50,000
Annual rent (payable at beginning of year)	$ 16,000
Maximum amount of guarantee	$ 27,000
Leaseback term	5 years
Incremental borrowing rate	12% per year
Date of sale	12/31/X4
Profit to Be Recognized at Date of Sale	
Sales price	$150,000
Less: Basis in property	50,000
Profit on sale	$100,000
Present value of annual rents	$ 64,598
Residual value guarantee—Gross amount	27,000
Profit to be deferred	$ 91,598
Profit to be recognized at date of sale	$ 8,402
Amortization of Deferred Profit	
Total deferred profit at 12/31/X4	$ 91,598
	$.8074

Present value of total rent at date of sale	$64,598		amortized for
Total annual rents	80,000	=	each $1 of rent
Annual amortization of deferred profit:	$16,000 × .8074	=	$12,918
Deferred profit at 12/31/X9	$ 27,000		

DISCUSSION

Although the guidance in ASC 840-40-25-4 through 25-5, 35-4, 55-79 through 55-80, 55-82 through 55-84, 55-86 through 55-88, 55-90 through 55-92, 55-94 is clear that a seller-lessee should defer profit on a sale-leaseback transaction equal to the present value of the minimum lease payments over the lease term and that such an amount should be amortized in proportion to rental expense over the lease term, it is unclear whether that amount should include a guarantee. In addition, even if a guarantee is included in deferred profit, it is unclear whether it should be included at its gross amount or at its present value. Those who supported including a guarantee at its gross amount, rather than reducing it to its present value, argued that because a guarantee is a contingent gain that is not resolved until the end of the lease term, it should not result in additional profit recognition at the inception of the lease term. Under the guidance in ASC 450, a contingent gain is not recognized until realized.

ASC 840-40-55-29 through 55-34 Accounting for Cross Border Tax Benefit Leases

BACKGROUND

Sale-leaseback transactions can be arranged so that both the seller-lessee and the buyer-lessor are entitled to tax deductions for the same depreciable asset. To accomplish that, the seller-lessee and the buyer-lessor must be located in different countries whose income tax laws differ as to which party is entitled to the deduction for a depreciable asset.

A typical example involves a U.S. entity as the seller-lessee and a foreign investor as the buyer-lessor. The transaction usually is structured as follows:

- A U.S. entity purchases a depreciable asset from a manufacturer and thus obtains title and tax benefits to be used in filing its U.S. taxes.

- The U.S. entity, which also is a manufacturer, enters into an agreement in the form of a leaseback for the ownership right with a foreign investor. The lease agreement includes an purchase option under which the U.S. entity will acquire the foreign investor's ownership right in the asset at the end of the lease term.

- The foreign investor pays the U.S. an amount of cash based on the asset's appraised value. The U.S. entity immediately transfers a portion of the cash to a third party trustee, which assumes the U.S. entity's obligation to make future payments on the lease, include payments for the purchase option. The cash retained by the U.S. entity is consideration for the tax benefits that the foreign investor in the foreign tax jurisdiction. The U.S.

entity may also agree to indemnify the third party trustee against certain events.

- The U.S. company agrees to indemnify the foreign investor only for a loss of tax benefits as a result of certain events such as the sale, loss, or destruction of the equipment or bankruptcy of the U.S. company, which can settle the obligation by buying a letter of credit from a bank in favor of the foreign investor.
- As a result of that transaction, the U.S. entity and the foreign investor have a tax basis in the same depreciable asset.

There were two views on the accounting for the net proceeds retained by the U.S. entity. Some viewed the net proceeds as income that should be recognized immediately. Others viewed the net proceeds as an adjustment of the cost of the equipment or as deferred income.

ACCOUNTING ISSUE

Should net proceeds retained by the U.S. entity (seller-lessee) in a tax benefit sale-leaseback transaction be reported as income immediately or as deferred that is amortized to income?

ACCOUNTING GUIDANCE

The timing of income recognition for cash received by the U.S. entity should be accounted for based on the individual facts and circumstances. However, immediate recognition is not appropriate if there is more than a remote possibility of a loss of the cash consideration as a result of contingencies, such as indemnification clauses.

The total consideration received by the U.S. entity is compensation for the foreign investor's tax benefits and the indemnification of the foreign investor or the third-party trustee. If the possibility of a loss is remote, the amount of income for the tax benefits that the seller-lessee recognizes immediately would be reduced as a result of the recognition of a liability in accordance with the requirement in ASC 460 for the indemnification agreement at inception.

ASC 840-40-55-37 through 55-41 Accounting for the Sale of Property Subject to the Seller's Preexisting Lease

BACKGROUND

A lessee under an operating lease of all or a portion of a property also may own an interest in that property. This might occur if, for example, the lessee has an investment in a partnership that owns the leased property. The lessee might have acquired the equity interest at or near the time the lease agreement was consummated.

The existence of both an operating lease and an equity interest in a property raises a question about whether a gain should be recognized if the lessee sells its equity interest in the property (or the partnership sells the property), but the lessee continues to lease the property under a preexisting operating lease. The question arises because a portion of the gain is deferred in other transactions in which owned property is sold and leased back.

ACCOUNTING ISSUES

1. Should the sale of a lessee's equity interest in a property be accounted for as a sale-leaseback transaction?
2. Should the amount of profit to be deferred be affected by the seller-lessee's prior ownership interest in the property?
3. Should the guidance in ASC 840-40-05-9 through 05-10, 15-4, 15-9 through 15-10, 25-9 through 25-14, 25-17, 50-1 through 50-2, 55-36, 55-49 through 55-77; ASC 980-840-25-1 through 25-3, 35-1 through 35-2 for sale-leaseback transactions apply to transactions involving real estate or real estate and equipment if a seller-lessee vacates and intends to sublease a property or exercises a renewal option subject to provisions in a preexisting lease?
4. Should the sale-leaseback guidance apply to transactions that involve property under the scope of ASC 840-40 if a preexisting lease is between parties under a seller's common control?

EITF CONSENSUS

1. a. A sale of an equity interest in a leased property should be accounted for as a sale-leaseback if the lease is modified in connection with the sale, excluding insignificant modifications.
   b. The sale-leaseback guidance in ASC 840-40 should be followed for all transactions that involve real estate and real estate.
   c. Profit on a sales transaction in which the preexisting lease is not modified significantly should be deferred and amortized into income in accordance with the guidance in ASC 840-40-25-3.
   d. A seller's prior ownership in a property should not affect the calculation of the amount of deferred profit, *regardless* of lease modifications.
2. The accounting for a transaction should not be affected by a seller-lessee's exercise of (a) a sublease provision contained in the preexisting lease or (b) a renewal option for a period within the original minimum lease term. However, a renewal option for a period not part of the original lease term is a new lease. The guidance in ASC 840-40 applies to such transactions. For example, if a lease has an initial term of ten years and a bargain renewal for an additional five years, the original minimum lease term would be 15 years, and the exercise of the renewal option would not affect the accounting. If, however, the renewal option were a fair value rental option, the minimum lease term would be ten years, and the exercise of the renewal would make the transaction subject to the guidance in ASC 840.
3. A lease between parties under common control should not be considered a preexisting lease. The guidance in ASC 840-40 thus applies to such transactions, with one exception. If the guidance in ASC 980, *Regulated Operations*, applies—that is, if one of the parties to the lease is a regulated enterprise and the lease has been approved by the appropriate regulatory agency—a lease between parties under common control is treated as a preexisting lease.

CHAPTER 54
ASC 845—NONMONETARY TRANSACTIONS

CONTENTS

Part I: General Guidance	54,001
ASC 845-10: Overall	54,001
Overview	54,001
Background	54,001
Accounting for Nonmonetary Exchanges and Transactions	54,002
Basic Principle	54,003
Gain or Loss	54,004
Illustration of the Major Provisions of ASC 845	54,004
Figure 54-1: Accounting for Nonmonetary Exchanges	54,005
Involuntary Conversion of Nonmonetary Assets to Monetary Assets	54,005
Disclosure	54,006
Part II: Interpretive Guidance	54,006
ASC 845-10: Overall	54,006
ASC 845-10-05-8, 15-5 through 15-9, 25-4 through 25-5, 30-15 through 30-16, 45-1, 50-3, 55-10, 55-12 through 55-17, 55-19 through 55-22, 55-24 through 55-26	
Purchases and Sales of Inventory with the Same Counterparty	54,006
ASC 845-10-05-10, 15-11, 30-17 through 30-20	
Barter Transactions	54,008
ASC 845-10-05-11, 15-12 to 15-17,15-20, 35-3 25-6 through 25-12, 30-12 through 30-14, 30-21 through 30-23, S30-2, 55-2, 55-27 through 55-37, 60-3, S99-3	
Exchanges Involving Monetary Consideration	54,010

GENERAL GUIDANCE

ASC 845-10: OVERALL

OVERVIEW

As a general rule, GAAP require that both monetary and nonmonetary exchanges be recorded based on the fair value inherent in the transaction. Certain exceptions exist, however, for nonmonetary transactions. Different accounting bases may be required for these transactions, depending on the unique characteristics of the exchange transaction.

BACKGROUND

The equity method guidance included in this chapter does not apply to the following types of transfers:

1. Transfers between a joint venture and its owners.
2. Capital contributions of real estate in return for an unconsolidated real estate investment (See ASC 970-323).
3. Transfers of real estate in exchange for nonmonetary assets other than real estate (See ASC 976-605 and 360-20-40).
4. Transfers of assets used in oil-and gas-producing activities (including either proved or unproved properties) in exchange for other assets also used in oil-and gas-producing activities (See ASC 932-360-40-7).
5. A deconsolidation of a subsidiary that is a business or nonprofit activity that is within the scope of ASC 810-10 (See ASC 810-10-40-3A).
6. A derecognition of a group of asserts that constitutes a business or nonprofit activity that is within the scope of ASC 810-10 (See ASC 810-10-40-3A).

Business transactions usually involve cash or monetary assets or liabilities that are exchanged for goods or services. These are identified as monetary transactions. Monetary assets or liabilities are fixed in terms of currency and usually are contractual claims to fixed amounts of money. Examples of monetary assets and liabilities are cash, accounts and notes receivable, and accounts and notes payable.

Some business transactions involve the exchange or transfer of nonmonetary assets or liabilities that are not fixed in terms of currency. These are identified as *nonmonetary transactions*. Nonmonetary assets and liabilities are those other than monetary assets and liabilities. Examples are inventory, investments in common stock, property, plant, and equipment, liability for advance rent collected, and common stock.

PRACTICE POINTER: Under certain circumstances, management's intent may affect the monetary/nonmonetary classification of an asset or liability. For example, a marketable bond being held to maturity qualifies as a monetary asset because its face amount is fixed in terms of currency. If the same bond were being held for speculation, however, it would be classified as a nonmonetary asset, because the amount that would be received when sold would not be determinable and therefore not fixed in terms of currency.

ACCOUNTING FOR NONMONETARY EXCHANGES AND TRANSACTIONS

An *exchange* is a reciprocal transfer between an enterprise and another entity that results in the enterprise's acquiring assets or services or satisfying liabilities by surrendering other assets or services or incurring other obligations. A reciprocal transfer of a nonmonetary asset is considered an exchange only if the transferor has no substantial continuing involvement in the transferred asset such that the usual risks and rewards of ownership of the asset are transferred.

A *nonreciprocal transfer* is a transfer of assets or services in one direction, either from an enterprise to its owners or another entity, or from owners or another entity to the enterprise (ASC Glossary). Examples of nonreciprocal transfers are:

- Declaration and distribution of a dividend
- Acquisition of treasury stock
- Sale of capital stock
- Conversion of convertible debt
- Charitable contributions

Basic Principle

In general, ASC 845 requires that accounting for nonmonetary transactions be based on the fair values of the assets or services involved, which is the same basis that ordinarily would be used for monetary transactions. The cost of a nonmonetary asset acquired in exchange for another nonmonetary asset is the fair value of the asset surrendered to obtain it. A gain or loss may be recognized in the exchange. The fair value of the asset received should be used to measure the cost if that amount is more clearly evident than the fair value of the asset surrendered. Similarly, a transfer of a nonmonetary asset to a stockholder or to another entity in a nonreciprocal transfer is recorded at the fair value of the asset transferred, and a gain or loss is recognized on the disposition of the asset (ASC 845-10-30-1).

Fair value is determined by referring to estimated realizable values in cash transactions of the same or similar assets, quoted market prices, independent appraisals, estimated fair values of assets or services received in exchange, and other available evidence. If one of the parties in a nonmonetary transaction could have elected to receive cash instead of the nonmonetary asset, the amount of cash that could have been received may be evidence of the fair value of the nonmonetary assets exchanged. For guidance on fair value measurement, see Chapter 49, *ASC 820—Fair Value Measurement*.

Fair value should be regarded as not determinable if major uncertainties exist about the realizability of the value that would be assigned to an asset received in a nonmonetary transaction. If the fair value of either the asset surrendered or the asset received is not determinable within reasonable limits, the recorded amount of the nonmonetary asset transferred from the enterprise may be the only available measure of the transaction (ASC 845-10-30-8).

If one of the parties in a nonmonetary transaction could have elected to receive cash instead of the nonmonetary asset, the amount of cash that could have been received may be evidence of the fair value of the nonmonetary assets exchanged.

ASC 845 involves accounting for the transfer of nonmonetary assets in a reciprocal transfer between an entity and another party. A reciprocal transfer qualifies as an exchange if the transferor has no substantial continuing involvement with the assets transferred. The risks and rewards of ownership must be transferred for an exchange transaction to take place.

ASC 845—Nonmonetary Transactions

While exchanges of nonmonetary assets generally are to be accounted for at fair value, there are three circumstances when an exchange is to be recorded based on the book value (less any reduction for impairment) of the net asset transferred. These are when:

- The fair value of the asset transferred or received is not determinable.
- The exchange is to facilitate a sale to a customer and it involves the exchange of a product held for sale in the ordinary course of business for another product to be sold in the same line of business.
- The exchange transaction lacks commercial substance.

An exchange has commercial substance if the entity's future cash flows are expected to change as a result of the transaction. An entity's future cash flows are expected to change if either (1) the amount, timing, or uncertainty of the future cash flows from the asset received differs significantly from the amount, timing, or uncertainty of the future cash flows from the asset transferred or (2) there is a significant difference between the entity-specific value of the asset received and the entity-specific value of the asset transferred. An asset's entity-specific value is its value to a particular entity, given the entity's intended use for that asset, rather than the asset's value as determined by the marketplace.

An exchange would not have commercial substance if such substance were based solely on cash flows as a result of achieving certain tax benefits, if the tax benefits arise solely from achieving a certain financial reporting result.

Gain or Loss

Gain or loss, when applicable, is recognized in nonmonetary transactions. A difference in the gain or loss for tax purposes and that recognized for accounting purposes may constitute a temporary difference in income tax provision (ASC 845-10-30-9).

The process of determining the appropriate amount of gain or loss, if any, to be recognized in nonmonetary exchanges is summarized in Figure 54-1.

Illustration of the Major Provisions of ASC 845

In all of the following cases, an enterprise is giving up nonmonetary Asset A, which has a recorded amount of $10,000.

Case 1: Asset A is exchanged for dissimilar nonmonetary Asset B, which is valued at $12,000. Entry to record:

Asset B	12,000	
Asset A		10,000
Gain on exchange		2,000

Explanation: Nonmonetary transaction is recorded at fair value and any gain or loss is recognized.

Case 2: Asset A is exchanged for similar productive (nonmonetary) Asset C, which is valued at $9,500. Entry to record:

Asset C	9,500	
Loss on exchange	500	
Asset A		10,000

Explanation: Exchange of similar assets is recorded at fair value; loss is recognized.

Case 3: Asset A is exchanged for similar productive (nonmonetary) Asset D, which is valued at $15,000. Entry to record:

Asset D	15,000	
Asset A		10,000
Gain on exchange		5,000

Explanation: Exchange of similar assets is recorded at fair value; gain is recognized.

Case 4: Asset A is exchanged for a similar productive (nonmonetary) Asset E, which is valued at $13,000; the transaction lacks commercial substance because it does not significantly alter future cash flows. Entry to record:

Asset E	10,000	
Asset A		10,000

Explanation: Exchange of similar assets is recorded at book value of asset surrendered because the transaction lacks commercial substance.

Case 5: Asset A is exchanged for a similar productive (nonmonetary) Asset F in a transaction that has commercial substance, but for which the fair value of neither asset can be reasonably determined. Entry to record:

Asset F	10,000	
Asset A		10,000

Explanation: Because fair value cannot be reasonably determined for either Asset A or Asset F, the acquired asset is recorded at the book value of the asset surrendered.

Figure 54-1: Accounting for Nonmonetary Exchanges

Involuntary Conversion of Nonmonetary Assets to Monetary Assets

When a nonmonetary asset is involuntarily converted to a monetary asset, a monetary transaction results, and ASC 605 requires that a gain or loss be recognized in the period of conversion (ASC 605-40-25-3). The gain or loss is the difference between the carrying amount of the nonmonetary asset and the proceeds from the conversion.

Examples of involuntary conversion are the total or partial destruction of property through fire or other catastrophe, theft of property, or condemnation of property by a governmental authority (eminent domain proceedings).

Gain or loss from an involuntary conversion of a nonmonetary asset to a monetary asset is classified as part of continuing operations, extraordinary items, disposal of a segment, etc., according to the particular circumstances (ASC 605-40-45-1). In addition, a gain or loss recognized for tax purposes in a period different from that for financial accounting purposes creates a temporary difference, for which recognition of deferred taxes may be necessary (ASC 740-10-55-66).

The involuntary conversion of a LIFO inventory layer at an interim reporting date does not have to be recognized if the proceeds are reinvested in replacement inventory by the end of the fiscal year (ASC 605-40-25-3).

OBSERVATION: This is the same treatment afforded a temporary liquidation at interim dates of a LIFO inventory layer that is expected to be replaced by the end of the annual period.

In the event the proceeds from an involuntary conversion of a LIFO inventory layer are not reinvested in replacement inventory by the end of the fiscal year, gain for financial accounting purposes need not be recognized, providing the taxpayer does not recognize such gains for income tax reporting purposes and provided that replacement is intended but not yet made by year-end (ASC 605-40-25-3).

Disclosure

Disclosure of the nature of the nonmonetary transaction, the basis of accounting for assets transferred, and gains or losses recognized are required in the financial statements for the period in which the transaction occurs (ASC 845-10-50-1).

PART II: INTERPRETIVE GUIDANCE

ASC 845-10: OVERALL

ASC 845-10-05-8, 15-5 through 15-9, 25-4 through 25-5, 30-15 through 30-16, 45-1, 50-3, 55-10, 55-12 through 55-17, 55-19 through 55-22, 55-24 through 55-26
Purchases and Sales of Inventory with the Same Counterparty

BACKGROUND

Companies sometimes enter into transactions to buy inventory from companies in the same line of business and to sell inventory in the form of raw materials, work-in-process (WIP), or finished goods to the same companies. Such purchase and sale arrangements may be structured under a single contract or under separate contracts.

The following guidance does *not* apply to inventory purchases and sales arrangements (*a*) accounted for as derivatives under the guidance in ASC 815 or (*b*) related to exchanges of software real estate. No guidance is provided as to whether transactions reported at fair value qualify for revenue recognition.

ACCOUNTING ISSUES

- To determine the effect of the guidance in ASC 845 on sale and purchase transactions of inventory with the same counterparty in the same line of business, under what circumstances should two or more inventory exchange transactions be considered to be one transaction?
- Are there circumstances under which nonmonetary exchanges of inventory in the same line of business should be recognized at fair value?

SCOPE

The following guidance applies to all inventory purchase and sale arrangements, including the following:

- Two or more inventory purchase and sale transactions between the same counterparties that are entered into with the intent of combining the transactions
- One inventory transaction that is legally dependent on the performance of another inventory transaction with the same counterparty. Such transactions are considered to have been made in contemplation of one another and would be considered to be a single exchange under the scope of the following guidance

An exchange of offsetting cash payments on invoices issued by counterparties in inventory purchase and sale transactions is not a factor in the determination whether those transactions should be considered as a single exchange transaction under the guidance in ASC 845-10.

ACCOUNTING GUIDANCE

For the purpose of determining the effect of the guidance in ASC 845 on sale and purchase transactions of inventory between two parties in the same line of business, two or more such transactions should be combined and accounted for as one transaction, because those purchase and sale transactions between the same two parties are entered into in contemplation of one another. The same guidance applies if an inventory transaction, such as a sale to a counterparty, legally depends on the counterparty's performance of another inventory transaction, such as a purchase from the same counterparty.

An inventory transaction that does *not* legally depend on the performance of another inventory transaction with the same counterparty should be evaluated based on the following factors, which are *not* determinative individually or all-inclusively, to determine whether those transactions were entered into in contemplation of one another:

— *The counterparties have a specific legal right of offset related to the inventory purchase and sale transactions.* The ability to offset transactions indicates there is a connection between them. It indicates that transactions that were entered into separately, actually were entered into in contemplation of one another. This indicator is more important for net settlement provisions related to specific inventory transactions identified by the counterparties than for those that are netted as part of a master netting agreement for all the transactions between the counterparties.

- *The counterparties have entered into the inventory purchase and sale transactions at the same time.* This indicates that the transactions were entered into in contemplation of one another.
- *The terms of inventory sale and purchase transactions between two counterparties are at off-market rates at the inception of the agreement.* Inventory transactions entered into under such terms indicate they are related to one another, and have been entered into in contemplation of another inventory transaction between the counterparties. This indicator is more important if the products' market prices are readily determinable, such as exchange traded commodities, than if the prices for those products are more flexible.
- *Relative certainty that reciprocal inventory transactions with the same party will occur.* If an entity enters into a sale transaction with a counterparty and the counterparty may, but is not obligated to, deliver an agreed amount of inventory. If that counterparty chooses to deliver its product to the entity, the entity is obligated to purchase the product. The more certain it becomes that the counterparty will deliver the agreed amount of inventory the more likely it becomes that the two transactions have been entered into in contemplation of one another.

Nonmonetary exchange transactions of finished goods inventory for raw materials or WIP inventory in the same line of business are *not* exchange transactions that will result in sales to customers other than the parties to the exchange in accordance with the guidance in ASC 845-10-30-3(b). Such a transaction should be accounted for at *fair value*, if (*a*) its fair value can be determined within reasonable limits *and* (*b*) the transaction has commercial substance. All other nonmonetary exchanges of inventory in the same line of business, such as an exchange of raw materials or WIP inventory for raw materials, WIP, finished goods inventory, or finished goods inventory for finished goods inventory, should be recognized at the *carrying amount* of the transferred inventory.

Inventory accounted for under the guidance for "purchases and sales of inventory with the same counterparty" should be classified as raw materials, WIP, or finished goods, in the same manner as it would be classified in the entity's external financial reporting

The amount of revenue and costs or gains and losses related to inventory exchanges recognized at fair value should be disclosed.

ASC 845-10-05-10, 15-11, 30-17 through 30-20 Barter Transactions

BACKGROUND

Entities sometimes exchange nonmonetary assets—equipment, for example—for barter credits. Such transactions may be entered into by the parties to the transaction directly, or the transactions may be arranged by a third party (a barter company) whose business is to match buyers with sellers.

Entities can use barter credits obtained in an exchange to purchase goods or services, such as advertising time, from the other party to the transaction, the barter company, or members of the barter company's exchange network. A barter contract may specify the goods and services that may be purchased, which can be limited to those available from the barter exchange network. Some barter transactions also require a payment of cash in addition to barter credits. Barter credits may expire on a specific date on which they lose their value.

ACCOUNTING ISSUES

- Should exchanges of nonmonetary assets for barter credits be accounted for in accordance with the provisions of ASC 845?
- If so, how should a gain or loss, if any, be determined and recognized?

ACCOUNTING GUIDANCE

1. The provisions of ASC 845 apply to exchanges of nonmonetary assets for barter credits. That guidance should be applied as follows:

    (1) It is assumed that the fair value of a nonmonetary asset exchanged for barter credits is more clearly evident than the fair value of the barter credits received. Therefore, barter credits should be reported at the fair value of the asset exchanged. That assumption may be overcome if:

    (a) The barter credits can be converted into cash in the near future as evidenced by past transactions, *or*

    (b) Independent quoted market prices can be used to determine the fair value of items to be received in exchange for barter credits.

    (2) Assume that the nonmonetary asset's fair value does not exceed its carrying amount unless persuasive evidence supports a higher value.

    (3) Recognize an impairment loss on barter credits if after the exchange it becomes apparent that:

    (a) The remaining value of the barter credits is less than their carrying amount.

    (b) It is probable that the entity will not use some, or all, of its barter credits before they expire.

    (4) If an operating lease is exchanged for barter credits, the lease's impairment should be measured as the excess of remaining lease costs (total of discounted rental payments and unamortized leasehold improvements) over the discounted amount of sublease rentals for the remaining term of the lease.:

DISCUSSION

Because of concerns that barter transactions were being used to defer losses that should have been recognized before an exchange occurred, an evaluation of (1) the impairment of a nonmonetary asset exchanged and (2) loss recognition prior to an exchange is required, if the fair value of the nonmonetary asset to be exchanged for barter credits is less than its carrying amount.

54,010 ASC 845—Nonmonetary Transactions

The presumption that the fair value of a nonmonetary asset exchanged be more clearly evident than the fair value of barter credits is required due to concerns about the objectivity of the valuation of barter credits.

ASC 845-10-05-11, 15-12 to 15-17,15-20, 35-3 25-6 through 25-12, 30-12 through 30-14, 30-21 through 30-23, S30-2, 55-2, 55-27 through 55-37, 60-3, S99-3
Exchanges Involving Monetary Consideration

BACKGROUND

The accounting guidance below applies to three types of exchange transactions of nonmonetary nonfinancial assets and monetary consideration (boot) for the following kinds of assets:

- Other nonmonetary nonfinancial assets;
- Real estate;
- A noncontrolling ownership interest in another entity.

SCOPE

The following guidance does not apply to:

- Transfers between a joint venture and its owners;
- Capital contributions of real estate for an unconsolidated real estate investment;
- Transfers of real estate in exchange for nonmonetary assets other than real estate;
- A deconsolidation of a subsidiary that is a business or a nonprofit activity under the scope of ASC 810-10;
- A derecognition of a group of assets that is a business or nonprofit activity under the scope of ASC 810-10.

ACCOUNTING ISSUES

Exchanges Involving Monetary Consideration

1. How much monetary consideration in a nonmonetary exchange would cause an entire transaction to be accounted for as a monetary exchange, which is not included under the scope of ASC 845?

Exchanges of Real Estate Involving Monetary Consideration

2. How should an exchange of similar real estate that is considered to be monetary because it includes boot that in excess of 25% of the fair value of the exchange be accounted for?

Monetary Exchange of a Nonfinancial Asset for a Noncontrolling Ownership Interest

3. If a nonmonetary exchange must be accounted for at fair value, should a full or partial gain be recognized if Entity A transfers a nonfinancial asset to Entity B in exchange for a noncontrolling ownership interest in Entity B?

ACCOUNTING GUIDANCE

Exchanges Involving Monetary Consideration

1. If an exchange of nonmonetary assets that would normally be recognized at historical cost includes boot, it should be accounted for as follows:

    (1) As a monetary exchange at fair value by both parties if boot is significant (i.e., at least 25% of the fair value of an exchange).

    (2) If boot is less than 25% of the fair value of an exchange, the recipient of boot should follow the guidance on pro rata gain recognition in ASC 845-10-30-6; the payer of boot does *not* recognize a gain. Fair value should be used only if it can be measured satisfactorily.

Exchanges of Real Estate Involving Monetary Consideration

2. An exchange of similar real estate with boot equivalent to 25% or more of the fair value of an exchange that is considered to be a monetary exchange under the guidance in Issue 1 above, should be allocated between the monetary and nonmonetary components of the transaction based on the relative fair values of the real estate assets exchanged at the time of the transaction.

Illustration of Accounting for an Exchange of Real Estate with Boot

Company A transfers real estate with a fair value of $500,000 and a net book value of $100,000 to Company B for $120,000 in cash, a note for $100,000, and real estate having a fair value of $280,000 and a net book value of $240,000. The initial investment requirement for full accrual profit recognition under ASC 360 is 20%. The terms of the note from Company B satisfy the continuing investment provisions necessary to apply the full accrual method. Interest on the note, which is considered fully collectible, is at a market rate. The fair values of the real estate transferred by both parties are readily determinable and realizable at the date of the exchange. Neither party has any continuing involvement with the real estate exchanged.

Allocation to Monetary and Nonmonetary Portions

Monetary portion:

$$\frac{\text{Total monetary consideration}}{\text{Total fair value of the exchange}} = \frac{\$220,000}{\$500,000} = 44\%$$

The monetary portion of the exchange is $120,000 in cash and a note for $100,000.

Nonmonetary portion:

$$\frac{\text{Fair value of real estate exchanged}}{\text{Total fair value of the exchange}} = \frac{\$280,000}{\$500,000} = 56\%$$

The nonmonetary portion of the exchange is real estate with a fair value of $500,000 for similar real estate with a fair value of $280,000 ($500,000 ×.56).

54,012 ASC 845—Nonmonetary Transactions

Company A (Receiver of boot)

Because the monetary portion of $120,000 in cash (more than 20% of the total consideration) and the $100,000 note meet the requirements for the buyer's initial and continuing investment, full accrual profit recognition is permitted on the monetary portion under FAS-66. Company A would recognize a gain as follows:

Monetary consideration	$220,000
Less: Company A's book value ($100,000) × .44	44,000
Profit recognized	$176,000

No gain is recognized on the nonmonetary portion, because two similar assets are exchanged. The basis for the new asset is as follows:

Net book value of real estate exchanged	$100,000
Pro rata portion of net book value retired ($100,000 ×.44)	44,000
	$56,000

Company B (Payer of boot)

Company B accounts for the monetary portion of the exchange at the amount of boot, $220,000, which represents an acquisition of real estate. No gain is recognized on the nonmonetary portion, because two similar assets are exchanged. The basis for the new asset is as follows:

Net book value of real estate exchanged	$240,000
Boot	220,000
	$460,000

Monetary Exchange of a Nonfinancial Asset for a Noncontrolling Ownership Interest

3. A monetary exchange of a financial asset for a noncontrolling ownership interest in the counterparty to an exchange should be accounted for as follows:

   a. Full or partial gain recognition is required in a monetary exchange that must be accounted for at fair value in which Entity A transfers a nonfinancial asset to entity B in exchange for a noncontrolling ownership interest in Entity B.

   b. If Company A has no actual or implied financial or other commitment to support Company B's operations, the amount of the gain recognized by Entity A, if applicable, may exceed the amount computed under 5(a) above. A commitment exists if the parties to the exchange have signed a binding, written agreement that specifies the agreement's principal provisions. A preliminary agreement does not qualify as a commitment for the purpose of this guidance if the principal provisions have not yet been negotiated, or are subsequently changed.

   c. The following transactions should be accounted for as a deconsolidation in accordance with the guidance in ASC 819-10-40-3A, except for a sale of in substance real estate, which should be accounted for based on the guidance in ASC 360-20 or ASC 976-605, or is a conveyance of oil and gas mineral rights, which should be accounted for based on the guidance in AC 932-60.

    (1) Entity A transfers a subsidiary that is a business or a nonprofit activity to Entity B in exchange for a noncontrolling interest in Entity B

    (2) Entity A transfers a group of assets that is a business or a nonprofit activity to Entity B in exchange for a noncontrolling interest in Entity B.

d. Exchanges of nonmonetary assets, other than those discussed in 5(c) above, for a noncontrolling ownerhip interest in another entity should be accounted for at fair value with recognition of a full or partial gain on the transaction.

e. If the fair value of a transferred asset is greater than its carrying value:

    (1) A *gain* for the difference should be recognized if the entity uses the cost method to accounts for the ownership received.

    (2) A *partial gain* should be recognized if the equity method is used to account for the ownership interest received.

    That amount should be calculated using the cost method reduced by a portion of the gain that is related to an economic interest retained in the transferred asset based on the guidance ASC 845-10-30-3. For example, if Entity A exchanged an asset with a fair value of $500,000 and a carrying value of $200,000 for a 20% economic interest in Entity B, the calculation of Entity A's gain would be $500,000 − $200,000 = $300,000 × .2 = $60,000. The gain would be $300,000 − $60,000 = $240,000. The amount that Entity A records for the ownership interest received in the exchange is partially based on its fair at the exchange date and partially based on the carryover of the asset surrendered.

f. If the fair value of an exchanged nonfinancial asset is less than its carrying value, the difference should be recognized as a *loss*.

CHAPTER 55
ASC 850—RELATED PARTY DISCLOSURES

CONTENTS

General Guidance	55,001
ASC 850-10: Overall	55,001
Overview	55,001
Background	55,001
Reporting and Disclosure Standards	55,002
Illustrations of Related Party Disclosures	55,003

GENERAL GUIDANCE

ASC 850-10: OVERALL

OVERVIEW

Financial statement disclosure of related party transactions is required by GAAP in order for those statements to fairly present financial position, cash flows, and results of operations.

BACKGROUND

A *related party* is one that can exercise control or significant influence over the management and/or operating policies of another party, to the extent that one of the parties may be prevented from fully pursuing its own separate interests.

Related parties consist of all affiliates of an enterprise, including (*a*) their management and their immediate families, (*b*) their principal owners and their immediate families, (*c*) their investments accounted for by the equity method (absent the election of the fair value option under ASC 825, Financial Instruments), (*d*) beneficial employee trusts that are managed by the management of the enterprise, and (*e*) any party that may, or does, deal with the enterprise and has ownership of, control over, or can significantly influence the management or operating policies of another party to the extent that an arm's-length transaction may not be achieved (ASC 850-10-05-3).

Transactions among related parties generally are accounted for on the same basis as if the parties were not related, unless the *substance* of the transaction is not arm's length. Substance over form is an important consideration when accounting for transactions involving related parties.

Common related party transactions include the following (ASC 850-10-05-4):

- Sales, purchases, and transfers of realty and personal property

- Services received or furnished (e.g., accounting, management, engineering, and legal services)
- Use of property and equipment by lease
- Borrowings and lendings
- Maintenance of bank balances as compensating balances for the benefit of another
- Intercompany billings based on allocation of common costs
- Filing of consolidated tax returns

> **OBSERVATION:** The Enron Corp. engaged in a number of related party transactions. These transactions were related to the financial improprieties that caused Enron's failure. Related party transactions are more likely when an entity is dealing with partnerships, particularly when these partnerships are located in tax havens and where there appears to be little economic justification for the partnership's existence. Regulators and standard-setters are focusing more resources on the proper disclosure of related party transactions; auditors and preparers of financial statements need to be aware of this heightened focus.

REPORTING AND DISCLOSURE STANDARDS

ASC 850 requires that material related party transactions that are not eliminated in consolidated or combined financial statements be disclosed in the financial statements of the reporting entity. Related party transactions involving compensation arrangements, expense allowances, and similar items incurred in the ordinary course of business, however, do not have to be disclosed (ASC 850-10-50-1).

If separate financial statements of an entity that has been consolidated are presented in a financial report that includes the consolidated financial statements, duplicate disclosure of the related party transactions is not necessary. Disclosure of related party transactions is required, however, in separate financial statements of (*a*) a parent company, (*b*) a subsidiary, (*c*) a corporate joint venture, or (*d*) an investee that is 50% owned or less (ASC 850-10-50-4).

Information required to be disclosed for material related party transactions is as follows (ASC 850-10-50-1):

- The nature of the relationship of the related parties
- A description of the transactions, including amounts and other pertinent information necessary for an understanding of the effects of the related party transactions, for each period in which an income statement is presented (related party transactions of no or nominal amounts must also be disclosed)
- The dollar amount of transactions for each period in which an income statement is presented; also, the effects of any change in terms between the related parties from terms used in prior periods

- If not apparent in the financial statements, (*a*) the terms of related party transactions, (*b*) the manner of settlement of related party transactions, and (*c*) the amount due to or from related parties

If the operating results or financial position of a reporting entity can be altered significantly by the effects of common ownership or management control of the reporting entity and one or more other entities, even if there are no transactions among any of the entities, the nature of the ownership or management control must be disclosed in the financial statements (ASC 850-10-50-6).

PRACTICE POINTER: The amount of detail disclosed for related party transactions must be sufficient for the user of the financial statements to be able to understand the related party transaction and its impact on the financial statements. Thus, all that is necessary may be disclosure of the total amount of a specific type of material related party transaction or of the effects of the relationship between the related parties. In other circumstances, however, more details may be required for the reader of the financial statements to have a clear understanding of the transaction.

One cannot assume that a related party transaction is consummated in the same manner as an arm's-length transaction. Disclosures or other representations of a material related party transaction in financial statements should not imply that the transaction was made on the same basis as an arm's-length transaction, unless the disclosures or representations can be substantiated (ASC 850-10-50-5).

Illustrations of Related Party Disclosures

Transaction between company and officers/directors During 20X5, the company purchased land and buildings adjoining one of its plants from two company directors for $750,000. The board of directors unanimously approved the purchase, with the two directors involved in the transaction abstaining.

Transaction between company and profit-sharing plan During 20X5, the company purchased land from one of its profit-sharing plans for $750,000. Department of Labor exemption was received prior to the transaction.

Lease between company and officer/owner Several years ago, the company leased land in upstate New York from John Doe, an officer and principal owner. The company constructed and furnished a residence on the property for use by the company's customers and distributors. The annual lease payment to Doe is $12,500, and the lease continues through December 31, 20X5. At that time, Doe has an option to purchase the residence and furnishings for $50,000 or to renew the lease at $10,000 per year for an additional five years.

Salary advance to officer During 20X5, the company made a $100,000 salary advance to John Doe, an officer, as part of a new employment contract that required Doe to relocate to Atlanta, Georgia. According to the terms of the contract, Doe is required to repay the loan at $20,000 per year for the next five years, beginning in 20X8.

CHAPTER 56
ASC 852—REORGANIZATIONS

CONTENTS

Part I: General Guidance	**56,001**
ASC 852-20: Quasi-Reorganizations	**56,001**
Overall	**56,001**
Background	**56,001**
Quasi-Reorganization	**56,002**
Accounting and Reporting	**56,002**
Accounting for a Tax Benefit	**56,004**
Disclosure	**56,004**
Illustration of Accounting for a Quasi-Reorganization	**56,004**
Part II: Interpretive Guidance	**56,006**
ASC 852-10: Overall	**56,006**
ASC 852-10-05-3 through 05-16, 10-1, 15-1 through 15-3, 25-1, 30-1, 45-1 through 45-2, 45-4 through 45-21, 45-26 through 45-27, 45-29, 50-2 through 50-4, 50-7, 55-3, 55-5 through 55-11, ASC 852-20-15-3; ASC 740-45-1 ASC 210-10-60-3	
Financial Reporting by Entities in Reorganization under the Bankruptcy Code	**56,006**
ASC 852-10-45-20	
An Amendment of AICPA Statement of Position 90-7	**56,021**

PART I: GENERAL GUIDANCE

ASC 852-20: QUASI-REORGANIZATIONS

OVERALL

When a struggling business reaches a turnaround point and profitable operations seem likely, a quasi-reorganization may be appropriate to eliminate an accumulated deficit from past unprofitable operations. The resulting financial statements have more credibility and may make it possible for the company to borrow money for its profitable operations. In addition, by eliminating the deficit in retained earnings, the possibility of paying dividends in the foreseeable future becomes more likely.

BACKGROUND

The specific criteria that must be met for a quasi-reorganization to be appropriate are:

- Assets are overvalued in the balance sheet.

- The company can reasonably expect to be profitable in the future if a restructuring occurs so that future operations are not burdened with the problems of the past.
- Formal shareholder consent is obtained.

Stockholders' equity usually is made up of the following:

- Capital contributed for stock, to the extent of the par or stated value of each class of stock presently outstanding
- Additional paid-in or contributed capital:
  — Capital contributed in excess of par or stated value of each class of stock, whether as a result of original issues, any subsequent reductions of par or stated value, or transactions by the corporation in its own shares
  — Capital received other than for stock, whether from shareholders or others (such as donated capital)
- Retained earnings (or deficit), which represents the accumulated income or loss of the corporation.

Generally, items properly chargeable to current or future years' income accounts may *not* be charged to contributed capital accounts. An exception to this rule occurs in accounting for quasi-reorganizations, in which case a one-time adjustment to contributed capital is appropriate.

Although the corporate entity remains unchanged in a quasi-reorganization, a new basis of accountability is established. Net assets are restated downward to their fair values, and stockholders' equity is reduced. Retained earnings (deficit) is eliminated by charging any deficit accumulated from operations and the asset adjustments to either (*a*) capital contributed in excess of par or (*b*) capital contributed other than for capital stock. Contributed capital accounts must be large enough to absorb the deficit in retained earnings, including adjustments made as part of the quasi-reorganization.

PRACTICE POINTER: Although the capital stock account may not be used to directly absorb a deficit in retained earnings, a corporation may reduce the par value of its existing capital stock and transfer the resulting excess to a capital contributed in excess of par account. This procedure frequently is used in a quasi-reorganization.

QUASI-REORGANIZATION

Accounting and Reporting

If a corporation restates its assets and stockholders' equity through a quasi-reorganization, it must make a clear report of the proposed restatements to its shareholders and obtain their formal consent (ASC 852-20-25-3).

Assets are written down to their fair values; if fair values are not readily determinable, conservative estimates are used (ASC 852-20-35-2). Estimates may also be used to provide for known probable losses prior to the date of the quasi-reorganization, when amounts are indeterminable (ASC 852-20-30-4).

> **PRACTICE POINTER:** Determination of the fair value of assets is a subjective process, requiring the use of different valuation and appraisal techniques for different asset categories.

If estimates are used and the amounts subsequently are found to be excessive or insufficient, the difference should be charged or credited to the capital account previously charged or credited and not to retained earnings (ASC 852-20-35-2).

The steps in the accounting procedure are as follows:

Step 1. All asset amounts to be written off are charged to retained earnings (ASC 852-20-25-4).

Step 2. After all amounts to be written off are recognized and charged to retained earnings, the negative (debit) balance is transferred to either *(a)* capital contributed in excess of par or *(b)* capital contributed other than for capital stock (ASC 852-20-25-4)

Capital contributed in excess of par value may have existed prior to the quasi-reorganization, or it may have been created as a result of a reduction of par value in conjunction with the quasi-reorganization.

Step 3. When a deficit in retained earnings is transferred to an allowable capital account, any subsequent balance sheet must disclose, by dating the retained earnings, that the balance in the retained earnings account has accumulated since the date of reorganization (ASC 852-20-50-2). For example:

Retained earnings, since July 1, 20X0 $1,234,567

The dating of retained earnings following a quasi-reorganization would rarely, if ever, be of significance after a period of ten years. There may be exceptional circumstances that could justify a period of less than ten years.

Step 4. New or additional shares of stock may be issued or exchanged for other shares or existing indebtedness. For example, stockholders may agree to subscribe to additional shares, or bondholders may agree to accept capital stock in lieu of principal or interest in arrears, to provide new cash for future operations. Accounting entries for these types of transactions are handled in accordance with GAAP. Consideration should include whether the issuance of new stock results in a change in control, in which case purchase accounting may be appropriate (ASC 852-20-25-6).

Step 5. Corporations with subsidiaries should follow the same procedures so that no credit balance remains in consolidated retained earnings after a quasi-reorganization in which losses have been charged to allowable capital accounts (ASC 852-20-25-4).

In those cases in which losses have been charged to the allowable capital accounts, instead of a credit balance in a subsidiary's retained earnings, the parent company's interest in such retained earnings is regarded as capitalized by the quasi-reorganization in the same way retained earnings of a subsidiary are capitalized by the parent on the date of its acquisition (ASC 852-20-25-4).

Step 6. The effective date of the quasi-reorganization from which income of the corporation is thereafter determined should be as close as possible to the date of formal stockholders' consent and preferably at the start of a new fiscal year (ASC 852-20-25-5).

Adjustments made pursuant to a quasi-reorganization should not be included in the determination of net income for any period.

Accounting for a Tax Benefit

Careful consideration must be given to the proper accounting for any tax attributes in a quasi-reorganization. Under ASC 740 (Income Taxes), tax benefits of deductible temporary differences and carryforwards as of the date of the quasi-reorganization ordinarily are reported as a direct addition to capital contributed in excess of par if the tax benefits are recognized in subsequent years. An exception may exist for entities that have previously adopted the predecessor standard to ASC 740 and effected a quasi-reorganization; in that instance, subsequent recognition of tax benefits may be included in income and then reclassified from retained earnings to capital contributed in excess of par (ASC 852-740-45-3).

Disclosure

Adequate disclosure of all pertinent information must be made in the financial statements. A new retained earnings account dated as of the date of the quasi-reorganization is established and reflected in subsequent financial statements.

Illustration of Accounting for a Quasi-Reorganization

The Centrex Company experienced losses in each of its first six years of operation. In May 20X5, the company acquired two patents on an advanced solarheating unit, which soon became the standard for the industry. The quarter ended September 30, 20X5, was profitable, and the patent and accompanying licensing agreements indicate that continuing profitability is quite likely.

Centrex is closely held and the stockholders have agreed in principle to a quasi-reorganization. Negotiations have been held with various creditors regarding capitalizing debts.

The balance sheet of Centrex at December 31, 20X5, appears as follows:

Assets:

Cash	$ 25,000
Accounts receivable (net)	410,000
Plant and equipment (net)	1,670,000

Other assets	80,000
Total assets	$2,185,000

Liabilities and Equity:

Accounts payable	$ 840,000
Notes payable—other	300,000
Equipment notes payable	240,000
Common stock	500,000
Paid-in capital in excess of par value—common stock	1,017,000
Retained earnings	(712,000)
Total liabilities and equity	$2,185,000

The stockholders and creditors have approved the following plan of informal reorganization effective January 1, 20X6:

1. The current shareholders will exchange their 100,000 shares of $5 par stock for 100,000 shares of $1 par stock.
2. The creditors have agreed to accept a new issue of 5% preferred stock valued at $300,000 for an equal amount of accounts payable.
3. The plant and equipment will be written down to its fair value of $1,100,000.
4. Accounts receivable of $70,000 will be written off as uncollectible.
5. Other assets will be written down to their fair value of $50,000.

The first step in a quasi-reorganization is to write down all assets to their fair values. In the example, the journal entry would be:

Retained earnings	670,000	
Plant and equipment ($1,670,000 - $1,100,000)		570,000
Accounts receivable		70,000
Other assets ($80,000 - $50,000)		30,000

Next, the change in the par value of the common stock is recorded:

Common stock	400,000	
Paid-in capital in excess of par value—common stock		400,000

The following journal entry records the new preferred stock issued for $300,000 of accounts payable:

Accounts payable	300,000	
5% Preferred stock		300,000

After all the quasi-reorganization adjustments are made, the deficit in retained earnings ($1,382,000) is eliminated against the paid-in capital—common stock—leaving a zero balance in retained earnings:

Paid-in capital—common stock	1,382,000	
Retained earnings ($712,000 + $670,000)		1,382,000

The Centrex Company balance sheet, after giving effect to the reorganization, appears as follows:

Assets:	
Cash	$25,000
Accounts receivable (net)	340,000
Plant and equipment (net)	1,100,000
Other assets	50,000
Total assets	$1,515,000
Liabilities and Equity:	
Accounts payable	$540,000
Notes payable—other	300,000
Equipment notes payable	240,000
5% Preferred stock	300,000
Common stock ($1 par)	100,000
Paid-in capital in excess of par value—common stock ($1,017,000 + $400,000 -$1,382,000)	35,000
Retained earnings since January 1, 20X5	-0-
Total liabilities and equity	$1,515,000

PART II: INTERPRETIVE GUIDANCE

ASC 852-10: Overall

ASC 852-10-05-3 through 05-16, 10-1, 15-1 through 15-3, 25-1, 30-1, 45-1 through 45-2, 45-4 through 45-21, 45-26 through 45-27, 45-29, 50-2 through 50-4, 50-7, 55-3, 55-5 through 55-11, ASC 852-20-15-3; ASC 740-45-1 ASC 210-10-60-3 Financial Reporting by Entities in Reorganization under the Bankruptcy Code

BACKGROUND

Entities experiencing severe financial distress may file for protection from creditors under Chapter 11 of the Bankruptcy Code. An entity filing for protection under Chapter 11 seeks to reorganize and to emerge from bankruptcy as a viable business. The primary objective of the reorganization is to maximize the recovery of creditors and shareholders by preserving the going concern value of the entity.

Legal Summary of the Reorganization Process

To begin the process of bankruptcy reorganization, an entity would file a petition with the Bankruptcy Court, an adjunct of the United States District Courts. The entity filing the bankruptcy petition typically prepares a reorganization plan, which it submits to the Court for confirmation. This plan specifies the treatment of the entity's assets and liabilities, and it may result in debt being forgiven. For the reorganization plan to be confirmed, the consideration to be received by parties in interest under the plan must exceed what would be received if the entity liquidated under Chapter 7 of the Bankruptcy Code. In most cases, the debtor has the exclusive right to file a reorganization plan during the first 120 days after the bankruptcy filing (this right is lost if the Court appoints a trustee).

In general, the provisions of a confirmed reorganization plan bind all parties connected with the entity. This includes (1) the entity itself (i.e., the debtor); (2) any entity issuing securities under the plan; (3) any entity acquiring assets under the plan; and (4) any creditor, stockholder, or general partner of the debtor. This is the case regardless of whether the claim of any of these parties is impaired by the reorganization plan and irrespective of whether the party accepted the plan.

The requirements that must be met for the Bankruptcy Court to approve a reorganization plan include the following:

- The technical requirements of the Bankruptcy Code have been met.
- In soliciting acceptance of the plan, the entity has provided adequate disclosures.
- A class of individuals whose claims are impaired might consent to the plan and yet have some individual members who dissent from this action. These dissenting members must receive at least as much under the plan as they would receive in a Chapter 7 liquidation.
- Priority claims under the terms of the Bankruptcy Code will be paid in cash.
- If the plan is confirmed, it is not likely to be followed by liquidation or further reorganization.
- At least one class of impaired claims, not including insiders, has accepted the plan.
- The plan proponent, typically the debtor, has obtained the consent of all parties with impaired claims or equity securities, or the plan proponent can comply with the "cram-down" provisions of the Bankruptcy Code. (This means that the plan can be forced on nonassenting creditors by the Bankruptcy Court.) The court can confirm a plan even if one or more parties with impaired claims or equity securities do not accept it. In order for the court to confirm a plan under these circumstances, the plan cannot unfairly discriminate against a nonconsenting class impaired by the plan, and it must treat nonconsenting classes in a fair and equitable manner.
    — A secured claim is treated in a fair and equitable manner if it remains adequately collateralized and if the present value of the payments it is to receive equals the amount of the secured claim when the plan becomes effective.
    — An unsecured claim is treated in a fair and equitable manner if the discounted assets it is to receive equal the allowed amount of the claim or if any claim junior to it will not receive or retain any assets.
    — An equity interest is treated in a fair and equitable manner if the discounted assets it is to receive equal the greatest of (1) any fixed liquidation preference, (2) any fixed redemption price, or (3) the value of such interest. Alternatively, the equity interest is treated fairly and equitably if no junior equity security interest will receive or retain any assets under the plan.

ACCOUNTING GUIDANCE

Accounting and Financial Aspects of the Reorganization Process

A central feature of the reorganization plan is to determine the reorganization value of the entity that seeks to emerge from Bankruptcy Court protection. The reorganization value is designed to approximate the fair value of the entity's assets, and it should conform with the amount that a willing buyer would pay for these assets.

The reorganization value is generally determined through the following steps:

Step 1:	Consideration of the amount to be received for assets that will not be needed by the reconstituted business
Step 2:	Computation of the present value of cash flows that the reconstituted business is expected to generate for some period into the future
Step 3:	Computation of the terminal value of the reconstituted business at the end of the period for which future cash flows are estimated

---

Illustration of Estimating Reorganization Value

ERT, Inc., is a debtor-in-possession operating under the protection of Chapter 11 of the Bankruptcy Code. In order to prepare a reorganization plan, ERT needs to estimate its reorganization value. ERT has $150,000 of cash above its likely needs as an ongoing business. (It is not unusual for entities operating under Chapter 11 protection to accumulate excess cash; these entities do not pay most claims during the period of time they are operating under Chapter 11 protection.) Also, ERT is expected to generate $40,000 of net cash flows per month, each year, during the first five years after it emerges from Chapter 11. ERT's terminal value is estimated to be $1,091,456. ERT's reorganization value of approximately $2,816,667 represents the $150,000 of excess cash on hand, the present value of receiving $40,000 per month for the next five years ($1,575,211 discounted at 18%), and the terminal value of the enterprise.

After the entity's reorganization value is determined, it is allocated in interest to parties in accordance with their respective legal priorities. Secured claims have first priority, to the extent of the value of their collateral. Following secured claims are those claims specifically granted priority under the provisions of the Bankruptcy Code. Finally, distributions are made to various classes of unsecured debt and equity interests in accordance with their respective legal priorities, or otherwise as the parties may agree.

Before the reorganization plan is submitted to creditors, equity holders, etc., these groups are provided with a disclosure statement. The disclosure statement must be approved by the Court, and it should contain adequate information for interested parties to make an informed decision as to the appropriateness of the reorganization plan.

The disclosure statement typically contains (1) a description of the reorganization plan, (2) historical and prospective financial information, and (3) a pro forma balance sheet that presents the reorganization value and the capital structure of the new entity. A valuation of the emerging entity is not required for the disclosure statement to be approved by the Bankruptcy Court. Normally, however, such a valuation would be performed unless (1) the reorganization value of the emerging entity exceeds its liabilities or (2) holders of existing voting shares will own a majority of the emerging entity.

Need for and Scope of Guidance

Before the issuance of the guidance in ASC 852-10-05-3 through 05-16, 10-1, 15-1 through 15-3, 25-1, 30-1, 45-1 through 45-2, 45-4 through 45-21, 45-26 through 45-27, 45-29; 50-2 through 50-4, 50-7; 55-3, 55-5 through 55-11; ASC 852-20-15-3; ASC 740-45-1 ASC 210-10-60-3; (SOP 90-7), there was no specific guidance for entities operating in reorganization proceedings. This led to wide diversity in practice.

That guidance applies to both (1) entities that are operating under Chapter 11 protection and that expect ultimately to emerge from such protection as a going concern and (2) entities that have emerged from Chapter 11 protection under a confirmed reorganization plan. It does not apply to (1) entities that restructure their debt outside of the Chapter 11 process, (2) entities that liquidate or that plan to do so, and (3) governmental entities.

Financial Reporting—Entity Operating under Chapter 11 Protection

For the most part, filing for Chapter 11 protection does not change the application of generally accepted accounting principles. One difference is that transactions or events that are directly associated with the reorganization proceedings should be kept separate from ongoing operations.

Balance Sheet Reporting

Prepetition liabilities (i.e., liabilities incurred by the enterprise before the Chapter 11 filing) may be subject to compromise. A liability is compromised when it ultimately is settled for less than its allowed amount. The *allowed* amount is that which is permitted by the Bankruptcy Court, even though such liabilities may not be paid in full. Prepetition liabilities subject to compromise should be separated from prepetition liabilities not subject to compromise (e.g., fully secured liabilities) and from postpetition claims. These two latter amounts are combined and reported as one amount. All liabilities should be reported at the amount allowed by the Bankruptcy Court, even though they ultimately may be settled for less than the allowed amount.

Some secured liabilities may be undersecured. An undersecured liability exists when the fair value of the collateral may be less than the allowed liability. In this case, the entire liability should initially be classified as a prepetition claim subject to compromise. The liability would not be reclassified unless it became clear that the secured claim in question would not be compromised. Certain prepetition liabilities may not become known until after the bankruptcy petition is filed. Those liabilities should be reported at the expected amount of the allowed claims (based on the framework of ASC 450-20. If the existence of the liability is at least reasonably possible, this information should be disclosed in the notes to the financial statements even if the amount of the prepetition liability cannot be estimated.

56,010 ASC 852—Reorganizations

In certain cases, the allowed amount of a prepetition liability may differ from its recorded amount. When this circumstance occurs, the carrying amount of the liability should be adjusted to the allowed amount. If unamortized debt discounts, premiums, or debt issue costs exist, these accounts are used in making the adjustment to record the liability at its allowed amount. Any resulting gain or loss is classified as a reorganization item and, as such, will be reported separately in the income statement.

Details of claims subject to compromise are to be reported in the financial statement notes. Finally, if a classified balance sheet is presented, claims not subject to compromise are to be categorized as current or noncurrent.

Illustration of Balance Sheet Presentation

Hale & Carter filed for protection from creditors under Chapter 11 of the Bankruptcy Code on February 15, 20X4. Its first set of annual financial statements prepared after this date is prepared on December 31, 20X4. The details of Hale & Carter's liabilities and stockholders' equity are as follows:

Prepetition liabilities subject to compromise

Secured debt, 12%, secured by a first mortgage on equipment (the fair value of the collateral is less than the claim)	$200,000
Senior subordinated secured notes, 16%	300,000
Subordinated debentures, 19%	200,000
Trade and other miscellaneous claims	100,000
Priority tax claims	50,000

Prepetition liabilities not subject to compromise

Secured debt, 11%, secured by a first mortgage on a building ($50,000 of principal due on 6/30/X5)	$700,000

Postpetition claims

Accounts payable—trade	$120,000
Short-term borrowings	180,000

Stockholders' equity

Preferred stock	$150,000
Common stock	100,000
Retained earnings (deficit)	(500,000)

In its December 31, 20X4, balance sheet, Hale & Carter reports total assets of $1,600,000. (The presentation of the asset side of the balance sheet for an entity operating under Chapter 11 does not present any unique issues.) The right-hand side of Hale & Carter's balance sheet would look as follows:

Liabilities and Shareholders' Deficit
Liabilities Not Subject to Compromise
    Current liabilities:

Short-term borrowings	$ 180,000
Accounts payable	120,000
Total current liabilities	$ 300,000
Noncurrent liabilities:	
11%, Long-term note (see Note xx)	$ 700,000

Liabilities Subject to Compromise		$ 850,000 (a)
Total liabilities		$1,850,000
Shareholders' (deficit):		
Preferred stock		$ 150,000
Common stock		100,000
Retained earnings (deficit)		(500,000)
Total liabilities & shareholders' deficit		$1,600,000

(a) Liabilities subject to compromise consist of the following:

Secured debt, 12%, secured by a first mortgage on equipment (the fair value of the collateral is less than the claim)	$200,000
Senior subordinated secured notes, 16%	300,000
Subordinated debentures, 19%	200,000
Trade and other miscellaneous claims	100,000
Priority tax claims	50,000
	$850,000

Income Statement

Items of revenue, expense, gain, or loss that occur because the entity is operating in reorganization proceedings are to be reported separately. However, under the provisions in ASC 225-20-45 as amended by ASC 360-10 and ASC 470-50-45-1, this requirement does not apply to an item required to be reported separately as a discontinued operation or as an extraordinary item.

The guidance in this pronouncement specifically addresses the treatment of three items on the income statement. First, professional fees related to the reorganization are to be recognized as incurred and categorized as a reorganization expense. Before this guidance was issued, some entities established a liability for professional fees upon filing for bankruptcy; other entities capitalized these fees when incurred and ultimately offset them against debt discharge when the reorganization plan was confirmed. Neither of those treatments is now acceptable. Second, interest expense is *not* a reorganization item. It should be reported only to the extent that interest is paid during the reporting period or to the extent that it will be an allowed claim. In many cases, the interest expense reported will be significantly less than contractual interest. Any difference between reported interest expense and contractual interest is to be disclosed. SEC registrants must disclose this difference on the face of the income statement. Third, any interest income above that which would normally be earned on invested working capital is to be reported as a reorganization item. Entities operating under Chapter 11 protection often generate large amounts of interest income. The entity continues to generate cash flows from operations, and payments under many liabilities are stayed by the bankruptcy proceedings.

Statement of Cash Flows

The guidance in this pronouncement provides that the most beneficial information that can be provided about an entity operating under Chapter 11 protection is the information presented in the statement of cash flows. Cash flows from operating, investing, and financing activities that relate to the reorganization should be shown separately. That treatment is more useful if an entity uses the direct method of preparing the statement. If the indirect method is used, a supplementary schedule (or a note) containing information on operating cash flows due to the reorganization proceedings must be provided.

Other Issues

A company presenting consolidated results may have one or more entities in reorganization proceedings. Assuming that this hypothetical company also has other entities that are not operating under Chapter 11 protection, condensed combined financial statements for the units operating under Chapter 11 must accompany the consolidated financial statements. Those units operating under Chapter 11 must present intercompany receivables and payables in the condensed combined financial statements. In addition, those entities that are not in reorganization proceedings must evaluate the propriety of reporting an intercompany receivable from a unit that is operating in Chapter 11.

In general, earnings per share for entities in reorganization are calculated in a manner similar to the calculation for any other entity. However, if it is probable that additional shares of stock or common stock equivalents will be issued under the reorganization plan, that fact should be disclosed.

Fresh-Start Reporting—Emergence from Chapter 11

For an entity emerging from Chapter 11 protection to employ fresh-start reporting, two conditions must exist. First, the value of the emerging entity's assets immediately before the reorganization plan is confirmed must be less than the amount of postpetition liabilities and prepetition allowed claims. Second, persons holding existing voting shares immediately before the reorganization plan is confirmed must receive less than 50% of the voting shares of the new entity. Note that the loss of control experienced by the former shareholders must be substantive and not temporary. Fresh-start reporting is to be applied as of the confirmation date, or at a later date when all material conditions precedent to the reorganization plan becoming binding have been resolved.

If an entity emerging from reorganization proceedings does not meet *both* of the criteria outlined in the previous paragraph, the entity is precluded from adopting fresh-start reporting. However, even in this case, the entity needs to ensure that (1) liabilities adjusted as a result of a confirmed reorganization plan are stated at present value and (2) any debt forgiveness received is reported as an extraordinary item.

Implementing Fresh-Start Reporting

In implementing fresh-start reporting, the reorganization value of the emerging entity should be assigned among the tangible and specifically identifiable intangible assets and liabilities of the entity in conformity with the guidance in ASC 805, Business Combinations Any excess of reorganization value over that which can be assigned to tangible and specifically identifiable intangible assets is reported as, if any, goodwill in accordance with the guidance in ASC 350-20-25-2. Goodwill as a result of the implementation of fresh-start reporting is not amortized, but is periodically evaluated for impairment in accordance with the guidance in ASC 350, (Intangibles—Goodwill and Other).

Deferred income taxes should be reported in conformity with GAAP. If deferred taxes cannot be recognized at the date of a plan's confirmation by eliminating the valuation allowance, tax benefits from preconfirmation net operating loss carryforwards and deductible temporary differences should be reported as a reduction of income tax expense.

An entity emerging from bankruptcy that applies fresh start reporting should follow the guidance in accounting standards that are *effective* when fresh-start reporting is adopted.

Transitioning to Fresh-Start Reporting

Before the confirmation date of the reorganization plan, the accounting should follow that which is required when an entity is operating under Chapter 11 protection. Any adjustments to the recorded asset and liability amounts that result from the adoption of fresh-start reporting would be reported in the predecessor entity's final statement of operations. Also, the effects of debt forgiveness are to be reported in the predecessor entity's final statement of operations. The adoption of fresh-start reporting gives rise to a new reporting entity, which has no retained earnings nor deficit when it begins operations. Any deficit of the predecessor entity would be eliminated before the new entity begins operations.

Disclosures Required by Fresh-Start Reporting

A number of disclosures are required for entities that are exiting Chapter 11 proceedings and are adopting fresh-start reporting. These disclosures are as follows:

- Adjustments to the historical amounts of assets and liabilities.
- The amount of debt that has been forgiven.
- The amount of prior retained earnings or deficit that is eliminated.
- Significant matters in determining reorganization value. These include the following:
  — *The method or methods used to determine reorganization value* This includes disclosing information such as discount rates, tax rates, the number of years for which cash flows are projected, and the method of determining terminal value.
  — *Sensitive assumptions* These are assumptions made where there is a reasonable possibility of divergence from the assumption that could materially affect the estimate of reorganization value.
  — *Assumptions about anticipated conditions that are expected to be different from current conditions (unless these differences are already apparent)*

Other Issues

If, for example, a calendar-year-end entity has its reorganization plan confirmed on June 30, 20X5, and adopts fresh-start reporting on July 1, 20X5, at December 31, 20X5, this new entity should not prepare comparative financial statements.

56,014 ASC 852—Reorganizations

The financial statements presented would be limited to capturing the activity of the new entity for the latter half of 20X5. It was believed that presenting comparative financial statements that straddle a confirmation date would be misleading; therefore, such statements should not be presented.

Illustration of Fresh-Start Reporting

Background

Edison, Inc., filed for protection from creditors under Chapter 11 of the Bankruptcy Code on March 1, 20X5. Edison's reorganization plan was confirmed by the applicable Bankruptcy Court on May 1, 20X5.

Reorganization Value

Edison's reorganization value immediately before the confirmation of the reorganization plan was as follows:

Cash in excess of normal operating requirements generated by operations	$ 85,000
Net realizable value expected from asset dispositions	130,000
Present value of discounted cash flows of the emerging entity	525,000 [1]
Terminal value	1,250,000 [2]
Reorganization value	$1,990,000

[1] The present value of discounting estimated yearly cash flows, $250,000, over the forecast period, 3 years, by the appropriate interest rate, 20%.
[2] Terminal value is determined via an independent business valuation.

Applicability of Fresh-Start Reporting

Holders of Edison's existing voting shares before the confirmation of the reorganization plan will receive less than 50% of the voting shares in the emerging entity (in fact, these former shareholders will have no interest in the new entity). This meets the first requirement for use of fresh-start reporting. The second requirement, that reorganization value must be less than total postpetition liabilities and allowed claims, is also met, as illustrated below:

Postpetition current liabilities	$ 400,000
Liabilities deferred pursuant to Chapter 11 proceeding	1,700,000
Total postpetition liabilities and allowed claims	$2,100,000
Reorganization value	(1,990,000)
Excess of liabilities over reorganization value	$ 110,000

Computing the Total Assets of the Emerging Entity

Total assets of the emerging entity are computed by subtracting assets that will be distributed before or simultaneously with the confirmation of the reorganization plan—in this case, the $85,000 of excess cash—from the new entity's reorganization value. Therefore, the total assets of Edison-New Entity at May 1, 20X6, are $1,905,000 ($1,990,000-$85,000).

Beginning Capital Structure—Emerging Entity

After consideration of the emerging entity's debt capacity, projected earnings to fixed charges, earnings before interest and taxes to interest, free cash flow to interest, etc., the following capital structure for the new entity has been agreed upon:

Capital Structure for the Emerging Entity

Postpetition current liabilities	$400,000
IRS note	75,000
Senior debt	610,000[1]
Subordinated debt	420,000
Common stock	400,000

[1] $100,000 due each year for the next five years, at 14% interest; $110,000 due in the sixth year.

Distributions to Be Received by Parties in Interest

Secured Debt—The company's $600,000 of secured debt was exchanged for $85,000 in cash, $400,000 of new senior debt, and $115,000 of subordinated debt. The senior debt carries an interest rate of 14%, and principal payments of $65,574 are due during each of the next five years (the first payment is due on June 30, 20X6). The final payment of $72,130 is due in the sixth year.

Priority Tax Claims—Payroll and withholding taxes of $75,000 are payable in five equal annual installments, with the first payment due on May 31, 20X7. The annual interest rate is 11%.

Senior Debt—The company's $400,000 of senior debt was exchanged for $150,000 of new senior debt, $175,000 of subordinated debt, and 15% of the new issue of voting common stock. The senior debt carries an interest rate of 14%, and principal payments of $24,590 are due during each of the next five years (the first payment is due on June 30, 20X6). The final payment of $27,050 is due in the sixth year. Payments under the subordinated debentures are due in equal annual installments over seven years. The first payment is due September 30, 20X7, and the interest rate is 17%.

Trade and Other Claims—The holders of $200,000 of trade and other claims received the following for their stake: (a) $60,000 of senior debt, (b) $70,000 of subordinated debentures, and (c) 10% of the new issue of voting common stock. The senior debt carries an interest rate of 14%, and principal payments of $9,836 are due during each of the next five years (the first payment is due on June 30, 20X6). The final payment of $10,820 is due in the sixth year. Payments under the subordinated debentures are due in equal annual installments over seven years. The first payment is due September 30, 20X7, and the interest rate is 17%.

Subordinated Debentures—The company's $425,000 of subordinated debt was exchanged for $60,000 of new subordinated debentures and 75% of the new issue of voting common stock. Payments under the subordinated debentures are due in equal annual installments over seven years. The first payment is due September 30, 20X7, and the interest rate is 17%.

Common Stock—Edison had 200,000 shares of $1 par value common stock outstanding immediately before the confirmation of its reorganization plan. None of these stockholders will have any interest in the emerging entity. Four hundred thousand shares of new voting common stock, $1 par value, will be issued. These shares will be issued as follows: (a) 60,000 shares to holders of the former entity's senior debt, (b) 40,000 shares to holders of trade and other claims from the former entity, and (c) 300,000 shares to holders of the former entity's subordinated debentures.

Plan of Reorganization—Recovery Analysis

It is necessary to prepare a schedule detailing what the claims of the parties in interest are, and how and to what extent these claims are being satisfied. This schedule facilitates the preparation of the journal entries necessary to implement fresh-start reporting. This type of schedule is included either as a note to the financial statements or as supplementary information to the financial statements.

The following points should be noted about this schedule:

1. All of Edison's liabilities, both prepetition and postpetition, and shareholders' equity accounts are listed in column (a) of the table.

2. Column (b), elimination of debt and equity, represents the difference between the claim held (column (a) amount) and the consideration received for the claim (total recovery listed in column (j)).

3. Columns (c)-(g) represent the book value, which at the date of fresh-start reporting would also equal fair value, of the various items of consideration issued to settle the Chapter 11 claims (e.g., surviving debt, cash, new secured debt).

4. Column (h), common stock percentage, represents the percentage of the voting shares of the emerging entity issued to various parties.

5. Column (i), the value of the common stock issued, is computed by multiplying the net assets of the emerging entity by the percentage of voting shares of common stock received. For instance, the emerging capital structure for Edison will have only $400,000 of common stock (a deficit or retained earnings is always eliminated as part of the fresh-start process). Multiplying this amount by the percentage of common stock received produces the common stock value. Also, although this is not the case for Edison, some entities will have a beginning balance in additional paid-in capital as a result of the fresh-start process.

6. Column (j), total recovery, represents the total of the various types of consideration received.

7. Column (k), total recovery percentage, is computed by dividing the total recovery amount (column (j)) by the amount of the claim.

Journal Entries—Needed to Implement Fresh-Start Reporting

Entry to record debt discharge:

Liabilities subject to compromise	$1,700,000	
Cash		$ 85,000
IRS note		75,000
Senior debt—current		100,000
Senior debt—long-term		510,000
Subordinated debt		420,000
Common stock—new		400,000
Gain on debt discharge		110,000 [1]

[1] The gain on debt discharge can be calculated as follows:
Using the recovery analysis schedule, column (b)—elimination of debt and equity, add the amounts in this column for liabilities that have been compromised. In the case of Edison, the $400,000 of senior debt was settled for $385,000, a $15,000 gain. In a similar fashion, there were $30,000 and $65,000 gains on the settlement of trade claims and subordinated debentures, respectively. The sum of these three amounts is $110,000.

EDISON, INC. PLAN OF REORGANIZATION RECOVERY ANALYSIS

	(a)	(b) Elimination of Debt and Equity	(c) Surviving Debt	(d) Cash	(e) IRS Note	(f) Senior Debt	(g) Subordinated Debt	(h) Common Stock Percentage	(i) Common Stock value	(j) Total Recovery	(k) Total Recovery Percentage
Postpetition liabilities	$400,000		$400,000							$400,000	100
Claim/Interest											
Secured debt	600,000			$85,000		$400,000	$115,000			600,000	100
Priority tax claim	75,000				$75,000					75,000	100
Senior debt	400,000	$(15,000)				150,000	175,000	15%	$60,000	385,000	96
Trade and other claims	200,000	(30,000)				60,000	70,000	10%	40,000	170,000	85
Subordinated debentures	425,000	(65,000)					60,000	75%	300,000	360,000	85
	1,700,000	(110,000)									
Common shareholders	200,000	(200,000)							0	0	0
Deficit	(535,000)	535,000						100%	$400,000		
	$1,765,000	$225,000	$400,000	$85,000	$75,000	$610,000	$420,000		$400,000	$1,990,000	

Entry to retire Edison's (old) common stock:

Common stock—old	200,000	
Additional paid-in capital		200,000

Entry to record the adoption of fresh-start reporting and to eliminate the deficit in retained earnings:

Inventory	50,000[1]	
Property, plant, and equipment	200,000[1]	
Reorganization value in excess of amounts allocable to identifiable assets	375,000[2]	
Gain on debt discharge	110,000[3]	
Additional paid-in capital	200,000[4]	
Goodwill		400,000[2]
Deficit		535,000[2]

[1] The fair values of inventory and property, plant, and equipment immediately before the confirmation of Edison's reorganization plan have increased by $50,000 and $200,000, respectively. To implement fresh-start reporting, the recorded values of these assets are written up to their fair values. Note that the staff of the SEC, in their interpretation of *Financial Reporting Release* Section 210 (ASR-25), believes that the recognition of reorganization value in the balance sheet of an emerging entity that meets the criteria for fresh-start reporting should be limited to no net write-up of assets.

[2] To eliminate goodwill and the deficit of the predecessor entity and to record the excess of the emerging entity's reorganization value over amounts allocated to tangible and identifiable intangible assets. These amounts are obtained from the Balance Sheet Worksheet (see next page).

[3] This amount represents the difference between Edison's allowed liabilities of $2,100,000 (see column (a) of Edison's plan of reorganization—recovery analysis) and the amount paid to settle these same liabilities, $1,990,000 (see column (j) of Edison's plan of reorganization—recovery analysis).

[4] The entry to additional paid-in capital is used to balance the entry. In this case, it represents the book value of Edison's former stockholders that is being forfeited as part of the reorganization plan.

Balance Sheet Analysis—Needed to Implement Fresh-Start Reporting

The table that follows illustrates the implementation of Edison's reorganization plan and the preparation of Edison's initial balance sheet as a reorganized entity.

Adjustments to Record Confirmation of Plan

ASSETS	Preconfirmation	Debt Exchange Discharge of Stock	Fresh Start	Edison, Inc.'s Reorganized Balance Sheet
Current Assets				
Cash	$ 120,000	$(85,000)	$50,000	$ 35,000
Receivables	250,000			250,000
Inventory	350,000			400,000
Assets to be disposed of valued at market, which is lower than cost	30,000			30,000
Other current assets	15,000			15,000
Total current assets	$ 765,000	$(85,000)	$50,000	$ 730,000
Property, plant, and equipment	500,000		200,000	700,000
Assets to be disposed of valued at market, which is lower than cost	100,000			100,000
Goodwill	400,000		(400,000)	0
Reorganization value in excess of amounts allocable to identifiable assets			375,000	375,000
Total assets	$1,765,000	$(85,000)	$225,000	$1,905,000

LIABILITIES AND SHAREHOLDERS' DEFICIT

Current Liabilities Not Subject to Compromise				
Short-term borrowings	$ 250,000			$ 250,000
Current maturities of senior debt		$ 100,000		100,000
Accounts payable-trade	150,000			150,000
Total current liabilities	$ 400,000	$ 100,000		$ 500,000
Liabilities Subject to Compromise				
Prepetition liabilities	1,700,000	(1,700,000)		0
IRS note		75,000		75,000
Senior debt, less current maturities		510,000		510,000
Subordinated debt		420,000		420,000
Total Liabilities	$2,100,000	$ (595,000)		$1,505,000
Shareholders' Deficit				
Common stock-old	200,000	(200,000)		-0-
Common stock-new		400,000		400,000
Additional paid-in capital		200,000	(200,000)	-0-
Retained earnings (deficit)	(535,000)	110,000	425,000[1]	-0-
Total liabilities in shareholders' deficit	$ (335,000)	$ 510,000	$-0-	$ 225,000
Total liabilities and shareholders' deficit	$1,765,000	$ (85,000)	$-0-	$ 225,000	$1,905,000

[1] Represents the net effect of the elimination of the deficit in retained earnings, via a $535,000 credit to this account, and the debt to retained earnings to eliminate the $110,000 gain on debt discharge.

ASC 852-10-45-20 An Amendment of AICPA Statement of Position 90-7

OVERVIEW

SOP 90-7 (Financial Reporting by Entities in Reorganization under the Bankruptcy Code) provides the primary guidance on financial reporting for entities that file for bankruptcy and expect to reorganize as a going concern under Chapter 11 of Title 11 of the United States Code. Under the guidance in ASC 852-10-05-3 through 05-16, 10-1, 15-1 through 15-3, 25-1, 30-1, 45-1 through 45-2, 45-4 through 45-21, 45-26 through 45-27, 45-29; 50-2 through 50-4, 50-7; 55-3, 55-5 through 55-11; ASC 852-20-15-3; ASC 740-45-1; ASC 210-10-60-3, entities in Chapter 11 that meet certain criteria are required to adopt fresh-start reporting. In addition, when such an entity first adopts fresh-start reporting, it is required under the guidance in ASC 852-10-45-20 to early adopt at that time changes in accounting principles, if any, that the emerging entity will be required to apply in its financial statements within the 12 months after having adopted fresh-start reporting.

Although new pronouncements issued in 1990 encouraged early adoption of those standards, the FASB has prohibited the early adoption of several recently issued standards. As a result, some have noted that the guidance in ASC 852-10-45-20 related to the early adoption of changes in accounting principles conflicts with the FASB's guidance regarding the adoption date of some recent pronouncements. The issue is, therefore, whether entities emerging from bankruptcy that apply fresh-start reporting should be permitted to continue following the guidance related to the early adoption of changes in accounting standards or whether such entities should be required to adopt new pronouncements based on their stated effective dates.

ACCOUNTING GUIDANCE

This guidance applies to entities that are required to apply fresh-start reporting under the guidance in SOP 90-7.

Recognition and Measurement

This guidance amends the guidance in ASC 852-10-45-20, which addresses the early adoption of changes in accounting principles. Consequently, entities emerging from bankruptcy that use fresh-start reporting should follow only accounting standards that are effective at the date the entity adopts fresh-start reporting, including standards eligible for early adoption if an entity elects to adopt early.

Amendment to SOP 90-7

SOP 90-7 is amended as follows: [Deleted text is ~~struck out~~.]

- Paragraph 38 (ASC 852-10-45-20)—fourth bullet *before* the effective date of FASB Statement No. 141 (revised 2007) (FAS-141R) (Business Combinations) and as amended by FAS-141(R).

  ~~Changes in accounting principles that will be required in the financial statements of the emerging entity within the twelve months following the adoption of fresh-start reporting should be adopted at the time fresh-start reporting is adopted.~~

CHAPTER 57
ASC 855—SUBSEQUENT EVENTS

CONTENTS

Part I: General Guidance	57,001
ASC 855-10: Overall	57,001
Overview	57,001
Background	57,001
Disclosure of Subsequent Events	57,002
Terminology	57,001
Recognition	57,002
Disclosure	57,003
Other Issues	57,003
ASU 2010-09 Update	57,004
Part II: Interpretive Guidance	57,004
ASC 855-10: Overall	57,004
ASC 855-10-S25-1, S99-2	
Issuance of Financial Statements	57,004

PART I: GENERAL GUIDANCE

ASC 855-10: OVERALL

OVERVIEW

The current authoritative guidance on disclosure of subsequent events (ASC 855) was derived primarily from the existing authoritative auditing guidance on subsequent events (i.e., AU Section 560). The FASB standard on subsequent events states that financial statement preparation, including the consideration of subsequent events, is the responsibility of the entity and its management.

> **OBSERVATION:** In addition to subsequent events, the FASB plans to issue a standard on evaluating the entity's going-concern status. Guidance on both subsequent events and going concern has historically resided exclusively in the auditing literature.

BACKGROUND

ASC 855 provides guidance on the accounting for events that occur after the balance sheet date but before the financial statements are issued or are available for issuance (ASC 855-10-05-1). First, this guidance includes defining the length of the period after the balance sheet date where events should be evaluated for possible recognition or disclosure in the financial statements. Second, the guidance indicates when events or transactions occurring after the balance sheet date should be recognized in the financial statements. Third, guidance is provided on the disclosures that should be made related to subsequent events.

The guidance in ASC 855 applies to evaluating all subsequent events, unless other applicable GAAP addresses subsequent events in a particular area. Examples of areas where other authoritative literature addresses subsequent events are contingencies, earnings per share, and uncertainty income taxes (ASC 855-10-15-5).

DISCLOSURE OF SUBSEQUENT EVENTS

Terminology

A subsequent event is an event or transaction that occurs after the balance sheet date but before the financial statements are issued or are available for issuance. Financial statements are issued when they are distributed to shareholders and other financial statements users and their form and format comply with GAAP (ASC Glossary). Financial statements are available to be issued when their form and format comply with GAAP, and all approvals necessary for release of the financial statements have been obtained. These approvals may be from management, the board of directors, and from significant shareholders (ASC Glossary).

> **PRACTICE POINTER:** In EITF Topic No. D-86, *Issuance of Financial Statements*, the staff of the U.S. Securities and Exchange Commission expressed its views on when financial statements are issued. The SEC views financial statements as being issued at the earlier of when they are widely distributed to all shareholders or are filed with the SEC.

There are two types of subsequent events. The first type (recognized, or Type I, subsequent events) provides additional evidence related to conditions that existed at the balance sheet date, including additional evidence relating to estimated amounts in the financial statements. The second type (non-recognized, or Type II, subsequent events) provides evidence about conditions that did *not* exist at the balance sheet date but that arose before the financial statements were issued or available for issuance (ASC Glossary).

An entity that plans to widely distribute its financial statements, including any public entity, is to evaluate subsequent events through the date the financial statements are issued. All other entities are to evaluate subsequent events through the date the financial statements are available to be issued (ASC 855-10-25-2).

Recognition

Subsequent events that provide additional evidence about events or conditions that existed at the balance sheet date, including additional evidence relating to estimated amounts in the financial statements, are to be recognized (recognized subsequent events, or Type I subsequent events). For example, the bankruptcy of a customer due to a deteriorating financial condition in the subsequent events period in an example of a Type I subsequent event. The entity would consider the customer's bankruptcy in establishing the year-end balance in the allowance for doubtful accounts. Also, settlement of litigation that existed at the balance sheet date during the subsequent event period would be considered in estimating any loss and liability related to the litigation in the year-end financial statements (ASC 855-10-55-1).

Subsequent events that provide evidence about conditions that arose after the balance sheet date but before the financial statements are issued or are available for issuance are not recognized in the financial statements; however, these events may be disclosed in the financial statements (non-recognized subsequent events, or Type II subsequent events) (ASC 855-10-25-3). These events, assuming they occurred after the balance sheet date and before the financial statements are issued or available for issuance, are examples of non-recognized subsequent events: (1) issuance of capital stock or debt, (2) a business combination, (3) settlement of litigation (where the litigation began after the balance sheet date), (4) a casualty loss, (4) changes in the fair value of assets or liabilities, (5) changes in foreign exchange rates, and (6) entering into significant commitments (ASC 855-10-55-2).

Disclosure

The entity must disclose the date through which subsequent events were evaluated, and whether that date is the date the financial statements were issued or the date the statements were available to be issued (ASC 855-10-50-1). Certain not-recognized (Type II) subsequent events may be of such significance that they must be disclosed in order to prevent the financial statements from being misleading. The determination of which non-recognized subsequent events need to be disclosed is a management judgment decision. If the entity decides to disclose a non-recognized subsequent event, both the nature of the event and an estimate of its financial effect, or a statement that an estimate of the financial effect is not possible, are to be disclosed (ASC 855-10-50-2).

If a non-recognized subsequent event is disclosed, the entity should consider providing pro-forma financial data related to the event. And, if the non-recognized subsequent event is very significant (e.g., a material acquisition), pro-forma data may be needed to adequately convey the nature and impact of the event. Pro-forma data should reflect the event as if it happened on the balance sheet date, and the optional form of the pro-forma presentation may be an additional column on the face of the balance sheet presenting pro-forma amounts (ASC 855-10-50-2).

Other Issues

Entities are sometimes required by the SEC or other regulatory agencies to reissue financial statements. Unless required by GAAP or regulatory requirements, events occurring between the date the financial statements were issued (or were available to be issued) (and the reissuance date are not to be included in the reissued statements. The date through which subsequent events have been evaluated is to be included in both the original and reissued financial statements (ASC 855-10-25-4 and ASC 855-10-50-4).

ASU 2010-09 Update

Accounting Standards Update (ASU) No. 2010-09 amends the guidance in ASC 855 on subsequent events in several ways:

- Definition of term "SEC Filer"—Defined in the Master Glossary as an entity that is required to file or furnish its financial statements with either of the following: (a) The Securities and Change Commission, or (b) with respect to an entity subject to Section 12(i) of the Securities Act of 1934, the appropriate agency under that section.
- Definition of term "Revised Financial Statements"—Defined in the Master Glossary as financial statements revised for either of the following reasons: (a) correction of an error, or (b) retrospective application of U.S. GAAP.
- Date through which subsequent events have been evaluated—ASC 855-10-50-1 is amended to require that an entity that is not required to file with the SEC should disclose: (a) the date through which subsequent events were evaluated, and (b) whether the date is the date the financial statements were issued or the date the financial statements were available to be issued.
- Revised financial statements—ASC 855-10-50-4 is amended to require that an entity that is not an SEC filer should disclose in its revised financial statements the dates through which subsequent events have been evaluated in: (a) issued or available to be issued financial statements, and (b) revised financial statements.

PART II: INTERPRETIVE GUIDANCE

ASC 855 SUBSEQUENT EVENTS

ASC 855-10: OVERALL

ASC 855-10-S25-1, S99-2 Issuance of Financial Statements

In response to inquiries as to when financial statements are considered to have been issued, the SEC staff announced that financial statements are issued as of the date they are distributed for "general use and reliance" in a form and format that complies with GAAP. Annual financial statements should include an audit report stating that the auditors complied with generally accepted auditing standards (GAAS) in completing the audit. Financial statements would be considered to have been issued when the annual or quarterly financial statements are widely distributed to a registrant's shareholders and other users of financial statements or filed with the Commission, whichever is earlier. The SEC staff's position is based on the view that in accordance with Rule 10b-5 12b-20 under the Securities Exchange Act of 1934 and General Instruction C(3) to Form 10-K, registrants and their auditors have a responsibility to issue financial statements that are not misleading as of the date they are filed with the Commission.

If a registrant that has widely distributed its financial statements or its auditor become aware that a transaction that existed at the date of the financial statements causes those financial statements to be materially misleading, the financial statements must be amended so that they are free of material misstatement or omissions before they are filed with the SEC. Registrants should also disclose the subsequent events, which should be evaluated by the auditors to determine how the events or transactions affect the auditor's report.

In addition, the SEC staff noted that the issuance of an earnings release should not be considered the issuance of financial statements, because its form and format do not comply with GAAP and GAAS.

CHAPTER 58
ASC 860—TRANSFERS AND SERVICING

CONTENTS

Part I: General Guidance	58,003
ASC 860-10: Overall	58,003
Overview	58,003
Background	58,003
Definitions	58,003
Objectives of the Accounting for Transfers and Servicing of Assets	58,004
Control Criteria and Transferor Accounting	58,005
Securitizations	58,007
Consolidation of Securitization Entities	58,007
Disclosures	58,008
ASC 860-20: Sales of Financial Assets	58,009
Recognition of Assets Obtained or Liabilities Incurred	58,009
Derecognition of Assets and Liabilities	58,009
Sale of a Participating Interest	58,009
Sale of an Entire Financial Asset Group or Group of Entire Financial Assets	58,010
Disclosures	58,010
ASC 860-30: Secured Borrowing and Collateral	58,011
Secured Borrowing and Collateral	58,011
Disclosures	58,012
ASC 860-40: Transfers to Qualifying Special Purpose Entities	58,012
ASC 860-50: Servicing Assets and Liabilities	58,012
Accounting for Servicing Assets and Liabilities	58,012
Initial Measurement of Servicing Assets and Servicing Liabilities	58,012
Subsequent Measurement of Servicing Assets and Servicing Liabilities	58,013
One-Time Option to Reclassify Available-for-Sale Securities	58,013
Disclosures	58,013
Extinguishment of Liabilities	58,014
Implementation Guidance	58,014
Measurement of Interests Held after a Transfer of Financial Assets	58,015
Illustration of Recording Transfers with Proceeds of Cash, Derivatives, and Other Liabilities	58,015
Participating Interests in Financial Assets That Continue to Be Held by a Transferor	58,016
Illustrations of Recording Transfers with Interests That Continue to Be Held by a Transferor	58,016
Part II: Interpretive Guidance	58,017
ASC 860-10: Overall	58,017

58,002 ASC 860—Transfers and Servicing

ASC 860-10-05-12 through 05-13, 05-22, 10-9, 10-12, 10-13, 10-22, 15-4, 35-5, 35-8, 35-10 through 35-12, 40-7, 40-9, 40-11, 40-12, 40-14, 40-24, 40-26, 40-27, 40-29, 40-31, 40-33, 40-40, 55-3, 55-4, 55-7 through 55-18, 55-24A, 55-25A, 55-27 through 55-33, 55-38 through 55-42; 55-46, 55-51, 55-54, 55-58, 55-59, 55-69 55-62 through 55-64, 55-66 through 55-70, 55-75 through 55-79; ASC 860-20-25-6, 35-2, 35-3, 35-5, 35-7, 35-8, 55-3 through 55-9, 55-11 through 55-16, 55-24, 55-25, 55-28, 55-31, 55-34 through 55-39, 55-60, 55-61, 55-101 through 55-107, ASC 860-30-15-2, 15-3, 25-9, 35-2, 35-3, 45-2, 45-3, ASC 860-40-05-6, 15-11, 15-15, 15-19 through 15-28, 40-11, 45-2, 45-4, 55-3, 55-11, 55-12, 55-14 through 55-16, 55-18 through 55-20, 55-23 through 55-25, 55-27 through 55-29; ASC 860-50-25-7 through 25-9, 30-2 through 30-9, 35-11 through 35-14, 35-15, 50-5; 55-4 through 55-11, 55-13 through 55-18; ASC 320-10-25-5, 25-18; ASC 405-20-55-5 through 55-9

A Guide to Implementation of Statement 140 on Accounting for Transfers and Servicing of Financial Assets and Extinguishments of Liabilities	58,017
ASC 860-10-05-11; ASC 860-20-35-10, 55-16	
Securitization of Credit Card and Other Receivable Portfolios	58,036
ASC 860-10-15-5, 40-40; ASC 815-10-40-2 through 40-3	
Accounting for Transfers of Assets That Are Derivative Instruments but That Are Not Financial Assets	58,039
ASC 860-20-25-11 through 25-13, 30-4,35-9, 55-41 through 55-42, 55-62 through 55-92; ASC 860-40-25-2; ASC 860-50-25-10	
Accounting for Changes That Result in a Transferor Regaining Control of Financial Assets Sold	58,040
ASC 860-10-S40-1, S99-1, 50-40-7 through 40-9; ASC 460-10-60-37	
Balance Sheet Treatment of a Sale of Mortgage Servicing Rights with a Subservicing Agreement	58,041
ASC 860-10-55-35, 40-24	
Definition of the Term *Substantially the Same for Holders of Debt Instruments*, as Used in Certain Audit Guides and a Statement of Position	58,043
ASC 860-10-55-3; ASC 310-20-25-20	
Accounting for Fees and Costs Associated with Loan Syndications and Loan Participations	58,045
ASC 860-10-55-13	
Sale of Bad-Debt Recovery Rights	58,046
ASC 860-10-55-71 through 55-72	
Sale of a Short-Term Loan Made under a Long-Term Credit Commitment	58,047
ASC 860-20: Sales of Financial Assets	58,049
ASC 860-20-25-11 through 25-13, 30-4, 35-9, 55-41 through 55-42, 55-62 through 55-92; ASC 860-40-25-2, 50-25-10	
Accounting for Changes That Result in a Transferor Regaining Control of Financial Assets Sold	58,049
ASC 860-20-35-6, 55-17 through 55-19	
Accounting for Accrued Interest Receivable under FAS-140 Securitizations	58,051
ASC 860-50: Servicing Assets and Liabilities	58,051
ASC 860-50-40-3 through 40-5	

Determination of What Risks and Rewards, If Any, Can Be Retained and Whether Any Unresolved Contingencies May Exist in a Sale of Mortgage Loan Servicing Rights	58,051
ASC 860-50-40-10, 50-11	
Sale of Mortgage Service Rights on Mortgages Owned by Others	58,053

PART I: GENERAL GUIDANCE

ASC 860-10: OVERALL

OVERVIEW

Transfers of financial assets take many forms and, depending on the nature of the transaction, the transferor may have a continuing interest in the transferred asset. Accounting for transferred assets in which the transferor has no continuing involvement with the transferred asset or with the transferee has been relatively straight forward and not controversial. Transfers of financial assets in which the transferor has some continuing interest, however, have raised issues about the circumstances in which the transfer should be considered a sale of all or part of the assets or a secured borrowing, and how transferors and transferees should account for sales of financial assets and secured borrowings.

ASC 860 establishes accounting and reporting standards for transfers and servicing of financial assets and extinguishments of liabilities based on the consistent application of the financial-components approach. For each party to a transfer, this approach requires the recognition of financial assets and servicing assets that are controlled by the reporting entity, the derecognition of financial assets when control is surrendered, and the derecognition of liabilities when they are extinguished. Specific criteria are established for determining when control has been surrendered in the transfer of financial assets. ASC 860 also contains specific guidance with respect to the accounting for separately recognized servicing assets and servicing liabilities. Finally, ASC 860 provides guidance with respect to the requirements for derecognizing financial assets and the initial measurement by the transferor of interests related to transferred financial assets.

PRACTICE POINTER: This chapter provides an overview of ASC 860. Because transfers of financial assets can be extremely complex transactions, practitioners encountering these transactions should seek the assistance of experts in analyzing the applicable accounting literature.

BACKGROUND

Definitions

The term *financial asset* is defined in ASC 860 as cash, evidence of an ownership interest in an entity, or a contract that conveys to one entity a right (*a*) to receive cash or another financial instrument from a second entity or (*b*) to exchange other financial instruments on potentially favorable terms with the second entity (ASC Glossary).

The term *financial liability* refers to a contract that imposes a contractual obligation on one entity (*a*) to deliver cash or another financial instrument to a second entity or (*b*) to exchange other financial instruments on potentially unfavorable terms with the second entity (ASC Glossary).

The term *transfer* refers to the conveyance of a noncash financial asset to someone other than the issuer of that financial asset. Examples are selling a receivable, putting it into a securitization trust, or posting it as collateral. It excludes the origination of the receivable, the settlement of the receivable, or the restructuring of the receivable into a security in a troubled debt restructuring. The *transferor* is the party that transfers a financial asset (or part of a financial asset or a group of financial assets) that it controls to another entity. The *transferee* is the entity that receives a financial asset from the transferor (ASC Glossary).

The term *servicing asset* refers to a contract to service financial assets under which the estimated future revenues from contractually specified servicing fees, late charges, and other ancillary revenues are expected to more than adequately compensate the servicer for performing the servicing. A service contract is either (1) undertaken in conjunction with selling or securitizing the financial assets being serviced or (2) purchased or assumed separately (ASC Glossary).

The term *servicing liability* refers to a contract to service financial assets under which the estimated future revenues from contractually specified servicing fees, late charges, and other ancillary revenues are not expected to adequately compensate the servicer for performing the servicing (ASC Glossary).

Objectives of the Accounting for Transfers and Servicing of Assets

Transfers of financial assets may take many forms, and accounting for those transfers in which the transferor has no continuing involvement with the transferred financial asset or with the transferee is uncontroversial. Accounting for transfers of financial assets in which the transferor has a continuing involvement with the assets or with the transferee, however, is less straightforward. Examples of continuing involvement include (ASC 860-10-05-4):

- Recourse or guarantee arrangements
- Servicing arrangements
- Agreements to purchase or redeem transferred financial assets
- Options written or held
- Pledges of collateral
- Arrangements to provide financial support
- Derivatives entered into contemporaneously with, or in contemplation of, the transfer
- The transferor's beneficial interests in the transferred financial assets

Issues raised by these types of transactions include the circumstances in which the transfers should be considered as sales of part or all of the assets or as secured borrowings and the accounting by transferors and transferees for sales and secured borrowings.

The FASB has stated two broad objectives in establishing standards for the transfer and servicing of financial assets and the extinguishment of liabilities. The first objective is for each party to the transaction to recognize only assets it controls and liabilities it has incurred, to derecognize assets only when control has been surrendered, and to derecognize liabilities only when they have been extinguished. (The term *derecognize* means the opposite of recognize, namely, to remove previously recognized assets or liabilities from the statement of financial position.) However, financial assets and liabilities may be disaggregated into components, which become separate assets and liabilities, as a result of a sale or transfer (ASC 860-10-05-5).

The second broad objective is that recognition of financial assets and liabilities not be affected by the sequence of transactions that result in their acquisition or incurrence unless the effect of those transactions is to maintain effective control over a transferred financial asset. For example, if a transferor sells financial assets and at the same time writes a put option on those assets, it should recognize the put obligation in the same manner as would an unrelated entity that writes an identical put option on assets it never owned. Certain agreements to repurchase or redeem transferred assets, however, are intended to maintain effective control over the assets and should be accounted for differently than agreements to acquire assets never owned (ASC 860-10-10-1).

Some entities use derivative financial instruments to offset the risks associated with changes in the value of the servicing assets and servicing liabilities. Those derivative instruments are required to be accounted for at fair value, with changes in their fair value being reported in current earnings.

ASC 860 provides guidance for determining whether or not financial assets can be derecognized when those assets are transferred. A transferor's beneficial interests are to be initially recognized at fair value when the transfer is accounted for as a sale.

CONTROL CRITERIA AND TRANSFEROR ACCOUNTING

ASC 860 provides guidance to determine whether the transferor has surrendered control over transferred financial assets. This determination requires the use of judgment and must consider the transferor's continuing involvement in the transferred assets as well as all arrangements or agreements made in connection with the transfer, even if they were not entered into at the time of the transfer (ASC 860-10-40-4).

Transferred financial assets may include the transfer of an entire financial asset, the transfer of a group of entire financial assets, or the transfer of a participating interest in an entire financial asset. A participating interest has the following characteristics (ASC Glossary):

1. From the date of transfer, it conveys proportionate ownership rights in an entire financial asset.

2. From the date of transfer, all cash flows received from the entire financial asset are divided proportionately based on the ownership shares of each participating interest holder.
3. The priority of each participating interest holder is equal, and no participating interest holder's interest is subordinated to the interest of another participating interest holder. Thus, no participating interest holder is entitled to receive cash before any other participating interest holder.
4. No party can pledge or exchange the entire financial asset without the agreement of all participating interest holders.

If a transfer of a portion of an entire financial asset does not meet the criteria for a participating interest, the transferor and transferee must account for the transfer as a secured borrowing (ASC 860-10-40-4B).

A transfer of an entire financial asset, a group of entire financial assets, or a participating interest in an entire financial asset is accounted for as a sale if the transferor surrenders control over those financial assets. The transferor has surrendered control if all of the following conditions are met (ASC 860-10-40-5):

1. The transferred financial assets have been isolated from the transferor (i.e., they are beyond the reach of the transferor and its creditors, even in bankruptcy).
2. Each transferee (or, if the transferee's sole purpose is to engage in securitization or asset-backed financing activities and is not allowed to pledge or exchange the assets it receives, each third-party holder of its beneficial interests) has the right to pledge or exchange the assets (or beneficial interests) it received, and no condition both (a) constrains the transferee (or third-party holder of beneficial interests) from taking advantage of its right to pledge or exchange and (b) provides more than a trivial benefit to the transferor.
3. The transferor, its consolidated affiliates, or its agents do not maintain effective control over the transferred assets or third-party beneficial interests related to the transferred assets. Examples of a transferor's effective control over the transferred financial assets include the following:
    a. An agreement that obligates the transferor to repurchase or redeem the assets before their maturity.
    b. An agreement that gives the transferor the unilateral ability to cause the holder to return specific financial assets other than through a cleanup call. (A cleanup call is an option held by the servicer or its affiliate to purchase the remaining transferred financial assets if the amount of outstanding financial assets or beneficial interests becomes burdensome in relation to the benefits of servicing (ASC Glossary).
    c. An agreement that permits the transferee to require the transferor to repurchase the transferred assets at a price that is so favorable to the transferee that it is probable that the transferee will require the transferor to repurchase them.

SECURITIZATIONS

Securitization refers to the process by which financial assets (such as loans and other receivables) are transformed into securities (ASC Glossary). Securitizations typically involve a transfer of assets to a securitization entity, through which the characteristics of those assets are changed (e.g., by credit enhancements or derivatives that alter the interest rate or currency characteristics of the original cash flows of the assets). The securitization entity issues beneficial interests in those assets to third-party investors. Entities enter into securitization transactions for a variety of reasons, for example, to obtain funding more economically or to change the characteristics of the assets transferred to achieve different regulatory or accounting treatment.

Transfers to a securitization entity should be evaluated under the control criteria, taking into consideration the nature of the entity, the transferor's rights under the arrangement, and the extent of interests that continue to be held by the transferor. For example, a transferor's right to reacquire specific assets held by the securitization entity indicates that the transferor has not relinquished effective control over the assets. Accordingly, the transferor may not account for the transfer of assets as a sale. If the criteria for a sale are not met, then both the transferor and transferee(s) should account for the transaction as a secured borrowing.

In situations where a transfer of assets in a securitization transaction qualifies as a sale, the transferor must recognize any interests it continues to hold (such as subordinated interests or servicing rights). Interest only strips, loans, other receivables, or other beneficial interests that can contractually be prepaid or otherwise settled in a manner that the holder would not recover substantially all of its recorded investment are measured like investments in debt securities and classified as either available-for-sale or trading in accordance with ASC 310 (ASC 310-10-35-45).

PRACTICE POINTER: The evaluation of control criteria for the transfer of assets to a securitization entity and the determination of the gain or loss to be recognized by the transferor are highly technical and much interpreted areas. Practitioners encountering these areas should seek the advice of experts.

Consolidation of Securitization Entities

ASC 810 establishes the term *variable interest entity*, which refers to an entity that has insufficient equity at risk or lack of a controlling financial interest. Specific conditions in ASC 810 must be evaluated to establish whether an entity is a variable interest entity and must therefore be consolidated by the entity determined to be the primary beneficiary. Many securitization entities are variable interest entities subject to ASC 810; however, the guidance in ASC 810 encompasses other types of entities as well. For more detail about this topic, see our discussion of ASC 810.

DISCLOSURES

ASC 860 includes various disclosure requirements related to continuing involvement in transferred assets. These disclosures are summarized as follows (ASC 860-10-50-1):

Condition Requiring Disclosure	Information Required to Be Disclosed
The transferor has continuing involvement with securitizations, asset-backed financing arrangements, and similar transfers that have been recorded as a sale.	
a. For each income statement presented	Characteristics of the transfer (e.g., a discussion of the transferor's continuing involvement)
	The nature and initial fair value of the assets obtained and the liabilities incurred in the transfer
	Gain or loss from the sale of transferred financial assets
	The level within the fair value hierarchy in which the fair value measurements fall
	Key inputs and assumptions used in determining the fair value of assets obtained and liabilities incurred as a result of the sale (e.g., discount rates, expected prepayments and credit losses, etc.)
	Any cash flows between a transferor and a transferee
b. For each statement of financial position presented, regardless of when the transfer occurred	Qualitative and quantitative information about the reasons for and risks related to the transferor's continuing involvement with the transferred financial assets, including how the transfer has changed the transferor's risk profile
	The entity's accounting policies for subsequently measuring assets or liabilities that relate to the transferor's continuing involvement
	Key inputs and assumptions used in determining the fair value of assets or liabilities (e.g., discount rates, expected prepayments and credit losses, etc.)

Condition Requiring Disclosure	Information Required to Be Disclosed
	Results of sensitivity testing: how the fair value of the transferor's interests in the transferred financial assets (including any servicing assets or servicing liabilities) would change given two or more unfavorable variations from the expected level for each key assumption (see previous disclosure)
	Information about the asset quality of transferred financial assets and any other assets that are managed together with them, separated between assets that have been derecognized and assets that continue to be recognized

The disclosures required by ASC 860 may be reported in the aggregate for similar transfers if separately reporting each transfer would not provide more useful information. A transferor must disclose how similar transfers are aggregated and must distinguish transfers that are accounted for as sales from those accounted for as secured borrowings (ASC 860-10-50-4A).

ASC 860-20: SALES OF FINANCIAL ASSETS

RECOGNITION OF ASSETS OBTAINED OR LIABILITIES INCURRED

Upon completion of a transfer of financial assets that meets the conditions required to be accounted for as a sale, the transferor must recognize any assets obtained or liabilities incurred in the sale, including the following (ASC 860-20-25-1):

1. Cash
2. Servicing assets
3. Servicing liabilities
4. In a sale of an entire financial asset or a group of entire financial assets, any of the following:
   a. The transferor's beneficial interest in the transferred financial assets
   b. Put or call options held or written
   c. Forward commitments
   d. Swapsd.

DERECOGNITION OF ASSETS AND LIABILITIES

Sale of a Participating Interest

Upon completion of a transfer of a participating interest that meets the conditions required to be accounted for as a sale, the transferor must (ASC 860-20-40-1A):

1. Allocate the previous carrying amount of the entire financial asset between the participating interest sold and the participating interest

maintained by the transferor, based on their relative fair values at the transfer date

2. Derecognize the participating interest(s) sold
3. Recognize and initially measure at fair value servicing assets, servicing liabilities, and any other assets obtained and liabilities incurred in the sale
4. Recognize any gain or loss on the sale in income
5. Report any participating interest(s) that continue to be held by the transferor as the difference between the previous carrying amount of the entire financial asset and the amount derecognized at the transfer date.

Sale of an Entire Financial Asset Group or Group of Entire Financial Assets

Upon completion of a transfer of an entire financial asset or a group of entire financial assets that meets the conditions required to be accounted for as a sale, the transferor must (ASC 860-20-40-1B):

1. Derecognize the transferred financial assets
2. Recognize and initially measure at fair value servicing assets, servicing liabilities, and any other assets obtained (including a transferor's beneficial interest in the transferred financial assets) and liabilities incurred in the sale
3. Recognize any gain or loss on the sale in income.

If the transferred financial asset had previously been accounted for as an available-for-sale security under ASC 320, the amount in other comprehensive income must be recognized in earnings when the transferred financial assets are derecognized on the transfer date.

DISCLOSURES

ASC 860-20 provides guidance on disclosures for securitizations, asset-backed financing arrangements, and similar transfers that both (1) are accounted for as a sale, and (2) result in the transferor maintaining a continuing involvement with the transferred financial assets. For each income statement presented, the entity must disclose all of the following (ASC 860-20-50-3):

1. The characteristics of the transfer including the following:
    a. A description of the transferor's continuing involvement
    b. The nature and initial fair value of the assets obtained and liabilities incurred in the transfer
    c. The gain or loss from sale of transferred financial assets.
2. The level within the fair value hierarchy in ASC 820 in which the initial fair value measurements fall
3. The key inputs and assumptions used in measuring the initial fair values
4. The valuation techniques used to measure fair value
5. Cash flows between a transferor and transferee

For each statement of financial position presented, an entity must disclose all of the following (ASC 860-20-50-4):

1. Sufficient qualitative and quantitative information about the transferor's continuing involvement with the transferred financial assets to permit financial statement users to assess the reasons for the continuing involvement and the risks related to the transferred financial assets

2. The entity's accounting policies for measuring assets and liabilities related to the continuing involvement

3. The key inputs and assumptions used in measuring the fair value of assets or liabilities related to the transferor's continuing involvement

4. A sensitivity analysis or stress test that shows the hypothetical change in the calculated fair values as a result of two or more unfavorable variations in the key assumption made in measuring fair values

5. A description of the objectives, methodology, and limitations of the sensitivity analysis or stress test

6. Information about the asset quality of transferred financial assets and any other financial assets that the entity manages together with them.

ASC 860-30: SECURED BORROWING AND COLLATERAL

SECURED BORROWING AND COLLATERAL

A debtor may grant a security interest in assets to a lender (identified below as the secured party) as collateral for its obligation under a borrowing. If collateral is transferred to the secured party, the arrangement is often referred to as a *pledge*. In some circumstances, a secured party is permitted to sell or repledge collateral it holds under a pledge.

Accounting for collateral by the debtor and the secured party depends on whether the secured party has the right to sell or repledge the collateral and whether the debtor has defaulted under the secured contract.

The following summarizes the accounting by both the debtor and the secured party for collateral transferred in a secured borrowing under several scenarios (ASC 860-30-25-5):

Scenario	*Accounting Requirements*
The secured party is permitted to sell or repledge the collateral.	*Debtor*—Reclassifies the asset and reports it separately from other assets not so encumbered.
	Secured party—Does not recognize the collateral as its asset.
The secured party sells or repledges the collateral.	*Debtor*—Continues to carry the collateral as its asset.

Scenario	Accounting Requirements
The debtor defaults under the contract secured by the collateral and is no longer entitled to the return of the collateral.	*Secured party*—Recognizes the proceeds from the sale of the collateral and records an obligation to return the asset. *Debtor*—Derecognizes the collateral *Secured party*—Recognizes the collateral as its asset at fair value (or, if the collateral has already been sold, derecognizes the obligation to return the collateral).

Disclosures

ASC 860 includes various disclosure requirements related to secured borrowing and collateral. These disclosures are summarized as follows (ASC 860-30-50-1):

Condition Requiring Disclosure	Information Required to Be Disclosed
Collateral	
1. Entity has entered into repurchase agreements or securities lending transactions.	Policy for requiring collateral or other security
2. Assets have been pledged and they are not reclassified and separately reported in the balance sheet.	The carrying amounts of both the assets and associated liabilities and their classifications
3. Collateral that can be sold or pledged has been accepted by the entity.	The fair value of the collateral Any amount of the collateral that has been sold or pledged A description of the sources and uses of the collateral
Secured Borrowings	
4. Financial assets have been transferred and accounted for as a secured borrowing.	The carrying amounts of both the assets and associated liabilities and their classifications

ASC 860-40: TRANSFERS TO QUALIFYING SPECIAL PURPOSE ENTITIES

The FASB has eliminated this ASC subtopic because of the perceived abuse of special purpose entities during the previous financial crisis.

ASC 860-50: SERVICING ASSETS AND LIABILITIES

ACCOUNTING FOR SERVICING ASSETS AND LIABILITIES

Initial Measurement of Servicing Assets and Servicing Liabilities

Servicing assets and servicing liabilities that are required to be separately recognized shall be initially measured at fair value. An entity is required to recognize a servicing asset or servicing liability each time it undertakes an obligation to service a financial asset by entering into a servicing contract in either of the following situations (ASC 860-50-25-1):

- A servicer's transfer of an entire financial asset, a group of entire financial assets, or a participating interest in an entire financial asset that meets the requirements for sale accounting.

- An acquisition or assumption of a servicing obligation that does not relate to financial assets of the servicer or its consolidated affiliates.

An entity that transfers financial assets to an unconsolidated entity in a transfer that qualifies as a sale and that classifies its retained securities as debt securities held-to-maturity in accordance with ASC 320 may either separately recognize its servicing assets or servicing liabilities or report those servicing assets or servicing liabilities together with the asset being serviced.

Subsequent Measurement of Servicing Assets and Servicing Liabilities

An entity may choose between two alternative methods of subsequent measurement for each class of separately recognized servicing assets and servicing liabilities—the amortization method and the fair value measurement method. Using the amortization method, servicing assets and servicing liabilities are amortized over the estimated service period and assessed for impairment or increased obligation based on fair value at each reporting period. Using the fair value measurement method, servicing assets and servicing liabilities are measured at their fair value each reporting date with changes in their fair value reported in earnings in the period in which the changes occur.

An entity must separately select, at the beginning of a fiscal year, either the amortization method or the fair value method for subsequent measurement for each class of servicing assets and servicing liabilities and must then apply the selected method to every servicing asset and servicing liability in a class. Classes of servicing assets and servicing liabilities are identified based on (*a*) the availability of market inputs used in determining the fair values, (*b*) an entity's method for managing the risks of its servicing assets and servicing liabilities, or (*c*) both (*a*) and (*b*). An election to use the fair value method for subsequent measurement for a class of servicing assets and servicing liabilities cannot be later reversed (ASC 860-50-35-3).

One-Time Option to Reclassify Available-for-Sale Securities

An entity may make a one-time election to reclassify available-for-sale securities as trading securities without calling into question the treatment of those securities under ASC 320. This election is limited to those available-for-sale securities that an entity intended to use to mitigate the income statement effects of changes in the fair value of servicing assets and servicing liabilities for which the entity has elected the fair value method of subsequent measurement.

Disclosures

ASC 860 includes various disclosure requirements related to transfers and servicing of financial assets. These disclosures are summarized as follows (ASC 860-50-50-2, 3, 4):

Condition Requiring Disclosure	Information Required to Be Disclosed
1. The entity has servicing assets or servicing liabilities.	Management's basis for determining its classes
	Description of risks and, if applicable, the instruments used to mitigate the income statements effect of changes in their fair value
	Amount of contractually specified servicing fees earned for each period Quantitative and qualitative information about the assumptions used to estimate the fair value
2. Servicing assets and servicing liabilities are subsequently measured at fair value.	For each class, the activity in the balance of servicing assets and the activity in the balance of servicing liabilities
3. Servicing assets and servicing liabilities are subsequently amortized.	For each class, the activity in the balance of servicing assets and the activity in the balance of servicing liabilities
	For each class, the fair value at the beginning and end of the period
	Risk characteristics used to stratify for purposes of measuring impairment
	Activity by class in any valuation allowance for impairment of recognized servicing assets

EXTINGUISHMENT OF LIABILITIES

A liability is considered extinguished if: (1) the debtor is relieved of its obligations as a result of having paid the creditor or (2) the debtor is legally released from its obligation. A liability must be extinguished before the debtor is permitted to derecognize the liability (ASC 405-20-40-1).

IMPLEMENTATION GUIDANCE

Appendix A of ASC 860 describes certain provisions of the standard in more detail and describes how they apply to certain types of transactions.

The specific areas for which implementation guidance is provided are as follows:

- Unit of account
- Participating interests in an entire financial asset
- Isolation beyond the reach of the transferor and its creditors
- Conditions that constrain a transferee
- Effective control over transferred financial assets or beneficial interests
- Changes that result in the transferor's regaining control of financial assets sold
- Measurement of interests held after a transfer of financial assets

- Participating interests in financial assets that continue to be held by a transferor
- Servicing assets and liabilities
- Securitizations
- Removal-of-accounts provisions
- Sales-type and direct financing lease receivables
- Securities lending transactions
- Repurchase agreements and "wash sales"
- Loan syndications
- Loan participations
- Banker's acceptances and risk participations in them
- Factoring arrangements
- Transfers of receivables with recourse
- Extinguishments of liabilities

The following illustrations highlight two of the most important aspects of ASC 860 for which implementation guidance is provided. These illustrations also provide a flavor of the type of implementation guidance included in ASC 860 for all of the areas listed above.

Measurement of Interests Held after a Transfer of Financial Assets

The financial-components approach recognizes that financial assets and liabilities are divisible into a variety of components. The approach requires accounting recognition of these different components, rather than treating a financial asset as an inseparable unit that has been entirely sold or entirely retained. This approach is applied in the following illustration, in which the primary transaction is the sale of loans for cash, but in which a separate financial asset is recognized for an interest rate swap, and a separate financial liability is recognized for the recourse obligation.

Illustration of Recording Transfers with Proceeds of Cash, Derivatives, and Other Liabilities

Fowler Company receives $2,610 in cash by selling loans with a fair value of $2,590 and a carrying amount of $2,500, undertaking no servicing responsibility. Fowler Company assumes a recourse obligation (valued at $120) to purchase delinquent loans. Fowler Company simultaneously enters into an interest rate swap agreement (valued at $100) with the transferee in which it receives fixed interest at an above-market rate and pays a floating rate.

The net proceeds and gain on the sale are determined as follows:

Net proceeds:	
Cash received	$2,610
Plus: Interest rate swap	100
Less: Recourse obligation	(120)
	$2,590

Carrying amount of loans		(2,500)
Gain on sale	$90	

The general journal entry to record the transfer and recognize related assets and liabilities is:

Cash	$2,610	
Interest rate swap	100	
Loans		$2,500
Recourse obligation		120
Gain on sale		90

Participating Interests in Financial Assets That Continue to Be Held by a Transferor

Interests in financial assets that continue to be held by the transferor are not included as part of the proceeds from the transfer and are measured at the date of the transfer by allocating the previous carrying amount to the components based on their relative fair values. The following illustration demonstrates these procedures in a situation in which a company sells loans with a recourse obligation, agrees to service the loans, and continues to hold an interest in the loans via an interest-only strip receivable.

Illustrations of Recording Transfers with Interests That Continue to Be Held by a Transferor

Anderson Company sells loans with a carrying amount of $2,600 to another entity for cash. Anderson Company agrees to service the transferred loans for the other entity and incurs a recourse obligation to repurchase any delinquent loans. Anderson Company also continues to hold an interest in the loans via an interest-only strip receivable.

Fair values are as follows: servicing asset, $90; recourse obligation, $150; interest-only strip receivable, $100. Anderson received $2,905 in cash.

The net proceeds are determined as follows:

Cash received	$2,905
Plus: Servicing assets	90
Less: Recourse obligation	(150)
Net proceeds	$2,845

This carrying amount is allocated to the loans sold and the servicing asset based on relative fair values as follows:

	Fair Value	Percentage of Total Fair Value	Allocated Carrying Amount
Loans sold	$2,845	97	$2,522
Interest-only strip-receivable	100	3	78
Total	$2,945	100	$2,600

The general journal entry to record the transfer is as follows:

Cash	$2,905	
Servicing asset	90	
Interest-only strip receivable	78	
Loans		$2,600
Recourse obligation		150
Gain		323

PART II: INTERPRETIVE GUIDANCE

ASC 860-10: Overall

ASC 860-10-05-12 through 05-13, 05-22, 10-9, 10-12, 10-13, 10-22, 15-4, 35-5, 35-8, 35-10 through 35-12, 40-7, 40-9, 40-11, 40-12, 40-14, 40-24, 40-26, 40-27, 40-29, 40-31, 40-33, 40-40, 55-3, 55-4, 55-7 through 55-18, 55-24A, 55-25A, 55-27 through 55-33, 55-38 through 55-42; 55-46, 55-51, 55-54, 55-58, 55-59, 55-69 55-62 through 55-64, 55-66 through 55-70, 55-75 through 55-79; ASC 860-20-25-6, 35-2, 35-3, 35-5, 35-7, 35-8, 55-3 through 55-9, 55-11 through 55-16, 55-24, 55-25, 55-28, 55-31, 55-34 through 55-39, 55-60, 55-61, 55-101 through 55-107, ASC 860-30-15-2, 15-3, 25-9, 35-2, 35-3, 45-2, 45-3,ASC 860-40-05-6, 15-11, 15-15, 15-19 through 15-28, 40-11, 45-2, 45-4, 55-3, 55-11, 55-12, 55-14 through 55-16, 55-18 through 55-20, 55-23 through 55-25, 55-27 through 55-29; ASC 860-50-25-7 through 25-9, 30-2through 30-9, 35-11 through 35-14, 35-15, 50-5; 55-4 through 55-11, 55-13 through 55-18; ASC 320-10-25-5, 25-18; ASC 405-20-55-5 through 55-9
A Guide to Implementation of Statement 140 on Accounting for Transfers and Servicing of Financial Assets and Extinguishments of Liabilities

ACCOUNTING GUIDANCE

Scope

Question 1: If a right to receive the minimum lease payments to be obtained under an operating lease is transferred, could that right be considered a financial asset within the scope of?

Answer: No. The guidance in ASC 860 does not apply to an unrecognized financial asset.

Question 2: Is a transfer of servicing rights that are contractually separated from the underlying serviced assets within the scope of ASC 860? For example, does the guidance in ASC 860 apply to an entity's conveyance of mortgage servicing rights that have been separated from an underlying mortgage loan portfolio that the entity intends to retain?

Answer: No. ASC 860-10-15-4 states that transfers of nonfinancial assets, for example, servicing assets are not addressed in ASC 860. See the discussion in ASC 860-50-40-3 through 40-5 (Determination of What Risks and Rewards, If Any, Can Be Retained and Whether Any Unresolved Contingencies May Exist in a Sale of Mortgage Loan Servicing Rights) for the treatment of servicing rights that have been separated from the underlying serviced assets.

ASC 860—Transfers and Servicing

Question 3: Is a debtor's conveyance of cash or noncash financial assets in full or partial settlement of an obligation to a creditor considered a transfer under the guidance in ASC 860?

Answer: No. A transfer involves the conveyance of a noncash financial asset by and to someone other than the originator of the financial asset.

Question 4: Does the guidance in ASC 860 address a reacquisition by an entity of its own securities by exchanging noncash financial assets (e.g., U.S. Treasury bonds or shares of an unconsolidated investee) for its common shares?

Answer: No. The guidance in ASC 860 does not address either investments by, or distributions to, owners.

Question 5: Do the provisions of ASC 860 apply to "desecuritizations" of securities into loans or other financial assets?

Answer: No. See the discussion in in ASC 320-10-25-18; ASC 860-10-55-34, 55-74 (The Applicability of FAS-115 to Desecuritizations of Financial Assets) for additional information.

Question 6: Are securitized stranded costs of a utility company a financial asset, and would the transfer of the asset be within the scope of ASC 860 ?

Answer: No. Securitized stranded costs do not meet the definition of a financial asset. The cash flows that arise from securitized stranded costs are the result of government regulation; they do not flow from a contract between two or more parties.

Question 7: Would a transfer of beneficial interests in a securitization trust that holds nonfinancial assets, such as securitized stranded costs or other similar rights by third-party investors, be within the scope of ASC 860?

Answer: Yes. In general, the beneficial interests in such a trust would be considered financial assets by third-party investors.

Question 8: Is a judgment from litigation a financial asset?

Answer: Generally not. However, a financial asset exists when a court judgment is reduced to contractually specified payment terms.

Question 9: Is a judgment from litigation a financial asset if it is transferred to an unrelated third party (i.e., would the transfer be within the scope of ASC 860)?

Answer: Yes, if the judgment is enforceable and has been reduced to a contractually specified payment schedule.

Question 10: Does the guidance in ASC 860 apply to a transfer of an ownership interest in a consolidated subsidiary by its parent if that consolidated subsidiary holds nonfinancial assets?

Answer: No. An ownership interest in a consolidated subsidiary denotes an interest in individual assets and liabilities. Some of these assets are nonfinancial in nature.

Question 11: This question was deleted because the concept of temporary control was eliminated by the guidance in ASC 360-10.

Question 12: Would the guidance in ASC 860 apply to a transfer of an investment in a controlled entity that has not been consolidated because that entity accounts for its investment at fair value (e.g., a broker-dealer or an investment company)?

Answer: Generally, yes. An entity that carries an investment in a subsidiary at fair value will realize its investment by transferring that investment, which is a financial asset, rather than by the realization of the underlying assets and liabilities, which might include nonfinancial assets.

Question 13: Is a transfer of an equity method investment within the scope of ASC 860?

Answer: Yes, unless the transfer is in substance a sale of real estate, as defined in FIN-43 (Real Estate Sales). The guidance in ASC 360, *Property, Plant and Equipment*; ASC 976, *Real Estate—Retail Land*, ASC 845, *Nonmonetary Transactions*), and ASC 845-10-05-11, 15-12 to 15-17, 15-20, 35-3 25-6 through 25-12, 30-12 through 30-14, 30-21 through 30-23, S30-2, 55-2, 55-27 through 55-37, 60-3, S99-3 (Exchanges Involving Monetary Consideration) for guidance.

Question 14: Is a forward contract on a financial instrument that must be (or may be) physically settled by the delivery of that financial instrument in exchange for cash a financial asset or liability, the transfer (or extinguishment in the case of a liability) of which would be within the scope of ASC 860?

Answer: Yes.

Question 15: Is a transfer of a recognized financial instrument that may be a financial asset or a financial liability at any point in time, such as during a forward or swap contract, subject to the provisions of both ASC 860-10-40-4, 40-5 and ASC 405-20-40-1?

Answer: Yes. Certain financial instruments (e.g., forwards or swaps) may ultimately prove to be either financial assets or liabilities. Therefore, transfers of these types of financial instruments must meet the requirements of both ASC 860-20-40-4, 40-5 (regarding assets) and ASC 405-20-40-1 (regarding liabilities) to be derecognized.

Question 16: Does the guidance in ASC 860 apply to a transfer of a recognized derivative instrument that is not a financial instrument?

Answer: Yes. The guidance in ASC 860 does apply if a derivative involves a nonfinancial liability (e.g., a written commodity option) at the date of transfer, because the guidance in ASC 860 applies to the extinguishments of all liabilities. Some derivatives have characteristics of both nonfinancial assets and nonfinancial liabilities (e.g., a commodity forward contract). In such cases, the guidance in ASC 860 does apply, but it does *not* apply if a derivative involves a nonfinancial asset (e.g., an option to purchase a commodity) at the date of transfer. However, the transfer of nonfinancial derivative instruments, subject to the requirements in ASC 815, should be accounted for using the guidance in ASC 860 (see ASC 815-10-40-2, 40-3; 860-10-15-5; 40-40 (Accounting for Transfers of Assets That Are Derivative Instruments but That Are Not Financial Assets) for additional discussion of this issue).

Control Criteria—Isolation

Question 17: What type of evidence is sufficient to provide reasonable assurance that transferred financial assets are isolated beyond the reach of the transferor and its consolidated affiliates under the guidance in ASC 860?

Answer: There must be reasonable assurance that the transferred financial assets could not be reached by creditors in bankruptcy or other receiver for the transferor or its consolidated affiliates, if any, included in the financial statements being presented and its creditors. The Audit Issues Task Force has issued guidance on evaluating legal interpretations in support of management's assertion that the isolation criterion has been met.

PRACTICE POINTER: Evaluating whether transferred assets are isolated beyond the reach of the transferor (and the transferor's creditors, even in bankruptcy) is primarily a legal judgment. Therefore, the auditor will typically not be able to evaluate management's assertion that transferred assets are appropriately isolated in the absence of a legal letter. The legal letter must not (1) restrict the auditor's reliance on the letter, (2) disclaim an opinion, (3) restrict its scope to facts and circumstances not applicable to the particular transfer, and (4) express its conclusions using conditional language, such as that contained in the Audit Issues Task Force's interpretation (e.g., "In our opinion, the transfer should be considered a sale . . . ").

PRACTICE POINTER: In evaluating whether transferred assets are isolated beyond the reach of the transferor (and the transferor's creditors, even in bankruptcy), a legal specialist should consider the following factors: (1) the structure of the transfer, (2) the nature of the transferor's continuing involvement, if any, with the transferred assets, (3) the type of insolvency or other receivership proceedings applicable to the transferor if it fails, and (4) other applicable legal factors.

Question 18: Is the requirement in ASC 860-10-40-5 (i.e., the isolation requirement) satisfied if the likelihood of bankruptcy is remote?

Answer: No. The focus is not on whether bankruptcy is remote, but whether the transferred financial assets would be isolated from the transferor in the event of bankruptcy.

Question 19: Are transferred financial assets isolated from the transferor in those cases in which the Federal Deposit Insurance Corporation (FDIC) would act as a receiver if the transferor failed?

Answer: Generally, yes. The FDIC cannot recover, reclaim, or recharacterize financial assets transferred by an insured depository institution if the transfer met all the requirements ASC 860 for sale accounting treatment, except the requirement that the transferred assets be legally isolated for the transferor's creditors. Finally, the Auditing Interpretation (the Use of Legal Interpretations As Evidential Matter to support Management's Assertion that a Transfer of Financial Assets Has Met the Isolation Criterion in ASC 860-10-40-5) was issue to help auditors assess when transferred assets would be beyond the reach of the FDIC.

Question 19A: Can financial assets transferred by an entity subject to possible receivership by the FDIC be considered isolated from the transferor (i.e., can the transfer meet the condition in ASC 860-10-40-4 and 40-5 if circumstances arise under which *the FDIC or another creditor* can require their return?

Answer: Yes. If an entity subject to possible receivership by the FDIC transfers financial assets, they are isolated from the transferor if the FDIC or another creditor cannot require that the financial assets be returned or can only require a return in receivership, after a default, and in exchange for payment of, at a minimum, principal and interest earned at the contractual yield to the date that investors paid. See Question 19C for guidance if a transferor can require that the transferred financial assets be returned.

Question 19B: Does the answer to Question 19A also apply to financial assets that an entity transferred subject to *the U.S. Bankruptcy Code*?

Answer: No. According to the guidance in ASC 860-10-55-19 through 55-23, transfers of financial assets by entities subject to the U.S. Bankruptcy Court meet the condition in ASC 860-10-40-4 and 40-5 if the transferred financial asset have been "put presumptively beyond the reach of the transferor and its creditors, even in bankruptcy . . . " That treatment differs from the treatment for receivership under the FDIC.

Question 19C: Can financial assets transferred by any entity be considered isolated from *the transferor* (i.e., can the transfer meet the condition in ASC 860-10-40-4 and 40-5 if circumstances can arise under which *the transferor* can require their return, only in exchange for payment of principal and interest earned (at the contractual yield) to the date investors are paid?

Answer: No, unless the transferor has the ability to require the return of the transferred financial assets solely from a contract with the transferee.

Question 19D: Which of the answers in questions 19A-19C applies to entities subject to possible receivership under jurisdictions other than the FDIC or the U.S. Bankruptcy Code?

Answer: It depends on the circumstances that apply to those entities. Under the guidance in ASC 860-10-55-24 and 55-25A, judgments about the isolation of transferred financial assets of entities that are subject to other possible bankruptcy, conservatorship, or other receivership procedures should be made in comparison to the powers of bankruptcy courts or trustees, conservators, or receivers in those jurisdictions. The same types of judgments may need to be made about the powers of a transferor and its creditors.

Question 20: Could a transfer from one subsidiary (the transferor) to another subsidiary (the transferee) of a common parent be accounted for as a sale for each subsidiary's separate-company financial statements?

Answer: Yes, if two conditions are met. First, the requirements of ASC 860-10-40-4 and 40-5, including the isolation requirement, must be met. Second, the financial statements of the transferee cannot be consolidated with the separate-company financial statements of the transferor.

Question 21: This question has been deleted because ASC 860-10-40-5 through 6A has amended the definition of proceeds in ASC 860 to include beneficial interests.

Control Criteria—Conditions That Constrain a Transferee

Question 22: Assuming that all of the other requirements of ASC 860-10-40-4, 5 are met, has a transferor surrendered control over transferred financial assets if the transferee, which is not an entity whose sole purpose is to engage in securitization or asset-backed financing activities is precluded from exchanging the transferred assets but obtains the unconstrained right to pledge them?

Answer: It depends. If the transferee is able to obtain most of the cash flows associated with the transferred financial assets either by transferring or pledging those assets, the transferee would have control over the transferred assets.

Question 22A: Entity A transfers a financial asset to Entity B which has a significantly limited ability to pledge or exchange the transferred assets and is not an entity whose sole purpose is to engage in securitization or asset-backed financing activities. The transferor receives cash for the transferred financial assets and has *no* continuing involvement with those assets. Does this transfer qualify under the requirements in ASC 860-10-40-5?

Answer: Yes. The requirements in ASC 860-10-40-5 would *not* be met if Entity B were *not* permitted to pledge or exchange the transferred financial asset and the transferor received a benefit from that limitation that is more than insignificant. However, if a transferor has any continuing involvement after a transfer to an entity that is not a securitization entity, the transferor should evaluate whether the requirements in ASC 860-10-40-5 have been met, in accordance with the guidance in ASC 860-10-40-15-6 through 15-7, 15-18.

Question 23: In certain loan participation agreements that involve transfers of participating interests, the transferor is required to approve any subsequent transfers or pledges of the interests in the loans held by the transferee. Would that requirement be a constraint that would prevent the transferee from taking advantage of its right to pledge or to exchange the transferred financial asset and, therefore, preclude accounting for the transfer as a sale?

Answer: It depends, and judgment clearly is necessary. A requirement that constrains the transferee from selling or pledging the transferred assets and that provides more than a trivial benefit to the transferor would result in sale accounting being precluded. In that case, the transferor has not given up control and should account for such transfers as secured borrowings. However, ASC 860 also indicates that a requirement to obtain the transferor's permission before selling or pledging the transferred assets—if such permission is not unreasonably withheld—typically does not constrain the transferee from selling or pledging the related assets.

Question 24: If a securitization entity issues beneficial interests in the form of Rule 144A securities and the holder of those beneficial interests may not transfer them unless an exemption from the 1933 U.S. Securities Act registration is available, do the limits on the transferability of the beneficial interests result in a constraint on the transferee's right to pledge or exchange those beneficial interests and, therefore, preclude sale accounting by the transferor?

Answer: It depends. The primary limitation on the sale of Rule 144A securities is that the buyer must be a sophisticated investor. If a large number of such investors exist, there would be no effective constraint on the transferee's right to pledge or exchange the asset.

Questions 24a through 30: These questions have been deleted because the concept of a qualifying special-purpose entity has been removed from ASC 860.

Question 31: Credit card securitizations often include a "removal-of-accounts provision" (ROAP) that permits the seller, under certain conditions and with trustee approval, to withdraw receivables from the pool of securitized receivables. Does a transferor's right to remove receivables from a credit card securitization preclude accounting for a transfer as a sale?

Answer: It depends on the rights that the transferor has under the ROAP. A ROAP that does not allow the transferor to unilaterally reclaim specific financial assets from the transferee does not preclude sale accounting.

Question 32: If a transferor is permitted to dissolve a securitization entity (e.g., through the beneficial interests that it holds) and reassume control of the transferred financial assets, is the transferor precluded from accounting for the transfer as a sale?

Answer: Yes. In this case, the transferor effectively maintains control over the assets through its ability to dissolve the securitization entity and reclaim the assets.

Questions 33 through 41: These questions have been deleted because the concept of a securitization entity has been removed from ASC 860.

Control Criteria—Effective Control

Question 42: Dollar-roll repurchase agreements (also called dollar rolls) are agreements to sell and repurchase similar but not identical securities. Dollar rolls differ from regular repurchase agreements in that the securities sold and repurchased, which are usually of the same issuer, are represented by different certificates, are collateralized by different but similar mortgage pools (e.g., conforming single-family residential mortgages), and generally have different principal amounts. Is a transfer of financial assets that are under a dollar-roll repurchase agreement within the scope of ASC 860?

Answer: Yes, if the dollar-roll repurchase agreement pertains to the transfer of securities that already exist.

Question 43: Does ASC 860-10-40-5 preclude sale accounting for a dollar-roll transaction that is subject to the provisions of ASC 860?

Answer: It depends. In order for sale accounting to be precluded, the transferred financial assets to be repurchased must be the same or substantially the same as the assets transferred. All of six characteristics discussed in ASC 860-40-24; ASC

860-10-55-35) must exist in order to meet the substantially-the-same requirement (see ASC 860-10-40-24 for further details).

Question 44: In a transfer of existing securities under a dollar-roll repurchase agreement, if the transferee is committed to return substantially the same securities to the transferor but that transferee's securities were to be announced at the time of transfer, would the transferor be precluded from accounting for the transfer as a secured borrowing?

Answer: No. The transferor is only required to obtain a commitment from the transferee to return substantially the same securities. The transferor is not required to determine that the transferee holds the securities that it is committed to return.

Question 45: ASC 860-10-40-24 states that to be able to repurchase or redeem financial assets on substantially the agreed terms, even in the event of default by the transferee, a transferor must at all times during the contract term have obtained cash or other collateral sufficient to fund substantially all of the cost of purchasing replacement financial assets from others. Would a transferor maintain effective control if, under the arrangement, the transferor is substantially overcollateralized at the date of transfer even though the arrangement does not provide for frequent adjustments to the amount of collateral maintained by the transferor?

Answer: No. If a mechanism does not exist to ensure that adequate collateral is maintained—even for a transaction that is substantially overcollateralized—sale accounting would not be precluded.

Question 46: ASC 860-10-40-24 requires that " . . . a transferor must at all times during the contract term have obtained cash or other collateral sufficient to fund substantially all of the cost of purchasing replacement financial assets from others." *Substantially all* is not specifically defined in ASC 860. Should entities interpret *substantially all* to mean 90% or more?

Answer: No. The FASB consciously decided not to provide a percentage test for the term *substantially all*. Judgment is required in interpreting this term, as well as interpreting the other criterion regarding whether the terms of a repurchase agreement fail to maintain effective control over the transferred asset.

Question 47: Does ASC 860 contain special provisions for differences in collateral maintenance requirements that exist in markets outside the United States?

Answer: No. The general provisions of ASC 860 apply. Therefore, the fact that some foreign markets typically do not require collateral for repurchase transactions would not preclude sale accounting.

Question 48: The example of effective control in ASC 860-10-40-5 states that the transferor maintains effective control over the financial transferred assets through "an agreement that both entitles and obligates the transferor to repurchase or redeem them before their maturity." What does the term *before maturity* mean in the context of the transferor that maintains effective control under the provisions of ASC 860?

Answer: ASC 860 does not define the term *before maturity*. However, in order for the agreement to be viewed as requiring repurchase or redemption before maturity, the remaining term in the life of the financial asset must be sufficient enough so that the asset could be sold again. That is, the remaining term must not be so short that a net cash payment would be made.

Question 49: How do different types of rights of a transferor to reacquire (call) transferred financial assets affect sale accounting under ASC 860?

Answer: Sale accounting is precluded if a transferor's right to reacquire (call) a transferred financial asset constrains the ability of a transferee to (or, if the transferee is an entity whose sole purpose is to engage in securitization or asset-backed financing activities and that entity is constrained from pledging or exchanging the assets it receives, each third-party holder of its beneficial interests) pledge or exchange the transferred financial assets (or beneficial interests) it received and provides more than a trivial benefit to the transferor.

In addition, ASC 860-10-40-5 precludes sale accounting if a transferor, its consolidated affiliates included in the financial statements being presented, or its agents, maintain effective control over transferred financial assets. For example, sale accounting is precluded if a right to reacquire a transferred financial asset results in either of the following:

1. The transferor, its consolidated affiliates included in the financial statements presented, or its agents, maintain effective control through an agreement that both entitles and obligates the transferor to repurchase or redeem the transferred financial asset before its maturity; or

2. The transferor, its consolidated affiliates included in the financial statements, or its agents, maintains effective control through an agreement that provides the transferor with both the unilateral ability to have the holder return the specific transferred financial assets and a more-than-trivial benefit attributable to that ability, other than through a cleanup call.

A unilateral right to reclaim specific transferred financial assets permits a transferor to maintain effective control and precludes sale accounting if the transferor has the unilateral right to reacquire the transferred financial assets and if that right provides the transferor with more than a trivial benefit. ASC 860-10-40-9 through 40-10, 40-33 through 40-34 states that "a call or other right conveys more than trivial benefit if the price to be paid is fixed, determinable or other otherwise potentially advantageous, unless because that price is so far out of the money or for other reasons it is probable when the option is written that the transferor will not exercise it. (See the table for extensive details regarding provisions for different types of rights of a transferor to reacquire (call) transferred assets.)

Question 50: In certain transactions, the transferor is entitled to repurchase a transferred, amortizing, individual financial asset that is not readily obtainable elsewhere when its remaining principal balance reaches some specified amount, for example, 30% of the original balance. Does FAS-140 permit such a transfer to be accounted for partially as a sale and partially as a secured borrowing?

Answer: If yes, a call enables a transferor to unilaterally force the holder of a transferred financial asset to return the remaining portion of the entire financial asset to the transferor and gives the transferor more than a trivial benefit, the transferor should not account for a transfer of the total financial asset for as a sale. Under the guidance in ASC 860, the provisions related to derecognition should be applied to a transfer of a total financial asset, a group of total financial assets, or a participating interest in a total financial asset. Further, accounting for a transfer of a total financial asset or a participating interest in a total financial asset partially as a sale and partially as a secured borrowing is prohibited. (See Question 49.)

Question 51: Would a transferor's contractual right to repurchase a loan participation that is not a readily obtainable financial asset preclude sale accounting?

Answer: Yes, based on the guidance in ASC 860-10-40-5, each transferee should have the right to pledge or exchange the assets it received and that a transferor cannot (a) restrict a transferee from using its right to pledge or exchange its assets and (b) receive more than a trivial benefit. A transferor's contractual right to repurchase a loan is a call option written by a transferee to the transferor. According to ASC 860-10-40-18, a freestanding call option may benefit the transferor and may restrict a transferee if the transferred financial assets are not readily in the marketplace. If a transferor's right to repurchase a financial asset is not freestanding but is attached to the loan and may be transferred with it, ASC 860-10-40-5 states that a transferor maintains effective control over the transferred financial asset.

Question 52: Deleted.

Question 53: Under the guidance in ASC 860, does a transfer of a debt security classified as held-to-maturity that occurs for a reason other than those specified in ASC 320-10-25-6, 25-9 (taint the entity's held-to-maturity portfolio?

Answer: It depends on how the transfer is handled. If the transfer of the debt security is treated as a sale, the entity's held-to-maturity portfolio would be tainted unless the transfer occurred for one of the reasons specified in (ASC 320-10-25-6, 25-9). If the transfer is accounted for as a secured borrowing, the held-to-maturity portfolio would not be tainted.

Question 54: Deleted the concept of a securitization entity is removed from ASC 860.

Question 55: Assuming that all of the other criteria of ASC 860-10-40-4 through 40-5) are met, is sale accounting appropriate if a cleanup call on a pool of assets in a qualifying SPE is held by a party other than the servicer? For example, sometimes the fair value of beneficial interests retained by a transferor of financial assets who is not the servicer or an affiliate is adversely affected by the amount of transferred financial assets declining to a "low level." If such a transferor has a call exercisable when assets decline to a specified low level, could that be a cleanup call?

Answer: No. Because the transferor is not the servicer or an affiliate of the servicer, the transferor's call on the assets in the qualifying SPE is not a cleanup call for accounting purposes. However, because the call option can only be exercised when the assets reach a certain pre-specified level, the transfer would be recorded as a partial sale (assuming the other provisions of ASC 860-10-40-4, 40-5 are met).

Question 56: In a securitization transaction involving not-readily-obtainable assets, may a transferor that is also the servicer hold a cleanup call if it "contracts out the servicing" to a third party (that is, enters into a subservicing arrangement with a third party) without precluding sale accounting?

Answer: Yes. This is due to the fact that from the SPE's perspective, the transferor remains the servicer. If the subservicer fails to perform under the contract, the transferor remains liable for servicing the assets. However, if the transferor sells the servicing rights to a third party, the transferor could not hold a cleanup call.

Measurement of Assets and Liabilities upon Completion of a Transfer

Question 57: Could a transferor's exchange of one form of beneficial interests in financial assets that have been transferred into a trust for an equivalent, but different, form of beneficial interests in the same transferred financial assets be accounted for as a sale under the guidance in ASC 860?

Answer: No. This type of arrangement definitely does not qualify for sale accounting, and it may not even meet the definition of a transfer in ASC 860. If the exchange is with a trust that originally issued the beneficial interests, a transfer has not occurred.

Question 58: Deleted because ASC 860 requires that derecognition provisions be applied to a transfer of the whole financial asset, a group of whole financial assets, or a participating interest in a whole financial asset. See the guidance in ASC 860-20-40-1; ASC 860-20-25-1 through 25-3; ASC 860-20-30-1 through 30-2).

Question 59: Deleted because a beneficial interest obtained in a transfer of a whole financial asset or a group of whole financial assets accounted for as a sale are considered to be proceeds of the sale and are recognized initially and measured at fair value under the guidance in ASC 860. **Question 60:** Deleted because a beneficial interest obtained in a transfer of a whole financial asset or a group of whole financial assets accounted for as a sale are considered to be proceeds of the sale and are recognized initially and measured at fair value under the guidance in ASC 860.

Question 61: An entity transfers debt securities to a qualifying SPE that has a predetermined life, in exchange for cash and the right to receive proceeds from the eventual sale of the securities. For example, a third party holds a beneficial interest that is initially worth 25% of the fair value of the assets of the qualifying SPE at the date of transfer. The qualifying SPE must sell the transferred securities at a predetermined date and liquidate the qualifying SPE at that time. In addition, the beneficial interests are issued in the form of debt securities, and prior to the transfer those securities are accounted for as available-for-sale in accordance with the guidance in ASC 320. Does the transferor have the option to classify the debt securities as trading at the time of the transfer?

Answer: Generally, no. ASC 320 securities held by the transferor after the transfer convey rights to the same cash flows as the ASC 320 securities held before the transfer. ASC 320 provides that transfers into and from the trading category should be rare. If, however, the transferred securities were not ASC 320 securities prior to the transfer, then the transferor would have the opportunity to decide the appropriate classification of the transferred assets at the date of the transfer.

Question 62: In certain transfers, the transferor retains an interest that should be subsequently accounted for under the guidance in ASC 325-40-05-1 through 05-2, 15-2 through 15-9, 25-1 through 25-3, 30-1 through 30-3, 35-1 through 35-13, 35-15 through 35-16, 45-1, 55-1 through 55-25, 60-7; ASC 310-20-60-1 through 60-2; ASC 310-30-15-5; ASC 320-10-35-38, 55-2 (Recognition of Interest Income and Impairment on Purchased Beneficial Interests and Transferor's Beneficial Interests in Securitized Financial Assets Obtained in a Transfer Accounted for as a Sale). If the transferred asset was accounted for as available-for-sale under the guidance in ASC 320 prior to the transfer, how should the transferor account for amounts in other comprehensive income at the date of transfer?

Answer: The application of that guidance should not result in recognition of earnings of an unrealized gain or loss that had been recognized in accumulated other comprehensive income before it is realized.

Question 63: Deleted because the concept of a securitization entity is deleted. Guidance is provided in Question 62 above.

Question 64: Assume an entity transfers a bond to a qualifying SPE for cash and beneficial interests. When the transferor purchased the bond, it paid a premium (or discount) for it and that premium (or discount) was not fully amortized (or accreted) at the date of the transfer. Would that existing premium or discount continue to be amortized (or accreted)?

Answer: Yes, but only to the extent a sale has not occurred because the transferor retained beneficial interests in the bond.

Question 65: Deleted because under the guidance in ASC 860 derecognition provisions must be applied to a transfer of the whole financial asset, a group of whole financial assets, or a participating interest in a whole financial asset. See the guidance in ASC 860-20-40-1; ASC 860-20-25-1 through 25-3; ASC 860-20-30-1, 30-2.

Question 66: Deleted because ASC 820, *Fair Value Measurement* defines fair value and establishes a framework for measuring fair value.

Question 67: Can the method used by the transferor for providing "recourse" affect the accounting for the transfer?

Answer: Yes. However, before evaluating the accounting treatment for the recourse provision, the transferor must first determine whether a sale has occurred. In some jurisdictions, the recourse provision may suggest that the transferred assets have not been appropriately isolated (i.e., the transferor and its creditors still have access to the assets). If a sale has occurred, the accounting depends on the manner in which the recourse provision is effected. The transferor may agree to reimburse the transferee for amounts not paid by debtors. The transferor would separately recognize a liability for this obligation. Alternatively, the transferor may retain a beneficial interest in the assets that is only receivable after other investors are paid. In such a manner, the transferor in essence retains credit risk. However, in this situation, no recourse liability is needed.

Question 68: What should the transferor consider when determining whether retained credit risk is a separate liability or a part of a retained beneficial interest in the asset?

Answer: If the transferor's liability is limited to a claim on its retained interest in the transferred assets, no separate liability is recognized. The transferor would recognize an asset valuation account for this recourse obligation on the date of transfer. However, if the transferor's obligation under the recourse provision could exceed its retained interest in the transferred assets, a separate liability is recognized.

Question 69: Deleted because the fair value practicability exception has been removed from ASC 860.

Question 70: Deleted because ASC 820 defines fair value and establishes a framework for measuring fair value.

Question 71: Deleted because the fair value practicability exception has been removed from ASC 860.

Question 72: Must a transferor recognize in earnings the gain or loss that results from a transfer of financial assets that is accounted for as a sale, or may the transferor elect to defer recognizing the resulting gain or loss in certain circumstances?

Answer: Sale accounting and the corresponding recognition of gain or loss is not optional if a transfer of financial assets meets the requirements in ASC 860 for sale accounting.

Question 73: Does ASC 860 require disclosures about the assumptions used to estimate fair values of the transferor's retained interests in securitized financial assets or of other assets obtained and liabilities incurred as proceeds in a transfer?

Answer: Yes, see the guidance in ASC 860-20-50-1 through 50-4.

Question 74: Deleted because a beneficial interest obtained in a transfer of a whole financial asset or a group of whole financial assets accounted for as a sale are considered to be proceeds of the sale and are recognized initially and measured at fair value under the guidance in ASC 860.

Question 75: How should a transferor initially and subsequently measure credit enhancements provided in a transfer if the balance that is not needed to make up for credit losses is ultimately to be paid by the transferor?

Answer: Credit enhancements are measured at the date of transfer by allocating previous carrying amounts between assets sold and retained interests, based on relative fair values. Credit enhancements provided by other parties are initially measured at the fair value of the enhancement that is expected to benefit the transferor. The guidance in ASC 860 does not address the subsequent measurement of credit enhancements—other existing authoritative literature should be consulted (e.g., ASC 310-10, Receivables—Overall).

Questions 76 and 77: Deleted because ASC 820 defines fair value and establishes a framework for measuring fair value.

Servicing Assets and Servicing Liabilities

Question 78: ASC 860-50-30-2 states that "typically, the benefits of servicing are expected to be more than *adequate compensation* to the servicer for performing the servicing . . ." (Emphasis added). What is meant by the term *adequate compensation*?

Answer: *Adequate compensation* means the amount of compensation necessary to attract an alternate servicing entity, if one becomes necessary. This amount is determined by the marketplace and includes a provision for normal profit.

Questions 79 through 86: Deleted because the fair value practicability exception has been removed from ASC 860.

Question 87: For sales of mortgage loans, is adequate compensation the same as normal servicing fees previously used in applying the guidance in ASC 948-10 and 948-360?

Answer: No. ASC 860 defines *adequate compensation* as the amount of compensation necessary to attract an alternate servicing entity, should one become necessary. That amount is determined by the marketplace, and includes a provision for normal profit. ASC 948 defines *normal servicing* fees as the amount that was typically charged for servicing a particular type of loan. Often, a normal servicing rate as formerly determined under the guidance in ASC 948 would exceed the definition of *adequate compensation* in ASC 860.

Question 88: Do the types of assets being serviced affect the amount required to adequately compensate the servicer?

Answer: Yes, since different asset classes require different levels of effort to service. The nature of the assets being serviced should be considered a factor in determining the fair value of a servicing asset or servicing liability.

Question 89: Does a contractual provision that specifies the amount of servicing fees that would be paid to a replacement servicer affect the determination of adequate compensation?

Answer: No. A contractually specified amount that would be paid to a replacement servicer could be more or less than adequate compensation.

Question 90: If market rates for servicing a specific type of financial asset change subsequent to the initial recognition of a servicing asset or servicing liability, does ASC 860 include any requirement to adjust the recorded asset or liability?

Answer: Yes. In terms of a servicing asset, a change in market rates may indicate that the asset is impaired. In terms of a servicing liability, a change in market values may increase the liability. Such an increase in the liability would be recorded as a loss in the income statement.

Question 91: Do additional transfers under revolving-period securitizations (e.g., home equity loans or credit card receivables) result in the recognition of additional servicing assets or servicing liabilities?

Answer: Yes. Servicing assets and liabilities arise from the sale of new receivables.

Question 92: The question and answer have been nullified by ASC 860, *Transfers and Servicing*, which provides specific guidance in its amendment to ASC 860-50-45-1 through 45-2, 25-1, 25-4, 30-1, 30-8, -35-1 through 35-5, 35-15.

Question 93: How should an entity account for rights to future income from serviced assets that exceed contractually specified servicing fees?

Answer: If the benefits to servicing are expected to exceed adequate compensation, the servicer should record a servicing asset, an interest-only strip, or both. For example, the servicer may be entitled to receive interest income from serviced assets that exceeds contractually specified servicing fees. This would represent a financial asset, not a servicing asset, and would effectively be an interest-only strip.

Question 94: Should a loss be recognized if a servicing fee that is equal to or greater than adequate compensation is to be received but the servicer's anticipated cost of servicing would exceed the fee?

Answer: No. Recognition of a servicing asset or a servicing liability depends on the marketplace, not on a servicer's cost of servicing.

Servicing—Other

Question 95: Should an entity recognize a servicing liability if it transfers all or some of a financial asset that meets the definition of a participating interest that is accounted for as a sale and retains an obligation to service the asset but is not entitled to receive a contractually specified servicing fee? Is the answer to this question affected by circumstances in which it is not customary for the transferor/servicer to receive a contractually specified servicing fee?

Answer: Yes. A servicer/transferor would be required to recognize a servicing at fair value if the benefits of servicing are less than adequate compensation.

Question 96: A selling entity (*a*) transfers a portion of a loan under a participation agreement that meets the definition of a participating interest and qualifies for sale accounting under FAS-140, (*b*) obtains the right to receive benefits of servicing that more than adequately compensate it for servicing the loan, and (*c*) and continues to service the loan, regardless of the transfer because it (the selling entity) retains part of the participated loan. In these circumstances, is the selling entity required to record a servicing asset?

Answer: Yes, the selling entity is required to record a servicing asset for the portion of the loans it sold. If the benefits of servicing are significantly greater than an amount that would be fair compensation for a substitute service provider, if one were to be required, the transferred portion does not meet the definition of a participating interest. Consequently, the transfer would not qualify for sale accounting.

Question 97: A transferor that sells mortgage loans that it originated in a transfer that is accounted for as a sale takes on the obligation to service them. Immediately thereafter the transferor enters into an arrangement to subcontract that obligation to another servicer. How should the transferor account for the obligation to service the loans in this situation?

Answer: The transferor should account separately for the two transactions. The sale of the mortgage loans and the obligation to service those loans should be accounted for in accordance with the guidance in ASC 860. The obligation to service the loans should be initially recognized and measured at fair value in accordance with the guidance in ASC 860-20-25-1 through 25-2, 401B. (A transferor's accounting for the subcontract with another servicer is not under the scope of the guidance in ASC 860, but should be accounted for under existing guidance).

Question 98: When servicing assets are assumed without cash payment, what is the appropriate offsetting entry to be made by the transferee?

Answer: If an exchange has occurred, the transaction should be recorded based on the facts and circumstances. On the other hand, if the investor is in substance making a capital contribution to the investee, the investee should recognize an increase in equity from a contribution by owner.

Question 99: ASC 860 requires that an entity separately evaluate and measure impairment of designated strata of servicing assets. If more than one characteristic exists for stratifying servicing assets, must more than one predominant risk characteristic be used?

Answer: No. Under the guidance in ASC 860-50-35-9, servicers are required to stratify servicing assets based on one or more predominant risk characteristics of the underlying financial assets.

Question 100: Under the guidance in ASC 860-50-35-9, a servicer is required to stratify servicing assets based on one or more of the predominant risk characteristics of financial assets. Should the strata selected by the servicer be used consistently from period to period?

Answer: Yes, generally the strata selected should be used consistently from period to period. If a significant change is made, it should be accounted for prospectively as a change in accounting estimate in accordance with the guidance in ASC 255 (Accounting Changes and Error Corrections).

Question 101: Under the guidance in ASC 860, the impairment of servicing assets must be recognized by a valuation allowance for an individual stratum. The valuation allowance should reflect changes in the measurement of impairment subsequent to initial measurement of impairment. Fair value in excess of the carrying amount of servicing assets for that stratum should not be recorded. How should an entity recognize subsequent increases in a previously recognized servicing liability?

Answer: The revised estimate of the liability should be recorded and a loss should be recognized in earnings. Similar to accounting for changes in the valuation allowance of an impaired asset, increases in the servicing obligation may be recovered, but the obligation should not be reduced below the amortized measurement of the initially recognized servicing liability.

Question 102: Deleted because the fair value practicability exception has been removed from FAS-140, as amended by FAS-166.

Question 103: Deleted because ASC 820 defines fair value and establishes a framework for measuring fair value.

Financial Assets Subject to Repayment

Question 104: If an entity recognizes both a servicing asset and the right to receive future interest income from serviced assets in excess of contractually specified servicing fees (an interest-only strip) in a transfer of a whole financial asset to an unconsolidated entity that meets the requirements for sale accounting, should the value of the right to receive future cash flows from ancillary sources (e.g., late fees) be included in measuring the servicing asset or in measuring the interest-only strip?

Answer: Yes, generally in the servicing asset. The value of the right to receive future cash flows from ancillary sources is included in the measurement of the servicing asset if the right to such future cash flow depends, as is customary, on servicing being performed satisfactorily. The value of the right to future cash flows from ancillary sources is generally not included in measuring the interest-only strip.

Question 105: Under the guidance in ASC 860-20-35-2, financial assets, except for instruments accounted for under the scope of ASC 815, that contractually can be prepaid or otherwise settled in such a way that the holder will not recover substantially all of its recorded investment must subsequently be measured like available-for-sale or trading debt securities in accordance with the guidance in ASC 320. Does this mean that those financial assets are included under the scope of ASC 320?

Answer: This depends on the form of the assets, but in either case, the measurement principles of ASC 320, including provisions for recognizing and measuring impairment, should be applied.

Question 106: Can a financial asset that can be contractually prepaid or otherwise settled in such a way that the holder would not recover substantially all of its recorded investment be classified as held-to-maturity if the investor concludes that prepayment or other forms of settlement are remote?

Answer: No. This is not a relevant factor in determining whether the provisions of ASC 860-20-35-2 apply to those financial assets.

Question 107: A transferor transfers mortgage loans in their entirety to a third party in a transfer that is accounted for as a sale but retains servicing. Afterward, the transferor enters into a subservicing arrangement with a third party. If the transferor's benefit of servicing exceeds its obligation under the subservicing agreement, should the difference be accounted for as an interest-only strip?

Answer: No. The transferor should account for the two transactions separately. The transfer of mortgage loans and the obligation to service the loans should be accounted for by the transferor in accordance with the guidance in ASC 860 and the contract with the subscriber should be separately accounted for under other guidance because it is not included in the scope of ASC 860).

Question 108: Can a debt security that is purchased late enough in its life that, even if prepaid, the holder would recover substantially all of its recorded investment, be initially classified as held-to-maturity?

Answer: Yes. A debt security can be classified as held-to-maturity if the conditions of ASC 320-10-25-1, 25-5; ASC 320-10-35-1 are met.

Question 109: May a loan (that is not a debt security), which when initially obtained could be contractually prepaid or otherwise settled in such a way that the holder would not recover substantially all of its recorded investment, be classified as held for investment later in its life?

Answer: Yes, if the following conditions are met: (1) it would no longer be possible for the holder not to recover substantially all of its recorded investment upon contractual prepayment or settlement and (2) the conditions for amortized cost accounting are met.

Question 110: Under the guidance in ASC 860-20-35-2 certain financial assets that are not in the form of debt securities are required to be measured at fair value like investments classified as available-for-sale or classified as trading under the guidance in ASC 320. How should instruments subject to provisions ASC 860-20-35-2 be evaluated for impairment?

Answer: All of the measurement principles of ASC 320 apply, including the recognition and measurement of impairment.

Question 111: Is a financial asset that is not a debt security under the guidance in ASC 320 subject to the requirements of ASC 860-20-35-2 because it is denominated in a foreign currency?

Answer: No. An entity is not required to measure such an investment like a debt security unless it has provisions that allow it to be contractually prepaid or otherwise settled in a way that the holder would not recover substantially all of its recorded investment, as denominated in the foreign currency.

Question 112: Is a note for which the repayment amount is indexed to the creditworthiness of a party other than the issuer subject to the provisions of ASC 860-20-35-2?

Answer: Yes, because the event that might cause the holder to receive less than substantially all of its recorded investment is based on a contractual provision, not on a default by the borrower.

Question 113: Can a residual tranche debt security in a securitization of financial assets using a securitization entity be classified as held-to-maturity?

Answer: The answer depends on the specific facts and circumstances. If the contractual provisions of the residual tranche debt security provide that the residual tranche can contractually be prepaid or otherwise settled so that the holder would not recover substantially all of its recorded investment, the residual tranche debt security should not be accounted for as held-to-maturity. On the other hand, if the only way the holder of the residual tranche would not substantially recover all of its recorded investment is via default of the borrower, then a held-to-maturity classification is acceptable if the conditions specified for that classification in ASC 320-10-25-1(c) and ASC 320-10-25-5(a) are met.

Secured Borrowings and Collateral

Question 114: Are the collateral recognition requirements of ASC 860-30-25-5 limited to transfers by or to broker-dealer entities, or do they apply to other types of borrowings?

Answer: The collateral recognition provisions of ASC 860-30-25-5 apply to the accounting for all transfers of financial assets pledged as collateral that are accounted for as secured borrowings.

Question 115: What is the proper classification by the transferor of securities loaned or transferred under a repurchase agreement that is accounted for as a secured borrowing if the transferee is permitted to sell or repledge those securities, and rights of substitution or termination are not granted to the transferor?

Answer: Pledged assets should be reported in the statement of financial position separately from other assets not so encumbered, but otherwise ASC 860 does not specify the classification or terminology to be used. ASC 860-50-55-22 illustrates possible classifications and terminology.

Question 116: What is the appropriate classification of liabilities incurred in connection with securities borrowing and resale agreement transactions?

Answer: ASC 860 does not specify classification or terminology to be used to describe liabilities by either the secured party or debtor in securities borrowing or resale transactions. Such liabilities should be separately classified.

Question 117: How should a transferor measure transferred collateral that must be reclassified?

Answer: The guidance in ASC 860-30-25-5, requires that transferred collateral that can be sold or repledged by a secured party be reclassified and reported separately by the transferor. However, it does not change the transferor's measurement of that collateral.

Question 118: Does ASC 860 provide guidance for the subsequent measurement of a secured party's obligation to return transferred collateral that the secured party recognized in accordance with the guidance in ASC 860-30-25-5?

Answer: No. ASC 860 generally does not address subsequent measurement of transferred financial assets or the obligation to return transferred collateral. The liability to return the collateral should be measured in accordance with other relevant authoritative literature.

Extinguishment of Liabilities

Question 119: Are liabilities extinguished by legal defeasances?

Answer: Yes, if the condition of ASC 405-20-40-1(b), is satisfied, which requires that the debtor has been legally released.

Question 120: How should a debtor account for the exchange of an outstanding debt instrument with a lender for a new debt instrument with the same lender but with substantially different terms? How should the debtor account for a substantial modification of a debt instrument?

Answer: ASC 405-20-40-1, permits derecognition of a liability only if it is extinguished by the debtor paying the creditor or the debtor being legally released as the primary obligor, either judicially or by the creditor.

Question 121: If an entity is released from being the primary obligor and it becomes a secondary obligor, should the entity recognize the resulting guarantee from being the secondary obligor in the same manner as a third-party guarantor?

Answer: Yes. The entity should recognize the guarantee in the same way it would have as a guarantor that had never been primarily liable.

Question 122: Does the guidance in ASC 860 address impairment of financial assets?

Answer: The guidance in ASC 860 does not address the subsequent measurement of assets and liabilities, except for servicing assets and servicing liabilities and interest strips, other beneficial interests, loans, other receivables, or other financial assets that contractually may be prepaid or settled otherwise so that the holder would not recover all of its recognized investment. Generally impairment should be measured by reference to other applicable authoritative guidance.

Question 123: Many securitization structures provide for a disproportionate distribution of cash flows to various classes of investors during the amortization period (referred to as a turbo provision). What effect do such provisions have on the accounting for transfers of financial assets under the guidance in ASC 860?

Answer: Distribution provisions that diverge from the stated ownership percentages of different parties do not affect whether (1) sale accounting is appropriate or (2) the transferred assets should be derecognized. Differential distribution provisions should be taken into consideration in determining the relative fair values of the portion of transferred assets sold and portions retained by the transferee.

ASC 860-10-05-11; ASC 860-20-35-10, 55-16
Securitization of Credit Card and Other Receivable Portfolios

BACKGROUND

Banks or other financial institutions form pools of receivables consisting of balances owed by credit card customers and transfer an interest in the receivables to a trust. A bank then sells undivided participation interests in the trust to investors. The trust is commonly referred to as a credit card securitization. It has a limited life that can be divided into two phases:

1. A reinvestment phase, during which all receivables generated by customers in the pool are kept by the trust while investors receive interest payments only
2. A liquidation phase, during which investors receive principal payments as well as interest

During the reinvestment phase, usually 18 to 36 months, the trust purchases additional credit card receivables as balances in the selected accounts increase.

Although the percentage of the bank's and investors' participation in the trust's assets may fluctuate up or down during this phase, as a result of charge and payment activities in the selected accounts, the investors' dollar investment in the trust remains constant, because proceeds from repayments (principal payments) allocated to the investors are reinvested in additional credit card receivables.

For example, the following illustrates such activity for a month.

	Credit Card Balances	Investors' Interest	Percentage
Total receivables in trust, 1/1	$1,000,000	$750,000	75.0
Repayments	(100,000)	(75,000)	75.0
Charges	80,000	75,000	93.8
Total receivables in trust, 1/31	$ 980,000	$750,000	76.5

In this example, a larger percentage of charges (93.8% instead of 75%) was allocated to the investors in order to maintain their $750,000 investment in the trust.

During the liquidation period, principal payments on receivables in the trust are allocated to investors, based on the terms of the agreement. The following methods are used:

- The *participation method,* which consists of:
  - *Fixed participation* Based on investors' interests in the receivables at the end of the reinvestment period.
  - *Preset participation* Based on a preset percentage that is higher than investors' participation interests at the end of the reinvestment period. (Results in a faster payout than the fixed participation method.)
  - *Floating participation* Based on investors' actual participation interests in the trust each month. (Interests will decline each month because of repayments.)
- The *controlled amortization method,* which is based on a predetermined monthly payment schedule; investors' interests are liquidated over a specified period. One of the three participation methods is used to allocate principal payments to investors. If principal payments are greater than the predetermined monthly payment, they are allocated to the bank and used to increase the investors' ownership interests. If allocated principal payments are less than the predetermined monthly payment, payments to investors are reduced by the deficiency. The deficiency is recovered in subsequent months if the amount allocated to investors exceeds the predetermined payments.

Credit losses on receivables in the trust generally are allocated to investors based on their actual floating participation interest (participation interests may fluctuate monthly because of an imbalance between charges and payments on accounts), regardless of the liquidation method. However, some form of credit enhancement, such as a third-party letter of credit that exceeds expected credit losses, may be used to mitigate losses allocated to investors.

ACCOUNTING ISSUES

1. Issues 1 and 2 have been nullified.
2. How should a gain or loss on transfer that is recognized as a sale be calculated?

ACCOUNTING GUIDANCE

1. This guidance has been nullified by the guidance in ASC 860, which as been amended by the guidance in ASC 860-10-35-4, 35-6, 05-8; ASC 860-20-25-5; ASC 460-10-60-35; ASC 860-20-55-46 through 55-48; ASC 860-50-05-2 through 05-4, 30-1 through 30-2, 35-1A, 35-3, 35-9 through 35-11, 25-2 through 25-3, 25-6, 50-5.

2. The guidance on the effect of the liquidation method was nullified by the guidance in ASC 860.

3. A gain, if any, on the sale of receivables should not exceed amounts related to existing receivables at the date of the sale. Amounts related to future receivables expected to be sold during the reinvestment period should *not* be included in the gain. (This guidance has been affirmed in ASC 860-50-25-9.) Based on information about certain transactions, some Task Force members noted that a gain on such transactions generally would not be significant, because the receivables sold have a relatively short life, the high cost of servicing credit card loans, and the yields required by the current interest rate environment. In addition, they noted that a transaction's terms should be reviewed to determine whether a loss should be recognized for costs expected to be incurred for all future servicing obligations, including costs for receivables not yet sold. Under the guidance in ASC 860, a servicer is required to recognize a servicing liability if the servicer expects that the costs of performing the service will exceed the benefits and the work is expected to be performed at a loss. Some members also observed that transaction costs related to sales of receivables may be recognized over the initial and reinvestment periods in a rational and systematic manner, unless a transaction results in a loss. (The was affirmed in ASC 860 and was not reconsidered in ASC 860-10-35-4, 35-6, 05-8; ASC 860-20-25-5; ASC 460-10-60-35; ASC 860-20-55-46 through 55-48; ASC 860-50-05-2 through 05-4, 30-1 through 30-2, 35-1A, 35-3, 35-9 through 35-11, 25-2 through 25-3, 25-6; 50-5, which amended the guidance in ASC 860.)

In addition, in accordance with the guidance in ASC 860), transaction costs for a past sale are not an asset and consequently should be included in a gain or loss. However, some of the transaction costs incurred at the beginning of a credit card securitization can qualify for asset recognition because they are related to future sales that will occur during the revolving period.

SUBSEQUENT DEVELOPMENT

The SEC Observer stated in July 1995 that the staff believes that above guidance also applies to securitizations of other types of receivables with similar arrangements.

> **OBSERVATION:** ASC 810-10, Consolidation of Variable Interest Entities, requires the consolidation of variable interest entities by an entity that absorbs a majority of a variable interest entity's expected losses or has the right to receive a greater part of a variable interest entity's expected residual returns or both.

> **OBSERVATION:** Although the guidance in ASC 860-50-35-3, 35-6 through 35-7; 50-5, which amends the accounting guidance in ASC 860 for separately recognized servicing assets and servicing liabilities, its guidance does not affect the guidance in this Issue. The FASB's decision in ASC 860-50-35-3, 35-6 through 35-7, 50-50-5 to replace the term *retained interests* with the term *interests that continue to be held by a transferor* is reflected in this Issue.

ASC 860-10-15-5, 40-40; ASC 815-10-40-2 through 40-3
Accounting for Transfers of Assets That Are Derivative Instruments but That Are Not Financial Assets

BACKGROUND

This Issue was raised because it was unclear how to account for transfers of *nonfinancial* assets that are accounted for as derivatives under the guidance in ASC 815. Transfers of such derivatives are excluded from the scope of ASC 860, which applies only to transfers of *financial* assets and financial liabilities, as defined in ASC *Glossary*).

ACCOUNTING ISSUE

How should transfers of nonfinancial assets that are accounted for as derivatives under ASC 815 be accounted for?

ACCOUNTING GUIDANCE

1. Transfers of nonfinancial assets (e.g., a forward contract to purchase gold requiring physical settlement) that are considered to be derivatives under the definition in ASC 815 should be accounted for by analogy to ASC 860. However, this guidance does not apply to contracts that may meet the definition of a derivative in ASC 815, for example, contracts issued by an entity in connection with stock-based compensation arrangements addressed in ASC 718 that are excluded from the scope of ASC 815-10-15-74.

2. If a derivative instrument could potentially be both a nonfinancial asset and a nonfinancial liability—for example, a commodity forward contract that is a nonfinancial derivative instrument—the instrument must meet the criteria in ASC 860 to qualify for derecognition.

A special purpose entity that receives nonfinancial assets in a transfer should not be accounted for as a securitization entity under the guidance in ASC 860.

58,040 ASC 860—Transfers and Servicing

ASC 860-20-25-11 through 25-13, 30-4, 35-9, 55-41 through 55-42, 55-62 through 55-92; ASC 860-40-25-2; ASC 860-50-25-10
Accounting for Changes That Result in a Transferor Regaining Control of Financial Assets Sold

BACKGROUND

According to the guidance in ASC 860-20-25-8, a transferor may regain control of financial assets previously accounted for as sold if the transferee no longer meets one of the conditions in ASC 860-10-40-4 through 40-5 that are required for sale accounting. Failure to meet the conditions in ASC 860-10-40-4 through 40-5 is usually a result of a change in law, or other circumstances. If such circumstances occur, a portion of the transferred financial assets may no longer meet the conditions of a participating interest or the transferor may regain control of a transferred financial asset that had been accounted for as a sale because one or more of the conditions in ASC 860-10-40-4 through 40-5 are no longer met. Under those circumstances, the transferor must account for the transferred financial assets as if they have been repurchased from the transferee in exchange for the liabilities assumed by the transferor. The transferor recognizes the transferred financial assets and liabilities at their fair value on the date the change occurs and thereafter reports the assets and the liabilities in its financial statements to the former transferee or other beneficial interest holders in those assets. The transferee derecognizes the transferred financial assets on that date and accounts for them as if they were sold in exchange for a receivable from the transferor. It is assumed in this Issue that the transferor does not consolidate the transferee. However, a transferor that subsequently consolidates an entity that had been involved in a transfer that was accounted for as a sale should apply current guidance.

ACCOUNTING ISSUES

1. How should a transferor account for retained beneficial interests if portions of the underlying assets that had been sold are rerecognized in accordance with the guidance in ASC 860-20-25-8 because the transferor's contingent call option on the transferred assets, such as a removal of accounts provision (ROAP), becomes exercisable? How much of a gain or loss should be recognized under those circumstances?

2. Are there any circumstances under which an allowance should be recorded for assets that are rerecognized at fair value in accordance with ASC 860-20-25-8?

3. How does the rerecognition of assets (or a portion thereof) sold in accordance with ASC 860-20-25-8 affect the accounting for a related servicing asset?

4. How should a transferor subsequently account for its interests, except for servicing assets, after the occurrence of an event that triggers the application of ASC 860-20-25-8?

ACCOUNTING GUIDANCE

1. When applying the guidance in ASC 860-20-25-8, a transferor should recognize no gain or loss in earnings related to its beneficial interests.

Such beneficial interests should be evaluated for impairment when applying that guidance and periodically thereafter. However, a transferor may recognize a gain or loss when exercising a removal of accounts provision (ROAP) or a similar contingent right related to a repurchased transferred financial asset that is not a derivative accounted for under the guidance in FAS ASC 815 and is not at-the-money. That is, the fair value of repurchased assets should not exceed or be less than the transferor's related obligation to the transferee.

2. A transferor should never recognize a loan loss allowance on a loan that does not meet the definition of a security when that loan is initially rerecognized under the guidance in ASC 860-20-25-8.

3. The accounting for a servicing asset related to a previously sold financial asset does not change if an event causing the application of ASC 860-20-25-8 occurs. The contractually required cash flows from the rerecognized assets continue to be paid to the securitization entity, which will use the proceeds to satisfy its contractual obligations, including those to beneficial interest holders. A transferor, as servicer, continues to be contractually required to collect the asset's cash flows for the benefit of the securitization entity and to service the asset in other ways. Therefore, a transferor should continue to recognize the servicing asset and evaluate it for impairment as required in ASC 860.

4. A transferor should not combine an interest in the underlying assets, other than the servicing asset, with rerecognized financial assets after an event occurs that requires the application of the guidance in ASC 860-20-25-8. A transferor's interest should be combined, however, with the underlying assets, if as a result of a subsequent event, the transferor recovers the financial assets from a transferee—for example, by exercising a removal of accounts provision or by consolidating an a securitization entity under GAAP, including ASC 810-10.

ASC 860-10-S40-1, S99-1, 50-40-7 through 40-9; ASC 460-10-60-37
Balance Sheet Treatment of a Sale of Mortgage Servicing Rights with a Subservicing Agreement

BACKGROUND

Mortgage servicers perform administrative services for mortgage investors for which they receive a fee. Among the services they perform are collection of mortgage payments, remittance of escrow taxes and insurance payments to the proper entities, and remittance of the net collections to the investor. The right to receive those fees is recognized in the mortgage servicer's financial statements as an asset referred to as "mortgage servicing rights." A mortgage servicer may sell the right to receive those fees, but may retain the obligation to service the mortgage through a subservicing agreement.

ACCOUNTING ISSUE

Should a transfer of mortgage servicing rights with a subservicing agreement be accounted for (*a*) always as a sale with a gain deferred, (*b*) always as a financing, or (*c*) based on the particular facts and circumstances of the transaction?

ACCOUNTING GUIDANCE

1. A sale of mortgage servicing rights with a subservicing agreement should be accounted for as a sale with gain deferred, if substantially all of the risks and rewards inherent in owning the rights have been effectively transferred to the buyer.

2. The transaction should be treated as a financing if substantially all risks and rewards have *not* been transferred. Risks and rewards associated with a seller performing purely administrative functions under a subservicing agreement would not necessarily preclude sales treatment.

3. Certain factors, if present, provide *conclusive evidence* that substantially all risks and rewards have *not* been transferred and thus preclude sales treatment. Certain other factors, if present, are *presumed to indicate* that substantially all risks and rewards have *not* been transferred. The presumption can be overcome only if there is sufficient evidence to the contrary. Those factors are in the following table:

Conclusive Evidence—No Sales Recognition	Must Be Overcome for Sales Recognition
• The seller/subservicer directly or indirectly guarantees a yield to the buyer.	• The seller/subservicer directly or indirectly provides financing or guarantees the buyer's financing. Nonrecourse financing would indicate that risks have not been transferred.
• The seller/subservicer is obligated to make payments of all or a portion of the subservicing fees to the buyer on a nonrecourse basis prior to receipt from the mortgagor.	• The terms of the subservicing agreement unduly limit the purchaser's ability to exercise the rights associated with ownership. An example is a subservicing agreement that is not cancelable by either party (although a reasonable noncancellation period is allowed).
• The seller/subservicer indemnifies the buyer for damages due to causes other than failure to perform its contractual duties.	• The buyer is a special-purpose entity without sufficient capital at risk.
• The seller/subservicer agrees to absorb losses on mortgage loanforeclosures not covered by government agencies or other guarantors, including absorption of foreclosure costs of managing foreclosed property.	
• Title to the servicing rights is retained by the seller/subservicer.	

There may be other factors that also indicate that the seller has not transferred substantially all risks and rewards associated with ownership to the buyer.

OBSERVATION: Under the provisions of ASC 460, a guarantor is required to recognize a liability for the obligation assumed at the inception of a guarantee.

OBSERVATION: Although the guidance in ASC 860-50-35-3, 35-6 through 35-7, 50-5 does not affect the guidance in this Issue, changes in the fair value of separately recognized servicing assets or servicing liabilities that are measured at fair value subsequent to adoption of that guidance should be included in earnings in the period in which the fair value changes occur. An additional change in the fair value of servicing assets or servicing liabilities, if any, from the last measurement date to a date of sale should be included in earnings at the date of sale.

SEC OBSERVER COMMENT

The SEC Observer noted that the SEC staff believes that if, in substance, a transaction transfers only a portion of the servicing revenue, substantially all the risks and rewards of ownership have not been transferred. Such a transaction should be accounted for under the guidance in ASC 470-10-25-1 through 25-2, 35-3.

DISCUSSION

The primary concerns were related to the transferor's continuing involvement with the loans and whether the risks and rewards have been transferred.

Those who believed that the determination of whether to account for the transaction as a sale or financing should be based on specific circumstances analogized to sale-leasebacks and to the specific criteria used to determine whether a transaction in ASC 470-10-25-1 through 25-2, 35-3 is a sale or financing. They also looked to SEC SAB-30 (Accounting for Divestiture of a Subsidiary or Other Business Operation) and SAB-82 (Certain Transfers of Nonperforming Assets) for guidance on factors that would help determine whether the transaction is a sale or a financing.

Each of the factors that provide conclusive evidence that the transaction is *not* a sale is related to aspects of the transferor's retention of risks and rewards of ownership that cannot be overcome. Although the list of presumptive evidence includes factors that also indicate retention of the risks and rewards of ownership, those factors, such as the buyer's ability to cancel the subservicing agreement, may be overcome.

ASC 860-10-55-35, 40-24
Definition of the Term *Substantially the Same for Holders of Debt Instruments*, as Used in Certain Audit Guides and a Statement of Position

BACKGROUND

The following discussion addresses whether two debt instruments are substantially the same. This guidance is designed to help classify various types of repurchase agreements as a sale or as a financing. For example, an entity may sell a debt instrument with an agreement to repurchase another debt instrument. If the debt instrument to be repurchased is substantially the same as the debt instrument that was sold, the transaction would be treated as a financing. Otherwise, the transaction would be treated as a sale.

ACCOUNTING GUIDANCE

Scope

The following guidance pertains to the sale and purchase, or the exchange, of debt instruments between two entities that both hold the debt instrument as an asset. The term *debt instrument* is defined broadly, including those instruments traditionally viewed as securities and those not classified as such. The debt instruments encompassed in this discussion include notes, bonds, debentures, money market instruments, certificates of deposit, mortgage loans, commercial loans, commercial paper, and mortgage-backed certificates. The following guidance does not apply in circumstances in which an entity originates or acquires a whole loan mortgage and then exchanges the loan for a participation certificate issued by a government-sponsored enterprise or agency (e.g., FHLMC, FNMA, or GNMA). However, exchanges of participation certificates are included within the scope of this guidance.

Conclusions

For debt instruments to be classified as substantially the same, all of six criteria must be met. This has the practical effect of making it quite difficult for two debt instruments to be viewed as substantially the same. The six criteria that must be met in order for two debt instruments to be classified as substantially the same are as follows:

1. The debt instruments must have the same primary obligor. However, if the debt instrument is guaranteed by a sovereign government, a central bank, or a government-sponsored enterprise or agency thereof, the debt must be guaranteed by the same party. Also, the terms of the guarantee must be identical.

2. Each debt instrument must be identical in form and type so that all provide the same risks and rights to their holders. For example, the following types of exchanges would not meet this criterion: (*a*) GNMA I securities for GNMA II securities, (*b*) loans to foreign debtors that are otherwise the same except for different U.S. foreign tax credits, and (*c*) commercial paper for redeemable preferred stock.

3. Each debt instrument must carry the same contractual interest rate.

4. In general, the debt instruments must have the same maturity. In the case of mortgage-backed pass-through and pay-through securities, the mortgages underlying the securities must have similar remaining weighted average maturities that result in approximately the same market yield. For example, an exchange of GNMA securities that have a high prepayment record for GNMA securities with a low prepayment record would not meet this criterion.

5. Mortgage-backed pass-through or pay-through securities must be collateralized by a similar pool of mortgages, such as single-family residential mortgages.

6. In general, each debt instrument must have the same unpaid principal amount. In the case of mortgage-backed pass-through or pay-through securities, the aggregate principal amounts of the mortgage-backed securities given up and the mortgage-backed securities reacquired must be within the accepted "good delivery" standard for the type of mortgage-backed security involved. These specific standards are promulgated by the Public Securities Association and are discussed in *Uniform Practices for the Clearance and Settlement of Mortgage-Backed Securities and Other Related Securities.*

Illustration of Applying Criteria

First Interstate Bank of Texas transfers its portfolio of mortgage-backed pass-through securities for a similar portfolio held by First Virginia Bank. At issue is whether this transfer of debt instruments would represent the transfer of instruments that are substantially the same.

Assume that criteria 2-4 and 6 are met. Criterion 5 also is met—both sets of mortgage-backed securities are collateralized by a similar pool of mortgages: single-family residential mortgages. However, criterion 1, which requires the debt instruments to have the same primary obligor, is not met; there is a different set of primary obligors on First Interstate's loans than on First Virginia's loans. Therefore, this transfer does not represent the transfer of debt instruments that are substantially the same.

ASC 860-10-55-3; ASC 310-20-25-20
Accounting for Fees and Costs Associated with Loan Syndications and Loan Participations

BACKGROUND

This Issue was discussed because some questioned the FASB staff's interpretation that the guidance in ASC 860 nullifies the previous conclusion that certain participations should be accounted for as "in-substance syndications."

ACCOUNTING ISSUES

1. Does the guidance in ASC 860 apply to loan participations even if they are considered to be in-substance syndications?

ACCOUNTING GUIDANCE

1. All loan participations should be accounted for under the provisions of ASC 860, which applies to all loan participations, even those having the characteristics of loan syndications.

2. All transactions structured legally as loan syndications, including those described as in-substance loan participations should be accounted under the provisions of ASC 310, Receivables.

DISCUSSION

58,046 ASC 860—Transfers and Servicing

The FASB staff explained that lenders sometimes structure transactions as loan participations rather than syndications because of the administrative difficulties of structuring a syndication. In a participation, the lender originates and funds the total loan but very shortly thereafter sells interests in the loan to other lenders, whereas in a syndication, several lenders initially fund the loan. The fees are the same in both transactions, but the lender in a participation has the credit and interest rate risk until other participants are found. Those who supported accounting for loan participations and loan syndications based on their legal form argued that ASC 860 applies to all transfers of financial assets and that it would be counterproductive to make exceptions to that requirement.

ASC 860-10-55-13
Sale of Bad-Debt Recovery Rights

BACKGROUND

A financial institution and another party enter into an agreement in which the financial institution sells the other party the right to receive the first $5 million collected on loans that had been previously written off by the financial institution. The other party (the buyer) pays the financial institution $5 million for that right and will receive a specified market rate of interest annually on $5 million reduced by loans recovered. The agreement continues until the buyer has recovered the $5 million. The buyer has no recourse to the financial institution and can use its own efforts to recover on the loans if dissatisfied with the financial institution's collection results.

ACCOUNTING ISSUES

Should the transaction be accounted for as:

- A sale of recovery rights and recognize a gain at the date of the transaction?
- A recovery of loans previously written off and recognized as a credit to the loan loss allowance?
- A borrowing secured by the potential recovery rights and recognized as a liability?
- A secured borrowing with the amount of proceeds received from the buyer considered in computing the current year's loan-loss provision?

ACCOUNTING GUIDANCE

The transaction is a secured borrowing. No conclusion was reached on whether proceeds received from a buyer should be considered in the current year's loan loss provision.

DISCUSSION

The following arguments supported the conclusion that the transaction is a secured borrowing:

- The transaction is similar to a nonrecourse financing or a funded guarantee.

- The buyer's stated annual return is more like a return on a financing transaction than a return on an equity transaction, because the buyer has no reward beyond recovery of the principal and interest.
- The buyer has no risk because, based on the institution's experience, the buyer will cover the principal and interest.
- The financial institution does not sell the buyer a right to recoveries on specific loans.
- Loans written off continue to be controlled by the financial institution, which has the incentive to make recoveries and limit the amount of interest paid.

ASC 860-10-55-71 through 55-72
Sale of a Short-Term Loan Made under a Long-Term Credit Commitment

BACKGROUND

A financial institution has made a 90-day short-term loan to a borrower under a five-year long-term credit commitment and subsequently transfers the short-term loan without recourse to a third party. Under the transfer agreement, the risk of loss on the short-term loan is legally transferred to the purchaser, while the transferor retains no obligation to repurchase the short-term loan. The financial institution may relend to the borrower under the long-term credit commitment when the short-term obligation matures, but may refuse to do so based on an evaluation of the borrower's credit or because the borrower does not satisfy a covenant under the long-term credit commitment.

ACCOUNTING ISSUE

Should a transfer of a short-term loan under a long-term credit commitment be accounted for as a sale or as a financing transaction?

ACCOUNTING GUIDANCE

1. A transfer of a short-term loan under the long-term credit commitment described above should be accounted for as a sale.
2. Loan covenants affect the accounting for a transfer as follows:
    a. A transfer of a short-term loan under a long-term credit commitment that includes a substantive *subjective* covenant should be accounted for as a sale.
    b. A transfer of a short-term loan under a long-term credit commitment that includes only *objective* covenants should be accounted for as a sale only if such objective covenants are substantive—that is, they specifically apply to the borrower and are expected to be meaningful and relevant in determining whether the long-term credit commitment obligates the financial institution to relend to the borrower.
3. Commitment fees received for long-term commitments should be recognized based on the guidance in ASC 310, Receivables.

EFFECT OF ASC 815

The guidance in ASC 815 applies if an analysis of the terms of a contract indicate that a put option qualifies as a derivative under the Statement.

EFFECT OF ASC 860

- The guidance in ASC 860 affirms the conclusion that a short-term loan under a long-term credit commitment to a third-party purchaser without recourse should be accounted for as a sale under the circumstances described. Such a transaction could meet the conditions for the surrender of control under the guidance in ASC 860-10-40-4 and 40-5 as Specific transactions should be evaluated based on the guidance in ASC 860-10-40-4 through 40-5.

- If a transaction discussed is accounted for as a transfer of a receivable with a put option, recognition of a sale is required if the transaction meets the conditions in ASC 860-10-40-4 through 40-5, would apply.

- The guidance in ASC 860-10-40-4 through 40-5 is amended to require that a transferor that effectively retains control over transferred financial assets be precluded from recognizing a sale on the transaction. Examples of when a transferor effectively retains control over transferred financial assets are included in ASC 860-10-40-4 and 40-5.

- The SEC Observer's concerns (see comment below) are partially resolved by the requirement in ASC 860-20-25-1, that a liability be recognized for a put obligation incurred or proceeds in such transactions if the put obligation does not prohibit sales accounting.

- The guidance in ASC 860 does not address a lender's refusal to relend to a borrower based on subjective or objective covenants. (See SEC Observer's Comment.) However, the put option's terms should be analyzed to determine whether the put meets the definition of a derivative in ASC 815. If a loan cannot be readily converted to cash and there is no market mechanism to enable the holder to settle the option in net cash, the put option may not meet the condition in ASC 815-10-15-83, which is further discussed in ASC 860-10-40-4 through 40-5.

- The recognition of commitment fees is not addressed in ASC 860 (FAS-140).

SEC OBSERVER COMMENT

The SEC Observer stated that he is uncomfortable with sales accounting and concerned about uncertainties related to the transaction, such as the accounting for commitment fees for long-term commitments under ASC 310, the classification of the loan by the borrower as short-term or long-term, and the probability of whether the financial institution will relend to the borrower.

DISCUSSION

Although the risk of loss has been transferred in this transaction, and the transferor has no contractual obligation to repurchase the short term loan receivable, the Issue is complicated by the fact that it deals with a short-term loan under a revolving long-term credit commitment. That is, if the transaction is viewed as a single loan that reprices periodically, the substance of the transaction is that the lender (transferor) either repays the transferee when the loan rolls over or the transferee agrees to purchase the additional portion of the loan.

To address concerns about the probability that the financial institution will relend to the borrower, the effect of loan covenants on the relending decision were discussed. The conclusion was based on a discussion of the following two types of financial-related covenants:

1. *Subjective covenants* Compliance is determined subjectively. For example, a provision that refers to a "material adverse change" may be evaluated differently by the parties to the agreement.

2. *Objective covenants* Compliance is determined objectively based on data such as financial ratios.

ASC 860-20: Sales of Financial Assets

ASC 860-20-25-11 through 25-13, 30-4, 35-9, 55-41 through 55-42, 55-62 through 55-92; ASC 860-40-25-2, 50-25-10
Accounting for Changes That Result in a Transferor Regaining Control of Financial Assets Sold

BACKGROUND

According to ASC 860-20-25-8, a transferor may regain control of financial assets previously accounted for as sold if the transferee no longer meets one of the conditions in ASC 860-10-40-4 through 40-5 that are required for sale accounting. Failure to meet the conditions in ASC 860-10-40-4 through 40-5 is usually a result of a change in law, or other circumstances. If such circumstances occur, a portion of the transferred financial assets may no longer meet the conditions of a participating interest or the transferor may regain control of a transferred financial asset that had been accounted for as a sale because one or more of the conditions in ASC 860-10-40-4 through 40-5 are no longer met. Under those circumstances, the transferor must account for the transferred financial assets as if they have been repurchased from the transferee in exchange for the liabilities assumed by the transferor. The transferor recognizes the transferred financial assets and liabilities at their fair value on the date the change occurs and thereafter reports the assets and the liabilities in its financial statements to the former transferee or other beneficial interest holders in those assets. The transferee derecognizes the transferred financial assets on that date and accounts for them as if they were sold in exchange for a receivable from the transferor. It is assumed in this Issue that the transferor does not consolidate the transferee. However, a transferor that subsequently consolidates an entity that had been involved in a transfer that was accounted for as a sale should apply current guidance.

ACCOUNTING ISSUES

1. How should a transferor account for retained beneficial interests if portions of the underlying assets that had been sold are rerecognized in accordance with the guidance in ASC 860-20-25-8 because the transferor's contingent call option on the transferred assets, such as a removal

of accounts provision (ROAP), becomes exercisable? How much of a gain or loss should be recognized under those circumstances?

2. Are there any circumstances under which an allowance should be recorded for assets that are rerecognized at fair value in accordance with ASC 860-20-25-?

3. How does the rerecognition of assets (or a portion thereof) sold in accordance with the guidance in ASC 860-20-25-8 affect the accounting for a related servicing asset?

4. How should a transferor subsequently account for its interests, except for servicing assets, after the occurrence of an event that triggers the application of ASC 860-20-25-8?

ACCOUNTING GUIDANCE

1. When applying the guidance in ASC 860-20-25-8 a transferor should recognize no gain or loss in earnings related to its beneficial interests. Such beneficial interests should be evaluated for impairment when applying the guidance in ASC 860-20-25-8 and periodically thereafter. However, a transferor may recognize a gain or loss when exercising a removal of accounts provision (ROAP) or a similar contingent right related to a repurchased transferred financial asset that is not a derivative accounted for under the guidance in ASC 815 and is not at-the-money. That is, the fair value of repurchased assets should not exceed or be less than the transferor's related obligation to the transferee.

2. A transferor should never recognize a loan loss allowance on a loan that does not meet the definition of a security when that loan is initially rerecognized under the guidance in ASC 860-20-25-8.

3. The accounting for a servicing asset related to a previously sold financial asset does not change if an event causing the application of ASC 860-20-25-8 occurs. The contractually required cash flows from the rerecognized assets continue to be paid to the securitization entity, which will use the proceeds to satisfy its contractual obligations, including those to beneficial interest holders. A transferor, as servicer, continues to be contractually required to collect the asset's cash flows for the benefit of the securitization entity and to service the asset in other ways. Therefore, a transferor should continue to recognize the servicing asset and evaluate it for impairment as required in ASC 860.

4. A transferor should not combine an interest in the underlying assets, other than the servicing asset, with rerecognized financial assets after an event occurs that requires the application of the guidance in ASC 860-20-25-8 A transferor's interest should be combined, however, with the underlying assets, if as a result of a subsequent event, the transferor recovers the financial assets from a transferee—for example, by exercising a removal of accounts provision or by consolidating an a securitization entity under GAAP, including ASC 810-10.

ASC 860-20-35-6, 55-17 through 55-19
Accounting for Accrued Interest Receivable under FAS-140 Securitizations

Question: How should the accrued interest receivable related to securitized and sold receivables be accounted for and reported under the guidance in ASC 860?

Answer: When credit card receivables are securitized, a pool of receivables is transferred to a trust and the trust receives the right to future collections of principal, finance charges, and fees. Assuming that the transfer of receivables meets the ASC 860 criteria for treatment as a sale, the transferor will carry on its balance sheet only its retained interests in the transferred receivables.

Some companies that securitize credit card receivables continue to recognize accrued interest receivable as an asset on their balance sheet, even thought the right to receive this accrued interest receivable has been transferred to the trust. The accrued interest receivable represents the investors' portion of the accrued fees and finance charges on the transferred credit card receivables. According to the final FSP that was recently issued, this accounting treatment is generally no longer acceptable.

Assuming that the securitization meets the requirements to be treated as a sale and the accrued interest receivable is subordinated, the accrued interest receivable should be considered one of the components of the sales transaction. The accrued interest receivable should be treated as retained beneficial interest. It is not acceptable to refer to the accrued interest receivable as "loans receivable," or as any other title that fails to communicate that the accrued interest receivable has been subordinated to the senior interests in the securitization.

The accrued interest receivable cannot be prepaid or settled in a manner in which the owner would suffer a significant loss of its investment. Therefore, the accrued interest receivable is not subsequently measured like an investment in debt securities that is treated as available-for-sale or trading under the guidance in ASC 320. The subsequent measurement of retained interests that cannot be prepaid or settled in a manner in which the owner would suffer a significant loss on its investment, including accrued interest receivable, is accounted for in accordance with ASC 450 (FAS-5, Accounting for Contingencies). ASC 450 provides guidance in providing for the uncollectibility of receivables including, as in this case, accrued interest receivable.

ASC 860-50: Servicing Assets and Liabilities

ASC 860-50-40-3 through 40-5
Determination of What Risks and Rewards, If Any, Can Be Retained and Whether Any Unresolved Contingencies May Exist in a Sale of Mortgage Loan Servicing Rights

BACKGROUND

A seller/transferor may provide a buyer/transferee with protection provisions in an agreement to sell or transfer servicing rights. Such provisions may include adjustment of the sales price for loan prepayments, defaults, or foreclosures occurring within a specific time period. In addition, most agreements include representations and warranty provisions that apply to eligibility defects discovered within a specific time period.

ACCOUNTING ISSUE

Is sales recognition precluded at the date title passes if the agreement includes any provision under which the seller retains specific risks, or could a sale be recognized at that date if:

- A seller can reasonably estimate and recognizes a liability for the costs related to protection provisions, or if
- A sales agreement provides for substantially all risks and rewards to irrevocably pass to the buyer, and the seller can reasonably estimate the minor protection provisions and recognizes a liability for that amount?

ACCOUNTING GUIDANCE

- A transfer of a right to service mortgage loans should be recognized as a sale if the following conditions have been met:
  — Title has passed.
  — Substantially all risks and rewards of ownership have irrevocably passed to the buyer.
  — The seller has retained only minor protection provisions that are reasonably estimable.
- A liability should be accrued for the estimated obligation associated with the minor protection provisions.
- A seller retains only minor protection provisions if:
  — The obligation related to those provisions does not exceed 10% of the sales price, and
  — Prepayment risk is retained for a maximum of 120 days.

DISCUSSION

Proponents of the view adopted by Task Force noted that authoritative pronouncements such as ASC 605, ASC 360, permit sales recognition when some risk has been retained by the seller. It also was argued that sufficient historical and projected information exists about the types of risks retained to enable a seller to estimate the effects of such uncertainties. In addition, provisions related to prepayment protection, early payment defaults, and investor approval are resolved within a short period of time, such as three months or less. The buyer's remedies usually are limited to a reduction of the sales proceeds for the disqualified portion, but the buyer cannot void the sale unless there is fraud. As a result, the seller can estimate the effect of the provisions.

The term *minor* was defined as 10% of the sales price to attain consistent application of the consensus. Ten percent was chosen as the maximum limit, because it is a common definition of minor found in the accounting literature, such as in lease accounting and pooling of interests. Ten percent also is considered a reasonable percentage of risk to be retained by the seller while recognizing a sale.

ASC 860-50-40-10, 50-11
Sale of Mortgage Service Rights on Mortgages Owned by Others

BACKGROUND

A company sells its portfolio of first-mortgage loans and retains the right to service the loans. Because there is a lag between the time the mortgage payments are collected and the time such payments are passed to the mortgage owners, the company invests that "float." As a result, the company can sell the mortgage servicing rights for cash or for participation in the future interest stream produced by the loans.

ACCOUNTING ISSUES

- Should a gain be recognized on the sale of mortgage servicing rights for a participation in the income stream of future interest?
- If so, how should the gain be measured?

ACCOUNTING GUIDANCE

- A gain should be recognized at the date of the sale.
- It is difficult to measure the gain if the sales price is based on the seller's participation in future payments; the accounting literature does not provide guidance on the upper limit of a computed sales price. All available information should be considered, including the gain that would be recognized if the servicing rights were sold for a fixed cash price.

DISCUSSION

It was discussed whether a gain should be calculated in the same way as on the sale of the related mortgage loan portfolio. It was noted that the difficulty in determining the upper limit of the sales price is the result of uncertainty about prepayments and the duration of the underlying mortgage loans. The question was raised whether the gain on this transaction, plus the gain on the sale of the mortgage loan portfolio, should be limited to the gain if the servicing rights were sold for a fixed cash price.

Appendices

APPENDIX A:
ASC 912—CONTRACTORS— FEDERAL GOVERNMENT

CONTENTS

General Guidance	59,001
ASC 912-10: Overall	59,001
Overview	59,001
Background	59,001
Cost-Plus-Fixed-Fee Contracts	59,001
Illustration of Percentage-of-Completion on CPFF Contract	59,002
Renegotiation	59,002
Terminated War and Defense Contracts	59,003
Government Contract Receivables	59,003
Disclosures	59,004

GENERAL GUIDANCE

ASC 912-10: OVERALL

OVERVIEW

Government contracts often include certain unique features, such as being based on the costs incurred by the contractor (i.e., cost-plus-fixed-fee) and being subject to renegotiation and termination.

BACKGROUND

Government contracts are usually performed under a cost-plus-fixed-fee arrangement, which provides for possible renegotiation if the contracting officer for the government believes that excess profits were made by the contractor. These contracts may also provide that the government may terminate the contract at its convenience. ASC 912 deals with both fixed-price and CPFF contracts. It addresses the problems involved in the termination of a government contract by the government; it does not cover terminations resulting from default of the contractor (ASC 912-10-15-3).

COST-PLUS-FIXED-FEE CONTRACTS

Cost-plus-fixed-fee (CPFF) contracts generally require the government to pay a fixed fee in addition to all costs involved in fulfilling the contract. The contract may include the manufacture of a product or only the performance of services, and the government may or may not withhold a specified percentage of the interim payments until completion of the entire contract. Furthermore, CPFF contracts usually are cancellable by the government. When such contracts are terminated, the contractor is entitled to reimbursement for all costs, plus an equitable portion of the fixed fee (ASC 912-605-25-27).

One of the main problems in accounting for CPFF contracts is determining when profits should be recognized. As a general rule, profits are not recognized until the right to full payment becomes unconditional, which is usually when the product has been delivered and accepted or the services have been fully rendered (completed-contract method).

When CPFF contracts extend over several years, however, the percentage-of-completion method is acceptable, provided that costs and profits can be reasonably estimated and realization of the contract is reasonably assured (ASC 912-605-25-5):

Illustration of Percentage-of-Completion on CPFF Contract

A company enters into a contract with the government that calls for a 20% profit on costs. The percentage-of-completion method is appropriate because costs and profits can be reasonably estimated.

Accumulated costs through the end of the third year of the contract totaled $1,200,000. Profits recognized in the first and second years of the contract were $100,000 and $75,000, respectively.

Profit recognized in the third year of the contract is computed as follows:

Accumulated costs to date	$1,200,000
CPFF percentage	20%
Estimated profit to date	$ 240,000
Profits recognized in previous years ($100,000 + $75,000)	(175,000)
Profit recognized in third year	$ 65,000

PRACTICE POINTER: When CPFF contracts involve the manufacture and delivery of products, the reimbursable costs and fees ordinarily are included in appropriate sales or other revenue accounts. When CPFF contracts involve only services, only the fees ordinarily should be included in revenues.

An advance payment by the government may not be offset as a payment on account, unless it is expected to be applied as such with reasonable certainty. In the event that an advance is offset, it must be disclosed clearly (ASC 912-210-45-1).

RENEGOTIATION

Renegotiation involves the adjustment of the original selling price or contract. Since the government makes renegotiation adjustments an integral part of a contract, a provision for such probable adjustments is necessary. A provision for renegotiation is based on the contractor's past experience or on the general experience of the particular industry, and it is shown in the income statement as a reduction of the related sales or income. If a reasonable estimate cannot be made, that fact should be disclosed in the financial statements or accompanying notes. The provision for renegotiation is reported as a liability in the balance sheet (ASC 912-405-25-1; 912-405-50-1). Classification as a current liability is appropriate if the criteria established in the ASC Glossary are met.

PRACTICE POINTER: In those unusual cases in which collection is not reasonably assured, it may be preferable to employ the installment-sale or cost-recovery method in accounting for a government contract.

When a provision for renegotiation is made in a particular year and the subsequent final adjustment differs materially, show the difference in the income statement of the year of final determination.

TERMINATED WAR AND DEFENSE CONTRACTS

ASC 912 deals with both fixed-price and CPFF contracts. It addresses the problems involved in the termination of a government contract by the government.

The determination of profit or loss on a terminated government contract is made as of the effective date of termination. This is the date that the contractor accrues the right to receive payment on that portion of the contract that has been terminated (ASC 912-605-25-20).

Although most government contracts provide for a minimum profit percentage formula in the event agreement cannot be reached, the amount of profit to be reported in the case of termination for the convenience of the government is the difference between all allowable costs incurred and the amount of the termination claim (ASC 912-605-25-32).

GOVERNMENT CONTRACT RECEIVABLES

A distinction should be made in the balance sheet between unbilled costs and fees and billed amounts (ASC 912-310-25-1).

In the case of terminated contracts, if a reasonable estimate of the termination claim for reporting purposes cannot be made, full disclosure of this fact should be made by note to the financial statements, which should describe the uncertainties involved (ASC 912-310-50-1).

Termination claims are classified as current assets if the criteria in the ASC Glossary are met. Prior to the termination notice, advances received are deducted from termination claims receivable for reporting purposes. Loans received on the security of the contract or termination claim are shown separately as current liabilities (ASC 912-310-45-3, 4). Material amounts of termination claims are classified separately from other receivables in the financial statements (ASC 912-310-50-2).

The cost of items included in the termination claim that are subsequently reacquired by the contractor is recorded as a new purchase, and the amount is applied as a reduction of the termination claim. These types of reductions from the termination claim generally are referred to as *disposal credits* (ASC 912-310-35-1; 912-310-25-1).

DISCLOSURES

When a significant portion of a company's business is derived from government contracts, such disclosure should be made in the financial statements or notes thereto, indicating the uncertainties involved and the possibility of renegotiation in excess of the amount provided. In addition, the basis of determining the provision for renegotiation should be disclosed (prior experience, industry experience, etc.) (ASC 912-275-50-1). Disclosure is required if 10% or more of an enterprise's revenue is derived from sales to the federal government, a state government, a local government, or a foreign government (ASC 280-10-50-42).

Termination claims are stated at the amount estimated as collectible, and adequate provision or disclosure should be made for items of a controversial nature (ASC 912-275-50-3).

APPENDIX B:
ASC 915—DEVELOPMENT STAGE ENTITIES

CONTENTS

General Guidance	60,001
ASC 915-10: Overall	60,001
Overview	60,001
Background	60,001
Accounting and Reporting Standards	60,002
Disclosure Standards	60,003
Table B-1: Disclosure Requirements for Development Stage Companies	60,004

GENERAL GUIDANCE

ASC 915-10: OVERALL

OVERVIEW

A development stage company is one for which principal operations have not commenced or principal operations have generated an insignificant amount of revenue. GAAP require that these entities issue the same financial statements as other enterprises and include additional disclosures.

BACKGROUND

A development stage company devotes most of its activities to establishing a new business. Planned principal activities have not commenced, or have commenced and have not yet produced significant revenue (ASC Glossary). Typical development stage activities include raising capital, building production facilities, acquiring operating assets, training personnel, developing markets, and starting production.

PRACTICE POINTER: ASC 915 does not provide guidance on what constitutes "significant" revenue; therefore, use judgment to determine whether a company is a development stage enterprise. An enterprise involved in the following activities can be said to be in the development stage (ASC 915-10-05-2):

- Financial planning
- Raising capital
- Exploring for natural resources
- Developing natural resources

- Research and development
- Establishing sources of supply
- Acquiring property, plant, equipment, and other operating assets
- Training personnel
- Developing markets

Once the company's primary attention is turned to routine, ongoing activities, it ceases to be a development stage enterprise. The point at which an enterprise ceases to be in the development stage is a matter of judgment and must be evaluated on a case-by-case basis.

ACCOUNTING AND REPORTING STANDARDS

A development stage company issues the same basic financial statements as any other enterprise, and such statements should be prepared in conformity with GAAP. Accordingly, capitalized or deferred costs are subject to the same assessment of realizability as for an operating enterprise (ASC 915-605-25-1; 915-810-35-1).

In the case of a subsidiary or a similar type of enterprise, the determination of expensing or capitalizing costs is made within the context of the entity presenting the financial statements. Thus, it would be possible to expense an item in the financial statements of a subsidiary and capitalize the same expense in the financial statements of the parent company. For example, if a subsidiary purchases a machine that will be used only for research and development, it would expense the cost of the item in the year of acquisition. The parent company could capitalize the same machine, however, if in its normal course of business such a machine has an alternative future use elsewhere in the company (ASC 915-810-35-1, 2).

A development stage company that is a subsidiary may change an accounting method to conform to the requirements of ASC 915. In this situation, the effect would be reflected generally in the established operating enterprise's consolidated financial statements that include the subsidiary (ASC 915-10-15-5).

OBSERVATION: Some observers have taken the position that development stage companies should be permitted to apply standards that are different from those of established operating enterprises. For example, because significant revenue has yet to be generated, some believe that operating costs during a start-up period should be capitalized rather than expensed and amortized over the early years of operations. The FASB took a position contrary to this view when it required development stage enterprises to present financial statements based on the same GAAP as established operating enterprises, with additional disclosures during the development stage.

ASC 915—Development Stage Entities **60,003**

DISCLOSURE STANDARDS

ASC 915 concentrates on establishing reporting and disclosure requirements for development stage companies. The required financial statements and additional information, summarized in Table B-1, are as follows (ASC 915-205-45-2):

- A balance sheet, presenting accumulated losses as "deficit accumulated during the development stage"
- An income statement, including revenues and expenses for each period being presented and also a cumulative total of both amounts from the company's inception. This provision also applies to dormant companies that have been reactivated at the development stage. In such cases, the totals begin from the time that development stage activities are initiated.
- A statement of cash flows, showing cumulative totals of cash inflows and cash outflows from the company's inception and amounts for the current period
- A statement of stockholders' equity, containing the following information:
    - The date and number of shares of stock (or other securities) issued for cash or other consideration and the dollar amount assigned
    - For each issuance of capital stock involving noncash consideration, a description of the nature of the consideration and the basis for its valuation

---

PRACTICE POINTER: A company can combine separate transactions of equity securities, provided that the same type of securities, consideration per equity unit, and type of consideration are involved and the transactions are made in the same fiscal period.

Modification of the statement of stockholders' equity may be required for a combined group of companies that form a development stage company or for an unincorporated development stage entity.

OBSERVATION: GAAP do not indicate the types of modifications that might be necessary. Therefore, judgment must be exercised in the preparation of financial statements of development stage enterprises.

- The financial statements are to be identified as those of a development stage company and contain a description of the proposed business activities (ASC 915-205-45-4).
- The financial statements for the first year that the company is no longer in the development stage shall indicate that in the prior year it was in the development stage. If the company includes prior years for comparative purposes, the cumulative amounts specified in 2 and 3 are not required (ASC 915-235-50-2).

Table B-1: Disclosure Requirements for Development Stage Companies

Category of Disclosure	Additional Information Required
Balance sheet	Accumulated losses during development stage, identified as "deficit accumulated during the development stage"
Income statement	Cumulative totals of revenues and expenses from the company's inception
Statement of cash flows	Cumulative totals of cash inflows and cash outflows from the company's inception
Statement of stockholders' equity	Date and number of shares of stock issued for cash and other consideration and dollar amounts assigned; nature of consideration and basis for valuation for each issuance of capital stock for noncash consideration
Notes to financial statements	Identification of enterprise as development stage and proposed line of business

APPENDIX C:
ASC 92X—ENTERTAINMENT

CONTENTS

Interpretive Guidance	61,001
ASC 924: Entertainment-Casinos	61,001
ASC 924-605: Revenue Recognition	61,001
ASC 924-605-25-2, 55-1 through 55-2, 65-1 (ASU 2010-16)	
Accruals for Casino Jackpot Liabilities	61,001

INTERPRETIVE GUIDANCE

ASC 924: Entertainment-Casinos

ASC 924-605: Revenue Recognition

ASC 924-605-25-2, 55-1 through 55-2, 65-1 (ASU 2010-16)
Accruals for Casino Jackpot Liabilities

BACKGROUND

Entities that earn their revenue from gaming activities classify slot machine jackpots as follows:

- "Nonprogressive" jackpots are *fixed* payouts that have been programmed into a slot machine based on certain combinations that are identified on the machine's payout table. Because in most jurisdictions a gaming entity is permitted to remove a machine paying such jackpots from the floor at any time, even if no fixed jackpots have been paid on that machine, a gaming entity is not required to make any payouts on such machines as long as a machine's payouts are within a preapproved percentage, which has been programmed into the machine.

- "Progressive" jackpots are payouts based on a percentage that is programmed into a slot machine and conforms to a machine's payout table, which increases as more customers play the machine. The amount that would be paid out the first time a slot machine is played or immediately after a jackpot has been paid out is referred to as the "base" amount of a progressive jackpot. Any amount paid above the base amount and until a customer wins a jackpot is referred to as the "incremental" amount of a progressive jackpot. The base amount of a jackpot is funded by the gaming entity while the incremental amount is funded by customers who play the machine. Therefore, in most jurisdictions, a gaming entity that removes a machine paying progressive jackpots from the floor is usually required to: (1) transfer the incremental amount to a different machine on the floor; or (2) award that amount in some sort of prize drawing. In some jurisdictions, a gaming entity that removes a progressive slot machine from the floor also has to retain and award the base amount of a progressive jackpot. In those circumstances, the gaming entity usually accrues a liability for the base amount before the jackpot has been won. However, some gaming entities also are accruing the incremental amount as a liability based a specific amount (e.g., five cents) per coin played by customers.

This Issue, which addresses how gaming entities should account for base jackpot liabilities if payment of a jackpot can be avoided, was discussed because some gaming entities are accruing a liability for progressive and nonprogressive base jackpots before a jackpot has been won. Those who support this approach base their view on the guidance in ASC 924-605-25-2, which states that "[b]ase jackpots shall be charged to revenue ratably over the period of play expected to precede payout." However, those who believe that a liability should not be accrued for a base jackpot's amount if the gaming entity is not required to make an award, as in a nonprogressive jackpot, cite the guidance in ASC 924-605-25-1, which states that "[r]evenue recognized and reported by a casino is generally defined as the win from gaming activities, that is, the difference between gaming wins and losses, not the total amount wagered."

SCOPE

The guidance applies to base jackpots and incremental amounts in progressive jackpots paid by entities that earn revenue from gaming activities.

ACCOUNTING GUIDANCE

A liability should *not* be accrued until an entity incurs an obligation to pay a base jackpot. An obligation to pay incremental amounts in progressive jackpots should be accounted for in the same manner as the obligation to pay a base jackpot because the same principle applies.

EFFECTIVE DATE AND TRANSITION

The guidance above is effective for fiscal years, and interim periods within those fiscal years, that begin on or after December 15, 2010. It should be applied through a cumulative-effect adjustment to retained earnings as of the beginning of the fiscal year in which it was adopted. Earlier application is permitted. However, an entity that chooses early adoption in a period other than the first reporting period in its fiscal year must apply the guidance *retrospectively* to the beginning of its fiscal year.

APPENDIX D:
ASC 93X—EXTRACTIVE ACTIVITIES

CONTENTS

Interpretive Guidance	62,002
ASC 930: Extractive Activities-Mining	62,002
ASC 930-330: Inventory	62,002
ASC 930-330-05-1, 25-1; ASC 930-10-15-2	
Accounting for Stripping Costs Incurred during Production in the Mining Industry	62,002
ASC 930-360: Property, Plant, and Equipment	62,003
ASC 930-360-35-1 through 35-2; ASC 930-805-30-1 through 35-2	
Mining Assets: Impairment and Business Combinations	62,003
ASC 930-715: Compensation-Retirement Benefits	62,004
ASC 930-715-05-2, 25-1, 45-1, 50-1; ASC 450-20-60-18; ASC 715-60-60-4	
Accounting for Estimated Payments in Connection with the Coal Industry Retiree Health Benefit Act of 1992	62,004
ASC 932: Extractive Activities-Oil and Gas	
ASC 932-10: Overall	62,005
ASC 932-10-S25-1, S50-2, S99-5; ASC 932-815-55-1 through 55-2	
Accounting for Gas-Balancing Arrangements	62,005
ASC 932-350: Intangibles-Goodwill and Other	62,007
ASC 932-350-50-12	
Application of FASB Statement No. 142, *Goodwill and Other Intangible Assets,* to Oil- and Gas-Producing Entities	62,007
ASC 932-360: Property, Plant, and Equipment	62,008
ASC 932-360-25-18	
Accounting for Suspended Well Costs	62,008
ASC 932-835: Interest	62,011
ASC 932-835-25-2	
Interest on Receivables and Payables: Accounting Interpretations of APB Opinion No. 21	62,011

INTERPRETIVE GUIDANCE
ASC 93X—EXTRACTIVE ACTIVITIES

ASC 930: Extractive Activities-Mining

ASC 930-330: Inventory

ASC 930-330-05-1, 25-1; ASC 930-10-15-2
Accounting for Stripping Costs Incurred during Production in the Mining Industry

BACKGROUND

Mining entities remove waste materials from a mine in order to extract ore from the ground. The costs of removing waste materials from a mine are referred to in the mining industry as stripping costs. Those costs may be incurred while a mine is under development, as preproduction stripping costs, and after production has begun, as post-production stripping costs. Mining entities generally capitalize stripping costs during the development stage as a component of a mine's depreciable cost, which includes costs related to building, developing, and constructing the mine. Amortization of costs related to preproduction begins when production begins and continues over the mine's productive life. A mine's production phase is defined in this Issue as the period when production begins and revenue is earned from the sale of minerals, regardless of the level of production. Because of a lack of authoritative literature on the accounting for stripping costs after production has begun, there has been diversity in practice in accounting for those costs. Some entities have been expensing those costs, others have been deferring them, and still others have been capitalizing and amortizing stripping costs during production.

ACCOUNTING ISSUE

How should entities in the mining industry account for stripping costs?

ACCOUNTING GUIDANCE

Stripping costs incurred by mining entities involved in finding and removing wasting natural resources, other than oil- and gas-producing entities accounted for under the guidance in ASC 932, are variable production costs. Those costs should be included in the costs of inventory produced during the period in which the stripping costs were incurred. The term "inventory produced" as used here means "inventory extracted."

> A mine's *production phase* is defined as follows in ASC 930-330-25-1:
>
> > The production phase of a mine is deemed to have begun when saleable minerals are extracted (produced) *from an ore body*, regardless of the level of production (or revenues). However, the production phase does not commence with the removal of de minimis saleable mineral material that occurs in conjunction with the removal of overburden or waste material for the purpose of obtaining access to an ore body.

The guidance discussed above does *not* apply to the accounting for stripping costs incurred during a mine's *pre-production phase*.

ASC 930-360: Property, Plant, and Equipment

ASC 930-360-35-1 through 35-2; ASC 930-805-30-1 through 35-2
Mining Assets: Impairment and Business Combinations

BACKGROUND

Some mining entities have been excluding estimated cash flows associated with a mining asset's economic value beyond its proven probable (VBPP) reserves and the effects of anticipated fluctuations in the minerals' future market prices over the period of cash flows when testing such assets for impairment in accordance with the guidance in ASC 360-10 and in making the purchase price allocation of business combinations. Both VBPP and an estimate of the future market price of the minerals are generally included in a mining asset's fair value.

VBPP is defined in the SEC's Industry Guide 7 (Using Cash Flow Information and Present Value in Accounting Measurements) as (1) *proven reserves*, for which quantity is computed from certain dimensions, such as workings or drill holes; for which quality is determined from detailed samplings; and the geologic character of which is well defined because of the close proximity of the sites for inspection, sampling, and measurement and (2) *probable reserves*, the quantity, grade, and quality of which is computed based on information similar to that used for proven reserves, but the sites for inspection, sampling, and measurement are farther apart. The degree of assurance is lower than that of proven reserves, but is high enough that continuity can be assumed between the points observed. Proven and probable reserves are distinguished based on the level of geological evidence and the subsequent confidence in the estimated reserves. In addition to information about VBPP, the SEC also requires registrants to complete a feasibility study before accepting a registrant's statement that mining assets are proven and probable reserves.

The guidance below applies to mining entities—which include entities that find and remove wasting natural resources—other than oil- and gas-producing entities under the scope of ASC 932-10.

ACCOUNTING ISSUES

1. Should VBPP be considered when an entity allocates the purchase price of a business combination to mining assets?
2. Should the effects of anticipated fluctuation in the future market price of minerals be considered when an entity allocates the purchase price of a business combination to mining assets?

ACCOUNTING GUIDANCE

The following guidance applies:

1. VBPP should be included in the value allocated to mining assets in the purchase price allocation of a business combination in the same manner

that a market participant would include VBPP in determining the asset's fair value.

2. The effects of anticipated fluctuations in the future market price of minerals should be included when the fair value of the mining assets is determined in a purchase price allocation. Estimates of those effects should be consistent with the expectations of marketplace participants—that is, available information, such as current prices, historical averages, and forward pricing curves should be considered. The assumptions should be consistent with the acquirer's operating plans for developing and producing minerals and should be based on more than one factor.

The cash flows associated with VBPP estimates of future discounted and undiscounted cash flows should be included in the evaluation of mining assets for impairment under ASC 360-10. In addition, estimated cash flows used to determine impairment should include estimated cash outflows necessary to develop and extract the VBPP.

The effects of anticipated fluctuations in the future market price of minerals should be included when estimating discounted and undiscounted cash flows used to determine impairment under ASC 360-10. Estimates of those effects should be consistent with the expectations of marketplace participants—that is, available information, such as current prices, historical averages, and forward pricing curves should be considered. The assumptions should be consistent with the acquirer's operating plans for developing and producing minerals and should be based on more than one factor.

ASC 930-715: Compensation-Retirement Benefits

ASC 930-715-05-2, 25-1, 45-1, 50-1; ASC 450-20-60-18; ASC 715-60-60-4
Accounting for Estimated Payments in Connection with the Coal Industry Retiree Health Benefit Act of 1992

BACKGROUND

The United Mine Workers of America (UMWA) and the Bituminous Coal Operators' Association, Inc. (BCOA) established four trusts (1950 and 1974 Pension and Benefit Trusts) to provide pension and health benefits for coal industry retirees and their eligible dependents.

In response to the financial crisis confronting the 1950 and 1974 Benefit Trusts, a commission was appointed to study the funding problem. Based on the results of that study, Congress approved the Coal Industry Retiree Health and Benefit Act of 1992 (the Act).

The Act created a new private plan called the United Mine Workers of America Combined Benefit Fund (Combined Fund), which would provide medical benefits beginning in 1993 to all beneficiaries in the 1950 and 1974 benefit plans who were receiving benefits as of July 20, 1992. The Combined Fund is described by the Act as a multiemployer fund under the Employee Retirement Income Security Act of 1974 (ERISA).

All companies that were party to a coal wage agreement will be responsible for payments to the Combined Fund. Those payments will be based on a formula determined by the Act, which will include assignment of beneficiaries, a per-beneficiary premium, and a percentage of the cost of unassigned beneficiaries (who are referred to as orphans). The premium to be charged will be determined by using the July 1, 1991, cost per individual based on payments required by the 1950 and 1974 Benefits Trusts.

ACCOUNTING ISSUE

How should an entity account for payments required by the Act?

ACCOUNTING GUIDANCE

The following guidance applies:

- Entities currently involved in operations in the coal industry should account for their obligation under the Act as (1) a participation in a multiemployer plan (on a pay-as-you-go basis) or (2) a liability. Entities that choose to account for the obligation as a liability should recognize the entire obligation as a loss under the provisions of ASC 450.
- Entities *not* currently involved in operations in the coal industry should account for the obligation as a liability and recognize the entire obligation as a loss under the provisions of SC 450.
- Entities accounting for the obligation as a loss under the provisions of ASC 450 should report the estimated loss as an extraordinary item.
- Disclosure about the effect of the Act should include information about the estimated amount of the total obligation and the entity's method of accounting for it.

FASB STAFF COMMENT

A member of the FASB staff stated that companies should not include the obligation imposed by the Act in the cumulative effect of a change in accounting principle when adopting the guidance in ASC 715, because this obligation is the result of legislation rather than the result of changing to an accrual method to account for the costs of postretirement benefits.

ASC 932: Extractive Activities-Oil and Gas

ASC 932-10: Overall

ASC 932-10-S25-1, S50-2, S99-5; ASC 932-815-55-1 through 55-2
Accounting for Gas-Balancing Arrangements

BACKGROUND

Partners in a gas well may arrange to share in the gas well's production. One partner, Entity A, may decide not to sell its share of the gas production because it does not have a customer or market conditions are unfavorable. In that situation, the other partner, Entity B, may agree to take Entity A's gas production and sell it. At a future date, Entity A will have the right to take more than its share of the gas production to make up for the extra amount taken ("the overtake") by Entity B. Alternatively, Entity B pays for the overtake, either in cash or with gas from another well. Such transactions are known as *gas-balancing arrangements*.

The two predominant methods used to account for those arrangements are the *entitlements method* and the *sales method*. The entitlements method assumes that each unit of gas is jointly owned by the well's partners. In the above scenario, Entity B would recognize revenue from sales only to the extent of its proportionate share of the gas sold, recording a payable to Entity A. Conversely, Entity A would recognize a receivable and a sale for the overtake. Under the sales method, Entity B would recognize sales revenue for the entire amount, recognizing no payable to Entity A, which would record no receivable or revenue currently. Under the sales method, the partners track the imbalance by making memorandum entries. The partners may not use the same accounting method, because each partner makes that choice independently.

To illustrate the difference between the two methods, consider a situation in which Entity A has a 40% interest and Entity B has a 60% interest in a gas well. Production of the entire well during November is 6,000 MCF (thousand cubic feet) and the price is $1.50 per MCF. The allocation of gas production and revenue according to the terms of the partnership agreement would be as follows:

	Percentage Interest	Gas Production	Revenue at $1.50/MCF
Entity A	40%	2,400MCF	$3,600
Entity B	60%	3,600MCF	5,400
Total	100%	6,000MCF	$9,000

Entity A gives up its share of the November production to Entity B. The accounting under the entitlements method and the sales method would be as follows:

	Entitlements Method			Sales Method		
	Entity A	Entity B	Total	Entity A	Entity B	Total
Cash received	$0	$9,000	$9,000	$0	$9,000	$9,000
Receivable	3,600	0	$3,600	0	0	0
Payable	0	($3,600)	($3,600)	0	0	0
Revenue	$3,600	$5,400	$9,000	$0	$9,000	$9,000

ACCOUNTING ISSUE

How should participants in a gas-balancing arrangement account for the transactions?

ACCOUNTING GUIDANCE

Although practice for accounting for gas-balancing arrangements is not uniform, to the question was referred to the AICPA's Committee on Regulated Industries because it is industry-specific and established practice exists.

EFFECT OF FAS-133

The terms of the arrangements discussed should be analyzed to determine whether an arrangement meets the definition of a derivative under the guidance in ASC 815. Even though the derivative may always have a zero value, the disclosures in ASC 815-30-50-1, would be required. Further, the option feature may not qualify for the exception for normal purchases and normal sales in ASC 815-10-15-13.

SEC OBSERVER COMMENT

The SEC Observer made the following comments:

- The SEC staff has not taken a position on which of the two methods is preferable.
- Under the entitlements method, the recorded receivable or liability should be valued at the lower of (*a*) the price at the time of production, (*b*) current market value, or (*c*) the contract price if there is a contract.
- Receivables should be recognized net of selling expenses.
- Registrants are required to disclose their accounting method and the amount of an imbalance in units and value, if significant.
- Management's Discussion and Analysis should include information about the effect of gas imbalances on operations, liquidity, and capital resources.

In addition, the SEC Observer noted that the same method should be used to account for gas imbalances consistently. An overtaker (Entity B) using the sales method that has insufficient reserves to offset the imbalance should recognize a liability for the shortfall at the current market prices; if a different price is specified in the contract, it should be used instead.

ASC 932-350: Intangibles-Goodwill and Other

ASC 932-350-50-12 Application of FASB Statement No. 142, *Goodwill and Other Intangible Assets*, to Oil- and Gas-Producing Entities

QUESTION

Does the scope exception, related to ASC 932 in ASC 350-10-15-4 apply to the balance sheet classification of and disclosures about drilling and mineral rights of oil- and gas-producing entities?

ACCOUNTING GUIDANCE

The scope exception in ASC 350-10-15-4 applies to the balance sheet classification of and disclosures about drilling and mineral rights of oil- and gas-producing entities that account for their operations under the provisions of ASC 932.

Because the accounting framework of ASC 932 is based on the level of an oil- or gas-producing entity's established reserves, rather than on whether its assets are accounted for as tangible or intangible assets, the scope exception in ASC 350-10-15-4 also applies to the disclosure provisions for drilling and mineral rights of oil- and gas-producing entities. However, if they choose, entities are permitted to provide information about their drilling and mineral rights in addition to the information required to be disclosed under the provisions of ASC 932-235).

The above guidance should *not* be applied analogously to other items included in ASC 350-10-15-4.

ASC 932-360: Property, Plant, and Equipment

ASC 932-360-25-18 Accounting for Suspended Well Costs

BACKGROUND

The guidance below addresses the accounting for costs of exploratory wells by entities that use the successful efforts method of accounting discussed in the FASB Accounting Standards Codification™ ASC 932 and amends that guidance.

The question is whether there are circumstances in which an entity can continue to capitalize costs related to exploratory wells beyond one year, even if *no* additional exploratory wells are necessary to justify major capital expenditures and the wells are under way or firmly planned for the near future. The guidance in ASC 932-360-35-17 states that the costs of drilling exploratory wells can be capitalized while determining whether proved reserves have been found. If such reserves are found, costs that have been capitalized are recognized as part of the entity's wells, equipment, and facilities. Otherwise, those costs should be expensed, net of salvage value.

Sometimes reserves are found but cannot be classified as proved reserves when drilling is completed, because additional geologic and engineering information is required. In addition, other matters, such as government approvals, sales contracts, and financing must be resolved to verify with "reasonable certainty" that the reserves can be recovered under "existing economic and operating conditions"—that is, based on prices and costs at the date of the estimate. In the past, the accounting guidance in ASC 932-360-35-6, 35-13, and 35-16 through 35-20 has been followed under such circumstances. Under that guidance, at least one of the following conditions had to be met in order to capitalize costs of major capital expenditures in an area in which reserves could not be classified as proved reserves:

- A discovery that a well has sufficient reserves to justify making additional capital expenditures towards its completion as a producing well
- Drilling of additional exploratory wells is in process or firmly planned for the near future

Otherwise, exploratory well costs had to be expensed. Capitalized costs related to exploratory wells *not* under the scope of ASC 932-360-35-13 and 35-20 had to be expensed if reserves could not be classified as proved reserves within one year from the date drilling was completed.

The issue of accounting for the costs of exploratory wells was raised because the manner in which oil and gas companies are performing their exploration activities has changed from that originally contemplated in the guidance in ASC

932-360-35-13 and 35-20. Exploration activities now frequently occur in more remote areas, go to greater depths, and are undertaken in more complex geological formations than previously. As a result, some believe that there is a need to extend the one-year capitalization period in which an entity can determine whether found reserves qualify for classification as proved reserves.

ACCOUNTING GUIDANCE

An entity should continue capitalizing exploratory well costs if (1) a well has sufficient reserves to justify its completion as a producing well and (2) the entity is making satisfactory progress in evaluating the reserves and the project's economic and operating viability.

Amendment of ASC 932 The guidance in ASC 932-360-35-16 through 35-18 is amended based on the above guidance, which is provided in ASC 932-360-25-18 for reserves that cannot be classified as proved reserves when drilling is completed. The guidance in ASC 932-360-35-13, 35-16 through 35-20 also applies to exploratory-type stratigraphic wells.

ASC 932-360-35-13 provides that the value of wells should be assumed to be impaired if the criteria in ASC 932-360-25-18 that have been incorporated in ASC 932-360-35-16 through 35-20 are *not* met or an entity has information that raises doubts about a project's economic or operational viability. In that case, capitalized exploration costs incurred, less salvage value, should be expensed. Further, it is required that exploratory well costs *not* continue to be capitalized based on an expectation that economic conditions will change or that technology will be developed to make a project economically or operationally viable.

The following guidance in ASC 932-360-35-19 provides indicators that should be considered along with other relevant facts and circumstances in determining whether an entity is making enough progress in its evaluation of reserves and a project's economic and operational viability:

- Commitment of appropriate personnel with appropriate skills is being made
- Costs are incurred to assess the reserves and their potential development
- The economic, legal, political, and environmental features of a potential development are being assessed
- Sales contracts (or active negotiations) with customers for oil and gas exist
- Agreements (or active negotiations) with governments, lenders and venture partners exist
- Outstanding requests for proposals for the development of the required facilities exist
- Firm plans, established timetables, or contractual commitments exist
- There is progress on contractual arrangements to permit future development
- Existing transportation and other infrastructure that is or will be available for the project has been identified.

The guidance in ASC 932-360-35-19 provides that long delays in assessing progress or in a development plan may raise questions about whether an entity should continue to capitalize exploratory well costs after the completion of drilling. Justification for the deferral of well exploration costs becomes more difficult the longer that process continues.

Under the guidance in ASC 932-360-35-20, capitalized exploratory costs associated with a well, net of salvage value, if any, should be expensed if activities have been suspended or the entity has *not* participated in substantial activities to assess the reserves or a project's development within a "reasonable" time period after drilling has been completed. Planning to undertake activities in the near future is *not* sufficient to continue capitalization. Brief interruptions of activities, however, should *not* affect continued capitalization.

DISCLOSURES

Under the amendment of ASC 932 in ASC 932-360-25-18 management is required to apply more judgment than previously was required in evaluating whether capitalized costs of exploratory wells meet the criteria for continued capitalization. Consequently, the following required disclosures in the notes to the financial statements are intended to provide financial statement users with information about how management is applying that judgment. The disclosures are not required in interim financial statements unless previous information has changed significantly, for example, if exploratory well costs capitalized for more than one year after the completion of drilling are found to be impaired at the most recent balance sheet date. These disclosures are:

- The amount of capitalized exploratory well costs awaiting the determination of proved reserves
- For each annual period that an income statement is presented, changes in capitalized exploratory well costs as a result of
  - Additions to wells awaiting determination of proved reserves
  - Transfer of costs to wells, equipment, and facilities because proved reserves were determined
  - Expensing of capitalized costs
- For exploratory well costs capitalized for a period longer than one year after the completion of drilling at the most recent balance sheet date
  - The amount of such costs and the number of projects to which they are related
  - An aging of the amount by year or by a range of years and the number of projects to which they are related
- For exploratory well costs that continue to be capitalized for a period longer than one year after the completion of drilling at the most recent balance sheet date
  - A description of the projects and activities *undertaken* to date to evaluate the reserves and the projects

— Remaining activities required to classify the related reserves as proved reserves

ASC 932-835: Interest

ASC 932-835-25-2 Interest on Receivables and Payables: Accounting Interpretations of APB Opinion No. 21

BACKGROUND

ASC 932-835-25-2 provides implementation guidance for ASC 835-30.

ACCOUNTING GUIDANCE

Question: Under the guidance in ASC 835-30, interest must be imputed for some rights to receive or to pay money on fixed or determinable dates. For example, a pipeline entity may make an advance payment to encourage exploration. The intent is for this advance payment to be satisfied by the delivery of future production. However, if future production is not sufficient to discharge the amount of the advance payment, there is an obligation to pay cash to settle the obligation. Does the guidance in ASC 835-30 apply to such advances?

Answer: No. The guidance in ASC 835-30 does *not* apply to amounts that will not be repaid in the future, but rather to amounts that will be applied to the purchase price of property, goods, or services. The advance described above fits this exclusion even though there is an obligation to pay cash if future production is not sufficient to settle the liability.

APPENDIX E:
ASC 9XX—FINANCIAL SERVICES

CONTENTS

Interpretive Guidance	63,002
ASC 942: Financial Services—Depository and Lending	63,002
ASC 942-310: Receivables	63,002
ASC 942-310-05-2, 35-1 through 35-4	
Income Recognition on Loans to Financially Troubled Countries	63,002
ASC 942-310-05-3, 25-2, 30-1 through 30-3, 35-5 through 35-7, 55-1	
Accounting for Foreign Debt/Equity Swaps	63,002
ASC 942-320: Debt and Equity	63,004
ASC 942-320-55-1 through 55-2	
Financial Institutions' Ability to Hold Mortgage Securities to Maturity	63,004
ASC 944: Financial Services-Insurance	
ASC 944-30: Acquisition Costs	63,005
ASC 944-30-25-1A through 25-2, 50-1, 55-1 through 55-1G; ASC 944-10-65-1	
Accounting for Costs Associated With Acquiring or Renewing Insurance Contracts	63,005
ASC 944-80: Separate Accounts	63,007
ASC 944-80-25-2 through 25-3, 25-12, ASC 944-80-65-1	
How Investments Held through Separate Accounts Affect an Insurer's Consolidation Analysis of Those Investments	63,007
ASC 944-605	
Revenue Recognition	63,009
ASC 944-605-25-9 through 25-11	
Situations in Which ASC 944-40-30-16 and ASC 944-605-35-2, 25-6 through 25-7 Permit or Require Accrual of an Unearned Revenue Liability	63,009
ASC 946: Financial Services-Investment Companies	
ASC 946-10: Overall	63,010
ASC 946-10-05-3, 15-4 through 15-5, 55-22 through 55-23, 55-25 through 55-71, 65-1; ASC 323-55-2 through 55-5, 55-7 through 55-9; ASC 810-15-2, 55-6, 55-8 through 55-1	
Clarification of the Scope of the Audit and Accounting Guide *Investment Companies* and Accounting by Parent Companies and Equity Method Investors for Investments in Investment Companies	63,010
ASC 946-605: Revenue Recognition	63,023
ASC 946-605-05-5 through 05-11, 25-4 through 7, 50-1	
Application of "Distribution Fees by Distributors of Mutual Funds That Do Not Have a Front-End Sales Charge," When Cash for the Right to Future Distribution Fees for Shares Previously Sold Is Received from Third Parties	63,023
ASC 946-605-25-8	

63,002 ASC 9XX—Financial Services

Distribution Fees by Distributors of Mutual Funds That Do Not Have a Front-End Sales Charge	63,025
ASC 946-830: Foreign Currency Matters	
ASC 946-830-05-1 through 05-2, 50-1 through 50-4, 55-1 through 55-8, 55-10 through 55-16, 45-1 through 45-5, 45-7 through 45-12, 45-14, 45-22 through 45-23, 45-25 through 45-29, 45-31, 45-34 through 45-39	
Foreign Currency Accounting and Financial Statement Presentation for Investment Companies	63,026

INTERPRETIVE GUIDANCE

ASC 942: FINANCIAL SERVICES—DEPOSITORY AND LENDING

ASC 942-310: Depository and Lending-Receivables

ASC 942-310-05-2, 35-1 through 35-4
Income Recognition on Loans to Financially Troubled Countries

BACKGROUND

Many bank loans to financially troubled countries meet the criteria for accrual of losses in accordance with the guidance in ASC 450. In those situations, banks should establish loan loss allowances by charges to income.

If a financially troubled country suspends interest payments, banks with outstanding loans from such a country should suspend the accrual recognition of interest income. Such financially troubled countries may later resume interest payments. Guidance on accounting by a creditor for the receipt of interest payments from a debtor that had previously suspended interest payments is included in the industry audit guide titled *Audits of Banks*.

ACCOUNTING GUIDANCE

When a country becomes current as to principal and interest payments and has normalized relations with the international financial markets, assuming the allowance for loan losses is adequate, the creditor may recognize interest on an accrual basis. Even if these conditions are met, the bank should not automatically return the loan to accrual accounting status. Some period of payment performance generally is necessary to make an assessment of collectibility before returning the loan to accrual status.

ASC 942-310-05-3, 25-2, 30-1 through 30-3, 35-5 through 35-7, 55-1
Accounting for Foreign Debt/Equity Swaps

BACKGROUND

Certain foreign countries, particularly those with rapidly developing economies, may experience periodic financial difficulties. These financial difficulties may call into question the ability of these countries to service debt that they have issued. As a method of dealing with these financial difficulties, foreign countries experiencing financial difficulties may permit U.S. lending institutions to convert dollar-denominated debt, issued by these same countries, into approved local equity investments.

Those foreign debt/equity swaps are generally structured as follows. First, holders of the U.S. dollar-denominated debt are credited with an amount of the local currency approximately equal to the amount of the outstanding debt. This conversion is performed at the official exchange rate, with a discount from the exchange rate imposed as a transaction fee. Second, the local currency credited to the lender must be used to make an approved equity investment—the currency can be used for no other purpose. Third, capital usually cannot be repatriated for several years. In some cases, it may be permissible to sell the investment. However, the proceeds from such a sale are generally subject to the same repatriation restrictions.

ACCOUNTING GUIDANCE

These types of foreign debt/equity swaps represent an exchange of a monetary asset for a nonmonetary asset. The transaction should be measured at its fair value on the date it is agreed to by both parties. Determining fair value for those types of transactions can be challenging. In some cases, the fair value of the equity investment received is unclear, and the fair value of the debt surrendered may be equally difficult to determine. It is not unusual for debt of foreign countries experiencing financial difficulty to be thinly traded.

Regarding the fair value of the exchange, both the secondary market value of the loan surrendered and the fair value of the equity investment/net assets received should be considered. The following factors should be considered in determining the fair value of the equity investment/net assets received:

- Similar transactions for cash
- Estimated cash flows from the equity investment or net assets received
- Market value (if available) of similar equity investments
- Currency restrictions, if any, that affect (*a*) dividends, (*b*) the sale of the investment, or (*c*) the repatriation of capital

If the fair value of the equity investment/net assets received is less than the recorded amount of the loan, the resulting difference should be reflected in income as a loss at the time the transaction is consummated. The amount of any resulting loss recognized should be charged against the allowance for loan losses and should include discounts, if any, from the official exchange rate that are taken as a transaction fee. This treatment is not affected even if some portion of the loan loss may have been due to changes in the interest rate environment (i.e., the fair value of the loan had declined due to an increase in interest rates). It is assumed that the causal factor leading to the debt/equity swap, which precipitates the loss, is the adverse financial condition of the foreign debtor.

Illustration of Loss on Debt/Equity Swap

Countries Bank, Inc., has a long-term $10 million dollar-denominated loan outstanding to the Mexican government. As a result of adverse financial conditions, the Mexican government is having difficulty making payments on the above loan. The Mexican government and Countries Bank have agreed to enter into a debt/equity swap. At the current exchange rate, 1 peso equals $.125; however, as a transaction fee, the exchange rate used for the swap is $.126. Therefore, Countries Bank receives 79,365,000 pesos in exchange for the $10 million of dollar-denominated debt (Countries Bank would have received 80 million pesos if the official exchange rate had been used; the difference is a transaction fee). Countries Bank will use those proceeds to purchase 50,000 shares of MexPower, a state-owned utility. MexPower is not publicly traded; however, a third party recently paid 140 million pesos for a 10% stake in MexPower (100,000 shares). The secondary market for the dollar-denominated debt issued by the Mexican government is thinly traded. Therefore, the fair value of this swap transaction will be measured by the fair value of the shares of MexPower received. Based on the recent cash transaction, the fair value of the MexPower shares received by Countries Bank is estimated to be 70 million pesos. In U.S. dollars, the fair value of Countries Bank's MexPower stake is $8.75 million (70 million pesos × .125). Therefore, Countries Bank will recognize a $1.25 million loss on this debt/equity swap ($10 million - $8.75 million).

OTHER ISSUES

With the exception of a discount from the official exchange rate imposed as a transaction fee, all other costs and expenses associated with the swap should be charged to income as incurred. Any discount from the official exchange rate has the effect of reducing the fair value of the equity investment received by the lender; therefore, such a discount is considered in determining the amount of any loss recognized by the lender as a result of the swap.

Because of the subjective nature of the valuation process, the fair value of the equity investment/net assets received might exceed the carrying amount of the loan. This apparent gain (or recovery of previous losses recognized on the loan) should not be recognized until the equity investment/net assets received are converted into unrestricted cash or cash equivalents.

A particular lender may have loans outstanding to a number of financially troubled countries. A loss recognized in a foreign debt/equity swap would be one piece of evidence suggesting that the allowance for loan losses, relating to loans outstanding to other financially distressed countries, should be increased.

ASC 942-320: Debt and Equity

ASC 942-320-55-1 through 55-2
Financial Institutions' Ability to Hold Mortgage Securities to Maturity

A policy statement issued by a federal regulator of financial institutions identified criteria for determining regulated financial institutions should consider mortgage derivative products to be *high-risk mortgage securities* that should be disposed of. That statement was later clarified to state that the existence of a bank examiners' authority to ask institutions to dispose of high-risk securities should not preclude institutions from classifying as held-to-maturity securities that are non-high-risk when acquired and when the institution has the ability and intent to hold such securities to maturity.

ASC 944: FINANCIAL SERVICES—INSURANCE

ASC 944-30: Acquisition Costs

ASC 944-30-25-1A through 25-2, 50-1, 55-1 through 55-1G; ASC 944-10-65-1 Accounting for Costs Associated with Acquiring or Renewing Insurance Contracts

BACKGROUND

When insurance entities, which are discussed in Financial Accounting Standards Board (FASB) Accounting Standards Codification™ (ASC) 944, *Financial Services—Insurance*, acquire or renew insurance contracts, they incur certain costs (e.g., agent and broker commissions, salaries of employees that are involved in functions related to underwriting and policy issues, medical and inspection fees, and other costs) that are referred to as "acquisition costs" and defined in the Glossary of ASC 944 as costs that "vary with and are primarily related to the acquisition of insurance contracts." Insurance entities recognize as assets costs meeting that definition and refer to them as deferred acquisition costs (DAC), which are amortized over time in proportion to revenues based on a contract's estimated gross profit or on its estimated gross margin. Costs that are not related to the acquisition or renewal of insurance contracts and that do not vary with those contracts (e.g., for administration or costs related to investments) are charged to expense as incurred.

There are diverse views in practice regarding which costs should be included in DAC. Some believe that only costs that are direct and incremental and related to the acquisition of new or renewal contracts should be included in DAC, while others believe that only a casual relationship is required for costs to meet the requirement that they "vary with and are primarily related to" the acquired contracts and that some costs (e.g., advertising) may be included in DAC.

SCOPE

The following guidance applies to insurance entities accounted for under the guidance in ASC 944 that incur costs in the acquisition of new and renewal insurance contracts.

ACCOUNTING GUIDANCE

The following is guidance related to the accounting for DAC:
- The entire amount of incremental direct contract acquisition costs incurred in transactions with employees or independent third parties should be deferred if the criteria for capitalization are met.
- Variable compensation paid to an employee should be considered part of the employee's overall compensation but only a prorated portion of

compensation that is related to successful contract acquisitions should be deferred as DAC.

- DAC should include the following:
  - Costs related to underwriting, policy issuance and processing, and medical inspection;
  - For activities performed by a contract sales force, only the portion of an employee's total compensation and fringe benefits that are directly related to the time the employee has spent performing activities related to contracts that were actually acquired and other costs related to those activities that would not have been incurred had the contract not been acquired; and
  - Medical and inspection fees paid to third parties that are related to successful contract acquisitions.
- Advertising costs should be capitalized only if they meet the requirements in ASC 340, *Other Assets and Deferred Costs*, for the capitalization of direct-response advertising. If so, costs related to direct-response advertising should be included in DAC for the purpose of classification, subsequent measurement, and premium deficiency calculation in accordance with the guidance in ASC 944.

RECURRING DISCLOSURES

Insurance entities should disclose the following information:

- The nature and type of **acquisition costs** capitalized;
- The method of amortizing capitalized acquisition costs; and
- The amount of acquisition costs amortized for the period.

TRANSITION METHOD, TRANSITION DISCLOSURES, AND EFFECTIVE DATE

Prospective application is required in fiscal years that begin after December 15, 2011 and interim periods within those fiscal years. However, *retrospective* application of the guidance is permitted, but not required. If an entity elects retrospective application, the guidance for retrospective application in ASC 250, *Accounting Changes and Error Corrections*, should be applied. Early adoption of the guidance is permitted, but should only be applied as of the beginning of an entity's annual reporting period to improve comparability with other entities that choose retrospective application.

An entity that chooses to apply the guidance prospectively should make one of the following transition disclosures instead of disclosing the information required in ASC 250-10-50-1(b)(2):

- A comparison of the amount of acquisition costs that an entity would have capitalized during the period immediately before adopting the guidance in this Issue if it had applied this guidance during that period to the amount that the entity had actually capitalized.

- A comparison of the amount of acquisition costs that an entity actually capitalized during the period in which the guidance in this Issue was adopted to the amount that the entity would have capitalized during that period if its previous policy related to the capitalization of DAC had been applied.

Entities that choose retrospective application of the guidance need *not* disclose the effect of a change in the current period as required in ASC 250-10-50-1(b)(2). However, those entities would have to disclose the information required in ASC 250-10-50-1 through 50-3.

Entities choosing retrospective application are permitted to make a reasonable estimate of the effect on prior years based on their specific circumstances and are not necessarily expected to redo their detailed capitalization, amortization, and premium deficiency calculations for every prior year if they have ways to reasonably estimate those amounts in accordance with the guidance in ASU 250-10.

When adopting the guidance discussed above an entity may elect not to capitalize costs that previously had not been capitalized.

ASC 944-80: Separate Accounts

ASC 944-80-25-2 through 25-3, 25-12, ASC 944-80-65-1
How Investments Held through Separate Accounts Affect an Insurer's Consolidation Analysis of Those Investments

BACKGROUND

Some life insurance products (e.g., variable annuity contracts) provide an investment return and sometimes also insure mortality risk. Separate accounts, which are not separate legal entities and are similar to mutual funds, are established by insurance companies to: (1) help pass through investment return risk; and (2) protect the assets that back the separate account component of a variable interest annuity contract from the insurance company's general creditors if the insurance company were to become insolvent. Separate accounts are accounting entities controlled by an insurance company that holds 100 percent of the separate account's assets. The insurance company cannot make investment allocation decisions for contract holders, but it has certain rights (e.g., voting on behalf of the contract holders).

Some separate accounts are required to file standalone financial statements and are considered to be investment companies. Although separate accounts that hold a majority interest in a mutual fund generally do not consolidate the mutual fund in their standalone financial statements, it is unclear whether that treatment is appropriate. In addition, in view of the issuance of FASB Accounting Standards Codificationtrade; (ASC) 810, *Consolidation* (FAS-160, *Noncontrolling Interests in Consolidated Financial Statements,* questions have been raised about the presentation of a noncontrolling interest if an investment was consolidated. Further, there are questions as to whether an insurer should combine its general account interest with its separate account interest in an investment in determining whether it has a controlling interest in the investment.

ACCOUNTING ISSUES

1. How should an insurer account for a majority owned investment in a mutual fund if the insurer's separate account holds a majority ownership interest?

2. If the conclusion is that an insurer should consolidate the mutual fund in issue 1, how should the consolidated mutual fund be presented in the insurer's financial statements?

3. How should an insurer account for a majority-owned investment in a mutual fund if its majority ownership is a result of a combination of interests held by its separate and general accounts, neither of which has a majority interest in the separate account on an individual basis?

SCOPE

The following guidance applies to an insurance company that holds a majority-owned investment in a voting-interest mutual fund through a separate account that meets all of the conditions in ASC 944-80-25-2 or through the combined interests of a separate account and a general account. However, the following guidance does *not* apply to an insurance company that has a majority interest in a mutual fund held through its general account.

The following guidance applies to investment funds that are considered to be variable interest entities (VIEs) under the guidance in Accounting Standards Update (ASU) 2009-17, *Consolidation (Topic 810): Improvements to Financial Reporting by Enterprises Involved with Variable Interest Entities*, which was issued in December 2009.

ACCOUNTING GUIDANCE

The following accounting guidance applies:

- An insurer that holds a majority interest in a mutual fund through its separate account or through a combination of its general and separate accounts is *not* required to consolidate the mutual fund if the general account does *not* hold a controlling interest in the fund on its own;

- An insurance entity that holds investments for the benefit of policyholders through its separate accounts should *not* be required to consider those investments as its own when applying the guidance in ASC 810-10, except if the holder of the separate account is a related party. In that case, the insurance entity should consolidate the separate account; (ASC 944-80-25-3)

- If consolidation is required, an insurance entity should include: (1) the portion of a fund's assets that represent the contract holder's interests as separate account assets and liabilities in accordance with the guidance in ASC 944-80-25-3; and (2) the remaining fund assets, including those owned by other investors, in the entity's general account on a line-by-line basis; (ASC 944-80-25-12)

- Noncontrolling assets should be classified as a liability or equity based on other guidance; (ASC 944-80-25-12) and
- Entities with arrangements that are not separate accounts are prohibited from applying this guidance to other investments by analogy.

EFFECTIVE DATE AND TRANSITION METHOD

This guidance is effective for fiscal years and interim periods that begin after December 15, 2010. *Retrospective* application is required to all prior periods on adoption. Early adoption is permitted. (ASC 944-80-65-1)

ASC 944-605: Revenue Recognition

ASC 944-605-25-9 through 25-11 Situations in Which ASC 944-40-30-16 and ASC 944-605-35-2 and 25-6 through 25-7 Permit or Require Accrual of an Unearned Revenue Liability

OVERVIEW

Under the guidance in FASB Accounting Standards Codification (ASC) 944-605-25-5, insurers are required to recognize revenue from universal life contracts in the period in which the contracts are assessed unless there is evidence that the amount assessed is for services that will be performed over more than one period. The guidance in ASC 944-605-25-6 through 25-7 states further that amounts assessed for services that will be performed in the future should be recognized as unearned revenue and recognized in income in the periods in which those services will be performed.

In the Basis of Conclusions section, the FASB argued against commentators' suggestions that revenue be recognized ratably over the life of a contract to show a "level pattern of service." The FASB's view was that revenue should be recognized according to a contract's terms and conditions, unless the substance of the agreement differs from the contract's terms. Here, the FASB stated again that amounts related to services that will be provided in the future should be deferred and recognized over the period during which the insurer will provide the service.

An assessed amount that is unearned would be assessed only in certain contract periods or in such a manner that the insurer would have current profits and incur future losses from a specific function of the contract. The FASB concluded that under those circumstances, specific assessments might result in the recognition of unearned revenue, but that it is necessary to consider the facts and circumstances of the particular situation to reach that conclusion. The issue of when insurers should recognize unearned revenue has been raised again because of diversity in the interpretation of ASC 944-605-25-8, which states:

> For a contract determined to meet the definition of an insurance contract . . . if the amounts assessed against the contract holder each period for the insurance benefit feature are assessed in a manner that is expected to result in profits in earlier years and losses in subsequent years from the insurance

benefit function, a liability should be established in addition to the account balance to recognize the portion of such assessments that compensates the insurance enterprise for benefits to be provided in future periods.

The guidance in ASC 944-605-25-8 also can be interpreted as limiting the circumstances in which insurers are required to recognize unearned revenue to those in which current profits will be followed by future losses.

ACCOUNTING GUIDANCE

The FASB staff believes that insurers should accrue an unearned revenue liability for amounts assessed to contract holders that represent compensation for services to be provided in future periods and that the situation discussed in ASC 944-25-8 does *not* restrict the recognition of unearned revenue for insurance benefit features of universal life contracts to situations in which profits are expected to be followed by losses. The requirement in ASC 944-605-30-16; ASC 944-605-35-2; ASC 944-605-25-6 through 25-7 is that an unearned revenue liability be accrued for "any amounts that have been assessed to compensate the insurer for services to be performed over future periods."

The FASB staff also stressed the need to consider the facts and circumstances of each situation. Further, the staff noted that if the amount of an insurance benefit liability is determined according to the guidance in ASC 944-605-25-8, unearned revenue liabilities accrued in accordance with the guidance in ASC 944-605-30-16; 944-605-35-2; 944-605-25-6 through 25-7 should be considered. For that purpose, an increase in the unearned revenue liability during a period should be excluded from amounts assessed against a contract holder's account balance for the period, and a decrease in the unearned revenue liability during a period should be included in that period's assessment.

ASC 946: Financial Services—Investment Companies

ASC 946-10: Overall

ASC 946-10-05-3, 15-4 through 15-5, 55-22 through 55-23, 55-25 through 55-71, 65-1; ASC 323-55-2 through 55-5, 55-7 through 55-9; ASC 810-15-2, 55-6, 55-8 through 55-12
Clarification of the Scope of the Audit and Accounting Guide Investment Companies and Accounting by Parent Companies and Equity Method Investors for Investments in Investment Companies

NOTE: The FASB has decided to delay the effective date of the guidance discussed below for an indefinite period of time. Entities that opted to adopt that guidance before the issuance its effective date was delayed were permitted, but not required, to continue applying that guidance. However, entities that had *not* yet adopted the guidance are prohibited from adopting it, except that a consolidated entity must apply the guidance in its standalone financial statements if that entity was formed or acquired after its parent company had early adopted the guidance and it had decided to continue following it.

ASC 946-10-65-1 has been amended as follows:

ASC 9XX—Financial Services **63,011**

The effective date of the pending content that links to this paragraph is delayed indefinitely. An entity that early adopted that pending content before December 15, 2007, is permitted but not required to continue to apply the provisions of the SOP. No other entity may adopt the provisions of that pending content that links to this paragraph, with the following exception. If a parent entity that early adopted the pending content that links to this paragraph chooses not to rescind its early adoption, an entity consolidated by that parent entity that is formed or acquired after that parent entity's adoption of that pending content must apply the provisions of that pending content in its standalone financial statements. If an entity that early adopted the pending contact that links to this paragraph voluntarily rescinds its early adoption as permitted by this paragraph, that entity shall account for that change according to the provisions of Subtopic 250-10.

The guidance in ASC 810-10-25-15 continues to be effective for entities that did *not* adopt that guidance.

DEFINITION OF AN INVESTMENT COMPANY

An investment company is defined as follows:

- An entity whose business purpose and activity is to invest in various investments, such as the securities of other entities, commodities, securities based on indices, derivatives, real estate, and other forms of investments, for current income, capital appreciation, or both, and has exit strategies for its investments. An investment company does *not* acquire or hold investments for strategic operating purposes and does *not* get benefits from its investees that are *not* available to noninvestors that are *not* related parties to the investees. An investment company: (1) sells its capital shares to investors; (2) invests the proceeds to achieve its investment objectives; and (3) makes distributions to its investors in the form of cash or ownership interests in its investees, income earned on investments, and proceeds realized on investments that have been disposed off, less expenses incurred by the investment company; or

- An entity, including one in a foreign jurisdiction, that is registered or regulated so that it is subject to the requirements of the 1940 Act, the Small Business Investment Company Act of 1958, or similar requirements, and is required to report its investments at fair value for regulatory or similar reporting purposes. Such entities include: (1) management investment companies; (2) unit investment trusts (UITs); (3) small business investment companies (SBICs); (4) business development companies (BDCs); (5) certain offshore funds; (6) separate accounts of insurance companies; and (7) common (collective) trust funds. To determine whether an entity is subject to reporting requirements sufficiently similar to those of the 1940 Act or the Small Business Investment Company Act of 1958, regulations related to the following should be considered: (1) registration requirements; (2) reporting and disclosure to investors; (3) the investment manager's and related entities' fiduciary duties; (4) investment diversification; (5) recordkeeping and internal controls; and (6) purchases and redemptions of shares at fair value.

The determination of whether an entity meets the definition of an investment company should be made when the entity is formed and should be reconsidered in each reporting period.

Activities Inconsistent with the Definition of an Investment Company

The following factors should be considered in determining whether an entity meets the definition of an investment company:

Business purpose. Under the definition, an investment company's business purpose is to invest for current income, capital appreciation, or both. How an entity presents itself to other parties may provide evidence about its business purpose. The business purpose of an entity that presents itself as a private equity investor whose objective is to invest for capital appreciation is consistent with the definition of an investment company. However, the business objective of an entity presenting itself as an investor for strategic operating purposes is *not* consistent with the definition. An entity's prior history of purchasing and selling investments, its offering memorandum, and other corporate partnership documents may provide information about an entity's business purpose.

An entity's activities, assets, and liabilities. To meet the definition of an investment company's business purpose, it should have *no* substantive activities other than its investment activities and *no* significant assets or liabilities other than those related to its investment activities.

Multiple substantive investments. An investment company should invest in and hold multiple substantive investments directly or through another investment company. An entity that has equity investments in other entities should organize those investees as separate legal entities, except for temporary investments as a result of foreclosure or liquidation of the original investment. However, an investment company is *not* required to hold multiple substantive investments at all times (e.g., while completing the entity's initial offering period, while identifying suitable investments, or during an entity's liquidation stage) as long as the entity plans to hold various substantive investments simultaneously.

Exit strategies. The following should exist for each investment:

- A potential exit strategy has been identified, even though a specific method has not yet been identified, such as whether an exit will occur through: (1) a sale of securities in a public market; (2) an initial public offering of equity securities; (3) a private placement of equity securities; (4) distributions to investors of ownership interests in investees; (5) sales of assets; or (6) holding a debt security to maturity.
- The expected time for exiting an investment has been determined in terms of an expected date or a range of dates. It is based on a milestone, the entity's limited life, or an entity's investment objective.

Not for strategic operating purposes. Since investment companies are prohibited from holding investments for strategic purposes, the following relationships and activities are *not* permitted:

- Acquiring, using, exchanging, or exploiting an investee's or its affiliate's technology, intangible assets, or processes;
- Significant sales or purchases of assets between the entity or its affiliates and an investee or its affiliates;
- Joint ventures between the entity or its affiliates and an investee or its affiliates;
- Other arrangements between the entity or its affiliates and an investee or its affiliates for joint development, production, marketing, or provision of products or services;
- Other transactions between the entity or its affiliates and an investee or its affiliates: (1) on terms unavailable to parties unrelated to the investee; (2) at a price not available to other market participants at that date; or (3) that correspond to a significant portion of an investee's or the entity's business activity or that of their affiliates; and
- The entity or its affiliates have disproportionate rights, exclusive rights, or rights of first refusal to purchase or acquire in other ways an investee's or its affiliate's assets, technology, products, or services, held temporarily as a result of a default related to an investment in a collateralized security. However, a right of first refusal to purchase or acquire a direct ownership interest in collateral as a result of a default related to an investment in a collateralized security is *not* inconsistent with the definition of an investment company.

Factors to Consider

When considering whether an entity meets the definition of an investment company, all of the following relevant facts and circumstances should be considered.

Number of substantive investors in an entity (pooling of funds). The fact that an entity has many investors who pool their funds in order to benefit from the entity's professional investment management provides significant evidence that the entity's business purpose is to invest for current income, capital appreciation, or both.

Level of ownership interests in investees. The entity's level of ownership interests in its investees and the significance of the investees to the total investment portfolio should be considered. It is more likely that an entity with minor levels of ownership in its investees is investing for current income, capital appreciation, or both, rather than for strategic operating purposes.

Substantial ownership by passive investors. If a substantial amount of an entity whose purpose is to invest for current income and capital appreciation is owned by passive investors rather than by principal investors who determine the entity's strategic direction or run its day-to-day operations, it is a significant indicator that the entity is investing for current income, capital appreciation, or both, rather than for strategic operating purposes.

Substantial ownership by employee benefit plans. Ownership of a substantial amount of an entity by employee benefit plans is a significant indicator that the entity is investing for current income, capital appreciation, or both, rather than for strategic operating purposes.

Involvement in the day-to-day management of investees, their affiliates, or other investment assets. An entity's involvement in investees' day-to-day management activities is an indicator that the entity is investing for strategic operating purposes and consequently would *not* meet the definition of an investment company. However, an investment company may occasionally become involved temporarily in an investee's day-to-day operations if the investee is having difficulties and the investment company steps in to maximize the value of its investment. If that involvement continues over an extended period of time, it may be an indicator that the entity made the investment for strategic operating purposes.

Provision of loans by noninvestment company affiliates of the entity to investees or their affiliates. If an affiliate of an investment company that is *not* an investment company provides a loan to an investee or its affiliate, depending on the arrangement's terms and conditions, it may be an indicator that the investment was made for strategic operating purposes. However, if *all* of the following conditions exist, such a loan may *not* be inconsistent with the definition of an investment company:

- The loan's terms are at fair value.
- The loan is not required as a condition of the investment.
- The loans are not made to most of the entity's investees or their affiliates.
- Making loans is part of the usual business activity of an affiliate that is *not* an investment company.

Compensation of investee's or its affiliate's management or employees depends on the entity's or its affiliate's financial results. If the compensation of an investee's or its affiliate's management or employees depends on the entity's or its affiliate's financial results, it is an indicator that the entity has made the investment for a strategic operating purpose. Options granted to acquire stock are an example of such compensation.

Directing the integration of operations of investees or their affiliates or the establishment of business relationships between investees or their affiliates. An entity's involvement with an investee's or its affiliate's integration of operations or the establishment of business relationships between investees or their affiliates, such as the creation of joint ventures or significant purchases or sales of assets or other transactions between an investee and its affiliate, is an indicator that the investment was made for strategic operating purposes.

Although none of the factors discussed are individually determinative as to whether an entity meets the definition of an investment company, some should be given more weight than others when the definition of an investment company is applied. Specifically, the indicators related to the number of an entity's investees and an entity's level of ownership interest in its investees provide more significant evidence about an entity's business purpose than the other factors discussed.

ASC 9XX—Financial Services **63,015**

ACCOUNTING BY PARENT COMPANIES AND EQUITY METHOD INVESTORS FOR INVESTMENTS IN INVESTMENT COMPANIES.

An investment company under the scope of this guidance may be: (1) a subsidiary of another entity; or (2) an investor in an investment company that has the ability to exercise significant influence over it and accounts for its investment under the equity method of accounting.

Overview. A parent company or an equity method investor that chooses to retain investment company accounting in its financial statements may do so only if *all* of the following conditions exist:

- A subsidiary or equity method investee under the scope of the Guide meets the definition of an investment company.
- The established policies of a consolidated group of a parent company that chooses to retain investment company accounting in consolidation follows established policies that distinguish the nature and type of the investment company's investments from the nature and type of the investments made by other entities in the consolidated group that are *not* investment companies. At a minimum, those policies should address the following:
  — The degree of the investment company's and its related entities' influence over the investment company's investees.
  — The extent to which the investment company's investees or their affiliates are in the same line of business as the parent company or its related parties.
  — The consolidated group's level of ownership interest in the investment company. The intent of this requirement is to prevent the consolidated group from selectively making investments in the investment company subsidiary that are similar to investments held by members of the consolidated group that are *not* investment companies and that would account for those investments by the equity method, consolidation, or the cost method.
- The purpose of the parent company's or equity method investor's investments are to earn current income, capital appreciation, or both rather than for strategic operating purposes.

The parent company or equity method investor (through the investment company) is investing for current income, capital appreciation, or both, rather than for strategic operating purposes. One of the requirements to retain investment company accounting in the financial statements of a parent company or an equity investor is that a parent company or an equity method investor should hold its investments for current income, capital appreciation, or both, rather than for strategic operating purposes. That requirement is *not* met if a parent company, an equity method investor, or their related parties have benefited or intend to benefit from relationships with their investees or the investees' affiliates that are not available to entities that are *not* investors and are *not* related parties to an investee. The following relationships or conditions violate that requirement:

- Acquiring, using, exchanging, or exploiting an investee's or its affiliate's technology, intangible assets, or processes;
- Significant sales or purchases of assets between the entity or its related parties and an investee or its affiliates;
- Joint ventures between the entity or its related parties and an investee or its affiliates;
- Other arrangements between the entity or its related parties and an investee or its affiliates for joint development, production, marketing, or provision of products or services;
- Other transactions between the entity or its related parties and an investee or its affiliates: (1) on terms unavailable to parties unrelated to the investee; (2) at a price not available to other market participants at that date; or (3) that correspond to a significant portion of the business activities of an investee or its affiliates, the parent company or equity method investor, or that of their related parties.
- An equity method investor or its related parties (not including insurance companies' separate accounts, trust funds, and other investments held by trust departments of financial institutions, and pension and profit-sharing trusts) have a *direct* investment in an investee or its affiliate enabling the investor to exercise significant influence over the investee or its affiliate.
- The parent company, equity method investor, or their related parties have disproportionate rights, exclusive rights, or rights of first refusal to purchase or acquire an investee's or its affiliate's assets, technology, products, or services in other ways.
- The parent company, equity method investor, or their related parties obtain tax benefits due to their ownership interest in the investment company and obtaining those benefits was a significant reason for making the investment.

Except for certain exceptions to be discussed below, a parent company or equity investor is considered to be holding an interest in an investee for strategic operating purposes, which results in a change in accounting, if transfers of investments, including, but not limited to, transfers made in exchange for cash or other consideration are made:

- From an investment company to its parent company, equity method investor, or to their related parties that are *not* investment companies; or
- From the parent company, equity investor, or their related parties that are *not* investment companies to the investment company.

The following transfers are the exceptions that would *not* lead to a conclusion that a parent company or equity method investor is investing for strategic operating purposes:

- Transfers in circumstances in which the investments and the effects of holding them would be reported in the same manner in the financial statements regardless of which party holds them.

- A transfer that is a pro-rata distribution of an investee's shares to an equity method investor in the investment company if: (1) the equity method investor is not able to initiate the distribution; and (2) the distribution of shares is a final liquidation of the investment company or the shares are publicly traded securities.
- Transfers that occur in rare situations between an investment company and its parent company, equity method investor, or their related parties if there have been: (1) significant changes in the facts and circumstances of the nature of the parent company's, equity method investor's, or their related parties' business activities that are unrelated to the investee or its affiliates; or (2) significant changes in the business activities of an investee or its affiliates that were *not* initiated or directed by the parent company, equity method investor, or their related parties so that retaining the investment in the investment company, parent company, equity method investor, or their related parties would lead to a conclusion that the investment company should *no* longer be accounted for under the Guide's scope.
- Immaterial and insignificant transfers in all respects, for example, in relation to: (1) a parent company's or equity investor's financial statements; (2) a parent company's or equity investor's interest in the investment company; and (3) the total investment portfolio of investment company subsidiaries and investees reported on the equity method.

Factors to Consider

The following factors should be considered in determining whether a parent company or equity method investor is investing in an investment company for strategic operating purposes:

- Involvement in the day-to-day management of investees, their affiliates, or other investment assets;
- Significant administrative or support services provided by the parent company, equity method investor, or their related parties;
- Financial guarantees or assets to serve as collateral provided by investees or their affiliates for borrowing arrangements entered into by the parent company, equity method investor, or their related parties;
- Compensation of an investee's or affiliate's management or employees depends on the parent company's, equity method investor's, or their related parties' financial results;
- Directing the integration of investees' or their affiliates' operations or the establishment of business relationships between investees or their affiliates;
- Active participation in an investee's or its affiliate's organization and formation; and
- Acquiring equity interests in an investment company in exchange for interests in investees.

GUIDANCE FOR EQUITY METHOD INVESTORS (THROUGH THE INVESTMENT COMPANY) THAT INVEST FOR CURRENT INCOME, CAPITAL APPRECIATION, OR BOTH, RATHER THAN FOR STRATEGIC OPERATING PURPOSES

Because an investment company may have a number of equity method investors, those investors should apply the guidance regarding the retention of investment company accounting in a parent company's or equity method investor's financial statements, based on their *own* facts and circumstances without regard to the relationships and activities of other investors in the investment company that are *not* related to the equity method investor. That is, some equity method investors in an investment may apply investment company accounting when applying the equity method in their financial statements while others may not. This guidance does *not* apply to investors that do not exercise significant influence over an investee, even though the guidance in ASC 323-30-S55-1, S99-1, and ASC 272-10-05-3 through 05-4; ASC 323-30-15-4, 35-3 provides that the equity method may be applied in certain situations in which an investor does not exercise significant control. Those investors should retain the specialized accounting for investment companies when applying the equity method to their investment in an investment company.

Changes in Status

An investment company's status as an entity that accounts for its transactions under the guidance in ASC 946 should be determined when the entity is formed. That determination should be reconsidered at each reporting period based on the guidance regarding the scope of ASC 946. If an entity's status changes (i.e., an entity previously not under the scope of the guidance in ASC 946 meets the requirements for investment company accounting or an entity that was under the scope of the guidance in ASC 946 no longer meets those requirements), the entity should adopt the appropriate accounting as of the date on which its status changed, rather than as of the reporting date. A change in status should be accounted for as follows:

- *Change from investment company accounting.* An entity that no longer meets the scope requirements under this guidance should stop accounting for its transactions in accordance with investment company accounting under the guidance in ASC 946 and report its changed status *prospectively* by accounting for its investments in accordance with other generally accepted accounting principles (GAAP) as of the date of the change in status using *fair value* as the carrying amount of the investments in conformity with investment company accounting *at the date of the change.*

- *Change to investment company accounting.* If there is a change in the status of an entity that previously had not met the scope requirements in this guidance to be accounted for in accordance with the the guidance in ASC 946, the effect of the change in status, which is the difference between the carrying amounts of the investments in conformity with the provisions of ASC 946 and their carrying amounts in accordance with other GAAP should be reported as of the date of the change as an adjustment to retained earnings in the period in which the change occurred.

- *Disclosure of change in status.* All entities that experience a change in status should disclose that fact in their financial statements. However, entities that change to investment company accounting from other GAAP should disclose the effect of the change in status on the financial statements in the period in which it occurred, including the effect of the change on the reported amounts of investments as of the date of the change in status and how that change has affected net income, change in net assets from operations (for investment companies) or change in net assets (for not-for-profit organizations), and related per share amounts. When making their initial investment in an investment company, a parent company or an equity method investor should make their initial determination whether to retain investment company accounting for that investment in their financial statements. The provisions in this guidance regarding the retention of investment company accounting in a parent company's or an equity method investor's financial statements should be reconsidered at each reporting period and may result in a change in status. A change in status should be accounted for as follows:

- *Parent company no longer meets the requirements for retention of investment company accounting.* If after the initial determination that a parent company should retain investment company accounting for a subsidiary in its financial statements, the parent company no longer meets the requirements in this guidance for retention of investment company accounting for *any* investment company subsidiary (or if an investment company subsidiary that previously had met the scope requirements under this guidance and had been consolidated in the parent company's financial statements no longer meets the scope requirements for investment company accounting under this guidance), the parent company should discontinue its retention of investment company accounting in its financial statements for *all* of its subsidiaries.

- *Equity method investor no longer meets the requirements for retention of investment company accounting.* If an equity method investor discontinues retention of investment company accounting in its financial statements for its investment in an investment company in accordance with this guidance after it had been determined that investment company accounting should be retained for that investee in the equity method investor's financial statements (or if an equity method investee that previously had met the scope requirements under this guidance and investment company accounting had been retained in the investor's financial statements for that investee no longer meets the scope requirements under this guidance for investment company accounting), the equity method investor should stop using investment company accounting to report its investment in *that* investment company and its equity method investments in *other* investment companies that meet both of the following conditions: (1) the equity method investor has the ability to exercise significant influence over the entity; and (2) the entity is managed by the same general partner, investment advisor, a party with an equivalent role, or a related party of that general partner, investment adviser, or party with an equivalent role for which investment company accounting is *not* permitted.

REPORTING A DISCONTINUANCE OF RETENTION OF INVESTMENT COMPANY ACCOUNTING

A parent company or an equity method investor that no longer retains investment company accounting for a subsidiary or investee in its financial statements in accordance with this guidance in should report a change in status *prospectively* by accounting for its investment in accordance with *other* GAAP as of the date of the change in status, rather than as of the reporting date, and should report the carrying amount of the investment at *fair value* in accordance with investment company accounting at the date of the change.

- *Adopting retention of investment company accounting.* If after an initial determination that a parent company does *not* meet the conditions in this guidance for retention of investment company accounting in its financial statements for a subsidiary or an equity method investor for its investee, a change in a parent company's or equity method investor's circumstances may result in the conclusion that investment company accounting should be retained in a parent company's or equity method investor's financial statements in accordance with this guidance. In that case, a parent company or equity method investor should change to the appropriate accounting as of the date of the change in status and should report the effect of that change as an adjustment to retained earnings in the period in which it occurred. The effect of that change equals the difference between the carrying amounts of the investments in accordance with the provisions of the Guide and the carrying amounts of the investments (or assets minus liabilities or consolidated investments) in accordance with GAAP other than that in ASC 946.

- *Disclosure of a change in status.* All entities that have a change in status should report that fact in their financial statements. Parent companies or equity method investors that had initially determined not to retain investment company accounting for their subsidiary or investee in their financial statements and that due to a change in circumstances have started to retain investment company accounting in their financial statements should disclose: (1) the effect of the change in status on the financial statements in the period in which the change occurred; (2) the effect of the change on the reported amounts of investments as of the date of the change in status; and (3) the related effects on net income, change in net assets from operations (for investment companies) or change in net assets (for not-for-profit organizations), and related share amounts.

DISCLOSURE REQUIREMENT

Disclosures About a Parent Company's Retention of Investment Company Accounting

Parent companies should disclose the following information if investment company accounting is retained for investment company subsidiaries in the parent company's consolidated financial statements:

- Retention of investment company accounting in the consolidated financial statements.
- As of each balance sheet date, the carrying amount (fair value) and cost of the portfolio of investment company subsidiaries for which investment company accounting has been retained.
- Disclosures about significant transactions between the parent company or its related parties and investees of the investment company or their affiliates, including:
  — The nature of the relationships.
  — A description of transactions for each of the periods for which income statements are presented and other information considered necessary to understand the effects of the transactions on the financial statements, such as the amount of gross profit (or similar measure) from the transactions.
  — The dollar amounts of transactions, such as sales and similar revenues, for each of the periods for which income statements are presented and the effects of a change, if any, in the method of establishing the terms of the transactions from that used in the preceding period.
  — Amounts due from or to investees or their affiliates as of the date of each balance sheet presented and, if not otherwise clear, the terms and manner of settlement.
- Gross unrealized total appreciation and total depreciation of investments in the investment company's investment portfolio for each balance sheet date.
- Net realized gains and losses from investments in the investment portfolio of investment company subsidiaries for which investment company accounting has been retained for each year an income statement is presented.
- Net increase (decrease) in unrealized appreciation (or depreciation) of the investment portfolio (change in unrealized amounts during the year) for each year an income statement is presented.
- The policy for distinguishing the nature and type of investments made by the investment company from the nature and type of investments made by other entities within the consolidated group that are *not* investment companies.

Disclosures about an Equity Method Investor's Retention of Investment Company Accounting

Equity method investors should disclose the following information if investment company accounting is retained in the financial statements:

- Retention of investment company accounting for an investment company in the equity method investor's financial statements.
- As of each balance sheet date, the carrying amount (fair value) and cost of the portfolio of equity method investees for which investment company accounting has been retained. Amounts disclosed should correspond to the equity method investor's proportionate interests in the portfolios of its equity method investees.
- Disclosures about significant transactions between the equity method investor or its related parties and investees of the investment company or their affiliates, including:
    - The nature of the relationships.
    - A description of transactions for each of the periods for which income statements are presented and other information considered necessary to understand the effects of the transactions on the financial statements, such as the amount of gross profit (or similar measure) from the transactions.
    - The dollar amounts of transactions, such as sales and similar revenues, for each of the periods for which income statements are presented and the effects of any change in the method of establishing the terms from that used in the preceding period.
    - Amounts due from or to investees or their affiliates as of the date of each balance sheet presented and, if not otherwise clear, the terms and manner of settlement.

Disclosures Related to Changes in Status Related to the Scope of ASC 946

The following information should be disclosed if in accordance with this guidance there is a change in the status of an investment company's qualification to be accounted for under the scope of ASC 946:

- The nature of and justification for the change in status.
- The disclosures required under this guidance related to the scope of ASC 946.

Disclosures Related to Changes in Status Regarding the Retention of Investment Company Accounting in the Financial Statements of a Parent Company and of an Equity Method Investor

The following information should be disclosed in accordance with this guidance:

- The nature of and justification for the change in status.
- The disclosures required under this guidance related to the retention of investment company accounting in the financial statements of a parent company and of an equity method investor.

EFFECTIVE DATE AND TRANSITION

See the Note above.

ASC 946-605: Revenue Recognition

ASC 946-605-05-5 through 05-11, 25-4 through 7, 50-1
Application of "Distribution Fees by Distributors of Mutual Funds That Do Not Have a Front-End Sales Charge," When Cash for the Right to Future Distribution Fees for Shares Previously Sold Is Received from Third Parties

BACKGROUND

Mutual fund shares referred to as "B shares" are usually sold by a fund's distributor without a sales commission (front-end load) on purchase. Rather, the distributor usually receives an asset-based fee on such shares, known as a 12b-1 fee, which is charged to investors over a period of six to eight years (12b-1 period). In addition, investors that redeem B-shares before the expiration of the 12b-1 plan period usually are charged an asset-based fee, known as a contingent deferred sales charge (CDSC), which also may be referred to as a back-end load or a sales charge. The amount of that fee declines over time until the 12b-1 plan period has expired. Fees related to shares previously sold by a distributor are referred to here as "Rights."

The 12b-1 fees are calculated periodically as a percentage of net asset value. The CDSC is calculated as a percentage of the current net assets or the original cost of shares being redeemed, whichever is less. Both fees are intended to compensate a fund's distributor for costs incurred in the form of sales commissions to broker-dealers, and for other costs related to the distribution of mutual fund shares, such as advertising, marketing, and financing costs. A distributor is usually a subsidiary of a fund's sponsor, but is a separate entity so that the distribution function is separate from the fund's investment advisory function and its record keeping and transaction services functions. However, if a fund replaces its distributor, the original distributor continues to receive 12b-1 fees and CDSC for shares it has sold.

Distributors sometimes sell their Rights to third parties and receive lump sum cash payments. The agreements may include provisions to protect buyers on default as well as indemnities in case a fund's independent board decides to terminate its 12b-1 plan. Under the guidance in "Distribution Fees by Distributors of Mutual Funds That Do Not Have a Front-End Sales Charge" which is discussed below, distributors are *not* permitted to recognize revenues on fees until cash is received. However, that guidance does *not* discuss the accounting for the receipt of cash from parties *other* than investors or the mutual fund. Consequently, some distributors have accounted for sales of Rights to third parties as sales of unrecognized financial assets. Others have recognized revenue on the receipt of cash from a third party for sales of Rights. Still others have accounted for such transactions as loans.

ACCOUNTING GUIDANCE

Question: How should a distributor account for cash received from a third party for a sale of Rights?

Answer: A distributor should recognize revenue on a sale of Rights when cash is received from a third party if the distributor has *no* recourse to those Rights or any continuing involvement with them. That is, neither the distributor nor any member of the consolidated group to which the distributor belongs: (1) retains an excessive interest in the risks and rewards related to the Rights sold; (2) guarantees or provides assurances related to a purchaser's rate of return on the Rights sold; or (3) can restrict the ability of a consolidated group or a mutual fund's independent board to remove, replace, or subcontract any of the entities or individuals that provide services to the fund. Deferred costs, if any, related to shares sold by a distributor to which the Rights pertain should be written off to earnings in the period in which revenue on the sale of those Rights is recognized.

This discussion is *not* intended to provide guidance to mutual funds, investors in mutual funds, or third party investors that obtain the Rights regarding how to account for those Rights. Mutual Funds should follow the accounting guidance provided in ASC 946-20-05-4, 05-7, 25-3, 30-2 through 30-5, 35-2 through 35-4, 45-2, 50-3. No analogies should be made to this guidance when accounting for other transactions.

Basis for Conclusions

This guidance is based on the following concepts:

- *Revenue recognition* If a distributor has *no* recourse or continuing involvement with Rights that have been sold, revenue recognition is appropriate when the distributor receives cash for the sale of those Rights because there is no uncertainty about the amount the distributor will receive on the sale. A sale of Rights is *not* analogous to sales of software as some have suggested because a distributor's right to receive 12b-1 fees or CDSC does *not* require the distributor to perform additional services to receive those Rights, which result from past services.

- *Continuing involvement* Services to investors performed by other members of a mutual fund's consolidated group are distinct and separable from a distributor's services and are *not* affected by the distributor's sale of Rights. However, a distributor maintains a continuing involvement if an arrangement includes the following provisions: (*a*) the distributor or any member of its consolidated group is required to perform future services in connection with the sale of the Rights, including actual or expected performance of a separate service with separate pricing that is a direct result of the transaction between the distributor and the buyer of the Rights, and (*b*) the distributor or any member of its consolidated group is permitted to participate in future risks or rewards in the Rights that are not proportionate to the portion of the Rights sold, for example, retention of risks or rewards of 60% when only 50% of the Rights have been sold.

- *Recourse* A distributor or its consolidated group would have recourse to a buyer that would preclude revenue recognition if an arrangement includes the following provisions:
  - The consolidated group must make a payment to the buyer if its independent board decides to change the nature of the Rights, for example, provisions related to the computation of fees and the timing of payments
  - The consolidated group must make a payment to the buyer if its independent board decides to change service providers such as the distributor, advisor, or transfer agent
  - The arrangement includes provisions that protect the buyer from risks related to fluctuations in a mutual fund's net asset value or to legal or regulatory risks that might result in termination of the 12b-1 plan
  - The arrangement restricts changes in a fund's investment objectives in accordance with the fund's prospectus or similar restrictions

Separate-Company Financial Statements

Revenue recognition in a distributor's separate-company financial statements is not affected if any member of the consolidated group that includes the distributor has a continuing involvement with a buyer as a result of the retention of a proportionate or pro rata interest. The provisions of this guidance apply to the determination of revenue recognition in a distributor's separate-company financial statements. For example, a distributor should recognize revenue in its separate-company financial statements when receiving cash from an arrangement in which a distributor transfers all or a pro rata interest in Rights to a member of its consolidated group that is *not* the distributor's subsidiary.

ASC 946-605-25-8 Distribution Fees by Distributors of Mutual Funds That Do Not Have a Front-End Sales Charge

BACKGROUND

Under Rule 12b-1 of the Investment Company Act of 1940, an investment company that sponsors a mutual fund can adopt a plan, known as a 12b-1 plan, which permits it to finance the cost of distributing its mutual fund's shares with the fund's assets, rather than charging a fee (front-end load) to investors when they purchase shares. Funds that have adopted such plans are known as no-load funds.

The fund usually enters into an agreement with a distributor, under which the distributor is paid a fee based on either an annual percentage of the fund's average net assets or an annual percentage of the fund's average net assets limited to actual costs incurred. Although distribution agreements usually continue from year to year, under the rules of a 12b-1 plan the agreement must be approved annually by the investment company's directors and may be terminated at any time with no penalty to the fund.

Because investors do not pay a front-end load, they are required to pay a contingent-deferred sales load (back-end load), which is a sales charge based on a percentage of the redemption proceeds or original cost, whichever is less, if the shares are held for less than a specified period. The percentage decreases (usually by 1% a year) until it is eliminated. The fee is deducted from the shareholder's proceeds on redemption and is paid to the distributor, even if the distribution agreement has been terminated.

When this Issue was discussed in 1985, distributors of mutual fund shares were recognizing distribution fees in income when they were received. Incremental direct costs related to distribution activities, such as sales commissions, were deferred and amortized over six years (the period shareholders would have to hold shares without incurring a fee on redemption). All other distribution costs were expensed as incurred. Because this method resulted in the deferral of a large amount of costs to future accounting periods (so they could be matched with future revenues), some in the industry suggested recognizing the discounted amount of the distribution fee in the period in which shares are sold.

ACCOUNTING ISSUE

Should fees that are expected to be received over a specified future period be recognized at a discounted amount when shares are sold, together with all related distribution costs, or on receipt with deferral of incremental direct costs?

ACCOUNTING GUIDANCE

Distributors should continue to recognize fees on receipt, defer incremental direct costs, and expense indirect costs when they are incurred.

DISCUSSION

The guidance is based on the conservative approach of recognizing revenue when a fee is realized and earned, which is consistent with the guidance in Statement of Financial Concepts No. 5, *Recognition and Measurement in Financial Statements of Business Enterprises*, (not included in the ASC).

ASC 946-830: Foreign Currency Matters

ASC 946-830-05-1 through 05-2, 50-1 through 50-4, 55-1 through 55-8, 55-10 through 55-16, 45-1 through 45-5, 45-7 through 45-12, 45-14, 45-22 through 45-23, 45-25 through 45-29, 45-31, 45-34 through 45-39
Foreign Currency Accounting and Financial Statement Presentation for Investment Companies

BACKGROUND

A number of U.S. investment companies offer closed-end single-country funds (e.g., the Germany Fund). Those funds typically adopt the U.S. dollar as their functional currency, even though many of the transactions of the fund are denominated in a different currency (e.g., the mark for the Germany Fund). The U.S. dollar is typically adopted as the functional currency because sales, redemptions, and dividends are paid to shareholders in U.S. dollars.

This pronouncement is designed to provide guidance to investment companies in computing and reporting foreign currency gains and losses in two types of investment transactions: (1) transactions involving securities denominated in or expected to be settled in a currency other than the U.S. dollar, and (2) investments in a currency other than the U.S. dollar. This Statement also provides guidance in handling other transactions (e.g., receivables and payables) denominated in a currency other than the U.S. dollar.

ACCOUNTING GUIDANCE

Scope

The provisions of this pronouncement apply to all investment companies subject to the provisions of ASC 946-830, Financial Services-Investment Companies. If a single-country fund invests in a country that is classified as "highly inflationary" in accordance with the guidance in ASC 830-10-45-11, the measurement and disclosure guidelines in this pronouncement may not apply.

> **PRACTICE POINTER:** This pronouncement does not specify the measurement and disclosure guidelines to follow if a single-country fund invests in a country classified as "highly inflationary." However, it seems reasonable to adapt the guidance on "highly inflationary" economies discussed in ASC 830 to the accounting for the single-country fund.

General Conclusions

The following conditions can give rise to a foreign currency gain or loss:

- The value of securities held, based on current exchange rates, differs from the securities cost.
- The amount of a receivable or payable at the transaction date differs from the amount ultimately received or paid upon settlement, or differs from the amount receivable or payable at the reporting date based on current exchange rates.
- The amount of interest, dividends, and withholding taxes at the transaction date differs from the amount ultimately received or paid, or differs from the amount receivable or payable at the reporting date based on current exchange rates.
- Expenses accrued at the transaction date(s) differ from the amount ultimately paid, or differ from the amount payable at the reporting date based on current exchange rates.
- Forward exchange contracts or foreign exchange futures contracts need to be marked to market.

All of those conditions result from changes in the exchange rate between the U.S. dollar and the foreign currency applicable to the fund. Before the settlement date of the transaction, a revaluation of securities, receivables, payables, etc., is classified as an unrealized gain or loss. When the transaction is settled (the cash flow occurs), the gain or loss is realized.

Differences between the amounts that were originally recorded and the amounts at which transactions are settled, or the amounts at which unsettled transactions are measured on the reporting date (based on the current exchange rate), are a function of changes in the exchange rate and changes in market prices. In recording the original transaction, the transaction at settlement, and the unsettled transaction at a reporting date, the reporting currency is used (i.e., typically the U.S. dollar).

The two components of gain/loss identified in the previous paragraph (changes in exchange rates and changes in market prices) must be separately identified, computed, and reported for all transactions other than for investments. Entities can choose to separately disclose the two components of gain/loss for investment transactions, or to combine these two elements.

Investments—Purchased Interest

Interest-bearing securities are often purchased between coupon dates. Accrued interest since the last coupon date is included in the purchase price of the security. The purchaser should recognize this accrued interest as interest receivable, measured on the basis of the spot exchange rate on the transaction date. If a reporting date intervenes before the purchased interest is received, the interest receivable is measured at the reporting date on the basis of the spot exchange rate on that date. After the settlement date, interest should be accrued on a daily basis using each day's spot exchange rate. If the exchange rate is relatively stable, however, interest can be accrued either weekly or monthly.

Illustration of the Accrual of Interest—Stable Exchange Rate

New Millennium Foreign Fund, a single-country closed-end fund, purchases an investment grade corporate bond for 1,000,000FC on December 1, 20X4. The interest rate is 8%, and the investment is purchased at face value. The semiannual interest payment dates are September 1 and March 1. The exchange rate at December 1, 20X4, is $.58 per FC. This transaction would be recorded at December 1, 20X4 (in the fund's functional currency, the U.S. dollar), as follows:

Investment in Corporate Debt (1,000,000 × $.58)	$580,000
Interest Receivable (1,000,000 × .08 × 3/12 × $.58)	11,600
Cash	$591,600

The exchange rate is relatively stable during December. New Millennium will accrue interest at December 31, 20X4, using the average exchange rate for December ($.57 per FC). The appropriate journal entry is as follows:

Interest Receivable (1,000,000 × .08 × 1/12 × $.57)	$3,800
Interest Income	$3,800

Investments—Marking to Market

As discussed previously, due to changes in both exchange rates and market values, the market value of a security at a valuation date (a reporting date) may differ from the amount at which the security was originally recorded on the transaction date. The two components of any unrealized gain or loss on securities *do not* have to be separately reported. However, the guidance in this pronouncement indicates that in many cases such separate reporting would provide valuable information to users of the fund's financial statements.

The two components—changes in exchange rates and changes in market prices—of any unrealized gains or losses can be computed as follows:

Unrealized foreign currency gain or loss

(Cost in foreign currency × Valuation date spot rate) - Cost in functional currency

Unrealized market value appreciation or depreciation

(Market value in foreign currency - Original cost in foreign currency) × Valuation date spot rate

In the above computations, weekly or monthly average exchange rates can be used if daily fluctuations in exchange rates are not significant. Also, if an entity holds a short-term security that is being carried at amortized cost, amortized cost should be substituted for market value in the above formulas.

Illustration of the Computation of Unrealized Gain

The New Millennium Foreign Fund purchases 1,000 shares of WMB Motors on December 1, 20X4, at a price of 40FC per share. The exchange rate on December 1, 20X4, is $.58 per FC. On December 31, 20X4, the market price of WMB Motors is 41FC per share, and the average exchange rate during December was $.57 (the exchange rate was relatively stable during the month). The two components of the unrealized gain recognized by New Millennium would be computed as follows:

Unrealized foreign currency gain or loss

(1,000 shares × 40FC per share × $.57) - (1,000 shares × 40FC per share × $.58) = ($400)

Unrealized market value appreciation or depreciation

[(1,000 shares × 41FC per share) - (1,000 shares × 40FC per share)] × $.57 = $570

PROOF:

(1,000 shares × 41FC per share × $.57) - (1,000 shares × 40FC per share × $.58) = $170

This proof is based on the following formula: (Market value in foreign currency × Valuation date spot rate) - (Cost in foreign currency × Transaction date spot rate)

Investments—Sale

A realized gain or loss on a security sale has two components: a realized exchange gain or loss and a realized market gain or loss. However, separately computing and displaying these two components is *optional*. If the entity chooses to report both pieces of the realized gain or loss, these amounts would be computed as follows:

Realized foreign currency gain or loss

(Cost in foreign currency × Sale date spot rate) - Cost in functional currency

Realized market gain or loss

(Sale proceeds in foreign currency - Original cost in foreign currency) × Sale date spot rate

Upon the sale of securities, a receivable is recorded based on the exchange rate on the trade date. Any change in the exchange rate between the trade date and the settlement date will be recognized as a gain or loss when the trade is settled.

Investments—Sale of Interest

An entity may sell an interest-bearing security between coupon dates. The difference between the recorded interest receivable and the foreign currency received, translated into the functional currency at the current exchange rate, represents a realized gain or loss.

Income—Interest

Interest on a security denominated in a foreign currency is to be accrued daily. First the interest is measured in the foreign currency, and then it is converted into the functional currency using the daily spot exchange rate. If the exchange rate is relatively stable, this calculation can be based on the average weekly or monthly exchange rate.

Interest receivable, which includes both accrued interest and purchased interest, is initially measured in the foreign currency. At the valuation date (which may be daily), the receivable is converted into the functional currency using the current exchange rate. The difference between the interest receivable, converted at the spot exchange date on the valuation date, and interest accrued in the foreign currency is the unrealized foreign currency gain or loss.

Income—Accretion and Amortization

Bonds are often purchased at a premium or a discount. Any such premium or discount should initially be amortized daily on a foreign currency basis. At maturity, the carrying value of the bond in the foreign currency will equal the foreign currency proceeds received. However, in most cases there will be a realized foreign currency gain or loss.

The purchase price of the bond, at the trade date, is converted into the entity's functional currency using that day's exchange rate. Daily amortization of discount or premium, in the entity's foreign currency, is converted into functional currency using the daily exchange rate (again, if exchange rates are relatively constant, a weekly or monthly average rate can be used). The sum of the purchase price of the bond (converted into functional currency on the trade date) plus (minus) amortization of the discount (premium) over the life of the bond (converted into functional currency at periodic spot rates) will produce the carrying value of the bond in the entity's functional currency. The proceeds received upon the expiration of the bond (its face value in foreign currency) is to be converted into the entity's functional currency using the exchange rate in effect on the maturity date. In most cases, the proceeds in functional currency will differ from the carrying value of the bond in functional currency. This is what gives rise to a foreign currency gain or loss.

Illustration of the Computation of a Foreign Currency Gain—Bond Expiration

The New Millennium Germany Fund purchased a 25,000,000 mark bond on October 1, 20X4, at 97%. The exchange rate on this date was $.56 per mark. The carrying value of this bond in U.S. dollars, the functional currency, on October 1, 20X4, is $13,580,000 (25,000,000 marks × 97% × $.56). Over the remaining life of this bond, New Millennium must amortize the discount of 750,000 marks. Based on the spot rates in effect when this discount was amortized, the functional currency amount of the discount amortization was $412,500. The spot exchange rate is $.59 on the bond's due date. Therefore, on the bond's due date the New Millennium Germany Fund will receive 25,000,000 marks, which is convertible into $14,750,000 (25,000,000 marks × $.59). The carrying value of the bond in U.S. dollars is $13,992,500 ($13,580,000 + $412,500). Therefore, New Millennium would have a realized foreign currency gain of $757,500.

Dividends

Dividend income on securities denominated in a foreign currency is to be recognized on the ex-dividend date. The amount of the dividend in foreign currency is to be converted into functional currency using the exchange rate on that date (DR, Dividend Receivable; CR, Dividend Income). The related Dividend Receivable account is to be translated daily at the spot exchange rate; differences that arise as a result of this process are unrealized gains or losses. When the dividend is received, the unrealized gain or loss account is reclassified as realized gain or loss.

Withholding Tax

In some cases, taxes are withheld from investment and dividend income at the source. These withheld amounts may or may not be reclaimable by the fund. If the tax withheld is not reclaimable, it should be accrued on each income recognition date if the tax rate is fixed and known. If the tax withheld is reclaimable, it should be recorded as a receivable and not as an expense. If the tax rate is not known or estimable, the expense (when the tax is not reclaimable) or the receivable (when the tax is reclaimable) is recorded on the date the (net) investment income is received. When the net investment income is received, the realized foreign currency gain or loss is computed on the gross income receivable and the accrued tax expense.

Expenses

Expenses should be accrued as incurred and translated into the functional currency using the exchange rate on the day the expense is incurred. The difference between the expense accrued in the functional currency and the related foreign currency accrued expense balance (a liability) translated into the functional currency using the exchange rate on the valuation date is the unrealized foreign currency gain or loss. When the expense is paid, the unrealized foreign currency gain or loss is reclassified as a realized gain or loss.

Receivables and Payables

Receivables and payables typically arise to record items of income and expense and to record the purchase or sale of securities. At each valuation date, all receivables and payables should be translated into the functional currency using the exchange rate on the valuation date. In most cases, there will be a difference between the amount of the receivable or payable translated at the valuation date and the functional currency amount that was recorded at various spot rates for income or expense items (or for purchases and sales of securities on different dates). This difference is an unrealized gain or loss. When a receivable or payable is settled, the difference between the amount received or paid (in functional currency) and the functional currency amount that was recorded at various spot rates for income or expense items (or for purchases and sales of securities on different dates) is a realized gain or loss.

Illustration of the Computation of a Foreign Currency Loss—Payables

The New Millennium Foreign Fund incurs the following expenses during December 20X4: 10,000FC on 12/7; 11,000FC marks on 12/14; 12,000FC on 12/21; and 13,000FC on 12/28. The spot exchange rates on these dates are $.55, $.59, $.57, and $.58, respectively. Therefore, the functional currency value of these expenses is $26,370 [(10,000FC × $.55) + (11,000FC × $.59) + (12,000FC × $.57) + (13,000FC × $.58)]. The exchange rate on December 31, 20X4, is $.58. Also, these expenses represent the December 31, 20X4, accrued expense balance. New Millennium's accrued expense balance, in its functional currency, is $26,680 at year-end. Therefore, New Millennium would have an unrealized (the liability is not yet settled) foreign currency loss of $310 ($26,680-$26,370).

Cash

Receipts of foreign currency (cash) are to be treated as if a foreign currency denominated security had been purchased. The foreign currency received is to be converted into the functional currency using the exchange rate on the day the cash is received. Every disbursement of foreign currency is to be treated as if a security had been sold. The functional equivalent of the foreign currency disbursed is to be credited (using specific identification, FIFO, or average cost to determine the amount of the functional currency to be released).

The acquisition of foreign currency does not result in a gain or loss. However, the disposition of foreign currency typically does result in a gain or loss. The gain or loss is measured as the difference between the functional currency equivalent on the date the foreign currency was acquired and the functional currency equivalent on the date the foreign currency is disbursed.

The functional currency equivalent of foreign currency held is to be computed on each valuation date. Any difference between this amount and the functional currency equivalent of the foreign currency on the date it was acquired is an unrealized gain or loss.

Forward Exchange Contracts

A *forward exchange contract* is an agreement between two parties to exchange two currencies at a specified rate on a specified date in the future. If a fund enters into a forward exchange contract, the contract is to be initially recorded at the forward rate and marked to market on a daily basis.

Unrealized gain or loss on these contracts is computed as follows: the foreign currency amount valued at the valuation date forward rate minus the amount to be received or paid at the settlement date. On the settlement date, the unrealized gain or loss is reclassified as realized gain or loss.

Financial Statement Presentation

A section of the Statement of Operations is titled "Realized and Unrealized Gain (Loss) from Investments and Foreign Currency." This section follows the presentation of investment income and investment expenses. All foreign currency gains and losses should be reported in this section. Gains or losses from non-investment transactions would have their own line item in the Statement: "Foreign currency transactions" (with separate line items for realized and unrealized gains and losses). If foreign currency gains and losses from investment transactions are computed separately, these amounts would be included in the line item "Foreign currency transactions" as well. If foreign currency gains and losses from investment transactions are not computed separately, they would be aggregated with market gains or losses from investment transactions and reported in the line item "Investments."

The Statement of Assets and Liabilities and the Statement of Changes in Net Assets should reflect the same unrealized and realized gain and loss components. It is permissible to combine (*a*) net realized gains and losses from investments with net realized gains and losses from foreign currency transactions and (*b*) net unrealized appreciation (depreciation) on investments with the net unrealized appreciation (depreciation) on the translation of assets and liabilities in foreign currencies.

The notes to the financial statements should disclose the entity's policy regarding the treatment of unrealized and realized gains or losses from investments. Otherwise these amounts do not have to be separately disclosed; however, such disclosure may provide useful information to financial statement users.

Certain taxes on foreign source income are not reclaimable. To the extent such taxes exist, the relevant amount should be deducted from the related amount of income. Either this reduction in the income amount is shown parenthetically on the face of the income statement or else a contra-account (to the income item) should be presented on the face of the income statement. Taxes that are based on the aggregate income or capital gains of the investment company are to be treated in a manner similar to income taxes.

Other Issues

Investing in foreign securities poses a number of risks. In addition to the foreign currency risks already discussed, risks related to liquidity, size, and valuation need to be monitored by management and considered for disclosure. Some foreign markets are illiquid. Therefore, quoted market prices may not necessarily be indicative of net realizable value. Some foreign markets are relatively small, and a fund may hold an investment that represents a sizable stake in the overall market. In these cases, quoted market prices may not be indicative of net realizable value. For the reasons previously discussed, determining the proper valuation of securities is sometimes subjective. The fund's board of directors has the ultimate responsibility for determining the fair values of securities.

64,001

APPENDIX F:
ASC 952—FRANCHISORS

CONTENTS

General Guidance	64,001
ASC 952-10: Overall	64,001
Overview	64,001
Background	64,001
ASC 952-605: Revenue Recognition	64,002
Franchise Fee Recognition	64,002
Individual Franchise Fees	64,002
Installment Method	64,003
Cost Recovery Method	64,003
Continuing Franchise Fees	64,003
Area Franchise Fees	64,003
Other Franchise Accounting Issues	64,004
Franchisee and Franchisor—Unusual Relationships	64,004
Tangible Assets Included in the Franchise Fee	64,005
Continuing Product Sales	64,005
Agency Sales	64,006
Expense Recognition	64,006
Repossessed Franchises	64,006
Business Combinations	64,007
Franchise Disclosures	64,007
Illustration of Accounting for Franchise Fee Revenue	64,007

GENERAL GUIDANCE

ASC 952-10: OVERALL

OVERVIEW

A franchise agreement transfers rights owned by the franchisor to a franchisee. The rights transferred for a specified period of time may include the use of patents, secret processes, trademarks, trade names, or other similar assets. The primary accounting issue associated with accounting for franchise fee revenue is the timing of the revenue recognition (i.e., determining when the franchise fee revenue is earned). Accounting standards prescribe specific criteria that must be met for revenue to be recognized. For further guidance on recognizing revenue other than franchise fees, see the Chapter 36, *ASC 605—Revenue Recognition*.

BACKGROUND

Payment for franchise rights may include an initial franchise fee and/or continuing fees or royalties. The agreement usually also provides for any continuing services that are to be rendered by the franchisor, and any inventory or purchases that may be required of the franchisee. In addition, the franchise agreement typically sets forth the procedure for cancellation, resale, or reacquisition of the franchise by the franchisor.

ASC 952-605: REVENUE RECOGNITION

FRANCHISE FEE RECOGNITION

Individual Franchise Fees

The two major accounting issues in revenue recognition of initial franchise fees are (1) the time the fee is properly regarded as earned and (2) the assurance of collectibility of any receivable resulting from unpaid portions of the initial fee.

OBSERVATION: These accounting issues are not unique to franchise accounting and merely represent an application of the principle of revenue realization. The realization principle requires that revenue be earned before it is recognized. GAAP require that the realization of revenue be recognized in the accounting period in which the earning process is substantially completed and an exchange has taken place. Revenue usually is recognized at the amount established by the parties to the exchange except for transactions in which collection of the receivable is not reasonably assured.

ASC 952 requires that revenue on individual franchise fees be recognized on the consummation of the transaction, which occurs when all material services or conditions of the sale have been substantially performed. Substantial performance by the franchisor occurs when the following conditions are met (ASC 952-605-25-1, 2):

- The franchisor is not obligated in any way (trade practice, law, intent, or agreement) to excuse payment of any unpaid notes or to refund any cash already received.
- The initial services required of the franchisor by contract or otherwise (e.g., training, site selection, etc.) have been substantially performed.
- All other material conditions have been met that affect the consummation of the sale.

The earliest that substantial performance is presumed to occur is when the franchisee actually commences operations of the franchise. This presumption may be overcome, however, if the franchisor can demonstrate that substantial performance occurs at an earlier date (ASC 952-605-25-3).

Another accounting issue involved in the recognition of individual franchise fees is the collectibility of any receivable resulting from unpaid portions of the initial franchise fee. An adequate provision for estimated uncollectible amounts from individual franchise fees must be established, if necessary. If the collection of long-term receivables from individual franchise fees is not assured reasonably, the cost recovery or installment sale accounting methods should be used to recognize revenue (ASC 952-605-25-7).

Installment Method

Under the installment method of accounting, each payment collected consists of part recovery of cost and part gross profit, in the same ratio that these two elements existed in the original sale. (For a more detailed discussion of the cost recovery and installment methods, see the chapter in this *Guide* titled "Installment Sales.")

Cost Recovery Method

The cost recovery method is used in situations in which recovery of cost is extremely uncertain. Initially, all amounts received are considered recoveries of cost. Once all cost has been recovered, any other collections are recognized as revenue.

Continuing Franchise Fees

Continuing franchise fees are consideration for the continuing rights granted by the franchise agreement and for general and specific services during the life of the franchise agreement. Continuing franchise fees are recognized as revenue when actually earned and receivable from the franchisee. This is true, even if the continuing franchise fee is designated for a specific purpose. If an agency relationship is established by the franchise agreement and a designated portion of the continuing franchise fee is required to be segregated for a specific purpose, however, the designated amounts are recorded as a liability. Any costs incurred for the specific purpose would be charged against the liability. All other costs relating to continuing franchise fees are expensed as incurred (ASC 952-605-25-12, 13).

In the event that the continuing franchise fees appear to be insufficient to cover the costs and reasonable profit of the franchisor for the continuing services required by the franchise agreement, a portion of the initial franchise fee, if any, is deferred and amortized over the term of the franchise. The amount deferred should be sufficient to cover all the costs of the continuing services plus a reasonable profit (ASC 952-605-25-4).

OBSERVATION: Apparently, ASC 952 assumes that continuing services required by the franchisor coincide with the term of the franchise and amortization should be based on the term of the franchise. An alternate approach would be to relate the amortization period to the period in which the continuing services will be provided by the franchisor, which may not necessarily be the entire term of the franchise.

Area Franchise Fees

Area franchises transfer franchise rights within a geographic area, permitting the opening of a number of franchise outlets. Accounting for revenue recognition from an area franchise is essentially the same as that for individual franchise fees. The only difference is that substantial performance of the franchisor may be more difficult to determine. The terms of the franchise agreement must be used to determine when substantial performance has occurred. In addition, it may be necessary to use the percentage-of-completion method of recognizing revenue in some franchise agreements. For example, an area franchise agreement may require the franchisor to provide specific initial services to any franchise opened in the area. In this event, the franchisor should estimate the number of franchises that are expected to be opened in the area and should recognize a portion of the total area franchise fee as substantial performance occurs for each franchise in the area. Thus, it is necessary to determine the cost of servicing each individual franchise within the area and the total cost of all individual franchises that are expected to be opened in the area. The next step is to determine the percentage of costs that have been substantially performed to the total costs of all individual franchises that are expected to be opened in the area. The resulting percentage is applied to the total initial area franchise revenue to determine the amount of area franchise revenue that can be recognized (ASC 952-605-25-5, 6).

> **PRACTICE POINTER:** The percentage-of-completion method of recognizing revenue on franchises should be used only in those situations in which costs can be estimated with reasonable reliability.

Estimates of the number of franchises that are expected to be opened in an area franchise are determined by reference to the significant terms and conditions of the franchise agreement (ASC 952-605-25-6).

If the franchisor's substantial performance under the terms of the franchise agreement is related to the area franchise, and not to the individual franchises within the area, revenue recognition occurs when all material services and conditions relating to the area franchise have been substantially performed. Thus, this type of area franchise is treated similarly to an individual franchise (ASC 952-605-25-5).

Any portion of the franchise revenue that is related to unperformed future services that may have to be refunded is not recognized by the franchisor until the right to refund has expired (ASC 952-605-25-5).

Other Franchise Accounting Issues

Franchisee and Franchisor—Unusual Relationships

Unusual relationships may exist between the franchisee and the franchisor, besides those created by the franchise agreement. For example, the franchisor may guarantee debt of the franchisee, or contractually control the franchisee's operations to the extent that an affiliation exists. In all these circumstances, all material services, conditions, or obligations relating to the franchise must be performed substantially by the franchisor before revenue is recognized (ASC 952-605-25-8).

> **OBSERVATION:** The above requirements for unusual relationships between the franchisee and franchisor relate to both individual and area franchises.

That is, substantial performance must occur before the franchisor may recognize any revenue.

The initial franchise fee is deferred if it is probable that the franchisor will acquire the franchise back from the franchisee because of an option or other understanding. In this event, the deferred amount is accounted for as a reduction of the cost of reacquiring the franchise when the option or understanding is exercised (ASC 952-605-25-9).

Tangible Assets Included in the Franchise Fee

In addition to the initial services of the franchisor, the initial franchise fee may include the sale of specific tangible property, such as inventory, signs, equipment, or real property. Thus, a portion of the initial franchise fee must be allocated to such tangible property. ASC 952 requires that the amount allocated be the fair value of the property. The fair value of the tangible property is recognized as revenue when title to such property passes to the franchisee, even though substantial performance has not occurred for other services included in the franchise agreement (ASC 952-605-25-10).

OBSERVATION: ASC 952 does not specify the date on which fair value of the tangible property must be determined. Ordinarily, fair value would be determined at the date of the franchise agreement, which usually establishes the date of the sale.

The franchise agreement may also allocate a portion of the initial franchise fee to specific services that the franchisor will provide. If the various services that the franchisor will provide are interrelated to the extent that objective segregation is impossible, ASC 952 prohibits the recognition of revenue for any specific service until all the services required under the franchise agreement have been substantially performed. If actual prices are available for a specific service through recent sales of the specific service, however, ASC 952 permits recognition of revenue based on substantial performance of that service. In other words, if the franchisor has established objective prices for specific service, a portion of the total franchise fee may be recognized upon completion of substantial performance of the specific services (ASC 952-605-25-11).

Continuing Product Sales

If the terms of the franchise agreement allow the franchisee to obtain equipment and supplies from the franchisor at bargain prices, a portion of the initial franchise fee must be deferred. That portion of the fee is either (*a*) the difference between the normal selling price of the equipment and supplies and the bargain purchase price or (*b*) an amount that will enable the franchisor to recover all costs and provide a normal profit. The deferred amount is accounted for as an adjustment of the initial franchise fee and an adjustment of the selling price of the bargain purchase items (ASC 952-605-25-14, 15).

> **PRACTICE POINTER:** The sale of equipment and supplies by the franchisor at normal selling prices, which should include a reasonable profit for the franchisor, is accounted for at the time the sale is complete. Find the amount of sale by reference to the franchise agreement; the cost of the sale is the cost of the equipment or supplies to the franchisor. If it is apparent that the franchisor is not making a reasonable profit on the equipment or supplies, then the rules for "bargain purchases" must be followed.

Agency Sales

Some franchise arrangements in substance establish an agency relationship between the franchisor and the franchisee. The franchisor acts as agent for the franchisee by reselling inventory, equipment, and supplies at no profit. ASC 952 requires that these transactions be accounted for on the franchisor's books as receivables and payables, and not as profit or loss items (ASC 952-605-25-16).

Expense Recognition

Direct franchising costs should be matched to their related franchise revenue in accordance with the accrual basis of accounting. This may necessitate the deferral of direct costs incurred prior to revenue recognition and the accrual of direct costs, if any, not yet incurred through the date on which revenue is recognized. Total direct costs that are deferred or accrued must not exceed their estimated related revenue (ASC 952-340-25-1, 2, 3).

Selling, general, administrative, and other indirect costs that occur on a regular basis regardless of the sales volume are required to be expensed when incurred.

Repossessed Franchises

In repossessing a franchise, the franchisor may or may not refund the consideration previously paid by the franchisee. If a refund is paid by the franchisor, the accounting treatment is equivalent to a cancellation of the original sale. Any revenue previously recognized is treated as a reduction of the revenue of the current period in which the franchise is reacquired (ASC 952-605-40-1).

> **PRACTICE POINTER:** Because substantial performance is required before any revenue is recognized, it is unlikely that a franchisor would grant a refund in the event that the revenue had already been recognized. Instead, it is more likely that the franchisor would enforce collection of any balance due rather than cancel the sale.

If a refund is not paid by the franchisor, the transaction is not considered a cancellation of the sale and no adjustment is made to the previously recorded revenue. If a balance is still owed by the franchisee, however, it may be necessary to review the allowance for uncollectible amounts for the transaction. Also, any deferred revenue on the original sale should be recognized in full (ASC 952-605-35-1).

Business Combinations

When a franchisor acquires the operations of one of its own franchises in an arm's-length transaction, ASC 952 requires that the acquisition be accounted for in accordance with ASC 805 (Business Combinations) (see theChapter 45, *ASC 805—Business Combinations.*

Franchise Disclosures

ASC 952 requires that the following disclosures be made in the financial statements or footnotes thereto:

- The nature of all significant commitments and obligations of the franchisor, including a description of the services that have not been substantially performed (ASC 952-440-50-1)
- If the installment or cost recovery method is being used to account for franchise fee revenue, the following must be disclosed (ASC 952-605-50-1):
  — The sales price of franchises being reported on the installment or cost recovery method
  — The revenue and related deferred costs (currently and cumulative)
  — The periods in which the franchise fees become payable The total revenue that was originally deferred because of uncertainties and then subsequently collected because the uncertainties were resolved
- If significant, separate disclosure for (*a*) initial franchise fees and (*b*) other franchise fee revenue (ASC 952-605-50-2)
- Revenue and costs related to non-owned franchises, as opposed to franchises owned and operated by the franchisor (ASC 952-605-45-1)
- If significant changes in the ownership of franchises occurs during the period, the following must be disclosed (ASC 952-605-50-3):
  — The number of franchises sold during the period
  — The number of franchises purchased during the period
  — The number of franchised outlets in operation during the period
  — The number of franchisor-owned outlets in operation during the period

The following disclosures, while not required, are considered desirable:

- A statement of whether initial franchise fee revenue will probably decline in the future because sales will reach a saturation point
- If not apparent in the financial statements, the relative contribution to net income of initial franchise fee revenue

---

Illustration of Accounting for Franchise Fee Revenue

Abbott (franchisor) enters into a franchise agreement with Martin (franchisee) that permits Martin to operate a fast-food restaurant under the name of Hot Dog Haven. Abbott operates a large number of restaurants under this name, and via franchises permits others to use the name in geographic areas where Abbott does not have its own operating units.

The initial franchise fee commitment is $10,000. Abbott receives $1,000 from Martin in 20X5 when the agreement is signed. Martin begins operations in 20X6 and is contractually obligated to pay Abbott 25% of the balance of the commitment each year from 20X6 through 20X9. Abbott considers the criteria for substantial performance to have been met in 20X6. Also, Abbott judges collection of the fee to be reasonably assured and makes an adequate allowance for uncollectible commitments based on the aggregate amount of all receivables from commitments to a large number of franchisees.

The agreement between Abbott and Martin also calls for Martin to pay Abbott 2% of total revenues each year as a continuing franchise fee. Abbott expects these amounts to adequately cover its costs of providing continuing service to Martin and to provide a reasonable profit on those costs. Martin reports revenue of $135,000 for 20X6.

General journal entries to record the above for Abbott for 20X5 and 20X6 are as follows:

20X5	Franchise fee receivable	9,000	
	Cash	1,000	
	Unearned franchise fee revenue		10,000
20X6	Unearned franchise fee revenue	10,000	
	Franchise fee revenue		10,000
	Cash ($9,000/4)	2,250	
	Franchise fee receivable		2,250
	Cash ($135,000 × 2%)	2,700	
	Franchise fee revenue		2,700

An entry identical to the second 20X6 entry will be made each year through 20X9. An entry similar to the third 20X6 entry will be made each year for 2% of Martin's revenue.

65,001

APPENDIX G:
ASC 954—HEALTH CARE ENTITIES

CONTENTS

Interpretive Guidance	65,001
ASC 954-280: Segment Reporting	65,001
ASC 954-280-45-1	
Meaning of the Term "Customer" as It Applies to Health Care Facilities under ASC 280	65,001
ASC 954-405: Liabilities	65,002
ASC 954-405-25-4 through 25-5; ASC 958-405-60-1	
Accounting for Costs of Future Medicare Compliance Audits	65,002
ASC 954-450: Contingencies	65,002
ASC 954-450-25-2, 65-1; ASC 954-720-25-1	
Health Care Entities: Presentation of Insurance Claims and Related Insurance Recoveries	65,002
ASC 954-605: Revenue Recognition	65,004
ASC 954-605-25-4, 45-4 through 45-5, 50-4, 55-1 through 55-4, 65-2; ASC 954-310-50-3, 55-1 through 55-3	
Health Care Entities: Presentation and Disclosure of Patient Service Revenue, Provision for Bad Debts, and the Allowance for Doubtful Accounts for Certain Health Care Entities	65,004
ASC 954-605-50-3, 65-1	
Health Care Entities: Measuring Charity Care for Disclosure	65,006

INTERPRETIVE GUIDANCE

ASC 954-280: Segment Reporting

ASC 954-280-45-1 Meaning of the Term "Customer" as It Applies to Health Care Facilities under ASC 280

BACKGROUND

Under the guidance in ASC 280, disclosure is required if 10% or more of an entity's revenue is derived from sales to a single customer. The disclosures should state that fact and should give the amount of revenue derived from each customer. A group of customers under common control is considered a single customer.

ACCOUNTING GUIDANCE

Question: Is an insuring entity (e.g., Blue Cross) considered a "customer" of a health care facility?

Answer: An insuring entity should *not* be considered a customer of a health care facility as the term *customer* is used in ASC 280. The fact that an insuring entity is

ASC 954—Health Care Entities

a paying agent for a patient does not make the insuring entity the customer of the health care facility. The paying entity does not decide which services to purchase and from whom those services will be purchased.

ASC 954-405: Liabilities

ASC 954-405-25-4 through 25-5; ASC 958-405-60-1
Accounting for Costs of Future Medicare Compliance Audits

Health care providers that have settled allegations of Medicare fraud with the U.S. government must commit under their settlement agreements to engage an independent organization annually for the following five years to test and report on their compliance with Medicare requirements. The issue is whether those entities may accrue a liability on settlement for costs related to that commitment.

A promise made in the settlement agreement to have future compliance audits creates a current duty and responsibility only if an obligating event has occurred, in accordance with the definition of a *liability* in paragraph 36 of Statement of Financial Concepts No. 6 (not in ASC), which would allow a provider little or no discretion to avoid incurring that cost. Entering into an agreement is not the obligating event for costs of a future compliance audit and therefore providers should *not* recognize a liability on the date of settlement.

ASC 954-450: Contingencies

ASC 954-450-25-2, 65-1; ASC 954-720-25-1
Health Care Entities: Presentation of Insurance Claims and Related Insurance Recoveries

BACKGROUND

Issues related to an insured entity's claims incurred under claims-made insurance and retroactive insurance contracts are codified in FASB Accounting Standards Codification™ (ASC) 720, *Other Expenses* (ASC 720-20). According to that guidance, it is inappropriate to offset prepaid insurance and receivables for expected recoveries from insurers against a recognized incurred but *not* reported liability or a liability incurred due to a past insurable event, unless the transaction meets the conditions in ASC 210-20-45. As a result of that guidance, liability claims and related anticipated insurance recoveries are usually recognized on a gross-basis.

Some constituents have asked whether the guidance in ASC 720-20 applies to health care entities because the language in ASC 954, *Health Care Entities*, has been interpreted by some to permit or require that insurance recoveries be netted against an organization's estimated accrual for medical malpractice claims.

ACCOUNTING ISSUE

How should health care entities record liabilities for medical malpractice and other similar claims and related insurance recoveries?

SCOPE

The following guidance clarifies that the requirements in ASC 210-20-45 apply to health care entities accounted for under the scope of ASC 954, which report medical malpractice claims and similar contingent liabilities, as well as related anticipated insurance recoveries on their balance sheets. In accordance with the guidance in ASC 210-20-45, entities are *not* permitted to offset anticipated insurance recoveries from third parties against conditional or unconditional liabilities.

ACCOUNTING GUIDANCE

Health care entities, similar to entities in other industries, should determine whether to present claims and insurance recoveries in the balance sheet on a gross or net basis based on the guidance in ASC 210-20-45, because a gross presentation shows that the entity is obligated on a claim even though an insurance company may be paying to defend the claim and may eventually pay for a portion of the claim or the total claim. In addition, a gross presentation of an insurance receivable required in ASC 210-20-45 is a better presentation of the retained credit risk if an insurer is unable to pay a claim.

If a health care entity will be indemnified by its insurer, a receivable should be recognized at the same time as the liability and should be measured on the same basis as the liability, conditional on a need for a valuation allowance for uncollectible amounts.

EFFECTIVE DATE, TRANSITION METHOD, AND TRANSITION DISCLOSURES

The following guidance should be followed:

- Adopt the guidance for fiscal years, and interim periods within those years, that begin after December 15, 2010. Early adoption is permitted.

- Record a cumulative-effect-adjustment to opening retained earnings (or unrestricted assets) as of the beginning of the period in which the guidance is adopted, if necessary.

- Calculate the cumulative-effect-adjustment as the difference between the following amounts: (1) the liability recognized in the balance sheet after the initial application of the above guidance that was not previously recognized; and (2) the receivable recognized in the balance sheet for expected insurance recoveries after the initial application of the above guidance.

- Provide the disclosures in ASC 250-10-50-1 through 50-3, in the period in which the guidance is adopted.

In addition, retrospective application of the guidance to all prior periods is permitted but not required. That treatment may be necessary in rare situations if the amount of the liability on a claim and the receivable from insurance are not completely offset.

ASC 954-605: Revenue Recognition

ASC 954-605-25-4, 45-4 through 45-5, 50-4, 55-1 through 55-4, 65-2; ASC 954-310-50-3, 55-1 through 55-3
Health Care Entities: Presentation and Disclosure of Patient Service Revenue, Provision for Bad Debts, and the Allowance for Doubtful Accounts for Certain Health Care Entities

BACKGROUND

In some cases in which a health care entity performs its services, it may be doubtful or not determinable whether the entity will be able to collect all or a portion of the amounts billed or billable. Sometimes, as in the case of charity care, a health care entity may recognize no revenue on such transactions.

It is practice in the health care industry to adopt a revenue recognition policy for billings to self-pay patients under which revenue is recognized at the gross amount charged with a relatively high provision for bad debt in accordance with the guidance in ASC 954-605-25-3. Under that revenue recognition policy, revenue for insured patients is recognized when the services are provided with adjustments for contractual discounts based on agreements with third-party payors or based on other arrangements. A provision for bad debt is usually recognized for deductibles and co-pays *not* expected to be collectible. The bad debt provision in those circumstances is usually classified as an expense, not as a reduction of revenue. The issue discussed is whether revenue should be recognized only if collectibility is reasonably assured.

SCOPE

The following guidance applies only to health care entities that recognize significant amounts of revenue from fees for patient services at the time the services are rendered without evaluating the collectibility of those fees. Entities that evaluate collectibity *before* recognizing revenue from fees for patient services are not affected by the following guidance.

ACCOUNTING GUIDANCE

Health care entities that recognize significant amounts of revenue from fees for patient services at the time the services are rendered without evaluating collectibility should present the provision for bad debts related to revenue recognized on fees for patient services as a deduction from revenue (net of contractual allowances and discounts) in the income statement, in a manner similar to the following:

Patient service revenue (net of contractual allowances and discounts)	$2,500,000
Provision for bad debts	250,000
Net patient service revenue less provision for bad debts	2,000,000
Premium revenue	50,000
Other operating revenue	500,000
Total revenue	$2,550,000

The following kinds of bad debts should be presented as operating expenses in a health care entity's income statement:

- Bad debts related to receivables from revenue other than revenue from patient services; and
- Bad debts related to receivables from patient service revenue if an entity recognizes revenue only for amounts that are expected to be collectible.

DISCLOSURES

A health care entity that recognizes significant amounts of revenue from patient services when the services are provided without evaluating a patient's ability to pay should disclose the following information by major payor revenue source for interim periods:

- The policy for evaluating collectibility in determining the timing and amount of revenue to be recognized for fees from patient services (net of contractual allowances and discounts); and
- The amount of revenue from fees for patient services (net of contractual allowances and discounts) before the provision for bad debts.

An entity's major payor sources of revenue should be identified in a manner that is consistent with the entity's management of its business (e.g., how the entity evaluates credit risk).

In addition, a health care entity should disclose qualitative and quantitative information about significant changes in its allowance for doubtful accounts related to accounts receivable from patients. The information may include significant changes in estimates and underlying assumptions, the amount of self-pay writeoffs, the amount of third-party payer writeoffs, and other unusual transactions that affect the allowance for doubtful accounts.

The required disclosures should be presented in interim and annual financial statements.

TRANSITION METHOD, TRANSITION DISCLOSURES, AND EFFECTIVE DATE

The guidance discussed above should be applied *retrospectively* in the income statement presentation of the provision for bad debts. The new disclosure requirements should be applied *prospectively*. It was noted that it should not be difficult for entities to adopt the requirement related to the income statement presentation of the provision for bad debts.

For *public entities,* the above guidance is effective for fiscal years and interim periods within those fiscal years that begin after December 15, 2011, but early adoption is permitted. For *nonpublic entities,* the above guidance is effective for the first annual period that ends after December 15, 2012, and interim and annual periods after that, but early adoption is permitted. Public entities include entities with public debt, including conduit bond obligors.

ASC 954-605-50-3, 65-1
Health Care Entities: Measuring Charity Care for Disclosure

BACKGROUND

Health care entities provide charity care, which is any service provided without the expectation of payment to patients that meet certain guidelines established by the health care entity. Under the guidance in ASC 954-605-25-10 through 25-11, no revenue should be recognized for charity care in the financial statements and judgment should be used to distinguish between bad debts and charity care, which should be based on established criteria. Under the guidance in ASC 954-605-50-3, an entity is required to disclose in the notes to the financial statements management's policy for charity care and the level of such care, which is determined based on a provider's rates, costs, units of service, or other statistical measurements. Some have asked whether the measurement of charity care disclosed in the financial statements should be standardized for improved comparability among health care entities.

ACCOUNTING ISSUE

How should a health care entities measure charity care?

SCOPE

The following guidance applies to entities that provide health care services.

ACCOUNTING GUIDANCE

Information about charity care disclosed in the financial statements of health care entities should be based on the entity's measurement of the direct and indirect costs of providing such services, which should be determined in a manner that is consistent with that used to report charity care to the IRS for regulatory purposes. Such information may be determined by various means, such as by using: (1) information from a cost accounting system; (2) reasonable techniques to estimate the cost of providing charity care, such as a calculation of a ratio of the cost of charity care to gross charges that would be multiplied by the amount of gross uncompensated charges related to charity care; or (3) other reasonable methods. Subsidies related to charity care, such as those from an uncompensated care fund or from gifts and grants, should be separately disclosed.

In addition to disclosing the costs of providing charity care, health care entities also should separately disclose the following information: (1) amounts received from various sources to compensate the entity for providing charity care; and (2) the method used to determine the costs of providing charity care.

EFFECTIVE DATE AND TRANSITION

The guidance discussed above is effective for fiscal years that begin after December 15, 2010, with early adoption permitted. The guidance should be applied *retrospectively*. In addition, the disclosures in ASC 250-10-50-1 through 50-3 should be made in the period of adoption.

APPENDIX H:
ASC 958—NOT-FOR-PROFIT ENTITIES

CONTENTS

Part I: General Guidance	66,002
ASC 958-10: Overall	66,002
Overview	66,002
Background	66,002
Financial Statements of Not-For-Profit Organizations	66,002
Financial Statements Required	66,003
Statement of Financial Position	66,004
Statement of Activities	66,006
Illustration of Format of Statement of Financial Position	66,006
Illustration of Format of the Statement of Activities	66,007
Statement of Cash Flows	66,008
Contributions Made	66,009
Accounting for Investments	66,009
Definitions and Applicability	66,009
Measurement and Recognition Standards	66,010
Disclosure Standards	66,011
Depreciation	66,012
Collections	66,012
Additional Disclosures for Collections	66,012
Contributions	66,013
Contributions Received	66,014
Contribution Standards Applicable Only to Not-for-Profit Entities	66,014
Conditional Promises	66,015
Accounting for Defined Benefit Postretirement Plans	66,015
Disclosures	66,016
Service Efforts	66,017
Business Combinations	66,018
Scope	66,018
Unique Features of NFP Combinations	66,019
Mergers	66,019
Disclosures: Mergers	66,020
Acquisitions	66,021
Identifying the Acquirer	66,021
Determining the Acquisition Date	66,021
Recognizing and Measuring Identifiable Assets, Liabilities, and Noncontrolling Interest	66,022
Exceptions to the General Recognition and Measurement Guidance	66,022
Contingencies	66,022

Income Taxes, Employee Benefits, and Indemnification Agreements	66,023
Reacquired Rights and Assets Held for Sale	66,023
Recognizing Goodwill or a Contribution Received	66,023
Noncontrolling Interests	66,024
Other Provisions of the Acquisition Method	66,024
Acquisition Achieved in Stages	66,025
Determination of the Measurement Period	66,025
Scope of the Acquisition Transaction and Acquisition-Related Costs	66,025
Financial Statement Presentation Issues	66,026
Subsequent Measurement	66,027
Disclosures: Acquisitions	66,027
ASC 958-20: Financially Interrelated Entities	66,030
Part II: Interpretive Guidance	
ASC 958-205: Presentation of Financial Statements	66,030
ASC 958-205-05-10, 45-21A, 45-28 through 45-32, 50-1A through 50-1B, 55-1, 55-31 through 55-53, 65-1	
Endowments of Not-for-Profit Organizations: Net Asset Classification of Funds Subject to an Enacted Version of the Uniform Prudent Management of Institutional Funds Act, and Enhanced Disclosures	66,030

PART I: GENERAL GUIDANCE

ASC 958-10: OVERALL

OVERVIEW

Historically, accounting principles for not-for-profit organizations have been fragmented into industry-specific pronouncements prepared by the AICPA and other groups. The result of this fragmentation is that the practices followed by the various types of organizations were inconsistent. The FASB has undertaken a broad project to address many of these inconsistencies and to attempt to improve the accounting and reporting of not-for-profit entities.

BACKGROUND

The primary source of GAAP for not-for-profit entities is ASC 958. Guidance is provided for the accounting for contributions received and made by all entities, as well as for the format and content of financial statements of all not-for-profit organizations. ASC 958 also establishes standards for accounting for business combinations involving NFP entities. Finally, ASC 958 requires not-for-profit entities to disclose information about depreciable assets and depreciation (ASC 958-360-05-1).

FINANCIAL STATEMENTS OF NOT-FOR-PROFIT ORGANIZATIONS

ASC 958 establishes standards for external financial statements of not-for-profit organizations. It requires not-for-profits to present a statement of financial position, a statement of activities, and a statement of cash flows. Operating cash flows of (*a*) unrestricted net assets, (*b*) temporarily restricted net assets, and (*c*) permanently restricted net assets must be disclosed separately in the statement of activities, and the statement of financial position must distinguish among these three classes of net assets. ASC 958 amends ASC 230 (Statement of Cash Flows), extending its provisions to not-for-profit entities (ASC 958-205-45-4). Not-for-profit entities are also required to disclose expenses by functional classification. Voluntary Health and Welfare Organizations (VHWO) are required, and Other Not-for-Profit Organizations (ONPO) are encouraged, to disclose expenses by natural classification as well (ASC 958-205-45-4).

Financial Statements Required

ASC 958 (*a*) specifies three financial statements that must be present in external financial reports and (*b*) standardizes the approach to the disclosure of operating cash flows from unrestricted, temporarily restricted, and permanently restricted net assets. ASC 958 reviews and discusses the fundamental concepts governing financial reporting; it emphasizes that general-purpose financial statements can be prepared to serve a wide range of user needs, including an assessment of management's stewardship responsibilities to safeguard entity assets and use them for authorized activities. ASC 958 further specifies that the user's primary informational needs include (ASC 958-205-05-4):

- Information about assets and liabilities
- Inflows and outflows of resources
- Cash flows
- Service efforts of the organization

Three financial statements are necessary to provide this information (ASC 958-205-45-4):

- Statement of financial position
- Statement of activities
- Statement of cash flows

ASC 958 also requires specific notes to the financial statements which complete the disclosures relevant to the information needs listed above.

ASC 958 also emphasizes that the disclosure requirements contained in all authoritative literature that do not specifically exempt not-for-profit entities remain in effect (ASC 958-205-45-5). Another noteworthy aspect of ASC 958 is that the degree of disaggregated fund information is not limited. Preparers have flexibility regarding the amount of detail provided, the order of line items, and the grouping of assets, liabilities, revenues, expenses, and gains. However, it is expected that the exercise of this flexibility will be similar to that used by business enterprises (ASC 958-205-45-1).

ASC 958 also deals with accounting for a *donor-restricted* endowment fund, which is an endowment fund created by a donor stipulating that the gift be invested in perpetuity or for a specified term. Gains and losses on investments in a donor-restricted endowment fund are classified as changes in unrestricted net assets, unless they are temporarily or permanently restricted by a donor's stipulation or by law that extends the donor's restriction to them (ASC 958-205-45-13, 17).

OBSERVATION: Gains and losses on restricted net assets are unrestricted unless the donor stipulates otherwise. Thus, in a permanent endowment, three possibilities exist:

---

1. Neither the donor nor law stipulates that the endowment restriction extends to gains and losses, in which case the gains and losses are unrestricted income.
2. The donor stipulates that gains and losses are to be used for some restricted purpose, often the same purpose for which the endowment income is restricted. In this case, the gains and losses are temporarily restricted income.
3. Either the donor or law stipulates that gains and losses become part of the endowment principal. In this case, the gains and losses are permanently restricted income. In situations in which an endowment cannot be sold (i.e., must be held in perpetuity), gains and losses on that security would be classified as permanently restricted income.

As a general rule (i.e., unless otherwise restricted by donor stipulation or law), losses on investments in a donor-restricted endowment reduce temporarily restricted net assets to the extent that donor-imposed temporary restrictions on net appreciation of the fund have not been met before the loss occurs. Further losses reduce unrestricted net assets (ASC 958-205-45-22). If losses reduce the assets of a donor-restricted endowment fund below the level required by donor stipulation or law, gains that restore the fair value of the assets to the required level are classified as increases in unrestricted net assets (ASC 958-205-45-24).

ASC 958 does not address issues related to measurement focus, basis of accounting, or measurement methods (ASC 958-205-15-1).

STATEMENT OF FINANCIAL POSITION

According to ASC 958, the objective of the statement of financial position is to present information about assets, liabilities, and net assets to facilitate analysis of credit, liquidity, ability to meet obligations, and the need to obtain external financing (ASC 958-210-05-2). In particular, ASC 958 emphasizes the need to distinguish between unrestricted assets and permanently or temporarily restricted assets. However, the focus of ASC 958 is on the organization as a whole, and therefore, the total amounts for assets, liabilities, and net assets must be reported (ASC 958-210-45-1).

The statement of financial position must provide information about the entity's liquidity. This disclosure can be accomplished (*a*) by sequencing assets in the order of diminishing liquidity or by current/noncurrent classification or (*b*) by sequencing liabilities according to their nearness to maturity (ASC 958-210-45-8).

Particular attention should be paid to disclosing which elements of the statement of financial position have donor-imposed restrictions on their use. Restrictions exist because assets cannot be used until a future period, because they may be used only for certain types of expenditures, or because only the investment income from the assets may be used. Internally imposed restrictions made by the governing board of an entity must also be disclosed. Preparers are given flexibility about where to show disclosures about restrictions: on the face of the statements or in notes to the statements (ASC 958-210-45-9, 10).

ASC 958 requires a not-for-profit entity to prepare a single, combined balance sheet with a net assets section distinguishing between classes of asset restrictions (ASC 958-205-45-15):

Net assets:

Unrestricted	$ xxx
Temporarily restricted	xxx
Permanently restricted	xxx
Total net assets	$ xxx
Total liabilities and net assets	$ xxx

While accounts may be maintained on a fund basis, the above example emphasizes that the reporting focuses on the nature of the restrictions and not on the particular fund in which an asset is carried.

PRACTICE POINTER: ASC 958 makes no recommendations about whether the statement of financial position should show assets and liabilities by fund. Indeed, the terms fund and fund balance are not used in ASC 958. In its discussion of the statement of activities, ASC 958 explicitly states that reporting by fund groups is not precluded, but is not a necessary part of external reporting. Accordingly, it seems clear that entities may prepare a statement of financial position that includes disaggregated fund groups, as long as those groups aggregate with net asset classes. It is also important to note that the statement of activities change in net asset class must articulate with the net assets shown on the statement of financial position. ASC 958 emphasizes that information should be simplified, condensed, and aggregated into meaningful totals, and that the statements should not be obscured by unnecessary fund or line item details.

ASC 958 requires that either the statements or the notes thereto give information describing the amount and nature of the various types of restrictions that exist within the major categories of *temporarily restricted* or *permanently restricted* assets. For example, disclosures must be made to show the amount of assets temporarily restricted as to time of availability or as to type of use allowed. Within the category of permanently restricted assets, differentiation should be made regarding assets of an endowment nature, which earn income, and assets that may be part of a collection (of art objects, historical treasures, etc.) (ASC 958-210-45-9). Entities may disclose board designations on unrestricted assets either on the face of the statements or in notes (ASC 958-210-45-11).

STATEMENT OF ACTIVITIES

The statement of activities is the operating statement for a not-for-profit entity, analogous to an income statement for a business. This statement combines the revenues, expenses, gains, and losses with the changes in equities. The statement should use the term *changes in net assets* or *changes in equities* to describe equity (ASC 958-205-45-1). ASC 958 sees net assets or equities as encompassing the whole of the net assets of the entity. The statement of activities must report the changes in total net assets and the change in each net asset class (ASC 958-225-45-1). Thus, an important dimension of reporting operations for not-for-profit entities by ASC 958 is the use of net asset classes. The requirement is to report changes in unrestricted, temporarily restricted, and permanently restricted net assets in the statement of activities. Therefore, the statement will contain sections for changes in unrestricted net assets (which includes revenues and gains), changes in temporarily restricted net assets (both inflows and outflows), and a line for total changes in net assets.

Illustration of Format of Statement of Financial Position

NFP Organization #1 Statement of Financial Position December 31, 20X5
(in thousands)

Assets:	
Cash and cash equivalents	$ 15
Accounts and interest receivable	425
Inventories and prepaid expenses	120
Contributions receivable	600
Short-term investments	300
Assets restricted to investment in land, buildings, and equipment	1,050
Land, buildings, and equipment	12,300
Long-term investments	43,600
Total assets	$58,410
Liabilities and net assets:	
Accounts payable	$ 500
Refundable advance	75
Grants payable	100
Notes payable	200
Annuity obligations	330
Long-term debt	900
Total liabilities	$ 2,105
Net assets:	
Unrestricted	$23,010
Temporarily restricted (Note B)	4,800
Permanently restricted (Note C)	28,495
Total net assets	56,305

Total liabilities and net assets $58,410

Illustration of Format of the Statement of Activities

NFP Organization #2 Statement of Activities for Year Ending June 30, 20X8
(in thousands)

Changes in unrestricted net assets:
  Revenues and gains:
    Contributions | $ 900
    Fees | 450
    Investment income | 25
    Other | 10
      Total unrestricted income | $ 1,385
Net assets released from restrictions:
    Program restrictions satisfied | $ 250
    Equipment acquisition restrictions satisfied | 200
    Time restrictions expired | 100
      Total assets released from restrictions | 550
      Total support | 1,935
Less: Expenses and losses:
    Program A | 600
    Program B | 750
    Management and administrative | 400
    Fund-raising expenses | 100
      Total expenses and losses | 1,850
      Increase in unrestricted net assets | 85
Changes in temporarily restricted net assets:
    Contributions | 650
    Investment income | 250
    Net assets released from restrictions | (110)
      Increase in temporarily restricted net assets | 790
Changes in permanently restricted net assets:
    Contributions | 310
    Investment income | 80
    Net realized and unrealized losses on investments | (550)
      Decrease in permanently restricted net assets | (160)
Increase in net assets | 715
Net assets, beginning of the year | 2,600

Net assets, end of the year	$ 3,315

ASC 958 states that the term *changes in net assets* or *change in equity* should be used in the statement (ASC 958-225-45-2).

PRACTICE POINTER: ASC 958 does not specifically state that the operating statement must be titled "Statement of Activities." The operating statement may be disaggregated into a "Statement of Unrestricted Revenues, Expenses, and Other Changes in Unrestricted Net Assets" (changes in unrestricted net assets in the previous illustration) together with a second statement, "Statement of Changes in Net Assets" (changes in temporarily and permanently restricted net assets in the previous illustration). ASC 958 unequivocally states, however, that the focus must be on net assets and the three major classes of restrictions: unrestricted, temporarily restricted, and permanently restricted.

The reporting of restricted resources is straightforward under ASC 958. When donor-restricted assets are received, they normally are reported as restricted revenues or gains. In cases in which the restrictions are met in the same period the resources are received, it is permissible to classify the receipts as unrestricted, provided the policy is disclosed and applied consistently (ASC 958-225-45-6). In addition, gains and losses on investments are unrestricted, regardless of the nature of the restrictions on the investment assets, unless the governing board determines that the law requires that such gains and losses be restricted (ASC 958-205-45-21). Finally, ASC 958 allows reporting of subtotals for operating and nonoperating items, expendable and nonexpendable items, or other terms as desired to provide additional detail within the three classes of net assets. This additional detail is not required, but preparers can make such distinctions as they deem necessary (ASC 958-225-45-9, 10).

ASC 958 allows the reporting of gains and losses as net amounts if they result from peripheral transactions, such as disposal of assets. In its basis for conclusion, the FASB clearly states that this approach should not be used for special events that are ongoing major activities (ASC 958-225-45-15).

STATEMENT OF CASH FLOWS

ASC 958 amends several sections of ASC 230 to require that not-for-profit organizations include a statement of cash flows in their financial statement package (ASC 230-10-15-2, 15-3, Glossary, 45-14, 45-25, 45-28, 45-29, 45-30, 50-4, 55-6). All these changes involve minor wording changes or additions to ASC 230 to clarify that ASC 230 is applicable to not-for-profit entities. As is the case for business entities, either the direct or indirect method may be used to present the cash flow information. The cash flow statement is best presented on an aggregated basis for the three classes of net assets; to do otherwise would result in a very detailed statement.

PRACTICE POINTER: The statement of cash flows as required by ASC 958 is essentially the same as that required by ASC 230 for business enterprises.

The only substantive difference is the substitution of "change in net assets" of the not-for-profit organization for "net income" of the business organization. For that reason, an illustration of the statement of cash flows is not presented here; see Chapter 7, *ASC 230—Statement of Cash Flows.*

CONTRIBUTIONS MADE

ASC 958 emphasizes full accrual and fair market value in providing guidance for contributions made. The fair market value emphasis is particularly evident in the directions given for accounting for contributions of nonmonetary assets. Contributions of nonmonetary assets are recognized as expenses and decreases in assets (or increases in liabilities) in the period made. Donors should find the most objective way possible to determine the fair market value of nonmonetary assets (ASC 720-25-30-1).

OBSERVATION: Absence of a definite valuation does not justify use of historical cost as a basis for recording the transaction.

Appraisals, present value of estimated cash flows, net realizable value, and quoted market prices are all acceptable ways of determining the fair market value of donated nonmonetary assets. If a present value technique is used to measure fair value of unconditional promises to give cash, subsequent accruals of the interest element shall be accounted for as contribution income by donees and contribution expense by donors. Not-for-profit organizations shall report the contribution increase as an increase in either temporarily or permanently restricted net assets if the underlying promise to give is donor restricted (ASC 958-310-35-6; 958-310-45-2).

ACCOUNTING FOR INVESTMENTS

Definitions and Applicability

The Codification establishes standards for certain investments in debt and equity securities. The term *securities* is defined as a share, participation, or other interest in property or in an enterprise of the issuer or an obligation of the issuer that has the following characteristics (ASC Glossary):

- It is represented by an instrument issued in bearer or registered form, or it is registered in books maintained to record transfers by or on behalf of the issuer.
- It is of a type that is commonly dealt in on securities exchanges or markets or, when it is represented by an instrument, commonly recognized as a medium for investment in any area in which it is issued or dealt in.
- It is one of a class or series, or by its terms is divisible into a class or series of shares, participations, interests, or obligations.

Equity securities represent an ownership interest in an enterprise (e.g., common and preferred stock) or the right to acquire (e.g., warrants, rights, call options) or dispose of (e.g., put options) an ownership interest at fixed or determinable prices. Convertible debt and preferred stock that by their terms either must be redeemed by the issuing enterprise or are redeemable at the option of the investor are not considered equity securities (ASC 958-320-55-3).

Debt securities represent a creditor relationship with an enterprise. Debt securities include U.S. Treasury securities, U.S. government agency securities, municipal securities, corporate bonds, convertible debt, commercial paper, securitized debt instruments and interest only and principal-only strips. Preferred stock that must be redeemed by the issuing enterprise or that is redeemable at the option of the investor, as well as collateralized mortgage obligations that are issued in equity form but are required to be accounted for as nonequity instruments regardless of how the instruments are classified, are considered debt securities. The term excludes option contracts, financial futures contracts, forward contracts, lease contracts, and swap contracts (ASC 958-320-55-1).

An equity security is deemed to have a readily determinable fair value if one of the following criteria is met:

1. Sales prices or bid-and-asked quotations for the security are available on a securities exchange registered with the Securities and Exchange Commission (SEC) or in the over-the-counter market. For over-the-counter market prices to qualify, they must be publicly reported by the National Association of Securities Dealers Automated Quotation (NASDAQ) system or by the National Quotation Bureau.

OBSERVATION: Restricted stock does not meet this criterion. The term *restricted stock* refers to equity securities for which sale is restricted at acquisition by governmental or contractual requirement, other than in connection with being pledged as collateral, except if that requirement terminates within one year or if the holder has the power by contract or otherwise to cause the requirement to be met within one year. Any portion of the security that can be reasonably expected to qualify for sale within one year is not considered restricted.

---

2. For an equity security traded only in a foreign market, that market is of a breadth and scope comparable to a U.S. market referred to in 1 above.
3. For an investment in a mutual fund, the fair value per share or unit is determined and published and is the basis for current transactions.

Measurement and Recognition Standards

The most important measurement and recognition requirement is that qualifying investments in equity securities (i.e., investments that have readily determinable fair values and are not accounted for by the equity method or consolidation) and all investments in debt securities are to be accounted for at fair value in the statement of financial position (ASC 958-320-35-1).

ASC 958 provides the following guidance for the income effects of measuring investments at fair value (ASC 958-320-45-1, 2, 3):

- Gains and losses on investments resulting from their measurement at fair value are to be reported in the statement of activities as increases or

decreases in unrestricted net assets, unless their use is temporarily or permanently restricted by donor stipulation or by law.
- Dividend, interest, and other investment income is to be reported in the period earned as increases in unrestricted net assets, unless the use of the assets received is limited by donor restrictions.
- Donor-restricted investment income is to be reported as an increase in temporarily restricted net assets or permanently restricted net assets, depending on the nature of the donor restriction.
- Gains and investment income that are limited to specific uses by donor restriction may be reported as increases in unrestricted net assets if the restrictions are met in the same reporting period as the gains and income are recognized (provided the organization has a similar policy for reporting contributions received, applies that policy consistently, and discloses that policy).

Disclosure Standards

The ASC 958 disclosure requirements can be separated into three classifications.

First, the following information related to the statement of activities is required (ASC 958-320-50-1):

- Composition of investment return, including at least the following components:
  — Investment income (e.g., dividends, interest)
  — Net realized gains or losses on investments reported at other than fair value
  — Net gains or losses on investments reported at fair value
- A reconciliation of investment return to amounts reported in the statement of activities, if the investment is separated into operating and nonoperating amounts and an explanation of how the amount included in operations is computed, including any changes in policy, used to make that classification

Second, the following information related to the statement of financial position is required (ASC 958-325-50-2):

- Aggregate carrying amount of investments by major type
- Basis for determining the carrying amount for investments other than equity securities with readily determinable fair values and all debt securities
- The method(s) and significant assumptions used to determine fair values
- The aggregate amount of the deficiencies for all donor-restricted endowment funds for which the fair value of the assets at the reporting date is less than the level required by donor stipulations or law

Third, for the most recent period for which a statement of financial position is presented, the nature of and carrying amount for each individual investment or group of investments that represents a significant concentration of market risk are required (ASC 958-320-50-3).

DEPRECIATION

Not-for-profit entities are required to recognize the cost of using up the future economic benefits or service potential of long-lived tangible assets by reporting depreciation on those assets. In addition, disclosure of the following items is required for those assets (ASC 958-360-35-1):

- Depreciation expense for the period
- Balances of major classes of depreciable assets by nature or function
- Accumulated depreciation by major class or in total
- A description of the methods of depreciation used

Depreciation is not required to be taken on works of art or historical treasures considered to have an indefinite service potential or an extraordinarily long useful life. Verifiable evidence should exist which indicates that (*a*) the historical treasures or works of art are of such value that they are worth preserving perpetually and (*b*) the entity has the capacity to preserve the undiminished service potential of the asset for an indefinite period, and is doing so (ASC 958-360-35-3).

COLLECTIONS

To be part of a collection, assets must be (ASC Glossary):

- Held for public exhibition, education, or research rather than held for financial gain
- Protected, preserved, and not used as collateral or otherwise encumbered
- Subject to a policy that requires the proceeds of collection items sold to be reinvested in collections

Entities are encouraged by ASC 958 to capitalize collections retroactively or on a prospective basis; however, capitalization is *optional*. Capitalization of selected items is not permitted (ASC 958-360-25-3). An entity that does not capitalize collections is required to disclose additional information.

Additional Disclosures for Collections

While capitalization of collections by donees is optional, ASC 958 requires that the financial statements disclose the cash flows associated with collections *whether the collection is capitalized or not*. The choice of capitalization policy affects the way that these cash flows are disclosed. If collections are capitalized, the cash consequences of collection activities are a result of routine transactions recorded in the ledger, and would appear in the statement of activities (ASC 958-360-45-5).

If collections are *not* capitalized, the cash consequences of collection activities appear in the statement of activities within a separate category called "changes in permanently restricted net assets." This category follows the revenue and expense categories. Substantial descriptive notes regarding the collections are required when collections are not capitalized. These disclosures must include the relative significance of the collection, along with the accounting and stewardship policies followed. In addition, the notes should indicate the values of items sold, lost, or destroyed. A line in the financial statements must refer to the collections note (ASC 958-360-50-6).

OBSERVATION: The note disclosures required for uncapitalized collections are extensive. They emphasize that readers of the financial statements must be made aware of the details of all significant changes in the collection. In particular, statement users must be advised regarding casualty losses, insurance recoveries, accounting policies, and managerial controls in place. The concept of *full disclosure* is very much in evidence in this standard.

CONTRIBUTIONS

ASC 958 provides guidance in accounting for contributions received and contributions given, promises to give cash or other assets, contributed services, collections of works of art, and gifts with donor-stipulated conditions. ASC 958 also specifies when to recognize the expirations of donor-imposed restrictions. ASC 958 standardizes the terminology used to describe the contributions and in the timing of recognition of income for the contributions received and expense for contributions given.

OBSERVATION: ASC 958 is consistent with the general trend toward a full accrual approach to the recognition of revenue and expenses, as well as an emphasis on fair market value as a basis for measuring nonmonetary transactions.

ASC 958 applies to contributions of cash, nonmonetary assets, and services, and to promises to give the same. It applies to exchange transactions in which the value received is substantially different from the value given. It does *not* apply to (*a*) bargained arm's-length transactions without a gift element or (*b*) transactions in which the entity is an intermediary or is acting in some form of agency capacity (ASC 958-605-15-6).

Also expressly excluded from the scope of ASC 958 are transactions that convey only contingent or indirect benefits, such as tax abatements. Transfers of assets from governments to businesses also are not covered by ASC 958 (ASC 958-605-15-6).

Contributions in ASC 958 include cash, assets, or services—or unconditional promises to give these in the future. The Statement emphasizes the word *promise* and requires verifiable documentary evidence that a promise has been made (ASC 958-605-25-8). It also distinguishes between donor-imposed *conditions* and donor-imposed *restrictions* to provide a basis for differentiating the way these items are reported. Imposing restrictions on how a gift is to be used does not delay recognition of income or expense. However, recognition of conditional gifts is delayed until the conditions are substantially met.

Contributions Received

ASC 958 generally requires that all unconditional contributions—whether assets, services, or reductions of liabilities—be measured at fair market value on the date received and be recognized currently as revenue or gains (ASC 958-605-25-2). ASC 958 takes the current recognition, fair value approach, which embraces the characteristics of relevance and reliability and the qualities of comparability and consistency that are discussed in FASB Concepts Statement No. 2 (Qualitative Characteristics of Accounting Information).

OBSERVATION: The FASB Statements of Financial Accounting Concepts are intended to provide conceptual guidance in selecting the economic events recognized and reported in financial statements. Concepts Statement No. 2 examines the characteristics of accounting information and is useful as a reference to understanding the importance attached to various concepts that are emphasized in the FASB Standards.

ASC 958 also provides guidance in accounting for donated services. In particular, it holds that donated services must create or enhance nonfinancial assets, or must be of a specialized nature, must be provided by individuals possessing those skills, and typically need to be purchased, before they can be included as revenue or gains in the operating statement (ASC 958-605-25-16). Thus, routine volunteer services requiring no particular expertise may not be reported as contribution revenue. Finally, ASC 958 requires explanatory footnotes that describe the programs or activities for which contributed services are used and other information that aids in assessing the success or viability of the entity (ASC 958-605-50-1).

Assets to be included in a collection are recognized as revenue or gains if they are capitalized, but may not be included in revenue or gains if they are not capitalized (ASC 958-605-25-19).

Contribution Standards Applicable Only to Not-for-Profit Entities

ASC 958 requires that not-for-profit organizations distinguish the use of assets and support as *unrestricted, temporarily restricted,* or *permanently restricted* (ASC 958-605-45-3, 4). This separation could be accomplished through fund accounting by having a different fund for each of the three classes of net assets. Support that is restricted by donors as being available only in future accounting periods is reported as restricted support (ASC 958-605-45-5).

Expiration of donor-imposed restrictions requires reclassification of net assets from restricted to unrestricted, or from a restricted to an unrestricted fund. ASC 958 provides guidance on financial statement format. Since restricted contributions are reported as support in the temporarily restricted class of net assets when first received, they are reclassified in the operating statement when restrictions lapse. ASC 958 requires that contributions to acquire fixed assets or contributions of plant assets be reported as restricted support over the life of the asset if (*a*) the donor restricts the use and disposition of the asset or (*b*) the donee has a policy of imposing a time restriction that expires over the life of the donated assets or the life of assets acquired with donated money (ASC 958-360-50-1; 958-605-45-6).

When restrictions lapse, recognition is required in the statement of activities. In general, a restriction expires when the period of the restriction has lapsed or when an expenditure for an authorized purpose is made. If an expense is incurred for a purpose for which both unrestricted and temporarily restricted net assets are available, the donor-imposed restriction is met (ASC 958-205-45-9).

Conditional Promises

Material gifts or promises subject to conditions present accounting problems regarding the appropriate time to recognize the gift revenue or expense. They may also create the need for additional note disclosures describing the nature of the conditions. ASC 958 requires that a promise to give be recognized when the conditions of the promise are substantially met (ASC 958-605-25-11). Conditional promises are essentially contingent events. If the contingent event (condition) is remote, it may be ignored and the promise accounted for as an unconditional promise. Otherwise, the gift is not recognized until the conditions have been substantially met. Although ASC 958 requires note disclosure by recipients of conditional promises, there is no similar requirement for the promisor.

Recognition problems also occur for donees when ambiguous wording makes it difficult to determine if conditions for recognition exist. Conditional promises are essentially contingent revenue for the donee. ASC 450 (Contingencies) prohibits recognition of contingent gains, and ASC 958 is consistent with ASC 450 in that regard (ASC 958-605-25-14). The donee need only prepare a note to the financial statements describing the nature and conditions of the promise and the amounts promised (ASC 958-310-50-4). Accrual of conditional promises is not permitted unless the probability that the condition will not lapse is remote. For unconditional promises, the notes to the financial statements should indicate the timing of the cash flows as well as amounts, and should disclose the balances in any allowances for uncollectibles (ASC 958-310-50-1).

ACCOUNTING FOR DEFINED BENEFIT POSTRETIREMENT PLANS

A not-for-profit entity may sponsor a defined benefit postretirement plan for its employees. The accounting requirements for these plans generally parallel those for business entities. The not-for-profit entity shall recognize in its statement of financial position the funded status of the benefit plan as the difference between the fair value of the plan assets and its benefit obligation. The aggregate status of all overfunded plans is recognized as an asset in the statement of financial position. The aggregate status of all underfunded plans is recognized as a liability in the statement of financial position. The asset is presented as a noncurrent asset. The liability is presented as a current liability, noncurrent liability, or a combination. The current portion is the amount by which the actuarial present value of benefits included in the benefit obligation payable in the next 12 months, or operating cycle if longer, exceeds the fair value of plan assets.

A not-for-profit entity shall recognize the gains or losses and the prior service costs or credits that arise during the period but are not recognized as components of net periodic benefit cost in accordance with ASC 715 (Compensation—Retirement Benefits). This disclosure shall be a separate line item or items in the changes in unrestricted net assets, apart from expenses. There is no requirement as to whether the separate line items are to be included within or outside the intermediate measure of operations or performance indicator, if one is presented (ASC 958-715-45-1).

> **PRACTICE POINTER:** AICPA guidance for certain types of health care organizations requires that certain items of other comprehensive income are reported outside the performance indicator.

The entity is required to reclassify to net periodic benefit cost a portion of the net gain or loss and prior service costs and credits previously recognized as a separate line item or items, and a portion of the transition asset or obligation remaining from the initial application of the previous guidance codified in ASC 715 and the recognition and amortization provisions of ASC 715. The contra adjustments are reported in the same line item or items within changes in unrestricted net assets, apart from expenses, as the initially recognized amounts. Net periodic benefit cost is reported by functional classification (ASC 958-715-45-2).

References throughout ASC 715 to accumulated other comprehensive income relate to unrestricted net assets for a not-for-profit entity (ASC 958-715-25-1). Any income tax effects are to be determined in accordance with the guidance in ASC 740 (Income Taxes).

Not-for-profit entities shall measure plan assets and benefit obligations as of the date of the fiscal year-end statement of financial position unless the exceptions described in the chapters on pension and other postretirement benefit plans apply (i.e., a consolidated subsidiary or an equity method investee).

Disclosures

Not-for-profit entities that sponsor defined benefit pension or other postretirement benefit plans need to disclose the following:

- For each annual statement of activities presented, the net gain or loss and the net prior service cost or credit recognized in the statement of activities apart from expenses
- Separate disclosure is required for amounts arising during the period and amounts reclassified as components of net periodic benefit cost during the period
- For each annual statement of activities presented, the net transition asset or obligation recognized as components of net periodic benefit cost for the period
- For each annual statement of financial position presented, the amounts that have not yet been recognized as components of net periodic benefit

cost, with separate disclosure of the net gain or loss, net prior service cost or credit, and net transition asset or obligation

- The amounts of net gain or loss, net prior service cost or credit, and net transition asset or obligation that arose previously and are expected to be recognized as components of net periodic benefit cost over the fiscal year that follows the most recent annual statement of financial position presented

- The amount and timing of any plan assets expected to be returned to the plan sponsor during the 12-month period, or operating cycle if longer, that follows the most recent annual statement of financial position presented

The above-mentioned disclosures are to be made separately for pension plans and other postretirement benefit plans.

SERVICE EFFORTS

One of the most important disclosures for not-for-profit organizations is information about service efforts. In health care entities, colleges and universities, and ONPOs, this disclosure is accomplished by arranging the statement of activities along functional lines. For VHWOs, this information traditionally has been contained in the Statement of Functional Expenses. Functional expense disclosure involves informing the statement users of the different types of expenses (e.g., salaries, rent, professional fees) incurred for the major types of programs or functions the entity conducts.

ASC 958 requires all not-for-profits to report expenditures by functional classification and encourages ONPOs, health care providers, and colleges and universities to also provide disclosure of expenses by natural classification (ASC 958-720-45-2, 15).

Health care providers, colleges and universities, and ONPOs can comply with the functional expense disclosure standards by reporting expenses by function in the statement of activities. VHWOs are required to show expenses by both functional and natural classifications (ASC 958-720-45-15). This must be done by showing, in a matrix-formatted statement, the amounts and types of expenses allocated to programs compared with the amounts spent on administration and fund-raising. The matrix format is accomplished by using multiple columns for each type of program or support expenditure while retaining line item expense categories in vertical format. This approach enables statement users to understand the basis of program expenditures and total expenditures and to compare the amounts of expenditures for programs with those for support.

OBSERVATION: Although an ONPO's disclosure of expenses in a functional-natural matrix is **not required** by ASC 958, any ONPO whose primary mission is to conduct public service, educational, research, or similar programs will have to disclose these data to fulfill the concept of full disclosure. ASC 958 has an expressed goal of describing the minimum disclosures necessary.

Preparers are expected to exercise their professional judgment and go beyond the minimum disclosures as needed.

Proper classification of expenditures between program and support is a fundamental disclosure principle. ASC 958 provides detailed guidance about the appropriate classification of items of a support nature. Supporting activities are divided into three categories: (1) management and general, (2) fund-raising, and (3) membership development (ASC Glossary).

OBSERVATION: ASC 958 specifies that membership development is an element of support activity and should be so reported.

Also, it is important to emphasize that much information about service efforts may not be presentable in the body of the financial statements. Accordingly, preparers should ensure that notes provide full disclosure of information describing service accomplishments, including program descriptions, statistical data relevant to program inputs and outputs, and narratives about accomplishments.

BUSINESS COMBINATIONS

ASC 958 also establishes standards for accounting for mergers and acquisitions involving not-for-profit entities. ASC 958 provides guidance on (1) determining whether a combination is a merger or an acquisition, (2) applying the carryover method in accounting for a merger, (3) applying the acquisition method in accounting for an acquisition, including determining the entity that is the acquirer, and (4) determining the appropriate disclosures. ASC 958 extends the requirements of ASC 350 to not-for-profit (NFP) entities, thereby improving the information provided by NFP entities about goodwill and other intangible assets (ASC 958-805-10-1; 958-805-05-1, 2, 4, 5).

Scope

ASC 958 provides guidance on accounting for a combination of NFP entities, which is a transaction or other event that results in a NFP entity initially recognizing another NFP entity, a business, or a nonprofit activity in its financial statements. ASC 958 applies to a combination that meets the definition of either a "merger" of NFP entities or an "acquisition" of a NFP entity (ASC 958-805-15-3; 958-805-05-1).

A "merger" of NFP organizations is a combination in which the governing bodies of two or more NFP entities cede control of those entities to create a new NFP entity. In contrast, an "acquisition" is a combination in which a NFP acquirer obtains control of one or more nonprofit activities or businesses. This is a particularly important consideration in applying ASC 958 because subsequent accounting for a merger is significantly different from that for an acquisition (ASC Glossary).

If the participating entities retain shared control of the new entity, they have not ceded their control. To qualify as a new entity (i.e., an acquisition), the combined entity must have a newly formed governing body. The new entity is often a new legal entity, although this is not a requirement. Control of a NFP entity is the direct or indirect ability to determine the direction of management and policies through ownership, contract, or otherwise (ASC Glossary).

> **PRACTICE POINTER:** Ceding control to a new entity is the sole definitive criterion for identifying a merger. One entity obtaining control over the other is the sole definitive criterion for an acquisition. Other characteristics, however, can be used to help identify a merger. Participating entities must consider all of the characteristics and other pertinent factors and make a professional judgment about whether (1) the governing bodies have ceded control of those entities to create a new entity, (2) one entity has acquired the other, or (3) another form of combination (e.g., the formation of a joint venture) has occurred (ASC 958-805-55-1, 2).

ASC 958 does not apply to the following (ASC 805-10-15-4):
- The formation of a joint venture;
- The acquisition of an asset or a group of assets that does not constitute either a business or a nonprofit activity;
- A combination between NFP entities, businesses, or nonprofit activities under common control; or
- A transaction or other event in which a NFP entity obtains control of another entity but does not consolidate that entity.

Unique Features of NFP Combinations

Combinations by NFP and business entities are similar in many ways, so much so that the same basic accounting method (i.e., the acquisition method) is appropriate for both (see the Chapter 45, *ASC 805—Business Combinations*, for a detailed discussion of the acquisition method of accounting). However, there are important differences between for profit and not-for-profit entities and those differences are reflected in the accounting for business combinations.

A fundamental difference between combinations for NFP and business entities is that a NFP entity lacks the type of ownership interests that business entities have and, as a result, negotiations in NFP mergers and acquisitions generally focus on the furtherance of the benefit for the public rather than on maximizing returns for equity holders. Many mergers and acquisitions by NFP entities do not involve a transfer of consideration. They are not fair value exchanges but rather are nonreciprocal transfers. This fundamental difference contributes significantly to ASC 958's requirement that different accounting methods apply to a merger of a NFP entity and an acquisition by a NFP entity. For an acquisition, those combinations result in a contribution of the acquiree's net assets to the acquirer, referred to in ASC 958 as "inherent contribution received," to distinguish it from other contributions received by a NFP entity.

MERGERS

The carryover method is required by ASC 958 for NFP mergers. Under the carryover method, the combined entity's initial set of financial statements carry forward the assets and liabilities of the combining entities, measured at their carrying amounts in the books of the combining entities at the merger date (ASC 958-805-25-6). In applying the carryover method, an entity recognizes neither additional assets nor additional liabilities that are not already recognized in the combining entities' financial statements before the merger (ASC 958-805-25-7). Exceptions are made to reflect a consistent method of accounting for the new entity if the merging entities used different methods and to eliminate the effects of intraentity transactions (ASC 958-805-30-2, 4).

The measurement date of a merger in ASC 958 is the actual merger date, defined as the date the combination becomes effective. The NFP entity that results from a merger is a new entity and, therefore, a new reporting entity. The history of the new entity begins at its inception and has no previous operations. Guidance on the measurement date and related presentation issues in ASC 958 is consistent with the merged entity's status as a new entity (ASC 958-805-30-1).

ASC 958 also provides additional guidance for applying the carryover method. For example, ASC 958 states how to make the classifications and designations that are required to apply other generally accepted accounting principles (GAAP), such as hedge accounting requirements. The new entity is to carry forward into the opening balances in its financial statements the merging entities' classifications and designations unless either of the following applies (ASC 958-805-25-9):

- The merger results in a modification of a contract in a manner that would change the previous classifications or designations; or
- Reclassifications are required to conform the accounting policies of the merging entities.

Disclosures: Mergers

ASC 958 outlines the following disclosure requirements for the new reporting entity that results from a NFP merger (ASC 958-805-50-2, 3, 4, 5):

- The name and a description of each merging entity;
- The merger date;
- The primary reasons for the merger;
- For each merging entity:
  — The amounts recognized as of the merger date for each major class of assets and liabilities and each class of net assets;
  — The nature and amounts of any significant assets or liabilities that GAAP does not require to be recognized;
- The nature and amount of any significant adjustments made to conform the individual accounting policies of the merging entities or to eliminate intraentity balances; and
- If the new entity is a public entity, the following supplemental pro-forma information:
  — If the merger occurs at other than the beginning of an annual period and the entity's initial financial statements cover less than an annual reporting period, the following information for the current reporting

period as if the merger had been at the beginning of the annual reporting period: (1) revenue; (2) for an entity subject to the *Health Care Organizations* Guide, the performance indicator; and (3) changes in unrestricted net assets, changes in temporarily restricted net assets, and changes in permanently restricted net assets.

— If the new entity presents comparative financial information in the annual reporting period following the year in which the merger occurs, the entity shall disclose the supplemental pro-forma information above for the comparable prior reporting period as though the merger date had been the beginning of that prior annual reporting period.

If disclosure of any of the above information is impracticable, the entity shall disclose that fact and explain why the information is not disclosed. The term "impracticable" as used in ASC 958 has the same meaning as in ASC 250 (Accounting Changes and Error Corrections) (ASC 250-10-45-9).

ACQUISITIONS

The acquisition method in ASC 958 is the same as the acquisition method described in ASC 805 for business entities. It contains additional guidance on items that are unique or especially significant to a NFP entity and eliminates any ASC 805 guidance that does not apply to NFP entities. ASC 958 guidance on identifying both the acquirer and the acquisition date is in substance the same as the guidance in ASC 805, but ASC 958 uses different terminology and adds some details unique to NFP entities (ASC 958-805-25-13).

Applying the acquisition method requires (ASC 958-805-25-13) the following:

- Identifying the acquirer;
- Determining the acquisition date;
- Recognizing and measuring the identifiable assets acquired, liabilities assumed, and any noncontrolling interest of the acquiree; and
- Recognizing and measuring goodwill or the contribution received.

Identifying the Acquirer

One of the combining entities must be designated as the acquirer in each acquisition (ASC 805-10-25-4). The former guidance in SOP 94-3, *Reporting of Related Entities by Not-for-Profit Organizations*, or the AICPA Audit and Accounting Guide *Health Care Organizations* should be used to identify the acquirer (ASC 958-805-25-15, 16).

Determining the Acquisition Date

The acquisition date is the date on which the acquirer obtains control of the acquiree (ASC 805-10-25-6). The acquisition date is generally the date that consideration is transferred, assets acquired, and liabilities assumed. This date is typically the closing date, although the acquisition date can precede the closing date if a contract or other written agreement indicates that control is obtained before the closing date. All relevant facts and circumstances are to be considered in determining the acquisition date (ASC 805-10-25-7).

Recognizing and Measuring Identifiable Assets, Liabilities, and Noncontrolling Interest

In ASC 958, the basic principles of recognizing and measuring identifiable assets, liabilities, and noncontrolling interest are as follows:

- As of the acquisition date, the acquirer recognizes separately from goodwill the identifiable assets acquired, liabilities assumed, and any noncontrolling interest in the acquiree. As a result, the acquirer may recognize certain assets and liabilities that the acquiree had not previously recognized (e.g., internally developed brand names, patents, and customer relationships).

- At the acquisition date, the acquirer shall classify or designate the identifiable assets acquired and liabilities assumed as required to subsequently apply other GAAP. The acquirer makes those classifications or designations based on the contractual terms, economic conditions, operating or accounting policies, and other pertinent conditions that exist at the acquisition date. There is an exception to this general rule: lease contracts and insurance contracts are classified by the terms that existed at the inception of the contract.

- The acquirer shall measure the identifiable assets acquired, liabilities assumed, and any noncontrolling interest at their fair value at the acquisition date.

Exceptions to the General Recognition and Measurement Guidance

The acquirer shall not recognize an acquired donor relationship as an identifiable intangible asset separately from goodwill (ASC 958-805-25-22). In addition, an acquirer that follows an accounting policy of not capitalizing "collections" (e.g., works of art and historical treasures) should not capitalize as an asset acquired works of art, historical treasures, etc. that it adds to its collection. If the work of art, historical treasure, etc. is purchased, the acquirer should decrease net assets in the statement of activities and present a cash outflow for investing activities. And if the work of art, historical treasure, etc. is contributed, the acquirer will not recognize the item as an asset or as contribution revenue (ASC 958-805-25-23). Finally, a conditional promise to give is only recognized if the underlying conditions have been substantially satisfied at the acquisition date, and assets that have already been transferred under a conditional promise are recognized as a liability (i.e., a refundable advance) unless the underlying conditions have been substantially satisfied (ASC 958-805-25-26).

Contingencies

In general, the acquirer shall recognize as of the acquisition date assets acquired and liabilities assumed that would be within the scope of ASC 450 (Contingencies), had they not been acquired or assumed in a business combination. If the fair value of an asset or a liability arising from a contingency can be determined during the measurement period, the acquirer should recognize the fair value of the asset or liability at the acquisition date (e.g., a warranty obligation). If the fair value of an asset or liability arising from a contingency is not determinable during the measurement period, an asset or liability would only be recognized if the ASC 450 criteria are met during the measurement period (i.e., probable that an asset existed or a liability has been incurred and the amount can be reasonably estimated).

Income Taxes, Employee Benefits, and Indemnification Agreements

The acquirer shall recognize and measure a deferred tax asset or liability arising from the assets acquired and liabilities assumed in an acquisition according to ASC 740.

The acquirer shall recognize and measure a liability or an asset, if any, related to the acquiree's employee benefit arrangements in according with other GAAP. Refer to the Chapter in this *Guide* covering ASC 715 for additional guidance on postemployment and postretirement benefits.

The seller in an acquisition by a NFP entity may contractually indemnify the acquirer for the outcome of a contingency or uncertainty related to all or part of a specific asset or liability. When the acquirer receives such an indemnity, the acquirer shall recognize an indemnification asset at the same time that it recognizes the indemnified item, measured on the same basis as the indemnified item, subject to the need for a valuation allowance for uncollectible amounts.

PRACTICE POINTER: If an indemnification asset is measured at fair value, no valuation allowance is needed because the risk related to uncollectibility is already included in determining the asset's fair value.

Reacquired Rights and Assets Held for Sale

In an acquisition an acquirer may reacquire a right that it had previously granted to the acquiree (e.g., the acquirer could have granted the acquiree a right to use technology under a technology licensing agreement). Such a reacquired right is recognized as an intangible asset at fair value. Fair value is based on the remaining contractual term of the transferred right, regardless of whether market participants would consider potential renewals in determining fair value.

At the acquisition date, the acquirer shall measure an acquired long-lived asset or disposal group that is classified as held for sale at fair value less cost to sell in accordance with ASC 360.

Recognizing Goodwill or a Contribution Received

ASC 958 differs most significantly from ASC 805 in the area of recognizing goodwill. Unlike business entities, some NFP entities are solely or predominantly supported by contributions and returns on investments (e.g., a soup kitchen). Other NFP entities are more like business entities and receive most, if not all, of their support from fees and services (e.g., a hospital that charges fees to help cover its costs). In general, the more a NFP entity is like a business, the more relevant information about goodwill is to the users of its financial statements.

ASC 958 recognizes that information about goodwill may be of limited use to the donors of a NFP entity in making decisions to provide resources to the entity. Accordingly, the standard requires an acquirer that expects the operations of the acquiree as part of the combined entity to be predominantly supported by contributions and returns on investments to recognize as a separate charge in its statement of activities the amount that would otherwise be recognized as goodwill at the acquisition date. The phrase "predominantly supported by" means that contributions and returns on investments are expected to be significantly more than the total of all other sources of revenues for the NFP entity (ASC 958-805-25-29).

Many acquisitions by NFP entities constitute an inherent contribution received because the acquirer receives net assets without transferring consideration. ASC 958 requires the acquirer to recognize such a contribution as a separate credit in its statement of activities on the acquisition date (ASC 958-805-25-31; 958-805-30-8, 9).

However, if the acquiree is not primarily supported by contributions and returns on investment, goodwill may be recognized as part of the acquisition. The goodwill amount to be recognized is computed as the excess of the purchase price over the fair value of the acquiree's net assets at the acquisition date. The acquisition price includes (1) consideration transferred (measured at fair value), (2) the fair value of any noncontrolling interest in the acquiree, and, (3) if the acquisition is achieved in stages, the fair value of the interest in the acquiree held by the acquirer on the acquisition date (ASC 958-805-25-28; 958-805-30-6). In some cases, an acquirer receives assistance from an unrelated third party in consummating an acquisition. Such assistance is included in the fair value of the consideration transferred by the acquirer (ASC 958-805-25-32). In addition, the acquirer may transfer contingent consideration. The fair value of such contingent consideration is included in determining the acquisition price (ASC 958-805-25-36). Finally, assets transferred where the acquirer retains control over the assets' future economic benefits are *not* to be considered as being transferred (ASC 958-805-25-33).

Noncontrolling Interests

ASC 958 requires that a recognized noncontrolling interest in another entity be measured at its fair value at the acquisition date. This is true whether the other entity is a business entity or another NFP entity. ASC 958 also provides guidance on and illustrates the presentation of a noncontrolling interest in a NFP entity's financial statements.

Other Provisions of the Acquisition Method

ASC 958 provides other guidance on applying the acquisition method in areas that are unique or especially significant for NFP entities, including the following:

- An acquisition achieved in stages;
- What constitutes the "measurement period";
- Determining what is part of the acquisition transaction;
- Acquisition-related costs;
- How to present in the statement of activities and the statement of cash flows various items that are unique to NFP entities, including an immediate charge to the statement of activities for amounts that otherwise would

be recognized as goodwill, and an immediate credit to the statement of activities for an inherent contribution received;
- Subsequent measurement.

Acquisition Achieved in Stages

An acquisition is achieved in stages when two or more transactions result in the acquirer obtaining control of the acquiree. For example, ABC Inc. might hold a 30% noncontrolling equity interest in XYZ Inc. and then acquire another 40% equity interest. Because ABC Inc. now holds a 70% equity interest in XYZ Inc., ABC now has control and that control was achieved in stages.

In an acquisition achieved in stages, the acquirer is to remeasure its equity stake in the acquiree at fair value at the acquisition date. In the preceding example, ABC Inc. would revalue its 30% stake in XYZ Inc. to fair value at the acquisition date. Any resulting gain or loss on the remeasurement would appear in ABC Inc.'s statement of activities. In addition, an entity subject to the AICPA Audit and Accounting Guide *Health Care Organizations* would include the gain or loss on remeasurement in the performance indicator (ASC 954-805-45-3).

Determination of the Measurement Period

If the accounting for an acquisition is incomplete by the end of the reporting period in which the acquisition occurred, the acquirer should account for the acquisition using provisional amounts. These provisional amounts are to be adjusted during the measurement period using additional information as to conditions that existed on the acquisition date. In addition, if additional information indicates that other assets and liabilities existed at the acquisition date they are to be recorded even if provisional amounts were not established. The measurement period ends when the acquirer obtains all the information it needs to account for the acquisition, but in no case shall the measurement period exceed one year from the acquisition date.

In determining whether information subsequently acquired provides information about the value of assets and liabilities as of the acquisition date or reflects transactions that occurred after the acquisition date, the acquirer should recognize that information received shortly after the acquisition date is more reliable than information received later. Changes to the provisional amounts recorded for assets and liabilities affect goodwill or, for those acquisitions where goodwill is not recognized, are recorded via a direct charge to the statement of activities. And, if the provisional amounts recorded for assets and liabilities are adjusted, amounts reported in prior-period statements are to be adjusted, including recomputing prior-period amounts for depreciation, amortization, etc. Finally, once the measurement period is over, adjustments related to the acquisition can only be recorded to correct errors.

Scope of the Acquisition Transaction and Acquisition-Related Costs

The acquirer and acquiree may have a relationship that precedes the acquisition transaction, or they may enter into a separate transaction during the acquisition negotiations. Any amounts exchanged that are not part of the consideration for the acquisition are to be accounted for separately. In particular, a transaction entered into primarily for the benefit of the acquirer is likely to be a separate transaction. Examples of separate transactions that are not part of the acquisition include the following (ASC 805-10-25-21; 958-805-25-7):

- A transaction to settle a preexisting relationship between the acquirer and acquiree;
- A transaction that compensates employees or former owners of the acquiree for future services;
- A reimbursement of the acquiree or its former owners for paying the acquirer's acquisition-related costs;
- A payment by a former owner of an acquired business that is unrelated to the acquiree.

Acquisition-related costs are costs incurred by the acquirer to consummate the acquisition. With one exception, acquisition-related costs are expensed as incurred. However, the costs to issue debt to fund an acquisition are accounted for in accordance with other applicable GAAP.

Financial Statement Presentation Issues

If the acquiree's operations are primarily supported by contributions and returns from investments, any excess of the acquisition price over the fair value of the net assets acquired is charged to the statement of operations in the period of the acquisition. A suitable line item description might be, "excess of consideration paid over net assets acquired in acquisition of Entity ABC" (ASC 958-805-45-4).

If the fair value of the net assets acquired exceeds the acquisition price, the acquirer has received an inherent contribution. Such an inherent contribution is to be recognized in the statement of activities. A suitable line item description might be "excess of assets acquired over liabilities assumed in donation of Entity ABC." For those entities where the AICPA Audit and Accounting Guide *Health Care Organizations* applies, whether the donation is included within the performance indicator depends upon whether the contribution is restricted or unrestricted. Unrestricted contributions are included within the performance indicator; temporarily are permanently restricted contributions are not (ASC 958-805-45-5).

The classification of the net assets associated with the inherent contribution depends on any restrictions imposed. Restrictions imposed on the net assets of the acquiree by a donor before the acquisition, or those imposed when the acquiree is donated to the acquirer are to be disclosed. Also, contributions restricted by donors are to be reported as restricted support even if the restrictions are satisfied in the period of the acquisition (ASC 958-805-45-6).

The use of assets by the acquirer to fund an acquisition may result in a change in net asset classifications. If assets restricted for the purchase of works of art are used to purchase an acquiree that has works of art, the acquirer should report the expiration of the restrictions either separately or in aggregate with other restrictions that have expired. And a transfer of unrestricted net assets to acquire assets that are either temporarily or permanently restricted results in a reclassification in the statement of activities (ASC 958-805-45-8, 9, 10).

In addition to the statement of activities, there are presentation issues that affect the statement of cash flows. The acquirer will report as a cash outflow in the investing activity portion of the statement the cash consideration transferred less the acquiree's cash balance. Noncash amounts and contributions received or transferred are to be disclosed as noncash transactions in accordance with the guidance in ASC 230 (ASC 958-805-45-11; 958-805-50-15).

Subsequent Measurement

Assets acquired or liabilities assumed in an acquisition are generally accounted for in accordance with other applicable GAAP. ASC 958 provides specific guidance in subsequently accounting for (1) reacquired rights, (2) indemnification assets, (3) contingent consideration, and (4) goodwill.

A reacquired right recognized as an intangible asset is to be amortized over the remaining contractual term. The gain or loss on any future sale of the reacquired right would consider the carrying value of the reacquired right.

The indemnification asset is to be measured at each future reporting date using the same (measurement) basis as the indemnified asset or liability, subject to any contractual limitation on the amount of the asset. The indemnification asset should only be derecognized when the acquirer collects the asset, sells the asset, or otherwise loses its right to the asset.

The amount of contingent consideration due may change because of subsequent business developments, say, meeting or failing to meet an earnings, share price, or other performance target. The acquirer is to remeasure the related asset or liability to fair value at the end of each reporting period until the contingency is resolved. Changes in the fair value of contingent assets and liabilities are included in the statement of activities (ASC 958-805-35-3).

The acquirer is to apply ASC 350 in accounting for goodwill and other intangible assets in future periods (ASC 958-805-35-5).

Disclosures: Acquisitions

ASC 958 requires extensive disclosures by the acquirer if an acquisition occurs either during the current period or after the current period but before the financial statements are issued or are available to be issued. However, if the accounting is incomplete for an acquisition occurring after the current period but before the financial statements are issued or are available to be issued, the acquirer should state the disclosures that could not be made and the reasons why (ASC 958-805-50-14).

The disclosures required by an acquirer as a result of an acquisition are as follows (ASC 958-805-50-8, 11, 12):

- The name and description of the acquiree;
- The acquisition date;
- If applicable, the percentage of voting equity ownership obtained;
- The primary reasons for the acquisition and how control was obtained;
- A description of the factors that make up the goodwill recognized or the separate charge recognized in the statement of activities for those ac-

quirees where goodwill is not recognized (i.e., acquirees whose support is primarily from contributions and returns on investment);
- The fair value of the consideration transferred (including by major class of consideration) at the acquisition date;
- For contingent consideration and indemnification assets, the amount recognized, a description of the arrangement and how any future payment is to be determined, and (if practicable) an undiscounted range of possible payment outcomes;
- For receivables acquired not subject to ASC 310-30, the receivables' fair values, gross contractual amounts, and cash flows expected to be collected, with these disclosures by major class of receivable;
- The amounts recognized as of the acquisition date for each major class of assets acquired and liabilities assumed;
- Assets and liabilities recognized as a result of contingencies, including the measurement basis (i.e., fair value or measured in accordance with ASC 450), and a description of the contingencies;
- If assets and liabilities related to contingencies are not recognized, any required disclosures from ASC 450 (e.g., the contingency is reasonably possible, or the contingency is probable but a reasonable estimate of the amount cannot be developed);
- Goodwill expected to be deductible for tax purposes;
- The dollar amount of "collectible" items (works of art, historical items, etc.) not recognized as an asset but rather recorded in the statement of activities as a decrease in the acquirer's net assets;
- The undiscounted amount of conditional promises to give acquired or assumed, with individual descriptions and amounts for each group of similar promises;
- For transactions with the acquiree that are not part of the acquisition: (1) a description of the transaction, (2) how the acquirer accounted for the transaction, (3) the amounts recognized for each transaction and the financial statement lines where these amounts appear, and (4) how the settlement amount was determined if the transaction settles a preexisting relationship;
- For transactions with the acquiree that are not part of the acquisition, the disclosure of (1) acquisition-related costs, (2) amounts recognized as an expense, and (3) the financial statement lines where these amounts appear;
- For those acquisitions involving an inherent contribution received, a description of why the transaction resulted in a contribution received;
- For those acquisitions where the acquirer owns less than 100% of the acquiree's equity interests, disclose (1) the fair value of the noncontrolling interests in the acquiree at the acquisition date and (2) the valuation technique and significant inputs used to determine fair value;

- For those acquisitions achieved in steps, disclose (1) the fair value of the acquirer's equity interest in the acquiree immediately before the acquisition date and (2) any gain or loss in revaluing the acquirer's equity interest and the line item in the statement of activities where this gain or loss appears;
- If the acquirer is a public entity, required additional disclosures are as follows:
  — The amounts included in the statement of activities attributable to the acquiree since the acquisition date for revenues, changes in unrestricted net assets, changes in temporarily restricted net assets, changes in permanently restricted net assets, and for entities subject to the AICPA Audit and Accounting Guide *Health Care Organizations* the performance indicator;
  — Selected pro-forma information as if all acquisitions during the period had occurred as of the beginning of the period, including revenues, changes in unrestricted net assets, changes in temporarily restricted net assets, changes in permanently restricted net assets, and for entities subject to the AICPA Audit and Accounting Guide *Health Care Organizations* the performance indicator;
  — If the acquirer presents comparative financial statements, selected pro-forma information as if all acquisitions during the period had occurred as of the beginning of the earliest period presented for comparative purposes, including revenues, changes in unrestricted net assets, changes in temporarily restricted net assets, changes in permanently restricted net assets, and for entities subject to the AICPA Audit and Accounting Guide *Health Care Organizations* the performance indicator.

If disclosure of any of the above information is impracticable, the entity shall disclose that fact and explain why the information is not disclosed. The term "impracticable" as used in ASC 958 has the same meaning as in ASC 250 (Accounting Changes and Error Corrections) (ASC 958-805-50-10).

In addition to the above disclosures, the acquirer is to disclose adjustments in the current period that relate to acquisitions in either the current or prior periods. The following items are to be disclosed for all material acquisitions and in the aggregate for immaterial acquisitions that are material when considered together (ASC 958-805-50-16):

- If the accounting for the acquisition is incomplete and provisional amounts are included in the financial statements, the following are to be disclosed:
  — The reasons that the accounting is incomplete;
  — The specific assets, liabilities, equity interests, or consideration amounts where the accounting is incomplete;
  — The nature and amount of any measurement-period adjustments recognized during the period;

- For each reporting period after the acquisition where a contingent consideration asset or liability continues to exist, the following are to be disclosed:
  — Any changes in the amounts recognized, including gains and losses on settlement;
  — Any changes in possible undiscounted outcomes and the reasons for these changes
  — A reconciliation of the beginning and ending goodwill balance.

ASC 958-20: FINANCIALLY INTERRELATED ENTITIES

ASC 958 requires a recipient organization to recognize at fair value an asset and liability instead of contribution revenue if the recipient organization accepts cash or other financial assets from a donor and agrees to use those assets, or disburse them and the return from investing the assets, or both, to a specified beneficiary (ASC 958-605-25-24). The specified beneficiary reports its interest in the assets held by the recipient organization as an asset and as contribution revenue (ASC 958-605-25-28). Exceptions to the above are situations in which the recipient organization is granted variance power (i.e., can redirect the use of funds) and in which the recipient and beneficiary organizations are interrelated (ASC 958-605-25-25, 27).

The Codification also specifies criteria for determining when the recipient organization and the specified beneficiary are considered interrelated organizations. These criteria are typically met by a not-for-profit organization and a related foundation (ASC Glossary).

PART II: INTERPRETIVE GUIDANCE

ASC 958-205: Presentation of Financial Statements

ASC 958-205-05-10, 45-21A, 45-28 through 45-32, 50-1A through 50-1B, 55-1, 55-31 through 55-53, 65-1
Endowments of Not-for-Profit Organizations: Net Asset Classification of Funds Subject to an Enacted Version of the Uniform Prudent Management of Institutional Funds Act, and Enhanced Disclosures

BACKGROUND

The Uniform Prudent Management Institutional Funds Act of 2006 (UPMIFA) is a model act that was adopted by the National Conference of Commissioners on Uniform State Laws (NCCUSL) to be used as a guideline by states enacting related legislation. It is a modernized version of the Uniform Management of Institutional Funds Act of 1972 (UMIFA) on which 46 states and the District of Columbia have based their primary laws that legislate the manner in which not-for-profit organizations (NFPOs) are required to invest and manage donor-restricted endowment funds.

UPMIFA provides new guidance for the designation of expenditures of a donor-restricted endowment fund, unless it is superseded by explicit donor conditions. While UMIFA dealt with the prudent spending of a fund's net appreciation, UPMIFA addresses the treatment of both the *original* gift and the *net appreciation* of a donor-restricted endowment fund. UPMIFA also replaces UMIFA's historic-dollar-threshold, which was defined in that act as the total fair value in dollars of: (1) the amount of the original endowment gift; (2) subsequent donations to the fund; and (3) "each accumulation made pursuant to a direction in the applicable gift instrument at the time the accumulation is added to the fund," below which an organization could not spend from a fund. Instead, UPMIFA provides guidance on what represents prudent spending while considering a fund's duration and preservation.

Under subsection 4(a) of UPMIFA, an endowment fund's assets are considered to be donor-restricted assets until the NFPO has designated them for disbursement, unless the gift instrument states otherwise. Some have raised questions about how that requirement in subsection 4(a) and the UPMIFA's changed focus from UMFIA's requirement of prudent spending (i.e., historical-dollar-threshold) to the detailed guidelines on what represents prudent spending, which requires consideration of an endowment fund's duration and preservation, would affect (a) the net asset classification of a donor-restricted endowment fund and (b) whether a *temporary* (i.e., time) restriction is imposed on the portion of a donor-restricted endowment fund that normally would be classified as "unrestricted net assets."

ACCOUNTING GUIDANCE

FASB Accounting Standards Codification (ASC) 958-205 provides the following guidance to NFPOs in states that have enacted a law based on UPMIFA:

- A portion of a donor-restricted endowment fund that has a *perpetual* duration should be classified as *permanently* restricted net assets. Based on the guidance in ASC 948-605-45-4, and ASC 958-205-45-21, the amount of an endowment fund that must be classified as permanently restricted is: (1) the amount that must be retained permanently in accordance with a donor's specific conditions; or (2) if there are *no* specified donor conditions, the portion of an endowment fund that must be permanently retained based on the NFPO's governing board's interpretation of the applicable law that should be applied on a consistent basis from year to year.

    Because legislation based on UPMIFA has only recently been enacted by many states and no case law currently exists for the interpretation of such legislation, it is not yet clear how a particular state will interpret and enforce that legislation. To help NFPOs understand the requirements of the applicable law in their particular states, the following sources of information may be consulted: (1) discussions of a state's legislative committee that have resulted in the law's adoption; (2) announcements from a state's Attorney General; (3) a consensus of scholarly lawyers in that state; or (4) similar information. The governing board of an NFPO in a state that has *not* enacted new legislation based on UPMIFA should interpret the requirements of UPMIFA consistently from year to year based on clarifying court decisions, additional guidance issued by their state's Attorney General, or similar developments.

In accordance with the guidance in ASC 958-205-45-17, 45-22, *permanently* restricted net assets should *not* be reduced by: (1) losses on a fund's investments, except as required by the donor, including losses related to specific investments required by the donor to be held in perpetuity; and (2) an NFPO's expenditures from the fund.

If the restriction discussed in subsection 4(a) of UPMIFA applies, classify as *temporarily* restricted net assets (i.e., time restricted) the portion of each donor-restricted endowment fund that is *not* classified as permanently restricted net assets until the NFPO has designated that amount for disbursement. Unless court decisions or interpretations of a state's Attorney General exist on when an amount is considered to be *appropriaated for expenditure*, for the purposes of this guidance, an amount is so designated when an expenditure has been approved. However, an expenditure that has been approved for disbursement in a *future* period is considered to occur when that period has been reached. An amount that has been appropriated for expenditure should be reclassified in *unrestricted net assets* because the time restriction for that amount has expired, unless that amount is also restricted for a specified purpose. If so, in accordance with the guidance in ASC 958-205-45-9, that amount would *not* be reclassified to unrestricted net assets until the purpose restriction also has been met. The guidance related to net asset classification in ASC 958-205-45-35, continues to apply to donor-restricted endowment funds under the guidance in UMIFA.

- Regardless of whether it is subject to an enacted version of UPMIFA, a NFPO is required to disclose information about the organization's *donor-restricted* and *board-designated* endowment funds to help users of its financial statements understand: (1) the classification and composition of net assets; (2) changes in the composition of net assets; (3) the organization's spending policies; and (4) related investment policies. At a minimum, the following information should be disclosed for each period for which a NFPO presents financial statements:

  — The governing board's interpretation of the law used to classify net assets of donor-restricted endowment funds.

  — The NFPO's spending policies (i.e., its policies for the designation of funds from endowment assets for disbursement).

  — The NFPO's investment policies for its endowments, including: (1) the organization's goals for returns and risk limits; (2) the relationship of those goals to its spending policies; and (3) the strategies used to achieve those goals.

  — The composition of the NFPO's endowment by net asset class at the end of the period, in total and by type of endowment fund, with donor-restricted endowment funds presented *separately* from board-designated endowment funds.

— A reconciliation of the beginning and ending balance of the NFPO's endowment, in total and by net asset class, including, at a minimum, the following line items, if applicable: (1) investment return, separated into investment income (e.g., interest, dividends, or rents) and net appreciation or depreciation of investments; (2) contributions; (3) amounts designated for disbursement; (4) reclassifications; and (5) other changes.

APPENDIX I:
ASC 962—PLAN ACCOUNTING

CONTENTS

Interpretive Guidance	67,001
ASC 962: Defined Contribution Pension Plans	67,001
ASC 962-310: Receivables	67,001
ASC 962-310-35-2, 45-2, 50-1, 65-1; ASC 962-325-55-16; ASC 310-10-50-5B, 50-7B	
Reporting Loans to Participants by Defined Contribution Pension Plans	67,001

INTERPRETIVE GUIDANCE

ASC 962: PLAN ACCOUNTING

ASC 962: Defined Contribution Pension Plans

ASC 962-310: Receivables

ASC 962-310-35-2, 45-2, 50-1, 65-1; ASC 962-325-55-16; ASC 310-10-50-5B, 50-7B
Reporting Loans to Participants by Defined Contribution Pension Plans

BACKGROUND

Loans to participants against assets in their plan accounts may be permitted under the provisions of some defined contribution pension plans. If so, some of the assets in a participant's account are liquidated to provide cash for the loan. The only collateral against the loan is the remaining balance in the participant's account, which would be offset if the participant defaults on the loan. In addition, because a plan has no recourse against a participant's personal assets, no assets would be returned to the plan if the participant defaults on the loan. The only consequence of default on a loan from a participant's account in a defined contribution plan is that the participant will be taxed on the unpaid balance of the loan.

Pension and welfare benefit plans are required to file an annual report, referred to as a Form 5500 filing, with the Department of Labor. Under that filing, defined contribution pension plans are required to report the plan's assets at "current value," which is defined as "fair market where available." Otherwise, the term "current value" means that fair value is "determined in good faith under the terms of the plan by a trustee or a named fiduciary, assuming an orderly liquidation at the time of determination." If a plan does not meet certain conditions, audited financial statements must be submitted with the filing. A difference, if any, between the valuation of the plan's assets in the Form 5500 filing and the audited financial statements must be reconciled in a note to the financial statements.

In accordance with the guidance in ASC 962, *Plan Accounting—Defined Contribution Pension Plans* (ASC 962-325-45-10), loans to participants must be reported as investments even though the nature of a loan is a receivable. In addition, under the guidance in ASC 962-325-35, most of a plan's investments, including loans made to participants, must be reported at fair value in accordance with the guidance in ASC 820, *Fair Value Measurements and Disclosures*. The fair value of a plan's investments is "the price that would be received to sell an asset or paid to transfer a liability in an orderly transaction between market participants at the measurement date." However, in practice, most defined contribution pension plans carry loans to participants at amortized cost, which is considered to be a good faith estimate of the fair value based on that definition.

Some believe that loans to participants should be valued based on the guidance in ASC 820 because it cannot be assumed that the outstanding principal balance of those loans is an estimate of their fair value. Others hold that doing so would require highly subjective assumptions about market interest rates and credit risk, which would result in information that is unreliable, not comparable, and not useful. Still others argue that the valuation of loans to participants based on the guidance in ASC 820, which might result in a value other than the unpaid balances of participants' loans, would be misleading to the participants and others (e.g., regulators) and would not be relevant because repayments of the unpaid balances of loans to participants are based on the original amounts of the loans, plus interest, less previous payments.

SCOPE

The following guidance applies to all loans to participants in defined contribution pension plans.

ACCOUNTING GUIDANCE

Participants' loans should be classified as notes receivable from participants in a defined contribution plan's financial statements and should be measured at the balance of the unpaid principal, plus accrued but unpaid interest, if any.

Recurring Disclosures

Additional recurring disclosures are not required for participant loans. In addition, the disclosure requirements about fair value in ASC 825, *Financial Instruments* (ASC 825-10-50-10 through 50-16), do not apply to loans to participants.

Loans to participants are exempt from making the disclosures about credit quality required in ASU 2010-10, *Receivables (Topic 310): Disclosures about the Credit Quality of Financing Receivables and the Allowance for Credit Losses*.

Transition Method, Transition Disclosures, and Effective Date

Employee benefit plans should apply the above guidance *retrospectively* to all prior periods presented. The guidance is effective for fiscal years that end after December 15, 2010.

APPENDIX J:
ASC 970—REAL ESTATE—GENERAL

CONTENTS

Part I: General Guidance	68,002
Overview	68,002
Background	68,002
Real Estate Costs and Initial Rental Operations	68,003
Preacquisition Costs	68,003
Illustration of Preacquisition Costs	68,004
Project Costs	68,004
Taxes and Insurance	68,004
Amenity Costs of Real Property	68,004
Ownership Not Retained by Developer	68,005
Ownership Retained by Developer	68,005
Incidental Operations of Real Property	68,006
Revisions of Estimates	68,006
Selling Costs	68,006
Project Costs	68,007
Prepaid Expenses	68,007
Period Costs	68,007
Rental Costs of Real Estate Projects	68,007
Initial Rental Operations	68,007
Operating Leases	68,008
Chargeable to Future Periods	68,008
Chargeable to the Current Period	68,008
Project Costs Related to Property, Plant, and Equipment	68,009
Project Costs	68,009
Illustration of Direct and Indirect Project Costs	68,009
Allocation of Capitalized Costs	68,010
Land Costs	68,010
Construction Costs	68,010
Abandonments and Changes in Use	68,010
Recoverability	68,011
Part II: Interpretive Guidance	68,011
ASC 970: General	68,011
ASC 970-340-25-1 through 25-2, 25-5 through 25-7, 35-3 through 35-4; ASC 970-720-25-1 through 25-2	
Accounting for Internal Costs Relating to Real Estate Property Acquisitions	68,011
ASC 970-360-25-1, 55-1 through 55-3	
Recognition of Receipts from Made-Up Rental Shortfalls	68,013
ASC 970-360-55-4 through 55-5	
Recognition by Homebuilders of Profit from Sales of Land and Related Construction Contracts	68,014

ASC 970—Real Estate—General

ASC 970-470-05-2 through 05-3, 25-1, 25-3, 55-2 through 55-14; ASC 460-10-60-40
    Accounting for Special Assessments and Tax Increment Financing Entities 68,015

ASC 974: Real Estate Investment Trusts 68,018
    ASC 974-323-25-1; ASC 974-840-25-1
    Accounting by a Real Estate Investment Trust for an Investment in a Service Corporation 68,018

ASC 978: Real Estate—Time Sharing Activities 68,020
    ASC 978-10-05-3 through 05-6, 15-3 through 15-6; ASC 978-230-45-1; ASC 978-250-35-1; ASC 978-310-05-2 through 05-3, 30-1 through 30-2, 35-1 through 35-6, 40-1 through 40-2; ASC 978-340-25-1 through 25-5, 40-1 through 40-2, 60-1; ASC 978-605-10-1, 15-1, 25-1 through 25-17, 25-19, 30-1 through 30-10, 55-1 through 55-25, 55-27 through 55-62, 55-64 through 55-95; ASC 978-720-05-2 through 05-4, 25-1 through 25-3; ASC 978-810-25-1; ASC 978-840-25-1 through 25-2
    Accounting for Real Estate Time-Sharing Transactions 68,020

PART I: GENERAL GUIDANCE

OVERVIEW

The authoritative literature establishes standards for the acquisition, development, construction, and selling and rental costs related to real estate projects. In addition, they cover accounting for initial rental operations and include rules for ascertaining when a real estate project is substantially completed and available for occupancy.

BACKGROUND

Real estate acquisition costs may be classified as (*a*) preacquisition costs and (*b*) postacquisition costs. Preacquisition costs are those that are incurred prior to the acquisition of the property, such as appraisals, surveys, legal fees, travel expenses, and costs to acquire options to purchase the property. Postacquisition costs are those that are incurred after the property has been acquired, such as development and construction costs. Postacquisition costs may be classified further as (*a*) direct costs, (*b*) indirect costs, (*c*) costs of amenities, and (*d*) incidental operational costs.

Direct costs are those that can be directly identified with the real estate project. Indirect costs may or may not be related to a specific real estate project. Indirect costs of several real estate projects may be allocated to each project on a reasonable allocation basis. Incidental operations of a real estate project occur during the development stage of the project and are intended to reduce the cost of the real estate project. Incidental operations do not include activities that result in a profit or return on the use of the real property.

Capitalized costs of a real estate project are allocated to the individual components within the project. The allocation usually is accomplished by the specific identification method, if the individual components within the project can be identified specifically. If specific identification is not possible, capitalized land cost and all other common costs, including common costs of amenities, are allocated based on the relative fair value of each land parcel benefited prior to any construction. Capitalized construction costs are allocated based on the relative sales value of each individual component within the real estate project. Individual components of a real estate project may consist of lots, acres, or some other identifiable unit.

Costs incurred to sell real estate projects may be accounted for as (*a*) project costs, (*b*) prepaid expenses, or (*c*) period costs, according to the accounting periods that are benefited.

Costs to rent real estate projects under operating leases are either chargeable to future periods or chargeable to the current period, according to whether their recovery is reasonably expected from future rental revenue.

REAL ESTATE COSTS AND INITIAL RENTAL OPERATIONS

Preacquisition Costs

Costs frequently are incurred before the actual date on which a parcel of real property is acquired. These costs are referred to as *preacquisition costs*. Practically any type of cost may be classified as a preacquisition cost if it is incurred prior to the date of acquisition of a parcel of real property. For example, the cost of an option to purchase real property at a future date is a preacquisition cost and usually is capitalized. If the option is not exercised on or before its expiration date, however, the option becomes worthless and should be expensed.

All other types of preacquisition costs are expensed when incurred, unless they can be identified specifically to the real property being acquired and (ASC 970-340-25-3):

- The preacquisition costs would be capitalized if the property were acquired.
- The acquisition of the property or an option to acquire the property is probable (e.g., the prospective purchaser is actively seeking to acquire the property and can obtain financing).

OBSERVATION: *Probable* implies that the property is available for sale, the purchaser is currently trying to acquire the property, and the necessary financing is reasonably expected to be available.

Thus, preacquisition costs of a real estate project consist of (*a*) unexpired options to purchase real property and (*b*) other costs that meet all of the above conditions. Preacquisition costs that do not qualify for capitalization should be expensed when incurred (ASC 970-340-25-4).

After a parcel of real property is acquired, preacquisition costs are reclassified as project costs. In the event that the property is not acquired, capitalized preacquisition costs shall not exceed the amount recoverable, if any, from the sale of options, developmental plans, and other proceeds. Capitalized preacquisition costs in excess of recoverable amounts are charged to expense (ASC 970-340-25-4).

Illustration of Preacquisition Costs

Omega Company incurred the following preacquisition costs related to a piece of property:

1. Option to purchase land parcel: $10,000
2. Architectural consultation concerning feasibility of constructing warehouse facility on land parcel: $14,000

Situation 1: At the end of the year in which the above costs were incurred, Omega was actively seeking financing for the land and warehouse facility. Management believes it is probable that financing will be found and the land will be purchased, after which time the warehouse facility will be constructed.

In this situation, the $10,000 option and the $14,000 feasibility study should be capitalized as preacquisition costs, to be reclassified as project costs when the land purchase and warehouse construction commence.

Situation 2: At the end of the year in which the above costs were incurred, preliminary results of the feasibility study were not optimistic. Omega has suspended its search for financing, pending the final outcome of the feasibility study. The company considers the probability of purchasing the land and constructing the facility as no more than reasonably possible, but is optimistic that it can sell the option for at least its $10,000 cost.

In this situation, the $10,000 option cost should be carried as an asset, but the $14,000 for the feasibility study should be expensed in the current period.

Project Costs

Taxes and Insurance

Property taxes and insurance are capitalized as project costs only during periods in which activities necessary to get the property ready for its intended use are in progress (ASC 970-340-25-8).

After real property is substantially completed and ready for its intended use, ASC 970 also requires that property taxes and insurance costs be expensed as incurred (ASC 970-340-25-8).

Amenity Costs of Real Property

Golf courses, swimming pools, tennis courts, clubhouses, and other types of amenities frequently are included in the overall plans of a real estate project. The ultimate disposition of an amenity, however, may vary from one real estate project to another. Thus, accounting for the costs of amenities is based on the developer's (management) ultimate plans for the disposition of the amenity. In this respect, a developer may decide to retain ownership of the amenity and to either (*a*) operate the amenity or (*b*) eventually sell the amenity. On the other hand, the developer may be required under the terms of the individual sales agreements to sell or otherwise transfer ownership of the amenity to the purchasers of the individual components within the project. In this event, the purchasers of the individual components within the project usually form an association for the purposes of taking title to the amenity and operating the amenity for the common benefit of all owners of individual components within the project.

Accounting for the costs of amenities under the provisions of ASC 970 is as follows:

Ownership Not Retained by Developer

When the ownership of an amenity is to be transferred to the individual components within the real estate project, the net cost of the amenity is accounted for by the developer as a capitalized common cost of the project. The capitalized common cost of an amenity is allocated to the individual components within the project that are expected to benefit from the use of the amenity. Thus, the total cost of each individual component in the project that benefits from the amenity will include a proportionate share of the costs of the amenity (ASC 970-340-25-9).

The developer's net cost or gain that is accounted for as a common cost (reduction) of the real estate project may include the sales price, if any, and all other proceeds, if any, from the transfer of the amenity, less the following items:

- Direct costs that clearly are identifiable to the amenity
- Indirect costs that clearly are related to the amenity
- The developer's cost of operating the amenity until the amenity is transferred to the individual components in the project in accordance with the sales contract or other contractual agreement
- Common costs of the project that are allocated appropriately to the amenity

If an amenity clearly benefits specific individual components within a real estate project, the common cost (reduction) of the amenity is allocated only to those specific individual components.

Ownership Retained by Developer

When a developer retains ownership of an amenity, the total cost of the amenity is capitalized as a separate asset. The total cost of an amenity includes direct costs, indirect costs, and the allocation of common costs, including operating results of the amenity prior to its date of substantial completion and availability for its intended use. Under ASC 970, however, the amount capitalized cannot exceed the estimated fair value of the amenity at its expected date of substantial completion. Any costs in excess of the estimated fair value of the amenity at the expected date of its substantial completion are accounted for as common costs of the real estate project (ASC 970-340-25-9).

After it is substantially completed and ready for its intended use, further revision of the final capitalized cost of an amenity is not permitted. This cost becomes the basis of the amenity for any future sale. The subsequent basis for determining gain or loss on the sale of the amenity is the capitalized cost of the amenity not in excess of its estimated fair value at its date of substantial completion, less any allowable depreciation to the date of the sale.

After its date of substantial completion and availability for its intended use, the operational results of an amenity that is owned by the developer shall be included in the developer's current net income (ASC 970-340-25-11).

Incidental Operations of Real Property

Incidental operations of a real estate project usually occur during the holding or development stage of the project and are intended to reduce the cost of the project. Incidental operations do not include activities that result in a profit or return from the proposed development of the real property. For example, revenue received from billboard advertisements placed on the property or miscellaneous concession income would be classified as incidental operations.

If the incremental revenue received from incidental operations exceeds the related incremental costs, the difference is accounted for as a reduction of the capitalized costs of the real estate project. Thus, when incidental operations of a real estate project result in a profit, the capitalized costs of the project are reduced by the amount of profit. Under ASC 970, however, the same does *not* hold true if the incidental operations result in a loss: if the incremental costs of incidental operations exceed the related incremental revenue, the difference is charged to expense when incurred (ASC 970-340-25-12). The guidance in ASC 970 on accounting for incidental operations does not apply to real estate time-sharing transactions.

Revisions of Estimates

Estimates are used extensively in the acquisition, development, and construction of a real estate project. As a result, revisions of estimated costs occur frequently, and past, present, and future accounting periods may be affected by the revisions.

Revisions of estimates that occur in the acquisition, development, and construction stages of a real estate project are accounted for as changes in accounting estimates (ASC 250). The effects of a change in accounting estimate are accounted for (*a*) in the period of change, if the change affects only that period or (*b*) in the period of change and future periods, if the change affects both. A change in an accounting estimate caused in part or entirely by a change in accounting principle should be reported as a change in accounting estimate. ASC 250 requires that disclosure be made in current period financial statements of the effects of a change in an accounting estimate on (*a*) income from continuing operations, (*b*) net income, and (*c*) related per share data (ASC 250-10-50-4). However, ordinary accounting estimates for uncollectible accounts or inventory adjustments, made each period, do not have to be disclosed, unless they are material (ASC 970-340-35-1).

Selling Costs

Costs incurred to sell real estate projects are accounted for as (*a*) project costs, (*b*) prepaid expenses, or (*c*) period costs.

Project Costs

Project costs are capitalized as part of the construction costs of the real estate project provided that both of the following conditions are met (ASC 970-340-25-13):

- They are incurred for tangible assets that are used as marketing aids during the marketing period of the real estate project, or for services performed in obtaining regulatory approval for real estate sales in the project.
- The costs incurred are reasonably expected to be recovered from sales.

PRACTICE POINTER: Costs to sell real estate that qualify as project costs, less recoverable amounts from incidental operations or salvage value, include legal fees for prospectuses, sales offices, and model units, with or without furnishings.

Costs to sell real estate projects that qualify as project costs become part of the capitalized cost of the project and are allocated to the individual components of the project as common costs.

Prepaid Expenses

Prepaid expenses, which are sometimes called *deferred charges,* are capitalized if:

- They are directly associated with the real estate project;
- The costs are likely to be recoverable from the sales of the project; and
- The full accrual method is not being used to account for sales.

The prepaid expenses are amortized over the period that is expected to benefit from the expenditure (ASC 970-340-25-15).

Advances on commissions and unused sales brochures are examples of costs to sell real estate projects that qualify as prepaid expenses.

Period Costs

Period costs are charged to expense in the period incurred because they do not meet the criteria for project costs or prepaid expenses. Costs to sell real estate projects that do not benefit future periods should be expensed in the period incurred as period costs. Grand opening expenses, sales salaries, sales overhead, and advertising costs are examples of period costs (ASC 970-340-40-1).

Rental Costs of Real Estate Projects

Initial Rental Operations

Initial rental operations commence when a real estate project is substantially completed and available for occupancy. A real estate project is considered *substantially completed and available for occupancy* when tenant improvements have been completed by the developer, but in no event later than one year after major construction activity has been completed, excluding routine maintenance and cleanup (ASC 970-605-25-2).

The actual rental operation of a real estate project shall commence when the project is substantially completed and available for occupancy. At this time, rental revenues and related operating costs are recognized on an accrual basis. Operating costs include amortization of deferred rental costs, if any, and depreciation expense (ASC 970-605-25-1).

Some portions of a real estate rental project may still require major construction for completion, and other portions of the same project may be substantially completed and available for occupancy. In this event, each portion should be accounted for as a separate project (ASC 970-340-25-17).

Operating Leases

Costs incurred to rent real estate projects under operating leases are either chargeable to future periods or chargeable to the current period.

Chargeable to Future Periods

If the costs can be identified to, and reasonably expected to be recovered from, specific revenue, such costs are capitalized and amortized to the periods in which the specific revenue is earned. If the costs are for goods not used or services not received, such costs are charged to the future periods in which the goods are used or services are received.

If deferred rental costs can be associated with the revenue from a specific operating lease, such costs are amortized over the lease term. The amortization period commences when the rental project is substantially completed and available for occupancy. If deferred rental costs cannot be identified with the revenue from a specific operating lease, such costs are amortized over the periods benefited. The amortization period commences when the rental project is substantially completed and available for occupancy (ASC 970-340-35-2).

PRACTICE POINTER: Expense unamortized rental costs that subsequently become unrecoverable from future operations when they are determined to be unrecoverable. For example, unamortized rental costs related to specific leases which have been, or will be, terminated should be charged to expense.

Chargeable to the Current Period

If the costs to rent real estate projects under operating leases do not qualify as chargeable to future periods, they are accounted for as period costs and expensed as incurred (ASC 970-340-25-16).

ASC 970—Real Estate—General **68,009**

PROJECT COSTS RELATED TO PROPERTY, PLANT, AND EQUIPMENT

Project Costs

Project costs of real estate projects may be direct or indirect. Direct costs that are related to the acquisition, development, and construction of a real estate project are capitalized as project costs (ASC 970-360-25-2).

Indirect costs of real estate projects that can be identified clearly to specific projects under development or construction are capitalized as project costs. Indirect costs that are accumulated in one account, but clearly relate to several real estate projects under development or construction, are allocated on a reasonable basis to each of the projects (ASC 970-360-25-3).

Indirect costs on real estate projects not under development or construction are expensed as incurred. In addition, indirect costs that cannot be identified clearly with specific projects such as general and administrative expenses are charged to expense when incurred (ASC 970-720-25-3).

Illustration of Direct and Indirect Project Costs

Zeta Co. incurs the following direct and indirect project costs for two major real estate construction projects, identified as L and M:

Direct project costs:	
Project L	$150,000
Project M	740,000
Indirect project costs:	
Identified with Projects L and M	270,000
Identified with projects not currently under development	145,000
General and administrative	250,000
Total	$1,555,000

The indirect costs associated with Projects L and M are allocable one-third to Project L and two-thirds to Project M.

Treatment of the $1,555,000 of project costs for the year is as follows (in thousands of dollars):

	Project L	Project M	Current Expense
Direct costs	$150	$740	
Indirect costs:			
Project L ($270 x 1/3)	90		
Project M ($270 x 2/3)		180	
Not allocable ($145 + $250)			$395
	$240	$920	$395

Allocation of Capitalized Costs

All capitalized costs of a real estate project are allocated to the individual components within the project. If practicable, ASC 970 requires that capitalized costs be allocated by the specific identification method. Under this method, capitalized costs are identified specifically with the individual components within the real estate project. However, if it is impractical to use the specific identification method to allocate capitalized costs, ASC 970 requires that allocations be made as follows (ASC 970-360-30-1).

Land Costs

Only capitalized costs associated with the land prior to any construction are allocated as land costs. Land costs prior to any construction include capitalized land costs and other preconstruction common costs related to the land, including preconstruction common costs of amenities.

Total capitalized land costs are allocated based on the relative fair value of each land parcel prior to any construction. A land parcel may be identified as a lot, an acre, acreage, a unit, or a tract.

Construction Costs

Capitalized construction costs are allocated based on the relative sales value of each individual structure or unit located on a parcel of land. In the event capitalized costs of a real estate project cannot be allocated by the specific identification method or the relative sales value method, the capitalized cost shall be allocated on area methods or other methods appropriate under the circumstances.

Abandonments and Changes in Use

Occasionally a real estate project is partially or completely abandoned, or there is a significant change in the use of the property in the project. Under the provisions of ASC 970, if part or all of a real estate project is abandoned, the related capitalized costs must be expensed immediately. The capitalized costs of an abandoned real estate project should not be allocated to other real estate projects (ASC 970-360-40-1).

The cost of land donated to a governmental authority for uses that will benefit the project is not accounted for as abandoned. Under this circumstance, the cost of the donated land is accounted for as a common cost of acquiring the project. Thus, the cost of the donated land is allocated to the other land in the project, based on the relative fair value of each parcel of land prior to construction of any buildings or structures (ASC 970-360-35-1).

After significant development and construction costs have been capitalized in a real estate project, there may be a change in the use of part or all of the land within the project. Under the provisions of ASC 970, capitalized costs incurred prior to a change in use of all or part of the land within a real estate project are charged to expense, except in the following circumstance:

> The enterprise has developed a formal plan that indicates that the change in use of the land will result in a higher economic yield than was originally anticipated. In this event, the maximum costs that can be capitalized must not

exceed the estimated value of the revised project at the date of substantial completion and availability for its intended use. Capitalized costs in excess of the estimated value of the revised project when substantially completed, if any, are charged to expense (ASC 970-360-35-2).

Recoverability

Real estate projects that are substantially complete and ready for their intended use are to be carried at the lower of carrying amount or fair market value less cost to sell (ASC 360-10-35-43).

Each individual project is analyzed separately to determine whether a write-down is necessary. An individual project is considered to consist of similar components within the real estate project, such as (*a*) individual residences, (*b*) individual apartments or condominiums, or (*c*) individual lots, acres, or tracts. Thus, a real estate project that includes 50 individual residences, 10 condominium buildings, 20 multifamily buildings, and 100 residential lots would be accounted for as four separate projects for the purposes of determining net realizable values. The net carrying amount of the 100 residential lots may exceed their net realizable value, while the individual net carrying values of the 50 individual residences, 10 condominium buildings, and 20 multifamily buildings may not exceed their individual estimated net realizable values (ASC 970-360-35-3).

PART II: INTERPRETIVE GUIDANCE

ASC 970: General

ASC 970-340-25-1 through 25-2, 25-5 through 25-7, 35-3 through 35-4; ASC 970-720-25-1 through 25-2
  Accounting for Internal Costs Relating to Real Estate Property Acquisitions

BACKGROUND

ASC 970-10-15-8 through 15-11; ASC 970-340-25-2 through 25-4, 25-8 through 25-17, 35-1; ASC 970-360-25-2 through 25-3, 30-1, 35-1 through 35-4, 40-1 through 40-2; ASC 970-605-21-1; ASC 970-720-25-3 provides guidance for the treatment of costs related to the acquisition, development, construction, sale, and rental of real estate projects. The costs addressed under that guidance include preacquisition costs and project costs. Under that guidance, preacquisition costs (e.g., for surveying, zoning studies, or obtaining an option on the property, which are incurred before its acquisition) (*a*) should be capitalized if they are related directly to the property, (*b*) would be incurred if the property were owned, and (*c*) should be capitalized only if it is probable that the property will be acquired or the purchaser will obtain an option to acquire the property.

Under the guidance in ASC 970-360-25-2 through 25-3, project costs are those that are "clearly associated with the acquisition, development and construction of a real estate project" and should be capitalized. Indirect project costs associated with more than one project also should be capitalized and allocated to the related projects.

This Issue has been raised because many real estate companies have full-time property acquisition departments that are involved in finding and acquiring properties and that perform services, such as appraisals and feasibility studies, which otherwise may be provided by outsiders. Because that existing guidance did not distinguish between the accounting for internal and external costs, the treatment of the costs of internal acquisition departments had been diverse—some companies capitalized those costs while others expensed them. Opinions also differed as to whether the existing guidance would apply to all real estate acquisitions or only to properties requiring further development and construction.

ACCOUNTING ISSUE

Should any costs incurred by an internal acquisitions department of a real estate entity to identify and acquire real estate properties be capitalized as part of the acquired property?

ACCOUNTING GUIDANCE

- Costs related to preacquisition activities that are incurred by a real estate entity's internal department to identify and acquire a property that will be classified as *nonoperating* when it is acquired should be *capitalized* as part of the cost of acquiring the property if the costs can be directly identified with the acquired property and were incurred *after* the acquisition was considered probable. If the entity later decides to classify the property as operating when it is acquired, capitalized costs should be expensed and additional costs should be expensed as incurred.

- Preacquisition costs incurred *internally* in connection with the acquisition of a property that will be classified as *operating* on acquisition should be *expensed* as incurred. However, if the entity later decides that the property should be classified as nonoperating when it is acquired, amounts that had already been expensed should *not* be capitalized as part of the cost of acquiring the property. An operating property is (*a*) a property on which major construction activities, not routine maintenance or cleanup activities have been substantially *completed* by the acquisition date; (*b*) a property that will be available for occupancy when tenant improvements are completed; or (*c*) a property that is already income producing. In addition preacquisition costs related to properties that are partially operating and partially nonoperating should be accounted for based on the guidance in ASC 970-360-25-17, which requires that the two components be accounted for as separate projects and that preacquisition costs incurred be allocated between the respective portions.

The FASB staff noted that guidance on distinguishing between external and internal costs is available in ASC 310-20-55-9 through 55-10. In addition, related guidance on accounting for a service corporation established by a real estate investment trust (REIT) is provided in ASC 974-323-25-1; 840-25-1, "Accounting by a Real Estate Investment Trust for an Investment in a Service Corporation," which is discussed below

DISCUSSION

- Although the original charge was to determine whether the accounting for preacquisition costs incurred by a real estate entity's internal property acquisitions department should differ from that for costs incurred for the same services provided by a third party, the final guidance is based on the guidance in ASC 970-360-25-3, which requires that (a) only costs that can be directly identified with a specific property be capitalized, that is, not all costs incurred to identify acquisitions are capitalizable, (b) the costs would be capitalizable if a property had already been acquired, and (c) it is probable that a property will be acquired. In addition, those who supported this guidance argued that there is no conceptual reason that the accounting for preacquisition costs incurred by an internal department should differ from costs incurred if the same services are provided by an unrelated third party.

  The decision that capitalization of preacquisition costs is appropriate only for properties that will be *acquired* was based on the view that those costs will be recovered over the life of the property through its revenue stream. The benefit of costs related to properties *not* acquired expires in the period in which the costs were incurred, because they will not be recovered from revenues earned in future periods.

- Internal costs related to the identification and acquisition of real estate properties that need further development (*nonoperating* properties) were distinguished from those incurred to identify and acquire *operating* real estate properties. Some argued that the acquisition of an operating property is similar to a business combination and should be accounted for based on the principles in ASC 815.

  The FASB staff, who supported the guidance, analogized to (a) the guidance on the capitalization of interest costs in ASC 835-20-25-5 through 25-6 under which capitalization ceases when the status of a property changes from nonoperating to operating and (b) the guidance in ASC 310 and ASC 840, both of which distinguish between the treatment of costs related to *originating* loans and leases and those related to *acquiring* existing loans or leases.

ASC 970-360-25-1, 55-1 through 55-3
Recognition of Receipts from Made-Up Rental Shortfalls

BACKGROUND

A public real estate syndication (buyer) purchases a newly constructed office building from a developer (seller). At the date of the sale, the buyer's general partner negotiates a master leaseback agreement with the seller for the building, which is only partially occupied. The agreement provides that the seller will lease vacant space for two years at a market rate and the buyer will pay the seller a reasonable fee, which is described as a fee in exchange for signing a master lease or as an escrowed portion of the purchase price. If a sublease meets certain conditions, the seller will not be required to make future lease payments on space the seller leases to others. The seller's rental payments would exceed the buyer's fee, if the seller is unable to lease the vacant space during the two-year lease period.

ACCOUNTING ISSUE

How should a buyer account for (*a*) a fee paid to the seller and (*b*) rental payments received from the seller?

ACCOUNTING GUIDANCE

A buyer should account for the fee paid to a seller and rental payments received from the seller as adjustments to the basis of the acquired property that will affect future depreciation.

The buyer's fee paid to the seller was considered by some, including the SEC Observer, to be an escrowed portion of the purchase price that is conditional on the seller's ability to rent the space.

EFFECT OF ASC 815

The guidance in ASC 815 applies if the agreement meets the definition of a derivative in ASC 815. However, usually the agreement would meet the scope exception in ASC 815-10-15-13 related to sales or service revenue of one of the parties to the agreement because the underlying is the syndicate's leasing rental revenue and consequently the accounting guidance above would not be affected.

ASC 970-360-55-4 through 55-5
Recognition by Homebuilders of Profit from Sales of Land and Related Construction Contracts

BACKGROUND

A homebuilder enters into a contract with a buyer to construct a single-family house on a lot owned by the homebuilder. The sales price stated in the contract does not distinguish between the sale of the lot and construction of the house. Title on the lot is not transferred to the buyer until completion of construction and closing.

If, instead, the house was built on a lot owned by the buyer, the homebuilder would be able to recognize profit on the construction of the house based on the percentage-of-completion method discussed in ASC 605-35-05-1 through 05-13, 15-6, 25-1 through 25-50, 25-54 through 25-88, 25-90 through 25-98, 45-1 through 45-2, 50-1 through 50-10, 55-1; ASC 210-10-60-2; ASC 460-1-60-10; ASC 910-20-25-5; ASC 912-20-25-1, "Accounting for Performance of Construction-Type and Certain Production-Type Contracts."

ACCOUNTING ISSUE

Should a builder recognize profit on the construction of a house on the builder's lot (*a*) separately for the construction of the house using the percentage-of-completion method regardless of the transfer of title on the lot or (*b*) for the construction of the house and sale of the lot when title passes at closing, based on the guidance in ASC 360-20; 976-605?

ACCOUNTING GUIDANCE

Profit recognition on the transaction should be recognized when the conditions for full accrual profit recognition in ASC 360-20-40-5 have been met. Until then, proceeds received for the land and construction of the house should be accounted for based on the deposit method discussed in ASC 360-20-55-17, 55-19.

DISCUSSION

This guidance is based on a strict application of the guidance in ASC 360-20-40-5. Under that guidance, profit should not be recognized under the full accrual method until a sale has closed; the buyer's initial and continuing investments meet the conditions in ASC 360-20-40; the seller's receivable cannot be subordinated to the buyer's other obligations, except for a first mortgage on the property or a loan, the proceeds of which will be used to pay the seller; and the seller has transferred the risks and rewards of ownership to the buyer and will have no continuing involvement with the property.

ASC 970-470-05-2 through 05-3, 25-1, 25-3, 55-2 through 55-14; ASC 460-10-60-40 Accounting for Special Assessments and Tax Increment Financing Entities

BACKGROUND

The construction of infrastructure or improvements may be financed by a municipality through special assessments or by a Tax Increment Financing Entity (TIFE), which is an independent taxing jurisdiction organized under various state statutes to issue bonds used to finance the construction, operation, and maintenance of roads and other capital infrastructure related to a specific project. For example, Company A owns land it wants to develop into an industrial park that requires roads, water, power, and all other infrastructure associated with such a development. Because the only entity receiving direct benefits is Company A, it might be considered unfair to levy an assessment payable by all members of the community. Instead, a TIFE is created to issue bonds to finance the construction and to levy assessments on users (in this case, Company A) to repay the debt and operate and maintain the infrastructure.

A TIFE established for a real estate development may repay a pro rata portion of the bonds as portions of the project are sold or if assessments surpass current tax rates. The entity (developer) provides the funds to repay the bonds or reduce future assessments. The bonds are generally nonrecourse to the sponsoring entity. If there is a default on a TIFE's bonds, however, the entity may be affected because the property would be subject to liens. In some states, such as California, the obligation for repayment of the debt remains with the property as it is sold to new owners. Some states set a minimum amount that must be repaid by the developer.

ACCOUNTING ISSUE

Should an entity that uses a TIFE to finance infrastructure construction recognize an obligation for special assessments or the TIFE's debt?

ACCOUNTING GUIDANCE

- There is a presumption that an entity (the property owner) should recognize an obligation if a special assessment or an assessment to be levied by a TIFE on each individual property owner is a fixed or determinable amount for a fixed or determinable period.
- The following factors indicate that an entity may be contingently liable for a TIFE's debt; recognition of a liability should therefore be evaluated under the provisions of ASC 450:
  - A shortfall, if any, in annual debt service obligations must be made up by the entity.
  - The entity has pledged assets.
  - A letter of credit or other means of supporting the TIFE's debt has been provided by the entity.
- There is a presumption that the TIFE's debt should be recognized as the entity's obligation if the entity is constructing facilities for its own use or operation and any of the criteria stated above is met.

OBSERVATION: An entity that has an interest in a variable interest entity and is required to absorb the majority of that entity's expected losses, or is entitled to receive most of the entity's expected residual returns, or both, is required to consolidate that entity in accordance with the guidance in ASC 810-10. ASC 810-10-05-10; 25-38 through 25-38G provides guidance for determining whether an entity has a controlling interest in a variable interest entity and on the consolidation of many special-purpose entities of the type used as TIFEs.

Illustration of Accounting for Special Assessments and TIFEs

A real estate developer organizes a TIFE to issue bonds for the construction of the infrastructure for a subdivision of homes. The infrastructure's assets become the property of the municipality when construction is completed. The company does not guarantee the TIFE's debt.

Case 1

Annual assessments are based on anticipated debt service requirements. Properties are taxed based on their stage of development. (That is, developed property is taxed at the maximum rate, undeveloped property is not taxed or taxed only to supplement shortfalls in the annual debt service requirement. If taxes collected on developed and undeveloped property are not sufficient to meet the obligation, an additional tax may be levied.)

Accounting. Because individual properties are assessed based on their rate of development, assessments are not fixed or determinable and no obligation need be recognized. The entity should, however, evaluate the recognition of an obligation under the guidance in ASC 450 if it is obligated to make up any shortfall in debt service requirements.

Case 2

The total assessment, which is based on the TIFE's annual debt service, is allocated equally to all lots in the development. In addition to their regular property taxes, property owners are assessed over the period that the debt is outstanding. When a portion of the property is sold, the developer must repay a pro rata portion of the TIFE debt or the purchaser must assume the obligation.

Accounting. The developer should recognize a liability because the amount of the assessment is fixed and determinable for a fixed or determinable period of time.

DISCUSSION

In the discussion of the treatment of TIFE debt by entities sponsoring infrastructure construction, it was determined that practice among such entities included recognition of a TIFE's debt and assets and treatment of a TIFE as a tax assessor (i.e., recording the annual tax assessments, user fees, or both as incurred in the assessment period).

The guidance in ASC 450-20-25-2, which requires recognition of a liability if it is probable that a loss will be confirmed by one or more events that will occur in the future and the amount is estimable is applied. Under the guidance in ASC 450, a property owner sponsoring an infrastructure project should account for a TIFE's debt as follows:

- *Debt recognized as a liability.* If assessments are fixed or determinable amounts for a fixed or determinable period, required payments can be estimated. In addition, payments are probable because the company is the primary obligor; the only way the company can avoid payment of the obligation is by selling the property. However, even when the property is sold, the entity has to satisfy the debt or reduce the selling price by the amount of debt assumed by the buyer.
- *Debt not recognized as a liability.* A TIFE's debt need not be recognized as an obligation if debt service requirements are met by other than fixed or determinable assessments, because the amount cannot be estimated. The following are examples:
  — Annual assessments whose rates depend on the land use category (developed or undeveloped)
  — Assessments computed based on the assessed value of the property
  — Normal property tax assessments
- *Debt may be a contingent liability.* A developer may remain contingently liable on a TIFE's debt. For example, in certain states, such as California, where the obligation remains with the property, the entity has to make up shortfalls in the annual debt service obligation. In other states, such as Colorado, an entity is required to guarantee a TIFE's debt. In those cases or if an entity guarantees a TIFE's debt by pledging assets, the entity has a

ASC 974: Real Estate Investment Trusts

ASC 974-323-25-1; ASC 974-840-25-1
Accounting by a Real Estate Investment Trust for an Investment in a Service Corporation

> **OBSERVATION:** Under the guidance in ASC 810-10, the consolidation of variable interest entities by an entity that absorbs a majority of a variable entity's expected losses or has the right to receive a greater part of the variable entity's expected residual returns or both is required. The following guidance does not apply to service corporations that are considered to be variable interest entities under the provisions of ASC 810-10, but it continues to apply to service corporations that are *not* variable interest entities.

BACKGROUND

To retain their favorable tax status (that is, be able to deduct dividends in arriving at taxable income), real estate investment trusts (REITs) may be established in the form of trusts, associations, or corporations, and may distribute a substantial amount of their taxable income to their shareholders annually. Because the Internal Revenue Code restricts the types of operating activities performed by a REIT to retain its qualification, some REITs have established service corporations (SCs) to perform certain services for the REIT or for third parties, such as property management, leasing services, and services involving the acquisition, development, construction, financing, or sale of real estate projects.

REITs are not permitted to own more than 10% of an SC's voting stock for federal income tax purposes. Consequently, a REIT may own a minimal interest in an SC's voting stock while holding a substantial interest in the SC's nonvoting preferred stock or nonvoting common stock, so that the REIT enjoys substantially all of the SC's economic benefits. A majority of an SC's voting stock is owned by the REIT's sponsors, officers, or affiliates. Generally, transfers of voting stock are not restricted. Owners of the majority of an SC's voting common stock generally contribute minimal amounts of equity to the SC.

ACCOUNTING ISSUES

1. Should an SC be considered an independent third party, as the term is used in ASC 310, when determining the amount of costs a REIT should capitalize for leasing services?

2. Should a REIT account for its investment in an SC on the cost method, the equity method, or the consolidation method, if the REIT receives substantially all of the economic benefits generated by the SC?

ACCOUNTING GUIDANCE

1. A REIT should not consider an SC to be an independent third party, regardless of how it accounts for its investment in the SC. A REIT should not capitalize costs for leasing services provided by the SC in excess of the amount of such costs that would have been capitalized under the provisions of ASC 840 if the REIT had incurred such costs directly.

2. A REIT should *not* account for its investment on the cost method if some or all of the following factors—which indicate the REIT's ability to exercise at least significant influence over an SC—exist:

    a. The SC's activities are performed primarily for the REIT.
    b. The REIT receives substantially all of the SC's economic benefits.
    c. The REIT can designate a seat on the SC's board of directors.
    d. Individuals serving on the REIT's board of directors also serve on the SC's board of directors.
    e. The REIT and SC share officers and/or employees.
    f. Owners of a majority of an SC's voting common stock contributed a minimal amount to the SC's equity.
    g. The SC's operations are influenced by the views of the REIT's management.
    h. The REIT can obtain the necessary financial information to account for its investment in the SC on the equity basis.

The decision whether to consolidate the SC or account for it on the equity basis depends on facts and circumstances.

If the application of the guidance on Issue 2 results in a change in the method of accounting for a REIT's investment in an SC, the change should be accounted for based on the guidance in ASC 250 for reporting a change in an entity's accounting.

DISCUSSION

1. This Issue initially was considered a secondary issue because the guidance might depend on the primary issue—the REIT's accounting for the SC. That is, if an SC provides leasing services to a REIT, guidance on the accounting for the REIT's investment in the SC would affect the amount of initial direct leasing costs capitalized by the REIT. Under the guidance in ASC 840, initial direct leasing costs are limited to (*a*) those that would be incurred in transactions with independent third parties to originate a lease and to (*b*) certain costs incurred by a REIT for specific activities related to obtaining a lease. If an SC is consolidated, the amount of leasing costs permitted under the guidance in ASC 310 would be limited to certain internal costs.

    During the discussion of a REIT's accounting for an investment in an SC, the SEC Observer expressed his discomfort with a conclusion that a REIT can capitalize fees paid to an SC that would not be capitalizable if the REIT had incurred those costs directly. The guidance was influenced by that view. It was also influenced by the fact that the decision on the method used by the REIT may be subject to judgment.

2. A REIT's voting interest in an SC is usually less than 10%. Under a strict interpretation of the guidance in ASC 323, a 20% or greater voting interest in an investee connotes significant influence. Because of a belief that a REIT often has significant influence over an SC's operations, even if it has less than a 20% voting interest in the SC, the list of factors was developed to indicate whether a REIT has significant influence and could overcome the 20% ownership presumption in ASC 323.

ASC 978 Real Estate—Time Sharing Activities

ASC 978-10-05-3 through 05-6, 15-3 through 15-6; ASC 978-230-45-1; ASC 978-250-35-1; ASC 978-310-05-2 through 05-3, 30-1 through 30-2, 35-1 through 35-6, 40-1 through 40-2; ASC 978-340-25-1 through 25-5, 40-1 through 40-2, 60-1; ASC 978-605-10-1, 15-1, 25-1 through 25-17, 25-19, 30-1 through 30-10, 55-1 through 55-25, 55-27 through 55-62, 55-64 through 55-95;ASC 978-720-05-2 through 05-4, 25-1 through 25-3; ASC 978-810-25-1; ASC 978-840-25-1 through 25-2
Accounting for Real Estate Time-Sharing Transactions

BACKGROUND

The volume of sales of interests in real estate time-sharing intervals has grown enormously. In addition, the variety of ways in which interests in time-sharing intervals are structured has increased. For example, interests in time-sharing intervals may be purchased for a fixed time, such as a specific week; for a floating time, such as a specific season; or in the form of points, vacation clubs, or fractional interests. Also, buyers may have the right to exchange their time-sharing intervals for other time periods and venues, as well as for other products, such as cruises, through a third-party exchange company. Some sellers of time-sharing intervals establish time-sharing special-purpose entities to which they transfer title in the real estate.

ACCOUNTING GUIDANCE

Scope

The following guidance applies to the accounting for *real estate* time-sharing transactions in which a seller:

- Passes title and ownership of the real estate to a buyer or special purpose entity (SPE) in a fee simple transaction without recourse
- Retains title and ownership of all or a portion of the real estate
- Passes to a buyer title and ownership of all or a portion of the real estate, which subsequently revert to the seller or are transferred to a third party

The following guidance also applies to transactions involving a time-share reseller.

Profit Recognition under ASC 360

Sellers should recognize revenue on sales of real estate time-sharing intervals in accordance with the guidance in ASC 360 for sales of real estate other than retail land sales. The guidance in ASC 360-20-40-37, through 40-38, 40-40 through 40-50, 40-56 through 40-64; ASC 460-10-60-3; ASC 840-10-25-60 regarding continuing involvement should be followed. Revenue may be recognized in accordance with the percentage-of-completion method if the criteria in ASC 360-20-40-50 have been met, but related selling and marketing costs should not be included in computing costs. Contract-for-deed arrangements qualify for profit recognition. Transactions in which title can revert to a seller, however, should be accounted for as operating leases.

Seller Identification of Projects and Phases

Time-share interval projects may be constructed in a single phase or in multiple phases. Under this guidance, sellers of time-sharing intervals are required to (*a*) define a project at its inception in terms of the number of phases to be developed and (*b*) to account separately for each phase of a project.

If the definition of a project or its phases changes because of significant changes in facts and circumstances related to the development of a project, that is, a change in the nature of a project, the change should be accounted for as a change in an accounting estimate by making an adjustment in the current period. Significant changes may include changes in sales prices or discount programs, changes in construction contract prices or inflation, temporary construction delays, design changes, or a seller's decision to significantly increase the proportion of a project's luxury units as compared to the number of standard units in the project. If a change in the definition of a project is *not* the result of a significant change in facts or circumstances in the project's development, such as a change in the number of phases into which a project is divided, which is a change in the way the project is accounted for but is *not* a change in the facts and circumstances of the project, the change should be accounted for as a cumulative effect of a change in the application of an accounting principle in accordance with the guidance in ASC 250-120-45-5 through 45-10.

Determination of Sales Value

Under the guidance in ASC 360, the *sales value* of a sale of real estate must be calculated in order to determine whether a buyer's initial and continuing investment is adequate for full accrual revenue recognition. To determine the sales value of a real estate sale, the stated sales price should be adjusted as follows:

- Reduce the stated sales price of a time-sharing interval by the difference between the amount paid by a buyer to a seller and the fair value of products or services a seller provides or is legally or otherwise committed to provide to a buyer as part of consummating a sale. Such products or services often are used as sales incentives and should be accounted for in accordance with the guidance in ASC 605-50-05-1, 15-2 through 15-3, 25-1 through 25-9, 45-1 through 45-11, S45-1, 55-1, 55-3, 55-5, 55-8 through 55-12, 55-14 through 55-15, 55-17 through 55-22, 55-24 through 55-25,

55-27 through 55-28, 55-30 through 55-31, 55-33 through 55-37, 55-40 through 55-44, 55-46 through 55-47, 55-49 through, 55-50, 55-52, through 55-53, 55-55 through 55-69, 55-71 through 55-72, 55-74 through 55-77, 55-79 through 55-95, 55-97 through 55-107, S99-1 ASC 330-10-35-13; ASC 908-360-55-1, Vendor's Income Statement Characterization of Consideration Given to a Customer (Including a Reseller) (discussed in Chapter 36), which differentiates between cash and noncash incentives. Noncash incentives should be accounted for as separate deliverables that have an associated cost of sales. Cash incentives should be accounted for as discounts of the stated sales prices.

- A seller may give a buyer a *cash* incentive in cash or by waiving a payment that the buyer would otherwise have to make, for example, payment for closing costs or for the first year of owners association maintenance fees. A *noncash* incentive is one that a buyer could purchase, such as a first-year membership in a time-share exchange program or a voucher for airline tickets. If a *noncash* incentive such as a voucher for airline tickets is provided free as an incentive to consummate a sale, the stated sales price of the time-sharing interval should be *reduced* by the fair value of the voucher, which should be recognized as a separate item in revenue.

    If a time-sharing interval is sold together with a membership in a time-share exchange program, however, and the first year of membership in the program is provided for free, the fair value of the fee for the exchange program should be accounted for as a *cash* incentive, because the buyer would otherwise have to pay the fee. In that case, the fair value of the fee for the exchange program should be deducted from the sales price and accounted for as a reduction of the seller's cost for fees instead of as a separate revenue item. Incentives do *not* include products or services that are included in future maintenance charges or other fees that a buyer pays for at market rates.

    Inducements provided by a seller to prospective buyers regardless of whether they make a purchase are considered to be selling costs, which should be accounted for in accordance with the guidance in the section on costs to sell time-sharing intervals.

- Increase the stated sales price for the purpose of determining sales value by fees charged to a buyer that are unrelated to financing, such as fees for document preparation. Fees that a seller collects for third parties, such as municipalities or taxing authorities, however, should *not* be added to the stated sales price and should *not* be included in a buyer's initial and continuing investment. Fees that are related to financing of time-share purchases, such as loan origination fees, should be accounted for as adjustments to the stated interest rate on financings, in accordance with the guidance in ASC 310. Sellers that offer buyers at the time of sale programs under which buyers can reduce their payments by prepaying their notes, or sellers that consistently make such offers during the term of buyers' notes should include estimated payment reductions in their calculations of sales value.

- Sellers that partially or fully finance buyers' time-sharing transactions at stated interest rates that are less than prevailing market rates for buyers with similar credit ratings in similar transactions should reduce the sales value and the amount of the note in accordance with the guidance in ASC 835.

Application of Test of Buyer's Commitment

When testing for the adequacy of a buyer's commitment under the guidance in ASC 360-20-40-5, sellers should reduce the amount of buyers' initial and continuing investments by the amount that the fair value of products or services offered to buyers as incentives exceeds the amount paid by a buyer for such goods or services. That requirement does not apply if a buyer does *not* receive the incentive until the buyer has met certain contractual obligations related to the purchase of a time-sharing interval. For example, a seller requires a buyer to make timely payments on a note for six months in order for the seller to pay the buyer's owners association fees in the second year. In that situation, a seller has to determine whether future performance meets the initial and continuing investment criterion for a buyer's commitment. To meet that criterion, a buyer's future payments required for eligibility to receive an incentive should at least equal the incentive's fair value. The required payments should equal the value of an incentive and interest on the amount *not* paid for the incentive.

When applying the criterion in ASC 360-20-40-5, a seller should reduce the measurement of a buyer's commitment by the amount that the fair value of an incentive exceeds the amount the buyer paid for the incentive if future performance is deemed *not* to be sufficient. If a portion of a buyer's down payment is considered to apply as a payment for an incentive because the buyer's future payment does *not* at least equal the fair value of the incentive, that amount should *not* be included in the buyer's initial and continuing investment.

Upgrade and Reload Transactions

In a *reload* transaction, an existing owner of a time-sharing interval purchases a new interval, which is accounted for as a separate transaction. The buyer must meet the commitment criterion in ASC 360-20-40-5 by making an additional cash payment or providing other consideration that qualifies. The buyer's initial and continuing investments from the initial transaction should *not* be included in measuring the buyer's commitment for the additional purchase.

In an *upgrade* transaction, a buyer modifies an existing time-share interval. In that case, the buyer's initial and continuing investments in the original transaction are included in determining whether the buyer meets the commitment criterion. The guidance in ASC 360 for profit recognition is applied to the sales value of the new interval.

Accounting for Uncollectibility

Receivables of interest and principal on sales of time-sharing intervals become uncollectible when a seller determines that less than the total amount of the note will be collected. Uncollectibility should be based on a seller's actual collection experience, regardless of who services the receivables, not based on amounts a seller receives as proceeds. In accounting for uncollectible receivables, sellers should:

- Recognize estimates of uncollectible receivables as a reduction of sales revenue when recognizing profit on sales of time-sharing intervals under the full accrual or the percentage of completion methods. To recognize the reduction in revenue on estimated uncollectible amounts accounted for under the relative sales value method, a corresponding adjustment is made to cost of sales and inventory by applying the cost-of-sales percentage.
- Charge uncollectible accrued interest income receivable to interest income when it is determined that a receivable is uncollectible.
- Consider modifications, deferments, or downgrades of receivables, which involve only modifications of the terms of notes receivable, as troubled debt restructurings, and account for them under the guidance in ASC 310. The allowance for uncollectible accounts should be charged when a recorded investment in a note receivable is reduced under the provisions of ASC 310. That treatment is necessary, because estimated losses were charged against revenue when a sale was recognized or was subsequently charged against revenue as a change in estimate. Direct costs associated with uncollectible receivables, such as collection costs, should be expensed as incurred.
- Account for assumptions of notes receivable as two separate activities with two different parties as follows:
  — Charge the allowance for uncollectible receivables with the remaining investment in the original note receivable, which becomes uncollectible when an arrangement with the original buyer is terminated.
  — Account for a time-sharing transaction with a new buyer in accordance with the profit recognition guidance in ASC 360.
- Account for the allowance for uncollectibles the same as for any receivables after the initial recognition of a sale when revenue is reduced for estimated uncollectibles, except that *no* bad debt expense is recognized.
- Evaluate receivables in each reporting period, and, at least quarterly, estimate the amount of ultimate collections and evaluate the adequacy of the allowance under the guidance in ASC 450. Adjust the allowance and current-period revenue through the account for uncollectibles, which is a contra-revenue account. Adjust cost of sales and inventory for a corresponding amount.
- Determine the amount of the allowance for uncollectibles by considering uncollectibles by year of sale and the aging of notes receivable and other

factors such as the location of timeshare units, contract terms, collection experience, economic conditions, and other qualitative factors.

- Adjust interest income if a gain or loss on a sale of a portfolio of receivables without recourse is attributable to a change in market interest rates between the date receivables were generated and the date they were sold. Adjust revenue for a gain or loss on the transaction attributable to other factors, such as a change in the perceived credit quality of the portfolio between the date receivables were generated and the date they were sold.

Accounting for Cost of Sales and Inventory

The following guidance applies only to transactions accounted for under the full accrual, percentage-of-completion, cost recovery, installment, or reduced profit revenue recognition methods discussed in ASC 360. It does *not* apply to transactions accounted for under the deposit method, which is also discussed in ASC 360.

Sellers should account for the cost of sales and time-sharing inventory by the *relative sales value method*, which is similar to a gross profit method. It is used to allocate inventory cost and to determine the cost of sales in conjunction with a sale. Under this method, cost of sales is calculated as a percentage of net sales using a cost-of-sales percentage, which is a ratio of total costs to the total remaining estimated time-sharing revenue. Different phases should be accounted for separately under this method. Common costs, including costs of amenities, should be allocated to inventory by the phase they will benefit.

Estimated total revenue, which is the actual amount to date, and expected future revenue, should include factors such as incurred or estimated uncollectibles, changes in sales prices or sales mix, repossession of intervals the seller may or may not be able to sell, effects of upgrade programs, and past or expected sales incentives to sell slow-moving inventory. Those estimates should be recalculated at least quarterly. The cost-of-sales percentage should be recalculated whenever estimated revenue or cost is adjusted based on newly estimated total revenue and total cost, including costs to complete, if any. The *effects* of changes should be accounted for prospectively in the period in which a change occurred so that the revised estimates will be reported in the balance sheet and in subsequent periods as if those estimates had been made at inception. The effects of changes should be disclosed in accordance with the guidance in ASC 250-10-50-4. The inventory balance in the balance sheet, estimated costs to complete the inventory, if any, is the pool of costs that will be charged against future revenue.

If the relative sales value method is used, inventory is *not* affected if a time-sharing interval is repossessed or reacquired, unless there is a change in expected uncollectibles. Sellers should test inventory for impairment based on the guidance in ASC 360-10.

Costs to Sell Time-Sharing Intervals

Costs incurred to sell time-sharing intervals should be expensed as (incurred unless the costs qualify for capitalization under this guidance.). Deferral of recognition until a sale transaction occurs, however, is permitted for costs that (*a*) are reasonably expected to be recovered from the sale of time-sharing intervals or from incidental operations and (*b*) are incurred for (1) tangible assets used directly during the selling period for the purpose of making sales (for example, model units and furnishings, sales property and equipment, and semi-permanent signs), and (2) services required to obtain regulatory approval of sales, for example, legal fees and costs of preparing, printing, and filing prospectuses. Such costs should be allocated proportionately to sale transactions based on the number of intervals available for sale in a project or phase to which those selling costs apply.

Other costs may be deferred until a sale occurs if they are (*a*) reasonably expected to be recovered from a sale of time-sharing intervals; (*b*) directly associated with sales transactions accounted for under the percentage of completion, installment, reduced profit, or deposit methods of accounting, such as commissions; and (*c*) incremental costs that a seller would *not* have incurred if a sales transaction had not occurred. Deferred selling costs should be expensed in the period in which the related revenue is recognized. Deferred selling costs related to sales contracts that are canceled before profit has been recognized on the transaction should be expensed in the period in which the cancellation occurred.

Costs of call centers and direct and incremental costs related to bringing potential buyers to tour a property should be expensed as incurred. Other costs that should be expensed as incurred are costs incurred for unsuccessful sales transactions and sales overhead, such as rent for on-site and off-site sales offices, utilities, maintenance, and telephone expenses. The cost of nonrefundable airline tickets purchased for potential buyers who will be touring a property should be expensed on the date of the visit.

Operations During Holding Periods

The holding period for time-sharing operations begins when intervals are available for sale, that is, when they are legally registered for sale as time-sharing intervals, which should be accounted for as inventory during holding periods and should *not* be depreciated. Operating costs during holding periods include (*a*) seller subsidies to an owners association and (*b*) maintenance and other costs related to time-sharing intervals held for sale.

Units rented in periods other than the holding period should be depreciated with rental activities accounted for under the guidance in ASC 840. In each reporting period, sellers should evaluate whether to continue classifying time-sharing intervals as held and available for sale.

During a holding period, revenue and costs of rental and other operations should be accounted for as incidental operations. If incremental revenue from incidental operations exceeds related incremental costs, the pool of inventory costs under the relative sales value method should be reduced by that excess amount. Estimates of future excess amounts should *not* be considered in calculations under the relative value method. Incremental costs that exceed incremental revenue should be expensed as incurred.

Costs related to rentals and other operations (for example, sampler programs and mini-vacations) during a holding period should be deferred if they are (*a*) directly related to rental activities during a holding period and are reasonably expected to be recovered from those activities and (*b*) incremental costs that a seller would not have incurred if a particular rental transaction had not occurred. Such deferred costs should be expensed or netted against inventory costs in the period in which a rental occurs.

Sampler Programs and Mini-Vacations

If a seller applies a portion of a buyer's payment for a sampler program or mini-vacation that has *not* been used in its entirety against the sales price of a time-sharing interval, the payment should be considered a part of the buyer's initial and continuing investment when evaluating the buyer's commitment. A seller should *not* include such a payment in a buyer's initial and continuing investments, however, if the buyer has fully used the sampler program or mini-vacation, even if legal documents state that the payment would be applied to the sales price.

Special Entities, Point Systems, Vacation Clubs, and Similar Structures

Interests in time-sharing intervals structured as special entities established to facilitate sales, point systems, vacation clubs, and variations of those structures, should be accounted for based on the guidance for profit recognition in ASC 360. The transactions should be evaluated primarily based on whether a seller has transferred title to an interest in a time-sharing interval without recourse and whether the seller has a continuing involvement with the buyer, and other requirements necessary to meet the profit recognition criteria in ASC 360. Profit should only be recognized if a time-sharing interval has been sold to an end user. No profit should be recognized on a transfer of time-sharing intervals to a special purpose entity (SPE), which should be considered to have no economic substance for balance sheet reporting purposes if it (*a*) was structured for legal purposes and (*b*) has no debt, and its only assets are the time-sharing intervals. Interests in an SPE not yet sold to end users should be presented in the balance sheet as time-sharing inventory. SPEs that do not meet the conditions in (*a*) and (*b*) above should be accounted for in the same manner as investments in other SPE's structures.

A seller, its affiliate, or a related party that operates a points program, vacation, or exchange program should be considered to have a continuing involvement with the buyer. A seller's accounting should be determined based on whether compensation for those services is set at prevailing market rates. If there is no compensation for the services, or if the fee is at below prevailing market rates, compensation should be imputed when a sale is recognized and charged against the sales value of the interval. Profit should be recognized under the guidance on continuing involvement in ASC 360. Revenue on those services should be recognized as it is earned.

Owners Associations

Until all time-sharing intervals have been sold, a seller is the owner of all unsold units and is required to pay the owners association dues or maintenance fees for those units. Also, sellers will frequently subsidize the operations of an owners association for a limited time rather than pay dues or maintenance fees on unsold units. Sellers' payments for maintenance fees should be expensed as incurred. Subsidies to an owners association also should be expensed. A seller that is contractually entitled to recover all or a portion of its subsidy to an owners association should recognize a receivable only if recovery is probable and the measurement of the receivable is reasonably reliable. A seller that is hired to manage an owners association for a fee should recognize that fee as revenue only if it is earned and realized or realizable. A seller that subsidizes an owners association's operations while acting as its manager should offset its revenue from fees on seller-owned intervals against its subsidy expense.

OBSERVATION: The guidance in the previous paragraph applies if a timeshare development's Owners Association (OA) is not consolidated in the seller's financial statements, but no guidance is provided regarding issues related to consolidation of an OA. Such guidance is provided in ASC 810.

Presentation and Disclosures

In its balance sheet, a seller should present gross notes receivable from time-sharing sales, a deduction from notes receivable for the allowance for uncollectibles, and a deduction from notes receivable for deferred profit under the guidance in ASC 360, if any.

Sellers of time-sharing intervals should make the following disclosures in their financial statements:

- The effects of changes in estimate in the relative sales value method, in accordance with the guidance in ASC 250-10-50-4.
- Maturities of notes receivable for each of the five years following the date of the financial statements and the total for all following years. The total of notes receivable balances displayed with various maturity dates should be reconciled to the amount of notes receivable on the balance sheet.
- The weighted average and range of stated interest rates of notes receivable.
- Estimated cost to complete improvements and promised amenities. Activity in the allowance for uncollectible accounts, including the balance at the beginning and end of the period, additions related to sales in the current period, direct write-offs charged against the allowance, and changes in estimates related to sales in prior periods. The same disclosures should be made for receivables with recourse, if applicable.

- Policies related to meeting the criteria for a buyer's commitment and collectibility of the sales price in ASC 360.

Changes in the amount of time-sharing notes receivable, including sales of those notes, should be reported as cash flows from operations in the statement of cash flows.

APPENDIX K:
ASC 976—REAL ESTATE—RETAIL LAND

CONTENTS

General Guidance	69,001
Overview	69,001
Background	69,001
Retail Land Sales	69,002
Profit Recognition	69,002
Profit Recognition—Full Accrual Method	69,002
Profit Recognition—Other Than Full Accrual Method	69,004
Percentage-of-Completion Method	69,004
Installment Sales Method	69,005
Deposit Accounting Method	69,005
Change in Accounting Method	69,005
Disclosure—Retail Land Sales	69,006

GENERAL GUIDANCE

OVERVIEW

The matching principle requires that revenue and related costs be recognized simultaneously in determining net income for a specific period. If revenue is deferred to a future period, the associated costs of that revenue are also deferred. Frequently, it may be necessary to estimate revenue and/or costs to achieve a proper matching.

GAAP require that the realization of revenue be recognized in the accounting period in which the earning process is substantially completed and an exchange has taken place. In addition, revenue usually is recognized at the amount established by the parties to the exchange, except for transactions in which collection of the receivable is not reasonably assured. In the event that collection of the receivable is not reasonably assured, the installment method or cost-recovery method may be used. Alternatively, collections may be recorded properly as deposits in the event that considerable uncertainty exists as to their eventual collectibility.

ASC 976 addresses the recognition of revenue from real estate sales and contains specialized accounting and reporting principles and practices.

BACKGROUND

ASC 976 provides guidance in accounting for retail land sales. The following items are *expressly* excluded from the provisions of ASC 976:

- Real estate projects that are not for sale or rent and are developed by an entity for its own use; this includes real estate reported in consolidated financial statements that was developed by one affiliated member of the group for use in the operations of another member of the group
- Initial direct costs of leases, including sales-type leases
- Direct costs that are related to commercial activities such as manufacturing, merchandising, or service-oriented activities
- Real estate rental periods of less than one month in duration

RETAIL LAND SALES

The development of a large tract of land, usually over several years, is typical for a company in the retail land sales industry. Master plans are drawn for the improvement of the property, which may include amenities, and all necessary regulatory approvals are obtained. Large advertising campaigns are held at an early stage, frequently resulting in substantial sales before significant development of the property. In most retail land sales, a substantial portion of the sales price is financed by the seller in the form of a long-term receivable secured by the property. Interest and principal are paid by the buyer over an extended number of years. In the event of default, the buyer usually loses his or her entire equity and the property reverts back to the seller. Frequently, the retail land sales contract or existing state law provides for a period in which the purchaser may receive a refund of all or part of any payments made. In addition, the seller may be unable to obtain a deficiency judgment against the buyer because of operation of the law. Finally, many project-wide improvements and amenities are deferred until the later stages of development, when the seller may be faced with financial difficulties.

Because of small down payments, frequent cancellations and refunds, and the possibility that the retail land sales company may not be financially able to complete the project, certain specific conditions must be met before a sale can be recognized.

Profit Recognition

ASC 976 requires that profit on all retail land sales within a project be recognized by a single accounting method. As conditions change for the entire project, the method of profit recognition changes in accordance with the provisions of ASC 976 (ASC 976-605-25-1). Profits on a retail land sales project are required to be recognized by (a) the full accrual method, (b) the percentage-of-completion method, (c) the installment sales method, or (d) the deposit method. Specific criteria must be met before a particular profit recognition method can be used.

Profit Recognition—Full Accrual Method

A retail land sales project must meet all of the following conditions for the full accrual method of accounting to be used for the recognition of profit (ASC 976-605-25-6):

- The down payment and all subsequent payments have been made by the buyer, through and including any period of cancellation, and all periods for any refund have expired.
- The buyer has paid a total of 10% or more, in principal or interest, of the total contract sales price.
- The seller's collection experience for the project or for prior projects indicates that at least 90% of the receivables in force for six months after the sale is recorded will be collected in full. A down payment of 20% or more is an acceptable substitute for this experience test.

OBSERVATION: Profit may be recognized before the end of six months if collection experience is based on a prior project. The six-month period is an eligibility test for the full accrual method of accounting.

The collection experience of a prior project may be used if (a) the prior project was similar in characteristics to the new project and (b) the collection period was long enough to determine collectibility of receivables to maturity dates.

- The seller's receivable for the property sold is not subject to subordination of new loans. However, subordination is allowed for construction of a residence, provided the project's collection experience for such subordinated receivables is approximately the same as that for those receivables that are not subordinated.
- The seller is not obligated to construct amenities or other facilities or to complete any improvements for lots that have been sold.

If all of the above conditions are met for the entire retail land sales project, the seller shall recognize profits by the full accrual method of accounting.

PRACTICE POINTER: The actual procedures that must be used to record retail land sales under the full accrual method of accounting are as follows:

- The total contract price of the retail land sale, before any deductions, is recorded as a gross sale. The total contract price includes the total amount of principal and interest that is expected to be received from the sale.
- The down payment on the sale is recorded. The difference between the total contract price of the retail land sale and the down payment is the gross receivable.
- The gross receivable is discounted at the date of sale to yield an amount at which it could be sold on a volume basis without recourse to the seller. The discount on the gross receivable is referred to as a "valuation discount."
- The valuation discount is amortized to income over the life of the retail land sales contract. The interest method should be used to produce a constant rate of amortization.

- An allowance for contract cancellations is established based on estimates of contracts that are not expected to be collected in subsequent periods. Canceled contracts are charged directly to the allowance account.

    For the purpose of determining the adequacy of the allowance for contract cancellations in subsequent periods, all receivables that do not conform to the criteria in the following table shall be considered uncollectible and the allowance account adjusted appropriately:

Percentage contract price paid	Delinquency period
Less than 25%	90 days
25% but less than 50%	120 days
50% and over	150 days

    If a buyer is willing to assume personal liability for his or her debt and apparently has the means and ability to complete all payments, the delinquency periods in the above table may be extended.

- The following items represent deductions from the gross sale to arrive at net sales for the period:
    - Valuation discount
    - Allowance for contract cancellations
    - Deferred portion of gross sale (to be matched with future work or performance of the seller)
- Cost of sales should be computed on net sales for the period.
- A sale that is made and canceled in the same reporting period should be included in, and also deducted from, gross sales or disclosed appropriately in some other manner.
- The unamortized valuation discount (discount on receivables) and the allowance for contract cancellations are shown on the balance sheet as deductions from the related receivables.
- Deferred revenue, less any related costs, is shown on the balance sheet as a liability. Deferred revenue should be recognized in future periods as the work is performed by the seller.

Profit Recognition—Other Than Full Accrual Method

Percentage-of-Completion Method

If the first four criteria for applying the full accrual method of accounting are met for the entire retail land sales project and the fifth criterion is not met (see "Profit Recognition—Full Accrual Method," above), the seller shall recognize profits by the percentage-of-completion method of accounting, provided the following additional criteria are met for the entire project (ASC 976-605-25-8):

- Progress on the entire project has passed the preliminary stages and tangible evidence exists to indicate that the project will be completed according to plans. Tangible evidence of such progress includes the following:
    - Funds have actually been expended.

- Work on project improvements has been initiated.
- Engineering plans and construction commitments pertaining to lots that have been sold are in existence.
- Access roads and amenities are substantially completed.
- There is no evidence of any significant delay to the project, and dependable estimates of costs to complete the project and extent of progress are reasonable.
• At the end of the normal payment period, it is reasonably expected that the property clearly will be useful for its intended purposes as represented by the seller at the time of sale.

If the above criteria are met for the entire project and the first four criteria for applying the full accrual method of accounting are met for the entire project, the seller recognizes profits on retail land sales by the percentage-of-completion method.

Installment Sales Method

If the first two criteria for applying the full accrual method of accounting are met for the entire project and the other three criteria are not met, the seller shall recognize profits by the installment sales method, provided the following additional criteria are met for the entire project (ASC 976-605-25-9):

- The current and prospective financial capabilities of the retail land sales company (seller) must reflect with reasonable assurance that the company is capable of completing all of its obligations under the sales contract and master plan.
- Indications of the seller's financial capabilities include (*a*) the sufficiency of equity capital, (*b*) borrowing capacity, and (*c*) positive cash flow from present operations.

If the above criteria are met for the entire project and the first two criteria for applying the full accrual method of accounting are met for the entire project, the seller shall recognize profits on retail land sales by the installment sales method.

Deposit Accounting Method

If a retail land sale does not meet the criteria for accounting by the full accrual method, the percentage-of-completion method, or the installment sale method, the seller shall account for all proceeds from retail land sales by the deposit method of accounting (ASC 976-605-25-2). Under the deposit method of accounting, the effective date of the sale is deferred and all funds received, including principal and interest, are recorded as deposits on retail land sales.

Change in Accounting Method

If a retail land sales entity has been reporting sales for the entire project by the deposit method and subsequently the criteria for the installment sales method, the percentage-of-completion method, or the full accrual method are met for the entire project, the change to the new method shall be accounted for as a change in accounting estimate (ASC 976-605-25-11). Thus, the effects of the change shall be accounted for prospectively in accordance with ASC 250 (Accounting Changes and Error Corrections). If the effects of the change in an accounting estimate are significant, disclosure of the effects on (a) income from continuing operations, (b) net income, and (c) the related per share data should be made in the financial statements of the period of change.

Initially, retail land sales may be accounted for by the installment sales method, and subsequently the criteria for the percentage-of-completion method may be met for the entire project. In this event, the percentage-of-completion method may be adopted for the entire project. The effects of the change to the percentage-of-completion method are accounted for as a change in accounting estimate and, if material, disclosure of the effects on (a) income before extraordinary items, (b) net income, and (c) related per share data should be made in the financial statements of the period of change.

In reporting the change from the installment sales method to the percentage-of-completion method, the following procedures should be observed:

- If required, the receivables should be discounted to their present values at the date of change in accordance with ASC 835 (Interest).
- The liability for the remaining future performance of the seller should be discounted to its present value at the date of the change.
- The amount of discount, if any, on the receivables and the amount of discount, if any, on the liability for remaining future performance by the seller are deducted from the unrealized gross profit on installment sales at the date of the change to arrive at the net credit to income resulting from the change.

Disclosure—Retail Land Sales

Retail land sales companies, diversified entities with significant retail land sales operations, and investors who derive a significant portion of their income from investments involved in retail land sales must disclose specific information in the financial statements, as follows (ASC 976-310-50-1):

- The maturities of the receivables from retail land sales for each of the five years following the date of the financial statements
- The amount of delinquent receivables and the method used to determine delinquency
- The weighted average and range of stated interest rates on receivables from retail land sales
- Estimated total costs and anticipated expenditures to improve major areas of the project from which sales are being made, for each of the five years following the date of the financial statements
- The amount of recorded obligations for improvements
- The method of recognizing profit

The effect of a change in accounting estimate, if the percentage-of-completion method is adopted for a retail land sales project originally reported using the installment method

70,001

APPENDIX L:
ASC 980—REGULATED OPERATIONS

CONTENTS

Interpretive Guidance	70,001
ASC 980-605: Revenue Recognition	70,001
ASC 980-605-25-1 through 25-4	
Accounting by Rate-Regulated Utilities for the Effects of Certain Alternative Revenue Programs	70,001
ASC 980-605-25-5 through 25-15; ASC 440-10-60-20	
Revenue Recognition on Long-Term Power Sales Contracts	70,003
ASC 980-605-25-17 through 25-18; ASC 980-350-35-3 through 35-5	
Revenue Recognition under Long-Term Power Sales Contracts That Contain Both Fixed and Variable Pricing Terms	70,008
ASC 980-715: Compensation-Retirement Benefits	70,011
ASC 980-715-25-4 through 25-7, 50-1; ASC 715-60-60-6	
Accounting for OPEB Costs by Rate-Regulated Enterprises	70,011

INTERPRETIVE GUIDANCE

ASC 980-605: Revenue Recognition

ASC 980-605-25-1 through 25-4
Accounting by Rate-Regulated Utilities for the Effects of Certain Alternative Revenue Programs

BACKGROUND

Utility customers generally are billed for their usage based on predetermined rates, which are regulated and approved by the utility's regulatory commission. The rates are set based on costs of service and are designed to recover the utility's allowable costs, which include a return on shareholders' investments.

Certain utility regulators have authorized the use of alternative revenue programs that reduce the volatility in the utility's earnings and have the following objectives:

- To protect the utilities, their investors, and their customers from unexpected fluctuations in sales and earnings caused by changes in weather patterns or by reduced demand because of conservation efforts
- To reward utilities for meeting certain goals

The following two major alternative revenue programs permit utilities to adjust future billings to consider certain past events:

Type A

Type A programs are intended to reduce the effects on a utility's revenue of differences between actual sales volume and estimated sales used to set base rates. Such differences may be caused by abnormal weather patterns, conservation efforts, and other external factors. For example, 50% more kilowatt hours of electricity may be used during a very hot summer, or user conservation efforts may result in decreased usage. Variations between forecasted revenue and actual usage may be adjusted by billing surcharges that are added to or deducted from base rates in future billings. For example, in a period following a hot summer, customers' billings would be increased by a surcharge. Surcharges are most commonly used to recover fuel costs that differ from estimated costs included in base rates. Under Type A programs, the utility recognizes revenue in the future when customers are provided with service at the base rate plus or minus a surcharge.

Type B

Type B programs involve incentive awards that are related to a utility's performance. Such programs commonly set goals that may be achieved by measurable improvement in a utility's effectiveness or efficiency of operations. Examples of such goals are controlling growth in demand, reducing costs, and reducing the number of customer complaints. Achievement of those goals may be measured subjectively and objectively and usually involves an audit by the regulatory authority. If the goals are achieved, Type B programs provide utilities with additional revenue. If they are not achieved, there may be penalties for the utility and refunds for its customers.

ACCOUNTING ISSUES

- What is the appropriate accounting for alternative revenue programs (Type A and Type B) of regulated utilities?
- Should the accounting for Type A and Type B programs be the same?

ACCOUNTING GUIDANCE

If the specific events that would allow a utility to bill additional revenues under Type A or Type B programs have occurred, a utility should recognize those additional revenues if all of the following conditions are met:

- The utility's regulatory commission has approved the additional revenue program, which allows the utility to adjust future rates automatically. Such adjustments are considered automatic even before the regulator has verified the adjustment to future rates.
- The utility can determine the amount of additional revenue for the period objectively, and recovery is probable.
- Additional revenues will be collected no later than 24 months from the end of the annual period in which they were recognized.

DISCUSSION

When this issue was discussed, industry practice was to recognize revenue and the related asset when the condition resulting in future billings occurred, the amount was known, and it was probable that it would be recovered.

The EITF was asked to consider when the economic benefit of alternative rate programs should be recognized in a utility's financial statements. Several alternatives were discussed. The following alternatives were considered:

Proponents of the view additional revenue should be recognized when the amount is known and realization is probable noted that the guidance in ASC 980-10-15-5 provides that regulated enterprises should follow GAAP, except if GAAP conflicts with the guidance in ASC 980. They argued that because ASC 980 does not specifically address that issue, GAAP for all entities should be followed in recognizing amounts to be received under those programs. Statement of Financial Accounting Concepts No. 5 states that revenue may be recognized when it is realized and has been earned. Assets are defined in Statement of Financial Accounting Concepts No. 6 as "probable future economic benefits obtained or controlled by a particular entity as a result of past transactions." Thus, this view supports recording the revenue and related asset in the year the earnings process and performance were completed, even though the surcharge billing occurs in the future.

ASC 980-605-25-5 through 25-15; ASC 440-10-60-20
Revenue Recognition on Long-Term Power Sales Contracts

BACKGROUND

Nonutility generators (NUGs) are entities that supply power to other entities (often rate-regulated utilities), usually under long-term sales contracts (20-30 years), or to builder/users for their own needs. Those entities are not regulated and generally would not be accounted under the guidance in ASC 980. However, accounting guidance NUGs is included in ASC 980-605 because many of the services provided by those entities are the same as those provided by regulated entities.

Long-term power sales contracts include pricing and terms that create practical issues in accounting, particularly in revenue recognition. Pricing arrangements may include the following:

- Specified prices per unit (e.g., per kilowatt hour or kwh) that increase, decrease, or remain fixed over the term of the contract
- Formula-based prices per kwh (e.g., a price determined annually based on the current cost of power from other sources or based on published rates)

A combination of those pricing arrangements is used in the following billing methods:

- Billings are based on a specified price schedule over the term of the contract, but at the end of the contract term, the NUG either makes or receives a payment so that total revenue recognized and payments made over the contract's term will equal the amount computed under an arrangement under which the pricing is based on a formula. The difference between the payments made and the amount calculated based on a formula pricing arrangement is (1) recorded in an interest-bearing tracker account, or (2) at a defined point in the life of the contract, the cumulative balance in the tracker account may be amortized to zero by adjusting subsequent billings.

- Billings are based on a specified price schedule but the NUG is required to make a payment if at the end of the contract term, the total revenue recognized and total payments received by the NUG under the specified rate schedule exceed the amount computed under a pricing arrangement based on a formula.

The discussion was based on the following three examples of long-term contracts:

Type 1 Contract

The customer (utility) is obligated to take or pay for all power made available by the NUG for the term of the contract (20 years). The price per kwh is specified and increases in years 11 to 20.

Type 2 Contract

The customer is obligated to take or pay for all power made available by the NUG for the term of the contract. Billings are based on specified prices per kwh that increase during the term. However, total payments over the term of the contract will be based on a formula used by the customer annually to compute its *avoided cost*, which is the cost that would have been incurred if power had been purchased from another source or had been self-generated (the source is specified in the contract). Over the term of the contract, the customer uses what is referred to as a "tracker account" to record its avoided cost and to offset actual billings against that amount. At the end of the contract, the tracker account is adjusted, if necessary, and may result in an additional payment to the NUG, if avoided cost is greater than actual billings, or in a refund to the customer, if billings exceed avoided cost.

Type 3 Contract

The contract is the same as a Type 2 contract, except the formula is used to limit the NUG's total revenue to the lesser of total avoided cost or total actual billings (i.e., an adjustment is made only if the customer's cost decreases).

SCOPE

Contracts that are considered to be leases are outside the scope of the following guidance and should be accounted for in accordance with the provisions of ASC 840, *Leases*.

ASC 980—Regulated Operations **70,005**

ACCOUNTING ISSUES

1. Should revenue on a power sales contract that provides for scheduled price changes (Type 1 contract) be recognized based on the price schedule or ratably over the term of the contract?

2. Should the accounting required for contracts described in Issue 1 change if the power sales contract provides that total revenues for the term of the contract be determined based on a separate, formula-based pricing arrangement (Type 2 contract)?

3. Should the accounting required for contracts described in Issue 1 change if the power sales contract provides that total revenues for the term of the contract be limited by a separate formula-based pricing arrangement (Type 3 contract)?

ACCOUNTING GUIDANCE

Contracts That Include Scheduled Price Changes

NUGs should account for Type 1 contracts as follows:

a. Recognize revenue at the lesser of

　i. The amount billable under the contract

　ii. An amount determined by the kwhs available to the customer during the period multiplied by the estimated average revenue per kwh over the term of the contract.

b. Determine the lesser amount annually based on the cumulative amount that would have been recognized under either method had it been applied consistently from the beginning of the contract.

Contracts That Determine or Limit Revenue Under Formula-Based Pricing

a. Recognize revenue for Type 2 and 3 contracts in each period based on a contract's separate formula-based pricing arrangement if *total* revenues billed under the contract are determined or limited by that arrangement, but not if the separate formula-based pricing arrangement is used only to establish liquidating damages.

b. Recognize a receivable only if (*a*) the contract requires the customer to pay the NUG for the difference between the amount billed and the amount calculated according to the formula-based pricing arrangement at the end of the contract, and (*b*) it is probable that the receivable will be recovered. A receivable occurs if the amount billed based on a formula exceeds the amounts billed.

Contracts That Meet the Definition of a Derivative

Long-term power sales contracts that meet the definition of a derivative in ASC 815 should be marked to fair value through earnings, unless a contract has been designated as a hedging instrument. Contracts that do not meet the definition of a derivative should be analyzed to determine whether they contain embedded derivatives that should be accounted for separately under the guidance in ASC

815. Otherwise, the guidance discussed above applies. Some contracts that meet the definition of a derivative may qualify for the normal purchases and normal sales scope exception in ASC 815-10-15-17(b). In that case, those contracts would be accounted for under the guidance discussed above.

DISCUSSION

1. The guidance on Issue 1 was based on two views. Under one view, revenue on a long-term power sales contract should be recognized as an amount that is billable under the contract. Under the second view, periodic revenue should be recognized based on estimated average revenue per kwh over the life of the contract.

   Proponents of the first view believed that the contracts are executory contracts under which customers have no obligation to pay unless the NUG makes power available to them.

   Under the second view, long-term power sales contracts are similar to operating leases and kwhs made available to customers annually are similar to property used by a lessee.

   The guidance on Issue 1 represents a compromise between those two views; it results in recognition of the most conservative amount of revenue, regardless of the method used. In addition, it attempts to associate revenue with the periods in which it was earned while allocating revenue more evenly over the term of the contract. That approach also addresses concerns about possible abuses or manipulation under the first approach; for example, structuring a contract to front-end revenue by charging higher rates in the early years, thereby recognizing revenue before it has been earned and distorting revenue recognized over the term of the contract.

2. Those who supported recognizing revenue on Type 2 and Type 3 contracts based on the avoided-cost formula believed that the tracker account used to monitor the cumulative difference between amounts billed and amounts calculated with the avoided-cost formula shifts the customer's substantial risk of changes in the utility's avoided cost to the NUG over the term of the contract. They further believed that the contract is in substance an arrangement under which a customer provides financing to the NUG in the early years and the NUG sells power to the customer at the avoided cost over the term of the contract. Although proponents of this view agreed that a power sales contract is not a lease, they argued that if a lease with escalating rents had an alternative calculation based on rents adjusted to, for example, the consumer price index, under the guidance in ASC 840, a lessor would be permitted to recognize revenue based on the CPI only in the early years of the lease.

   A working group met with industry representatives to discuss the characteristics of contracts similar to those referred to above as Type 2 and Type 3 contracts, except that they also may have some of the characteristics of Type 1 contracts. All those contracts use a tracking account. They were described as Category A and Category B contracts in the working group's discussions. Some contracts under Category A use a tracking account only to measure liquidated damages if the NUG does not perform under the contract. Revenue is not limited to avoided cost, and the NUG can retain all amounts billed if it performs under the contract. Another type of contract in this category has specified rates in the early years of the contract and fluctuating rates based on avoided cost in the later years. A balance of billings over avoided cost in the tracker account in the early years of the contract is forgiven over the years when rates are based on avoided cost. If the NUG performs over the contract term, the tracker account is amortized to zero. Industry representatives believed that the economic substance of Category A contracts is the same as for Type 1 contracts in Issue 1. That is, the NUG keeps all amounts billed, but here the customer has the additional security that the NUG will perform. They argued that because the NUG's total revenue is not determined by or limited to revenues based on the avoided-cost formula and the tracker account is used only to determine liquidation damages, if necessary, revenue on this category should not be based on the avoided-cost formula. Rather, revenue on those contracts should be recognized the same as for contracts in Issue 1.

In Category B contracts, which measure total revenue on a contract based on the avoided-cost formula, the tracker account is used to accumulate the difference between billings and actual annual avoided cost. The balance of the tracker account must be settled at the end of such contracts with the customer paying no more than total actual avoided cost. The economic substance of such contracts is that the NUG takes on the risk that there will be unexpected changes in avoided-cost projections over the term of the contract or that the projections of avoided cost on which the contract's rates were based were inaccurate. Although they have adequate cash flows, NUGs that recognize revenue based on avoided cost in this category of contracts incur losses in the early years of a contract, because avoided cost is too low to cover the NUG's financing and construction costs. In contrast, actual amounts billed on the contract are based on avoided costs over the long term and always exceed annual avoided cost in the early years and reverse in later years.

Under the guidance, revenue on Type 2 and 3 contracts must be recognized based on avoided cost, because that amount represents revenue earned in each period. Because the NUG's *total* revenue on Type 3 contracts is determined by or limited to total revenue based on the avoided-cost formula over the *term* of the contract, revenue recognition based on the avoided-cost formula also best represents revenue earned over the term of the contract.

70,008   ASC 980—Regulated Operations

ASC 980-605-25-17 through 25-18; ASC 980-350-35-3 through 35-5
Revenue Recognition under Long-Term Power Sales Contracts That Contain Both Fixed and Variable Pricing Terms

BACKGROUND

The following guidance addresses contracts that consist of fixed and variable pricing arrangements, which were not considered under the guidance in ASC 980-605-25-5 through 25-15; ASC 440-10-60-20 discussed above. For example, billings under such contracts are based on a stated price schedule for a certain period of time, such as the first ten years of a 30-year contract, with billings at a variable rate for the remainder of the contract. Unlike the contracts discussed above, total revenues billed under the contracts addressed under the following guidance are not limited by a tracker account that the NUG maintains to record the difference between a utility's avoided costs and amounts that can be billed under the contract, with the difference, if any, repaid at the end of the contract. *Avoided energy cost* is the cost that a utility would have incurred had it purchased the power from another source or had the power been self-generated.

Power sales contracts negotiated on a competitive basis by NUGs prior to developing and constructing a power generation facility usually are long-term contracts (20 to 30 years) that are intended to minimize the NUG's financial risk. Although the contracts usually provide for payments based on both an energy and a capacity component, the following discussion applies only to the energy component, which is arrived at through a complex formula that represents the utility's avoided energy cost.

NUGs generally price long-term powers sales contracts to recover expected fixed and variable costs and to earn a reasonable rate of return. Rates must be sufficiently firm to assure financing for construction of the facility. Utilities are motivated by cost so they usually seek rates that agree with their estimated long-range avoided costs. Most of the contracts addressed here were negotiated in California in the early to mid-1980s. The initial terms of the contracts were at fixed or scheduled prices based on avoided cost to guarantee a revenue stream. It was expected at that time that avoided costs would increase significantly over the term of the contracts (30 years). In reality, avoided costs have decreased.

ACCOUNTING ISSUE

How should NUGs recognize revenue on long-term power sales contracts that consist of separate, specified terms for (*a*) a fixed or scheduled price per kwh for one period of the contract and (*b*) a variable price per kwh (which is based on market prices, actual avoided costs, or formula-based pricing arrangements), for a different portion of the contract, if total revenues billable under the contract over its entire term are not determined or limited by a tracker account or other form of adjustment?

ACCOUNTING GUIDANCE

The contracts addressed here should be divided and accounted for as follows:

- Revenue earned during the contract period in which prices are fixed or scheduled should be recognized in accordance with the guidance discussed above for contracts that include scheduled pricing changes, that is, at the lesser of (*a*) the amount billable under the contract or (*b*) an amount based on the kwh made available during the period multiplied by the estimated average revenue per kwh over the term of the contract. The lesser amount should be determined annually based on the cumulative amounts that would have been recognized had each method been applied consistently from the beginning of the term of the contract.

- During the contract period in which variable prices are used, revenue should be recognized as billed, in accordance with the contract's provisions for that period.

Revenue for the entire contract should be recognized based on the guidance for Issue 1 of ASC 980-605-25-5 through 25-15; ASC 440-10-60-20 discussed above if the contractual terms during the separate fixed and variable portions of the contract do not approximate the expected market rates at the inception of the contract.

Such contracts should be reviewed periodically to determine whether they are profitable or whether immediate loss recognition is required. Premiums related to a contractual rate in excess of current market rates should be amortized over the remaining portions of the respective periods of long-term power sales contracts acquired in purchase business combinations. For example, a premium resulting from an above-market rate related to the fixed or scheduled portion of a contract would be amortized over the remaining portion of that period of the acquired contract.

DISCUSSION

The approach adopted accounts for each phase of the contract separately. Proponents believed that revenues earned during each contract period are not affected by revenues in another contract period. They argued further that total revenues under the contracts discussed here are not the sum of revenues earned in each period of the contract. They noted that the guidance for Issue 1 of ASC 980-605-25-5 through 25-15; ASC 440-10-60-20 discussed above specifically states that it applies only to contracts with scheduled price changes that are determined by the contract and do not require estimating a utility's future avoided cost. They argued that if they had wanted NUGs to recognize level revenues over the contract term, such estimates would have been required for formula-based contracts discussed in ASC 980-605-25-5 through 25-15; ASC 440-10-60-20 discussed above, which usually are based on avoided cost.

Market rates are used in the variable-rate period of the contracts. Proponents analogized to the revenue recognition practices of oil or natural gas producers who enter into long-term contracts and recognize revenue as billed at current market prices on delivery. Similar accounting is followed by the mineral extractive industries and for agricultural commodities.

70,010 ASC 980—Regulated Operations

Illustration of Revenue Recognition on Long-Term Power Sales Contracts with Fixed and Variable Pricing Terms

Highpower Resources Co. has entered into a ten-year contract to provide energy. There is no tracker account. During the first five years of the contract, the rates are fixed at amounts stated in the contract; for the following five years, rates are at the utility's actual avoided energy cost. It is expected that actual avoided costs in the second half of the contract will be higher than those at the time the contract is entered into. Actual avoided costs decrease over the contract term. Annual demand is 1 million kwh per year.

The following energy rates are used in years 1-5 (the fixed portion of the contract):

Year 1	$.06
Year 2	.07
Year 3	.08
Year 4	.09
Year 5	.10

Actual avoided energy costs in years 6-10 are as follows:

Year 6	$.041
Year 7	.038
Year 8	.035
Year 9	.031
Year 10	.027

Revenue recognition during the fixed portion of the contract

1. Calculate the estimated average rate per kwh:

$$\frac{\text{Total revenue per kwh based on contract}}{\text{Number of years}} = \frac{\$.4}{5} = \$.08$$

2. Calculate the cumulative amounts using estimated revenue that is based on the average rate and that is the billable amount. Recognize the amount that results in a lower cumulative amount had each method been applied consistently from the beginning of the contract term. (For example, in year 4, recognizing $90,000 at the billable rate results in the lower cumulative amount of $300,000; had $90,000 been recognized at the average rate, the resulting cumulative amount would be $320,000.)

Cumulative Amounts

Estimated	Avg. Rate	Avg. Rate	Billable Rate	Revenue Recognition
Year 1	$.08	$ 80,000	$ 60,000	$ 60,000
Year 2	.08	160,000	130,000	70,000
Year 3	.08	240,000	210,000	80,000
Year 4	.08	320,000	300,000	90,000
Year 5	.08	400,000	400,000	100,000

Revenue recognition during the variable portion of the contract

Recognize revenue based on actual avoided energy costs.

Actual Avoided	Energy Cost	Revenue Recognition
Year 6	$.041	$41,000
Year 7	.038	38,000
Year 8	.035	35,000
Year 9	.031	31,000
Year 10	.027	27,000

ASC 980-715: Compensation-Retirement Benefits

ASC 980-715-25-4 through 25-7, 50-1; ASC 715-60-60-6
Accounting for OPEB Costs by Rate-Regulated Enterprises

BACKGROUND

Like other entities, rate-regulated entities were required to apply the provisions of ASC 715-60 for fiscal years beginning after December 15, 1992. Under that guidance postretirement benefits are considered to be deferred compensation arrangements, which involve an exchange of a promise of future benefits for current services performed by employees. The guidance in ASC 715-60 requires recognition of an obligation over the employees' related service period associated with providing future postretirement benefits to retired employees.

Before the guidance in ASC 715-60 became effective, most companies, including regulated entities, were accounting for costs of other postretirement benefits (OPEB costs) on a pay-as-you-go or cash basis. OPEB costs were paid and recognized in the period in which they were incurred. Rate regulators generally permitted including such costs in rates when they were paid. On adoption of the guidance in ASC 715-60, regulated entities not only had to accrue postretirement benefit obligations in their financial statements in the current period, but also had to either recognize a transition obligation relating to prior service costs immediately or amortize that obligation over the employees' average remaining service period, or 20 years, whichever is longer. Therefore, costs recognized under the guidance in ASC 715-60 would be significantly higher than those recognized on a cash basis.

As rate-regulated entities were getting ready to adopt the guidance in ASC 715-60 for financial reporting, the question arose as to how costs recognized under the requirements of that guidance would affect OPEB costs included in rates. If regulators were to permit entities to include in rates all of the costs under the guidance in ASC 715-60 (including amortization of the transition obligation), the costs reported in the entity's financial statements and the costs included in rates would not differ. In this case, no deferral of costs or recognition of a regulatory asset would be necessary. However, if regulated entities were not allowed by the applicable regulator to include in rates, the entire amount of the costs charged to customers under the guidance in ASC 715-60, some questioned whether regulated entities would have sufficient evidence to meet the criteria in ASC 980-340-251 and 40-1 for deferral of the difference between the amount charged in rates and the total cost recognized in the financial statements under the guidance in ASC 715-60. Under the guidance in ASC 980-340-251 and 40-1, all or part of an incurred cost that would otherwise be charged to expense may be capitalized as a regulatory asset if two conditions are met: (*a*) it is probable that by including the cost in rates charged to customers the capitalized cost will be recovered from future revenues and (*b*) future revenue will result in recovery of a previously incurred cost instead of providing for similar levels of future costs.

ACCOUNTING ISSUES

1. What additional criteria or evidence does a rate-regulated entity need in order to meet the requirements in ASC 980-340-25-1, 40-1 for recognition of a regulatory asset related to costs under the guidance in ASC 715-60 for which rate recovery has been deferred?

2. Should the conclusions reached apply to discontinued plans under the guidance in ASC 715-60?

3. If a rate-regulated entity initially fails to meet the regulatory asset recognition criteria, should a regulatory asset be recognized in a subsequent period when the criteria are met?

ACCOUNTING GUIDANCE

The following guidance is limited to accounting for regulatory assets related to costs accounted for under the guidance in ASC 715-60 by regulated entities that apply the guidance in ASC 980).

1. Recognition of a regulatory asset should be based on the following guidelines:

    a. *No* regulatory asset should be recognized for costs under the guidance in ASC 715-60 if a regulator continues to include OPEB costs of a continuing plan in rates on a pay-as-you-go basis.

    [It was noted that OPEB costs should be included in current rates, because they represent current costs of providing the regulated service or product that must be recovered through rates under the provisions of ASC 980.]

    b. A regulatory asset related to a continuing plan should be recognized for the difference between costs under the guidance in ASC 715-60 and OPEB costs included in rates if:

    (1) It is probable that at least the amount of the regulatory asset will be recovered from future revenues that include the cost in rates, and

    (2) All of the following criteria are met:

    (a) Deferral of costs under the guidance in ASC 715-60 and subsequent inclusion of those deferred costs in the entity's rates is allowed by the entity's regulator under a rate order, which includes a policy statement or generic order that applies to entities in the regulator's jurisdiction.

(b) Annual costs under the guidance in ASC 715-60, including amortization of the transition obligation, will be included in rates within approximately five years of adopting the guidance in ASC 715-60. Conversion to full accrual accounting may occur in steps, but additional amounts should not be deferred longer than approximately five years.

(c) The regulator's authorized period for combined deferral and recovery of the regulatory asset should not be longer than approximately 20 years from adoption of the guidance in ASC 715-60. If a regulator requires a deferral period that exceeds 20 years, only the proportionate amount of costs that will be recovered within 20 years should be recognized as a regulatory asset.

(d) For each year, the percentage by which rates increase under the regulatory recovery plan should not exceed the percentage by which rates increased in the immediately preceding year. That criterion is similar to that for phase-in plans discussed in ASC 980-340-25-3. This criterion would be met by recovering the regulatory asset in rates on a straight-line basis.

c. *Transition requirement* The guidance discussed above applies to rate-regulated entities that elect to immediately recognize the transition obligation in accordance with the guidance in ASC 715-60 (nd to entities that elect to delay recognition of the transition obligation and amortize it in accordance with the guidance in ASC 715-60.

d. *Disclosure* Rate-regulated entities should disclose the following information about costs recognized under the guidance in ASC 715-60 in their financial statements:

(1) A description of the regulatory treatment of OPEB costs

(2) The status of any pending regulatory action

(3) The amount of any costs recognized under the guidance in ASC 715-60 that have been deferred as a regulatory asset at the balance sheet date

(4) The expected period of recovery of deferred amounts through rates.

2. A regulatory asset of a discontinued plan related to costs recognized under the guidance in ASC 715-60 should be recognized if it is probable that an amount at least equal to the deferred asset will be included in rates and recovered in future revenues within approximately 20 years after adopting the guidance in ASC 715-60. During that period, rate recovery may continue on a pay-as-you-go basis. For the purpose of this guidance, a discontinued plan is one in which employees do not earn additional benefits for future service (it has no current service costs).

3. A rate-regulated entity that initially does not meet the criteria for recognizing a regulatory asset but that meets the criteria in a subsequent period should recognize a regulatory asset for the cumulative difference between costs under the guidance in ASC 715-60 and OPEB costs included in rates since the date the guidance in ASC 715-60 was adopted.

DISCUSSION

1. This Issue was discussed because of concerns about the recoverability of a regulatory asset for costs recognized under the guidance in ASC 715-60 through rates in future periods. The underlying premise of ASC 980-340 is that rates charged to current customers include current costs of providing the regulated service. However, ASC 980-340-25-1, 40-1 provides for situations in which some costs may be deferred because they are not recovered in rates in the same period in which they are recognized in the financial statements. Some believed that the judgmental criteria in ASC 980-340-25-1,40-1 are adequate and analogized to accounting for pensions, compensated absences, and taxes by rate-regulated entities.

However, others were concerned about the changing regulatory environment and questioned the probability that capitalized costs would be recovered. They were concerned whether regulators would permit including costs recognized under the guidance in ASC 715-60 in rates because such costs are noncash expenses that represent estimates of costs that will be incurred in the future. Generally, rates charged by regulated entities include costs incurred to provide services in the current period. A further concern was related to the extended time period for recovery of the liability recognized under the guidance in ASC 715-60 including the transition obligation, which is related to prior service and could be amortized over more than 20 years.

The concerns about recoverability were resolved by adding criteria that would tighten the requirements in ASC 980-340-25-1, 40-1 and by requiring that costs recognized under the guidance in ASC 715-60 be fully included in rates within approximately 20 years from adoption of the guidance in ASC 715-60. Those who supported a 20-year recovery period for the regulatory asset argued that the period should not be shorter for rate-regulated entities than for other entities and that at the end of that period, regulated entities would present costs recognized under the guidance in ASC 715-60 in their financial statements in the same manner as other entities.

Another concern was that regulated entities may *backload* the recovery of the regulatory asset for costs under the provision of ASC 715-60. For example, if a portion of costs recognized under the guidance in ASC 715-60 is deferred during the first five years, but the asset will not be recovered through rates until years 16 to 20, there was a concern about the probability of recovery.

That concern was dealt with by adopting the requirement for phase-in plans under the guidance in ASC 980-340, which requires a decreasing or steady percentage increase in rates over the recovery period. It was decided not to differentiate between entities that elect immediate recognition of the transition obligation and those electing to amortize it in accordance with the requirements of ASC 715-60, because the transition method elected would not affect the entity's revenues, net income, or equity during the recovery period if the entity meets the criteria for recognizing a regulatory asset. Although the regulatory asset of an entity that elects immediate recognition of the transition obligation would be larger than that of an entity that elects to recognize it over approximately 20 years, both entities would be recovering the cost through rates based on this guidance.

2. It was considered whether a regulated entity with a discontinued OPEB plan—a plan having a transition obligation related to employees' prior service but no current service costs—should be prohibited from recording a regulatory asset like an entity with a continuing plan, if OPEB costs are included in rates on a pay-as-you-go basis. The question was raised because of concerns that significant amounts of current period operating costs would continue to be deferred over long periods if OPEB costs were to be recovered through rates on a pay-as-you-go basis. Those who supported permitting recognition of a regulatory asset in this situation argued that unlike a continuing plan, which may have increasing deferrals over 30 to 40 years, no current costs would be deferred. Therefore, they did not object to pay-as-you-go recovery if deferred costs will be recovered through rates within approximately 20 years after adoption of the guidance in ASC 715-60.

3. Those who supported recognizing a regulatory asset for an incurred cost when it meets the criteria in ASC 980-340-25-1, 40-1—even though the criteria were not met when the cost was incurred—believed that the asset is created by the regulator's rate action rather than by incurring the cost. They referred to paragraph 180 in Statement of Financial Accounting Concepts No. 6 (not in ASC), which states that "[t]he ultimate evidence of the existence of assets is the future economic benefit, not the cost incurred." They argued that a regulatory asset should be recognized when it becomes probable that it will be recovered in future rates, even if recovery occurs in a period other than the one in which the cost was incurred. Another argument was that recognition of a regulatory asset when its recovery becomes probable is consistent with a balance sheet approach to financial reporting.

APPENDIX M:
ASC 985—SOFTWARE

CONTENTS

Part I: General Guidance	71,002
ASC 985-20: Costs of Software to Be Sold, Leased, or Marketed	71,002
Overview	71,002
Background	71,002
Computer Software to Be Sold, Leased, or Otherwise Marketed	71,002
Computer Software Costs	71,003
Technological Feasibility	71,004
Including Detail Program Design	71,004
Not Including Detail Program Design	71,005
Computer Software Costs That Must Be Capitalized	71,005
Amortization of Capitalized Computer Software Costs	71,005
Inventory Costs	71,005
Periodic Evaluation of Capitalized Computer Software Costs	71,006
Financial Statement Disclosure	71,006
Part II: Interpretive Guidance	
ASC 985-605: Revenue Recognition	71,006
ASC 985-605-05-1, 05-3, 15- 2 through 15-4, 25-1 through 25-19, 25-21 through 25-31, 25-33 through 25-41, 25-44 through 25-89, 25-91 through 25-107, 55-2, 55-28, 55-127 through 55-129, 55-131 through 55-133, 55-136 through 55-144, 55-146 through 55-148, 55-150 through 55-151, 55-154 through 55-160, 55-162 through 55-168, 55-170 through 55-179, 55-181 through 55-184, 55-205 through 55-210	
Software Revenue Recognition	71,006
ASC 985-605-05-4, 55-121 through 55-125 Application of ASC 985-605	
Software Revenue Recognition, to Arrangements That Include the Right to Use Software Stored on Another Entity's Hardware	71,014
ASC 985-605-15-3 Applicability of ASC 985-605	
Software Revenue Recognition, to Non-Software Deliverables in an Arrangement Containing More-Than-Incidental Software	71,015
ASC 985-605-15-3 through 15-4A, 25-10, 50-1, 55-211 through 55-236, 65-1	
Applicability of ASC 985-605 to Certain Arrangements That Include Software Elements	71,016
ASC 985-705: Cost of Sales and Services	**71,018**
ASC 985-705-S25-1, S99-1	
Accounting for the Film and Software Costs Associated with Developing Entertainment and Educational Software Products	71,018

PART I: GENERAL GUIDANCE

ASC 985-20: COSTS OF SOFTWARE TO BE SOLD, LEASED, OR MARKETED

OVERVIEW

Accounting for computer software has resulted in significant accounting issues, particularly when that software is developed internally. Similar to research and development costs and start-up costs of a new entity, computer software costs are elusive and often difficult to identify and measure. The major issue for internally developed software is the distinction between costs that should be expensed immediately and those that should be capitalized and amortized over some period in the future.

BACKGROUND

The role of computer software in our economy has increased rapidly over the past 20 years and its role is likely to continue to grow in the future. Some entities develop computer software for sale to other parties. These entities need guidance on recognizing revenue from the sale of computer software. Entities that sell computer software also need guidance on accounting for the costs of developing, such software.

Other entities do not sell computer software, but they use software internally in the operation of their businesses. Such software may be purchased externally or developed internally. These entities need guidance on accounting for the costs of computer software used in the operation of their businesses, particularly the software that is developed internally.

ASC 985 provides guidance on accounting for the costs of developing computer software for those entities that plan to sell that software. Generally, accounting for such software parallels accounting for research and development costs. To the point of establishing technological feasibility, costs are expensed as incurred. Once technological feasibility is established, it is evident that the particular software can be produced in accordance with design specifications. After that point, all costs incurred in developing the computer software product should be capitalized. The development costs of a computer system that improves an enterprise's administrative and selling procedures are not considered R&D costs. Costs incurred for internally developed computer software products that are used in the enterprise's own R&D activities, however, are considered R&D and should be accounted for accordingly.

COMPUTER SOFTWARE TO BE SOLD, LEASED, OR OTHERWISE MARKETED

ASC 985 applies to those costs incurred in purchasing or internally developing and producing computer software products that are sold, leased, or otherwise marketed by an enterprise. The costs covered by ASC 985 may be incurred (*a*) for separate computer software products or (*b*) for integral parts of computer software products or processes. ASC 985 does *not* cover those costs incurred for computer software that is (*a*) produced by an enterprise for others under a contractual arrangement or (*b*) created for the internal use of an enterprise (ASC 985-20-15-3).

Under ASC 985, the terms *computer software product, software product*, and *product* are used interchangeably to mean either (*a*) a computer software program, (*b*) a group of programs, or (*c*) a product enhancement. A product enhancement represents improvement to an existing product that significantly improves the marketability or extends the estimated useful life of the original product. A product enhancement almost always involves a new design or redesign of the original computer software product (ASC 985-20-15-4).

ASC 985 does not apply to research and development assets acquired in a business combination, or in a combination of not-for-profit entities. Those assets are recognized and measured at fair value in accordance with ASC 805 and ASC 958. However, ASC 985 does apply to any costs incurred after the date of a business combination for computer software to be sold, leased, or otherwise marketed, whether internally developed and produced or purchased (ASC 985-20-15-2).

The primary activities that are involved in the creation of a computer software product are the (*a*) planning function, (*b*) design function, and (*c*) production function. The planning function of a computer software product generally includes preliminary product specifications and design and the development of production and financial plans for the product. In addition, the planning function should include a marketing analysis and a marketing plan for the product. The planning function should generate sufficient documentation and detail information for an enterprise to make a determination of the overall feasibility of the proposed computer software product.

The design function of a computer software product includes the product design and the detail program design. The production of a product master generally involves coding, testing, and the development of training materials. Coding is the process in which the requirements of the detail program design are converted into a computer language. Testing includes the steps necessary to determine whether the computer software product works in accordance with its design specifications and documentation.

Computer Software Costs

ASC 985 specifies that all costs incurred in establishing the technological feasibility of a computer software product that is to be sold, leased, or otherwise marketed by an enterprise are research and development costs, which must be accounted for as required by ASC 730 (Research and Development). Thus, until technological feasibility is established in accordance with ASC 985, all costs incurred through the purchase or internal development and production of a computer software product that is to be sold, leased, or otherwise marketed are accounted for as R&D costs and expensed in the period incurred (ASC 985-20-25-1).

The development costs of a computer system that improves an enterprise's administrative or selling procedures are not considered R&D costs. All costs incurred for internally developed computer software products used in an enterprise's own R&D activities, however, are charged to expense when incurred, because the alternative future use test does not apply to such costs (ASC 730-10-25-4).

Production costs incurred for integral parts of a computer software product or process are expensed, unless (*a*) technological feasibility has been established for the computer software product or process and (*b*) all research and development activities have been completed for the other components of the computer software product or process (ASC 985-20-25-4).

Technological Feasibility

Technological feasibility is established upon completion of all of the activities that are necessary to substantiate that the computer software product can be produced in accordance with its design specifications, including functions, features, and technical performance requirements. Thus, all planning, designing, coding, and testing activities that are required to substantiate that the computer software product can be produced to meet its design specifications must have been completed before technological feasibility is established (ASC 985-20-25-2).

Under ASC 985, the method of establishing the technological feasibility of a computer software product depends on whether the process of creating the computer software product includes a detail program design or not. The minimum requirements for establishing the technological feasibility of a computer software product are discussed below (ASC 985-20-25-2).

Including Detail Program Design

If the process of creating the computer software product includes a detail program design, the following criteria establish the technological feasibility of a computer software product (ASC 985-20-25-2):

- An enterprise must complete the product design and detail program design for the computer software product and establish that it has available the necessary skills, hardware, and software technology to produce the product.

- An enterprise must substantiate the completeness of the program design and its consistency with the product design by documenting and tracing the detail program design to the product specifications.

- An enterprise must identify the high-risk development issues in the computer software product through review of the detail program design; if any uncertainties relating to the high-risk development issues are discovered, they must be resolved through coding and testing. High-risk development issues that may be encountered in the production of a computer software product may include novel, unique, or unproven functions and features, and/or technological innovations.

Not Including Detail Program Design

If the process of creating the computer software product *does not* include a detail program design, the following criteria establish the technological feasibility of a computer software product (ASC 985-20-25-2):

- An enterprise must complete a product design and a working model of the computer software product.
- An enterprise must substantiate the completeness of the working model and its consistency with the product design by testing the model.

Computer Software Costs That Must Be Capitalized

After technological feasibility has been established, ASC 985 specifies that all costs incurred for a computer software product that is sold, leased, or otherwise marketed by an enterprise shall be capitalized. Thus, the costs of producing product masters for a computer software product, including costs for coding and testing, are capitalized, but only after technological feasibility has been established (ASC 985-20-25-3).

Production costs for computer software that is to be used as an integral part of a product or process are capitalized, but only after (*a*) technological feasibility has been established for the software and (*b*) all R&D activities for the other components of the product or process have been completed.

Capitalization of computer software costs is discontinued when the computer software product is available to be sold, leased, or otherwise marketed. Costs for maintenance and customer support are charged to expense when incurred or when the related revenue is recognized, whichever occurs first (ASC 985-20-25-6).

OBSERVATION: Under ASC 985, the amount of costs that an enterprise is required to capitalize depends primarily on its choice of production methods. Thus, an enterprise may control the amount of computer software costs that it capitalizes by establishing technological feasibility at a designated time during the production process.

Amortization of Capitalized Computer Software Costs

Amortization of capitalized computer software costs, on a product-by-product basis, begins when the product is available to be sold, leased, or otherwise marketed. Periodic amortization, on a product-by-product basis, is equal to the greater of (*a*) the amount computed by the straight-line method over the estimated useful life of the product or (*b*) the amount computed by using the ratio that current gross revenues bear to total estimated gross revenues (including current gross revenues) (ASC 985-20-35-1).

Inventory Costs

Inventory costs are capitalized on a unit-specific basis and charged to cost of sales when the related revenue from the sale of those units is recognized.

Inventory costs include duplicate copies of the computer software product made from the product master, documentation, training materials, and the costs incurred for packaging the product for distribution (ASC 985-330-25).

Periodic Evaluation of Capitalized Computer Software Costs

Unamortized computer software costs that have been capitalized previously in accordance with ASC 985 are reported at net realizable value on an enterprise's balance sheet. Net realizable value is determined on a product-by-product basis and is equal to the estimated future gross revenues of a specific product, less estimated future costs of completing and disposing of that specific product, including the costs of performing maintenance and customer support on a product-by-product basis as required by the terms of the sale.

The excess of any unamortized computer software costs over its related net realizable value at a balance sheet date shall be written down. The amount of write-down is charged to periodic income. Capitalized costs that have been written down as a charge to income shall not be capitalized again or restored in any future period (ASC 985-20-35-4).

FINANCIAL STATEMENT DISCLOSURE

The total amount of unamortized computer software costs that is included in each balance sheet presented shall be disclosed in the financial statements. The total amount of computer software costs charged to expense shall be disclosed for each period for which an income statement is presented. The total amount of computer software costs charged to expense shall include amortization expense and amounts written down to net realizable value (ASC 985-20-50-1).

All computer software costs that are classified as R&D costs shall be accounted for in accordance with ASC 730. These costs may include the costs of planning, product design, detail program design, and the costs incurred in establishing technological feasibility of a computer software product (ASC 730-10-50-1).

PART II: INTERPRETIVE GUIDANCE

ASC 985-605: Revenue Recognition

ASC 985-605-05-1, 05-3, 15- 2 through 15-4, 25-1 through 25-19, 25-21 through 25-31, 25-33 through 25-41, 25-44 through 25-89, 25-91 through 25-107, 55-2, 55-28, 55-127 through 55-129, 55-131 through 55-133, 55-136 through 55-144, 55-146 through 55-148, 55-150 through 55-151, 55-154 through 55-160, 55-162 through 55-168, 55-170 through 55-179, 55-181 through 55-184, 55-205 through 55-210; ASC 985-20-60-3; ASC 450-10-60-12; ASC 605-35-15-3; ASC 730-10-60-5 **Software Revenue Recognition**

BACKGROUND

This pronouncement provides guidance on when and the amount of revenue that should be recognized from a sale, lease, or licensing of computer software.

Software arrangements may be limited to providing a license for a single software product or, at the other end of the spectrum, they may consist of the delivery of software or a software system that requires significant production, modification or customization. The following guidance does *not* apply to sales of products that contain software that is incidental to the product being sold.

SCOPE

The scope of the following guidance applies to all entities and to the following transactions and activities, unless there is a scope exception that is discussed below:

1. Licensing, selling, leasing, or marketing software in other ways.
2. Software and elements, such as software products, upgrades, enhancements, services, or postcontract customer support (PCS), related to software under an arrangements that includes software that is more-than-incidental to the products or services of the total arrangement. The following are some, but not all, indicators that software is more-than-incidental to an arrangement's products or service as a whole:
   a. The marketing effort focuses on the software or it is sold separate.
   b. The vendor provides PCS.
   c. The vendor incurs significant costs discussed under the scope of ASC 985-20.

   A service is included under the scope of the following guidance if the service would not function without the software under the arrangement.

3. Offers of more-than-insignificant discounts with the following characteristics on future purchases :
   a. The discounts are in addition to a range of discounts included in the pricing of an arrangement's other elements.
   b. The discounts are in addition to a range of discounts usually given on comparable transactions.
   c. The discounts are significant.

   Determining whether an additional discount is significant requires judgment. There is a presumption that the existence of more-than-insignificant discounts or other concessions in an arrangement constitutes an offer of an additional element or elements.

4. Arrangements to deliver software or a software system, alone or together with other products that require significant production, modification, or software customization. Software arrangements that include services that are not essential to any of the arrangement's elements or that would be additional to the price of the arrangement (see ASC 985-605-25-78) should be accounted for separately.

The guidance does not apply the following transactions and activities:

1. Arrangements for products or services including software that is incidental to the total arrangement.

2. Leases of software that include property, plant, or equipment (tangible products) if the software is incidental to the tangible product as a whole, or if the tangible product's software and nonsoftware components work together to enable the tangible product to perform its essential function.
3. Marketing and promotional activities that are not unique to software transactions, such as:
    a. Insignificant discounts on future purchases offered in a software arrangement.
    b. Discounts that are not given in addition to discounts usually given in comparable transactions.
4. Nonsoftware components of tangible products.
5. Software components of tangible products that are sold, licensed, or leased with tangible products whose software and nonsoftware components work together to enable the tangible product to perform its essential function.
6. Undelivered elements related to software essential to the ability of the tangible product discussed in (5) (above) to function.

ACCOUNTING GUIDANCE

If the sale of computer software involves significant customization, modification, or production, the transaction should be accounted for as a long-term contract. In all other cases, revenue should be recognized when the following four conditions are met:

1. Persuasive evidence of an arrangement exists.
2. Delivery has occurred.
3. The vendor's price is fixed or determinable.
4. Collectibility of the selling price is probable.

Evidence an Arrangement Exists

Some entities require a written contract to support the sale of computer software. If the entity customarily uses written contracts to support the sale of software, such a written contract—signed by both parties to the contract—must exist to confirm that a sale arrangement exists. If written contracts are not typically used to support the sale of computer software, other evidence that a sale arrangement exists must be present. Other evidence might include a purchase order from the customer or an electronic order. Even if all the other criteria for software revenue recognition specified in this pronouncement are met, a sale should not be recorded unless there is persuasive evidence that a sales arrangement exists.

Delivery Has Occurred

In most cases, delivery is deemed to have occurred at the transfer of the product master or, in cases where the product master is not transferred, at the transfer of the product master, or a first copy. The one exception to this general rule is when the amount of revenue is a function of the number of copies shipped. In this case, revenue is recognized as copies are delivered to the user or reseller. Sometimes the delivery mode for software is electronic dissemination. In those cases, delivery is deemed to have occurred when the buyer: (1) takes possession of the software by downloading it, or (2) has been provided with the access codes necessary to download the software. In addition, if there is uncertainty as to whether the customer has accepted the software, license revenue should be deferred until such acceptance occurs.

Delivery has not occurred until the software is delivered to the customer's place of business or to an intermediate site designated by the customer. In some cases in which a customer specifies an intermediate site as the delivery point, a substantial portion of the revenue is not due until the vendor moves the software from the intermediate site to another location designated by the customer. In those cases, revenue is not recognized until the software is delivered to that other site.

A delivery agent, acting for a vendor, may distribute software to customers. Revenue is not recognized when the vendor delivers the software to the delivery agent. Rather, revenue is recognized when the delivery agent has delivered the software to the customer.

Software may contain authorization keys, which prohibit unauthorized access to the software. The possession of those keys is what allows a customer to access the software. Typically, delivery of a software key is not a prerequisite to a vendor's recognition of revenue.

Price Is Fixed or Determinable and Collectibility Is Probable

A number of situations indicate that the selling price is not fixed or determinable. In those cases, revenue is recognized as payments from customers become due. Situations where the selling price is not fixed or determinable are as follows:

- The selling price is a function of the number of copies distributed or the number of users of the product.
- In general, the presence of extended payment terms exists.
- A significant portion of the license fee is not due until after the expiration of the license period or not due until more than 12 months from the sale date. However, such payment terms are not a problem if the vendor has a history of successfully collecting the sales price using such payment terms, without making concessions.
- The sale includes a cancellation period. The selling price is not fixed or determinable until the cancellation period lapses.

Before revenue can be recognized, collectibility also must be reasonably assured. If a right of return exists, the requirements for revenue recognition in ASC 605-15 must be met.

Additional criteria must be met when the sale is to a reseller. For example, the following four situations suggest that the sale price may not be fixed or determinable, or that collectibility is not reasonably assured:

71,010 ASC 985—Software

1. The vendor's payment is substantially contingent on the reseller's success in distributing the software to end users.
2. The reseller's financial situation may be such that it is unable to make fixed or determinable payments to the vendor until it collects cash from its customers.
3. Uncertainties about the number of copies to be sold by the reseller may preclude reasonable estimates of future returns.
4. The vendor provides the reseller protection against future price changes, and there are significant uncertainties about the vendor's ability to maintain its selling price.

Computer Software—Multiple Elements

Note: See ASC 605-25-15-3A, 25-2, 30-2, 30-5, 30-6A through 30-6B, 30-7, 50-1 through 50-2, 55-1, 55-3, 55-7, 55-12, 55-25, 55-29, 55-32, 55-34, 55-36 through 55-47, 55-52, 55-54, 55-6A through 55-57, 55-61, 55-69, 55-75 through 55-6B, 55-93, 65-1, "Revenue Arrangements with Multiple Deliverables" for updated guidance on (1) how a vendor should determine whether an arrangement that involves multiple deliverables should be accounted for as more than one unit of accounting, (2) how to measure consideration on such an arrangement and (3) how to allocate that consideration the arrangement's separate units of accounting.

The sale of computer software often includes other elements in addition to the software itself. Other elements might include a service that cannot function without the software element of an arrangement, the delivery of enhancements/upgrades, services of various types, and post-contract support (PCS). If a sales contract includes multiple elements, revenue should be allocated to the multiple elements based on vendor-specific objective evidence (VSOE) of the relative fair values of each element. Separate prices stated within the contract that apply to each element are often not indicative of relative fair values.

OBSERVATION: This pronouncement originally limited VSOE to two criteria:

---

1. The price charged when the same element was sold separately
2. For an element not yet being sold separately, the price set for the separate element by an appropriate level of management and where it is probable that the price would not change before the separate element is introduced into the marketplace.

Those two criteria were viewed by many as too restrictive as to what constitutes VSOE. The effective date of this provision was deferred by SOP 98-4 (not in ASC) and it was subsequently permanently eliminated Although the two original limitations on what constitutes VSOE have been eliminated from this pronouncement, entities must still allocate fees received in a multiple element arrangement based on the relative fair values of each element. Those fair values must be supported by VSOE. If VSOE is insufficient to support unbundling of the total fee, the entire fee must be deferred.

In general, if VSOE of relative fair values does not exist, revenue recognition should be deferred until the earlier of (1) the date on which VSOE of relative fair values exists, or (2) the date when all elements under a contract have been delivered. There are four exceptions to this general guidance:

1. If the only undelivered element is PCS, the entire fee is to be recognized ratably.
2. If the only undelivered element are services that do not involve significant production, modification, or customization, the entire fee is to be recognized over the period that the service is performed.
3. If the software sale is essentially a subscription, the entire fee is to be recognized over the subscription period.
4. If the fee is based on the number of copies sold of more than one product, it is often not clear how many of each product will be sold. In most cases, revenue cannot be recognized because total revenue allocable to each software product is not known.

Collectibility may be a problem when software is delivered in installments. The collectibility criterion is not met if the portion of the fee allocated to units already delivered is subject to forfeiture if other elements of the software package are not delivered. In evaluating whether revenue allocated to units already delivered is subject to forfeiture, the focus is on management's intent and not just on the terms of the legal contract. That is, if management typically refunds fees already paid if other elements of the software sale are not delivered, the collectibility criterion is not met even if management is not legally required to provide such refunds.

Multiple Software Elements—Rights to Upgrades and Enhancements

A vendor may deliver a software package and promise to provide upgrades or enhancements to that software as those upgrades/enhancements subsequently become available. The purchase price is allocated between the current software product and the right to future upgrades/enhancements based on VSOE. Some customers may choose not to exercise their right to the upgrade/enhancement. If sufficient evidence exists to estimate the number of customers who will not exercise the upgrade/enhancement right, revenue allocated to this right should be reduced.

Vendors may deliver software and a promise to provide additional software in the future. Again, the fee should be allocated between the current software product and the right to additional software based on VSOE. Unlike the situation of upgrades/enhancements, the fee allocated to the additional software is not reduced for any customers not expected to take delivery of the additional software.

Often the promise to provide customers with future versions of software is, in essence, a subscription agreement. For example, the vendor may promise to deliver all new products that comprise a certain "family" of software that are developed over some number of future years. In the case of subscription agreements, no revenue is allocated to individual software products. Rather, all of the revenue is recognized over the life of the subscription agreement, beginning on the date of delivery of the first product.

Multiple Software Elements—Postcontract Customer Support

Software is often sold with a promise, either contractual or implied by the vendor's normal business practices, to provide postcontract customer support (PCS). An example of postcontract customer support is telephone support (e.g., a help desk maintained by the vendor). Revenue is to be allocated between the software product and the PCS based on the fee to be received if the PCS was sold separately. This fee is best estimated by referring to the rate charged for such service at renewal (i.e., the renewal rate). Revenue allocated to PCS is to be recognized ratably over the PCS period.

In cases where the sale of software includes multiple elements (including PCS), there may not be the VSOE needed to allocate the fee across the multiple elements. In those cases, if the PCS represents the only undelivered element, the entire software fee should be recognized ratably over:

- The PCS contract period if the vendor is contractually obligated to provide these services.
- The estimated period over which the vendor will provide PCS if the vendor's obligation to provide these services is implied based on its past actions.

In some cases, PCS revenue can be recognized along with the initial licensing fee at delivery of the software product if all of the following conditions are met:

- The PCS fee is included with the initial licensing fee.
- The term of the PCS included with the initial license is for one year or less. This criterion is not violated if the vendor provides telephone support for more than one year, if the vendor's past history indicates that the majority of the telephone support will be provided in the first year after the sale.
- The estimated cost of providing the PCS during this period is insignificant.
- Unspecified upgrades/enhancements offered during the PCS period have historically been, and are expected to continue to be, minimal and infrequent.

If PCS revenue is recognized on delivery of the software product, the estimated costs of providing PCS are to be accrued on this date. The estimated costs of providing PCS include the costs of providing software upgrades/enhancements.

Multiple Software Elements—Services

The sale of software may include the provision of future services (non-PCS related) in addition to the software product itself. These services might include installation, consulting, and training. The vendor must determine whether the service elements qualify for separate accounting treatment as the services are performed. If not, the entire purchase price (for both the software and services) is to be accounted for using contract accounting. To conclude that the service element of the contract can be accounted for separately, the following criteria must be met:

- The fair value of the service element of the contract must be supported by sufficient VSOE.
- The ability to use the software (i.e., functionality) must not depend on the service.
- The price of the contract would be expected to vary based on the inclusion or exclusion of the service.

If the service qualifies for separate accounting, revenue allocated should be recognized as the service is performed. If no pattern of performance is obvious, revenue is recognized over the period during which the service is to be performed.

There may be instances in which there is not sufficient VSOE to allocate the sale price between the software product and the services included. If the only undelivered element of the sale is the service and if the service does not involve significant production, modification, or customization, the entire purchase price is recognized as services are performed.

Software is more likely to be functional without any additional services being rendered if the software is viewed as off-the-shelf software. If the software is not off-the-shelf, or if significant modifications to off-the-shelf software are necessary to meet the customer's functionality, no element of the arrangement would qualify as accounting for a service. Rather the entire purchase price, both for the software and for any services, would be accounted for using contract accounting.

Factors that indicate that the service element of the arrangement is essential to the functionality of the software are as follows:

- The software is not off-the-shelf.
- The services to be rendered include significant modifications to off-the-shelf software.
- It is necessary to build complex interfaces for the customer to use the vendor's software in its own environment.
- The customer's obligation to pay for the software is tied to the completion of the services.
- Customer acceptance criteria (i.e., milestones) affect the realizability of the software-license fee.

Multiple Software Elements—Contract Accounting

Software or software systems that require significant production, modification, or customization do not meet the criteria for separate accounting for the service element. In those cases, contract accounting must be applied. Contract accounting is implemented using either the percentage-of-completion method or the completed-contract method. Guidance on applying those methods is provided in Chapter 36, *ASC 605—Revenue Recognition*, of this Guide.

In applying the percentage-of-completion method, both input and output measures of the degree to which the software project is complete can be used. A typical input measure is labor hours incurred. Labor hours incurred provides a good measure of progress toward completion for software projects that are labor intensive (e.g., customization of core software). Milestones toward completion of the software project are examples of output measures. A good example of useful output measures of progress to date is the completion of tasks that trigger independent review.

ASC 985-605-05-4, 55-121 through 55-125
Application of ASC 985-605, Software Revenue Recognition, to Arrangements That Include the Right to Use Software Stored on Another Entity's Hardware

BACKGROUND

Instead of licensing software that is installed on a customer's hardware, some software companies and entities referred to as application software providers (ASPs) are offering customers access to software applications without taking possession of the software. Under such arrangements, the customer can access software—which is installed on a vendor's or a third party's hardware—over the Internet or over a dedicated line. This type of storage or access service is known as hosting.

The form of such arrangements consists of a right to (1) use software and (2) store software on hardware owned by a vendor or a third party. Customers in those arrangements may not have a license to the software and may not be able to access the software through a different host. ASPs consider themselves to be service providers that deploy, host, and manage application solutions for rent.

Although the terms of hosting arrangements may differ significantly, the following guidance applies to arrangements in which a customer purchases a software license as well as a right to store and access the software. It is assumed that payment occurs at the inception of the arrangement.

ACCOUNTING ISSUES

1. Should the guidance in ASC 985-605 apply to arrangements that require a vendor to host the software?
2. Does the guidance in ASC 985-605 apply to arrangements in which a customer can choose to take delivery of the software?
3. If the answer to Issue 2 is affirmative, when does delivery occur and how does a vendor's obligation to host the software affect revenue recognition?

ACCOUNTING GUIDANCE

1. The guidance in ASC 985-605 applies to the software element of a hosting arrangement if
    a. The customer has a contractual right to take physical possession of the software at any time during the hosting period without significant penalty, and

b. It is feasible for the customer to run the software on its own hardware or to contract for a hosting arrangement with a third party that is unrelated to the vendor or the host.

Arrangements that do not give those options to a customer are accounted for as *service arrangements*, which are not included under the scope of ASC 985-605.

2. If a customer in a hosting arrangement can choose whether to take physical possession of the software as discussed above, delivery occurs when the customer is able to takes possession of the software. Service arrangements could include multiple elements that would affect the allocation of revenue.

3. The Task Force noted that if the guidance in ASC 985-605 applies to software in a hosting arrangement, revenue for the portion of the fee allocated to the software portion of the arrangement should be recognized on delivery only if *all* of the revenue recognition requirements under that guidance are met. This would include the requirement for vendor-specific objective evidence of fair value and that the portion of the fee allocated to the software cannot be forfeited, refunded, or be subject to any other concession. The portion of the fee allocated to the hosting arrangement would be recognized as the service is provided. In addition to the software and the hosting service, arrangements under this guidance that are accounted for under the guidance in ASC 985-605 also may include other elements, such as specified or unspecified upgrade rights.

The following guidance applies to the accounting for costs of developing software for hosting arrangements:

a. The provisions of ASC 985-20 apply to software development costs incurred by vendors that sell, lease, license, or market to others software that is accounted for under the guidance in ASC 985-605.

b. The provisions of ASC 350-40 apply to the development costs of software accounted for under the scope of ASC 985-605 if it is used only to provide services and is not sold, leased, licensed, or marketed to others.

c. The provisions of ASC 985-20 also apply to software development costs if in the process of developing or modifying the software, a vendor develops a substantive plan to sell, lease, license, or market the software to others.

ASC 985-605-15-3 Applicability of ASC 985-605, Software Revenue Recognition, to Non-Software Deliverables in an Arrangement Containing More-Than-Incidental Software

BACKGROUND

This question has been raised because there is diversity in practice in the application of the provisions of ASC 985-605, Software Revenue Recognition, in arrangements that include non-software deliverables, such as hardware, in addition to software that is more than incidental to the products or services as a whole. The guidance in ASC 985-605-15-3 includes the following indicators that software is more than incidental: (*a*) the company's marketing focuses on the software and or it is sold separately, (*b*) the vendor provides postcontract customer support, and (*c*) the vendor incurs significant costs that are accounted for under the scope of ASC 985-20 (Accounting for the Costs of Computer Software to Be Sold, Leased, or Otherwise Marketed). There has been some confusion, because the guidance in ASC 985-605-15-3 through 15-4 states that revenue related to property, plant, or equipment included in a lease of software should be accounted for under the guidance in ASC 840-10, Leases, but the guidance in ASC 985-605-25-5 discusses accounting for revenue from software arrangements with *multiple elements* and states that "all additional products and services specified in the arrangements" should be accounted for under the guidance in ASC 985-605.

ACCOUNTING ISSUE

Should non-software deliverables included in an arrangement that contains software that is more than incidental to the products or services as a whole be included under the scope of ASC 985-605?

ACCOUNTING GUIDANCE

Software and software-related elements are included under the scope of ASC 985-605 in arrangements that include software that is *more than incidental* to the products or services as a whole. Software-related elements include software products and services, such as upgrades and enhancements and postcontract customer support (PCS), as well as non-software deliverables that require a software deliverable for their functionality. Unrelated equipment that does not require a software deliverable for its functionality is not considered to be software-related and should be *excluded* from the scope of ASC 985-605.

ASC 985-605-15-3 through 15-4A,25-10, 50-1, 55-211 through 55-236, 65-1
Applicability of ASC 985-605 to Certain Revenue Arrangements That Include Software

BACKGROUND

The guidance in ASC 985-605, Software Revenue Recognition, applies to products or services that contain software that is "more than incidental" to the products or services as a whole and requires that the selling price of separate deliverables in an arrangement that includes multiple elements be based on vendor-specific objective evidence (VSOE). Certain transactions under the scope of ASC 985-605 include software-enabled devices, which are sold only with other deliverables and result in a revenue pattern that is *not* based on the economics of the transaction because VSOE cannot be determined for those devices.

Some constituents have suggested that the model in ASC 985-605 should be amended to exclude some transactions that include software-enabled devices that may *not* have been considered when that guidance was written.

ACCOUNTING ISSUES

1. Should the measurement criteria or the scope of ASC 985-605 be modified?
2. If so, how should the scope of ASC 985-605 be modified?

SCOPE

The following guidance applies to arrangements with multiple elements that include both hardware and software elements. However, hardware elements of a tangible product are never accounted for under the scope of software revenue recognition guidance

ACCOUNTING GUIDANCE

1. The scope of the guidance in ASC 985-605-15-3 should be amended by deleting the existing subparagraph 3b and amending ASC 985-605-15-3c to include a service that cannot function without the software element of an arrangement.

2. This guidance amends the guidance in ASC-985-605-15-4 to *exclude* application of the guidance in ASC 985-605 to the following transactions and activities in addition to those already listed:

    a. Leases of software that include property, plant, or equipment (tangible products) if the software is incidental to the tangible product as a whole, or if the tangible product's software and nonsoftware components work together to enable the tangible product to perform its essential function. (ASC 985-605-15-4b)

    b. Nonsoftware components of tangible products. (ASC 985-605-15-4d)

    c. Software components of tangible products that are sold, licensed, or leased with tangible products whose software and nonsoftware components work together to enable the tangible product to perform its essential function. (ASC 985-605-15-4e)

    d. Undelivered elements related to software essential to the ability of the tangible product discussed in the previous bullet to function. (ASC 985-605-15-4f)

3. A vendor should consider all of the following factors to determine whether software components that function together and are delivered with a tangible product are necessary for the tangible product to perform its basic function:

    a. There is a rebuttable presumption that a software product is essential to a tangible product's ability to perform its function if the tangible product is rarely sold without the software element.

    b. If a vendor sells products that perform similar functions, such as different models of similar products, the products should be considered to be the same products for the evaluation of factor (a) if the only difference between similar products is that one includes software that the other does not.

c. If a vendor sells software separately as well as tangible products containing the same software, it should not be presumed that the software is not essential to the tangible product's functionality because the vendor also sells the software separately.
   d. The fact that a software element may not be embedded in a tangible product does not mean that it is not considered to be essential to that product's functionality.
   e. Nonsoftware elements of a tangible asset must contribute significantly to a product's essential function. That is, a tangible product should not only be a means of delivering software to a customer. (ASC 985-605-15-4A)

A vendor that has entered into an arrangement that includes software deliverables, which are under the scope of ASC 605-25, and nonsoftware deliverables, which are not under the scope of ASC 605-25, should allocate consideration under that arrangement to the nonsoftware and software deliverables as a group based on the guidance in ASC 605-25-15-3A. If a nonsoftware deliverable includes software deliverables that are considered to be essential to a tangible product's ability to perform its function and the arrangement includes more than one software deliverable, a portion of the consideration on the arrangement should be allocated to the software deliverables as a group based on the guidance in ASC 605-25-15-3A and should be separated and allocated further based on the this guidance. In addition, software contained in a tangible product that is *not* essential to that product's ability to perform its function as well as nonessential software and other deliverables under an arrangement (other than the nonsoftware components of a tangible product) related to the nonessential software also are included in the scope of this guidance. An undelivered element related to a deliverable under the scope of this guidance and to a deliverable excluded from the scope of this guidance should be separated into (a) a software deliverable, which is under the scope of this guidance, and (b) a nonsoftware deliverable, which is not under the scope of this guidance. (ASC 985-605-25-10(f))

DISCLOSURE

A vendor should disclose the information required under the guidance in ASC 605-25 for arrangements that apply to multiple elements that may or many not be under the scope of ASC 985-605.

ASC 985-705: Cost of Sales and Services

ASC 985-705-S25-1, S99-1 Accounting for the Film and Software Costs Associated with Developing Entertainment and Educational Software Products

BACKGROUND

Games incorporating audio, film, graphics, and interactive software technology on CD-ROM are entertainment and educational software (EE) products, which may include film content taken from an existing film or film developed specifically for the software product. The development of such products by both motion picture companies and software companies differs from the development of software for business applications or operating systems; production costs are a significant component of multimedia entertainment product costs.

Motion picture companies had been capitalizing costs related to EE products as inventory and amortizing them over the product's expected revenue stream under the provisions of FAS-53 (not in ASC). In addition, motion picture companies were not applying the guidance in ASC 720-35 on reporting for advertising costs. Motion picture companies considered EE products to be entertainment products similar to films for the following reasons: (*a*) the products usually use previously developed or simple software, so technological feasibility is reached at the beginning of the project, and (*b*) the software content often is minimal. In contrast, software companies have been expensing film production and software costs under the provisions of ASC 605-25. Some software companies were accounting separately for costs related to the film content under the provisions of FAS-53 (not in ASC) and costs related to the software content under the provisions of ASC 605-25.

ACCOUNTING ISSUE

How should companies developing EE products account for related film and software costs?

SEC OBSERVER COMMENT

At the May 1996 meeting, the SEC Observer announced that based on the educational session presented by a working group from the motion picture and software industries the SEC staff believes that EE products that are sold, licensed, or otherwise marketed should be accounted for based on the requirements of ASC 605-25. Therefore, subsequent to May 23, 1996, SEC registrants should account for film costs related to those products under the provisions of ASC 605-25, not under the provisions of FAS-53. In addition, registrants should expense exploitation costs incurred subsequent to May 23, 1996, unless they qualify for capitalization under the provisions in ASC 720-35. Registrants that previously capitalized all costs incurred in the development of EE products should restate prior-period financial statements to account for software development costs, in accordance with the provisions of ASC 605-25, if the related amounts are material. The SEC staff's views are not intended to apply to costs incurred to produce computer generated special effects and images used in products exhibited in theaters or licensed to television stations.

Accounting Resources on the Web

The following World Wide Web addresses are just a few of the resources on the Internet that are available to practitioners. Because of the evolving nature of the Internet, some addresses may change. In such a case, refer to one of the many Internet search engines, such as Google (http://www.google.com) or Yahoo (http://www.yahoo.com).

Accounting Research Manager   http://www.accountingresearchmanager.com

AICPA   http://www.aicpa.org

American Accounting Association   http://aaahq.org

CCH Integrated Solutions   http://cchgroup.com/

CCH Learning Center   http://cch.learningcenter.com

FASAB   http://www.fasab.gov

FASB   http://www.fasb.org

Federal Tax Law   http://www.taxsites.com/federal.html

Fedworld   http://www.fedworld.gov

GASB   http://www.gasb.org

Government Accountability Office   http://www.gao.gov

House of Representatives   http://www.house.gov

International Accounting Standards Board   http://www.iasb.org/Home.htm

IRS Digital Daily   http://www.irs.gov/

Library of Congress   http://www.loc.gov

National Association of State Boards of Accountancy   http://www.nasba.org

Office of Management and Budget   http://www.whitehouse.gov/omb/

ProSystem fx Engagement   http://www.tax.cchgroup.com/Engagement/default

Public Company Accounting Oversight Board   http://www.pcaobus.org

Securities and Exchange Commission   http://www.sec.gov

Thomas Legislative Research   http://thomas.loc.gov